New York Real Estate

FOR SALESPERSONS

5TH EDITION

Custom Edition for New York Real Estate Institute

BILL PLUNKETT

HONDROS LEARNING™
4140 Executive Parkway
Westerville, Ohio 43081
www.hondroslearning.com

Published 2015. Printed in the United States of America

18 17 16 15 1 2 3 4
978-1-59844-256-4

The publisher makes every reasonable effort to ensure the accuracy and completeness of the information in this book and to provide appropriate citation of source material. Due to the dynamic nature of the material and the possibility of human or mechanical error, the reader is encouraged to refer to original sources as the ultimate authority on this subject. Please keep in mind that the examples presented in this text are for demonstration purposes only. Actual values may vary greatly in different regions, states, and cities.

For more information on, or to purchase, our products, please call 1-866-84LEARN or visit www.hondroslearning.com

A Letter from the President

Dear Students,

Welcome to the New York Real Estate Institute, your first step in becoming a successful Real Estate Salesperson. I would like to take this opportunity to introduce myself and explain why NYREI graduates are more successful Real Estate professionals than any other school in New York.

My name is Richard Levine and I am the President of NYREI, the leading provider of real estate education in New York.

We understand that our students have very busy, diverse schedules and that is why we allow you to create your own class schedule. Classes are given 7 days a week, including nights and weekends. You can start your classes whenever it is convenient for you. There are 20 independent classes that you can take in any order (you do not have to wait for Class Session 1 as shown on the class schedule on the following page). The classes add up to 75 hours. NY State requires you to take a minimum of 67.5 hours.

In addition to the classroom sessions, you can also can sign up for the Online course for review or to complete your hours. For more information please contact sales@nyrei.com.

NYREI typically offers the school test every Monday as well as a night test and weekend test for your convenience (if needed, it is possible to take the test on a different day). NY State gives their test every Tuesday. To help you prepare for the school and state exams, we offer many options including:

- Cram For The Exam Book – can be purchased in office or shipped to you for a small fee.
- Online Practice Exams
- Tutoring – group sessions for the school and state exams are available every week.

For more information please visit http://www.nyrei.com/examprep/

NYREI offers Continuing Education Courses online. The Continuing Education Courses are available to everyone, and if you have your real estate license you get continuing education credit for the course.

In addition, NYREI is the only school that offers daily job recruitment and job placement assistance with a sponsoring broker.

Note: For the most current Package information and additional information including detailed information on all the courses and seminars we offer, please visit our web site at **www.NYREI.com**.

Sincerely,

Richard Levine, President of NYREI

NYREI AT A GLANCE

NYREI State Certified and **New York State Exam**

Thank you, for choosing the **New York Real Estate Institute.**

OUR CLASSES ARE INDEPENDENT MODULES: One of the unique features of our school is that you may start at any point in the course. There are 20 independent classes consisting of 75 hours. You can take classes in any sequence (you do not have to start with class #1), and you can take the same class twice, however you will not receive duplicate credit.

ATTENDANCE: The N.Y. State Department of State allows a student to be absent for only 7.5 hours of the course. *They strictly audit attendance records.* If you have not met the minimum required 67.5 hours, under no circumstances will you be allowed to take the NYREI State Certified Exam. We will check and verify your hours of attendance prior to the school test and alternate test.

COURSE DEADLINE: Starting from your first class you will have 4 months to complete the course and school exam, otherwise you may extend the course for an additional charge of $150 for 2 months. Please try and complete in the time allotted.

NOTE TO ALL STUDENTS: STUDENTS MUST SIGN IN FOR ALL CLASSES AND SIGN THE ATTENDANCE SHEET TO GET CREDIT FOR CLASSES!

BELOW IS YOUR REGISTRATION NUMBER FOR FUTURE REFERENCE.

IF YOU MISPLACE YOUR SCAN CARD JUST ENTER
YOUR REGISTRATION NUMBER ON THE KEYPAD.

KEEP A RECORD OF YOUR ATTENDANCE. HOURS CAN BE CHECKED ONLINE BY CLICKING "VERIFY HOURS" ON THE HOMEPAGE.

Class Schedule

Please record the date of each class you attended in the box below:

Session	Topic	Date Attended
1 **1A**	The Independent Contractor or Employee Real Estate License Law	
2	Law of Agency 1: Relationships with Sellers, Buyers, Tenants and Landlords between Brokers, Agents, and Third Parties	
3	Law of Agency 2: Disclosure and Listing Forms	
4	Law of Agency 3: Other Types of Disclosure and Antitrust Laws	
5	Easements and Liens	
6 **6A**	Deeds Real Estate Closings	
7	Estates and Interests	
8	Land Use Regulations	
9 **9A**	Construction Basics Environmental Issues and Property Concerns	
10 **10A**	The Valuation Process and Pricing Properties Real Estate Math	
11	Human Rights and Fair Housing	
12 **12A**	Contracts and Contract Preparation Leases	
13	Overview of Real Estate Finance	
14	Mortgage Basics	
15 **15A**	Municipal Agencies Property Insurance	
16 **16A**	Real Estate Taxes and Assessments Income Tax Issues in Real Estate	
17	Condominiums and Cooperatives	
18	Property Management	
19	Commercial and Investment 1	
20	Commercial and Investment 2	

Real Estate Exam Prep Available from NYREI

Everything you need to pass your Real Estate Salesperson or Brokers Exam

Online Practice Exams

Get instant access to one of the best Real Estate Exam Prep Guides on the net. Our challenging and easy to use sample tests will help you prepare for your Salesperson or Broker exam. $49.99

Kristen's Real Estate Exam Pass Book

If you're concerned about passing your New York State real estate licensing exams, this is the book for you! It addresses both school and state requirements for salesperson and broker candidates.

Acclaimed teacher Kristen Bacorn believes real estate should never be boring or overly complex. In this book, she offers a fun, easy way to learn essential real estate concepts. $75 - with shipping ($10)

Cram For The Exam Book

Essential study guide designed to help you pass both NYREI School and New York State real estate salesperson exam.

Pick up your textbook any time at our New York location or have us ship it to you ($10 shipping fee - shipping within US only.). $25 - with shipping ($10)

State Tutoring

Worried about passing the NY State Real Estate Salesperson Licensing Test? Put your fears aside - you have come to right place! We have many well-known outstanding real estate trainer, that have put together an independent 2-hour tutoring session (Note that this is group private tutoring and not the same as the NYREI tutoring given each week) $75

CompuCram® Exam Prep

Get instant online access (for six months) to the only complete Exam Prep system that integrates Flash Cards, Matching and Fill-In-The-Blank vocabulary tools, practice testing and comprehensive simulated exams into an "all-in-one" solution. CompuCram® guides students each step of the way based on their initial pre-assessment and the work completed during each session.

Regardless of how students use CompuCram® to prepare for the test, they receive continuous feedback via the revolutionary new Readiness Indicator – ensuring that they pass the first time. $79

School Tutoring

Worried about passing the NYREI Real Estate Salesperson Licensing Test? NYREI School tutoring is available weekly (schedule located on salesperson schedule). $45

Private Tutoring

Get your REAL ESTATE License with the help of a professional! Our instructors provide expert tutoring that teaches you what you need to know to pass the New York School Exam and NY State Test to become a Licensed Real Estate Salesperson.

For more information contact sales@nyrei.com

NYREI State Certified and New York State Exam
WHAT YOU NEED TO KNOW

OFFICE HOURS:
Monday - Friday 8:30 AM - 7:00 PM (except Friday until 5:00 PM)
Saturday - Sunday 8:30 AM - 4:00 PM

BUILDING HOURS:
Monday - Friday 6:00 AM - 8:00 PM
Saturday 6:00 AM - 6:00 PM - ONLY ENTRY into the building is at the 35th Street entrance!
Sunday 8:00 AM - 4:00 PM - ONLY ENTRY into the building is at the 35th Street entrance!

NYREI STATE CERTIFIED EXAM: The New York Department of State requires that you take and pass the NYREI State Certified Exam in order to obtain a New York Real Estate Salesperson License. You must complete the minimum required 67.5 hours of the 75 hour course (**NO EXCEPTIONS**) to be eligible to take the NYREI State Certified Exam. You do NOT have to register for the NYREI exam, just go to the assigned classroom and scan-in. The test consists of 75 questions, 65 is passing and you will be given 1 hour and 30 minutes to complete the exam. You will be graded immediately after taking the test and will receive your completion certificate. If you fail to pass the exam you will be allowed to take one make-up exam.

NEW YORK STATE EXAM: Please read Department of State web site very carefully!!!

The state exam is typically offered every Tuesday at 9:00 AM, 11:00 AM and at 2:00 PM (except holidays) at 123 Williams St. (212-417-2154). Subways (4/5 to Fulton St.; N/R to Cortlandt St.; 2/3 Fulton St. and walk east about 1 block). You are now required to make an online reservation in order to take the state exam. **WE URGE YOU TO MAKE YOUR RESERVATION NOW.** Go to http://www.nyrei.com and click link for Dept. of State and then link for Real Estate Salesperson Exam Online Reservation in order to make your reservation or go here http://www.dos.state.ny.us/lcns/realestate/index.html. There are other locations within the state that you can take the exam. You may take the New York State exam before taking the NYREI exam and you can take both exams before you have a sponsoring broker, however, you cannot be licensed until your broker signs your license application. You must register with a broker within 2 years of passing the New York State exam. If you have not registered with a broker within that time, you will have to re-take the state exam. However, your school completion certificate does not expire. Also, your permanent License and Pocket Card will be sent to your broker's office, no license will be sent to your home.

YOU MUST HAVE TWO #2 PENCILS FOR BOTH THE NYREI AND STATE EXAMS. Also, calculators are permitted if they are silent, nonprinting, and do not contain an alphabetic keyboard. PDA's and cellular phones are not allowed.

CRAM FOR THE EXAM: $25.00 ($30.00 for non-student)

Your guide to passing the New York Real Estate Salesperson Exam. Need a quick way to prepare? Why spend more time then needed? Here you have a directed review in an easy-to-study format. You can do a comprehensive review in only a few hours. Increase your chances of passing both exams dramatically!

For Registration or additional information, **call 212-967-7508** or go **online at www.nyrei.com**

Table of Contents

Table of Contents

Table of Contents

PREFACE

Real estate has, and will always be, a prized possession. And the ability to buy and sell real estate at will is part of the American dream. Since real estate is a key indicator of our economy and because most people consider a real estate purchase one of the biggest decisions they will make in their lives, it is no wonder quality real estate professionals are in high demand.

This edition has been completely reorganized to meet the salesperson 75-hour prelicensing requirements effective July 1, 2008. Each chapter has been revised and updated to reflect changes outlined in the new curriculum, and material is presented in a logical sequence to help easily transition from one topic to the next. There have been added in some chapters new laws that are now currently in effect

It should also come as no surprise that real estate education is continually being reviewed and updated so students are prepared to enter the professional world armed with the knowledge they need to be ethical, professional, and, of course, successful.

New York Real Estate for Salespersons is a new and thorough treatment of real estate principles and practices for pre-licensing students in New York. The text covers the fundamentals of the real estate profession that are needed to fulfill the new **75-hour curriculum** requirement in New York. Students are introduced to everything from real estate law to property management—all the information future real estate professionals need to pass the state licensing and school exam.

The author team for New York Real Estate Salesperson consists of veteran instructors and real estate professionals, as well as subject and industry subject matter experts. This text was written with the understanding that every student brings a different level of experience and learning style to the classroom. It is easy to use and easy to understand, ensuring all students can successfully master New York's pre-licensing requirements, and begin a fulfilling career as a real estate professional.

Using this Text

This text was designed to give you the information you need to successfully enter the real estate industry in New York State. Contained here are the **principles and practices of real estate,** as well as a **complete review of important topics present on the New York real estate licensing exam.**

Whether used in the classroom or for self-study, you will find the information presented in a clear and concise manner. Key terms, examples, chapter summaries, reinforce concepts presented throughout each chapter.

About the Author

Bill Plunkett has been a Licensed Real Estate Agent since 1990. He is also a member of the National Association of REALTORS®, New York State Association of REALTORS®, and Long Island Board of REALTORS®. Since 2007 he has been affiliated with the Prudential Douglas Elliman organization. He still works real estate on a referral basis with a partner, Tim Castor, Associate Broker of Prudential Douglas Elliman.

In 2000 Bill Plunkett was certified as a New York state instructor. Since January 2002, he has compiled a complete Real Estate program for Hofstra University. It included the 45-hour pre-licensing course, for Real Estate Salesperson and Broker, including the exam, also a continuing education course. All have been accepted by New York Department of State Division of Licensing Services.

In 2004 Bill has made the teaching of the courses his primary goal at the New York Real Estate Institute. His focus has been the incorporation of not only the laws and ethics of the industry as a whole, but also the inclusion of real-world experiences faced by salespeople and brokers. This information has come from his own experiences, as well as other sales professionals in the industry. This approach, he feels, benefits students by providing a realistic view of what to expect in their real estate careers.

In addition to comprehensive training, Bill has designed and maintained on a regular basis his own website to assist students in their careers. Including helpful links, as well as the most recent information, www.bprei.com is a valuable tool for all of his students.

He personally wishes all of you the warmest regards for an exciting, rewarding and successful real estate career.

Acknowledgements

The revised edition of the New York Real Estate for Salespersons would not have been possible without the aid and assistance of many people. First there are the brokers and agents who gave so much to evaluating the text to make sure it would flow for the students to read and comprehend. The students who were givien copies to read not knowing it was to be put in the book. They all gave a very honest opinion.

The author would also like to thank for his understanding and support in this project **Richard A. Levine,** president New York Real Estate Institute.

A special thank you to the following for their comments, suggestions, and expertise:

Patricia E. Cardinale: *Broker/Owner 30 years Merrick, N.Y.*

Dorothea Carr: *Associate Broker, TechValley Homes*

Robin Carlson MS Ed

Tom Carvetta: *Supt. Mgr., Kaufman Arcade, West 36th Street, New York, NY*

Tim Castor: *Associate Broker, Prudential Douglas Elliman*

Timothy Detty: *Certified General Appraiser*

Vince Dibartolo: *Licensed Property & Casualty*

John Dilanni: *Associate Broker, Realty USA*

Lisa Durand: *Mortgage originator, Albany Funding Inc.*

Laura Farrell: *Broker, L. Newman Real Estate*

Marian Fraker-Gutin: *Past President of LIBOR 1994 &2005, Past President of MLSLI 1983-84*

Jeanne Heran: *Esquire: Attorney at Law*

J. Chris Jones: *B.S. Accounting*

Stephen Kaufman: *President, Kaufman Organization*

Kevin Kurland: *President, Kurland Realty New York City*

Stephen Love: *Chief Operating Officer, Ardor Realty*

Fanny Montalvo: *Vice President Client Services, Fenwick, Keats Goodstein*

Kevin Magioncalda: *New York Real Estate Institute*

Nancy Mosca: *Instructor, RE Associate Broker, EXIT Kingdom Realty, Forest Hills, N.Y. & EXIT Realty Landmark, New York, N.Y.*

Barbara Schultis: *Managing Director of Sales, Long Beach & Merrick Branches, Prudential Douglas Elliman Real Estate*

Sandy Todd Schwartz, Esq : *Schwartz, Levine & Kaplan, PLLC*

Paul Semanek: *Associate Broker, Realty USA*

Bill Seto: *Principal Broker, Goldmark Realty, Inc.*

Erin Sheridan: *Associate Broker, Pro Realty of N.Y. Inc.*

Jim Speer: *Vice President, Operations Multiple Listing Service of Long Island, Inc.*

Joseph Sullivan: *Broker, Prudential Manor Homes*

Olinda Turturro: *Associate Broker and Director of Recruiting, BondNewYork*

Jeanne Warzek: *Associate Broker, Coldwell Banker Prime Properties*

A very special thank you has to go to **Jerome H. Blue**, *President Bluestone Developers, Inc.* Uniondale, New York 11556, Former Commissioner of New York State Division of Human Rights. Without his help the Fair Housing chapter would not be as complete. Thank you Jerry.

There are also two people who are owed a lot of thanks by every real estate agent in New York State.

A special thanks go out to **Carol Gallo-Turschmann**, LIBOR's Commission Escrow Sub Committee Chair and NYSAR's Commission Escrow Working Group Vice Chair, who worked tirelessly for years spearheading the efforts on both the state and local level to make sure that this bill became law!

There is another person who deserves a thank you and that is LIBOR Commission Escrow Act Sub Committee Vice Chair **Lou Gutin**, who single-handedly brought life back into this legislation which was all but dead just a few years ago.

Also to **Laura Melcher**, Manager, Editorial Development, REALTOR.org, NATIONAL ASSOCIATION OF REALTORS®, the author would like to especially thank her for all her help in putting the material from the NAR in the book.

INTRODUCTION TO THE REAL ESTATE PROFESSION

CONGRATULATIONS!!!

You have just taken the first step to your new life and career. You will find that real estate has many benefits. You will be dealing in one of the biggest markets selling or renting. The people you are going to meet, either professionals like yourself, or buyers and sellers. You will have the satisfaction of helping people reach their goals whether it is residential or commercial real estate. You are also going to find out many new avenues of your life, either professionally or personally. As you grow into your new life you will have an understanding on how to help people and the rewards that will come from it. As you study the book and prepare to take your tests, there are more avenues to travel. We will try and give some of the answers you may have. The real estate profession has expanded and offers one of the widest career selections in the business world today. Helping people buy and sell homes, office buildings, industrial property and corporation farmland, property management, land development, mortgage banking, urban planning, real estate counseling, appraisal and research are all aspects of a career in real estate.

Becoming a Real Estate Professional

According to New York State law, *a real estate license and affiliation with a broker* are necessary to act as an agent for someone who wants to buy or sell real estate. This license is all encompassing—it allows you sell or rent, commercial, industrial, residential, property management, industrial. There is one license issued in New York for real estate.

What You Will Do as a Salesperson

With your salesperson license working under the sponsorship of a licensed broker, you may perform activities for other people. Examples could be listing and selling property, renting or managing property, and relocating, buying property at an auction.

You will study other fields of real estate to learn about specialized areas. You may want to become a broker and open your own firm, you can look toward a management position. You will become active in community projects, either school board, PTA, or any opportunity that will help gain the exposure you need. Within residential and commercial real estate, there are a number of specialties. Single-family, multi-family, condominiums, and co-ops are examples of residential specialties. Commercial, industrial, and farm properties also have their own sub-categories.

Advantages and Rewards of a Career in Real Estate

A career in real estate provides flexibility and freedom to set your own pace. Income directly reflects your efforts, with no limits on what astute, hard-working men and women can earn. Successful people in real estate are goal-oriented, persevering, self-motivated, ambitious and people-oriented. The rewards of a real estate career are a potential for high earnings, status in the community, autonomy, time freedom, helping people, the intellectual challenge and the satisfaction from those accomplishments.

Working in real estate allows for independence and choices of environment in which to work, such as affiliation with a large or small firm as a listed salesperson. With more experience and upon passing of an additional exam, becoming a real estate broker is the next step. Brokers can own their own businesses and employ other salespeople.

The Contrast of the Broker and Salesperson

Salespersons will work full-time for a minimum of two years to obtain their broker license. Salespersons must work under the supervision and sponsorship of a licensed broker. Brokers may own and operate their own company or elect to work under the supervision of a licensed broker as a associate broker. New York law prohibits associate brokers or salespersons to be partners, stockholders in a brokerage company. If you have three years experience as a property manager, investor, developer or combining any of these you may apply for the broker license without becoming a salesperson first. It is always wise to check with the DOS to see if your requirements will be accepted.

Careers in Real Estate

When most people think of the real estate profession, salespersons and brokers usually come to mind. While these people often have the greatest visibility, there are many other aspects of, and careers in, real estate. Even though this textbook focuses on earning a real estate salesperson's license, it is important to know the other options available for those interested in real estate.

There are tremendous numbers of opportunities for real estate licensees to move into other related fields. In addition to the brokerage and sales side of the real estate business, careers are also available in:

- Finance
- Property management
- Construction
- Trade associations
- Government work
- Appraisal
- Development
- Title work
- Education

Finance

New York ranks in the top five for the highest number of financial institutions, including savings and loan associations, mutual savings banks, and commercial banks. These institutions have a constant need for highly trained people to fill real estate-related positions.

In addition to taking and approving mortgage loan applications, financial institutions need people who can help manage loan portfolios, appraise properties, and assess risk. There are also opportunities in banks for people with title experience and familiarity with the national secondary mortgage market.

Mortgage companies are also looking for people with many of these same skills. Mortgage brokers, real estate trusts, endowments, private lenders, and government agencies devoted to real estate finance (such as the FHA and VA) offer additional opportunities for interesting careers that involve real estate and finance.

Appraisal

Real estate appraisal offers many career opportunities. Appraisers can work for financial institutions, developers, property managers, or government agencies. In addition to a good understanding of real estate, an appraiser must have a good understanding of appraisal methods.

To become a licensed real estate appraiser in New York, a person must meet specific requirements such as age, reputation, experience, and education.

Property Management

Property management companies in agency relationships with property owners and property managers owe property owners the same **fiduciary duties** of *obedience*, *loyalty*, *disclosure*, *confidentiality*, *accountability*, and *reasonable care* owed to all clients. A property manager or property management company is a *general agent* because of the broad range of duties performed whereas a real estate salesperson is classified as a *special agent* because duties are restricted to *one area* of performance.

Among other things, property managers are responsible for:

- Setting rents that cover all expenses associated with operating the building while still returning a profit.
- Maintaining a plan for the maintenance and rehabilitation of the building so it produces the greatest amount of rental income for as long as possible
- Protecting the building from loss
- Insulating the owner from liability with appropriate insurance policy recommendations

Development

Real estate development offers a range of career opportunities. Land development is the process of acquiring large tracts of land at a low cost per acre, then subdividing and improving them with streets, sewers, and utilities so they can be resold at a higher cost per front foot (for lots) or per square foot (for buildings).

Land is developed for residential, commercial, industrial, and other uses. Once the appropriate amenities are in place and necessary zoning obtained, lots can be sold as bare land ready for a structure to be built, or with houses or buildings already in place.

Typically, residential developers:

- Make a feasibility study of the prospective development
- Execute an option or purchase agreement for a large tract of land
- Obtain the necessary zoning changes
- Obtain early financing from financial institutions or through syndication
- Install improvements, such as streets, sewer, water, electricity, and gas lines
- Arrange for amenities like parks, playgrounds, golf courses, swimming pools, etc.
- Take care of legal arrangements, such as deeds and title evidence, for each lot
- Market and sell the individual lots
- Construct buildings

Title Work

Real estate title work is a growing field. More and more brokers and attorneys, as well as banks, are entering the title market. New regulations are making it easier for companies to provide homebuyers with more than one service as long as there is proper disclosure. Title work is a natural extension of many other real estate service businesses.

There are several functions within the area of title work with career potential including research, escrow, and insurance.

Urban Planning

Urban planning is thriving in New York. And those who have experience in real estate can benefit from the many opportunities available. Typically, those involved in urban or city planning are concerned with the orderly growth and development of a city. Ensuring adequate and appropriate resources for the city's housing, business, industry, transportation, distribution, recreation, culture, comfort, convenience, health, and welfare of its population are all within the city planner's realm.

Putting Your Prelicensing Education to Use

Whether you choose to go into real estate sales or another real estate-related career, you'll find the knowledge and insight you gain from studying for and obtaining a real estate license are well worth the effort. You'll feel confident as you pursue your career goals, and demonstrate to your employer your ambition and foresight.

Real estate is one of the few careers where pure ability is all that matters. Many brokers use performance as their only employment test and rate desire as their most important criterion. If you are good with people and perform well, then you're a coveted individual in an industry where performance and personal service go hand in hand.

Personal Considerations

There are a number of factors to take into account when choosing the best path for a real estate career. After confirming your preference for a real estate sales career over a career in another aspect of real estate, you must then select a broker with whom you will work.

There are many factors to consider when choosing a broker. These factors include different levels of training and staff support, as well as different compensation plans. You will see there are many forms the broker-salesperson relationship can take.

What's Next?

Once you complete your pre-licensing coursework, and take and pass the state licensing exam, what's next? Now is the time to **choose a broker**. Choosing a broker is one of the most important decisions you will make. You will want to listen carefully and ask questions when talking with prospective brokers. The three main areas to consider include:

1. Level of training offered by the broker.
2. Services, like support staff, offered to agents whether you work in the office or from home.
3. Payment arrangement

These areas are important to all agents, especially those just starting in the field. Let's take a closer look at each area.

Level of Training

Training varies widely from broker to broker and consists of everything from assistance with completing contracts, forms, and other documents, to how to close a transaction. Many large brokerages use standardized training programs and require all new licensees to complete them. These training sessions cover a broad range of topics including how to sell yourself and your company to prospective clients. This can be very helpful in obtaining new listings. Some will assign you phone time, or even assign a mentor to walk you through some processes and procedures.

Typically, smaller brokerages do not have formal training programs, but they still offer assistance. This type of arrangement usually gives you direct contact with the broker, allowing you to profit directly from his experience. To find the right brokerage, decide which level of training you are most comfortable with and what best suits your individual needs.

Support Services

Support services are tools available to help you do your job effectively and efficiently. Typical support services include:

- Technical support
- Administrative support
- Help with advertising

Compensation Plan

Compensation plans vary from office to office. Smaller brokerages have more flexibility when it comes to determining commission splits. They may be able to offer you a 40/60 or 50/50 split. National franchises, on the other hand, may have to adhere to guidelines set by corporate offices.

Some firms may allow you to keep 100% of your commission and charge you a monthly fee instead—even if you do not have a closing in a particular month. As you can see, there are pros and cons to both the split and keeping your entire commission. Luckily, many brokerages offer choices in the middle. You will want to do extensive research and ask many questions to find the compensation plan right for you and your income requirements.

Professional Considerations

Again, there are a number of real estate career choices available to you. You have many decisions to make even after you decide to begin your career as a real estate salesperson. There are many specializations within real estate sales, as well as professional organizations you can join, and many professional designations you can achieve.

Specializations within Real Estate Sales

Although there are a few laws specific to one type of property or another, the New York real estate license requirements apply uniformly to all types of real estate. The main obstacles in moving from one specialization to another are the special terminology for a particular kind of real estate and finding a broker willing to act as a mentor in helping you learn what is needed to be competent and successful in a highly specialized area.

Residential Properties

Residential properties include single-family homes, multi-family residences, condominiums, and cooperatives.

Single-Family Residential Properties. The majority of new licensees begin their work in the single-family residential market. Most brokers actively recruit salespersons to work in this area since there are more single-family homes on the market than any other type of property.

From the perspective of new licensees, beginning in single-family home sales is a logical choice since they probably know at least a few people who may be in the market for a home—whether to live in or for investment purposes. Further, many people may have some familiarity with this area of real estate through personal experience. Finally, there is less technical knowledge required to become competent in this area.

Multi-Family Residential Properties. Multi-family residential properties can be anything from a simple twin-single (or double or duplex) to a large apartment building. The typical buyer in this category is an investor rather than a homebuyer.

Condominiums and Cooperatives. While not exactly the same, these types of properties are similar to both single-family and multi-family residences. There are special rules for how each operates, and you should be familiar with these before listing and selling them.

Commercial Properties

Commercial properties include office buildings, stores, hotels, and other buildings used for commercial purposes. Those dealing in commercial properties are usually involved in sales and in other aspects of brokerage like leasing and leasebacks, property management, appraisal, and even construction and financing.

Property Management

This area involves the operation of property as a business. Both residential and commercial property owners can have property management responsibilities such as renting, rent collection, and maintenance.

Industrial Properties

People involved with industrial brokerage must be familiar with many of the same areas needed for commercial properties. Typically, a person will specialize in commercial *and* industrial properties because there is less demand for industrial services only, and a high level of experience and expertise is required.

Farm Properties

This area of specialization is waning due to the decline in the number of family-run farms and the widespread sale of farmland for other uses. Although, in some parts of the country, the buying and selling of farmland is thriving and requires the expertise of a licensee familiar with the unique attributes of farm property.

Professional Organizations

As a real estate professional, you can choose to join one or more of many national, state, and local professional organizations. Besides the networking opportunities, knowledge sharing, and professional growth, each organization has its own benefits.

National Association of REALTORS®

Founded in 1908, *the primary organization real estate licensees join is the* **National Association of REALTORS® (NAR®)**. To be a full member of the NAR®, a person must be licensed in an individual state and must join a local real estate board that is a member of the **New York State Association of REALTORS®**, which is in turn a member of the NAR®.

Any person who has a real estate license is a *real estate licensee* and must abide by the ***Code of Ethics and Standards of Practices***, which was first published in 1913 and is often referred to as simply the *Code of Ethics*. For a copy of the *Code of Ethics and Standards of Practice*, visit the NAR's® Web site at www.realtor.org.

It is important to note a real estate licensee is ***not*** automatically a **REALTOR®.** Only those who join the National Association of REALTORS® may use the term REALTOR® because it is a registered trademark of the NAR®.

Membership in the NAR® is not mandatory *unless* your sponsoring broker is also a member. Even though membership is not mandatory, many licensees choose to join to take advantage of the benefits of membership, including:

1. Participation in the **Multiple Listing Service (MLS®)**.
2. The right to use the trademarked term, **REALTOR®**.
3. Political and legislative voice at all levels of government defending the interests of the real estate industry.
4. Education and training that allow agents to earn professional designations.
5. Real estate business publications.
6. The use of standardized real estate forms.

The **MLS®** *is a service whereby local member brokers agree to share listings, and further agree to share commissions on properties sold jointly*. The MLS generally consists of online computer services.

Association of Real Estate License Law Officials (ARELLO)

ARELLO was founded in 1930 to facilitate the exchange of information and cooperation among regulators and policy makers in the area of real property. Back then this concept existed as a handful of individuals around a table License Law officials on state commissions established ARELLO in 1930. The first laws were passed in California. Through the efforts of ARELLO each state now has licensing laws. Each state has adopted legislation to protect the public. ARELLO has created standards and approves distance learning and continuing education for many states, including New York. For more information, see: www.arello.org

ARELLO Mission, Purpose, and Goals

Mission: Support jurisdictions in the administration and enforcement of real estate license laws to promote and protect the public interest

Vision: The essential link for making regulation better.

Core Purpose: To promote excellence in real estate regulation.

Core Values: We value...

- Protection of the public interest;
- Freedom from undue influence;
- The exchange of information and the creation of knowledge; and
- An inclusive community, with cooperation among regulators and jurisdictions.

National Association of Real Estate Brokers

Another professional organization is the *National Association of Real Estate Brokers* (NAREB), comprised mostly of minority brokers. Members of the NAREB use the term Realtist. Members agree voluntarily to follow the NAREB Code of Ethics in addition to the NAR® Code of Ethics.

Women's Council of REALTORS®

The *Women's Council of REALTORS®* (WCR®) is devoted to addressing the issues, needs, and concerns of women in the real estate profession. The WCR® was originally formed in response to discrimination that kept women from full participation in the NAR®, but now the WCR® is affiliated with the NAR®.

Besides joining the NAR® or other professional organizations, you may also want to consider joining your local Chamber of Commerce, a civil service club, and other local organizations that allow you to network. This is especially important when first starting in the real estate industry.

Professional Designations

Professional designations signify experience and expertise in real estate. Each designation has its own criteria. So, as you begin thinking about areas of specialization, also think about how you can earn the corresponding professional designation.

NAR® Designations and Certifications

- **Accredited Buyer Representative® (ABR)** can be earned by a member of the NAR® who completes an extensive classroom training program on buyer agency practices and procedures, passes a written exam, and submits evidence of practical experience as a buyer representative.
- **Accredited Buyer Representative Manager® (ABRM)** is geared to real estate brokers, office/franchise owners, and managers who have or wish to incorporate buyer representation into their daily practice.
- **Accredited Land Consultants (ALC)** are the recognized experts in land brokerage transactions of five specialized types: 1. farms and ranches, 2. undeveloped tracts of land, 3. transitional and development land, 4. subdivision and wholesaling of lots, and 5. site selection and assemblage of land parcels.
- **Accredited Residential Manager (ARM)** is given by the NAR's® Institute of Real Estate Management (IREM) to those who specialize in managing residential properties.
- **At Home with Diversity Certification (AHWD)** relays to the public that those certified have been professionally trained in and are sensitive to a wide range of

cultural issues, inviting a wide volume of business from a variety of cultures.

- **Certified International Property Specialist (CIPS)** focuses specifically on the "international" market. The network is comprised of 1,500 real estate professionals from 50 countries who deal in all types of real estate.
- **Certified Property Manager (CPM)** is awarded by the NAR's® Institute of Real Estate Management (IREM) to real estate property managers.
- **Certified Real Estate Brokerage Manager (CRB)** is given by the Real Estate Brokerage Manager's Council to those who complete required coursework, which varies by experience.
- **Certified Residential Specialist (CRS)** is given by the Residential Sales Council of the NAR® to those who complete CRS courses and who have closed a certain number of transactions.
- **Counselor of Real Estate (CRE)** is given by the NAR's® American Society of Real Estate Counselors to asset managers and others. Membership is by invitation only.
- **e-PRO®** is a training program presented entirely online to certify real estate agents and brokers as Internet Professionals.
- **General Accredited Appraiser (GAA)** is given by the NAR's® Appraisal Section to those with 1,000 hours of appraisal experience and 60 hours of appraisal coursework above state mandates.
- **Graduate, Realtor Institute (GRI)** is often the first designation a REALTOR® achieves. The designation is awarded by the NAR® to agents who have completed 90 hours of coursework on topics like marketing and real estate law.
- **Performance Management Network (PMN)** is a REALTOR® designation focusing on the idea that to enhance your business you must enhance yourself. The curriculum covers topics like negotiating strategies and tactics, networking and referrals, business planning and systems, personal performance management, and cultural differences in buying and selling.
- **Residential Accredited Appraiser (RAA)** is given by the NAR's® Appraisal Section to those with 1,000 hours of appraisal experience and 45 hours of appraisal coursework above state mandates.
- **REALTOR® Association Certified Executive (RCE)** is for association executives interested in demonstrating commitment to the field of REALTOR® association management.
- **Real Estate Professional Assistant SM (REPA)** is a comprehensive two-day certificate course that provides an intensive introduction to the real estate business and to the specific ways support staff can become valuable assets to their employers. Every administrative employee in the brokerage office, from listing secretary to the personal assistant, will benefit tremendously from this quick-start program.
- **Resort and Second-Home Property Specialist (RSPS)** is for agents specializing in resort and second-home markets. The RSPS core certification requirements include the NAR® Resort and Second-Home Market Course and the RLI Tax-Deferred (1031) Exchange Course. RSPS applicants will also choose from nine different electives including courses from the NAR® Education Matrix and the NAR® Resort Symposium held every 18 months.
- **Society of Industrial and Office Realtors® (SIOR)** is a designation available to members of this NAR®-affiliated organization, and is concerned primarily with the sale of factories, warehouses, and other industrial properties.
- **Transnational Referral Certification** prepares real estate professionals to make and receive compensated referrals using the Transnational Referral system developed by the International Consortium of Real Estate Associations (ICREA).

Other Designations and Certifications

The NAR® is not the only professional organization that awards designations and certifications. In fact, you would probably be surprised by the number of organizations that award professional designations. Let's look at several of those.

- **ASA Senior Member**, **ASA Senior Residential Member**, and **ASA Fellow** are offered by the *American Society of Appraisers* (ASA) to members who meet its criteria.
- **Certified Commercial Investment Member (CCIM)** is awarded by the *CCIM Institute* and is a recognized expert in commercial and investment real estate.
- **Commercial Specialist Designation (CSD)** is given to agents who successfully complete coursework designed to give residential agents a look at the commercial side of real estate.
- **Distinguished Real Estate Instructor (DREI)** is awarded by the *Real Estate Educators Association* (REEA) and shows excellence among real estate instructors.
- **IFAS Senior Member** and **IFAC Appraiser-Counselor** are designations offered by the *National Association of Independent Fee Appraisers* (NAIFA) to members who meet its criteria.
- **Member Appraisal Institute (MAI)** is the highest designation offered by The Appraisal Institute to members who meet its criteria.
- **New Home Specialist Designation (NHSD)** is given to agents who successfully complete the coursework designed for those who want to make their mark in the lucrative, but increasingly competitive, field of new builds.
- **Property Management Specialist Designation (PMSD)** is given to agents who successfully complete coursework designed to enhance property management skills and knowledge of acquisitions, financing, leasing, ethics, and legal issues.
- **Real Estate Cyberspace Specialist Designation (RECS)** is earned by becoming a member of the *Real Estate Cyberspace Society,* taking a Selling in Cyberspace course, and completing an individual practicum. The designation distinguishes the recipient as a professional who is proficient in computer and Internet disciplines as well as one who stays current with industry advances and services.
- **Real Property Administrator (RPA)** is awarded to property managers for completing courses offered by the *Building Owners and Managers Institute International*, an independent institute affiliated with *Building Owners and Managers Association*.
- **Residential Specialist Designation (RSD)** is given to agents who successfully complete coursework designed to help new agents avoid many common mistakes.
- **Senior Real Estate Specialist (SRES)** is a designation of the *Senior Advantage Real Estate Council* (SAREC) aimed at those interested in the "over 55" client niche and those looking to enhance their status from "salesperson" to that of "counselor."

ALWAYS REMEMBER!

What would you attempt to do

If you knew you could not fail

unknown

SUMMARY

1. New York State law requires anyone who, for a fee, sells, lists, leases, exchanges, negotiates, or otherwise deals in the real estate of others, must be licensed. *Exceptions* to the license law: 1. attorneys licensed to practice in New York, 2. building supervisors or maintenance workers, 3. persons acting in any capacity under the judgment or order of a court, 4. property owners, 5. public officers, and 6. tenants' associations and nonprofit corporations.

2. Licensed real estate sales professionals *obtain listing contracts from sellers*, then *search for ready, willing, and able buyers for properties they have listed*. You can also choose to *work with buyers and show them properties listed by other brokers.* **Advantages** to real estate sales are unlimited compensation potential, controlling your time, minimum office time, and the potential to own your own brokerage with additional training, education, and experience. **Disadvantages** are possible non-steady income, seasonal/cyclical real estate swings, and the need to work evenings and weekends.

3. **Three main areas to consider when choosing a broker**: 1. *level of training offered*, 2. *broker services*, and 3. *compensation structure*. Training can include assistance with completing contracts, forms, etc., phone time, and advice on how to close a sale. *Services* may include support staff, advertising, and staff to answer the phone. *Commission* splits vary, but may increase if you pay for your own supplies, services, fees, etc.

4. **Areas of specialization** within real estate sales include *residential* (single-family residences, multi-family residences, condominiums, cooperatives), *commercial* (including property management), *industrial*, and *farm* properties.

5. Real estate licensees must join the National Association of REALTORS® (NAR®) and affiliated state and local boards *if their broker is a member*. Benefits to joining include access to the Multiple Listing Service (MLS®) and use of the term REALTOR®. Only members may use the term REALTOR® because it is a registered trademark of the NAR®. *Realist* is the term used by members of the National Association of Real Estate Brokers. Professional designations can be earned by licensees who meet the requirements of different organizations.

6. People who enjoy working in real estate but desire a more predictable income might consider one of the many alternative real estate careers, which can be less susceptible to real estate cycles. Real estate is one of the few careers where ability is all that matters. If you can perform well, and you are good with people, then you have a good chance of succeeding in real estate.

1

The Independent Contractor or Employee

In This Session

Most real estate licensees operate as independent contractors, not as employees of the broker; however, the distinction is important. Whether a salesperson is legally considered an employee or an independent contractor affects both the business relationship and taxation issues.

You'll learn:

- Differentiate between employees and independent contractors
- Identify the criteria that must be met to be classified as an independent contractor
- Describe state and federal laws related to independent contractors

Key Terms

- Employee
- Independent Contractor
- Statutory Employee
- Statutory Non-employees

Broker Supervision of Salesperson

The supervision of a real estate salesperson by a licensed real estate broker, required by subdivision (d) of **Section 441 of the Real Property Law**, shall consist of regular, frequent and consistent personal guidance, instruction, oversight and superintendence by the real estate broker with respect to the general real estate brokerage business conducted by the broker, and all matters relating thereto. The broker and salesperson shall keep written records of all real estate listings obtained by the salesperson, and of all sales and other transactions effected by, and with the aid and assistance of, the salesperson, during the period of his association, which records shall be sufficient to clearly identify the transactions and shall indicate the dates thereof. Such records must be submitted by the salesperson to the Department of State with his application for a broker's license. IRS independent contractor laws differ from New York. Under IRS codes there is no legal duty to supervise an independent contractor. The IRS made an exception in its regulations for real estate salespersons and brokers. The IRS regulations allow the independent contractor relationship and tax regulations to apply to licensed real estate salespersons and brokers.

Independent Contractor or Employee

Most real estate licensees operate as independent contractors – not as employees of the broker. It is sometimes difficult to classify a worker as an employee or independent contractor. From the Internal Revenue Service and New York law view, the most important principal of the independent contractor relationship is in which the employer does not have the right to control the details of the workers performance. Other issues to consider when determining independent contractor status include:

- When and where to do the work
- What tools or equipment to use
- Who to hire or assist with the work
- Where to purchase supplies and services
- If the worker has work hours set by his employer
- If the worker is paid by the job
- What work must be performed by an individual
- What order or sequence to follow

How the independent contractor or employee is paid directly affects the classification. If the worker is an employee then the worker's employer must withhold federal, state, and Social Security taxes. The employer would have to pay federal and state unemployment taxes, and give the worker a W-2, W-3, and form 940.

If the worker is classified as an independent contractor, then the employer will not have pay any of the taxes and no money is taken from the worker's paycheck. If the worker earns $600.00 or more, the employer must file only a form 1099MISC with the IRS to report the earnings. The worker must also pay self-employment taxes.

When licensees work for a real estate broker, their employment is classified in one of four ways:

1. **Independent contractor.** The worker does not work under the direct supervision of his employer.
2. **Employee.** Trade or profession of worker is holding employee status.

3. **Statutory employee.** The work, trade, or profession of worker is as legal statutes hold employee status.
4. **Statutory non-employee.** The trade or profession of this worker is written into legal statutes as holding non-employee status. Worker who holds this status under law are classified as independent contractor.

Internal Revenue Code Section 3508[a][b]

According to IRS code, real estate salespeople are statutory non-employees, therefore independent contractors. The real estate agent must be licensed and all monies received are for services must be related to output or sales not the number of hours worked. The law states there must be a written agreement between the sales associate and the broker and it must clearly define that the licensee is not an employee for federal ax purposes. The independent contractor agreement must be reviewed every 12-15 months to ensure compliance. The agreement cannot be signed under duress or undue influence by either party.

Independent Contractor and New York Law

There are two specific codes found in New York law directing the operation of independent contractor relationships:

Supervision by Broker

Regulation 175.21 Supervision of salesperson by broker

(a) The supervision of a real estate salesperson by a licensed real estate broker, required by subdivision l(d) of Section 441 of the Real Property Law, shall consist of regular, frequent and consistent personal guidance, instruction, oversight and superintendence by the real estate broker with respect to the general real estate brokerage business conducted by the broker, and all matters relating thereto.

(b) The broker and salesperson shall keep written records of all real estate listings obtained by the salesperson, and of all sales and other transactions effected by, and with the aid and assistance of, the salesperson, during the period of his association, which records shall be sufficient to clearly identify the transactions and shall indicate the dates thereof. Such records must be submitted by the salesperson to the Department of State with his application for a broker's license.

(c) Participation in the general real estate brokerage business as a licensed real estate salesperson shall consist of active service under the supervision of a licensed real estate broker for at least 35 hours per week for 50 weeks in each year required for qualification under the law.

Records to be Maintained

Regulation 175.23 Records of transactions to be maintained

(a) Each licensed broker shall keep and maintain for a period of three years, records of each transaction effected through his office concerning the sale or mortgage of one- to four-family dwellings. Such records shall contain the names and addresses of the seller, the buyer, mortgagee, if any, the purchase price and resale price, if any, amount of deposit paid on contract, amount of commission paid to broker or gross profit realized by the broker if purchased by him for resale, expenses of procuring the mortgage loan, if any, the net commission or net profit realized by the broker showing the disposition of all payments made by the broker. In lieu thereof each broker shall keep and maintain, in connection with each such transaction a copy of (1) contract of sale, (2) commission agreement, (3) closing statement, (4) statement showing disposition of proceeds of mortgage loan.

(b) Each licensed broker engaged in the business of soliciting and granting mortgage loans to purchasers of one to four family dwellings shall keep and maintain for a period of three years, a record of the name of the applicant, the amount of the mortgage loan, the closing statement with the disposition of the mortgage proceeds, a copy of the verification of employment and financial status of the applicant, a copy of the inspection and compliance report with the Baker Law requirements of FHA with the name of the inspector. Such records shall be available to the Department of State at all times upon request.

Noncompliance

If sales associates are not deemed independent contractors they will not be able to file schedule C of the federal income tax form 1040 and deduct the expenses associated with the industry. This key reason is why new sales associates should retain accountants that have real estate knowledge.

If sales associate is not classified as an independent contractor, rather an employee, it will cost the employer a large amount of money. Because of this the employer will have to pay all employment taxes.

Elements of the Independent Contractor Relationship

Several elements are present in every relationship with an independent contractor. These elements help provide clear classification of the relationship between the employing firm and the independent contractor. When we limit our view to the realm of real estate, these characteristics can be more firmly defined. Common characteristics of the broker-independent contractor relationship include:

- Compensation is paid only for output without regard for the number of hours worked
- Compensation is paid without any deductions for taxes, and the independent contractor is solely responsible for the payment of the taxes to the appropriate agencies
- Salespersons determine their own work hours, depending on the needs of their clients
- Brokers can provide an office and supplies, but salespersons are responsible for expenses incurred.
- Salespersons are free to engage in outside employment.
- The broker may direct and supervise, but does not fully control the actions of the salesperson
- The agreement may be terminated by either the salesperson or the broker at any time
- Law also requires a written agreement, executed by both parties without duress or undue influence by either party

When Looking for a Broker

You've done your research about different professions; evaluated your strengths, weaknesses, interests, and goals; and are now ready to launch your new career in real estate. One of the first decisions you will need to make is selecting a brokerage affiliation – one that will help you establish your career and support you while you

INDEPENDENT CONTRACTOR RELATIONSHIP AGREEMENT

AGREEMENT, this day of , 200 , by and between ______________________________residing at ____ (hereinafter referred to as the "Sales Associate") and ____ having a principal place of business at ____ (hereinafter referred to as the "Broker").

WITNESSETH:

WHEREAS, Sales Associate and Broker are each respectively duly licensed pursuant to Article 12-A of the Real Property Law of the State of New York, and WHEREAS, the parties hereto have freely and voluntarily entered into this Agreement, without duress.

NOW, THEREFORE, in consideration of the mutual promises herein contained, it is hereby agreed as follows:

1. Sales Associate is engaged as an independent contractor associated with the Broker pursuant to Article 12-A of the Real Property Law and shall be treated as such for all purposes, including but not limited to Federal and State Income taxation, withholding tax regulations, Unemployment Insurance and Workers' Compensation coverages.

2. Sales Associate (a) shall be paid a commission on Sales Associate's gross sales, if any, without deduction for taxes, which commission shall be directly related to sales or other output; (b) shall not be entitled to a draw against commissions; (c) shall not receive any remuneration related to the number of hours worked; and (d) shall not be treated as an employee with respect to such services for Federal and State Income tax purposes.

3. Sales Associate shall be permitted to work such hours as Sales Associate may elect to work.

4. Sales Associate shall be permitted to work out of Sales Associate's residence or the offices of Broker or any other location in the sole discretion of Sales Associate.

5. Sales Associate shall be free to engage in outside employment.

6. Broker may provide office facilities and supplies for the use of Sales Associate. All other expenses, including but not limited to automobile, travel, and entertainment expenses shall be borne by Sales Associate.

7. Broker may offer initial training and hold periodic sales meetings. The attendance by Sales Associate at such sessions shall be at the option of Sales Associate.

8. Broker may offer a group insurance plan, and if Sales Associate wishes to participate therein all premiums shall be paid by Sales Associate.

9. Broker may elect, but shall be under no obligation, to assign leads to Sales Associate on a rotating basis. Sales Associate shall be responsible for procuring Sales Associate's own leads.

10. Broker and Sales Associate shall comply with the requirements of Article 12-A of the Real Property Law and the regulations pertaining thereto. Such compliance shall not affect Sales Associate's status as an independent contractor nor shall such compliance be construed as an indication that Sales Associate is an employee of Broker for any purpose whatsoever.

11. This contract and the association created thereby may be terminated by either party hereto at any time upon notice given by one party to the other.

12. For purposes of this Agreement the term "Broker" shall include individual real estate brokers, real estate brokerage companies, real estate brokerage corporations and any other entity acting as a principal broker and the term "Sales Associate" shall include real estate sales associates and real estate brokers, who, as real estate licensees, associate with and place their real estate license with a principal broker.

13. Sales Associate hereby agrees to and hereby assigns to Broker irrevocably and without the necessity of any additional consideration, all of Sales Associate's right, title and interest in any copyright rights or other intellectual property rights in any property listing posted by Sales Associate in the MLS system or otherwise provided to the MLS. Such right, title and interest shall be deemed assigned as of the moment of creation without any further action on the part of either party. During and after the term of this independent contractor agreement, Sales Associate shall confirm such assignment by executing and delivering such assignments or other instruments and take any action necessary to enable Broker to secure, protect, enforce and defend its copyrights in such data and/or content.

http://www.nysar.com/members/legal/indcontr.asp 4/14/2008

Source: New York State Association of REALTORS®, Inc.

14. This Agreement shall be governed and construed in accordance with the laws of the State of New York.

15. No waiver of any of the provisions of this agreement or any of the rights or remedies of the parties hereto shall be valid unless such waiver is in writing, signed by the party to be charged therewith.

16. Whenever in this Agreement any notices are required to be given, such notices shall be in writing and shall be sent by registered mail or certified mail, return receipt requested, to the party entitled to receive the same.

17. This Agreement and all of its terms, covenants and provisions insofar as applicable, shall be binding upon and inure to the benefit of the parties hereto, their respective heirs, executors, administrators, successors and assigns.

IN WITNESS WHEREOF, the individual parties hereto have hereunto set their hands and seals, and any corporate party has caused this instrument to be signed by a corporate officer and caused its corporate seal to be hereunto affixed, all as of the day and year first above written.

____
Sales Associate

(SEAL) ______________________
Broker

*Optional clause for inclusion in Independent Contractor Agreement

"The parties acknowledge that Broker has elected to maintain membership as a REALTOR with an affiliated Board of the New York State and National Association of REALTORS. Associate agrees to maintain individual membership status in the Board of Realtors and Associate agrees to adhere to the REALTOR Code of Ethics."

ACKNOWLEDGMENTS

STATE OF NEW YORK)

COUNTY OF) ss:

On the day of in the year 20 , before me the undersigned, a Notary Public in and for said State, personally appeared . , personally known to me or proved to me on the basis of satisfactory evidence to be the individual whose name is subscribed to the within instrument and acknowledged to me that he executed the same in his capacity, and that by his signature on the instrument, the individual, or the person upon behalf of which the individual acted, executed the instrument.

____
Notary Public
STATE OF NEW YORK)
COUNTY OF)

On the day of in the year 20 , before me the undersigned, a Notary Public in and for said State, personally appeared , personally known to me or proved to me on the basis of satisfactory evidence to be the individual whose name is subscribed to the within instrument and acknowledged to me that he executed the same in his capacity, and that by his signature on the instrument, the individual, or the person upon behalf of which the individual acted, executed the instrument.

____
Notary Public

grow your skills, experience, and business. In fact, this is one of the most important decisions you will make, because the company you select to first "hang your license" with can make or break your real estate career. Entry into the real estate field depends on education, training and interests. Most people begin as sales trainees in a brokerage firm. Other possibilities include office assistant, listing or rental agent, assistant in a department of a large real estate organization. No matter what field you are going into, you must be focused and ask questions. As you will be interviewed by brokers you should interview them also.

When you are face to face with a broker in negotiating an employment contract, remember to stay motivated and professional. Ask questions you feel are important

QUESTION TO ASK BROOKER

- What is the specific focus of the firm: Sales, Leasing? Is it local or part of a franchise? Any other offices?
- What is the commission or fee schedule and what is the commission split for sales agents?
- What are the specific duties, i.e, floor time, phone duty, and so on?
- Are you a member of the MLS? What are the start-up fees, including training if there is any?
- What types of leads will there be, if any?
- What is expected with regard to the first six months or year?
- What specifically will the broker and company do to assist me with my goals?
- Most importantly, what type of training is there? You are looking for formal training, not once in awhile.

These are only a few suggestions when talking to broker. It would be a good idea if you think of anything, ask. Don't assume.

SUMMARY

1. Most real estate licensees operate as independent contractors and not as employees of the broker. The factors that determine whether the relationship is contract or employee are: the amount of control, direction, and supervision the broker has over the services being performed.
2. Licensees working for a broker can be classified in one of four ways: 1. statutory employee, 2. statutory non-employee, 3. independent contractor, or 4. employee.
3. The two major differences between the four classifications are: 1. who directs activities and 2. who pays payroll taxes. Independent contractors decide how to accomplish a given task; the payer determines the desired end result. Employees are directed by employers who determine the result and how they want it to be achieved. Statutory employees are independent contractors who are classified as employees for Social Security and Medicare taxes. Statutory non-employees are treated as independent contractors provided they meet specific criteria.
4. Three categories of common law rules determine whether the relationship between a worker and business is that of an employee or independent contractor: 1. behavioral control, 2. financial control, and 3. type of relationship of the parties.
5. Independent contractors must make sure they meet the criteria for claiming independent contractor status; otherwise, the business and licensee could face fines and penalties from the IRS.

1-A

Real Estate License Law

In This Session

In this session, you'll learn about real estate licensing law in general and the New York State agencies that regulate real estate licensees. You'll understand why a license is necessary and who must be licensed, and you'll also be able to distinguish between brokers and salespersons. The information in this session is the foundation for your new career

You'll learn:

- List the different types of real estate license categories.
- Identify the types of real estate broker licenses.
- Explain the requirements to become a real estate broker or salesperson.
- Explain a broker's responsibility to the salesperson.
- Identify acts that could warrant the suspension or revocation of a license.

- Administrative Discipline
- Article 12-A
- Article 78 Proceeding
- Associate Broker
- Blind Ad
- Broker
- Commingling
- Continuing Education
- Dual Agent
- Dual Licensure
- Escrow
- Exemption
- Irrevocable Consent
- Kickback
- Listing Agreement
- Misdemeanor
- Multiple Listing Service
- Net Listing Agreement
- Office Manager
- Pocket Card
- Real Estate Appraiser
- Real Estate Salesperson
- Reciprocity
- Revocation
- Sponsoring Broker
- Suspension
- Violation

New York Department of State

The New York State Department of State's **Division of Licensing Services** plays an important role for consumers, occupational licensees, applicants and the business community in New York State. The Division is responsible for the licensure, registration and/or regulation of the following:

- Real estate brokers and salespersons
- Apartment information vendors
- Apartment sharing agents
- Real estate appraisers
- Notaries public
- Home inspectors

The mission of the Division is to protect the health, safety and welfare of consumers; to provide efficient processing and examination services to license applicants; and to provide accurate information and qualified licensees to the business community.

Most of the laws pertaining to salespersons and brokers is contained in **Article 12-A** of the Real Property Law. Other laws, rules and regulations cover the licensure process. As referenced in the previous paragraph New York authority is to protect the public. The purpose is to protect the public from dishonest dealings with brokers or salespeople. They are subject to administrative discipline by the Department of State.

License Categories

The three real estate license categories in New York are:

- Broker.
- Associate broker.
- Salesperson.

A **real estate broker** means *any person, firm, limited liability company or corporation, who, for another and for a fee, commission or other valuable consideration, lists for sale, sells, at auction or otherwise, exchanges, buys or rents, or offers or attempts to negotiate a sale, at auction or otherwise, exchange, purchase or rental of an estate or interest in real estate, or collects or offers or attempts to collect rent for the use of real estate.* Real estate brokers supervise and are responsible for associate brokers and salespersons under their sponsorship.

An **associate real estate broker** is *a licensed broker who chooses to work under the name and supervision of another broker licensed to do business as an individual, partnership, corporation, or trade name*. When an individual applies for the associate broker's license, his supervising broker must sign the association statement. The associate broker also retains the right to be licensed as a broker under a separate broker's license, which can be registered as an individual, partnership, trade name, limited liability company, or corporation. Associate brokers follow the same rules as salesperson except they must use the words "associate broker."

A **real estate salesperson** is *any person who performs the acts of a broker, but does so only when associated and sponsored by a licensed broker.*

Office Manager

As of July 2008, an **office manager** may be a licensed associate real estate broker who by choice elects to work as an office manager under the name and supervision of an individual broker or another broker who is licensed under a partnership, trade name, limited liability company, or corporation. The office manager retains his license as a real estate broker, but operates under the provisions of a salesperson. He may elect to retain a separate broker's license under an individual, partnership, trade name, limited liability company (LLC), or corporation. **Someone licensed as a salesperson cannot manage an office.**

General Licensing Qualifications

In order to become licensed in New York, prospective real estate salespersons or brokers must meet several qualifications.

- Article12-A specifically states applicants must have fair knowledge of the English language. Dictionaries are not permitted during the licensing exam.
- Requirements for a **broker license** must be 20 years of age, a U.S. citizen or lawfully admitted permanent resident. No person shall be entitled to a license as a real estate salesperson under this article unless he or she is over the age of 18 years.
- No person shall be entitled to a license as a real estate broker or real estate salesperson under this article who has been convicted in this state or elsewhere of a felony, or who has not subsequent to such conviction received executive pardon therefore or a certificate of good conduct from the parole board, to remove the disability under this section because of such conviction

Age Requirements

No person shall be entitled to a license as a real estate broker unless he or she is 20 years of age or over. No person shall be entitled to a license as a real estate salesperson under this article unless he or she is over the age of 18 years.

Education and Experience

In the event the applicant shall obtain **salesperson license** they must have attended and successfully completed **75 hours** of an approved real estate course.

In determining competency for **broker license,** the department shall require proof that the person being tested to qualify to apply for a broker's license a fair understanding of the general purposes and general legal effect of deeds, mortgages, land contracts of sale, and leases, a general and fair understanding of the obligations between principal and agent, as well as of the provisions of this section. The applicant must also furnish proof that he has attended for at least **120 hours** and has successfully completed a real estate course or courses approved by the Secretary of State.

Applicants for broker or salesperson must also pass the state licensing exam.

New York Licensure Examination

Potential licensees must first register online with the Department of State (**http://www.dos.state.ny.us/lcns/realestate/index.html**) before an exam appointment may be scheduled. The exam can be taken at any time during the

> **eAccessNY**
>
> Before taking the real estate licensing examination, applicants must first register with eAccessNY, the state's licensing management system (http://www.dos.state.ny.us/lcns/realestate). Registration is simple and takes only a few minutes. After registering, applicants can:
>
> - Schedule a broker or salesperson licensing examination at one of the exam centers. (Walk-ins are not permitted.)
> - Use a credit card to pay the required examination fee.
> - See exam results.

licensing course. To take the real estate salesperson or broker examination at any of the exam centers, applicants are required to schedule an online appointment and are required to prepay a $15 examination fee. Walk-in exams are no longer permitted. All applicants are fingerprinted at the test site prior to taking the exam. Applicants should bring a silent calculator and a government-issued photo ID; acceptable forms are:

- Driver's license.
- Certificate of U.S. citizenship
- United States INS-issued ID.
- United States passport.
- State-issued ID.

The licensing exam is multiple choice and is based on the 75-hour prelicensing curriculum all applicants are required to take. Exam results are reported as pass/fail. A passing score is 70 percent. You will now be able to view your scheduled exam details or exam results and apply for your salesperson license online. The results can also be obtained online through your account at eAccessNY. If a potential licensee fails the exam, they may take it over as many times as needed, and pay the $15.00 fee. Persons with disabilities who require accessibility information should call 518-473-2731. Persons who require testing modifications should not schedule an exam and should instead call 518-473-2731.

> ***Note:* While you must complete the required 75 hours of prelicensing education before applying for a real estate salesperson license, you are NOT required to complete the required education before taking the state licensing examination. However, keep in mind that the questions on the exam are based on the topics covered in the 75-hour course.**

Examination Sites

Albany Exam Site
Alfred E. Smith State Office Building
80 South Swan Street
Albany, New York 12239

Binghamton Exam Site (State Office Building)
44 Hawley Street, 15th Floor
Binghamton, NY 13901

Buffalo Exam Site (State Office Building)
65 Court Street
Main Floor Hearing Room, Part 5
Buffalo, NY 14202

Franklin Square Exam Site (VFW Hall)
68 Lincoln Road, Basement
Franklin Square, NY 11010

Hauppauge Exam Site (Perry Duryea State Office Building)
250 Veterans Memorial Highway
Basement Conference Room
Hauppauge, NY 11788

Newburgh Exam Site (Orange Ulster BOCES Adult Educational Center)
Federal Building, 471 Broadway, 2nd Floor
Newburgh, NY 12550

New York City Exam Site
123 William Street, 19th Floor
New York, NY 10038

Plattsburgh Exam Site (Clinton County Community College)
Lake Shore Drive, Route 9 South
Plattsburgh, NY 12901

Requirements for Licensure

If any of the transactions are for others and you are compensated:

1. Offering or listing real estate for sale
2. Buying or offering to buy real estate
3. Offering or selling any real property
4. Renting, leasing
5. Selling or purchasing real estate at an auction
6. Performing any business in regard to condominium and cooperative property
7. Selling a business where the real estate transferred is greater than the business
8. Showing or discussing with anyone regarding any real property.

Licensing Exemptions

Certain individuals or groups may be exempt from real estate licensure:

1. **Attorneys** licensed to practice in New York. Note: Attorneys who establish brokerages with real estate salespersons must obtain a license, but are not required to take pre-licensing courses or the New York licensing exam, and are exempt from license renewal requirements.
2. **Building supervisors** or **maintenance workers**. Those who are hired as employees—not independent contractors—of an owner and who perform tasks on the owner's behalf, such as collecting rent or showing apartments, are not considered to be agents and therefore are not required to be licensed.
3. Persons acting in any capacity **under the judgment or order of a court**. Examples include administrators, executors, guardians, and trustees in bankruptcy cases.
4. **Property owners**. Persons dealing with their own property may engage in a real estate transaction without a license.
5. **Public officers**. While acting in official capacity, public officers do not need a real estate license.
6. **Tenants' associations and nonprofit corporations**. Agencies include residential neighborhoods and rural preservation companies authorized by the commissioner of the New York Department of Housing and Community Renewal or by the New York City Housing Authority to manage residential property owned by the state or the city.

In addition to these state exemptions, New York City has additional licensing exemptions. Tenant associations and non-profit corporations responsible for enforcing housing maintenance codes to manage residential property owned or managed by the City are exempt from New York licensing requirements.

Applying for a Salesperson's License

Application must be filed with the Department of State and must contain:

- Name and residence address of the applicant
- Name, business address of broker with whom the salesperson will associate; a statement of association; and signature by the sponsoring broker
- There are also questions regarding responsibility for child support
- Attendance and successful completion of an approved, qualified real estate program of at least 75 hours
- Proof of completion of and passing a written salesperson's examination

New York Real Estate Salesperson Application

UNIQUE ID NUMBER
(for office use only)

EFF. DATE

FEE
$50

NYS Department of State
Division of Licensing Services
P.O. Box 22001
Albany, NY 12201-2001

Real Estate Salesperson Application

Read the Instruction Sheet for details before completing this application form. You must answer each question and TYPE or PRINT responses in ink.

APPLICANT'S LAST NAME | FIRST NAME | M.I. | SUFFIX

HOME ADDRESS - NUMBER AND STREET (PHYSICAL ADDRESS REQUIRED, P.O. BOX MAY BE ADDED TO ENSURE DELIVERY) | APT/UNIT

CITY | STATE | ZIP+4 | COUNTY

DAYTIME TELEPHONE NUMBER
( )

SOCIAL SECURITY NUMBER (SEE PRIVACY NOTIFICATION)

E-MAIL ADDRESS (THIS ADDRESS WILL BE APPLICANT'S USER ID FOR ON-LINE ACCOUNT) HAS THIS E-MAIL ADDRESS CHANGED SINCE TAKING EXAMINATION? ☐ YES ☐ NO

BUSINESS NAME (EXACTLY AS IT APPEARS ON THE BROKER'S LICENSE) | OFFICE LICENSE/UNIQUE ID NUMBER (BEGINS WITH 1099, 1039 OR 39)

BUSINESS ADDRESS WHERE APPLICANT WILL BE PERMANENTLY STATIONED - NUMBER AND STREET

☐ LOCATION IS PRINCIPAL OFFICE
☐ LOCATION IS BRANCH OFFICE

CITY | STATE | ZIP+4 | COUNTY

1 Background Data

YES NO

1. What is your date of birth? ____________
2. Have you ever applied for or been issued a real estate broker's or salesperson's license in this state? ____ ____
   → **IF "YES,"** in what year? ____________ Under what name? ____________
   LICENSE/UNIQUE ID NUMBER (if applicable) ____________
3. Have you ever been convicted in this state or elsewhere of any criminal offense that is a misdemeanor or a felony? ____ ____
   → **IF "YES,"** you must submit with this application a written explanation giving the place, court jurisdiction, nature of the offense sentence and/or other disposition. You must submit a copy of the accusatory instrument (*e.g.,* indictment, criminal information or complaint) and a Certificate of Disposition. If you possess or have receive a Certificate of Relief from Disabilities, Certificate of Good Conduct or Executive Pardon, you must submit a copy with this application.
4. Are there any criminal charges (misdemeanor or felonies) pending against you in any court in this state or elsewhere? ____ ____
   → **IF "YES,"** you must submit a copy of the accusatory instrument (*e.g.,* indictment, criminal information or complaint.)
5. Has any license or permit issued to you or a company in which you are or were a principal in New York State or elsewhere ever been revoked, suspended or denied? ____ ____
   → **IF "YES,"** you must provide all relevant documents, including the agency determination, (if any).

(For Office Use Only – Revenue Unit)

Source: New York State Department of State

DOS-0022 (Rev. 6/08)

PAGE 1 OF 3

Real Estate Salesperson Application

2 Certification of Satisfactory Completion

____
(Name of School)

Real Estate Salesperson Course (Code) # S-______________

This certifies that ______________ (Name of Student) has satisfactorily completed a 75-hour salesperson qualifying course in real estate approved by the Secretary of State in accordance with the provisions of Chapter 868 of the Laws of 1977; that attendance of the student was in compliance with the law and that a passing grade was achieved on the final examination.

The course was completed on ______________.

Authorized Signature

X ______________ *Date* ______________

(School Seal)

3 Child Support Statement — *You must complete this section. If you do not complete it, your application will be returned.*

"X" A or B, below

I, the undersigned, do hereby certify that (You *must* "X" A or B, below):

A. [ ] **I am not under obligation to pay child support**. (SKIP "B" and go directly to **Applicant Affirmation**).

B. [ ] I am under obligation to pay child support (You must "X" any of the four statements below that are true and apply to you):

[ ] I do *not* owe four or more months of child support payments.

[ ] I am making child support payments by income execution or court approved payment plan or by a plan agreed to by the parties.

[ ] My child support obligation is the subject of a pending court proceeding.

[ ] I receive public assistance or supplemental social security income.

4 Applicant Affirmation — I affirm, under the penalties of perjury, that the statements made in this application are true and correct. I further affirm that I have read and understand the provisions of Article 12-A of the Real Property Law and the rules and regulations promulgated thereunder.

____
Applicant Print Name

X ______________________________ *Date* ______________
Applicant's Signature

Real Estate Salesperson Application

5 DMV Consent Section — IMPORTANT Information Regarding Your Photo ID

The Department of State produces photo ID cards in cooperation with the NYS Department of Motor Vehicles (DMV). If you have a current NYS Driver License or Non-Driver ID card, please provide your 9-digit DMV ID Number in the space provided below. Then read the informed consent and sign this form. If you do not have a current NYS photo Driver License or Non-Driver ID card, please have your photo taken at any nearby DMV office BEFORE you complete this application. For more details, refer to our enclosed notice, "Request for Photo ID."

INFORMED CONSENT

I authorize the NYS Department of State and the NYS Department of Motor Vehicles (DMV) to produce an ID card bearing my DMV photo. I understand that DMV will send this card to the address I maintain with the Department of State. I also understand that the Department of State and DMV will use my DMV photo to produce all my subsequent ID Cards for as long as I maintain my license/registration with the Department of State.

DMV ID # ___/___/___ - ___/___/___ - ___/___/___

X ____________________ ____________

Applicant's Signature *Date Signed*

6 Association Statement — I am sponsoring this application in accordance with the Real Property Law, §441.1(d).

Broker License/Unique ID number ____________________

Broker Print Name ____________________

Broker Signature ____________________ Date ____________

Please remember to include with this application any required explanations and statements along with your application fee (checks should be made payable to NYS Department of State).

It is important that you and/or your broker update any changes to your business address through your online account so you can continue to receive renewal notices and any other notifications pertinent to your license.

Types of Broker Licenses

There are six classes of licensure for which DOS offers for real estate brokers.

Broker License	Class	Description
Individual Broker	35	Conducts business under his own name. This type of license does not allow any association with a firm or company.
Associate Broker	30	Works under the name and supervision of another licensed broker.
Trade Name Broker	37	Operates the business as a sole proprietorship and does business using a business name, not a personal name.
Partnership Broker	32	Multiple brokers can apply to conduct business under a partnership name. Each individual must be a licensed real estate broker and submit an application.
Corporate Broker	31	A real estate brokerage can conduct business under the name of a corporation as long as the broker is an officer of the corporation, and was an officer before licensing. Corporate officers cannot be licensed as salespeople or associate brokers within the corporation; **they must be licensed as a broker.**
Limited Liability Company (LLC) or Limited Liability Partnership (LLP)	49	A member or manager of an LLC or LLP who completes the requirements for broker licensure can conduct business as a real estate brokerage under the LLC or LLP name.

Applying for a Broker's License

In order for the Department of State to grant a broker's license, the application is divided into several parts.

- Application must be filed with the Department of State and should contain:
  - Name and residence address; or if co-partnership, LLC, or corporation, the name and residence address of each of the members or officers.
  - The address of the place of business.
  - Provide background data regarding age, criminal record if any, associate broker applicant must have sponsoring broker sign the application or whether they are an attorney.
- Length of time engaged in the real estate business and detailing the accumulated points earned for experience as a salesperson. Must have **3,500 points.** Individuals claiming equivalent experience in general real estate along information about relevant employment history must have **5,250 points.**
- Proof of completion and passing a written broker's examination
- Must have completed 120 hours of qualified real estate coursework (75 hours salesperson education and 45 hours broker education) and two years experience as a licensed salesperson or three years qualifying experience.

Real Estate Broker/Associate Broker Application
Licensed Salespersons Activity Only

PAGE ___ OF ___

APPLICANT NAME (ENTER NAME EXACTLY AS SHOWN ON APPLICATION PAGE 1) **License/Unique ID Number**

Instructions for Completing Supplement A

You must accumulate a minimum of **3500** points* to qualify for a broker's license based on experience as a real estate salesperson. Applicants must also be licensed as a real estate salesperson for a minimum period of two years*.

1. In the Number of Transactions Performed column, enter the amount of your activity for each category.
2. Multiply the number of transactions performed by the point value indicated to arrive at the points earned for that category.
3. Add the points earned for each category to arrive at your total points.
4. Enter the total figure on the Total Qualifying Points Line. This is your final qualifying points earned.

*Except those using combined experience.

You must also complete the experience report on the other side of this page to report your qualifying experience. Points earned for that experience must be calculated below.

Category	*Point Value X*	*Number of Transactions Performed*	=	*Total Points Earned*
Residential Sales:				
1. Single Family, condo, co-op unit, multi family (2 to 8 unit), farm (with residence, under 100 acres)	250 X	______	=	______
2. Exclusive listings	10 X	______	=	______
3. Open listings	1 X	______	=	______
4. Binders effected	25 X	______	=	______
5. Co-op unit transaction approved by seller and buyer that fails to win Board of Directors approval	100 X	______	=	______
Residential Rentals:				
6. Rentals or subleases effected	25 X	______	=	______
7. Exclusive Listings	5 X	______	=	______
8. Open Listings	1 X	______	=	______
9. Property Management - Lease renewal	2 X	______	=	______
- Rent collections per tenant/per year	1 X	______	=	______
Commercial Sales:				
10. Taxpayer/Storefront	400 X	______	=	______
11. Office Building	400 X	______	=	______
12. Apartment Building (9 units or more)	400 X	______	=	______
13. Shopping Center	400 X	______	=	______
14. Factory/Industrial warehouse	400 X	______	=	______
15. Hotel/Motel	400 X	______	=	______
16. Transient garage/parking lot	400 X	______	=	______
17. Multi-unit commercial condominium	400 X	______	=	______
18. Urban commercial development site	400 X	______	=	______
19. Alternative sale type transaction	400 X	______	=	______
20. Single-tenant commercial condo	250 X	______	=	______
21. Listings	10 X	______	=	______
Commercial Leasing:				
22. New Lease - aggregate rental $1 to $200,000	150 X	______	=	______
23. New Lease - aggregate rental $200,000 to $1 million	250 X	______	=	______
24. New Lease - aggregate rental over $1 million	400 X	______	=	______
25. Renewal - aggregate rental $1 to $200,000	75 X	______	=	______
26. Renewal - aggregate rental $200,000 to $1 million	125 X	______	=	______
27. Renewal - aggregate rental over $1 million	200 X	______	=	______
28. Listings	10 X	______	=	______
Commercial Financing (includes residential properties of more than four units):				
29. $1 to $500,000	200 X	______	=	______
30. $500,000 to $5,000,000	300 X	______	=	______
31. Over $5,000,000	400 X	______	=	______
Miscellaneous:				
32. Sale vacant lots, land (under 100 acres)	50 X	______	=	______
33. Sale vacant land (more than 100 acres)	150 X	______	=	______
34. Other, must be fully explained	___X	______	=	______
Total Qualifying Points	➢			______

Source: New York State Department of State

DOS-036A (Rev. 6/08)

Maintaining a License

Licensees must have a thorough understanding of the laws and regulations. The DOS will not accept any excuse for a violation.

License and Pocket Card

The Department of State, in cooperation with the Department of Motor Vehicles, prepares, issues, and delivers license and **pocket card** containing *a photo ID, name, business address of the licensee, and for salespersons, the name, and address of the affiliated broker*. Such cards are to be carried at all times and must be shown on demand. Licensees who cannot produce their pocket card when asked are in violation of New York license law and are subject to reprimand and even suspension of their license. Lost or destroyed cards can be replaced by the Secretary of State for a $10.00 fee.

The broker license must be displayed at all times. Salesperson licenses do not have to be displayed but must be kept in a safe and accessible place.

Changes in Name, Status, or Location

Any broker who relocates his principal or branch office must notify the Department of State within five days in writing of the new principal business address for himself and the licensees working under him. A broker who fails to notify the Department of a change of address could have his license suspended. Brokers then cross out the former address on their license and also salesperson and associate brokers. The broker will print the new address on all licenses, complete a broker change of address form, send it to DOS with a $10.00 fee. Each salesperson and associate broker submits a change of address and pays $10.00 fee.

Branch Offices

Any physical location other than the main office maintained for business use to meet with clients or customers on a regular basis may be considered a branch office. A broker can have any number of branch offices throughout New York; however, each one must have its own branch office license. They can be supervised by an associate broker office manager. The fee is $150.00 for each branch office.

Fees for Licensure

A broker pays $150.00 fee and a salesperson $50.00 fee for each 2 year term.

Changes of Association

If a real estate salesperson shall leave the service of a real estate broker, the real estate broker shall file a termination of association notice on such form as secretary may designate. The salesperson's license may be endorsed to a new sponsoring broker upon the establishment of a new record of association filed with the Department of State. The fee for filing a record of association shall be $20.

Termination of Association Form

Source: New York State Department of State

SALESPERSON OR ASSOCIATE BROKER UNIQUE ID NUMBER

SALESPERSON OR ASSOCIATE BROKER NAME - PRINT LAST NAME FIRST

PLEASE TYPE OR PRINT CLEARLY

1. Sponsoring broker's business name as it appears on license — SPONSORING BROKER'S BUSINESS NAME
2. Business address — NUMBER AND STREET; CITY STATE ZIP COUNTY
3. Date of termination of association. — MONTH DAY YEAR

X SALESPERSON'S OR ASSOCIATE BROKER'S SIGNATURE

X SPONSORING BROKER'S SIGNATURE

DATE SIGNED

SPONSORING BROKER'S UNIQUE ID NUMBER

OS-0020 (Rev. 3/07)

SAMPLE

Change of Association Form

Source: New York State Department of State

SALESPERSON OR ASSOCIATE BROKER UNIQUE I.D. NO.

NAME OF SALESPERSON OR ASSOCIATE BROKER — PRINT LAST NAME FIRST

1. New business name as it is to appear on his/her license
2. Business address where salesperson or associate broker will be stationed — NUMBER AND STREET; CITY STATE ZIP COUNTY
3. Is this a branch office? YES* NO — *IF YES, SPECIFY BRANCH OFFICE UNIQUE I.D. NUMBER AS IT APPEARS ON THE LICENSE:
4. Starting date of new association (if applicable) — MO DAY YEAR
5. Previous sponsoring Broker's name

X *Sponsoring Broker's Signature*

X *Salesperson's or Associate Broker's Signature*

DOS-0021 (Rev. 3/07)

Dual Licensure

When real estate licensees hold more than one license at a time, it is **dual licensure**. Instances when this may occur are when a broker wishes to also be an associate broker with another firm; or, when a salesperson wishes to work with more than one broker. It is important to note that associate brokers and salespersons who wish to be dual licensed must obtain a statement from each sponsoring broker acknowledging each licensure

License Renewal

Real estate licenses expire after a term of two years. Licensees must file an application with the Department of State for license renewal. One or two months before renewal the DOS sends the sponsoring broker a renewal notice. Licensees may renew online or by mail. If licensees do not renew by the expiration date, they have a two year grace period from that date to renew. They may not function in real estate during this time. If licensees allow the time period to lapse they must retake and pass the exam also complete the continuing education requirements

Continuing Education

In order to renew, a licensee must complete 22.5 hours of approved continuing education courses in the two years prior to renewal. Coursework must provide at least **three hours** of instruction on fair housing or discrimination in the sale or rental of real property

Some licensees are exempt from taking continuing education courses, including:

- Attorneys who hold a license and are admitted to the New York State bar. However, attorneys must obtain a broker's license if they hire salespeople or associate brokers to assist them.
- Brokers with more than 15 years of consecutive licensure before July 1, 2008 and who are actively engaged in the real estate business. Any broker who allows his license to lapse is no longer exempt.

Reciprocity

License **reciprocity** is *when states agree to allow licensees from other states to sell real estate in their own by accepting the licensee's out-of-state course credits or license level.* Currently, there are 10 states offering reciprocity, including:

Arkansas	Broker only—two years licensure and current. (Business and Residence must be in Arkansas.)
Colorado	Broker and Associate Broker. Current licensure. (Business and residence addresses must be in Colorado). Colorado Associate Brokers must submit a salesperson application and $50 fee, along with their certification and irrevocable consent form.
Connecticut	Broker and Sales—current licensure only. (Business and Residence must be in Connecticut.)
Georgia	Broker and Sales—current licensure only (business and residence must be in Georgia). Must have obtained their license by passing Georgia exam.
Massachusetts	Broker only—two years licensure and current. (Business and Residence must be in Massachusetts.)
Mississippi	Broker and Salesperson—current licensure only (business and residence must be in Mississippi). Must have obtained their license by passing Mississippi exam.
Oklahoma	Broker and Sales—two years licensure and current. (Business and Residence must be in Oklahoma.)
Pennsylvania	Broker and Salesperson —current licensure only. (Business and Residence must be in Pennsylvania.)
West Virginia	Broker and Sales—current licensure only. (Business and Residence must be in West Virginia.)

All need **current** certification (dated within six months, from the Real Estate Commission where license was obtained), completed application, irrevocable consent form, and the appropriate fee.

Applicants seeking a reciprocal real estate salesperson's license must be sponsored by their home-state broker who must hold a current New York State broker's license.

Applicants seeking a corporate real estate broker's license must file said corporation in the New York State Corporations Bureau at 41 State Street, Albany, NY 12231, as a foreign corporation.

Licensed real estate brokers and salespersons in states outside New York can apply to do business in New York, as long as the state in which they do business is a reciprocating state. They are not required to have an office in the state of New York; however, out-of-state licensees must file an application and sign an **irrevocable consent** form, which *subjects them to the jurisdiction of the courts of the state of New York.*

Other Licenses Pertaining to Real Estate

There are other licenses related to real estate. None require a salesperson or broker license. **Licensees should be wary in engaging other activities that may pose a conflict of interest inherent in each of the licenses.**

1. **Apartment information vendor** – License fee is $400.00 per year. They furnish information regarding the location and availability of residential property.
2. **Apartment sharing agent** – License fee is $400.00 per year. They arrange and coordinate meetings between owners, who want to share their housing with others (roommates).
3. **Appraiser** – Estimates the value of real property. There are four licenses:
   - NYS Appraiser Assistant
   - NYS licensed Real Estate appraiser
   - NYS Certified Residential Appraiser
   - NYS Certified General Appraiser

   The license term is for two years. Appraiser assistant fee is $250.00 per term all other levels are $300.00 per term.
4. **Home inspector** – Individual who inspects real property. They usually perform a home inspection for the buyer. To obtain the license they must complete 100 hours of course work and 40 hours of supervised field work and pass a NYS exam. The fee is $250.00 for a 2-year term.
5. Mortgage Banker and Mortgage Broker licenses are discussed more fully in the chapters pertaining to the Mortgage section.

Place of Business and Signage

Except as otherwise provided in this article, each licensed real estate broker shall have and maintain a definite place of business within this State, and shall conspicuously post on the outside of the building in which said office is conducted a sign of a sufficient size to be readable from the sidewalk indicating the name and the business of the applicant as a licensed real estate broker, unless said office shall be located in an office, apartment or hotel building, in which event the name and the words "licensed real estate broker" shall be posted in the space provided for posting of names of occupants of the building, other than the mail box.

Where the applicant for a real estate broker's license maintains more than one place of business, the broker shall apply for and the department shall issue a supplemental license for each branch office so maintained upon payment to the Department of State for each supplemental license so issued the same fee prescribed in this article for a license to act as a real estate broker. Each such branch office shall be under the direct supervision of the broker to whom the license is issued, or a representative

- This form is to be used by a corporate applicant if the applicant is a foreign corporation.
- Nonresident individuals and partnerships must use the form on the other side of this sheet.
- This form must be signed by either the president, vice president, secretary or treasurer of the foreign corporation.

STATE OF NEW YORK
DEPARTMENT OF STATE
Division of Licensing Services

Uniform Irrevocable Consent and Designation
Foreign Corporation

This irrevocable consent and designation is made by ______________________________,
(Name of Corporation)

a corporation incorporated under the laws of the State of ____________________ on the __________ day of __________ 20 ____ , with its principal office at ______________________________.

______________________________ hereby irrevocably submits to the
(Name of Corporation)

jurisdiction of the courts of the State of New York and, further, hereby irrevocably designates the Secretary of State of the State of New York as its agent upon whom may be served any summons, subpoena or other process naming the corporation in any action or special proceeding commenced in the State of New York.

By this consent and designation, the corporation agrees that service of process upon the Secretary of State shall be, in all respects, as valid and binding as if personal service had been made upon the corporation within the State of New York.

IN WITNESS HEREOF, this consent and designation is signed by an authorized officer this __________ day of __________ 20 ______.

____
(Name of Corporation)

By: ______________________________
(Signature)

Name: ______________________________

Title: ______________________________

State of ______________________________

County of ______________________________

On this __________ day of __________ 20 ___ before me personally came ______________________________ to me known, and who, being duly sworn, did depose and say that (he)(she) resides in ______________________________ and that (he)(she) is the
(State)

______________________________ of the corporation described in and which executed the above instrument,
(Title)

and that, by order of the board of directors of the corporation, (he)(she) has executed the above document for and on behalf of the corporation by signing (his)(her) name thereto.

____
Notary Public

DOS-17 (Rev. 3/08)

Source: New York State Department of State

- This form is to be used by nonresident individuals and nonresident partnerships.
- Foreign corporations must use the form on the other side of this sheet.
- This form must be signed by all the partners of the foreign partnership.

STATE OF NEW YORK
DEPARTMENT OF STATE
Division of Licensing Services

Uniform Irrevocable Consent and Designation
Individual and Partnership

(I)(we) ____,
(Name of Individual or Partners)

doing business under the name ____,
hereby irrevocably submit(s) to the jurisdiction of the courts of the State of New York, and, further, hereby irrevocably designate(s) the Secretary of State of the State of New York as (my)(our) agent upon whom may be served any summons, subpoena or other process naming (me)(the partnership or any partner) in any action or special proceeding commenced in the State of New York.

By this consent and designation, (I)(we) agree that service of process upon the Secretary of State shall be, in all respects, as valid and binding as if personal service had been made upon (me)(the partnership and each of the partners) within the State of New York.

IN WITNESS HEREOF, this consent and designation is signed by (me) (us) this ____________________ day of ____________________ 20 ________.

Signed: ______________________________

Address: ______________________________

Signed: ______________________________

Address: ______________________________

Signed: ______________________________

Address: ______________________________

State of ____________________

County of ____________________

On this ____________ day of ____________, 20 ______ before me personally came ____________________ ______________________________ to me known and known to me to be the person(s) who (is) (are) named in and who executed the foregoing instrument, and (he)(she)(they) duly acknowledged that (he)(she)(they) executed the same.

DOS-17 (Rev. 3/08)

____
Notary Public

broker of a corporation or partnership or manager of a limited liability company holding such license, or a duly appointed office manager. Such fee shall accompany such application and shall be non-refundable.

For purposes of this subdivision, the principal residence of a real estate broker or salesperson shall not be deemed a place of business solely because such broker or salesperson shall have included the residence telephone number in his business cards.

Broker Supervision

The supervision of a real estate salesperson by a licensed real estate broker, required by subdivision l(d) of §441 of the Real Property Law, shall consist of regular, frequent and consistent personal guidance, instruction, oversight and superintendence by the real estate broker with respect to the general real estate brokerage business conducted by the broker, and all matters relating thereto.

Compensation

No real estate salesperson shall receive or demand compensation of any kind from any person, other than a duly licensed real estate broker with whom he is associated, for any service rendered or work done by such salesperson in the appraising, buying, selling, exchanging, leasing, renting or negotiating of a loan upon any real estate.

Kickbacks

No real estate broker shall pay any part of a fee, commission or other compensation received by the broker to any person for any service, help or aid rendered in any place, by such person to the broker in buying, selling, exchanging, leasing, renting or negotiating a loan upon any real estate including the resale of a condominium unless such a person be a duly licensed real estate salesperson regularly associated with such broker or a duly licensed real estate broker or a person regularly engaged in the real estate brokerage business in a state outside of New York; or is exempt from the license law.

Lawsuits for Compensation

No person, co-partnership, limited liability company or corporation shall bring or maintain an action in any court of this State for the recovery of compensation for services rendered in the buying, selling, exchanging, leasing, renting or negotiating a loan upon any real estate without alleging and proving that such person was a duly licensed real estate broker or real estate salesperson on the date when the alleged cause of action arose.

Advertising

The Department of State spells out rules brokers must follow related to advertising, including:

- All advertisements placed by a broker must indicate that the advertiser is a broker and give the name of the broker and his telephone number. Ads that do not contain this information are **blind ads**.
- All advertisements placed by a broker which state that property is in the vicinity of a geographical area or territorial subdivision must include as part of such advertisement the name of the geographical area or territorial subdivision in which such property is actually located.

The Department of State also has rules regulating licensees' business cards. Contact the DOS for further information regarding any advertisement which you may not understand the legal boundaries.

Advertising Guidelines for Business Cards

Understanding that a business card is a form of advertisement, it must conform to the general advertising standards. It must be truthful and not misleading. To avoid consumer confusion, a business card must include at least the following information:

- The name and address of the brokerage as licensed by the Department of State (or the branch office if the salesperson is associated with one).
- The individual's full name, as licensed.
- Type of license held (Licensed Real Estate Broker, Licensed Real Estate Salesperson, or Licensed Associate Real Estate Broker).
- The firm's business telephone number.

The inclusion of additional information is permissible, (business titles, business e-mail address, specialization, trade affiliations or accreditations), providing the information is true and not misleading.

A licensee may include his or her home e-mail address, cell and/or home telephone numbers, provided that there is a notation that such are residence numbers, and further that such use is not extended to any activity that would constitute branch office operation.

Internet Advertising

The Association of Real Estate License Law Officials (ARELLO) provides guidelines for New York licensees. *These ARELLO Best Practices Internet Guidelines, last updated in 2001, are intended only for educational purposes for member jurisdictions and licensees. Licensees advertising on the Internet should seek competent legal advice as to whether their web sites comply with local, state and national regulations.* This paper details ARELLO's proposed cross-jurisdictional "best practices" guidelines on Internet regulatory issues as they pertain to the real estate industry in order to:

1. Create a framework of real estate consumer protection against: online fraud, misrepresentation, and deceptive practices and services from licensed and unlicensed individuals and firms; and
2. Provide regulatory guidelines that each jurisdiction can use to create any specific regulations concerning online real estate activities that it deems necessary, in a manner that is consistent with the operation and nature of the Internet and that will minimize cross-jurisdictional regulatory conflict, confusion, and inefficiencies; and
3. Provide standards of online behavior for all licensees and licensed firms that when followed, will enhance online real estate consumer protection; and
4. Provide a framework for licensed firms to create their own Internet Policies and Procedures that addresses and enforces appropriate online licensee behavior.

ARELLO does not seek to discourage licensees from using the full power and innovative possibilities of the Internet in their business. Instead, it seeks to encourage that use by establishing guidelines whose use can minimize the need for regulatory provisions.

Reprinted with official permission from ARELLO.

Blind Ads

When a broker advertises property for sale without disclosing the fact she is a licensed real estate broker, or when a broker attempts to mislead the public into believing a property is for sale by owner, she has placed a **blind ad**. **Blind ads are illegal in New York.** For example, if broker Judy includes only a phone number on a sign she places in front of a client's home, she is placing a blind ad, which is illegal.

Unlicensed Real Estate Assistants

In today's real estate market many agents find the use of an unlicensed assistant very useful and helpful. The assistants can do much of the paperwork and other matters that do not require a license. This will free up the licensee to look for new clients and buyers. Remember unlicensed assistants may not do anything that requires a license. Some of the activities they may perform according to the DOS are answer phones, take messages, arrange appointments, write ads for broker approval, prepare flyers for open houses, compile CMA material, assemble documents for closing.

Unlicensed assistants should not discuss real estate with customers or clients or show any property either for sale or rent (apartments). They can be paid directly by the broker or salesperson. If compensated on the completed transaction, they must be licensed.

Death of a Broker

A license issued to a real estate broker who was, at the time of his death, the sole proprietor of a brokerage office may be used after the death of such licensee by his duly appointed administrator or executor in the name of the estate pursuant to authorization granted by the surrogate under the provisions of the Surrogate's Court Procedure Act for a period of not more than 120 days from the date of death of such licensee in order to complete any unfinished realty transactions in the process of negotiation by the broker or his salespersons existing prior to his decease. There shall be endorsed upon the face of the license, after the name of the decedent, the words "deceased", the date of death and the name of the administrator or executor under whose authority the license is being used. The period of 120 days may be extended upon application to the Secretary of State, for good cause shown, for an additional period not to exceed 120 days. A license expiring during such period or extension shall be automatically renewed and continued in effect during such period or extension. No fee shall be charged for any such license or renewal thereof.

Required Disclosure Property Condition Disclosure

Except as is provided in section 463, every seller of residential real property pursuant to a real estate purchase contract shall complete and sign a property condition disclosure statement as prescribed by subdivision two of this section and cause it, or a copy thereof, to be delivered to a buyer or buyer's agent prior to the signing by the buyer of a binding contract of sale. A copy of the property condition disclosure statement containing the signatures of both seller and buyer shall be attached to the real estate purchase contract. Nothing contained in this article or this disclosure statement is intended to prevent the parties to a contract of sale from entering into agreements of any kind or nature with respect to the physical condition of the property to be sold, including, but not limited to, agreements for the sale of real property "as is".

Exemptions to Property Condition Disclosure

A property condition disclosure statement shall not be required in connection with any of the following transfers of residential real property:

1. A transfer pursuant to a court order, including, but not limited to, a transfer order by a probate court during the administration of a decedent's estate, a transfer pursuant to a writ of execution, a transfer by a trustee in bankruptcy or debtor-in-possession, a transfer as a result of the exercise of the power of eminent domain, and a transfer that results from a decree for specific performance of a contract or other agreement between two or more persons;

2. A transfer to mortgagee or an affiliate or agent thereof by a mortgagor by deed in lieu of foreclosure or in satisfaction of the mortgage debt;
3. A transfer to a beneficiary of a deed of trust;
4. A transfer pursuant to a foreclosure sale that follows a default in the satisfaction of an obligation that is secured by a mortgage;
5. A transfer by a sale under a power of sale that follows a default in the satisfaction of an obligation that is secured by a mortgage;
6. A transfer by a mortgagee, or a beneficiary under a mortgage, or an affiliate or agent thereof, who has acquired the residential real property at a sale under a mortgage or who has acquired the residential real property by a deed in lieu of foreclosure;
7. A transfer by a fiduciary in the course of the administration of a descendant's estate, a guardianship, a conservatorship, or a trust;
8. A transfer from one co-owner to one or more other co-owners;
9. A transfer made to the transferor's spouse or to one or more persons in the lineal consanguinity of one or more of the transferors;
10. A transfer between spouses or former spouses as a result of a decree of divorce, dissolution of marriage, annulment, or legal separation or as a result of property settlement, agreement incidental to a decree of divorce, dissolution of marriage, annulment or legal separation;
11. A transfer to or from the state, a political subdivision of the state, or another governmental entity;
12. A transfer that involves newly constructed residential real property that previously had not been inhabited;
13. A transfer by a sheriff; or
14. A transfer pursuant to a partition action.

Revision

If a seller of residential real property acquires knowledge which renders materially inaccurate a property condition disclosure statement provided previously, the seller shall deliver a revised property condition disclosure statement to the buyer as soon as practicable. In no event, however, shall a seller be required to provide a revised property condition disclosure statement after the transfer of title from the seller to the buyer or occupancy by the buyer, whichever is earlier.

Remedy

In the event a seller fails to perform the duty prescribed in this article to deliver a disclosure statement prior to the signing by the buyer of a binding contract of sale, the buyer shall receive upon the transfer of title a credit of $500 against the agreed upon purchase price of the residential real property.

Duty of an Agent

An agent representing a seller of residential real property as a listing broker shall have the duty to timely inform each seller represented by that agent of the seller's obligations under this article. An agent representing a buyer of residential real property, or, if the buyer is not represented by an agent, the agent representing a seller of residential real property and dealing with a prospective buyer, shall have the duty to timely (in any event, before the buyer signs a binding contract of sale) inform such buyer of the buyer's rights and obligations under this article. If an agent performs the duties and obligations imposed upon him or her pursuant to this section, the agent shall have no further duties under this article and shall not be liable to any party for a violation of this article

NYS Department of State
Division of Licensing Services
P.O. Box 22001
Albany, NY 12201-2001
(518) 474-4429
www.dos.state.ny.us

Property Condition Disclosure Statement

Name of Seller or Sellers: ______________________________

Property Address: ______________________________

____

General Instructions:

The Property Condition Disclosure Act requires the seller of residential real property to cause this disclosure statement or a copy thereof to be delivered to a buyer or buyer's agent prior to the signing by the buyer of a binding contract of sale.

Purpose of Statement:

This is a statement of certain conditions and information concerning the property known to the seller. This Disclosure Statement is not a warranty of any kind by the seller or by any agent representing the seller in this transaction. It is not a substitute for any inspections or tests and the buyer is encouraged to obtain his or her own independent professional inspections and environmental tests and also is encouraged to check public records pertaining to the property.

A knowingly false or incomplete statement by the seller on this form may subject the seller to claims by the buyer prior to or after the transfer of title. In the event a seller fails to perform the duty prescribed in this article to deliver a Disclosure Statement prior to the signing by the buyer of a binding contract of sale, the buyer shall receive upon the transfer of title a credit of $500 against the agreed upon purchase price of the residential real property.

"Residential real property" means real property improved by a one to four family dwelling used or occupied, or intended to be used or occupied, wholly or partly, as the home or residence of one or more persons, but shall not refer to (a) unimproved real property upon which such dwellings are to be constructed or (b) condominium units or cooperative apartments or (c) property on a homeowners' association that is not owned in fee simple by the seller.

Instructions to the Seller:

a. Answer all questions based upon your actual knowledge.
b. Attach additional pages with your signature if additional space is required.
c. Complete this form yourself.
d. If some items do not apply to your property, check "NA" (Non-applicable). If you do not know the answer check "Unkn" (Unknown).

Seller's Statement:

The seller makes the following representations to the buyer based upon the seller's actual knowledge at the time of signing this document. The seller authorizes his or her agent, if any, to provide a copy of this statement to a prospective buyer of the residential real property. The following are representations made by the seller and are not the representations of the seller's agent.

GENERAL INFORMATION

1. How long have you owned the property? .... ______
2. How long have you occupied the property? .... ______
3. What is the age of the structure or structures? .... ______
   Note to buyer – If the structure was built before 1978 you are encouraged to investigate for the presence of lead based paint..
4. Does anybody other than yourself have a lease, easement or any other right to use or occupy any part of your property other than those stated in documents available in the public record, such as rights to use a road or path or cut trees or crops? .... ☐ Yes ☐ No ☐ Unkn ☐ NA
5. Does anybody else claim to own any part of your property? *If Yes, explain below* .... ☐ Yes ☐ No ☐ Unkn ☐ NA

____

Property Condition Disclosure Statement

6. Has anyone denied you access to the property or made a formal legal claim challenging your title to the property? *If Yes, explain below* .... ❒ Yes ❒ No ❒ Unkn ❒ NA

7. Are there any features of the property shared in common with adjoining landowners or a homeowner's association, such as walls, fences or driveways? *If Yes, describe below* ..... ❒ Yes ❒ No ❒ Unkn ❒ NA

8. Are there any electric or gas utility surcharges for line extensions, special assessments or homeowner or other association fees that apply to the property? *If Yes, explain below* ..... ❒ Yes ❒ No ❒ Unkn ❒ NA

9. Are there certificates of occupancy related to the property? *If No, explain below* .... ❒ Yes ❒ No ❒ Unkn ❒ NA

ENVIRONMENTAL

Note to Seller:

In this section, you will be asked questions regarding petroleum products and hazardous or toxic substances that you know to have been spilled, leaked or otherwise been released on the property or from the property onto any other property. Petroleum products may include, but are not limited to, gasoline, diesel fuel, home heating fuel, and lubricants. Hazardous or toxic substances are products that could pose short or long-term danger to personal health or the environment if they are not properly disposed of, applied or stored. These include, but are not limited to, fertilizers, pesticides and insecticides, paint including paint thinner, varnish remover and wood preservatives, treated wood, construction materials such as asphalt and roofing materials, antifreeze and other automotive products, batteries, cleaning solvents including septic tank cleaners, household cleaners and pool chemicals and products containing mercury and lead.

Note to Buyer:

If contamination of this property from petroleum products and/or hazardous or toxic substances is a concern to you, you are urged to consider soil and groundwater testing of this property.

10. Is any or all of the property located in a designated floodplain? *If Yes, explain below* ..... ❒ Yes ❒ No ❒ Unkn ❒ NA

11. Is any or all of the property located in a designated wetland? *If Yes, explain below* ...... ❒ Yes ❒ No ❒ Unkn ❒ NA

12. Is the property located in an agricultural district? *If Yes, explain below* .... ❒ Yes ❒ No ❒ Unkn ❒ NA

13. Was the property ever the site of a landfill? *If Yes, explain below* .... ❒ Yes ❒ No ❒ Unkn ❒ NA

Property Condition Disclosure Statement

14. Are there or have there ever been fuel storage tanks above or below the ground on the property? ❑ Yes ❑ No ❑ Unkn ❑ NA
   - If Yes, are they currently in use? ❑ Yes ❑ No ❑ Unkn ❑ NA
   - Location(s) ______
   - Are they leaking or have they ever leaked? *If Yes, explain below* ❑ Yes ❑ No ❑ Unkn ❑ NA

15. Is there asbestos in the structure? *If Yes, state location or locations below* ❑ Yes ❑ No ❑ Unkn ❑ NA

16. Is lead plumbing present? *If Yes, state location or locations below* ❑ Yes ❑ No ❑ Unkn ❑ NA

17. Has a radon test been done? *If Yes, attach a copy of the report* ❑ Yes ❑ No ❑ Unkn ❑ NA

18. Has motor fuel, motor oil, home heating fuel, lubricating oil or any other petroleum product, methane gas, or any hazardous or toxic substance spilled, leaked or otherwise been released on the property or from the property onto any other property? *If Yes, describe below* ❑ Yes ❑ No ❑ Unkn ❑ NA

19. Has the property been tested for the presence of motor fuel, motor oil, home heating fuel, lubricating oil, or any other petroleum product, methane gas, or any hazardous or toxic substance? *If Yes, attach report(s)* ❑ Yes ❑ No ❑ Unkn ❑ NA

STRUCTURAL

20. Is there any rot or water damage to the structure or structures? *If Yes, explain below* ❑ Yes ❑ No ❑ Unkn ❑ NA

21. Is there any fire or smoke damage to the structure or structures? *If Yes, explain below* ❑ Yes ❑ No ❑ Unkn ❑ NA

22. Is there any termite, insect, rodent or pest infestation or damage? *If Yes, explain below* ❑ Yes ❑ No ❑ Unkn ❑ NA

23. Has the property been tested for termite, insect, rodent or pest infestation or damage? ❑ Yes ❑ No ❑ Unkn ❑ NA
   If Yes, please attach report(s)

24. What is the type of roof/roof covering (slate, asphalt, other)? ______
   - Any known material defects? ______
   - How old is the roof? ______

Property Condition Disclosure Statement

- Is there a transferable warrantee on the roof in effect now? *If Yes, explain below* ..... ❒ Yes ❒ No ❒ Unkn ❒ NA

25. Are there any know material defects in any of the following structural systems: footings, beams, girders, lintels, columns or partitions? *If Yes, explain below* .... ❒ Yes ❒ No ❒ Unkn ❒ NA

MECHANICAL SYSTEMS AND SERVICES

26. What is the water source? *(Circle all that apply)* .... well, private, municipal, other: ______
    - If municipal, is it metered? .... ❒ Yes ❒ No ❒ Unkn ❒ NA
27. Has the water quality and/or flow rate been tested? *If Yes, describe below* .... ❒ Yes ❒ No ❒ Unkn ❒ NA

28. What is the type of sewage system? *(Circle all that apply)* .... public sewer, private sewer, septic, cesspool
    - If septic or cesspool, age? .... ______
    - Date last pumped? .... ______
    - Frequency of pumping? .... ______
    - Any known material defects? *If Yes, explain below* .... ❒ Yes ❒ No ❒ Unkn ❒ NA

29. Who is your electrical service provider? .... ______
    - What is the amperage? .... ______
    - Does it have circuit breakers or fuses? .... ______
    - Private or public poles? .... ______
    - Any known material defects? *If yes, explain below* .... ❒ Yes ❒ No ❒ Unkn ❒ NA

30. Are there any flooding, drainage or grading problems that resulted in standing water on any portion of the property? *If Yes, state locations and explain below* .... ❒ Yes ❒ No ❒ Unkn ❒ NA

31. Does the basement have seepage that results in standing water? *If Yes, explain below* .... ❒ Yes ❒ No ❒ Unkn ❒ NA

Are there any known material defects in any of the following? *If Yes, explain below. Use additional sheets if necessary* ....

32. Plumbing system? .... ❒ Yes ❒ No ❒ Unkn ❒ NA
33. Security system? .... ❒ Yes ❒ No ❒ Unkn ❒ NA
34. Carbon monoxide detector? .... ❒ Yes ❒ No ❒ Unkn ❒ NA

Property Condition Disclosure Statement

35. Smoke detector? ❐ Yes ❐ No ❐ Unkn ❐ NA
36. Fire sprinkler system? ❐ Yes ❐ No ❐ Unkn ❐ NA
37. Sump pump? ❐ Yes ❐ No ❐ Unkn ❐ NA
38. Foundation/slab? ❐ Yes ❐ No ❐ Unkn ❐ NA
39. Interior walls/ceilings? ❐ Yes ❐ No ❐ Unkn ❐ NA
40. Exterior walls or siding? ❐ Yes ❐ No ❐ Unkn ❐ NA
41. Floors? ❐ Yes ❐ No ❐ Unkn ❐ NA
42. Chimney/fireplace or stove? ❐ Yes ❐ No ❐ Unkn ❐ NA
43. Patio/deck? ❐ Yes ❐ No ❐ Unkn ❐ NA
44. Driveway? ❐ Yes ❐ No ❐ Unkn ❐ NA
45. Air conditioner? ❐ Yes ❐ No ❐ Unkn ❐ NA
46. Heating system? ❐ Yes ❐ No ❐ Unkn ❐ NA
47. Hot water heater? ❐ Yes ❐ No ❐ Unkn ❐ NA

____

____

____

____

48. The property is located in the following school district _______________ ❐ Unkn

Note: Buyer is encouraged to check public records concerning the property (e.g. tax records and wetland and floodplain maps).

The seller should use this area to further explain any item above. If necessary, attach additional pages and indicate here the number of additional pages attached.

____

____

____

____

____

____

____

____

Property Condition Disclosure Statement

Seller's Certification:

Seller certifies that the information in this Property Condition Disclosure Statement is true and complete to the seller's actual knowledge as of the date signed by the seller. If a seller of residential real property acquires knowledge which renders materially inaccurate a Property Condition Disclosure Statement provided previously, the seller shall deliver a revised Property Condition Disclosure Statement to the buyer as soon as practicable. In no event, however, shall a seller be required to provide a revised Property Condition Disclosure Statement after the transfer of title from the seller to the buyer or occupancy by the buyer, whichever is earlier.

Seller's Signature

X ______________________________ *Date* ______________

Seller's Signature

X ______________________________ *Date* ______________

Buyer's Acknowledgment:

Buyer acknowledges receipt of a copy of this statement and buyer understands that this information is a statement of certain conditions and information concerning the property known to the seller. It is not a warranty of any kind by the seller or seller's agent and is not a substitute for any home, pest, radon or other inspections or testing of the property or inspection of the public records.

Buyer's Signature

X ______________________________ *Date* ______________

Buyer's Signature

X ______________________________ *Date* ______________

Suspension or Revocation of Licenses

If a broker's license is suspended or revoked, then all salespeople working for him are suspended as well. In this case, salespersons may change their association or wait until their broker's suspension is lifted in order to once again practice real estate. If a license is revoked, the licensee must wait one year before reapplying.

The Department of State may revoke the license of a real estate broker or salesperson or suspend the same, for such period as the department may deem proper, or in lieu thereof may impose a fine not exceeding $1,000 payable to the Department of State:

- Misstating information on license applications e.g.: not checking correct boxes, age, criminal record etc.
- Violating any provision of article 12-A
- Making a false promise to try and influence or induce someone to sign a contract.
- Committing fraud or fraudulent practices These are acts meant deceive or misrepresent giving one person an advantage over another.
- Demonstrating untrustworthiness or in competency to be a real estate broker or salesperson
- Failing to complete continuing education in the required time allowed.
- Knowingly making willful misrepresentation on several bases:
    - Intentional misrepresentation (active fraud) that is making a false statement of a material fact
    - Intentional concealment (constructive fraud) failing to disclose a material fact.
    - Negligent misrepresentation. Making a false statement about a material fact the broker did not know but should have known to be false.
- **Commingling funds** A real estate broker shall not commingle the money or other property of his principal with his own and shall at all times maintain a separate, special bank account to be used exclusively for the deposit of said monies and which deposit shall be made as promptly as practicable.
- Paying any part of a fee, commission, or other compensation received to another party for any service.
- Paying **kickbacks**, which is *paying part of the proceeds of a sale to another party that helped secure the sale, but is unlicensed.*
- Placing a sign on a property without the owner's consent.
- Offering a property for sale or lease without the owner's consent.
- Attempting to negotiate the sale, exchange, or lease of property already under an exclusive listing with another broker. A licensee may not interfere with another brokers listings
- Failing to provide a list of multiple listing service participants, if a member of a MLS.
- Retaining any form of information upon termination of association. When a licensee terminates with a broker they must turn over all information, whether received from the broker, or obtained by them. They may keep copies of all documents for their reference.
- Failing to immediately provide a duplicate original of any instrument to parties involved in a real estate transaction.
- Failing to keep adequate records. Brokers must maintain records in the sale or mortgage of 1-4 unit properties. Records must be maintained for **three years.**

- Establishing an exclusive listing agreement with an automatic renewal of contract New York prohibits automatic renewals. All listings must be resigned or extended. The seller and agent sign the forms to renew the listing.
- Accepting services of another broker's employee without their broker's knowledge. A broker may not pay another broker's salesperson without the knowledge of the salesperson's broker.
- Failing to advise potential buyers and sellers of the rights and obligations of the agency relationship. Licensees must make clear their position regarding the party for whom they are working in a real estate transaction, seller, buyer, or both. In regard to residential 1-4 units, licensees must have sellers and buyers sign specific mandated disclosure forms.
- A real estate broker shall not directly or indirectly buy for himself property listed with him, nor shall he acquire any interest there in without first making his true position clearly known to the listing owner.

  Before a real estate broker buys property for a client in the ownership of which the broker has an interest, he shall disclose his interest to all parties to the transaction.

  Before a real estate broker sells property in which he owns an interest, he shall make such interest known to the purchaser.
- Failing to remit funds held for a client.
- Entering into a **net listing agreement** in *which the seller sets a net amount acceptable for the property; if the actual selling price exceeds that amount, the broker is entitled to keep the excess as commission.*
- Soliciting the sale, lease, or listing of a property in a cease-and-desist zone.
- Practicing law without a license. In all legal matters licensees should recommend that buyers and sellers consult and attorney. Legal matters:
  - Drawing legal documents such as mortgages or deeds.
  - Giving an opinion or advice regarding a title.
  - Giving any opinion or advice regarding any document or anything that can be taken as legal advice.
- Violating any discrimination law regarding the sale, rental or advertisement of housing or commercial space.
- Receiving compensation from more than one party in a transaction, without the others' consent.
- Receiving or demanding compensation from any person other than the broker for work done in the appraising, buying, selling, exchanging, leasing, renting, or negotiating of a real estate loan.

Notice of Complaint and Hearing

When the DOS receives a complaint it will notify the licensee in writing and seek a response. If there is no response, they will assign an investigator. Before the Department of State revokes, suspends, or fines a licensee, it notifies the licensee in writing of the charges at least 10 days prior to the set date of the hearing. This allows the licensee to be heard by counsel. If the licensee is a salesperson, the broker is also notified of the charges.

The DOS may also impose a fine not to exceed $1,000. Violation of the license law is a misdemeanor and is punishable by a fine of up to $1,000 or a year in jail.

An appeal of a decision that the DOS makes may be heard through a proceeding under the NYS Civil Practice Law and Rules (CPLR) called an **Article 78 proceeding**. This is the method for appeals against agencies such as the DOS.

Case Studies Cited by the Department of State

Article 12-A of the Real Property Law grants to the Department of State the authority to regulate real estate brokers and salespersons. Real Property Law & sect;441-c provides, in part, that the Department of State may revoke, suspend, fine or reprimand a real estate broker or salesperson if that licensee is found to have, among other things, violated any provision of Article 12-A of the Real Property Law, engaged in fraud or fraudulent practices, or demonstrated untrustworthiness or in competency. As the Court of Appeals stated in *Matter of Gold v. Lomenzo*, 29 NY2d 468, 329 NYS2d 805, 811 (1972), "the Legislature intended the Secretary of State to be vested with a wide discretion in determining what should be deemed untrustworthy conduct."

In fact, even if a licensee engaged in conduct unrelated to his or her activities as a real estate broker or salesperson, that conduct can still act as the basis for and be considered by the Department of State in bringing a disciplinary proceeding against that licensee for engaging in untrustworthy behavior.

For example, in *Eich v. Shaffer*, 136 AD2d 701, 523 NYS2d 902 (2nd Dept. 1988), the Department of State held, after a disciplinary proceeding, that a finding by the New York State Department of Insurance petitioner violated his duties as an insurance broker and thereby demonstrated untrustworthiness and in competency, was a sufficient basis for determining petitioner guilty of untrustworthiness with reference to his license as a real estate broker. In confirming that determination, the Appellate Court stated that it was "proper for the [Secretary] of State to base her determination that the petitioner was untrustworthy to act as a real estate broker within the meaning of Real Property Law §441-c on his misdeeds as an insurance broker." *Eich,* 523 NYS2d at 904.

Eich followed the holding in *Dovale v. Patterson,* 85 AD2d 601, 444 NYS2d 694 (2nd Dept. 1981), in which the Court stated that "(a)lthough the actions underlying the disciplinary charges are not acts for which petitioner's license as a real estate broker was required, they may be considered in determining petitioner's untrustworthiness and incompetency as a broker." *Dovale,* 444 NYS2d at 695. In *Dovale*, the Court upheld the Department of State's revocation of petitioner's real estate broker's license based upon his regularly engaging in the practice of submitting fraudulent contracts and loan applications to banks in order to obtain larger mortgages than might otherwise be available.

Finally, in *Fogel v. Department of State,* 209 AD2d 615, 619 NYS2d 104 (2nd Dept. 1994), the Court held that the Department of State properly denied the renewal of petitioner's real estate salesperson's license.

Real Estate Brokers and Salespersons and the Unauthorized Practice of Law

Source: New York Department of State

Article 12-A of the Real Property Law provides for the licensure of real estate brokers and salespersons. A licensee is statutorily held to standards of competency and trustworthiness. Failure to abide by such standards can result in the suspension or revocation of the license. The New York State Department of State has long considered the unlawful practice of law by a real estate broker or salesperson as grounds for disciplinary action. Its interpretation of what constitutes unlawful practice has been guided by relevant provisions of the Judiciary Law and by the seminal case of *Duncan & Hill Realty, Inc. v. Department of State,* 62 A.D.2d 690, (4th Dept. 1976), app dismissed, 45 N.Y.2d 821, 381 N.E.2d 608, 409 N.Y.S.2d 210 (1978). Judiciary Law sect;478 prohibits the practice of law by non-attorneys, the purpose of which is to protect the public from the dangers of legal representation and advice given by persons not trained, examined, and licensed for such work.

Jemzura v. McCue, 45 A.D.2d 797, 357 N.Y.S.2d 167 (3rd Dept. 1974), app dismissed 37 N.Y.2d 750, 337 N.E.2d 135, 374 N.Y.S.2d 624 (1975). Section 484 of the Judiciary Law additionally provides that "no natural person shall ask or receive, directly or indirectly, compensation for...preparing deeds, mortgages, assignments, discharges, leases or any other instruments affecting real estate...unless he has been regularly admitted to practice, as an attorney or counselor..." A violation of either of these sections is a misdemeanor. See, Judiciary Law sect;485. It may be prosecuted by the attorney general, or, upon leave of the supreme court, by a bar association. See, Judiciary Law sect;476-a. Additionally, should a real estate broker or salesperson be found to have engaged in such unlawful practice, the Department will take independent action against such broker's license.

In *Duncan & Hill*, the court upheld the Department of State's determination that a real estate broker who was not a licensed attorney demonstrated untrustworthiness and incompetence in violation of Real Property Law sect;441-c, finding that, when he prepared documents that included detailed mortgage terms he had devised, he engaged in the unauthorized practice of law.

The court went on to state:

> *It is for this reason that real estate brokers and agents must refrain from inserting in a real estate purchase offer or counteroffer any provision which requires the exercise of legal expertise. Thus it is not proper for such a broker to undertake to devise the detailed terms of a purchase-money mortgage or other legal terms beyond the general description of the subject property, the price and the mortgage to be assumed or given. A real estate broker may readily protect himself from a charge of unlawful practice of law by inserting in the document that it is subject to the approval of the respective attorneys for the parties. Moreover, a real estate broker or agent who uses one of the recommended purchase offer forms...or one recommended by a joint committee of the bar association and realtors association of his local county, who refrains from inserting provisions requiring legal expertise and who adheres to the guidelines agreed upon by the American Bar Association and the National Association of Real Estate Brokers, above noted, has no need to worry about the propriety of his conduct in such transactions.*
>
> *Duncan & Hill, supra, 62 AD2d at 701, 405 N.Y.S.2d at 345.*

Under these circumstances, a real estate broker or salesperson who prepares a simple fill-in-the-blanks purchase and sale contract can avoid the unlawful practice of law by **including in the contract a condition making it subject to approval by each party's attorney.** Alternatively, brokers and salespersons can utilize a fill-in-the-blanks form that has been approved by a joint committee of the bar association and realtors association of his or her county. Such an approved form would only require that the real estate brokers and salespersons fill in non-legal provisions such as the names of the parties, the date and location of the closing, a description of the property, the consideration for sale and any other relevant facts. The brokers and salespersons would not be permitted to develop and "legal terms." Further, since the contract establishes significant legal rights and obligations, it should clearly and prominently indicate on its face that it is a legally binding document and clearly and prominently recommend that the parties seek advice and counsel from their lawyers prior to affixing their signature to the document.

Brokers and salespersons must refrain, even with respect to these approved contracts, from providing legal advice to their clients. Nor may they discourage the parties from seeking advice from their attorneys.

Brokers and salespersons may not add provisions to the approved contracts unless they make the entire contract subject to and conditioned upon the review and approval of each party's attorney. In addition, brokers and salespersons may prepare purchase and sale contracts, subject to the above conditions, only as an incident of the purchase and sale of real estate and may not charge a separate fee for preparation of the contract or share in the fees of attorneys for preparation or review of these contracts.

SUMMARY

1. Real estate activity in New York is regulated by the **New York Department of State** (DOS). The **New York State Real Estate Board** operates under the DOS and sets rules and regulations for salespeople and brokers, and establishes continuing education requirements. The **Secretary of State** can set rules regarding clients' accounts, records maintenance, contracts and more. The **New York Division of Licensing Services** is responsible for the licensing, regulation, and registration of real estate brokers and salespeople. These bodies share responsibility for implementing and enforcing license laws.
2. The three categories of real estate licenses are: broker, associate broker, and salesperson. A **broker** is *licensed to represent a party in a real estate transaction for compensation*. A broker's license can be held by an individual or a business. A **real estate salesperson** is *a licensed agent associated with a broker and may perform most of the acts of a broker on his or her behalf.*. A salesperson's license must be held by a broker. An **associate broker** is *a licensed broker working under the supervision of another broker*. Note: An **office manager** may be *a licensed associate real estate broker who works as an office manager under the name and supervision of another broker*. The six different licenses for which real estate brokers can apply are: individual, associate, trade name, partnership, corporate, and Limited Liability Company or partnership.
3. Real estate sales license exam requirements include 18 or older (20 for broker); honest, truthful and good reputation; not convicted of a felony; be a U.S. citizen or lawful alien, be in compliance of child support laws; *educational:* 75 hours of real estate coursework (120 hours for broker); *broker affiliation* must be secured before submitting application; *completed application, application fee, and copies of transcripts*; *additional fee to take exam*.
4. New York provides exemptions to licensing requirements to: attorneys admitted to the New York State Bar, building supervisors or maintenance workers, persons acting in any capacity under the judgment or court order, property owners, public officers, and tenant associations and nonprofit corporations. **Reciprocity** is when states agree to allow licensees from other states to sell real estate in their own, by accepting the licensee's out-of-state credentials. Out-of-state licensees may practice in New York as long as they are from one of the 10 reciprocating states and sign an **irrevocable consent** subjecting them to the jurisdiction of the New York courts.
5. Licenses are issued by the Department of State and sent to the broker. A broker's license must be displayed; salespersons' licenses are kept on file. Salespeople cannot practice real estate in New York without a license issued by the Department of State. Licensees are required to produce a **pocket card** on demand.
6. Operating a brokerage in New York requires more than obtaining a broker's license. Brokers must abide by strict regulations pertaining to their place of business, branch offices, compensation, supervisory responsibilities, and advertising.

7. Licensees must complete 22.5 hours of **continuing education** coursework within two years prior to their license renewal. The coursework must include at least three hours of fair housing or discrimination in the sale or rental of real property. Licensees must complete an application form and submit a license renewal fee to renew their license. They must be in good standing and meet child support obligations,. If a licensee's license lapses, they have two years to renew and take continuing education or they must retake a written exam to re-qualify.

8. Licensees are required by Article 12-A of the New York Licensing Law to follow certain laws and requirements. If they fail to do so, their license could be suspended or revoked. **Suspension** means *a license is withdrawn for a certain and specified period of time* and may call for a condition to be met before reactivation is permitted. **Revocation**, an application for a new license must be submitted after one year from revocation. Any licensee in violation of any Acts found in Article 12-A is guilty of a **misdemeanor**. The hearing process for licensee suspension or revocation is set forth by the DOS and affects a broker and everyone working for him.

2/3/4

Law of Agency

In These Sessions

These sessions focus on the duties and responsibilities of an agent to those for whom and with whom they work.

You will learn:

- Describe ways in which an agency relationship is created.
- Identify legal forms of agency in New York.
- Define different types of agency relationships.
- Explain circumstances that may terminate the agency relationship.
- Identify the fiduciary duties an agent owes to a client.

Key Terms

- Accountability
- Actual Fraud
- Agency
- Agency Disclosure Form
- Agency Relationship
- Antitrust
- Brokerage
- Broker's Agent
- Broker Protection Clause
- Brokerage
- Buyer Broker Contract
- Buyer's Agent
- Client
- Confidentiality
- Consensual Dual Agency
- Constructive Fraud
- Cooperating Broker
- Customer
- Designated Agency
- Disclosure
- Dual Agency
- Estoppel
- Exclusive Agency
- Exclusive Right To Sell
- Expressed Agency
- Fiduciary Duties
- Fiduciary Relationship
- First Substantive Contact
- Fraud
- General Agent
- Implied Agency

Law of Agency 1: Relationships with Sellers, Buyers, Tenants and Landlords between Brokers, Agents, and Third Parties

What Is Agency?

Agency is when one person hires another individual to act on their behalf. Real estate brokers and salespersons are commonly referred to as agents. In real estate it is a relationship between licensees and buyers, sellers, landlords or tenants. The person hired on another's behalf is the **agent**. The person who hires the agent is the **principal/client**. The agency relationship is always consensual, meaning both parties enter into it willingly.

Agency is a *relationship of trust created when one party (such as a seller, buyer, landlord, or tenant) gives another (a real estate licensee) the right to represent him in dealings with third parties.* The party granting the right of representation in a real estate transaction is known as the principal in the relationship. The licensee, or agent, is a fiduciary of the principal and is in a position of trust and loyalty to the principal. There is a distinction between the duties owed by the agent to a client and how a customer is treated. The client is who the agent owes all undivided loyalty, gives advice regarding their real property, and whose interest is above all others. The customer is given and owed fair and honest treatment by the agent, meaning any questions regarding the property that can be disclosed, without breeching the fiduciary duties owed to the principal must be answered truthfully. **The agent *represents* the principal, and *works with* the customer.**

Importance of Agency Law and Possible Legal Ramifications to Licensees

Agency law is increasingly vital for all real estate agents. While most of the laws have remained the same for so long, the principles have changed dramatically over the years. Many buyers, sellers and even professionals still wrongly believe that selling agents represent the buyer, when in fact they may be subagents of the seller. Some of the common causes of legal action regarding agency issues are:

- Lack of appropriate disclosure of agency relationship.
- Breach of fiduciary duties by sellers' agents or subagents in dealing with third parties.
- Conflict of interest arising out of buyer-customer becoming interested in broker's listing.

Key Terms

- Listing Agreement
- Loyalty
- Misrepresentation
- Negligence
- Net Listing
- Nonsolicitation Orders
- Obedience
- Offer of Compensation
- Open Listing
- Ostensible Agency
- Price Fixing
- Principal
- Procuring Cause
- Renunciation
- Revocation
- Self-Dealing
- Stigmatized
- Subagent
- Tie-In Arrangement
- Undisclosed Dual Agency
- Undivided Loyalty

- Insufficient knowledge on the part of the agent regarding duties owed to sellers or buyers.
- Agents buying property for themselves and not disclosing the fact.
- Misrepresentation of any kind.

Fiduciary Relationships

The relationship between an agent and a principal is described as a fiduciary relationship, one of trust and confidence. The term means a **"position of trust."** The agent owes his fiduciary duties only to the principal, but always owes fairness and honesty to third parties. The fiduciary duties include:

Obedience

The agent must act with obedience and obey all legal and reasonable instructions from the client. The principal can not ask an agent to perform any act that would be illegal. If this occurs the broker must reject the agency. Reasonable care also must be adhered to by the agent. If a seller asks that his home not be shown because of a sickness in the family, the agent must obey. The buyer broker may have instructions not to reveal the name of the buyer; the agent must obey these instructions.

Obedience.
Loyalty.
Disclosure.
Confidentiality.
Accountability.
Reasonable care.

Loyalty

The duty of loyalty dictates the agent must always put the principal's interests above those of other persons, including the agents. Agents must always work their hardest to serve the best interests of the principal. The agent may not work for anyone adverse to the principal's interest or for personal interest. The seller's agent must try to obtain the highest price and best terms, the buyer's agent to obtain the lowest price. The agent may never take advantage of a position to profit at the principal's expense.

Disclosure

Agents must pass on to the principal all facts or information the broker obtains that could affect the principal's decisions. A broker must present every offer to the seller, all information regarding the offer any terms, price or conditions, even if there is a contract Agents must give their principals all material facts so they may be able to make informed decisions.

Confidentiality

An agent may not disclose any confidential information learned from a principal. The fiduciary relationship the agent owes is faith, trust, and confidentiality. If a seller should tell an agent anything in confidence, the agent may not repeat it to anyone without the seller's permission. For example, if sellers tell you they will take a lower price than listed, this can not be told to anyone without their authorization. If sellers give you permission to disclose any confidential matter, it is wise to get it in writing. This way there will be no misunderstandings in the future. This duty lasts forever.

Accountability

Brokers must report all funds entrusted to them. The license law requires copies of all documents must be given to all affected by the document. Broker's are prohibited from commingling (mixing) the funds of their principal with their personal funds. All funds must be placed in an escrow account, separate from the broker's funds.

Reasonable Skill, Care, and Diligence

Agents when offering their services assert that they have the skill and training to perform the services that they offer. Agents must cautiously exercise these traits to which all is entitled. If a principal suffers loss due to an error or negligence on the agent's behalf, the agent will be held liable.

Scope of Authority

The brokerage contract expresses the agent's authority. The principal is the one who controls the extent of authority given to an agent. The two classes of agents are general and special. The main difference between the two is the authority the principal gives to the agent and the services they provide.

General Agent

A **general agent** is *empowered to represent the principal in a specific range of matters.* An example is a property manager, who may collect rent, evict, enter into leases, and perform many activities for the principal concerning a specific property or properties. A power of attorney can express this agency, but is not always needed. A general agent may bind the principal to any contract within the scope of the agent's authority.

Special Agent

A **special agent** is *authorized to represent the principal in one specific matter.* A real estate broker is usually a special agent. If hired by a seller through the listing agreement, the broker's duties are to find a ready, willing, and able buyer for the seller. The broker can market the property but cannot make decisions on behalf of the seller regarding price or any special conditions or terms.

Duties of the Principal to the Agent

Under the agency, the principal is obligated to the agent for honesty, compensation, and repayment. The agency would clearly set out the parameters for the compensation to be paid to the agent and how it will be earned.

A principal in an agency should not impede the agent's effort to market and show the property, without just cause. The agency was created for service and the principal should expect the agent to show the property at all times.

A listing agreement might provide that for compensation the seller will pay the broker a set percentage of the accepted sale price of the property, when a ready, willing, and able buyer is produced.

An agent should not be held liable if the principal withholds information that causes the agent to make incorrect statements to third parties. If an agent is found liable to third parties for a principal's misrepresentation to the agent, the agent is entitled for any repayment that may have caused the agent financial harm.

Agent's Responsibility to Third Parties

The broker and principal are the first parties in the agency. All other parties are considered third parties. Even though the agent's primary responsibility is to the principal, the agent also has obligations to third parties. The agent may not engage in any form of misrepresentation to a third party The agent must disclose any material fact of which they have knowledge or should have had knowledge concerning the property. An agent can not disclose any confidential information to any third party that could injure the principal. The agent must deal fairly and honestly with third parties.

Examples of disclosure to third parties include:

- If there is a problem regarding a wet basement.
- If there is an unresolved boundary dispute (i.e., encroachment or encumbrance).
- If there were previous damage even though corrected must be disclosed (i.e., a fire in the kitchen or pests).

An agent may be held liable for not disclosing or concealing the information from buyers. Agents must always be careful on how they answer questions from third parties. The agent must be sure the third party understands if what they are saying is an "opinion" or a "fact." A statement that is meant as your opinion is permitted as long as they understand it is only your "opinion." Agents must be sure that anything said is not construed as a statement of fact but just an opinion.

Misrepresentation and Nondisclosure

A broker can be held liable for any misrepresentation or nondisclosure of any material fact that can affect any party in the transaction. These acts also violate the broker's obligation to deal fairly and honestly with third parties. The misstatements do not have to be intentional. A real estate agent can be held liable for misrepresentations if they knew or should have known it to be false. Most complaints will come from buyers.

Misrepresentations impose liability on several bases:

- **Intentional misrepresentation** (active fraud). Knowingly making a false statement about a material fact.
- **Intentional concealment** (constructive fraud). Knowingly failing to disclose a material fact.
- **Negligent nondisclosure**. Failure to disclose for lack of exercising adequate care in obtaining information about the property.
- **Negligent misrepresentation**. Making a false statement about a material fact that the broker did not know but should have known to be false.
- **Negligent advice**. Giving incorrect professional advice when the agent should have known the advice was wrong and not referring the parties to experts.

Active fraud imposes liability on an agent for knowingly making a false statement with the intention to deceive a buyer. A fact is considered material if it would affect a reasonable buyer's decision to buy or how much to pay. (The buyer claimed agent misrepresented home to be in perfect condition upon further inspection workmanship was deemed unsuitable.)

Constructive fraud imposes liability for intentionally concealing known material defects from a buyer, especially if the buyer is unable or unlikely to discover them without assistance. The agent made a statement thinking it to be true, but later learned it was wrong without correcting it. (An agent received two estimates for repair on a window. One estimate did not include structure damage, the other did. The agent gave the estimate without the damage.)

Negligent nondisclosure for failure to exercise reasonable care to discover a material defect and disclose to the buyer. The decision imposed on a seller's agent to disclose such defects to the buyer even if they do not ask and no fiduciary relationship exist.

(A broker can be held liable for misrepresenting a property's boundary lines by telling the buyers what the seller told him and not verifying it.)

Negligent misrepresentation making false statements the agent did not know were false or that a reasonable observation would have revealed it untrue. (An agent writes a listing saying a home is connected to sewer system, when in fact it is not.)

Self-dealing can occur when broker has an *undisclosed interest in a property.* The broker must disclose his interest in a property to the principal and any other party to the transaction. Illegal self-dealing includes listing property, buying the property, and collecting commission. (A broker takes a listing and tells the homeowners he has a buyer but at a lower price. The homeowners in need of the sale accept the offer. Later they find that it was a friend of the broker and he put up the money for the home.)

Negligent advice giving incorrect professional advice when the agent should have known it was wrong. (An agent advises a buyer they do not need a financing contingency in the purchase agreement would be held liable for negligent advice.)

Agency and Brokerage

Brokerage is *the business of bringing buyers and sellers together and assisting in the sale of real estate.* A brokerage firm can be owned by a single licensed broker or more than one licensed person such as a partnership or corporation. A single license firm is independent if not affiliated with national or local franchise. Being part of a franchise allows the broker to use the franchise's trade name, reputation, and referral services. The broker still owns and operates the firm.

Creation of Agency

An agency relationship can be created by either a written or oral agreement between the agent and the principal. It can also be implied from the words or actions of either party. But for the best way to ensure that all parties have a clear understanding of the agency, it is in everyone's best interest to create the agreement with a written document.

The most common method of creating an agency is with an **express agreement** (either spoken or written). The written agreement creates an express agency between seller and broker. A typical example is the **listing agreement.** With this form of agreement, the seller authorizes the broker to find a buyer or tenant for their property. An agency agreement is formed between a buyer/tenant and broker by the use of a form called **buyer agency agreement.** This type of agency makes the buyer/tenant the principal and the seller is the customer.

Implied Agency

An agency also could be *created by the words or actions of the principal and agent indicating that they have agency.* This would be an **implied agency.** For example, if a broker helps a seller with pricing the home, or any other means necessary to show it properly, the agent shows the property to buyers, acting as though there is an agency this could be considered an implied agency. There is also the **estoppel** and **ratification** when someone claims to be to be an agent but there is no agreement and principal does not stop them and accepts a sales agreement by signing it. That is ratifying the previously implied agency. Licensees should be careful regarding these types of agencies; New York courts do not easily enforce implied real estate agreements

Broker's Compensation

The broker's fee is specified in the listing agreement, management agreement, or rental agreement with the principal and is **always subject to negotiation.** It is a violation of federal and state laws for any person or organization to recommend any schedule of commission. It is illegal for any brokers to conspire to set a standard commission rate. This is called "price fixing" and violates the antitrust laws. A percentage of the final sales price generally pays the brokers. They may also charge a flat fee.

The commission is usually considered earned when a broker brings a ready, willing, and able buyer to the seller, or the seller should accept an offer from the buyer that could be less than the list price, e.g., if the list price is $100,000, the offer is $90,000, and the seller accepts it, the broker has earned the commission.

Many listings will have an **"as, if, and when" clause**. This could state that the commission which is now earned and payable shall be deferred until closing of title or earlier termination of the sale. If the seller should default, the broker is entitled to the commission. Compensation by both parties is permissible with informed consent by both parties.

Compensation to Salespersons

The sales associate and broker by agreement set the amount of the compensation split. Under the general commission split, the entire commission is paid to the broker. The broker will then pay a portion to the agent who sold the property and a portion to the agent who listed the property. Some firms will use an incentive program, that is, they will increase the percentage to each agent for the sale of the property raising the dollar volume. Remember the commission split is always negotiable between the broker and sales associate.

Commission Window Breakdown

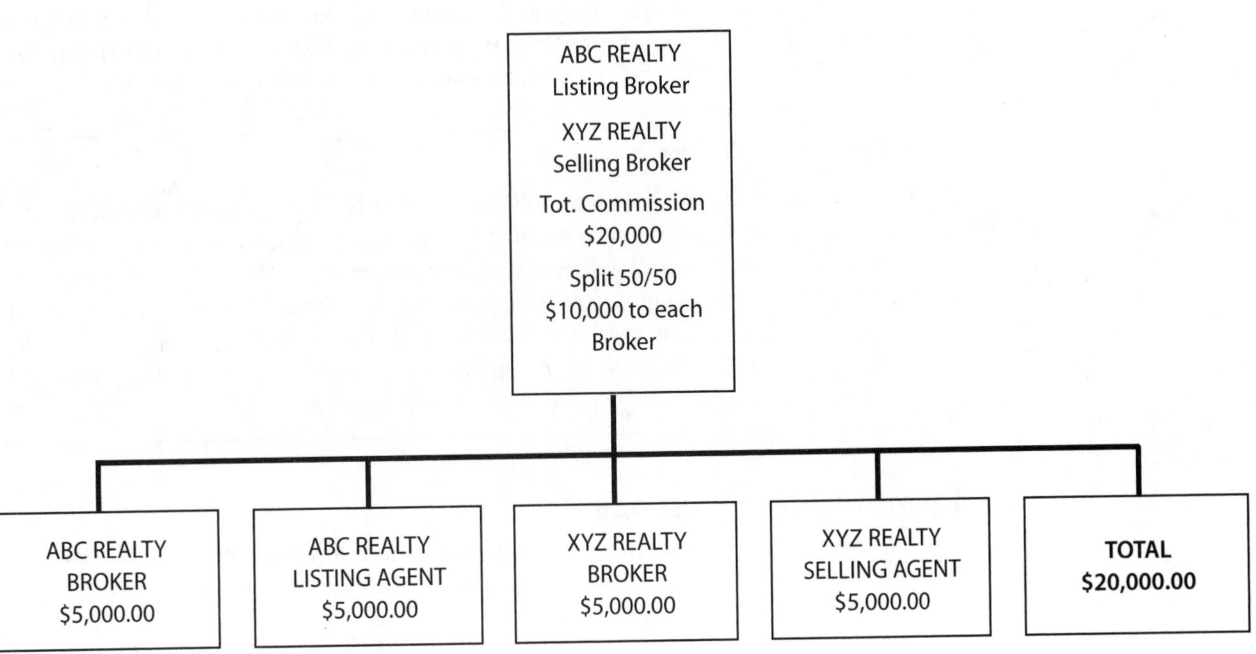

This would be the way a general split is done. Using a 50/50 split, the commission could have been at a total of 6%. The listing broker keeps 3%; the selling broker receives 3%. Or another way, the listing broker keeps 3.5% and puts out 2.5% for the selling agent. The buyer broker compensation is determined at time of listing. It could be 0%, 1%, negotiable, or the same 3% as the selling agent. This is a sample; there are many other variables for commission splits.

Net Listing

One type of listing arrangement is the net listing. This is when a seller sets a net amount they want, and everything over that amount is the broker's commission. This type of listing is always illegal in New York. One of the broker's duties is to give the owner the fair market value of their property. A net listing leaves open the opportunity for the broker to take advantage of the seller, by putting their interest before the owner.

Commission for Cooperating Brokers

The commission paid to the listing broker by the owner is then shared with the selling broker on a prearranged basis. This is most commonly done when the home is put on multiple listing services. Some listing firms will offer two forms of cooperating commissions. One share is payable to a subagent of the seller, another payable to a buyer agent as a cooperative who does not represent the seller. A salesperson may accept compensation from a former broker for fees earned while still associated with that broker.

Referral Fees

In New York referral fees are legal, as long as such fees are paid to the broker *with the informed consent of the person being referred.* Firms will pay a referral fee to the agent from other locations when they refer either a buyer or seller. As with all commissions, the percentage of the fee is always negotiable; there is no standard fee. If an agent refers a buyer to another firm, there will be a referral form filled out so each party knows the percentage and agreement of payment. When the transaction is finalized, the broker to whom the party was referred will send the referring broker a check for the fee. That broker will then split with the agent who referred the party

FRANCHISE COMPANY

Real estate franchises are ever expanding. Many firms are joining franchises for the simple reason they offer name recognition and services on a nationwide or even global network. The franchisee pays for the right to use the name of the franchise, including their operating procedures. With the usual commission split the broker will pay the sales agent the agreed upon split. In franchises, the firm will deduct a percentage of the fee from the agents' total check. New licensees should always ask what the franchise fee is when interviewing. This way there will be no misunderstandings.

Termination of Agency

We have discussed how an agency is created and the responsibilities associated with the agency, also how we earn the commission and the splits. Terminating an agency can be for:

- Expiration of the terms (e.g., the listing expires).
- Death or incompetence of either party.

- Mutual agreement by both parties.
- Bankruptcy.
- Completion or fulfillment of the purpose (e.g., the property sells and closes).
- Revocation of the broker's license.

An exception to the rule allowing a principal to revoke an agency agreement is that a principal does not have the right to revoke an agreement if the **agency is coupled with an interest.** That means the agent has a financial or security interest in the property that is the subject of the agency. For example, if a listing agreement provides the real estate broker will invest money to improve the property, the seller cannot revoke the broker's agency. Also, an agency coupled with an interest is not terminated by the death, incompetency, or bankruptcy of the principal.

Agency Creation and Alternatives

The agent is someone authorized to represent a principal in a transaction. Agency relationships between a broker and seller are usually created through the listing agreement, where the broker will be the agent of the seller. Other agency terms can be:

- Subagent
- Single agent
- Seller's agent
- Broker's agent
- Buyer agent
- Dual agent
- Designated agent

Subagent/Subagency

Subagency can be created when the broker and seller agree through multiple listing service that other members of MLS will also be working for the seller.

Agents that accept the offer of **subagency** *owe the same fiduciary responsibilities to the seller as the listing broker does.* Whether the agent is from the listing broker's office or from any other office, the same obligations apply to them. For example, John works for ABC Realty. He takes a listing and informs the seller of subagency. He puts it on MLS and any agent from any office that sees the listing and accepts the offer of subagency will owe the seller the same fiduciary duties that John and anyone from his office owe to the seller.

Single Agent

A **single agent** can represent *either the seller or buyer, but never both.* Whoever the agent should represent they are the ones the fiduciary is owed. The other parties in the transaction are treated as customers or third parties; they are still owed fair and honest dealings always.

Seller's Agent

A **seller's agent** is an agent who is *engaged by a seller to represent the seller's interests.* The seller's agent does this by securing a buyer for the seller's home at a price and on terms acceptable to the seller. A seller's agent has, without limitation, the following fiduciary duties to the seller: Reasonable care, undivided loyalty, confidentiality, full disclosure, obedience, and duty to account. A seller's agent does *not* represent the interests of the buyer. The obligations of a seller's agent are also subject to any specific provisions set forth in an agreement between the agent and the seller. In dealings with the buyer, a seller's agent should:

- Exercise reasonable skill and care in performance of the agent's duties.
- Deal honestly, fairly and in good faith.
- Disclose all facts known to the agent materially affecting the value or desirability of property, except as otherwise provided by law.

Broker's Agent

A **broker's agent** is *an agent that cooperates or is engaged by a listing agent or a buyer's agent (but does not work for the same firm as the listing agent or buyer's agent) to assist the listing agent or buyer's agent in locating a property to sell or buy, respectively, for the listing agent's seller or the buyer agent's buyer.* The broker's agent does *not* have a direct relationship with the buyer or seller, and the buyer or seller cannot provide instructions or direction directly to the broker's agent. The buyer and the seller, therefore, do *not* have **vicarious liability** for the acts of the broker's agent. The listing agent or buyer's agent does provide direction and instruction to the broker's agent and, therefore, the listing agent or buyer's agent will have liability for the acts of the broker's agent.

Buyer's Agent

A **buyer's agent** is *an agent who is engaged by a buyer to represent the buyer's interests.* The buyer's agent does this by negotiating the purchase of a home at a price and on terms acceptable to the buyer. A buyer's agent has, without limitation, the following fiduciary duties to the buyer: Reasonable care, undivided loyalty, confidentiality, full disclosure, obedience, and duty to account. A buyer's agent does *not* represent the interests of the seller. The obligations of a buyer's agent are also subject to any specific provisions set forth in an agreement between the agent and the buyer. In dealings with the seller, a buyer's agent should:

- Exercise reasonable skill and care in performance of the agent's duties.
- Deal honestly, fairly and in good faith.
- Disclose all facts known to the agent materially affecting the buyer's ability and/or willingness to perform a contract to acquire seller's property that are not inconsistent with the agent's fiduciary duties to the buyer.

Difference Between Subagent and Broker's Agent

The main distinction between a subagent and a broker's agent comes down to vicarious liability. In a subagency, the owner will accept the vicarious liability of all subagents or seller's agents working through the listing broker. In a broker's agency, the broker will accept the vicarious liability of the agents, called broker's agents. The listing itself is not changed except for the person accepting the liability. All agents showing the property still owe the owner the full fiduciary relationship.

Dual Agency

A real estate broker may represent *both the tenant and the landlord or the seller and the buyer if all parties to the transaction give their informed consent in writing.* In such a **dual agency** situation, the agent will not be able to provide the full range of fiduciary duties to the principal or customer. The obligations of an agent are also subject to any specific provisions set forth in an agreement between the agent, and the tenant and landlord. An agent acting as a dual agent must explain carefully to both the landlord and tenant that the agent is acting for the other party as well. The agent should also explain the possible effects of dual representation, including that by consenting to the dual agency relationship the landlord and tenant are **giving up their right to undivided loyalty.** A landlord and tenant should carefully consider the possible consequences of a dual agency relationship before agreeing to such representation. There are states that have outlawed dual agency; Florida being the first state to do so. There will be more discussion regarding this and other agencies with regard to the agency disclosure forms.

Dual Agency with Designated Sales Agents

If the buyer and the seller or tenant and the landlord provide their informed consent in writing, the principals and the real estate broker who represents both parties as a dual agent may designate a sales agent to represent the buyer and another sales agent to represent the seller to negotiate the purchase and sale of real estate. A sales agent works under the supervision of the real estate broker. With the informed consent in writing, the designated sales agent for the tenant will function as the tenant's agent representing the interests of and advocating on behalf of the tenant and the designated sales agent for the landlord will function as the landlord's agent representing the interests of and advocating on behalf of the landlord in the negotiations between the tenant and the landlord. A designated sales agent cannot provide the full range of fiduciary duties to the landlord or tenant. The designated sales agent must explain that like the dual agent under whose supervision they function, they **cannot provide undivided loyalty.** A landlord or tenant should carefully consider the possible consequences of a dual agency relationship with designated sales agents before agreeing to such representation.

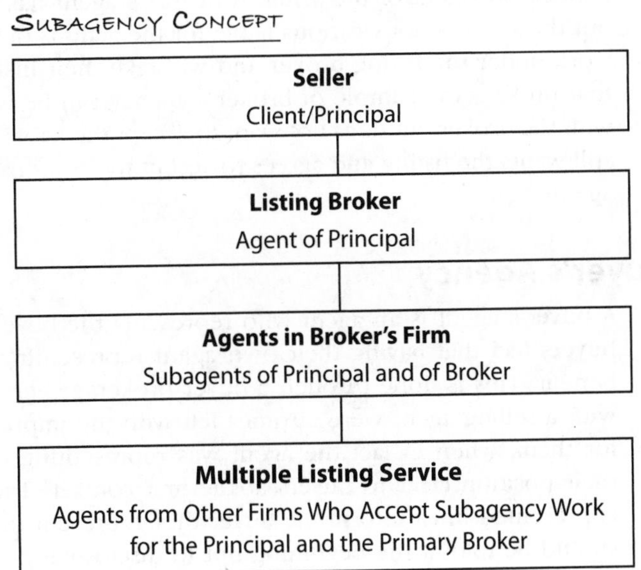

Subagency, Buyer Agent, or Dual Agent

You now have an idea of different types of agents. It is up to the licensee or the policy of the firm to decide with whom they wish to represent.

Subagency

Subagency is created when the broker and seller decide that other agents will represent the owner. This is done by means of multiple listing service. With the creation of buyer agency and other alternatives, owners do not have to put their property on MLS. The owner now has the option to accept subagency or reject it when signing the listing.

When other agents accept subagency, they are working through the listing broker and become the owner's subagent, as do all the agents affiliated with the brokers' office. The agents working for the broker and all subagents owe the client the same fiduciary duties. All these agents still must deal fairly and honestly with all third parties, and disclose any and all material or latent defects. The great advantage for an owner regarding subagency is that there are more agents with more potential customers to be shown their property. What principals should be made aware during subagency is the term **vicarious liability**. It means *one person is responsible for the actions of another person.* The principal can be held liable for the actions of agents or subagents in cases of misrepresentation or any act that will cause damage to third parties. Section 442 of Real Property Law indicates a broker is vicariously liable for a salesperson's deeds only if the broker had knowledge of the offense or gained profit from it after having knowledge.

Broker's Agent

A broker's agent is a cooperating broker who is an agent of the listing broker but is not a subagent of the seller. A broker's agent has fiduciary duties to the seller, but the seller is not vicarious liable for the actions of broker's agents. These agents work under the listing broker and will take their instructions and directions from that broker. An example of broker's agency can be when a seller list his property with the broker but does not want to accept the liability of other agents. The broker still wants the listing and agrees to accept the responsibility for the actions of other agents.

Buyer's Agency

A buyer's agent is an agent who represents the buyer who is the principal. Some buyers feel that having their own agent representing them provides much better benefit. This is done through a buyer brokerage agreement. Buyers when dealing with a selling agent were at times left with the impression the agent was working for them, when in fact the agent was representing the seller. Agents must make their position clear to buyers at the first contact. The agent when the disclosure is presented must inform the buyer they represent the seller. The buyer customer should be told at the beginning not to disclose any information to the agent they do not want the seller to know. In this manner there can be no misunderstanding. Agents should answer any question from a buyer that they are permitted to answer. Buyers should expect agents to answer all questions pertaining to the property. They cannot expect the agent to answer questions that would be deemed confidential, e.g., if the sellers have to sell for any particular reason, or if they must move quickly. This would give the buyer an advantage over the seller. The buyer can also expect the agent to comply with all fair housing and discrimination laws. The buyer's agent has the same standard – they must be fair and honest with the seller.

With a buyer brokerage agreement the agency is turned so that the agent represents the buyer and the seller is now the customer. Even though the buyer is the agent's principal, the agent must deal fairly and honestly with the seller and sellers' agent. Payment in buyer brokerage is done by different means.

The buyer will pay the agent a fee when they purchase a home; this is established in the buyer broker agreement. Other means of payment can be through multiple listing service when the listing broker offers cooperating compensation to the buyer broker. In this case, the buyer will not pay a fee and the deal is simplified. If the broker is going to be paid by the buyer, the listing agent must be notified and the split arrangement can be adjusted. The buyer broker can also receive an up-front nonrefundable fee credited at the closing. If the buyer broker is being paid directly from the buyer, the seller and seller's agent are notified and the buyer's agent rejects cooperating commission.

A buyer's agent must make his status clear when showing a property. He must notify the listing agent immediately that he is acting as a buyer's broker. This way the seller can be notified who will be showing the property. In some cases the owner may want the listing agent to be present for the showing.

The types of buyer agency agreements can be:

- **Open buyer-agency agreement.** This agreement permits the buyer to deal with a number of other agents. The buyer only pays the agent who finds the house.
- **Exclusive buyer-agency agreement.** The buyer is legally bound to pay the fee to the agent regardless of who finds the property. This is similar to the exclusive right to sell listing agreement.
- **Exclusive-agency buyer-agency agreement.** The broker is entitled to compensation if he is the one who locates the property and brings about the sale. With this agreement, the buyer can find a property on his own without being obligated to pay a fee.

Dual Agency

In New York, dual agency is legal and permissible with timely and informed consent of both parties. In this case the agent must have the signed disclosure from both parties. The agent represents *both the buyer and seller in the same transaction and owes both fiduciary duties.* Because the seller and buyer both have conflicting interest the agent *cannot give undivided loyalty to either party.* Dual agency situations can arise with in-house sales if a buyer-client represented by one of the broker's agents becomes interested in the broker's listing. The agents who are subagents of the listing broker must be careful of their obligations to the seller. Even with informed and signed consent from both parties, the agent must be wary not to disclose any information to either party that would give one party an advantage over the other. The agent must remember that both parties are adverse to each other in the transaction. The seller wants the highest price and the buyer wants the lowest.

Unintended or **undisclosed dual agency** is *unlawful can pose serious problems for the broker.* Failure to disclose dual agency whether intentional or unintentional violates license law and agency law, jeopardizing any commission due. This situation may also call for recession of the deal, leaving the broker open to civil suit. It is no defense to claim that it was done with good intentions to help both buyer and seller.

Company policies could allow for dual agency representation for in-house sales. The seller client should be informed when signing the listing that dual agency may happen. A buyer's agent showing a listing from his firm to his buyer client might be a dual agent. Agents must be very careful when representing either buyer or seller; they have to understand the serious implications of dual agency.

Consensual dual agency can work with informed consent and written acknowledgement of dual agency. A licensee may not engage in dual agency without informed consent of both parties and the broker. Agents must realize the hazards of dual agency, as the agent trying to represent both parties must understand the situations that can arise in which the agent might unintentionally compromise one principal in favor of the other. Agents must warn buyers to avoid accidental undisclosed dual agency by not saying anything they would not tell the seller, as their fiduciary obligation requires the agent to tell the seller.

As of January 1, 2011, it is possible to get advance informed consent from a consumer for dual agency or for dual agency with designated sales agents through the Agency Disclosure Form, which is covered in Session 3.

Designated Agency

The Department of State has approved an alternative by which in-house dual agency can be handled in a brokerage firm. When the firm's buyer/client expresses interest in a property listed with the firm, according to New York law, the broker can designate one agent to represent the buyer and another agent to represent the seller. This is done with full disclosure and informed consent of the seller and the buyer. If designated agents are appointed, the firm continues as dual agent representing both the buyer and seller in the same transaction. The broker must still supervise the designated agents. When designated agency is formed both the seller and buyer will not have full fiduciary duties available as if it was a single agency. Designated agents must represent the best interests of the party they each represent. Both agents must speak with their client confidentially. The agents should refrain from disclosing any personal information they obtain, provided it does not violate their duty to deal fairly and honestly with a customer. The fiduciary of *undivided loyalty cannot be delivered by either the designated sales agent or the broker.*

Article 12-A or other regulations are not violated as long as both parties sign the disclosure form. The agent will explain the benefits of appointing a designated agent for the buyer and another for the seller. If they both agree, designated agents are appointed.

As of January 1, 2011, it is possible to get advance informed consent from a consumer for dual agency or for dual agency with designated sales agents through the Agency Disclosure Form, which is covered in Session 3.

Law of Agency 2: Disclosure and Listing Forms

3

Agency Disclosure

Article 12-A, Section 443 of the New York State Real Property Law requires real estate licensees who are acting as agents of buyers or sellers or landlords and tenants of property to advise the potential buyers or sellers or landlords and tenants with whom they work of the nature of their agency relationship and the rights and obligations it creates. This disclosure will help consumers to make informed choices about their relationship with the real estate broker and its sales associates.

Throughout the transaction, someone may receive more than one disclosure form. The law requires each agent assisting in the transaction to present this disclosure form. According to New York Real Property Law, Section 443 applies to **all residential real property transactions**, including multi-family buildings, condominiums, and cooperatives. Prior to January 1, 2011, written disclosure was required only for residential property with one- to four-unit dwellings and did not include condos and co-ops. The current law does not cover vacant land, even if a dwelling is expected to be built there.

First Substantive Contact

The law states the disclosure form must be presented to sellers, buyers, landlords, or tenants at the first substantive contact. **First substantive contact** would be considered *when the agent meets face to face with either the client or customer.*

Examples of first contact could be when a buyer meets an agent for the first time or an agent doing an open house when buyers are walking through the home if they stop and ask any questions regarding the property. This is considered first contact or meeting a buyer at a home for the first time. The agent when taking a listing has to understand all disclosure forms must be presented to the principal before the listing agreement is signed.

At any rate, the form must be presented and signed before entering into any listing agreement or a buyer agency agreement.

Licensees and the Disclosure Forms

Licensees must be fully aware of the disclosure forms and the meanings of each. They must explain these forms to either seller or buyer, and explain their role in each instance. They must also give sellers or buyers the explanation of their fiduciary duties and how it pertains to each. The agent's fiduciary must be understood by each. Sellers must understand even if the agent represents them the agent always owes fair and honest dealings with third parties. The same is true when working with buyers as clients. The agent owes fair and honest dealings to sellers. The form must be explained to each party and signed prior to any agreement being signed (i.e., a listing agreement). There are two separate disclosure forms: One for buyer/seller and one for landlord/tenant.

Note that the Agency Disclosure Form that became effective as of January 1, 2011 allows for agents to obtain **advance informed consent to dual agency** and **dual**

agency with designated sales agents. This gives the agent permission to act as a dual agent for that consumer without having to go back at a later time and present a second Agency Disclosure Form in the event that the agency relationship were to change.

The only fundamental difference between the revised forms that are effective as of January 1, 2011, and the previous version is the addition of this section on the last page with the other acknowledgments:

> **For advance informed consent to either dual agency or dual agency with designated sales agents complete section below:**
>
> **( ) Advance informed consent dual agency.**
>
> **( ) Advance informed consent to dual agency with designated sales agents.**

Refusal to Sign the Disclosure Form

There may be times when someone does not want to sign the form. Generally sellers will always sign; buyers maybe reluctant to sign. If the seller, buyer, landlord or tenant refuses to sign an acknowledgment of receipt pursuant to this subdivision of Real Property Law, the agent shall set forth under oath or affirmation a written declaration of the facts of the refusal and shall maintain a copy of the declaration for not less than three years. The agent may then proceed to show the property.

Declaration by Real Estate Licensee pursuant to Section 443(3)(F) of Real Property Law

State of New York

County of ________________

__________________________(name of licensee) do hereby swear and affirm under penalties of perjury:

1. I am the principal broker / associate broker / licensed salesperson affiliated with ____________ ____________(name of firm). I make this statement in compliance with Section 443(3)(f) of the New York Sate Real Property Law.

2. On______________, 20____, I presented to __________________________ (name of buyer or seller) the disclosure notice required under Section 443 of the Real Property Law. A true copy of the actual disclosure form presented to him/her is attached to this affirmation.

3. Although I indicated to the buyer/seller that New York State Law required that I request that he/she sign to acknowledge receipt of the disclosure notice, he/she refused to sign the acknowledgement to the disclosure form when presented. The reason given for this refusal was as follows:

____

____

Dated ______________, New York

____________________, 20____.

____

Print Name Below Signature of Licensee

Because certain information is needed to complete the form, the licensee should make good notes about the time, date, and reasons for refusal to sign. Once the agent completes the declaration, he maintains a copy and gives a copy to his broker that must keep it on file for three years.

New York State
DEPARTMENT OF STATE
Division of Licensing Services
P.O. Box 22001
Albany, NY 12201-2001

Customer Service: (518) 474-4429
www.dos.state.ny.us

New York State Disclosure Form for Buyer and Seller

THIS IS NOT A CONTRACT

New York State law requires real estate licensees who are acting as agents of buyers or sellers of property to advise the potential buyers or sellers with whom they work of the nature of their agency relationship and the rights and obligations it creates. This disclosure will help you to make informed choices about your relationship with the real estate broker and its sales agents.

Throughout the transaction you may receive more than one disclosure form. The law may require each agent assisting in the transaction to present you with this disclosure form. A real estate agent is a person qualified to advise about real estate.

If you need legal, tax or other advice, consult with a professional in that field.

Disclosure Regarding Real Estate Agency Relationships

Seller's Agent

A seller's agent is an agent who is engaged by a seller to represent the seller's interests. The seller's agent does this by securing a buyer for the seller's home at a price and on terms acceptable to the seller. A seller's agent has, without limitation, the following fiduciary duties to the seller: reasonable care, undivided loyalty, confidentiality, full disclosure, obedience and duty to account. A seller's agent does not represent the interests of the buyer. The obligations of a seller's agent are also subject to any specific provisions set forth in an agreement between the agent and the seller. In dealings with the buyer, a seller's agent should (a) exercise reasonable skill and care in performance of the agent's duties; (b) deal honestly, fairly and in good faith; and (c) disclose all facts known to the agent materially affecting the value or desirability of property, except as otherwise provided by law.

Buyer's Agent

A buyer's agent is an agent who is engaged by a buyer to represent the buyer's interests. The buyer's agent does this by negotiating the purchase of a home at a price and on terms acceptable to the buyer. A buyer's agent has, without limitation, the following fiduciary duties to the buyer: reasonable care, undivided loyalty, confidentiality, full disclosure, obedience and duty to account. A buyer's agent does not represent the interest of the seller. The obligations of a buyer's agent are also subject to any specific provisions set forth in an agreement between the agent and the buyer. In dealings with the seller, a buyer's agent should (a) exercise reasonable skill and care in performance of the agent's duties; (b) deal honestly, fairly and in good faith; and (c) disclose all facts known to the agent materially affecting the buyer's ability and/or willingness to perform a contract to acquire seller's property that are not inconsistent with the agent's fiduciary duties to the buyer.

Broker's Agents

A broker's agent is an agent that cooperates or is engaged by a listing agent or a buyer's agent (but does not work for the same firm as the listing agent or buyer's agent) to assist the listing agent or buyer's agent in locating a property to sell or buy, respectively, for the listing agent's seller or the buyer agent's buyer. The broker's agent does not have a direct relationship with the buyer or seller and the buyer or seller can not provide instructions or direction directly to the broker's agent. The buyer and the seller therefore do not have vicarious liability for the acts of the broker's agent. The listing agent or buyer's agent do provide direction and instruction to the broker's agent and therefore the listing agent or buyer's agent will have liability for the acts of the broker's agent.

Dual Agent

A real estate broker may represent both the buyer and seller if both the buyer and seller give their informed consent in writing. In such a dual agency situation, the agent will not be able to provide the full range of fiduciary duties to the buyer and seller. The obligations of an agent are also subject to any specific provisions set forth in an agreement between the agent, and the buyer and seller. An agent acting as a dual agent must explain carefully to

DOS-1736-a (Rev. 11/10)

Source: New York State Department of State

both the buyer and seller that the agent is acting for the other party as well. The agent should also explain the possible effects of dual representation, including that by consenting to the dual agency relationship the buyer and seller are giving up their right to undivided loyalty. A buyer or seller should carefully consider the possible consequences of a dual agency relationship before agreeing to such representation. A seller or buyer may provide advance informed consent to dual agency by indicating the same on this form.

Dual Agent with Designated Sales Agents

If the buyer and seller provide their informed consent in writing, the principals and the real estate broker who represents both parties as a dual agent may designate a sales agent to represent the buyer and another sales agent to represent the seller to negotiate the purchase and sale of real estate. A sales agent works under the supervision of the real estate broker. With the informed consent of the buyer and the seller in writing, the designated sales agent for the buyer will function as the buyer's agent representing the interests of and advocating on behalf of the buyer and the designated sales agent for the seller will function as the seller's agent representing the interests of and advocating on behalf of the seller in the negotiations between the buyer and seller. A designated sales agent cannot provide the full range of fiduciary duties to the buyer or seller. The designated sales agent must explain that like the dual agent under whose supervision they function, they cannot provide undivided loyalty. A buyer or seller should carefully consider the possible consequences of a dual agency relationship with designated sales agents before agreeing to such representation. A seller or buyer may provide advance informed consent to dual agency with designated sales agents by indicating the same on this form.

This form was provided to me by ______________________ (print name of licensee) of ______________________ (print name of company, firm or brokerage), a licensed real estate broker acting in the interest of the:

(____) Seller as a (check relationship below)

(____) Seller's agent

(____) Broker's agent

(____) Buyer as a (check relationship below)

(____) Buyer's agent

(____) Broker's agent

(____) Dual agent

(____) Dual agent with designated sales agent

For advance informed consent to either dual agency or dual agency with designated sales agents complete section below:

(____) Advance informed consent dual agency

(____) Advance informed consent to dual agency with designated sales agents

If dual agent with designated sales agents is indicated above: ______________________ is appointed to represent the buyer; and ______________________ is appointed to represent the seller in this transaction.

(I) (We) ______________________ acknowledge receipt of a copy of this disclosure form: signature of {   } Buyer(s) and/or {   } Seller(s):

______________________ ______________________

______________________ ______________________

Date: ______________________ Date: ______________________

DOS-1736-a (Rev. 11/10)

FORM FOR APARTMENT

New York State
DEPARTMENT OF STATE
Division of Licensing Services
P.O. Box 22001
Albany, NY 12201-2001

Customer Service: (518) 474-4429
www.dos.state.ny.us

New York State Disclosure Form for Landlord and Tenant

THIS IS NOT A CONTRACT

New York State law requires real estate licensees who are acting as agents of landlords and tenants of real property to advise the potential landlords and tenants with whom they work of the nature of their agency relationship and the rights and obligations it creates. This disclosure will help you to make informed choices about your relationship with the real estate broker and its sales agents.

Throughout the transaction you may receive more than one disclosure form. The law may require each agent assisting in the transaction to present you with this disclosure form. A real estate agent is a person qualified to advise about real estate.

If you need legal, tax or other advice, consult with a professional in that field.

Disclosure Regarding Real Estate Agency Relationships

Landlord's Agent

A landlord's agent is an agent who is engaged by a landlord to represent the landlord's interest. The landlord's agent does this by securing a tenant for the landlord's apartment or house at a rent and on terms acceptable to the landlord. A landlord's agent has, without limitation, the following fiduciary duties to the landlord: reasonable care, undivided loyalty, confidentiality, full disclosure, obedience and duty to account. A landlord's agent does not represent the interests of the tenant. The obligations of a landlord's agent are also subject to any specific provisions set forth in an agreement between the agent and the landlord. In dealings with the tenant, a landlord's agent should (a) exercise reasonable skill and care in performance of the agent's duties; (b) deal honestly, fairly and in good faith; and (c) disclose all facts known to the agent materially affecting the value or desirability of property, except as otherwise provided by law.

Tenant's Agent

A tenant's agent is an agent who is engaged by a tenant to represent the tenant's interest. The tenant's agent does this by negotiating the rental or lease of an apartment or house at a rent and on terms acceptable to the tenant. A tenant's agent has, without limitation, the following fiduciary duties to the tenant: reasonable care, undivided loyalty, confidentiality, full disclosure, obedience and duty to account. A tenant's agent does not represent the interest of the landlord. The obligations of a tenant's agent are also subject to any specific provisions set forth in an agreement between the agent and the tenant. In dealings with the landlord, a tenant's agent should (a) exercise reasonable skill and care in performance of the agent's duties; (b) deal honestly, fairly and in good faith; and (c) disclose all facts known to the tenant's ability and/or willingness to perform a contract to rent or lease landlord's property that are not consistent with the agent's fiduciary duties to the buyer.

Broker's Agents

A broker's agent is an agent that cooperates or is engaged by a listing agent or a tenant's agent (but does not work for the same firm as the listing agent or tenant's agent) to assist the listing agent or tenant's agent in locating a property to rent or lease for the listing agent's landlord or the tenant agent's tenant. The broker's agent does not have a direct relationship with the tenant or landlord and the tenant or landlord can not provide instructions or direction directly to the broker's agent. The tenant and the landlord therefore do not have vicarious liability for the acts of the broker's agent. The listing agent or tenant's agent do provide direction and instruction to the broker's agent and therefore the listing agent or tenant's agent will have liability for the acts of the broker's agent.

Dual Agent

A real estate broker may represent both the tenant and the landlord if both the tenant and landlord give their informed consent in writing. In such a dual agency situa-

DOS-1735-a (Rev. 11/10)

Source: New York State Department of State

tion, the agent will not be able to provide the full range of fiduciary duties to the landlord and the tenant. The obligations of an agent are also subject to any specific provisions set forth in an agreement between the agent, and the tenant and landlord. An agent acting as a dual agent must explain carefully to both the landlord and tenant that the agent is acting for the other party as well. The agent should also explain the possible effects of dual representation, including that by consenting to the dual agency relationship the landlord and tenant are giving up their right to undivided loyalty. A landlord and tenant should carefully consider the possible consequences of a dual agency relationship before agreeing to such representation. A landlord or tenant may provide advance informed consent to dual agency by indicating the same on this form.

Dual Agent with Designated Sales Agents

If the tenant and the landlord provide their informed consent in writing, the principals and the real estate broker who represents both parties as a dual agent may designate a sales agent to represent the tenant and another sales agent to represent the landlord. A sales agent works under the supervision of the real estate broker. With the informed consent in writing of the tenant and the landlord, the designated sales agent for the tenant will function as the tenant's agent representing the interests of and advocating on behalf of the tenant and the designated sales agent for the landlord will function as the landlord's agent representing the interests of and advocating on behalf of the landlord in the negotiations between the tenant and the landlord. A designated sales agent cannot provide the full range of fiduciary duties to the landlord or tenant. The designated sales agent must explain that like the dual agent under whose supervision they function, they cannot provide undivided loyalty. A landlord or tenant should carefully consider the possible consequences of a dual agency relationship with designated sales agents before agreeing to such representation. A landlord or tenant may provide advance informed consent to dual agency with designated sales agents by indicating the same on this form.

This form was provided to me by ______________________________ (print name of licensee) of ______________________ (print name of company, firm or brokerage), a licensed real estate broker acting in the interest of the:

(____) Landlord as a (check relationship below)

(____) Landlord's agent

(____) Broker's agent

(____) Tenant as a (check relationship below)

(____) Tenant's agent

(____) Broker's agent

(____) Dual agent

(____) Dual agent with designated sales agent

For advance informed consent to either dual agency or dual agency with designated sales agents complete section below:

(____) Advance informed consent dual agency

(____) Advance informed consent to dual agency with designated sales agents

If dual agent with designated sales agents is indicated above: ______________________________ is appointed to represent the tenant; and ______________________________ is appointed to represent the seller in this transaction.

(I) (We) ____ acknowledge receipt of a copy of this disclosure form: signature of { } Landlord(s) and/or { } Tenant(s):

______________________________ ______________________________

______________________________ ______________________________

Date: ______________________________ Date: ______________________________

DOS-1735-a (Rev. 11/10)

Different Forms

For the purpose of explaining the listing and other forms used besides the agency disclosure form, these forms are supplied by the Multiple Listing Service of Long Island. Each agent should check with their office or local board for forms related to them.

Exclusive Right to Sell Agreement

With the **exclusive right to sell listing agreement**, the *property is listed with only one broker.* If anyone should sell the property during the term of the agreement the broker is legally entitled to the commission. This agreement, like all other listings, must have a termination date. New York prohibits automatic extension of listings. All listing extensions must be renewed in writing. As part of Article 12-A of New York Property Law, Section 443 the Agency Disclosure form must be presented and signed.

Exclusive Agency Agreement

In an **exclusive agency listing**, the *property is listed with one broker*. If the broker sells the property or if the listing is part of multiple listing service and any broker or agent from a participating firm should sell the property, they are entitled to the commission. If the owner sells the property to anyone not generated from any broker/agent they owe no commission.

Upon listing with the excusive right to sell or exclusive agency, the agent must explain each listing and the differences and give the owners the right to choose. The owners must initial or sign near each of the explanations to prove they were given the explanations and choice.

Open Listing Agreement

In an **open "listing,"** the *seller allows the property to be shown by as many brokers as they can give it to.* Under this type, the broker affecting the sale earns a commission. If the owner sells the property to someone not generated by any broker, they owe no commission. In an open, the same rules of disclosure apply. Agents should be wary of this arrangement, since no documents are signed. Very rarely will a seller sign any form expressing the agent's role. Licensees should check with their broker on office policies regarding open listings.

Exclusive Right to Rent Agreement

This listing is similar to the exclusive right to sell. In this, the contract is between a landlord/lessor and a broker in the rental of residential property. If the owner or anyone else rents the property, the listing broker is entitled to his fee. With this agreement, as with other exclusive right to sell or exclusive agency agreements, the New York agency disclosure is mandated.

Exclusive Buyer Agency Agreement

With this form of agreement, the buyer is the principal/client and the seller/owner is the customer or third party. As with the other exclusive listings, the agent owes all fiduciary duties to the buyer, but also owes the third party "fair and honest dealings." This agreement must clearly spell out the obligations of each party. The listing should spell out exactly what the criteria for the buyer are, the commission for the agent, and the listing expiration.

LONG ISLAND MULTIPLE LISTING SERVICE REALTORS MLX

RESIDENTIAL PROPERTY DATA SECTION (PDS)

EQUAL OPPORTUNITY LENDER

★Means Required Information *Broker Load *(Y or N)* *ML #

LOCATION

Street #: Street Dir: *Street Name: St Suffix:
*Town: *Zone: *Zip: Zip + 4:
Sec/Area: Cross St:
*School District Name:
School District #: District: Section: Block:
Lot: Zoning: Cul-de-sac *(Y or N)*:
*Waterfront *(Y or N)*: Water Frontage: Waterfront Desc.: *Waterview *(Y or N)*:
Bulkhead *(Y or N)*: Docking Rights: Beach Rights *(Y or N)*: *Adult Community *(Y or N)*: Minimum Age:

PRICE & DATES

*Listing Price: *Taxes (w/o exempt.): Additional Village Taxes:
*Listing Date: *Exp Date:

HOME CHARACTERISTICS

*Style: *Rooms: *Bedrooms: *Baths-Full: *Baths-Half:
*# Families: *Detached/Att *(Det-Att-Sd)*: *# Kitchens: *Eat In Kitchen *(Y or N)*:
*Dining Room: *Den/Family Rm *(Y or N)*: *Office *(Y or N)*: *Attic *(Y or N)*: Handicap Access *(Y or N)*:
Handicap Access Desc.:
Approx int Square Footage: *Basement *(Crawl-Full-Part-None-Opt)*: Finished Bsmt *(P-Y-N)*:
*# Fireplaces: W/W Carpet *(Y or N)*: Wood Floors: *(Y or N)*: *Approx. Year Built: *New Construction: *(Y or N)*:
Skylight: Appearance:
Floor Description:
Bsmt/Subfloor:
*1st Floor:
2nd Floor:
3rd Floor:

EXTERIOR

*Construction: Garage: Garage Type: Driveway *(PTY-PVT-N)*:
Deck: Patio: Porch:
*Pool *(AG-IG-N)*: Pool Desc.:
Inground Lawn Sprinklers: Tennis Court *(Y or N)*: Tennis Court Desc.:
*Lot Size: *Lot Sq. Footage:
Building Size:

APPLIANCES

*Stove: *Refrigerator: *Washer: *Dryer: *Dishwasher:

UTILITIES

*Fuel: *Heat: # Heating Zones: Sewer *(Y or N)*: Separate Hot Water Heater:
*A/C *(# or CAC)*: CAC # Zones Water *(Public-Well)*:

OWNER/BROKER

*Owner: *Phone #:
*Seller Agency Compensation: *Buyer Agency Compensation:
*Broker Agency Compensation: Agency *(Enter A If Agency)*: *Exclusions *(Y or N)*: *Negotiate Direct *(Y or N)*:
Occupancy:
Show Instructions:
Lockbox *(Y or N)*: Owner Financing *(Y or N)*

REMARKS

Remarks:
*Directions:
Property Desc.: *(No Contact info, Status, etc.)*

MISCELLANEOUS

Rent Income: *Also For Rent *(Y or N)*: Rental Price:
Renting Broker Compensation:
Items Excluded In Sale:
*Supersedes *(Y or N)*: Supersedes ML #: Foreclosure *(Y or N)*:

OPEN HOUSE

Broker Open House Start Date: Broker Open House End Date:
Broker Open House Time: Broker Open House Note:
Consumer Open House Start Date: Consumer Open House End Date:
Consumer Open House Time: Consumer Open House Note:

SIGNATURES

Owner Signature ____________ Owner Signature ____________
Address ____________ Email Address ____________
Home Phone ____________ Other Phone ____________
Date ____________ MLS Office Name ____________
Listing Agent ____________ Co-Listing Agent ____________

RESIDENTIAL PROPERTY DATA - 6R REV. 03/2007 Subsidiary of Long Island Board of Realtors, Inc.

REALTOR'S COPY (1st Part) OWNER'S COPY (2nd Part) Page 1 of 2
REALTOR'S COPY

Source: Multiple Listing Service of Long Island.

ML#______________________ Property Address____

List Price________________________________

LISTING AGREEMENT FOR REAL PROPERTY
EXCLUSIVE RIGHT TO SELL

Commission Rates for the Sale, Lease or Management of Property Shall be Negotiated between the BROKER[1] and the Owner

EMPLOYMENT

1. The BROKER agrees to act as a special limited agent for the Owner(s) for the sole purpose of finding a Purchaser and/or Tenant to buy and/or rent the property described in the PROPERTY DATA SECTION hereinafter called PDS at the price and conditions set in the PDS. The PDS is incorporated herein by reference.
2. The parties agree that the BROKER represents the owner as seller's agent and shall cooperate with other licensed real estate brokers who are Participants in the Multiple Listing Service of Long Island, Inc. (MLSLI) (Cooperating Brokers). The owner acknowledges the BROKER must cooperate with agents who represent buyers. Such buyer's agents represent the interests of the prospective buyers only. In addition to cooperating with buyer's agents the owner authorizes the BROKER to work with seller's agents and/or broker's agents as indicated by the compensation offered in paragraph 6. The compensation to be paid to a cooperating broker representing a buyer should be inserted in paragraph 6 of this agreement.
3. The Owner(s) authorizes the BROKER to enter the information set forth in the PDS, and any photographs, images, graphics and video recordings of the owner's property whether taken by BROKER'S agent, supplied by owner or otherwise (listing content), into a listing content compilation owned by MLSLI. The Owner understands and agrees that said compilation is exclusively owned by MLSLI who alone possesses the right to publish said compilation in any media form it deems appropriate including, the World Wide Web. MLSLI may license, sell, lease and commercially utilize its compilation. Among other uses MLSLI may license or sell the listing content to aggregators who will aggregate the listing content and resell the same. Such aggregated content shall not contain any personal information about the owner other than the owner's name. If any photograph, image, graphics or video recordings were created by the owner and are delivered to BROKER for use in the MLSLI compilation by virtue of such delivery and the execution of this agreement the owner(s) hereby irrevocably assign and Transfers to BROKER any and all copyright rights and other intellectual property rights in the foregoing.
4. BROKER agrees to use its experience and knowledge to determine the appropriate marketing plan for the property. The Owner(s) grants to the BROKER full discretion to determine an appropriate marketing plan for the property.
5. The owner shall not offer nor show their property for sale or rent to any prospective buyers or tenants but shall refer all such prospective buyers or tenants to the BROKER, nor shall the owner negotiate the sale or rental of the property with a buyer unless the BROKER participates in such negotiations.

COMPENSATION

6. A. The Owner(s) hereby agrees to pay the BROKER a total commission in the amount of _____% of the selling price Or $_______ or in the case of a rental by separate agreement. Said commission shall be shared with Cooperating Brokers as follows:
   If the Cooperating Broker is a Seller's Agent _____% of the selling price Or $_______.
   If the Cooperating Broker is a Broker's Agent _____% of the selling price Or $_______.
   If the Cooperating Broker is a Buyer's Agent _____% of the selling price Or $_______.
   B.Said total commission shall be earned and payable under any of the following conditions:
   (a) If the BROKER or Cooperating Broker produces a buyer ready, willing and able to purchase the property on the terms and conditions set forth in the PDS;
   (b) If through the BROKER's or Cooperating Broker's efforts a buyer and the owner(s) reach an agreement upon all the essential terms of a transaction.
   (c) If the property is sold or rented during the term of this Agreement whether or not the sale or rental is a result of the BROKER'S efforts and even if the property is sold as a result of the efforts of the Owner(s) or any other broker or agent not acting under this agreement.
   (d) If the BROKER or Cooperating Broker is the procuring cause of a transaction.
7. The above compensation shall be paid to the BROKER in the event that the owner enters into a contract of sale to sell the property or actually sells the property within a period of ___________ days after the termination of the agreement to any person (buyer) who has been shown the property during the term of this agreement. This paragraph shall not apply if the Owner(s) has in good faith relisted the property with another broker after the expiration of this Agreement and prior to the commencement of negotiations with such buyer.

GOOD FAITH

8. In the event the Owner(s) signs a binder/contract of sale during the term of this employment agreement, the parties agree that the expiration date set forth below shall be extended until the time that said contract of sale is fully performed or until such time as said contract fails to be performed either by its terms or because of the default of one of the parties. Nothing herein contained is intended to reduce the term of this Agreement.
9. The Owner(s) agrees at all times to act in good faith to assist the BROKER in the performance of the BROKER'S obligations and to fully cooperate with the BROKER in the BROKER'S efforts to find a buyer for the property and complete the transaction contemplated by this agreement..

RENTAL OF THE PROPERTY

10. Should the Owner(s) desire to rent the property or any portion thereof during the term of this agreement, the parties shall modify this agreement so as to specify the amount of the rent desired by the Owner(s); the terms of the rental; the amount of commission to be paid to the BROKER.
11. In the event the tenant purchases the real property described in the PDS during the term of the tenancy or during the occupancy of the tenant where such occupancy exceeds the original term, the Owner(s) agrees to pay the BROKER the total commission set forth in paragraph 6 hereof.

TERM OF AGREEMENT

12. This agreement shall commence on the date set forth below and shall terminate at midnight on ____________.

MISCELLANEOUS PROVISIONS

13. Any notices required to be given under this agreement shall be in writing and may be given to the party by hand delivery of such notice, confirmed facsimile or by certified or ordinary mail.
14. ALL ORAL OR PRIOR AGREEMENTS BETWEEN THE PARTIES ARE HEREBY MERGED INTO THIS AGREEMENT AND THE PARTIES AGREE THAT THEIR RELATIONSHIP SHALL BE GOVERNED SOLELY BY THIS AGREEMENT AND NOT BY ANY OTHER PRIOR ORAL OR WRITTEN REPRESENTATIONS OR AGREEMENTS. The parties agree that no change, amendment, modification or termination of this agreement shall be binding on any party unless the same shall be in writing and signed by the parties hereto subsequent to the date of this agreement.
15. The Owner(s) understands and agrees that neither the Long Island Board of Realtors, Inc. nor the MLSLI are parties to this agreement and that the BROKER is not an agent for either of said organizations and has no authority to make any representation, agreement or commitment with respect to either of said corporations other than those contained in the printed portions hereof.

REAL PROPERTY LAW 294-b NOTICE

16. Effective January 1, 2009, Broker Shall have the rights set forth in Real Property Law Section 294-b. Notice be given to the seller that:

AT THE TIME OF CLOSING, YOU MAY BE REQUIRED TO DEPOSIT THE BROKER'S COMMISSION WITH THE COUNTY CLERK IN THE EVENT THAT YOU DO NOT PAY THE BROKER HIS OR HER COMMISSION AS SET FORTH HEREIN. YOUR OBLIGATION TO DEPOSIT THE BROKER'S COMMISSION WITH THE COUNTY CLERK MAY BE WAIVED BY THE BROKER.

INDEMNITY

17. In the event any claim or action is commenced against the BROKER or a cooperating broker as a result of the BROKER or cooperating broker obeying the lawful instructions of the Owner(s), then, and in such event, the Owner(s) hereby agrees to defend, indemnify and hold harmless the BROKER or cooperating broker in any such claim or action. Owner shall have the right to select counsel in such event, subject to the approval of the BROKER and/or cooperating broker, which approval shall not be unreasonably withheld.
18. With respect to the provisions of this agreement relating to compensation (Paragraph 6) and indemnity (Paragraph 17) cooperating brokers shall be third party beneficiaries of this agreement.

PROPERTY CONDITION DISCLOSURE

19. The Seller is required by law to complete and sign a Property Condition Disclosure Statement and cause it, or a copy thereof, to be delivered to a buyer or buyer's agent prior to the signing by the buyer of a binding contract of sale.
20. A copy of the Property Condition disclosure Statement containing the signatures of both the buyer and the seller must be attached to the real estate purchase contract.
21. If prior to closing or possession by the buyer the seller acquires knowledge which renders materially inaccurate a Property Condition Disclosure Statement previously provided, the seller must deliver a revised Property Condition Disclosure Statement to the buyer as soon as practicable.
22. If the seller fails to so deliver a Property Condition Disclosure Statement, the buyer will be entitled to a credit in the amount of $500 against the purchase price of the property upon the transfer of title.

EXPLANATIONS

23. An "EXCLUSIVE RIGHT TO SELL" listing means that if you, the Owner(s) of the property find a buyer for your house, or if another broker finds a buyer, you must pay the agreed commission to the present broker.
24. An "EXCLUSIVE AGENCY" listing means that if you, the Owner(s) of the property find a buyer, you will not have to pay a commission to the broker. However, if another broker finds a buyer, you will owe a commission to both the selling broker and your present broker.

EQUAL OPPORTUNITY IN HOUSING

25. The parties agree that the above listed property is to be marketed in compliance with all Federal, State, Municipal and Local Laws concerning discrimination in housing.

[1] Wherever the word broker is capitalized (BROKER) in this agreement, it is intended to describe the real estate broker who is a party and signatory to this agreement and no other broker.

Owner Signature ______________________ Owner Signature ______________________

Owner Resident Address ______________ City/Town ______________ State ______________ Zip ________

Home Phone ______________ Other Phone ______________ Email Address ______________

Date ______________________ MLS Office Name ______________________

Listing Agent ______________________ Co-Listing Agent ______________________

MLS LI-C-CEA (11/08) ©Multiple Listing Service of Long Island Inc. PAGE 2 OF 2 Subsidiary of Long Island Board of Realtors, Inc.

REALTOR'S COPY

LONG ISLAND MULTIPLE LISTING SERVICE REALTORS MLS

CONDO-COOP-HOA PROPERTY DATA SECTION (PDS)

EQUAL OPPORTUNITY LENDER

*** Means Required Information** *Broker Load (Y or N) ☐ *ML # ☐

LOCATION

Street #: ☐ Street Dir: ☐ *Street Name: ☐ St Suffix: ☐
Unit #: ☐ *Town: ☐ *Zone: ☐ *Zip: ☐ Zip + 4: ☐
Cross St: ☐ Development: ☐
*School District Name: ☐ School District #: ☐ District: ☐
Section: ☐ Block: ☐ Lot: ☐ Building: ☐
Tax Unit # ☐ *Waterfront (Y or N): ☐ Waterfront Desc.: ☐ *Waterview (Y or N): ☐
Bulkhead (Y or N): ☐ Docking Rights: ☐ Beach Rights (Y or N): ☐ *Adult Community (Y or N): ☐ Minimum Age: ☐

PRICE & DATES

*Listing Price: ☐ *Taxes (w/o Exempt.): ☐ Additional Village Taxes: ☐
Common Charges: ☐ Maintenance: ☐
Deductible %: ☐ Heating: ☐ Management: ☐
Insurance: ☐ Sewer: ☐ Electric: ☐
Reserve: ☐ Fees: ☐ Other Fees: ☐
*Listing Date: ☐ *Exp Date: ☐
Finance Restrictions: ☐

HOME CHARACTERISTICS

*Type Ownership (Condo, Co-op, Homeowner's Assoc): ☐
*Model Name: ☐ Detached/Att (Det-Att-Sd): ☐ # Floors in Building: ☐
Unit on Floor #: ☐ # Floors in Unit: ☐ *Rooms: ☐ *Bedrooms: ☐ *Baths-Full: ☐ *Baths-Half: ☐
*Kitchen Type (None, Combo, Eik, Eff): ☐ *Dining Room: ☐ *Basement (Crawl-Full-Part-None-Opt): ☐
Finished Bsmt (P-Y-N): ☐ Approx Int. Square Footage: ☐ # Fireplaces: ☐ W/W Carpet (Y or N): ☐ Wood Floors: ☐ Cable (Y or N): ☐
Elevator (Y or N): ☐ *Approx. Year Built: ☐ *New Construction (Y or N): ☐ Appearance: ☐
Handicap Access (Y or N): ☐ Handicap Access Desc.: ☐ *Smoking (Y or N): ☐
*1st Floor Description: ☐
2nd Floor Description: ☐

EXTERIOR

*Construction: ☐ Garage: ☐ Gar. Type: ☐ Parking Spaces: ☐ Parking Charges: ☐
Patio/Terrace (Y or N): ☐ *Pool (AG-IG-N): ☐ Pool Description: ☐
Amenities: ☐
Auxiliary Rooms: ☐ Pets (Y or N): ☐ Tennis Court (Y or N): ☐
Tennis Court Desc.: ☐

APPLIANCES

*Stove: ☐ *Refrigerator: ☐ *Washer: ☐ *Dryer: ☐ *Dishwasher: ☐

UTILITIES

*Fuel: ☐ *Heat: ☐ *A/C (# or CAC): ☐ CAC # Zones: ☐

OWNER/BROKER

*Owner: ☐ *Phone #: ☐
*Seller Agency Compensation: ☐ *Byuer Agency Compensation ☐ *Broker Agency Compensation: ☐
Agency (Enter A If Agency): ☐ *Exclusions (Y or N): ☐ *Negotiate Direct (Y or N): ☐ Occupancy: ☐
Show Instructions: ☐ Lockbox (Y or N): ☐ Owner Financing (Y or N): ☐

REMARKS

Remarks: ☐
*Directions: ☐
Property Desc.: (No Contact info, Status, etc.) ☐

MISCELLANEOUS

*Also For Rent (Y or N): ☐ Rental Price: ☐ Renting Broker Compensation: ☐
Items Excluded In Sale: ☐
*Supersedes (Y or N): ☐ Supersedes ML #: ☐ Foreclosure (Y or N): ☐
President Board/Managing Agent: ☐
Managing Agent Phone #: ☐ Bylaws Attached (Y or N): ☐

OPEN HOUSE

Broker Open House Start Date: ☐ Broker Open House End Date: ☐
Broker Open House Time: ☐ Broker Open House Note: ☐
Consumer Open House Start Date: ☐ Consumer Open House End Date: ☐
Consumer Open House Time: ☐ Consumer Open House Note: ☐

SIGNATURES

Owner Signature ______ Owner Signature ______
Address ______ Email Address ______
Home Phone ______ Other Phone ______
Date ______ MLS Office Name ______
Listing Agent ______ Co-Listing Agent ______

SAMPLE

CONDO-COOP-HOA PROPERTY - LI-10 REV. 3/2007 REALTOR'S COPY Page 1 of 2 Subsidiary of Long Island Board of Realtors, Inc.

Source: Multiple Listing Service of Long Island

EXCLUSIVE RIGHT TO REPRESENT
(Buyer Broker Agreement)

Date__________________________

This agreement made by and between ____with offices at ____ (hereinafter referred to as "BROKER") and the person or persons who are named below and signed this agreement residing at (hereinafter referred to as "CLIENT").

1. Whenever the term BUYER is used in this Agreement, the same shall be construed to mean the CLIENT who executed the Agreement as well as any other person, firm, limited liability company or corporation acting for the BUYER or on the BUYER'S behalf.

EXCLUSIVE EMPLOYMENT

2. The BUYER hereby retains BROKER for the purpose of locating residential real property[1] to be purchased by BUYER in the State of New York, in the following locations:

under terms and conditions acceptable to BUYER.

3. The BUYER agrees to work exclusively with the BROKER and agrees not to retain or utilize the services of any other real estate broker or to negotiate with any owner in connection with the purchase of residential real property during the entire term of this Agreement.

4. If the BUYER enters into a contract to purchase residential real property in the aforesaid counties during the term of this contract, the BUYER agrees to pay the BROKER a commission of $__________ or __________% of the purchase price if the property is listed with a real estate broker or $ __________ or __________% of the purchase price if the property is not so listed. Said commission shall be deemed earned at the time the buyer enters into a contract of sale for the purchase of said residential real property but shall not be payable until closing of title or the failure of the transaction to close because of the buyer's acts or omissions.

5. The commission set forth in paragraph 4 above shall be payable by the BUYER to the BROKER in the event the BUYER enters into a contract to purchase residential real property in one of the aforesaid counties within ______ days after the expiration of the term of this Agreement where the BUYER was first introduced to said property by the BROKER. This paragraph shall not apply if the BUYER has in good faith signed an Exclusive Right to Represent Agreement with another BROKER after the expiration of this Agreement and prior to the commencement of negotiations with the Seller of such property.

6. If the BUYER leases real property which was first shown to the BUYER during the term of this contract or for a period of ______ days after the expiration of the term of this contract, BUYER agrees to pay a commission of ____________________ to the BROKER.

7. If BUYER leases any such property and then purchases the same during their occupancy thereof, then in addition to the commission set forth in paragraph 6 above, the BUYER agrees to pay an additional commission at the time that the BUYER exercises such option or any successor in interest to the BUYER or assignee of the BUYER exercises such option, of________________ .

8. BUYER and BROKER agree that the commission set forth in paragraph 4 above may be included in the purchase price and paid on behalf of the BUYER by the seller should the seller so agree. However, in such event, BUYER shall remain responsible for the payment of same if the seller does not pay the commission.

9. Client shall pay BROKER a non-refundable retainer fee of $__________ at the time of signing this Agreement which amount shall be credited against and commission due the BROKER hereunder.

SERVICES PROVIDED BY BROKER

10. The BROKER shall only have such duties as are specifically set forth in this Agreement. If the BUYER desires any other services to be performed by the BROKER, the BUYER shall enter into a written agreement for such services with the BROKER. Absent such a written agreement, the BUYER shall be foreclosed from enforcing any oral or implied agreement with respect to claimed obligations of the BROKER not set forth in this Agreement. The BROKER undertakes to do the following:

a. To use reasonable efforts to locate property which would meet the BUYER'S desired with respect to residential real property.

b. To accurately and faithfully provide to the BUYER any and all information actually known by the BROKER concerning any property for which the BUYER has expressed an interest to purchase.

c. To advise the BUYER of the BROKER'S opinion of the range of the fair-market value of residential real property to which the BROKER has introduced the BUYER. The BUYER understands and agrees the BROKER does not warrant the accuracy of such opinion and, if the opinion is not accurate, the BROKER shall only be liable to the BUYER in the event the BROKER has been guilty of gross negligence in formulating such opinion, or has acted in Bad Faith.

d. To negotiate with owners of real property on behalf of the BUYER and to act in the BUYER'S best interest in such negotiations.

11. The BUYER is hereby put on notice that in dealing with the BROKER they are dealing with one particular agent of said BROKER. The BUYER understands the BROKER has other agents in addition to the agent with whom the BUYER is dealing. The BUYER is hereby made aware and hereby agrees the BROKER, either through an agent other than the agent with whom the BUYER is working or the same agent with whom the BUYER is working, has the right to present offers to the owner of a property made by other buyers in competition with the offer or offers being made by the BUYER. The BUYER understands and agrees in such a case, there is no obligation created by this Agreement which requires such agent to reveal to the BUYER the amount, terms or conditions of any competing offer. No obligation is created by this Agreement for the agent who is working for the BUYER to ascertain whether or not other agents working with other buyers are negotiating on a property upon which the BUYER is negotiating. In the event the BROKER'S agent acquires actual knowledge of such a competing offer, the BROKER'S sole obligation shall be to continue to advise the BUYER of the BROKER'S estimate of the fair market value of the property; to submit to the owner or the owner's agent, all offers made by the BUYER; and to report to the BUYER all information which the seller or seller's agent authorizes the BROKER to disclose to the BUYER. To the extent any law or regulation contravenes this section of the Agreement, the BUYER hereby waives the same and agrees to the terms and conditions set forth above.

Source: Multiple Listing Service of Long Island.

SERVICES NOT PROVIDED BY THE BROKER

12. The BROKER shall not undertake any of the following NOR SHALL the BUYER make any claim or bring any action, proceeding or complaint based upon the BROKER'S failure to do any of the following:

a. Counsel the BUYER on legal matters, express opinions or perform any other services or do any action which would constitute the practice of law.

b. Inspect or issue an opinion concerning the physical condition of the property, the need for repair, the existence of water damage, termite or other infestation, asbestos, Radon or Lead Paint. Specifically, the buyer is advised that they cannot rely on any statement contained in any listing agreement, multiple listing form or oral or written statement concerning the condition of residential real property expressed to the BUYER by the BROKER. **This Agreement places upon the BUYER the absolute obligation to obtain information concerning the condition of residential real property from sources other than the BROKER. The BROKER recommends the BUYER hire an engineer or qualified home inspector duly licensed by the State of New York for the purpose of ascertaining the physical condition of the property.**

c. Research, ascertain or give advice or opinions concerning applicable zoning, building department, health department, fire regulations or other regulatory matters effecting the property or improvements located thereon and its compliance with laws, codes and regulations.

d. Provide or give opinions concerning surveys diagramming the property.

e. Give tax or financial advice with respect to the purchase, sale or ownership of the property.

f. Review any public records concerning the property including, but not limited to, documents on file with the county clerk's office of the county in which the property is located, Federal, State or local court offices and records in any town or village in which said property is located.

g. Searching for, discovering or giving opinions concerning environmental conditions affecting the property or the locale in which the property is located including, but not limited to, the location of toxic sites, underground infiltration of pollutants, asbestos, buried oil tanks and any other conditions which are not readily observable upon the property. In the event the BUYER has any question with respect to environmental conditions or problems affecting the property or the locale in which the property is located, the BUYER hereby specifically undertakes to hire the necessary environmental experts and consultants to satisfy themselves concerning such environmental conditions. **Under no circumstances is the BUYER entitled to rely on any statement or representation of the BROKER with respect to environmental conditions whether said statement is oral or in writing.**

h. Search, review or discover any public or private record revealing crime scenes, sex offenders or other matters.

13. **Notwithstanding the provisions of paragraph 12 above, the BROKER hereby agrees to truthfully and honestly disclose to the BUYER any and all information affecting both the property and the locale within which the property is located of which the BROKER has actual knowledge.**

14. Governing Law: This Agreement will be governed by and construed in accordance with the law of the State of New York.

ARBITRATION

15. Any dispute between the parties arising out of this agreement where the amount in dispute is greater than Six Thousand ($6,000) Dollars shall be resolved by arbitration before one arbitrator. The arbitration shall be held in any county in which the real estate, which is the subject matter of this agreement, is located. The arbitration shall be governed by the rules of the National Arbitration and Mediation and judgment on the award rendered by the arbitrator may be entered in any court having jurisdiction thereof.

16. In any action, proceeding or arbitration to enforce any provision of this Agreement or for damages caused by default, the prevailing party shall be entitled to reasonable attorney's fees, costs and related expenses, such as expert witness fees, fees paid to investigators, fees paid to arbitration tribunals and arbitrator's fees.

MISCELLANEOUS

17. The parties acknowledge and agree that neither LIBOR nor MLSLI are parties to this Agreement and that BROKER is not an agent of either of said organizations and has no authority to make any representation, agreement or commitment with respect to either of said organizations other than those contained in the printed portion hereof.

18. All notices, requests, demands and other communications hereunder shall be in writing and shall be deemed duly given if delivered or mailed, first class, postage prepaid, certified, registered or express mail, return receipt requested. Either party may change that party's address for purposes hereof by giving written notice of such change of address to the other party herein in the manner herein provided for the giving of notice. A notice given by counsel shall be deemed to be notice by the party represented by such attorney.

19. This Agreement may be executed in counterparts with the same force and effect as if all the signatures were on one document. It is not necessary that all parties sign all or any one of the counterparts, but each party must sign at least one counterpart for this Agreement to be effective.

20. This Agreement may be amended only by an instrument in writing signed by the parties hereto.

21. Neither party may waive any of its rights or any obligation of the other party or any provision of this Agreement except by an instrument in writing signed by that party.

22. This Agreement contains the entire understanding of the parties with respect to the subject matter of the agreement, and it supersedes all prior understandings and agreements, whether written or oral, and all prior dealings of the parties with respect to the subject matter herein.

23. This agreement shall commence on ______________________ and terminate at midnight ________ days thereafter on ______________________ .

[1]Residential real property means property improved by a one to four family dwelling or vacant land which can be so improved.

IN WITNESS WHEREOF, the parties have signed this Agreement as of the date first above written.

______________________________, BROKER ______________________________, BUYER

______________________________ ______________________________, BUYER

PRINT BROKER'S NAME

______________________________, AGENT

____

PRINT AGENT'S NAME

LONG ISLAND MULTIPLE LISTING SERVICE REALTORS MLS

RENTAL PROPERTY DATA SECTION (PDS)

EQUAL OPPORTUNITY LENDER

*** Means Required Information** *Broker Load *(Y or N)* *ML #

LOCATION

Street #: Street Dir: *Street Name: St Suffix:
Apt #: *Town: *Zone: *Zip: Zip + 4:
Cross St: *School District Name:
School District #: District: Section: Block:
Lot: *Waterfront *(Y or N)*: Waterfront Desc.: *Waterview *(Y or N)*:
Bulkhead *(Y or N)*: Docking Rights: Beach Rights *(Y or N)*: *Adult Community *(Y or N)*: Minimum Age:

PRICE & DATES

*Listing Price:
*Listing Date: *Exp. Date:

TERMS

Terms: Lease *(Y or N)*: Option to Buy *(Y or N)*:
Rental Type *(i.e. Month-Month, 1 year, etc.)*: Security Deposit:
Pets *(Y or N)*: Permit #: Permit Exp. Date:

CHARACTERISTICS

*Style: *(i.e. Colonial, Apt. in House, Apt. in Building, etc.)*: *Rooms: *Bedrooms:
*Baths-Full: *Baths-Half: *Kitchen Type *(Combo, Eik, Eff, Share, None)*:
*Basement *(Crawl-Full-Part-None-Opt)*: Finished Bsmt *(P-Y-N)*: *# Fireplaces: Carpet *(Inc-Allowed)*:
Furnished *(Y or N)*: Approx Int. Square Footage: Approx. Year Built: Wood Floors *(Y or N)*:
Appearance: Handicap Access *(Y or N)*: *Smoking *(Y or N)*:
Handicap Access Desc:
Bsmt/Subfloor Desc:
1st Floor Description:
2nd Floor Description:
3rd Floor Description:

EXTERIOR

*Construction: Parking Facilities: Deck:
Patio: Porch: Fence *(Y or N)*: Private Entrance: *(Y or N)*:
*Lot Size: *Lot Sq Footage: *Pool *(AG-IG-N)*:
Pool Desc.: Tennis Court *(Y or N)*:
Tennis Court Desc.:

APPLIANCES

Stove *(Included, Hp, Allow)*: Refrigerator *(Included, Allow)*: Washer *(Included, Allow)*:
Dryer *(Included, Allow)*: Dishwasher *(Included, Allow)*:

UTILITIES/CARE

A/C *(Included, Allow)*: CAC # Zones:
Cable *(Included, Allow)*: Heat *(Included, Not Included Partial)*:
Gas *(Included, Not Included Partial)*: Electric *(Included, Not Included Partial)*:
Water *(Included, Not Included Partial)*: Sewer *(Included, Not Included Partial)*:
Garbage Removal *(Included, Not Included Partial)*: Separate Thermostat *(Y or N)*:
Pool Care *(Included, Not Included Partial)*: Ground Care *(Included, Not Included Partial)*:
House Keeping *(Included, Not Included Partial)*:

OWNER/BROKER

*Owner: *Status / Showing Phone:
*Agency Offered:
*Listing Broker Compensation: Agency *(Enter A if Agency)*: *Exclusions *(Y or N)*:
*Negotiate Direct *(Y or N)*: Compensation Paid By: Occupancy:
Show Instructions: Lockbox *(Y or N)*:

REMARKS/MISC

Remarks:
*Directions:
Ad Text: *(Enter public remarks or advertising text here)*
*Supersedes *(Y or N)*: Supersedes ML #:

SIGNATURES

I/We hereby acknowledge receipt of a copy of this contract.

OWNER SIGNATURE ______ OWNER SIGNATURE ______
ADDRESS ______ EMAIL ADDRESS ______
HOME PHONE ______ OTHER PHONE ______
DATE ______ MLS OFFICE NAME ______
LISTING AGENT ______ CO-LISTING AGENT ______

The Owner(s) and the Broker understand that they must market the property in accordance with federal, state and local laws concerning discrimination in housing.

RENTAL PROPERTY DATA – 8 REV 02/2008 © Multiple Lising Service of Long Island Inc. Subsidiary of Long Island Board of Realtors, Inc.
MW

SAMPLE

Source: Multiple Listing Service of Long Island.

ML#________________________ Address____

LISTING AGREEMENT FOR REAL PROPERTY
EXCLUSIVE RIGHT TO LEASE

Commission Rates for the Sale, Lease or Management of Property
Shall be Negotiated between the BROKER[1] and the Landlord.

EMPLOYMENT

1. The BROKER agrees to act as a special limited agent for the Landlord(s) for the sole purpose of finding a Tenant to rent the property described in the PROPERTY DATA SECTION hereinafter called PDS at the price and conditions set in the PDS. The PDS is incorporated herein by reference.
2. The parties agree that the BROKER represents the Landlord as a Landlord's agent and shall cooperate with other licensed real estate brokers who are Participants in the Multiple Listing Service of Long Island, Inc. (MLSLI) (Cooperating Brokers). The Landlord acknowledges the BROKER must cooperate with agents who represent tenants (tenant's agents). Such tenants' agents represent the interests of the prospective tenants only. In addition to cooperating with tenant's agents the Landlord authorizes the BROKER to work with Landlord's agents and/or broker's agents as indicated in paragraph 6.
3. The Landlord(s) authorizes the BROKER to enter the information set forth in the PDS, and any photographs, images, graphics and video recordings of the Landlord's property whether taken by BROKER'S agent, supplied by Landlord or otherwise (listing content), into a listing content compilation owned by MLSLI. The Landlord understands and agrees that said compilation is exclusively owned by MLSLI who alone possesses the right to publish said compilation in any media form it deems appropriate including, the World Wide Web. MLSLI may license, sell, lease and commercially utilize its compilation. Among other uses MLSLI may license or sell the listing content to aggregators who will aggregate the listing content and resell the same. Such aggregated content shall not contain any personal information about the Landlord other than the Landlord's name. If any photograph, image, graphics or video recordings were created by the Landlord and are delivered to BROKER for use in the MLSLI compilation by virtue of such delivery and the execution of this agreement the Landlord(s) hereby irrevocably assign and Transfers to BROKER any and all copyright rights and other intellectual property rights in the foregoing.
4. BROKER agrees to use its experience and knowledge to determine the appropriate marketing plan for the property. The Landlord(s) grants to the BROKER full discretion to determine an appropriate marketing plan for the property.
5. The Landlord shall not offer nor show their property for rent to any prospective tenants or but shall refer all such prospective tenants to the BROKER, nor shall the Landlord negotiate the rental of the property with a tenant unless the BROKER participates in such negotiations.

COMPENSATION

6. A. In addition to tenant's agents the Landlord(s) also authorizes BROKER to work with Cooperating Brokers as:
   (check the appropriate space or spaces)
   Landlord's Agent _____ (represents the Landlord)
   Broker's Agent _____ (represents the listing broker)
   (If you check one of the above, such agency shall be offered in addition to Tenant's Agency)

   B. The BROKER shall be paid its commission by the tenant and not the Landlord except in the case where the Landlord delivers possession of the premises to a tenant without first being informed in writing by the BROKER that the BROKER'S commission has been paid. In such event, the Landlord shall pay the BROKER'S commission. The BROKER'S commission is _______________. (Insert the total commission.)

   C. Said BROKER'S commission shall also be be earned and payable by the Landlord under any of the following conditions:
   (a) If the BROKER or Cooperating Broker produces a tenant ready, willing and able to lease the property on the terms and conditions set forth in the PDS and the Landlord refuses to lease the premises or fails to deliver possession of the premises after the Landlord has approved the qualifications of the tenant;
   (b) If through the BROKER'S or Cooperating Broker's efforts a tenant and the Landlord(s) reach an agreement upon all the essential terms of a transaction and the Landlord refuses to lease the premises or fails to deliver possession of the premises;
   (c) If the property is rented during the term of this Agreement whether or not the rental is a result of the BROKER'S efforts and even if the property is rented or sold as a result of the efforts of the Landlord(s) or any other broker or agent not acting under this agreement and the landlord has allowed the tenant possession of the premises without being informed by the BROKER in writing that the BROKER'S commission has been paid by tenant;
   (d) If the BROKER or Cooperating Broker is the procuring cause of a transaction.
7. The above compensation shall be paid to the BROKER in the event that the Landlord enters into a lease or rental agreement or actually leases or rents the property within a period of __________________ (   ) days after the termination of the agreement to any person who has been shown the property during the term of this agreement. This paragraph shall not apply if the Landlord(s) has in good faith relisted the property with another broker after the expiration of this Agreement and prior to the commencement of negotiations with such Tenant.

LANDLORDS'S REPRESENTATIONS AND OBLIGATIONS

8. The Landlord represents that all legal requirements including, but not limited to, rental permits, certificate of occupancies or other governmental permits, to create and maintain the rental unit which is the subject of this Agreement have been obtained by Landlord and are currently valid. The Landlord(s) agrees at all times to act in good faith to assist the BROKER in the performance of the BROKER'S obligations and to fully cooperate with the BROKER in the BROKER'S efforts to find a tenant for the property and complete the transaction contemplated by this agreement.

TERM OF AGREEMENT

9. This agreement shall commence on the date set forth below and shall terminate at midnight on ____________________.

MISCELLANEOUS PROVISIONS

10. Any notices required to be given under this agreement shall be in writing and may be given to the party by hand delivery of such notice, confirmed facsimile or by ordinary mail.
11. ALL ORAL OR PRIOR AGREEMENTS BETWEEN THE PARTIES ARE HEREBY MERGED INTO THIS AGREEMENT AND THE PARTIES AGREE THAT THEIR RELATIONSHIP SHALL BE GOVERNED SOLELY BY THIS AGREEMENT AND NOT BY ANY OTHER PRIOR ORAL OR WRITTEN REPRESENTATIONS OR AGREEMENTS. The parties agree that no change, amendment, modification or termination of this agreement shall be binding on any party unless the same shall be in writing and signed by the parties hereto subsequent to the date of this agreement.
12. The Landlord(s) understands and agrees that neither the Long Island Board of Realtors, Inc. nor the MLSLI are parties to this agreement and that the BROKER is not an agent for either of said organizations and has no authority to make any representation, agreement or commitment with respect to either of said corporations other than those contained in the printed portions hereof.

ARBITRATION

13. Any dispute between the parties or a Cooperating Broker appointed pursuant to the authority granted by this agreement and arising out of this agreement where the amount in dispute is greater than small claims court jurisdiction shall be resolved by arbitration before one arbitrator. This paragraph shall not apply if all of the parties to such dispute are REALTORS. The arbitration shall be held in the county in which the real estate, which is the subject matter of this agreement, is located. The arbitration shall be governed by the rules of the National Arbitration and Mediation and judgment on the award rendered by the arbitrator may be entered in any court having jurisdiction thereof. Nothing herein contained is intended to deny any Party, or Cooperating Broker from applying to the Courts for injunctive relief such as is provided in CPLR 2701.

ESCROW AND RECOVERY OF FEES

14. If, for any reason, the BROKER is not paid a commission which is payable by the Landlord on the due date or there is a dispute concerning such payment or all or part of such payment, the Landlord(s) shall deposit with the Long Island Board or Realtors, Inc. an amount equal to the compensation set forth herein or the disputed amount, as the case may be. If the Landlord's attorney is holding money in an escrow account to which the Landlord is entitled, or over which the Landlord has control, the Landlord shall direct the attorney to make the deposit herein required to the extent of such monies. The said monies shall be held by the Long Island Board of Realtors, Inc. in escrow until the parties' rights to the escrow monies have been determined (i) by the written agreement of the parties, (ii) by an award of an arbitrator, (iii) by judgment or (iv) by some other process to which the parties agree in writing.
15. In any action, proceeding or arbitration to enforce any provision of this Agreement, including but not limited to the above escrow provision, or for damages caused by default, the prevailing party shall be entitled to reasonable attorney's fees, costs and related expenses, such as expert witness fees, fees paid to investigators, fees paid to arbitration tribunals and arbitrator's fees. Paragraphs 14 and 15 hereof shall be deemed to be incorporated into the terms of any lease executed by the Landlord(s) with a buyer/tenant procured by BROKER or a Cooperating Broker in their performance of this agreement.

INDEMNITY

16. In the event any claim or action is commenced against the BROKER or a Cooperating Broker as a result of the BROKER or Cooperating Broker either obeying the lawful instructions of the Landlord(s) or relying upon any representation made by the Landlord in this Agreement, then, and in such event, the Landlord(s) hereby agrees to defend, indemnify and hold harmless the BROKER or Cooperating Broker in any such claim or action. Landlord shall have the right to select counsel in such event, subject to the approval of the BROKER and/or Cooperating Broker, which approval shall not be unreasonably withheld.
17. With respect to the provisions of this agreement relating to compensation, (Paragraph 6), arbitration (Paragraph 13), escrow and recovery of fees (Paragraphs 14 & 15) and indemnity (Paragraph 16) Cooperating Brokers shall be third party beneficiaries of this agreement.

EXPLANATIONS

18. An "EXCLUSIVE RIGHT TO LEASE" listing means that if you, the Landlord(s) of the property find a tenant for your house, or if another broker finds a tenant, you must pay the agreed commission to the present broker.
19. An "EXCLUSIVE AGENCY" listing means that if you, the Landlord(s) of the property find a tenant, you will not have to pay a commission to the broker. However, if another broker finds a tenant, you will owe a commission to both the leasing broker and your present broker.

EQUAL OPPORTUNITY IN HOUSING

20. The parties agree that the above listed property is to be marketed in compliance with all Federal, State, Municipal and Local Laws concerning discrimination in housing.

[1] Wherever the word broker is capitalized (BROKER) in this agreement, it is intended to describe the real estate broker who is a party and signatory to this agreement and no other broker.

Owner Signature ______________________ Owner Signature ______________________

Address ______________________ Email Address ______________________

Home Phone ______________________ Other Phone ______________________

Date ______________________ MLS Office Name ______________________

Listing Agent ______________________ Co-Listing Agent ______________________

LISTING AGREEMENT - LI-8C REV 02/08 ©Multiple Listing Service of Long Island Inc. PAGE 2 OF 2 Subsidiary of Long Island Board of Realtors, Inc.

OFFICE EXCLUSIVE CERTIFICATION

Date: ______________________

TO MULTIPLE LISTING SERVICE OF LONG ISLAND, INC.
300 SUNRISE HIGHWAY, WEST BABYLON, N.Y. 11704

I hereby certify that I have given ______________________
(Name of Realtor Office)

an exclusive listing on my property at ______________________
(Address of Property)

______________________, a copy of which is attached hereto. Said office has explained the advantages of The Multiple Listing Service, however, for personal reasons I direct that this property not be published in The Multiple Listing Service.

The exclusive listing runs from ______________________ to
(Beginning Date)

______________________.
(Expiration Date)

____
Owner

____
Owner

____
Salesperson Name (Print)

____
Firm Name

____
Office Address

____
Office Phone

FOR SERVICE USE ONLY:

ROSTER #: ____________

CODE: ____________

BRANCH: ____________

MLS - LI - 2 (4/93)

Office Exclusive Certification

Source: Multiple Listing Service of Long Island.

REPORT OF CHANGE
IN LISTING CONTRACT

______ YES ______ NO The following changes have been entered into the computer. (REMINDER: There is a charge for these changes to be entered at the service office.)

TOWN................................ ZONE ....

ML Number................................ Listing Realtor................................

Addr of property................................ Style ....

Owner ....

It is agreed between the parties that the following changes are to be made in the original listing agreement dated .... 20 .... concerning the above mentioned property.

_____ 1. List price (LP$) has been changed to: $ ....

.... 20.......
Day Month Year
Signature Date

....
Owner

....
Owner

_____ 2. Address of property corrected to: ....

_____ 3. Taxes changed to: ....

_____ 4. New picture for zone book.

_____ 5. Premises will be available for occupancy on .... 20 ....

_____ 6. The following additional information is to be included in the herein mentioned listing agreement ....

....

....

....

_____ 7. Expiration date (XD) of listing agreement is amended to: .... 20.......
Day Month Year

.... 20.......
Day Month Year
Signature Date

....
Owner

....
Owner

The above changes in the herein mentioned listing agreement are effective immediately. **Owner hereby acknowledges receipt of a copy of this Report of Change in Listing Contract which they are entitled to under the law.**

Above changes are agreed to by the Listing Realtor. ....
Listing Realtor

By ....

Office Phone #: ....

MLS-LI-5 (2/93)

.... 20.......
Day Month Year

Source: Multiple Listing Service of Long Island.

WITHDRAWAL FORM

______ YES ______ NO The following changes have been entered into the computer. (REMINDER: There is a charge for these changes to be entered at the service office.)

DATE OF WITHDRAWAL ____________________ ML NO. ________________ ZONE __________

Supplemental agreement to original listing contract dated ______________________________________
(Date of Listing)
and due to expire on __________________________________.
(Expiration Date)

IN CONSIDERATION OF THE WITHDRAWAL of the property located at:

____

Listed under said Multiple Listing Contract, it is mutually understood and agreed between the parties hereto that ____ as owner(s), represents that:
Name(s) of Owner(s)

1. there are no negotiations pending with anyone for the sale, lease, or exchange of said property; and
2. that this withdrawal is void if negotiations are pending at the time of said withdrawal; and
3. the owner(s) agrees that, should said property be sold, leased, or exchanged before ______________, by
month / day / year

    a. the owner(s), or
    b. any Realtor-Participant in the Multiple Listing Service of Long Island, Inc., or
    c. any other broker; or
    d. through any other source

   THAT SAID OWNER(s) WILL PAY THE COMMISSION THAT WOULD BE DUE UNDER THE SAID MULTIPLE LISTING CONTRACT, IN ACCORDANCE WITH THE TERMS THEREOF.

4. the said owner(s) further agrees that, should the property be offered again for sale, lease, or exchange before __________________.
month / day / year

   the owner(s) agrees to relist the property with the present listing broker in the Multiple Listing Service of of Long Island, Inc.

BY: __________________________________ __________________________________
(Authorized Representative) (Owner)

FIRM: ________________________________ __________________________________
(Owner)

MLS - LI - 3 (4/93)

Source: Multiple Listing Service of Long Island.

Office Exclusive and Other Forms Pertaining to Listings

The office exclusive is when the seller does not want his home on the multiple listing service and directs the agent not to do so for whatever reason. Agents must explain the benefits of MLS and obey sellers' wishes. There are forms for this and transaction and withdrawal also report of change forms. Agents must be aware of all forms and when to use them.

Cooperating Brokers

There are all different types of broker/agents that can be considered when referring to cooperative. They can be subagents, dual agents, buyer's agents. The agents work with each other to sell a property. Sales can be by a seller's agent from the same firm or another real estate company, working as subagents of the listing broker and seller. Cooperative sales are given through a multiple listing service. It can also be a buyer's agent from another firm who represents the buyer. Whenever an agent requests to show a property, they must make their position clear at the outset if they are a subagent or buyer's agent.

Listing Protection

Most exclusive listing agreements contain a clause or paragraph immediately following the compensation paragraph, that should the owner sell or enter into a contract during a specified period of time following the expiration of the listing. The broker is still owed the commission. The paragraph could look like this:

COMPENSATION

The Owner(s) hereby agrees to pay the BROKER a total commission in the amount of _____% of the selling price Or $_______ or in the case of a rental by separate agreement. Said commission shall be shared with Cooperating Brokers as follows:

If the Cooperating Broker is a Seller's Agent _____% of the selling price Or $_______.

If the Cooperating Broker is a Broker's Agent _____% of the selling price Or $_______.

If the Cooperating Broker is a Buyer's Agent _____% of the selling price Or $_______.

Said total commission shall be earned and payable under any of the following conditions:

(a) If the BROKER or Cooperating Broker produces a buyer ready, willing and able to purchase the property on the terms and conditions set forth in the PDS;

(b) If through the BROKER's or Cooperating Broker's efforts a buyer and the owner(s) reach an agreement upon all the essential terms of a transaction.

(c) If the property is sold or rented during the term of this Agreement whether or not the sale or rental is a result of the BROKER'S efforts and even if the property is sold as a result of the efforts of the Owner(s) or any other broker or agent not acting under this agreement.

(d) If the BROKER or Cooperating Broker is the procuring cause of a transaction.

The above compensation shall be paid to the BROKER in the event that the owner enters into a contract of sale to sell the property or actually sells the property within a period of __________ days after the termination of the agreement to any person (buyer) who has been shown the property during the term of this agreement. This paragraph shall not apply if the Owner(s) has in good faith relisted the property with another broker after the expiration of this Agreement and prior to the commencement of negotiations with such buyer.

Regulation 175.7

In addition to Section 443 of the New York Real Property law requiring disclosure of an agency relationship, Regulation 175.7 of the codified rules has a direct correlation in satisfying the disclosure obligation. Regulation 175.7 requires agents to make clear for which party he is acting. In addition, the regulation limits compensation from more than one party in a transaction except when full disclosure and consent is granted by all parties. The requirement for the agent to make clear his relationship and to not receive undisclosed and non-consented compensation from more than one party is not limited to residential transactions, but applies to all real estate transactions.

Agents Changing Their Position

With the written consent of the principal, agents may change their roles after having established a agency with the seller as a client, a seller subagent-client relationship, or a buyer's agent-client association.

- **Seller client-agent to dual agent.** An agent working for a seller to represent them may know of another agent in the same firm who represents a buyer client. This buyer may have interest in the property. The seller's agent must approach the seller about possible dual agency with the buyer. Seller and buyer may accept the dual agency relationship. The brokerage firm now becomes dual agent for the buyer and seller. The broker may assign designated agents. The agency is disclosed with informed consent in writing accepted by all parties.
- **Buyer client-agent to dual agent.** As with the previous example of seller client to dual agent, it would be the same except the roles are reversed from seller to buyer. As with any type of change in the agency make up, all parties must agree and the proper disclosures must be signed to verify it.

Your Role and Explaining Agency Disclosure Form

Licensees must thoroughly discuss the agency relationship and whom they represent. Agents must clarify client and customer roles and explain the fiduciary responsibilities to the client. They must also explain to the client the services they offer and that by law they must deal fairly and honestly with third parties. They also must explain to sellers and buyers by law they have certain consumer rights.

The licensee should explain the document and answer questions they may have. There are now two separate disclosure forms. One form is for the Buyer and Seller and another form for the Landlord and Tenant. The agent must explain the different sections if any of the parties do not understand what they are being asked to sign. First the agent should make clear that **the form is not a contract.** It is a state mandated form to explain their consumer rights. If need be, the agent can go over each paragraph and explain the meaning of seller's agent, buyer's agent, broker's agent, dual agent, and dual agent with designated sales associate. The agent will fill in the spaces required to be filled in and ask for the signature.

Licensees must be careful to make sure the form is presented at **first substantive contact.** This could be when holding open house buyers want information on the property, disclosure form must be presented. If buyers are just walking around and do not discuss the property the form does not need to be presented. When taking a listing the first formed to be signed is the agency disclosure. If an agent is entering into a buyer agency form is first to be signed. Licensees must be careful in maintaining their records. Part 175.23 of Rules affecting brokers and salespersons states: Each licensed broker shall keep and maintain for a period of three years, records of each transaction effected through his office concerning the sale or mortgage of one- to four-family dwellings.

Agent Record Keeping

New licensees must start their career with the habit of keeping records. Everything must be documented and saved. In today's world of so many electronic devices, paper and pen are becoming obsolete. Agents should use any form of documentation they are comfortable with, as long as the firm allows. First, this could help if any problems arise in the future. The agent will have the documentation to dispute any claims of irregularity. Record keeping is the backbone of any agent's career. Agents must make notes of any conversations with buyers or clients. These notes will help the agent to take better care of the parties they are working with.

When working with buyers, the first thing an agent will do is write the necessary information, e.g., name, phone, address, also the criteria of what they are looking to purchase, type of home, how many bedrooms, approx. price, etc. With this information now the agent can start the search and also make an appointment for the buyer to see the properties. Part of the records should include any property that is shown, the date, and any brief remark from the buyer. Properties suggested to buyers must be written down so agents will have the information if they are called by the buyer. This will enable the agent to better find the right properties. Any phone calls to or from a seller or buyer should be written on their form, the purpose of the call, and other information. Agents must realize they will be dealing with many people during the course of one day. It will be almost impossible to remember every face or name after they have been working for just a little while. This is the fundamental reason for keeping notes: You do not want to try and remember something from a week ago. All it takes is one mistake answering a seller's or buyer's question wrong because you had no record of the conversation to ruin your credibility. Besides just keeping notes, agents should get in the habit of calling all their sellers buyers on a timely basis. This may help prevent any misconception or error later in the transaction.

Nonsolicitation Orders and Cease and Desist Zones

A **nonsolicitation order** is a directive to all real estate brokers and real estate salespersons. The nonsolicitation order directs that *all brokers and salespersons must refrain from soliciting listings for the sale of residential property within a designated geographic area.* A nonsolicitation order prohibits any and all types of solicitation directed at or toward homeowners in the designated geographic area. The types of solicitation that are prohibited include but are not limited to letters, postcards, telephone calls, door-to-door calls, handbills, and postings in public areas. In addition, a nonsolicitation order may contain such other terms or conditions as the Secretary of State may determine are, on balance, in the best interest of the public, which shall include but not be limited to the affected owners and licensees. This topic is discussed further in the session on Fair Housing.

Law of Agency 3: Other Types of Disclosure and Antitrust Laws

Disclosure Obligations

Licensees in certain situations will be required to make other forms of disclosures to either sellers or buyers. Some disclosures, such as the Residential Lead Based Paint Disclosure, are discussed in Environmental Issues session.

Stigmatized Property

1. Notwithstanding any other provision of law, it is not a material defect or fact relating to property offered for sale or lease, including residential property regardless of the number of units contained therein, that:

   (a) an owner or occupant of the property is, or was at any time suspected to be, infected with human immunodeficiency virus or diagnosed with acquired immune deficiency syndrome or any other disease which has been determined by medical evidence to be highly unlikely to be transmitted through occupancy of a dwelling place; or

   (b) the property is, or is suspected to have been, the site of a homicide, suicide or other death by accidental or natural causes, or any crime punishable as a felony.

2. (a) No cause of action shall arise against an owner or occupant of real property, or the agent of such owner or occupant, or the agent of a seller or buyer of real property, for failure to disclose in any real estate transaction a fact or suspicion contained in subdivision one of this section.

   (b) Failure to disclose a fact contained in subdivision one of this section to a transferee shall not be grounds for a disciplinary action against a real estate agent or broker licensed pursuant to this article.

   (c) As used in this section, the terms "agent," "buyer" and "seller" shall have the same meanings as such terms are defined in §443 of this article.

3. Notwithstanding the fact that this information is not a material defect or fact, if such information is important to the decision of the buyer to purchase or lease the property, the buyer may, when negotiating or making a bona fide offer, submit a written inquiry for such information. The buyer or the agent of the buyer shall provide the written request to the seller's agent or to the seller if there is no seller's agent. The seller may choose whether or not to respond to the inquiry. The seller's agent, with the consent of the seller and subject to applicable laws regarding privacy, shall report any response and information to the buyer's agent or to the buyer if there is no buyer's agent. If there is no seller's agent, the seller shall inform the buyer's agent, or the buyer if there is no buyer's agent, whether or not the seller chooses to provide a response.

4. This section shall preempt any local law inconsistent with the provisions of this section.

Electrical Services

Any person, firm, company, partnership, or corporation offering to sell real property to which no utility electric service is provided shall provide written notice to the prospective purchaser or to the prospective purchaser's agent, clearly indicating this fact. Such notice shall be provided prior to accepting a purchase offer.

Utility Surcharge

Any person, firm, company, partnership, or corporation offering to sell real property against which an electric or gas utility surcharge is assessed for the purpose of defraying the costs associated with an electric or gas line extension, or for the purpose of defraying the costs associated with related facilities, shall provide written notice to the prospective purchaser or the prospective purchaser's agent, stating as follows: "This property is subject to an electric and/or gas utility surcharge." In addition, such notice shall also state, the type and purpose of the surcharge, the amount of the surcharge and whether such surcharge is payable on a monthly, yearly or other basis. Such notice shall be provided by the seller prior to accepting a purchase offer.

Uncapped Well Disclosure

Any person, firm, company, partnership or corporation offering to sell real property on which uncapped natural gas wells are situated, and of which such person, firm, company, partnership or corporation has actual knowledge, shall inform any purchaser of the existence of these wells prior to entering into a contract for the sale/purchase of such property.

Agricultural Districts

When any purchase and sales contract is presented for the sale, purchase, or exchange of real property located partially or wholly within an agricultural district established pursuant to the provisions of article 25-AA of the Agriculture and Markets Law, the sales contract includes agricultural district disclosure form.

Megan's Law: What Must Licensees Know?

In 1996, Congress modified the Violent Crime Control and Law Enforcement Act to require released sex offenders to register with their local law enforcement agencies and to require that they register their addresses with local law enforcement agencies. These agencies, in turn, can make these addresses available to the public. The federal law required all states to enact their own Megan's Laws by September 1997. New York Court of Appeals in January 2000 dismissed a lawsuit, *Glazer v. LoPreste,* brought against the sellers and salespeople by the buyers because they weren't told that a convicted sex offender lived across the street. The court ruled that under the doctrine of caveat emptor, neither the sellers nor the salespeople had a duty to disclose this information, since there was no active concealment and the information was available to the buyers in newspapers.

New Law Bans Sex Offenders from Holding a Real Estate License

Up until recently, a person with any conviction of any type of misdemeanor, including sex-related offenses, could obtain or hold a real estate license. However, the loophole with the old law has finally been closed. State Senator Charles J. Fuschillo, Jr. and the Long Island Board of Realtors (LIBOR) recently announced a new law that prohibits all convicted sex offenders from obtaining or holding a real estate license in New York State. The legislation, which was just signed into law by

Governor David Paterson, will help prevent dangerous sex offenders from gaining access to the homes of New York families. In the past, the loophole allowed many sex offenders initially charged with felonies to plead their cases down to misdemeanors and still lawfully keep, or obtain their license.

Senator Fuschillo (8th District), Chairman of the Consumer Protection Committee, who sponsored the bill is quoted as saying, “No one I know would want to give a registered sex offender the key to their house. Before this law went into effect, convicted sex offenders could hold real estate licenses and gain access to the homes of numerous New Yorkers who had their houses on the market.” This new law is just a commonsense measure that adds another layer of protection for residents of New York State.

The new law (S. 1531, Chapter 430) is already in effect. Previously, while the state prohibited people convicted of a felony, including felony sex crimes, from being licensed as a real estate broker or salesman, those convicted of misdemeanor sex offenses were not automatically prohibited from obtaining or holding a realtor’s license.

The new law makes it illegal for a convicted misdemeanor sex offender to acquire or hold a license to sell real estate. Under the state penal law, misdemeanor level sex offenses include sexual misconduct, sexual abuse in the second degree, forcible touching, unlawful imprisonment in the second degree, and hate crimes.

The new law also requires persons who already hold a real estate license in New York State to report any felony or misdemeanor sexual convictions within five days of conviction. Previously, licensed real estate agents were not required to report if they were convicted of a sex crime until the next time they sought to renew their real estate license, which occurs every two years.

Reprinted with permission of the Multiple Listing Service of Long Island.

New York City Bedbug Disclosure

To address the issue of bedbug infestation, Article 4 - Extermination and Rodent Eradication in the Administrative Code of the City of New York was amended in 2010. The new law requires owners and landlords of property within the City of New York to disclose bedbug infestation history of property before it is leased, as indicated below.

§ 27-2018.1 *Notice of bedbug infestation history.*

a. For housing accommodations subject to this code, an owner shall furnish to each tenant signing a vacancy lease, a notice in a form promulgated or approved by the State Division of Housing and Community Renewal that sets forth the property’s bedbug infestation history for the previous year regarding the premises rented by the tenant and the building in which the premises are located.

b. Upon written complaint, in a form promulgated or approved by the Division of Housing and Community Renewal, by the tenant that he or she was not furnished with a copy of the notice required pursuant to subdivision a of this section, the Division of Housing and Community Renewal shall order the owner to furnish the notice.

Owner's Notice to Tenant Disclosure of Bedbug Infestation

State of New York
Division of Housing and Community Renewal
Office of Rent Administration
Web Site: www.nysdhcr.gov

NOTICE TO TENANT
DISCLOSURE OF BEDBUG INFESTATION HISTORY

Pursuant to the NYC Housing Maintenance Code, an owner/managing agent of residential rental property shall furnish to each tenant signing a vacancy lease a notice that sets forth the property's bedbug infestation history.

Name of tenant(s):

Subject Premises:

Apt. #:

Date of vacancy lease:

BEDBUG INFESTATION HISTORY
(Only boxes checked apply)

[ ] There is no history of any bedbug infestation within the past year in the building or in any apartment.

[ ] During the past year the building had a bedbug infestation history that has been the subject of eradication measures. The location of the infestation was on the ______________ floor(s).

[ ] During the past year the building had a bedbug infestation history on the ____________ floor(s) and it has not been the subject of eradication measures.

[ ] During the past year the apartment had a bedbug infestation history and eradication measures were employed.

[ ] During the past year the apartment had a bedbug infestation history and eradication measures were not employed.

[ ] Other: ____.

Signature of Tenant(s): ____________________________ Dated: ______________

Signature of Owner/Managing Agent: ________________________ Dated: ______________

DBB-N (9/10)

Source: New York State Division of Housing and Community Renewal.

Licensee's Responsibilities

Think back to your obligation to treat everyone honestly and fairly even if no fiduciary relationship exists. As an agent, you are responsible for what you know and what you should know. Remember that you're not an expert in pest control, but when you're on your first walk-through with a seller, you should be on the lookout for tell-tale signs of insect infestation or damage. Sellers should be asked if they know of any problems, the same way you would ask about water damage, etc.

You are obligated to disclose material facts about the condition of the property to a buyer even if a seller claims that such disclosure violates his or her agency relationship and the fiduciary obligations of loyalty, obedience, or confidentiality. Your response should be to remind sellers that you told them at the first listing appointment you must treat everyone fairly and honestly. Are bedbugs a material fact? That could be an argument that ends up in court. Remember, though, that "disclosure" of facts important to the transaction will keep you out of trouble.

Enforcement Protocols for Bed Bug Complaints: What Property Owners Should Know

From the New York City Department of Health and Mental Hygiene's website, here is how New York City's enforcement protocols work when it receives a bed bug complaint:

1. **An Inspection by the Department of Housing Preservation and Development**

   When a complaint is made to 311 about bed bugs in a residential building, a housing inspector from the Department of Housing Preservation and Development (HPD) may conduct an inspection. The inspector examines places where bed bugs are commonly found, such as on and around mattresses, beds and headboards, as well as other potentially infested areas as directed by the tenant.

   If the HPD inspector finds bed bugs, the property owner is issued an HPD Notice of Violation ordering that the condition be addressed.

2. **A Commissioner's Order from the Health Department**

   When a Notice of Violation is issued by HPD, the property owner also receives an Order of the Commissioner from the Health Department.

   The Commissioner's order tells property owners what must be done to address the bed bug problem. For example, owners must hire a licensed pest management professional (exterminator) to treat the infestation. To prevent the spread of bed bugs, owners must also inspect and, where necessary, treat apartments next to and above and below infested units, and keep a record of all treatments conducted.

   When these actions have been taken, property owners must notify HPD that the problem has been corrected through HPD's violation certification process.

3. **Enforcement for Persistent Problems**

   Beginning in 2011, to better support the prevention and control of bed bugs, New York City took a stronger approach to enforcement by expanding what it requires of property owners who persistently fail to comply with Housing and Health Codes.

   Where bed bugs persist, or occur in multiple apartments in the same building, the Health Department will issue an Order of the Commissioner requiring that property owners take several additional steps.

For example, owners will be ordered to develop and distribute to tenants a building-wide Pest Management Plan. They will be required to notify tenants that bed bugs have been found in the building, and to provide guidance on how to prevent and control infestations. In addition, to prove that bed bug infestations have been treated, owners must have their licensed exterminator complete an Affidavit of Correction of Pest Infestation.

Owners that fail to provide these documents in a timely way to the Health Department will be issued a Notice of Violation and will have to appear at a hearing before the City's Environmental Control Board where fines may be levied.

Samples of the forms and orders mentioned above are available from the New York City Department of Health and Mental Hygiene's website: http://www.nyc.gov/html/doh/bedbugs/html/info/enforcement.shtml

Commission Escrow Act

After more than 20 years of striving for a law that would protect their rightfully earned commissions, New York State REALTORS® got their wish when Governor David Paterson signed the Commission Escrow Act into law on August 8, 2008. The law went into effect on January 1, 2009.

The act expands the affidavit of entitlement to include a provision requiring the seller to deposit unpaid commissions with the county clerk until it has been decided whether the broker is entitled to the commission called for under the written contract of brokerage agreement. The act does not create a lien against the seller's property. REALTORS® are required to satisfy numerous requirements in order to comply with the act before the seller is required to deposit unpaid commissions. The Commission Escrow Act is located in Section 294-b of the Real Property Law. The act only applies to the sale of residential real property, a condominium or an interest in a cooperative apartment. The act does not apply to vacant, commercial or leased property. Furthermore, the act does not invalidate the transfer of real property, nor does it create a lien on the seller's property (even though the county clerk files it in the lien docket) Lastly, the seller is only going to be required to deposit disputed commissions into escrow if there was a closing (passage of title, stock certificates and/or proprietary lease. It must be emphasized that the statute specifically states that only the "duly licensed real estate broker" can file the affidavit of entitlement.

The first requirement that brokers must fulfill is that the provisions of the act are only applicable when the executed agreement contains the following statement in clear and conspicuous bold face type.

> **"At the time of closing, you may be required to deposit the broker's commission with the county clerk in the event that you do not pay the broker his or her commission as set forth herein. Your obligation to deposit the broker's commission with the county clerk may be waived by the broker."**

If the executed agreement does not contain this disclosure, the seller is not bound by the obligations set forth in the act.

As you can see this must be executed to the letter of the law. There will be seminars and courses to outline the very specific details that must be adhered to. This is just a brief overview of the scope of this law, brokers and new licensees should avail themselves to all information so they can properly and professional take advantage of the new law. There will be new listing agreements to reflect the change in the new

[Individual Broker]

AFFIDAVIT OF ENTITLEMENT TO COMMISSION FOR COMPLETED BROKERAGE SERVICES

STATE OF NEW YORK)
) ss:
COUNTY OF _______________)

____ being duly sworn, deposes and says:

1. I am a duly licensed real estate broker in the State of New York. I have produced a person ready, willing and able to purchase all or part of a piece of real property or an interest in a cooperative apartment pursuant to a written contract of brokerage employment with the owner thereof. This person or another acting on his or her behalf has subsequently contracted to purchase such real property or an interest in a cooperative apartment pursuant to such contract of brokerage employment.

2. I make this affidavit in accordance with Section 294-b(2) of the Real Property Law.

(i) My name is ____
and my license number is ____________________________________

(ii) The name of the seller or person responsible for the commission is
____.

(iii) The name of the person authorizing the sale on behalf of the seller (if other than the seller) is ______ ______________________________ and the date of such authorization is __________ ____.

(iv) The brokerage employment agreement was written and a copy thereof is attached hereto, which pursuant to Section 294-b(5)(j) of the Real Property Law contains the following statement to the seller in clear and conspicuous boldface type: "AT THE TIME OF CLOSING, YOU MAY BE REQUIRED TO DEPOSIT THE BROKER'S COMMISSION WITH THE COUNTY CLERK IN THE EVENT THAT YOU DO NOT PAY THE BROKER HIS OR HER COMMISSION AS SET FORTH HEREIN. YOUR OBLIGATION TO DEPOSIT THE BROKER'S COMMISSION WITH THE COUNTY CLERK MAY BE WAIVED BY THE BROKER."

(v) The real property or interest in a cooperative apartment involved is situated in the County of _______ ______________________ and State of New York and is described as follows:
____
____
____.

(vi) The commission is due and unpaid is ______________________________ ($).

Source: New York State Department of State

(vii) The brokerage services performed and applicable dates are as follows:

Date	Service Provided
____________	____
____________	____
____________	____
____________	____
____________	____
____________	____
____________	____
____________	____
____________	____
____________	____

3. The Broker has not waived the seller's obligation to deposit the broker's commission with the county clerk in the event the seller does not pay the Broker's commission as set forth herein. By the filing of this affidavit and its service upon the seller, the Broker is putting the seller on notice that if the Broker does not receive the compensation called for under the terms of the attached written contract at or prior to the delivery of the deed or delivery of the stock certificate and/or proprietary lease, the lesser of the net proceeds of the sale or the amount of the unpaid portion of the compensation agreed to in such written contract of brokerage employment shall be deposited by the seller at the time of the delivery of the deed or the delivery of the stock certificate and/or proprietary lease, with the county clerk of the county set forth in paragraph 2(v), pursuant to Section 294-b(5)(a) of the Real Property Law. Furthermore, if the seller fails to make such deposit with said county clerk, the seller may be responsible for paying the broker's costs and reasonable attorney fees pursuant to Section 294-b(5)(h) of the Real Property Law.

____
[BROKERS SIGNATURE AND PRINTED NAME]

Sworn to before me this
____ day of ____________, 20__.

____

law. Brokers and agents must become familiar with the way they must be filled out and explained.

Reprinted with permission of the Multiple Listing Service of Long Island.

Commission Escrow Act Compliance Checklist

- Written contract of broker employment (listing agreement) contains mandatory disclosure (as shown above) in a clear and conspicuous boldface type.
- Broker has performed duties under listing agreement (advertising, open house, negotiations etc.), procured a purchaser, and a binding purchase contract has been executed by both the seller and the purchaser.
- Broker completes an affidavit of entitlement including those brokerage services performed pursuant to the listing agreement. Broker attaches the signed copy of the written contract of brokerage employment and the broker then signs the affidavit of entitlement in front of a public notary who then notarizes the affidavit.
- Broker (or a representative) files the original affidavit of entitlement (with listing agreement attached) in the county clerk's office where the property is located. Broker should have at least two copies time stamped by the county clerk (one to serve on seller and one for broker's file). Be sure to call county clerk first to inquire as to filing fees and what form of payment county clerk accepts. It is also recommended that broker ascertain the location of the seller and determine whether seller will be able to be served within five days of filing the affidavit.
- Seller is served within five days of filing the affidavit either personally or via registered/certified mail return receipt requested at address of seller found on listing agreement (this is not necessarily the address of the subject property). If filing within five days of closing, must serve seller personally (can be done at closing but not after).
- Broker must also attach $25 fee made payable to county clerk for deposit of funds in a form acceptable to the county clerk.
- If entire commission is not paid at closing, seller must deposit disputed funds with county clerk at the time of the recording of the deed/stock certificate/ proprietary lease.
- Broker initiates action within 60 days of deposit or else seller can ask for return of funds from county clerk.
- Broker must initiate legal action within six months of deposit or will lose any claim for commission.

Antitrust Laws and the Real Estate Industry

Under federal and New York antitrust laws, independent real estate brokerage firms, franchisees, boards, or MLS services cannot combine to fix commission rates. Each brokerage firm is free to set its own fee schedule and to negotiate different charges with clients. Any agreement between two or more different firms to set a standard commission rate is s violation of antitrust laws. Licensees must be aware of the serious consequences regarding violating antitrust laws. Whether it is discussions about price fixing, group boycotting, market allocation agreements, or tie-in arrangements, these are very serious laws and the penalties can be very severe.

History of Antitrust Laws

Source: Federal Trade Commission

Free and open markets are the foundation of a vibrant economy. Aggressive competition among sellers in an open marketplace gives consumers – both individuals and businesses – the benefits of lower prices, higher quality products and services, more choices, and greater innovation. The FTC's competition mission is to enforce the rules of the competitive marketplace – the antitrust laws. These laws promote vigorous competition and protect consumers from anticompetitive mergers and business practices. The FTC's Bureau of Competition, working in tandem with the Bureau of Economics, enforces the antitrust laws for the benefit of consumers.

Congress passed the first antitrust law, the Sherman Act, in 1890 as a "comprehensive charter of economic liberty aimed at preserving free and unfettered competition as the rule of trade." In 1914, Congress passed two additional antitrust laws: the Federal Trade Commission Act, which created the FTC, and the Clayton Act. With some revisions, these are the three core federal antitrust laws still in effect today.

The antitrust laws proscribe unlawful mergers and business practices in general terms, leaving courts to decide which ones are illegal based on the facts of each case. Courts have applied the antitrust laws to changing markets, from a time of horse and buggies to the present digital age. Yet for over 100 years, the antitrust laws have had the same basic objective: to protect the process of competition for the benefit of consumers, making sure there are strong incentives for businesses to operate efficiently, keep prices down, and keep quality up. The Sherman Act outlaws "every contract, combination, or conspiracy in **restraint of trade**," and any "monopolization, attempted monopolization, or conspiracy or combination to monopolize.

The Sherman Act imposes criminal penalties of up to $100 million for a corporation and $1 million for an individual. The Clayton Act addresses specific practices that the Sherman Act does not clearly prohibit. The Federal Trade Commission Act bans "unfair methods of competition" and "unfair or deceptive acts or practices."

Both the FTC and the U.S. Department of Justice (DOJ) Antitrust Division enforce the federal antitrust laws. In some respects their authorities overlap, but in practice the two agencies complement each other

- **Price fixing** is an agreement (written, verbal, or inferred from conduct) among competitors that raises, lowers, or stabilizes prices or competitive terms. Generally, the antitrust laws require that each company establish prices and other terms on its own, without agreeing with a competitor.
- **Market division or customer allocation** plain agreements among competitors to divide sales territories or assign customers are almost always illegal.
- **Group boycott** any company may, on its own, refuse to do business with another firm, but an agreement among competitors not to do business with targeted individuals or businesses may be an illegal boycott, especially if the group of competitors working together has market power. For instance, a group boycott may used to implement an illegal price-fixing agreement. In this scenario, the competitors agree not to do business with others except on agreed-upon terms, typically with the result of raising prices.
- **Tie-In arrangements** can occur when a broker as a condition of a sale tells the buyer they must use a certain mortgage company as a condition of the buyer agency agreement. This would be illegal.

Summarizing Antitrust Issues

Real estate licensees in New York must observe all federal and state antitrust laws and court precedents. The findings and conclusions of a 1972 lawsuit, *United States v. Long Island Board of REALTORS®, Inc.* established the following precedent for the association and its members:

- Broker's fees are to be negotiated between members and the consumer.

- Information regarding fees agreed upon by a broker with a client can be published in the MLS and the amount of compensation offered to cooperating brokers may also be published.
- A broker receiving a fee from a client must pay the cooperative broker the agreed amount.
- Changes to an agreed upon commission or fee must be agreed upon by both the listing and selling broker.

Further, the lawsuit concluded associations and boards of REALTORS® cannot:

- Fix commission rates or encourage members to have or publish a standardized fee or commission.
- Reference a suggested fee in any educational course.
- Place limitations on a board member in negotiations with his client regarding fees or commissions.
- Take any form of action against a member for not adhering to a standard fee schedule.
- Have rules prohibiting a member from conducting business with another member.
- Structure membership fees for an association, board, or MLS that are not related to the costs of operating the organization.
- Decline acceptance of any listing of property for submission to the MLS due to the rate of commission or fee established in the listing.

Code of Ethics

The antitrust laws do not prohibit professional associations from adopting reasonable ethical codes designed to protect the public. Such self-regulatory activity serves legitimate purposes, and in most cases can be expected to benefit, rather than to injure, competition or consumers. In some instances, however, ethical rules may be unlawful if they unreasonably restrict the ways professionals may compete. For example, a mandatory code of ethics that prevents members from competing on the basis of price or on terms other than those developed by the trade group can be an unreasonable restraint on competition.

Several antitrust cases have challenged realtor board rules that restricted access to Multiple Listing Services (MLS) for advertising homes for sale. The MLS system of combining the home listings of many brokers has substantial benefits for home buyers and sellers. The initial cases invalidated realtor board membership rules that excluded certain brokers from the MLS because access to the MLS was considered key to marketing homes. More recently, FTC enforcement actions have challenged MLS policies that permit access but more subtly disfavor certain types of brokerage arrangements that offer consumers a low-cost alternative to the more traditional, full-service listing agreement. For instance, some brokers offer a limited service model, listing a home on the local MLS for a fee while handing off other aspects of the sale to the seller. The FTC has challenged the rules of several MLS organizations that excluded these brokers from popular home sale web sites. These rules limited the ways in which brokers could conduct their business and denied home sellers the benefit of having different types of listings.

Antitrust Compliance

The **National Association of REALTORS®** has printed a brochure and class regarding antitrust.

YOU SAID WHAT?

An Antitrust Compliance Brochure

This brochure has been prepared by the Risk Management Committee of the National Association of REALTORS® to supplement the REALTOR® association's long standing antitrust compliance program. Its purpose is to assist members in applying these principles in their individual offices when confronting issues raised by the presence of new business models offered by competitors.

Real estate is and always has been a very competitive business. The multitude of firms that are active in the business in most markets, the entrepreneurial spirit that is a trademark of the sales people who make up the bulk of the industry, and the relative easy entry into the real estate business combine to insure competition. Over the years the real estate business has benefited from that aspect by seeing the different possible business models employed by competitors. Successful innovations take root and spread among the industry. Less successful ones fall by the wayside.

Our industry finds itself in another period where new business models are being introduced. That increases challenges and competition, just as new models have in the past. The law and our Code of Ethics serve to assure that consumers have the complete and accurate information they need to make their marketplace decisions. In the end, consumers decide which business methods will prevail and survive and which will fail. That, of course, is the heart of the REALTOR® association's antitrust compliance program.

One of the bedrock principles of antitrust compliance is that neither associations nor their members collectively set the price of services provided by real estate professionals. That is a decision that is made independently by each firm. The firm's sales associates must take care to present pricing policies to prospective clients in a manner that is consistent with the fact that the fees or prices are ***independently established***. This means they should never respond to a question about fees by suggesting that all competitors in the market follow the same pricing practices or to a policy of the local board or association of REALTORS® that supposedly prohibits or discourages price competition.

Never say things that could be understood to suggest a conspiracy or falsely disparage a competitor:	***Focus on the positive aspects of doing business with you and the services which distinguish your firm***:
• This is the rate every firm charges. • I'd like to lower the commission, but no one else in the MLS will show your house unless the commission is X%. • I have to charge you this rate because this is the rate the Board of REALTORS® set for all real estate agents. • Before you decide to list with XYZ Realty you should know that because they are "discount" brokers, members of the association won't show their listings.	• I have a marketing program that gets results. Let me explain my sixty day marketing plan and all it includes. • Our company has been in business for Y years and has serviced thousands of clients with the highest professionalism. We choose to charge X% and our clients have chosen to pay X% because of the service provided. • Yes, our company charges a commission of A% and company 2 charges a commission of B%, but at the same time you are comparing commission rates, Mr. Seller, be sure to compare services, in order to get an apples-to-apples analysis. • I appreciate your comments, my interest is in helping you meet your goals by getting you the best price, in the quickest amount of time, with the least amount of problems. Let me show you how I do it. • I am proud of my company's reputation for professionalism and getting things done. Let me show you some of our sales *(or whatever)* statistics that prove we do what we say.

Additionally, the obligations of a member of the REALTOR® association impose a higher standard with regard to the statements made about competitors. Article 15 of the REALTOR® Code of Ethics states,

REALTORS® shall not knowingly or recklessly make false or misleading statements about competitors, their businesses, or their business practices.

The National Association's Professional Standards Committee has said the Article logically flows from the REALTOR®'s duty established in Article 12 "to present a true picture in ... representations." This includes comparisons with competitors, and comments or opinions offered about other real estates professionals. While the Article is not intended to limit or inhibit the free flow of the commercial and comparative information that is often of value to potential users of the many and varied services that REALTORS® provide, it does require a good faith effort to ensure that statements and representation are truthful and accurate.

The path to managing this risk is really consistent with the philosophy of the REALTOR® organization. By focusing on the positive and presenting it honestly, the potential risks posed by the antitrust laws will be minimized and you will not only have avoided that legal and ethical liability, but you will probably elevate yourself and your firm in the eyes of the most important audience, the people who are going to be selecting you to represent them in the sale or purchase of their home.

Excerpts from Antitrust and Real Estate for REALTORS® and REALTOR-ASSOCIATE®s (5th ed.) and Professionalism in Real Estate (2003).

Additional Resources:
Avoiding Antitrust Risk (a REALTOR Magazine Toolkit)
http://www.realtor.org/rmotoolkits.nsf/pages/brokerrisk17?OpenDocument
Antitrust and the Real Estate Brokerage Firm (The Letter of The Law)
http://www.realtor.org/LetterLw.nsf/pages/0802antitrust?OpenDocument
Please note: Both of the foregoing articles are in the members-only section of Realtor.org
REALTOR® Code of Ethics
http://www.realtor.org/mempolweb.nsf/pages/code?opendocument

SUMMARY

1. **Agency** *is the relationship between a principal and a party representing their interests*. Brokerage is a business concept based on bringing parties together for the purpose of a transaction.
2. A listing agreement or buyer (or tenant) representation agreement is considered an employment contract and creates an agency relationship.
3. When a salesperson takes a listing or enters into a buyer (or tenant) representation agreement, that salesperson is acting on behalf of the broker. Any agreement the salesperson is involved with putting together is an agreement between the broker and the seller (or landlord) or buyer (or tenant). The salesperson is a subagent of the broker and the broker's principal, the seller/ landlord or buyer/tenant. A **subagent** *owes fiduciary duties to his principal, the broker, and the broker's principal*.
4. Listing agreements and buyer (or tenant) agreements can be exclusive or non-exclusive. **Exclusive listing agreements** *are exclusive right to sell and exclusive agency*. **Open listing agreements** *are non-exclusive*. **Net listing agreements** *are **not** permitted in New York. When a buyer exclusively engages a broker it is known as* **buyer brokerage**.
5. In New York, exclusive right to sell and exclusive agency listing agreements must include a definite expiration date. In addition, no listing agreement may "automatically" extend or renew according to New York law.
6. Most exclusive listing agreements contain a broker protection clause that covers a certain period after the listing expires. A **broker protection clause** *provides the broker is still entitled to a commission if the property is sold during that time period under certain circumstances.*
7. For in-company transactions the scenarios are: single agency, where either the buyer/tenant or seller/landlord is a customer; or dual agency. In dual agency, when both parties in a transaction are clients of the brokerage, all licensees in the brokerage are dual agents; or, a salesperson can be designated to more fully represent the client's position. In designated agency, the broker is a dual agent.

8. Listing brokers commonly extend an offer to outside brokerage firms to sell (or rent) the listing to outside buyers (or tenants) through an offer of cooperation. Listing brokers in their offer of cooperation additionally specify an offer of compensation. The selling (or renting) broker bringing a buyer (or tenant) to a transaction may be compensated for representing the listing broker's seller (or landlord). In this case the buyer (or tenant) would be a customer. Listing brokers may limit their compensation to brokers who represent a buyer (or tenant) either exclusively or non-exclusively. Or, the listing broker could offer to compensate both.
9. Through their own independent business decision, brokers establish the types of agency relationships their brokerage firm offers. The choices, usually incorporated into the firm's company policies on agency, are *seller/landlord agency exclusively, buyer/tenant agency exclusively, seller/landlord* and *buyer/tenant agency, consensual dual agency* - either for all licensees affiliated with the brokerage, or with designated agents.
10. *Brokers could be held accountable for actions taken by his licensees as well as cooperative licensee(s), which is called* **vicarious liability**. Vicarious liability means one person is responsible for the actions of another. In some cases the broker may be subject to pay damages or have action taken on the part of DOS in the form of fines or other reprimand. Liability could move upward to the principal.
11. Using broker's agents is a method used to eliminate vicarious liability that could potentially affect the principal. The concept of a broker's agent stops the liability with the broker. The broker's agent is not a subagent of the seller or buyer, but is engaged and works directly for the broker. The broker's agent owes the same fiduciary duty to the broker's principal that the broker does.
12. Section 443 of Article 12-A of the New York Real Property Law requires that in the sale and rental of residential properties, written disclosure of an agency relationship by the agent is required. Section 443 requires a specific written agency disclosure form that details consumer choices in agency relationships and representation. The agency disclosure form is written documentation that affirms agency disclosure has taken place and that informed consent of the party for a specific relationship has been given.
13. There is specific timing which triggers agents to perform disclosure. The triggering events of agency disclosure are substantive contacts. An agency disclosure form must be presented and consented to by the prospective seller or buyer at the earliest substantive contact.
14. Regulation 175.7 of the codified rules requires an agent to *make clear for which party he is acting*. In addition the regulation limits compensation from more than one party in a transaction except when full disclosure and consent has been received from all of the parties. The requirement for the agent to make clear his relationship and to not receive undisclosed and non-consented compensation from more than one party is not limited to residential transactions, but applies to all real estate transactions.
15. After an initial relationship is formed between a broker and a principal, the broker could: change his relationship with the buyer/tenant and work with them as a customer; become a dual agent for the buyer/tenant and seller/landlord; or become a dual agent with designated agents for the buyer/tenant and seller/landlord. Changing agency relationships is permissible as long as the agent reviews the disclosure form, discusses the revised relationship, and obtains informed consent for the new relationship.
16. If a party refuses to sign an agency disclosure form, the agent can carry on the relationship described during agency disclosure as long as at the earliest point in time following the substantive contact he completes a declaration form of which a copy must be provided to the broker and kept on file for three years.
17. New York City landlords are required to inform new tenants in writing of whether the apartment has suffered a bedbug infestation within the past year, or if there has been a bed bug problem in the building during that time. This is accomplished through the use of form DBB-N – Owner's Notice to Tenant Disclosure of Bedbug Infestation History.
18. Antitrust issues in real estate include *price-fixing, group boycotts, market allocation agreements,* and *tie-in arrangements*. Discussing commission rates among competitors is potentially an antitrust violation. Commission rates are set independently by each broker. Therefore, there can be no standardized rate among competitors or members of any organization. Licensees should know what to do in situations that could lead to occurrences potentially punishable as a felony.

5

Easements and Liens

In This Session

When someone has a claim or right concerning property but does not have the right to possess the property, they are said to have a nonpossessory interest. Real estate agents should be aware of any nonpossessory interest that could affect a property with which they are dealing. The two primary examples of nonpossessory interests discussed in this session are easements and liens.

You'll learn:

- Different types of easements and who benefits from them.
- How easements may be created.
- The difference between easements and licenses.
- The difference between encumbrances and encroachments.
- Various types of liens.
- The impact of liens on property.
- Adverse possession and the requirements necessary for it.

CAUTION: We've mentioned throughout this textbook that a real estate licensee must never give legal advice. The topics in this session are presented so that you have a well-rounded understanding of real property law as it affects real estate transactions. You should always advise parties to seek legal representation on these issues.

Key Terms

- Adverse Possession
- Dominant Tenement
- Easement
- Easement Appurtenant
- Easement by Condemnation
- Easement by Express Grant
- Easement by Implication
- Easement by Necessity
- Easement by Prescription
- Easement for Light and Air
- Easement in Gross
- Encroachment
- Encumbrance
- General Lien
- Involuntary Lien
- License
- Lis Pendens
- Mechanic's Lien/Materialman's Lien
- Mortgage
- Nonpossessory Interest
- Party Wall Easement
- Right of Way
- Servient Tenement
- Specific Lien
- Subordination Agreement
- Tax Lien
- Voluntary Lien

Easements

An **easement** is a *right to use another person's real property for a particular purpose.* An easement creates limited rights for the easement holder related to the land surface, its airspace, or subsurface. An *easement that grants access to property* is commonly referred to as a **right of way** (ROW). Like a lien, an easement is considered an **encumbrance**, since it *encumbers (burdens) a real property owner's title*.

Easements can be either:

- **Public** (e.g., for power lines) or **private** (e.g., for access to a landlocked parcel).
- Put into a **deed** before a transfer of property occurs or created separately as an **agreement** between the parties.
- Classified as **easements in gross** or **easements appurtenant**.

Easements in Gross

An **easement in gross** involves a *specific parcel of land and benefits a person or company* (called the **dominant tenant**) *not a piece of land.* The *burdened land* is called a **servient tenement**. Easements in gross are most commonly held by the government and public utilities for commercial purposes, for example, a utility easement that a power company has to place power lines over someone's property or that a municipality has to place sewer lines under the surface.

Easements in gross that belong to companies can be assigned to others. For example, if Phone Company A has an easement in gross to place underground lines, they could assign or sell the easement rights to Cable Company B.

Easements in gross can also be granted for noncommercial purposes, for example, an easement that allows access to a public beach. These types of easements, called **personal easements in gross**, generally may not be conveyed or assigned to someone else and end when the dominant tenant dies.

Easements Appurtenant

An **easement appurtenant** involves *two separately deeded parcels that are owned by different parties. This type of easement burdens one piece of land* (called the **servient tenement**) *for the benefit of the other piece of land* (called the **dominant tenement**). An easement appurtenant can be either:

- **Affirmative**, which *allows someone to do something* (e.g., allowing someone to cross property to reach property with no road access) or
- **Negative**, which *prevents someone from doing something* (e.g., forbidding a property owner from damming a small stream that runs through his property if it will deprive property owners downstream of the water).

EXAMPLE:

D has an easement appurtenant across neighbor S's property. The easement permits D to cross S's land for the benefit of D's land. Therefore, D's land is the dominant tenement and S's land is the servient tenement.

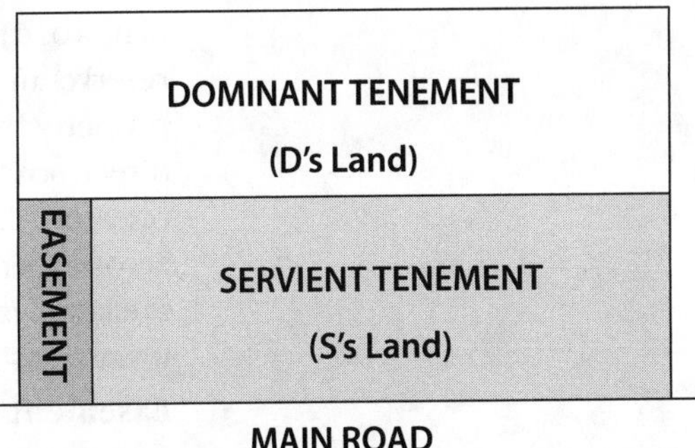

Appurtenances are rights that go with real property (e.g., air rights), so an easement appurtenant is a *right that goes with land ownership*. A recorded easement (either in a deed or as a separate document) gives notice to third parties, and so usually causes the easement to transfer with the property, which means the easement *runs with the land*. When title is transferred, the new owner owns the easement (if the dominant tenement) or takes title subject to the burden of the easement (if the servient tenement).

Light Rights

An **easement for light and air**, or view easement, is considered *a negative appurtenant easement in that the dominant tenant can prevent the servient tenant from doing something on the land because it could impact the dominant land*. These easements are most frequently seen in relation to solar panels, view restrictions, and aviation. With the use of solar panels becoming more common, the right to light is becoming more of an issue. Many states have passed solar easement laws, zoning laws or building codes (which may require owners to place certain restrictions or covenants in deeds) geared toward solar issues. Under the statutes of some states, the landowner who first establishes solar panels for power generation has the right to unobstructed and continued use. This means that a neighbor cannot do anything on the property that would interfere with the neighbor's solar panels, such as planting trees or erecting a structure that could interfere with the light.

New York law does not generally recognize a homeowner's right to a view or right to light

Establishing Easements

Easements can be created a number of ways:

- **Easement by express grant** means *a landowner divides land and includes deed language, so the seller retains an easement across his former land*. This can also be part of the deed transfer or be in a separate document conveying only the easement.
- **Easement by implication** is *created by law when land is divided, and there is a long-standing apparent use reasonably necessary for the enjoyment of the land*. This is also called an implied easement. Generally, easement by implication arises when a tract of land was originally held by one owner and divided into two or more parcels. The original owner would keep an ingress or egress, which is a means to enter or exit property.

  For example, X owned a large piece of land with a long driveway leading from the main road to her house. X sold the south half of her land (the part beside the main road) to Y, and kept the north half (the part with her house on it). X did not reserve an easement for herself in the deed to Y. Although she could reach her property by a winding back road, the driveway across Y's parcel was much more direct, so X just went on using the driveway as she always had. Y filed a lawsuit to prevent X from using it. The court ruled that X had an easement by implication across Y's parcel. X's use of the driveway was obvious and well-established when the land was divided. Although the driveway was not the only access to X's parcel, it was reasonably necessary for the enjoyment of her property.

- **Easement by necessity** (sometimes called easement **of** necessity) is a *special easement that arises if land would be completely useless without the easement, even if there is no long-standing apparent use*. An example is a **landlocked** property with no access. For a court to assign an easement by necessity, the claimant does not have to prove the use was long-established and obvious at the time of the sale, but must prove an easement is strictly necessary (not just reasonably necessary) to use the land; if there is another way to access the land, easement by necessity will not be assigned. This type of easement is not automatic and usually not granted to owners of vacant land.
- **Easement by prescription** is *created by open and notorious, hostile and adverse use of another person's land for a specific time as indicated by state law.* Open and notorious use of the land means the use must be obvious and unconcealed, so if the landowner is kept reasonably informed about the property, she would be aware of the use. Hostile and adverse is use without the owner's permission and against his interests. If the owner gives permission, there is no easement by prescription. In New York, to claim easement by prescription, continuous use for **ten years** is required. It does not require constant use, just regular use considered normal for that type of property. Easement by prescription does not convey title, however. A court would be required to make that decision.

  Note also that an easement by prescription can rarely be acquired against government property, nor can a negative easement, such as an *easement for view,* be created by prescription.
- **Easement by condemnation** *occurs through the government's power of eminent domain*. Just as the power of eminent domain allows the government to take title to private property for a public use, the same power allows government entities to impose easements upon private property. These easements are usually for the purpose of future rights of way, visibility, safety, and expansion of existing roadways or utilities and require payment of just compensation to the servient tenant.
- **Party wall easement** is *when a wall is shared between two connected properties*. The ownership of the wall is split between the two, and each has an appurtenant easement in the other half of the wall. An agreement should be expressed in writing outlining the ownership of the wall between the two parties. Each owner shares in the building and maintenance costs of the wall.

Recording Easements

Easements can be created voluntarily or involuntarily. When easements are created voluntarily, the parties involved should put the easement in writing. A document granting an easement should be drawn up and signed just like a deed and should be **recorded in the public records** in the county where the property is located to ensure that anyone who buys the land has notice of the easement. If the buyer doesn't have notice, the easement probably won't run with the land, which has the potential for conflict.

For example, D and S are neighbors. D asks S for an access easement allowing D to cross S's property. S agrees, but the easement agreement is never put in writing. Six months later, S changes his mind and tells D to keep off his land. D cannot enforce the easement right because it was only an oral agreement. Instead, suppose S signed a document granting D the easement. Now, if S has a change of mind, D has an enforceable right.

As a real estate agent, you can imagine how important it is to know what easements are attached to a property. For example, what if your buyer purchased property because it was large enough to build an in-ground pool, only to discover a gas utility easement across the middle of the backyard when applying for a pool permit?

It should be possible to discover existing easements from a number of public sources. Even if you don't perform that research yourself, at the very least, you need to be able to explain to your clients any easements that show up on a title abstract, where that gas utility easement would have likely appeared.

CASE IN POINT

In 1994, a hotel in Montauk, Suffolk County, filed a lawsuit to regain access for its guests to footpaths to the beach after a property owner erected fences. The court had to decide whether or not the property abutting the beach was encumbered by an easement allowing access to the water. The history of the property was traced back to an 1879 sale of the land from the Montauk Indians. In 1904, the owners filed a plan for landscaping the property in the land records. The plaintiffs in this lawsuit claimed that language in that recorded map and in their deeds included an express grant of easement over that property to get to the beaches. The judge eventually ruled that the map and deeds did create an easement that could not be eliminated by the current property owners, the servient tenant in this case. The fences were ordered to be removed.

ENCROACHMENT OR ENCUMBRANCE?

An **encroachment** is *a physical object intruding onto a neighbor's property*. A driveway that extends two feet over a property line is an example of an encroachment. Another common example is a tree limb that extends over a property line. Although most encroachments are unintentional, they are a form of trespassing in the eyes of the law. If a neighbor sues, the court can order removal of the encroachment or payment of damages to the neighbor by the encroacher, but the owner of the encroached upon property does ***not*** have the right to destroy the encroachment.

An encroachment is ***not*** an encumbrance because it is not a right or interest that is held. However, the encroacher could get an easement from the neighbor to allow the encroachment.

Terminating Easements

Easements can be terminated in several ways:

- **Release**. A document *all parties sign releasing the easement holder's interest in the property*. Easement releases should always be recorded. For example, Ellen has an easement by necessity to access the road from her house from Tom's property. A road is built that abuts Ellen's property, so she releases her easement to use Tom's property. If the release is recorded, the person to whom Ellen sells her property would have no right to use Tom's property.

- **Merger.** *Uniting two or more separate properties by transferring ownership of all properties to one person*. If one person owns the property, both the dominant tenement and the servient tenement, the easement is terminated by merger. If the land is later divided again, the easement no longer exists and must be recreated if desired.
- **Abandonment**. The failure *to occupy and use property, which may result in a loss of rights*. An easement ceases to exist if the owner abandons it. Non-use alone, however, is not enough for abandonment. There must be an act or statement that clearly expresses the owner's intention to abandon the easement.
- **Prescription**. Loss of easement by prescription occurs after *ten years of non-use*. If an easement owner does not use the property for ten years, it can be lost by prescription.
- **Failure or Expiration of Purpose**. An easement terminates when *the purpose for which it was created no longer exists.* For example, an electric company's easement for power lines across a farmer's property can end from failure or expiration of purpose if the company removes the lines. Likewise, an easement can be terminated if the property is involuntarily destroyed. For example, if a dock is destroyed by a hurricane and rebuilt, a previous easement to use it is not automatic; it must be recreated.
- **Court Action.** An easement may be terminated through a quiet title action in the courts. For example, Ellen has an easement by necessity to access the road from her house from Tom's property. A road is built that abuts Ellen's property, but she wants to continue to use the easement since it's more convenient. Tom could go to court to have the easement terminated. Of course, when it's in the hands of a court, termination is not guaranteed.

LICENSES

A **license** is *temporary, revocable, non-assignable permission to enter another's land for a particular purpose*. A license is ***similar*** to an easement because it grants permission to use another's property. Unlike an easement, a license does ***not*** create an interest in property and is not considered an encumbrance. Some other differences are:

- Easements are usually for an indefinite period of time, while licenses are often temporary.
- Easements are created by written agreement or action of law, but licenses may be created by oral contract.
- Easements run with the land, but licenses do not have to.
- Easements cannot be revoked, whereas licenses may be revoked at any time, except where the licensee makes a substantial financial commitment in reliance on the license.
- A license cannot be assigned and becomes invalid if the licensee dies.

Liens

A **lien** is not only *a financial interest in property; it is also a financial encumbrance*. Liens are typically security for a debt that gives the creditor, or lien holder, the right to foreclose on the debtor's property if the debt is not paid. In **foreclosure**, the *property is sold and the lien holder collects the amount of the debt from the proceeds of the foreclosure sale*. A lien can be:

- **General**, which means it attaches *to all property, personal and real, owned in the county by the debtor*, or
- **Specific**, which means it *attaches only to specific property*.

Liens may also be either voluntary or involuntary.

Voluntary Liens

Voluntary liens are placed against property *with consent of the owner*. The most common form of a voluntary lien is a mortgage or, similarly, a home equity line of credit.

Mortgages

Mortgages are written *instruments that use real property to secure payment of a debt*. Without a debt, there can be no mortgage. A mortgage is a powerful incentive for an owner to pay since it represents a potential transfer of title to the mortgagee in case of default. A mortgage is a *voluntary, specific* lien.

Involuntary Liens

Involuntary liens arise by operation *of law without consent of the property owner*. These liens are created to protect a landowner's creditors.

Mechanic's and Materialman's Liens

Mechanic's liens and **materialman's liens** are liens *claimed by someone who performed work on real property and was not paid*. The property serves as security for payment if the property owner does not pay contractors, subcontractors, laborers, or materialmen for improvements to their property. If a property owner does not pay the bills, the holder of this lien can force the sale of the property and collect the debt from the proceeds. A party can file a mechanic's or materialman's lien without going to court.

In New York, a mechanic's lien refers broadly to any work performed or materials used to improve a property. If the work was on a single-family residence, the lien must be filed within four months of when the labor was completed or the material supplied. The deadline is eight months for other properties. A mechanic's lien is good for **one year**, although it can be renewed. These are *involuntary, specific* liens.

This law even applies to real estate brokers who are owed commission for the negotiation of a long-term commercial lease. According to New York Lien Law § 10, a broker can file a lien for unpaid commission up to eight months after the commission is due.

Tax Liens

Tax liens are *liens on property to secure the payment of taxes*. **Property taxes** create an *involuntary, specific* lien against real estate. A property tax lien could result from ad valorem taxes assessed by local entities such as municipalities and school districts to raise revenue, or special assessment taxes to pay for specific improvements that only affect specific property owners. Unpaid **federal income taxes** also create liens on real property. Income tax liens are *involuntary, general* liens, and so unlike other tax liens, these can be attached to personal property as well. Other types of tax liens include:

- **Estate tax liens.** When a person dies, estate tax is administered to the estate of the deceased. The taxable estate is calculated by subtracting allowable deductions from the gross estate. A person's estate can include life insurance, annuities, and property. Deductible expenses from the estate can include funeral costs, debts, charity, and a state death tax, if applicable. An estate tax is an *involuntary, general* lien.

- **Corporation franchise tax lien.** Corporations operating in New York are required to pay an annual state tax based on net profit. If the corporation fails to pay the corporation franchise tax, the outstanding amount becomes a lien on corporate assets. Remedy action of the state includes attachment of the assets as well as foreclosure and dissolution of the corporation. In the latter event, the business could no longer operate legally in New York. A corporation franchise tax lien is an *involuntary, general* lien.

Judgment Liens

Judgment liens are liens *against a person's property through court action*. At the end of a lawsuit, if it is determined that one party owes the other money, a judgment is entered. The winner of the lawsuit (judgment creditor) may claim a lien against the other party's (judgment debtor) real property or other personal assets.

To claim a lien, the judgment creditor obtains a certificate of judgment from the court issuing the judgment and files it in the county where the judgment debtor owns real property. A judgment lien attaches to all of a debtor's real property in each county where the certificate is recorded. It is valid for ten years from the judgment date and renewable for ten more years. Judgment liens are generally *involuntary, general* liens.

Judgment liens that are created by a **confession of judgment** are *voluntary, general* liens. A confession of judgment is when someone who owes money permits judgment to be entered against him or her by written statement without necessity of legal proceedings. An example of this would be an IOU that a borrower gives to a lender in exchange for money.

Attachment Liens

Attachment liens are liens intended *to prevent transfer of property pending the outcome of litigation.* When a plaintiff files a lawsuit, there is a danger that before a judgment is entered, the defendant may sell all property, making a judgment worthless. To prevent this, at the outset of a lawsuit, a plaintiff can ask the court to issue an order of attachment. The order directs the sheriff to seize personal property or to create an *involuntary lien against real and/or personal property*.

A notice of a pending suit, called a **lis pendens**, may also be recorded. Although this is not a lien, it can *serve notice to potential buyers that there is a lawsuit pending*, and the outcome may affect the title to the subject property.

Lien Classification

Type of Lien	Voluntary	Involuntary	General (against individual, all property, personal or real)	Specific (against specific real property)
Property Tax Lien		X		X
IRS Tax Lien		X	X	
Estate Tax Lien		X	X	
Corporation Franchise Tax Lien		X	X	
Mortgage Lien	X			X
Mechanic's Lien		X		X
Judgment Lien		X	X	
Attachment Lien		X	X	X

Impact of Liens

Lien Priority

It is not unusual for real estate to have several liens against it at the same time (e.g., mortgage, mechanic's lien, and property tax lien). Sometimes, the total owed for the liens is more than the land will bring at a sale, so there is an order of priority for paying off liens after foreclosure. Generally, liens are paid in the order they were attached to the land. A helpful phrase to remember is this: "first in time, first in line." In other words, the creditor who has the first lien recorded on the property will be the first to be paid in a forced sale and will get every cent that's owed to him. If there is money left over, the second recorded lien holder will be paid, and so on down the line. If there is a third lien holder, for example, but the proceeds from the sale of the property only covered the amount owed to the first two lien holders, that third lien holder would get nothing.

An important exception are **property tax liens**, which are *superior to all other liens*. No matter when a property tax lien is placed on a property, it will always be paid *before* any other liens when the property is sold. This is the reason that many mortgage lenders prefer to maintain an escrow account to cover property taxes. The lender is assured that the property taxes will be paid, thus keeping themselves in line as the first position in the priority of liens. Under certain circumstances, a lien recorded by the Internal Revenue Service for **unpaid federal income taxes** may be able to jump ahead of a recorded mortgage lien or other lien, though not ahead of a property tax lien.

Sometimes a lender is willing to change its order of priority with a **subordination agreement**. With this contract, a *lender voluntarily puts its lien in a lower order of priority*. This is usually done if the lender is sure the property is worth enough to pay off the additional liens *and* the mortgage.

Transferring Property With Liens

Liens against property do not prevent a property's transfer, nor does a transfer nullify the lien. The buyer takes the property **subject to the liens**, which means *the buyer takes the property with the lien obligation, but without being personally liable.* The buyer must keep paying the liens to keep the property, but loses the equity only in the event of default. The creditor cannot hold the new owner personally responsible for these debts because the new owner did not assume the debts. In most real estate transactions, sellers clear their titles of all liens before closing. There are a number of ways in which the debtor could do this:

- The necessary funds could be withheld at settlement to pay off the debt, and a record of satisfaction of the lien should be recorded in the public records to protect the new owner.
- If the seller owes more on the property than the sale of it will generate, the seller might have to come to the settlement table with a check to discharge the additional debt.
- If it's a general lien against the property owner, the creditor could agree to release the property that's being sold if the debtor has other collateral or to switch the lien to a property that the debtor will acquire.

Adverse Possession

Adverse possession is when *someone acquires the title to someone else's real property through open, notorious, hostile (adverse), and continuous use of it for a specific period of time as determined by state law.* Adverse possession does *not* apply to government-owned land. Adverse possession, also known as **title by prescription**, is similar to easement by prescription, but instead of acquiring an easement or an interest in the property, the actual title is acquired.

In the State of New York, the time required to claim adverse possession, like easement by prescription, is **ten years.** A claim of adverse possession in New York generally requires that the property is cultivated or improved or protected by a substantial enclosure. Adverse possession does not automatically convey title; a court must make the decision to award the land.

Title to large parcels of property through adverse possession is not that common. It's more likely to come into play over a disputed property line. For example, homeowner Joe put up a fence that enclosed a small portion of his neighbor's property. Over the years, he planted trees and bushes and enjoyed the use of the property. Twenty years later when the neighbor's property was sold, the new owners discovered that the fence was actually on their property. When the new owners removed the fence, Joe sued to claim title to that specific portion of the property through adverse possession.

SUMMARY

1. **Encumbrances** are *nonpossessory interests in property*; a person can have a claim or right to a property without actually possessing it. Thus, they burden a property. Two common encumbrances are easements and liens.
2. **Easements** are the right *to use another's property for a particular purpose*. Two types are easements appurtenant and easements in gross. **Easements appurtenant** *burden one parcel of land* (the servient tenement) *for the benefit of another piece of land* (the dominant tenement). **Easements in gross** burden *one parcel of land for the benefit an individual or a corporation* (the dominant tenant), such as a utility company.
3. Easements are created by express grant, express reservation, implication, necessity, agreement, or prescription. Easements are terminated by release, merger, abandonment, prescription, or failure or expiration of purpose.
4. An **encroachment** is *a physical object intruding onto a neighbor's property.* Although most encroachments are unintentional, they are a form of trespassing in the eyes of the law. An encroachment is *not* an encumbrance because it is not a right or interest that is held.
5. A **license** is *temporary, revocable, non-assignable permission to enter another's land for a particular purpose.* A license is *similar* to an easement because it grants permission to use another's property. Unlike an easement, a license does *not* create an interest in property and is not considered an encumbrance.
6. **Liens** are *nonpossessory interests and financial encumbrances*. Liens are classified as **voluntary** or **involuntary**, and as **general** (attaches to all property) or **specific** (attaches only to the property that incurred the debt). Common liens are mortgages, tax liens, mechanic's liens, judgment liens, and attachment liens. Mechanic's liens are placed on property when owners do not pay contractors, subcontractors, laborers, or materialmen for improvements to their property, and are good for one year. Tax liens are placed on property when owners do not pay property taxes, federal income taxes, estate taxes, or corporate franchise taxes. Judgment liens are court-ordered liens. **Attachment liens** are liens intended *to prevent transfer of property pending the outcome of litigation* and may involve a notice of **lis pendens** to *serve notice to potential buyers that there is a lawsuit pending.*
7. Lien holders can **foreclose** on property in the event of default or lack of payment. This *forces the property to be sold and the proceeds to be used to repay the debt*. The priority in which liens are paid is generally based on the order in which liens are recorded. The only exception is a **tax lien**, *which takes priority* over all other liens.
8. **Adverse possession** is when *someone acquires title to someone else's real property through open, notorious, hostile (adverse), and continuous use of it for a specific period of time as determined by state law.* Adverse possession does *not* apply to government-owned land. In the State of New York, the time required to claim adverse possession or easement by prescription is **ten years**.

6

Deeds

In This Session

Deeds are important real estate documents. Much of the discussion about deeds involves the practice of law, so it is not an area in which licensees can advise clients or customers. However, a real estate licensee must be familiar with deeds since a real estate transaction culminates in the delivery and acceptance of a properly drafted deed.

You'll learn:

- The purpose of a deed.
- Essential elements of a valid deed.
- How to distinguish among the different forms of deeds.
- About a property's legal description.
- Methods of transferring title.

Key Terms

- Acknowledgment
- Adverse Possession
- Bargain and Sale Deed
- Block and Lot
- Consideration
- Conveyance
- Dedication
- Deed
- Devise
- Delivery and Acceptance
- Executor
- Foreclosure
- Full Covenant and Warranty Deed
- Grant
- Grantee
- Grantor
- Habendum Clause
- Involuntary Alienation
- Metes and Bounds
- Plat
- Quitclaim Deed
- Referee's Deed
- Sheriff's Deed
- Survey
- Voluntary Alienation

Deeds

A **deed** is *an instrument that conveys a grantor's interest, if any, in real property.* A *deed can also be referred to as a* **conveyance**. The deed is the *document* used by a real property owner to transfer all or part of the interest in the property to another and is mere evidence of title.

Title is the *actual lawful ownership of real property and refers to holding the bundle of rights conveyed.* Title is *not* a document, but rather *a theory* pertaining to ownership. The deed is written proof of the rights conveyed to the owner, but having title to the land is what must be held to actually "own" it. **Equitable title** is an interest in property created on the execution of a valid sales contract, whereby actual title will be transferred by deed at a future date, such as at the closing. Having equitable title is *not* the same as having actual title, but the person who holds equitable title still enjoys certain rights and privileges.

Essential Elements of a Valid Deed

For a deed to be valid in New York, it must be **in writing**, as required by the Statute of Frauds, and it must include the following elements:

1. **Competent grantor.** *A person who wishes to grant or convey land, is of sound mind for the purposes of entering a contract, and has reached the age of majority, which in New York is 18.*
2. **Identifiable grantee.** The *person to whom the interest in real property is to be conveyed and identified in such a way to reasonably separate this person from all others in the world.* This would include getting proper and complete full names of the grantee(s), as well as designations, such as Jr., Sr., etc. If the deed is to be recorded, New York requires both the grantor and the grantee to be identified by address.
3. **Act of conveyance.** A clause in the deed that *states the grantor intends to convey title to the land.* Also called the *granting clause*, these words *identify the document as one that involves the transfer of interest from one person to another.* The wording of the deed must communicate a definite and clear intent by the grantor to part with the subject land. The words "give, grant, bargain, sell, and convey" leave no doubt as to the intent of the grantor.
4. **Consideration.** *Anything of value such as money, goods, services, or promises, given to induce another person to enter into a contract.* To be valid, a deed must contain a clause acknowledging the grantor did, in fact, receive some type of consideration for the land. In New York, the actual price paid need not be recited, but the full consideration must be stated when the deed is signed by a fiduciary, such as an executor, or by a referee in cases involving public sale, such as foreclosure.
5. **Legal description.** The legal description of the property being conveyed should be thorough and complete. The test of a valid property description is the ability to identify and distinguish that property from any and all other parcels of land.
6. **Habendum clause.** Often included after the granting clause, it *describes the type of estate granted and must always agree with the granting clause.* The clause is easy to identify; it begins with, "to have and to hold."
7. **Limitations.** How property may or may not be used, such as a deed restriction; must be noted.
8. **Exceptions and reservations.** Anything that affects the property, such as an easement; must be expressly noted on the deed. These are also known as "subject to" clauses.

9. **Signatures.** A deed must contain the **signatures** of all grantors. While it's not a requirement of a valid deed, to ensure they are in fact receiving a "good" title, grantees should always require **acknowledgement**, which means *the party signing the deed declares before a public official, such as a notary public or judge, that it was signed voluntarily and the signature is genuine*. Grantees do not need to sign the document.
10. **Delivery and acceptance.** Even when a deed has been properly executed, it has no legal effect until there has been **delivery** *of the deed by the grantor with the intention of transferring title* and **acceptance** *by the grantee receiving the land*. This delivery and acceptance must take place while the grantor is alive, or it has no legal effect. Delivery may be made directly to the grantee, or representing agent, such as an attorney or real estate broker. Once a deed is delivered and accepted, the grantee holds title to the land. Title cannot be re-conveyed by destroying the deed or returning it to the grantor. If the grantee wishes to give the land back, she would have to execute a new deed transferring title back to the original grantor.

RECORDING DEEDS

Usually, a final step after delivery and acceptance is filing the document in the county clerk's office where the property is located. Deeds are ***not*** required to be recorded to be valid; an unrecorded deed may in fact be valid, but it does not protect the grantee against challenges. Recording a deed makes its existence clear to third parties as part of the public record and also insures against lost documents. (Note that recording an invalid document does ***not*** make it valid.) In addition to the elements required to create a valid deed, these elements must be present in order to record the deed:

- A public official, such as a notary public, must serve as a legal witness to the grantor's **acknowledging signature**.
- A **certificate of the address of grantee** *ensures that tax authorities are informed as to where to send tax bills***.** To record a deed, New York requires both the grantor and grantee be identified by address.
- There should be evidence of **real estate transfer tax** (in most states and some local governments), which is often in the form of a stamp.

Types of Deeds

There are many types of deeds based on the various warranties contained within the document. Further, a deed may have several variations depending on the purpose for which it was drawn.

In New York, the full covenant and warranty deed, the bargain and sale deed, and the quitclaim deed are used most frequently.

Full Covenant and Warranty Deed

A **full covenant and warranty deed** *contains the strongest and broadest form of guarantee of title of any type of deed and provides the greatest protection of any deed to the grantee*. In this type of deed, the grantor makes various covenants, or warranties. These warranties are legal promises that the grantee will enjoy full and unencumbered ownership. A full covenant and warranty deed usually contains these covenants:

- **Covenant of seizin**. Assures the grantee that the grantor holds the title specified in the deed being conveyed.
- **Covenant of right to convey**. States the grantor owns the land and has the right to convey it. The covenant of right to convey usually follows the covenant of seizin.
- **Covenant against encumbrances**. Assures the grantee that the property is free of encumbrances not recited as exceptions in the deed.
- **Covenant of quiet enjoyment**. Ensures the grantee can possess the land without claims of title from others and will not be disturbed in the use of quiet enjoyment of the land because of a defect in title.
- **Covenant of further assurances**. Requires the grantor to remedy any defects in the title being conveyed and any errors or deficiencies in the deed itself.
- **Covenant of warranty forever**. Provides the grantor will defend the grantee's interest against all lawful claims of title. The covenant of warranty forever is the most important of all covenants because it is the best form of warranty for protecting the grantee.

Bargain and Sale Deed

A **bargain and sale deed** *implies that the grantor owns the property and has a right to convey it, but there are no warranties with it.* A **bargain and sale deed with covenants** (sometimes called a special warranty deed) is a guarantee that the grantor has not encumbered the property in any way except what is stated in the deed. Grantors are willing to warrant *only the time they owned the property, but not for previous owners*. A bargain and sale deed with covenants is frequently used for transactions in the New York City area.

Quitclaim Deed

A **quitclaim deed** makes no warranties regarding the title, if any, held by the grantor. Instead, it *conveys any interest in a parcel of land the grantor has at the time the deed is executed.* It conveys whatever right, title, or interest the grantor holds in the property without representation that there is any interest at all. Also known as a deed of release, quitclaim deeds are often used to remedy **clouds on a title**, which is when someone *may have a claim on the title*.

Judicial Deeds

Judicial deeds *result from some sort of court order and generally contain no covenants or warranties, although ownership is implied*. They could contain the covenant that the grantor has done nothing to encumber the property, however. The name of the deed being used reflects the role of the person executing the deed:

- **Executor's deed**, used to convey property of the deceased
- **Administrator's deed**, the person appointed by the court to convey property of the deceased
- **Guardian's deed**, used to convey property by a court-appointed representative
- **Sheriff's deed**, used in sheriff's sale at foreclosure
- **Referee's deed**, used in bankruptcy or foreclosure proceedings

Sample Warranty Deed

FORM S 301 – Warranty Deed with Lien Covenant

© NATIONAL LEGAL SUPPLY, INC. 126 Sheridan Ave., Albany, N.Y. 12210

N.Y.S. TAX $494.00

C07011

This Indenture

Made the 19th *day of* July *Nineteen Hundred and* Ninety-One

Between ERIC C. DAVIS and SHARON A. DAVIS, husband and wife, presently residing at 20 Venezio Avenue, Albany, New York, 12203,

LIBER 2441 PAGE 145

*part*ies *of the first part, and*

PAULINE D. SMITH and KATHERINE DiIANNI, residing at 2217 Highland Glen Road, Westwood, Ma., 02090, as joint tenants with rights of survivorship

*part*ies *of the second part,*

Witnesseth *that the part*ies *of the first part, in consideration of* ONE AND 00/100 ------------------------------ *Dollar* ($ 1.00) *lawful money of the United States,* and other good and valuable consideration *paid by the* parties *of the second part, do hereby grant and release unto the part*ies *of the second part,* their heirs *and assigns forever, all*

THAT LOT, PIECE OR PARCEL OF LAND with the buildings thereon, situate, lying and being in the Town of Guilderland, County of Albany and State of New York, known and distinguished as Lot 179 and a portion of Lot 178 as shown on a map entitled "Revised Resubdivision No. 3 of Section I, Westlawn, Guilderland, Albany County, New York" made by Keis and Holroyd, Consulting Engineers, dated December, 1949, and recorded in the Albany County Clerk's Office on the 24th day of December, 1949, in Drawer 142, as Map #2555, and bounded with reference to said Map as follows:

On the East by the west line of Venezio Avenue, as shown on said map, 80 feet along the same; on the South by the south line of Lot 179 as shown on said map, 125 feet along the same; on the West by the west lines of Lots 179 and 178 as shown on said map, 80 feet along the same, and on the North by a line parallel to and distant northerly 33 feet from the north line of Lot 179 as shown on said map, 125 feet along the same.

SUBJECT to all covenants, conditions, easements and restrictions of record affecting said premises.

BEING the same premises conveyed to the parties of the first part herein by Robert J. Bain and Deborah J. Bain, his wife, by deed dated the 25th day of October, 1984, and recorded in the Albany County Clerk's Office on the 26th day of October, 1984, in Liber 2271 of Deeds at page 297.

RECEIVED $ 494.00 RE- JUL 19 1991 TR- AL- COUN-

OFFICE OF ALBANY COUNTY CLERK ALBANY, N.Y. JUL 19 2 46 PM '91

SAMPLE

Source: John DiIanni, Associate Broker Realty USA

LIBER 2441 PAGE 146

Together *with the appurtenances and all the estate and rights of the part* ies *of the first part in and to said premises,*
To have and to hold *the premises herein granted unto the part*ies *of the second part,* their heirs *and assigns forever.*

And *said* parties of the first part *covenant as follows:*

First, *That the part*ies *of the second part shall quietly enjoy the said premises;*

Second, *That said* parties of the first part *will forever* **Warrant** *the title to said premises.*

Third, *That, in Compliance with Sec. 13 of the Lien Law, the grantors will receive the consideration for this conveyance and will hold the right to receive such consideration as a trust fund to be applied first for the purpose of paying the cost of the improvement and will apply the same first to the payment of the cost of the improvement before using any part of the total of the same for any other purpose.*

In Witness Whereof, *the part*ies *of the first part ha*ve *hereunto set* their *hand*s *and seal*s *the day and year first above written.*

IN PRESENCE OF

Eric C. Davis L.S.
Sharon A. Davis L.S.
L.S.
L.S.

State of New York
County of ALBANY } **ss.**

On this 19th *day of* July *Nineteen Hundred and* Ninety-One *before me, the subscriber, personally appeared*

ERIC C. DAVIS and SHARON A. DAVIS

*to me personally known and known to me to be the same person*s *described in and who executed the within Instrument, and* they *acknowledged to me that* they *executed the same.*

William N. Young
Notary Public.
WILLIAM N. YOUNG, JR.
Notary Public, State of New York
Qualified in Albany County
No. 4503497
Commission Expires May 31, 1993

Tax Map No. ______
Tax Billing Address ______

STATE OF NEW YORK)
COUNTY OF ALBANY)
Recorded in DEEDS
~~As Shown Hereon and~~
Examined
Thomas G. Clingan
THOMAS G. CLINGAN
ALBANY COUNTY CLERK

Deed

WARRANTY WITH LIEN COVENANT

ERIC C. DAVIS and
SHARON A. DAVIS

TO

PAULINE D. SMITH and
KATERINE DiIANNI

Dated, July 1991

STATE OF NEW YORK

COUNTY OF ______ *SS.*

RECORDED ON THE

day of ______ *A.D. 19* ______

at ______ *o'clock* ______ *M.*

in LIBER ______ *of DEEDS*

at PAGE ______ *and examined*

CLERK

Record & Return
David I. Bacon
61 Columbia St
Albany NY 12210

Legal Descriptions

Although street addresses are useful for the purpose of locating property, they do not provide an accurate description of land boundaries for the property. Therefore, real property must be identified by its **legal description,** the *description of the property that provides the ability to identify and distinguish that property from any and all other parcels of land.* Many documents in real estate, including deeds and mortgages, require a legal description to be valid.

There are various methods for providing a legal description: The metes and bounds system and the block and lot system are most common in New York. A property's legal description may be based on one or both of these methods.

Metes and Bounds System

With the **metes and bounds system**, *a licensed surveyor describes a property's boundaries in terms of distance (metes) and compass direction (bounds).* The surveyor starts at an easily identifiable point of beginning (POB) and works clockwise to define the boundary until he ultimately returns to the point of beginning.

The selection of the POB is perhaps one of the most important aspects of the metes and bounds description. The POB should be easily identifiable and well established, usually a point on a road. Once the POB is identified, the surveyor sights the direction of the next **marker**, which is a *fixed physical object used as a reference point.* Most markers are permanent physical objects such as rods, sometimes called **pins**, that have been driven into the ground to be used as reference points.

Monument System

In the past, the system similar to metes and bounds system was used but instead of using markers or pins placed by surveyors, the marker or monument might have been an object such as a tree, a rock, a wall, or even a specific bend in a river.

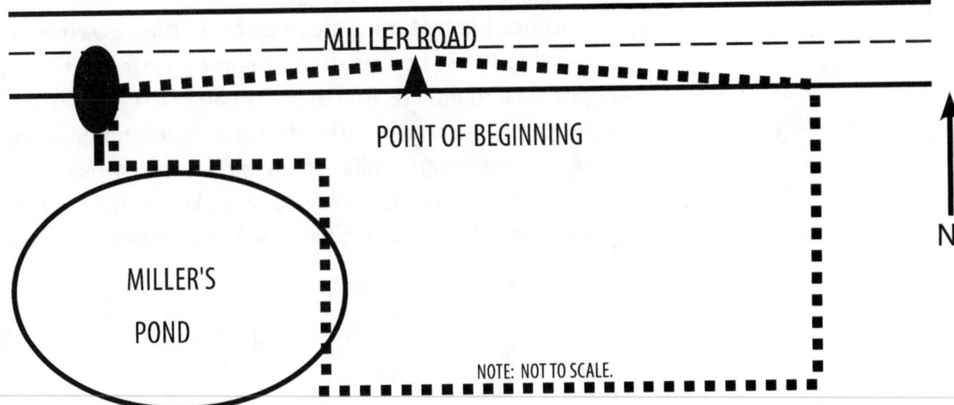

Sample Metes and Bounds Survey *Beginning at the pin in the center of Miller Road, go SE 300 feet at an angle until the edge of the road meets another pin; then due south 250 feet to a pin at the adjoining property's fence; then, go due west 350 feet to a pin at the edge of Miller's Pond; then, north 200 feet to another pin; due west 100 feet to a pin near the base of an old oak tree; then due north to a pin at the edge of the road; then NE at an angel to the point of beginning at the pin in the center of Miller Road.*

Block and Lot System

The **block and lot system** is a legal description used for **platted property**, which is *land that has been subdivided into blocks and lots.* To find the exact location of a parcel, one consults a **plat of subdivision**, a *detailed survey map of a subdivision recorded in the county where the land is located*. This plat map may also be called a plot plan or recorded plat. The plat map indicates unique numbers for each lot in each block of the particular subdivision. A legal description using this system might be: "Lot No. 105 as shown on said plan, as found in Plan Book (or liber) Volume 88, page 23." So the legal description indicates both the location of the lot and the location of the plot plan in the public records.

In New York, this system is more typically referenced as **section, block, and lot**, which may be written in a legal description as SEC, BLK, LOT. The legal description of each lot may be further defined using the metes and bounds system.

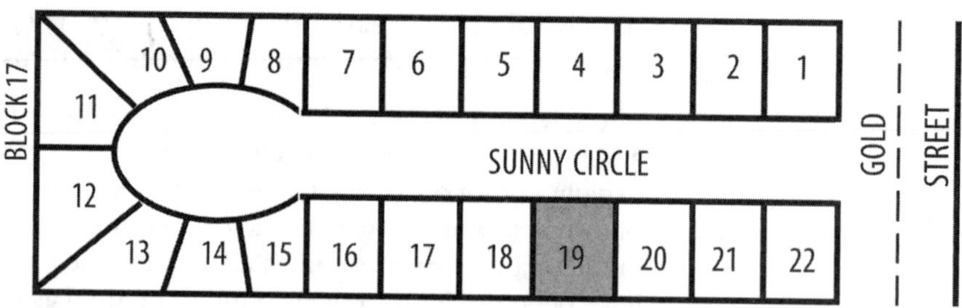

Sample Subdivision Plat Map *Golden Valley Estate, Block 17, Lots 1–22.*

Government Survey System

Another type of legal description is the **government survey system,** sometimes referred to as the **rectangular survey system**. This system is based on intersecting principal meridians (north-south) and base lines (east-west) designated throughout much of the country. Using the meridians and base lines, land is divided into six-mile by six-mile squares called **townships**. Each township contains 36 square-mile **sections**, and each section contains 640 acres. While this method is *not* used in New York, there are some elements associated with this system that are important to remember:

- 1 township = 36 sections
- 1 section = 640 acres = 1 square mile
- 1 square mile = 640 acres
- 1 acre = 43,560 square feet

Methods of Transferring Ownership

The process of *transferring ownership interests in property* is called **alienation**. In New York, title to real property may be transferred numerous ways: Voluntary alienation, involuntary alienation, or devise or descent.

Voluntary Alienation

Voluntary alienation, the most common way to transfer ownership of land, is *an action that the property owner undertakes of his free will.* It may be accomplished in a number of ways:

- **Sale** of property, in which the owner agrees to hand over the title in exchange for consideration; usually completed with a **deed**.
- **Gift** of a deed, in which the owner may transfer title without receiving something of value from the recipient.
- **Dedication** of private property for public use, for example, a developer who dedicates land for streets within a new subdivision or someone who dedicates land for a park to a municipality.
- **Grant**, as when the government transfers the title to land to an individual. Historically, government **land grants** were issued to public companies to build railroads and to colleges and universities. A more recent example includes grants still available in Alaska to individuals who want to create homesteads on the land. The evidence of such title may be referred to as a **land patent**.

Involuntary Alienation

Involuntary alienation is the *transfer of title in an interest in real property against the will of the owner, or without action by the owner.* It may be accomplished in a number of ways:

Eminent Domain

Eminent domain is *the government's constitutional power to take private property for public use, as long as the owner is paid just compensation.* The actual act of taking private property for public use through eminent domain is known as **appropriation** or **condemnation**. Most frequently, it is the federal, state, and local governments; utility companies; and school districts that exercise the right to eminent domain. In order for the property to be transferred, the courts must rule that the recommended use will benefit the public's greater good. In New York, when private property is condemned through the right of eminent domain, the landowner has the right to challenge the compensation offered.

Foreclosure

If a landowner *defaults on debts secured by real property, the property can be transferred without consent* through **foreclosure**. When a property is foreclosed, it is sold and the proceeds from the sale are applied to the owner's debt. Default on a mortgage loan is the most common reason for foreclosure; however, unpaid taxes, liens, and judgments can also result in foreclosure.

Adverse Possession

Possession and use of property can mature into title. Acquiring title to land by **adverse possession** requires *open and notorious, hostile and adverse, exclusive,* *and continuous use* of another's land for a designated period of time, which is **ten years** as defined by the laws of the State of New York.

Accession

Accession is the *acquisition of title to land by its addition to real estate already owned, through human actions or natural processes.* Accession gives property owners the right to everything produced by their land. Sometimes this addition to one person's land can result in an involuntary alienation of another person's land.

- Land bordering bodies of water may acquire additional land through **accretion**, which is simply *the gradual addition to dry land by the forces of nature.* The *land added through accretion* is known as **alluvion**.
- **Avulsion** is *when land is lost due to sudden acts of nature such as floods or earthquakes.*
- **Reliction** is *when a body of water gradually recedes, exposing land that was previously underwater.*

Devise or Descent

Another way that property transfers is *upon the death of the owner*. There are two ways this happens:

Devise

When someone dies *with a will,* he is said to die **testate**. In the will, the *testator* or *testatrix* (the deceased) may have named an **executor** (or executrix for a female*) to carry out the provisions of the will,* including disbursement of land. If no executor or executrix was named, the court appoints an administrator with the responsibility of carrying out the decedent's wishes. To *transfer land through a will* is to **devise** it, thus *heirs who are left the land* are **devisees**. The process by which the deceased's property is distributed is called **probate**. Probate occurs under the supervision of the surrogate court in the county where the decedent lived.

Descent

When someone dies *without a will,* he is said to die **intestate**. In these instances, property descends by **intestate succession** to the *natural heirs of the deceased.* Natural heirs include spouses, children, and relatives. The Statute of Descent and Distribution lists those persons in a close enough degree of kinship to be considered natural heirs. If a property owner dies intestate and there are *no heirs or creditors, the property would revert to the state* through the process of **escheat**.

SUMMARY

1. The **deed** is the *document used by the owner of real property to transfer all or part interest in the property to another*. The deed is *mere evidence* of title; it does not necessarily prove ownership of property. **Title** is *the actual lawful ownership of real property and refers to holding the bundle of rights conveyed.* Title is not a document, but rather a *theory* pertaining to ownership.

2. For a deed to be **valid** in New York, it must be **in writing** and include these elements:
   1. Competent grantor
   2. Identifiable grantee
   3. Act of Conveyance, or granting clause
   4. Consideration
   5. Legal description
   6. Habendum clause ("to have and to hold")
   7. Limitations, such as deed restrictions
   8. Exceptions and reservations, such as liens
   9. Grantor's signature
   10. Delivery of the deed and acceptance by the grantee

   A deed does *not* have to be recorded in the county clerk's office to be valid; to be recorded, however, the deed must be **acknowledged by the grantor** and witnessed by a notary public or other official.

3. There are several forms of deeds. In New York, the *full covenant and warranty deed*, the *quitclaim deed,* and the *bargain and sale deed* are used most frequently. A **full covenant and warranty deed** *contains the strongest and broadest form of guarantee of title of any type of deed and provides the greatest protection of any deed to the grantee.* In this type of deed, the grantor makes various legal promises, or covenants, including the: **Covenant of seizin** (assures the grantee that the grantor holds the title to convey); **covenant of right to convey** (states the grantor owns the land and has the right to convey); **covenant against encumbrances** (assures the grantee the property is free of encumbrances not recited as exceptions in the deed); **covenant of quiet enjoyment** (ensures the grantee can possess the land without claims of title from others and will not be disturbed in the use of the land); **covenant for further assurances** (requires the grantor to remedy any defects in the title being conveyed and any errors or deficiencies in the deed itself); and **covenant of warranty forever** (provides the grantor will defend grantee's interest against unlawful claims of title).

4. Other deeds may or may not include warranties but are still a valid way to transfer title to real property: **Bargain and sale deed with covenants** (implies the grantor holds title to the property and has not encumbered the property); **quitclaim deed** (conveys any interest in a parcel of land the grantor has at the time the deed is executed); **judicial deed** (someone empowered by the court to exercise judicial power to convey the land in question, such as an executor, guardian, administrator, sheriff, or referee).

5. A **legal description** is required for a deed. The two methods used in New York are the **metes and bounds system** (a surveyor starts at an easily identifiable point of beginning and describes the property's boundaries, moving clockwise, in term of direction and distances, ultimately returning to the point of beginning) and the **block and lot system** (description states only the property's lot and block number in a particular subdivision plat book). In New York, this is more commonly the section, block, and lot system.

6. Another type of legal description is the **government survey system**, sometimes referred to as the **rectangular survey system**. This system, which is *not* used in New York, divides land into six-

mile by six-mile squares called **townships**. Each township contains 36 square-mile **sections**, and each section contains **640 acres**. One acre is equal to **43,560 square feet**.

7. There are several methods of transferring ownership. **Voluntary alienation** *occurs when title to land is voluntarily transferred.* Title may be transferred voluntarily through sales, gifts, dedications, and grants. **Involuntary alienation** *occurs when title is transferred without the owner's consent.* Title may be transferred involuntarily through eminent domain, foreclosure, adverse possession, and natural processes such as accretion or avulsion.

8. When a landowner dies *with a will* (**testate**), the deceased's property is distributed through the process of **probate.** To transfer land through a will is to **devise** it. When a landowner dies *without a will* (**intestate**), property descends by **intestate succession** to the natural heirs of the deceased. If there are no heirs or creditors, the property *passes to the state* through **escheat**.

6-A

Real Estate Closings

In This Session

A ready, willing, and able buyer is found; the sales contract is drawn up; and both parties have fulfilled their obligations under the agreement. Finally, closing can occur. At the closing, the buyer receives the deed for the purchase and the seller receives payment for the property. This session looks at the steps necessary to hold a closing and provides some background on related concepts.

You'll learn:

- The purpose of the public records system.
- The significance of a marketable title.
- The documents necessary for closing.
- Which closing costs are paid by a buyer and by a seller.
- How to calculate prorations.

Key Terms

- Abstract of Title
- Actual Notice
- Chain of Title
- Closing Disclosure
- Closing Statement
- Cloud on the Title
- Constructive Notice
- Credits
- Debits
- Marketable Title
- Proration
- Real Estate Settlement Procedures Act (RESPA)
- Reconciliation
- Settlement Statement
- Survey
- Title
- Title Insurance
- Title Search

Evidence of Marketable Title

When conveying real property, the seller is generally expected to deliver a **marketable title**, *a title that is free and clear from undisclosed encumbrances or other defects that would expose a purchaser to litigation or impede a purchaser's ability to enjoy the property or to later sell the property easily.* A **title search** of the public records, also known as a title examination, is necessary to *determine ownership and the quality of the title prior to conveyance*. If a marketable title cannot be produced, a closing may have to be postponed.

Public Records

The public records system is a way to provide **notice** so that the public is able to determine who holds an interest in any piece of property. Recording documents in the public records of the county clerk's office where the property is located allows property owners to defend their estate, right, or interest against third parties claiming a subsequent interest. Although there is no legal requirement to record a real estate document, such as a deed or title, an unrecorded document is likely to be unenforceable against a third party claiming a subsequent right or interest in the property. In New York, a recorded deed takes precedence over any prior unrecorded deed, and so it is in all parties' best interests to record deeds.

The concept of *constructive notice* provides this protection. A person is considered to have **constructive notice** of something when *it should be known*, even if it is not. Since the public records are available for anyone's inspection, *everyone is considered to have constructive notice of the contents of recorded documents*. The burden of discovery rests with the general public. Furthermore, the law expects a buyer or lender to search the public record for his or her own protection. This results in **actual notice**, which exists *when individuals have actual knowledge of a fact*. Actual notice includes what someone personally saw, heard, read, or observed.

Chain of Title

The **chain of title** is a *clear and unbroken chronological record of the ownership of a specific piece of property*. Tracing the chain of title simply means tracing the successive conveyances of title, starting with the current deed and going back a suitable number of years. Each owner is linked to the *previous* owner and the *subsequent* owner through deeds, forming a chain of title as disclosed in the public records. In New York, chains of title, if unbroken, date all the way back to a grant from the King of England.

A *gap in the chain of title* creates uncertainty, which is referred to as a **cloud on the title**, also called color of title. A cloud on the title could be something simple, for example, Sue Jones buys a house. She gets married and is now Sue Smith. When she sells the house, the grantor name on the deed is Sue Smith. This creates a break in the chain of title.

Suit to Quiet Title

A **suit to quiet title** may be required to close any missing links and remove the cloud on the title. This is a *lawsuit filed to determine and resolve problems of instruments conveying a particular piece of land.* The purpose of this suit is to clear a particular, known claim, title defect, or perceived defect. In New York, this is accomplished through an **Article 15 proceeding** (Article 15 of Real Property Actions and Proceedings). To close the gap and clear the cloud on the title, the court may issue a quitclaim deed or a judicial deed.

Abstract of Title

A title search, usually performed by an abstractor or a title company, starts with the chain of title and results in the creation of an **abstract of title,** *a summarized chronological history of title to a property, listing all recorded documents that affect the title.* A title abstractor will examine records of deeds, taxes, special assessments, liens, judgments, mortgages, and other encumbrances that have ever affected the property, even if the encumbrance has been removed or satisfied. An abstract of title does *not* ensure the validity of the title, and there is no guarantee associated with this type of title evidence, so the homeowner or lender does not have any recourse if title defects are discovered later. In rare occasions, an abstract could be accepted in place of title insurance if a satisfactory **letter of opinion** from an attorney is issued regarding the quality of the title.

Title Insurance

Title insurance *protects lenders (and sometimes property owners) against loss due to disputes over ownership of a property and defects in the title not found in the search of the public record.* Further, title insurance protects lenders and property owners from claimants not listed in the insurance policy, including defects in the public record such as forged documents, improper deeds, undisclosed heirs, errors in a property's legal description, and other mistakes. Title insurance does not generally cure defects, although a title company could potentially purchase the property and fix the problem. More commonly, it simply insures against losses (up to the coverage amount specified in the policy) due to title defects other than those specifically excluded. It may require the title company to go to court if necessary and defend its policyholder against any claim against the ownership of the land. A title insurance policy, generally paid for with a one-time premium, may have different insureds:

- **Mortgagee's policies.** The mortgagee (lender) may have a policy to protect its interests in the property. The mortgagee's policy is for the loan amount outstanding at the time a claim is paid. The owner's policies and the mortgagee's policies typically coincide, so the title insurance issuer is not paying twice on the same claim.
- **Owner's policies.** Owner's fee title insurance policies are issued in the name of the property owner. Coverage runs from the time of purchase for as long as the policyholder owns the property. When the property is sold, the new buyer must purchase a new policy and be named beneficiary to collect on a claim from a title defect.
- **Leasehold policies.** A less common type of title insurance is the leasehold policy. Lessees typically obtain this type of insurance when a substantial amount of money is invested in a property, such as for a building owned on leased land.
- **Easement policies.** Another less common type of title insurance is the easement policy, which *protects an easement owner's interests across another's property.*

Real Estate Settlement Procedures Act

The **Real Estate Settlement Procedures Act** (RESPA) of 1974 requires mortgage lenders, mortgage brokers, or servicers of home loans to *provide borrowers with pertinent and timely disclosures of the nature and costs of the real estate settlement process.* Its purpose is to regulate settlement and closing procedures and to protect borrowers. The Act does not apply to loans used to finance the purchase of 25 acres or more, vacant land, or transactions where the buyer assumes, or takes subject to, an existing loan. The U.S. Department of Housing and Urban Development (HUD) enacted **Regulation X**, which implements RESPA. As a real estate professional, you should know that RESPA:

- Prohibits kickbacks and fees for services not performed during closing.
- Requires brokers and lenders to disclose affiliated business relationships without obligating parties to use suggested referrals.
- Sets limits on the amount of escrow reserves a lender can hold or require a buyer to deposit in advance to cover real estate taxes, real estate insurance premiums, and other similar costs.

Truth In Lending Act

- Requires a **Loan Estimate** of closing costs be given to the buyer within three business days of applying for a loan.
- Requires use of the **Closing Disclosure** for all federally-related residential loans on properties intended for occupancy by one to four families.
- Requires the buyer receives the **Closing Disclosure** three days before the closing.

Consumer Financial Protection Bureau

The **Home Loan Toolkit** provides a step-by-step guide to help consumers understand the nature and costs of real estate settlement services, define what affordable means to them, and find their best mortgage. The toolkit features interactive worksheets and checklists, conversation starters for discussions between consumers and lenders, and research tips to help consumers seek out and find important information.

The toolkit is designed to replace an existing booklet that creditors currently must provide to mortgage applicants, which was initially developed by the Department of Housing and Urban Development, called the "HUD Settlement Booklet".

The Closing

A **closing** is *the final step in a real estate transaction when the transfer of real property ownership from seller to buyer occurs, according to the terms and conditions in a sales contract*. In most real estate transactions, two closings take place simultaneously:

- **The closing of the buyer's mortgage loan and disbursement of funds.** At the closing, sellers are paid the balance of the purchase price, and existing liens, such as a mortgage, are satisfied. Typically, buyers pay the balance of the purchase price with a combination of a mortgage loan and personal funds.
- **The closing of the sale and transfer of title.** Before a real estate transaction closes, all conditions and contingencies of the sales contract must be met. Once all parties are satisfied the conditions and contingencies have been met, the deed can be executed and delivered, thus transferring title to the new owner.

Participants at the Closing

A closing is usually a face-to-face meeting of all interested parties. The sales contract typically identifies when and where the closing takes place. Closings are generally held at the title company's office, the broker's office, the lending institution, or at one of the participating attorney's offices. The closing may be conducted by an attorney, a broker, or a title company representative, sometimes called a *closing agent.* Each participant in the closing has a distinct role:

- **Buyers** attend to pay for and receive title to the property.
- **Sellers** attend to grant their property to the buyers and receive payment.
- The **buyer's and seller's attorneys** are present to review all closing documents to ensure they are in their clients' best interests.
- **Real estate agents** are there to fulfill their fiduciary obligation to their clients to account for all monies transacted.
- A **mortgage company representative** examines all loan documents and makes sure the property for which a mortgage is being issued has a clear title, prepares the settlement statement, and disburses funds to the seller.
- **Title company representatives** review the documents and, once satisfied, deliver evidence that the title is insured.

A Broker's Role at Closing

In some areas, it is customary for brokers to step out of the picture once they have brought about a meeting of the minds and turn things over to attorneys for the seller and buyer. In other areas, brokers remain involved all the way through closing, advising the client and remaining in contact with all parties involved to ensure everything needed to close the transaction is in place. Brokers attend a final walk-through with buyers on the day of closing or immediately prior to it. Even though brokers are not typically responsible for actually conducting the closing, a broker is fulfilling the fiduciary obligations of care and accountability by ensuring the closing transaction follows the terms as outlined in the written sales contract.

Regardless of the extent of the broker's participation, the broker's commission is paid at the closing. Prior to the closing, the broker submits a commission statement to the participating attorneys or closing agent and a check is cut to the broker(s) for commission earned. The broker(s) is then responsible for distributing the commission to his agents and to any cooperating agents according to their agreement.

Typical Closing Documents

One of the most important documents necessary to prepare for a real estate closing is the **sales contract**. The terms of the sales contract dictate the requirements of the closing, including the necessary documents. For example, if the transaction involves the *transfer of personal property* from the seller to the buyer, a **bill of sale** may be required. While not every document is applicable for every closing, several documents or forms are typically presented and reviewed as part of the closing process.

Deed. A **deed** is *an instrument that conveys a grantor's interest, if any, in real property.* At closing, the seller (the grantor) provides a new signed deed to the buyer (the grantee). To be properly executed, the grantor must *deliver* the deed with the intention of transferring title. Once the grantee *accepts* the deed, she holds title to the land.

Survey. In some transactions, either the buyer or the buyer's lender will require a survey to ensure the property description is accurate. A **survey** is the *process of determining the physical size and boundaries of a property.* If the mortgage company requires a survey, the buyer usually bears the cost of it. In certain counties in New York, however, the seller pays for it.

Mortgage documentation. Since buyers generally do not have ready cash on hand to purchase property, most real estate transactions require some sort of financing, which involves multiple documents:

- The financing instrument, typically a **promissory note**, is a written promise to repay the money owed and is signed by the borrower.
- The security instrument, usually a **mortgage**, provides security for the debt by creating a voluntary lien against the property. The buyer is required to sign this and give it to the lender as security for repayment of the note. The mortgage must be recorded at the county recorder's office in the county where the property is located to ensure constructive notice to the public and establish lien priority.
- If the seller still has a mortgage on the property, the buyer's lender typically brings a check in the payoff amount made out to the seller's mortgagee. Once the seller's lender is paid, that lender issues a **satisfaction of mortgage**, which should be recorded as evidence that the lien has been released. According to NY law, lenders have 45 days after the request from the mortgagor to record the satisfaction of mortgage.

Homeowners insurance. Lenders require homeowners insurance policies be sufficient to replace the home or reimburse the mortgage amount *in the event of a fire or other disaster.* Depending on the location of the property, **flood insurance** may also be required.

Property inspection reports and certificates of occupancy. Lenders require a pest inspection, while buyers may also require a home inspection. Other inspections that may be required by a buyer or lender include structural integrity, septic systems/soil/waterflow (referred to as percolation or perc tests), and radon gas, among others. Some municipalities may require a certificate of occupancy as evidence that the property is inhabitable.

FORMS REQUIRED BY NEW YORK STATE

- **New York Transfer Tax Return.** All transfers of real property in the state of New York require the use of **Form TP 584**, officially titled the *Combined Real Estate Transfer Tax Return, Credit Line Mortgage Certificate, and Certification of Exemption from the Payment of Estimated Personal Income Tax* form. Among other things, this form is used to transmit the New York State transfer tax and to exempt New York State residents from owing state capital gains tax on the sale of property. Form TP 584 must be signed by both buyer and seller at closing before the deed can be recorded.
- **Real Property Transfer Report.** The New York State Office of Real Property Services (ORPS) requires that **Form RP-5217**, *Real Property Transfer Report,* accompany the deed when it is recorded. This form documents the details of the property transfer so that property tax records can be updated.

The Closing Disclosure

The **Closing Disclosure**, formerly known as the HUD 1 Settlement Statement, *itemizes all expenses and costs paid by the buyer and seller to close the real estate transaction. The disclosure also provides pertinent information concerning features of the mortgage loan.* It is generally prepared by the buyer's and seller's attorneys or title or bank representatives prior to closing. While real estate licensees do not typically prepare settlement statements, it is advisable to be familiar with them so that clients' questions may be addressed. The Truth In Lending Act requires the use of the standardized five (5) page **Closing Disclosure** for all federal-related residential loans.

Closing Disclosure

This form is a statement of final loan terms and closing costs. Compare this document with your Loan Estimate.

Closing Information

Date Issued	4/15/2013
Closing Date	4/15/2013
Disbursement Date	4/15/2013
Settlement Agent	Epsilon Title Co.
File #	12-3456
Property	456 Somewhere Ave Anytown, ST 12345
Sale Price	$180,000

Transaction Information

Borrower	Michael Jones and Mary Stone 123 Anywhere Street Anytown, ST 12345
Seller	Steve Cole and Amy Doe 321 Somewhere Drive Anytown, ST 12345
Lender	Ficus Bank

Loan Information

Loan Term	30 years
Purpose	Purchase
Product	Fixed Rate
Loan Type	☒ Conventional ☐ FHA ☐ VA ☐ ____________
Loan ID #	123456789
MIC #	000654321

Loan Terms

Loan Terms		Can this amount increase after closing?
Loan Amount	$162,000	**NO**
Interest Rate	3.875%	**NO**
Monthly Principal & Interest *See Projected Payments below for your Estimated Total Monthly Payment*	$761.78	**NO**
		Does the loan have these features?
Prepayment Penalty		**YES** • **As high as $3,240** if you pay off the loan during the first 2 years
Balloon Payment		**NO**

Projected Payments

Payment Calculation	**Years 1-7**	**Years 8-30**
Principal & Interest	$761.78	$761.78
Mortgage Insurance	+ 82.35	+ —
Estimated Escrow *Amount can increase over time*	+ 206.13	+ 206.13
Estimated Total Monthly Payment	$1,050.26	$967.91

Estimated Taxes, Insurance & Assessments *Amount can increase over time* *See page 4 for details*	$356.13 a month	**This estimate includes** ☒ Property Taxes ☒ Homeowner's Insurance ☒ Other: Homeowner's Association Dues *See Escrow Account on page 4 for details. You must pay for other property costs separately.*	**In escrow?** **YES** **YES** **NO**

Costs at Closing

Closing Costs	$9,712.10	Includes $4,694.05 in Loan Costs + $5,018.05 in Other Costs – $0 in Lender Credits. *See page 2 for details.*
Cash to Close	$14,147.26	Includes Closing Costs. *See Calculating Cash to Close on page 3 for details.*

CLOSING DISCLOSURE PAGE 1 OF 5 • LOAN ID # 123456789

Closing Cost Details

Loan Costs	Borrower-Paid At Closing	Borrower-Paid Before Closing	Seller-Paid At Closing	Seller-Paid Before Closing	Paid by Others
A. Origination Charges	**$1,802.00**				
01 0.25 % of Loan Amount (Points)	$405.00				
02 Application Fee	$300.00				
03 Underwriting Fee	$1,097.00				
04					
05					
06					
07					
08					
B. Services Borrower Did Not Shop For	**$236.55**				
01 Appraisal Fee to John Smith Appraisers Inc.					$405.00
02 Credit Report Fee to Information Inc.		$29.80			
03 Flood Determination Fee to Info Co.	$20.00				
04 Flood Monitoring Fee to Info Co.	$31.75				
05 Tax Monitoring Fee to Info Co.	$75.00				
06 Tax Status Research Fee to Info Co.	$80.00				
07					
08					
09					
10					
C. Services Borrower Did Shop For	**$2,655.50**				
01 Pest Inspection Fee to Pests Co.	$120.50				
02 Survey Fee to Surveys Co.	$85.00				
03 Title – Insurance Binder to Epsilon Title Co.	$650.00				
04 Title – Lender's Title Insurance to Epsilon Title Co.	$500.00				
05 Title – Settlement Agent Fee to Epsilon Title Co.	$500.00				
06 Title – Title Search to Epsilon Title Co.	$800.00				
07					
08					
D. TOTAL LOAN COSTS (Borrower-Paid)	**$4,694.05**				
Loan Costs Subtotals (A + B + C)	$4,664.25	$29.80			

Other Costs	Borrower-Paid At Closing	Borrower-Paid Before Closing	Seller-Paid At Closing	Seller-Paid Before Closing	Paid by Others
E. Taxes and Other Government Fees	**$85.00**				
01 Recording Fees Deed: $40.00 Mortgage: $45.00	$85.00				
02 Transfer Tax to Any State			$950.00		
F. Prepaids	**$2,120.80**				
01 Homeowner's Insurance Premium (12 mo.) to Insurance Co.	$1,209.96				
02 Mortgage Insurance Premium (mo.)					
03 Prepaid Interest ($17.44 per day from 4/15/13 to 5/1/13)	$279.04				
04 Property Taxes (6 mo.) to Any County USA	$631.80				
05					
G. Initial Escrow Payment at Closing	**$412.25**				
01 Homeowner's Insurance $100.83 per month for 2 mo.	$201.66				
02 Mortgage Insurance per month for mo.					
03 Property Taxes $105.30 per month for 2 mo.	$210.60				
04					
05					
06					
07					
08 Aggregate Adjustment	– 0.01				
H. Other	**$2,400.00**				
01 HOA Capital Contribution to HOA Acre Inc.	$500.00				
02 HOA Processing Fee to HOA Acre Inc.	$150.00				
03 Home Inspection Fee to Engineers Inc.	$750.00			$750.00	
04 Home Warranty Fee to XYZ Warranty Inc.			$450.00		
05 Real Estate Commission to Alpha Real Estate Broker			$5,700.00		
06 Real Estate Commission to Omega Real Estate Broker			$5,700.00		
07 Title – Owner's Title Insurance (optional) to Epsilon Title Co.	$1,000.00				
08					
I. TOTAL OTHER COSTS (Borrower-Paid)	**$5,018.05**				
Other Costs Subtotals (E + F + G + H)	$5,018.05				
J. TOTAL CLOSING COSTS (Borrower-Paid)	**$9,712.10**				
Closing Costs Subtotals (D + I)	$9,682.30	$29.80	$12,800.00	$750.00	$405.00
Lender Credits					

CLOSING DISCLOSURE

PAGE 2 OF 5 • LOAN ID # 123456789

Calculating Cash to Close

Use this table to see what has changed from your Loan Estimate.

	Loan Estimate	Final	Did this change?	
Total Closing Costs (J)	$8,054.00	$9,712.10	**YES**	• See **Total Loan Costs (D)** and **Total Other Costs (I)**
Closing Costs Paid Before Closing	$0	– $29.80	**YES**	• You paid these Closing Costs **before closing**
Closing Costs Financed (Paid from your Loan Amount)	$0	$0	**NO**	
Down Payment/Funds from Borrower	$18,000.00	$18,000.00	**NO**	
Deposit	– $10,000.00	– $10,000.00	**NO**	
Funds for Borrower	$0	$0	**NO**	
Seller Credits	$0	– $2,500.00	**YES**	• See Seller Credits in **Section L**
Adjustments and Other Credits	$0	– $1,035.04	**YES**	• See details in **Sections K and L**
Cash to Close	$16,054.00	$14,147.26		

Summaries of Transactions

Use this table to see a summary of your transaction.

BORROWER'S TRANSACTION

K. Due from Borrower at Closing		**$189,762.30**
01	Sale Price of Property	$180,000.00
02	Sale Price of Any Personal Property Included in Sale	
03	Closing Costs Paid at Closing (J)	$9,682.30
04		
Adjustments		
05		
06		
07		
Adjustments for Items Paid by Seller in Advance		
08	City/Town Taxes to	
09	County Taxes to	
10	Assessments to	
11	HOA Dues 4/15/13 to 4/30/13	$80.00
12		
13		
14		
15		
L. Paid Already by or on Behalf of Borrower at Closing		**$175,615.04**
01	Deposit	$10,000.00
02	Loan Amount	$162,000.00
03	Existing Loan(s) Assumed or Taken Subject to	
04		
05	Seller Credit	$2,500.00
Other Credits		
06	Rebate from Epsilon Title Co.	$750.00
07		
Adjustments		
08		
09		
10		
11		
Adjustments for Items Unpaid by Seller		
12	City/Town Taxes 1/1/13 to 4/14/13	$365.04
13	County Taxes to	
14	Assessments to	
15		
16		
17		
CALCULATION		
Total Due from Borrower at Closing (K)		$189,762.30
Total Paid Already by or on Behalf of Borrower at Closing (L)		– $175,615.04
Cash to Close ☒ From ☐ To Borrower		**$14,147.26**

SELLER'S TRANSACTION

M. Due to Seller at Closing		**$180,080.00**
01	Sale Price of Property	$180,000.00
02	Sale Price of Any Personal Property Included in Sale	
03		
04		
05		
06		
07		
08		
Adjustments for Items Paid by Seller in Advance		
09	City/Town Taxes to	
10	County Taxes to	
11	Assessments to	
12	HOA Dues 4/15/13 to 4/30/13	$80.00
13		
14		
15		
16		
N. Due from Seller at Closing		**$115,665.04**
01	Excess Deposit	
02	Closing Costs Paid at Closing (J)	$12,800.00
03	Existing Loan(s) Assumed or Taken Subject to	
04	Payoff of First Mortgage Loan	$100,000.00
05	Payoff of Second Mortgage Loan	
06		
07		
08	Seller Credit	$2,500.00
09		
10		
11		
12		
13		
Adjustments for Items Unpaid by Seller		
14	City/Town Taxes 1/1/13 to 4/14/13	$365.04
15	County Taxes to	
16	Assessments to	
17		
18		
19		
CALCULATION		
Total Due to Seller at Closing (M)		$180,080.00
Total Due from Seller at Closing (N)		– $115,665.04
Cash ☐ From ☒ To Seller		**$64,414.96**

CLOSING DISCLOSURE

PAGE 3 OF 5 • LOAN ID # 123456789

Additional Information About This Loan

Loan Disclosures

Assumption
If you sell or transfer this property to another person, your lender
☐ will allow, under certain conditions, this person to assume this loan on the original terms.
☒ will not allow assumption of this loan on the original terms.

Demand Feature
Your loan
☐ has a demand feature, which permits your lender to require early repayment of the loan. You should review your note for details.
☒ does not have a demand feature.

Late Payment
If your payment is more than *15* days late, your lender will charge a late fee of *5% of the monthly principal and interest payment.*

Negative Amortization (Increase in Loan Amount)
Under your loan terms, you
☐ are scheduled to make monthly payments that do not pay all of the interest due that month. As a result, your loan amount will increase (negatively amortize), and your loan amount will likely become larger than your original loan amount. Increases in your loan amount lower the equity you have in this property.
☐ may have monthly payments that do not pay all of the interest due that month. If you do, your loan amount will increase (negatively amortize), and, as a result, your loan amount may become larger than your original loan amount. Increases in your loan amount lower the equity you have in this property.
☒ do not have a negative amortization feature.

Partial Payments
Your lender
☒ may accept payments that are less than the full amount due (partial payments) and apply them to your loan.
☐ may hold them in a separate account until you pay the rest of the payment, and then apply the full payment to your loan.
☐ does not accept any partial payments.
If this loan is sold, your new lender may have a different policy.

Security Interest
You are granting a security interest in
456 Somewhere Ave., Anytown, ST 12345

You may lose this property if you do not make your payments or satisfy other obligations for this loan.

Escrow Account
For now, your loan
☒ will have an escrow account (also called an "impound" or "trust" account) to pay the property costs listed below. Without an escrow account, you would pay them directly, possibly in one or two large payments a year. Your lender may be liable for penalties and interest for failing to make a payment.

Escrow		
Escrowed Property Costs over Year 1	$2,473.56	Estimated total amount over year 1 for your escrowed property costs: *Homeowner's Insurance* *Property Taxes*
Non-Escrowed Property Costs over Year 1	$1,800.00	Estimated total amount over year 1 for your non-escrowed property costs: *Homeowner's Association Dues* You may have other property costs.
Initial Escrow Payment	$412.25	A cushion for the escrow account you pay at closing. See Section G on page 2.
Monthly Escrow Payment	$206.13	The amount included in your total monthly payment.

☐ will not have an escrow account because ☐ you declined it ☐ your lender does not offer one. You must directly pay your property costs, such as taxes and homeowner's insurance. Contact your lender to ask if your loan can have an escrow account.

No Escrow		
Estimated Property Costs over Year 1		Estimated total amount over year 1. You must pay these costs directly, possibly in one or two large payments a year.
Escrow Waiver Fee		

In the future,
Your property costs may change and, as a result, your escrow payment may change. You may be able to cancel your escrow account, but if you do, you must pay your property costs directly. If you fail to pay your property taxes, your state or local government may (1) impose fines and penalties or (2) place a tax lien on this property. If you fail to pay any of your property costs, your lender may (1) add the amounts to your loan balance, (2) add an escrow account to your loan, or (3) require you to pay for property insurance that the lender buys on your behalf, which likely would cost more and provide fewer benefits than what you could buy on your own.

CLOSING DISCLOSURE PAGE 4 OF 5 • LOAN ID # 123456789

Loan Calculations

Total of Payments. Total you will have paid after you make all payments of principal, interest, mortgage insurance, and loan costs, as scheduled.	$285,803.36
Finance Charge. The dollar amount the loan will cost you.	$118,830.27
Amount Financed. The loan amount available after paying your upfront finance charge.	$162,000.00
Annual Percentage Rate (APR). Your costs over the loan term expressed as a rate. This is not your interest rate.	4.174%
Total Interest Percentage (TIP). The total amount of interest that you will pay over the loan term as a percentage of your loan amount.	69.46%

Questions? If you have questions about the loan terms or costs on this form, use the contact information below. To get more information or make a complaint, contact the Consumer Financial Protection Bureau at **www.consumerfinance.gov/mortgage-closing**

Other Disclosures

Appraisal
If the property was appraised for your loan, your lender is required to give you a copy at no additional cost at least 3 days before closing. If you have not yet received it, please contact your lender at the information listed below.

Contract Details
See your note and security instrument for information about
- what happens if you fail to make your payments,
- what is a default on the loan,
- situations in which your lender can require early repayment of the loan, and
- the rules for making payments before they are due.

Liability after Foreclosure
If your lender forecloses on this property and the foreclosure does not cover the amount of unpaid balance on this loan,

☒ state law may protect you from liability for the unpaid balance. If you refinance or take on any additional debt on this property, you may lose this protection and have to pay any debt remaining even after foreclosure. You may want to consult a lawyer for more information.

☐ state law does not protect you from liability for the unpaid balance.

Refinance
Refinancing this loan will depend on your future financial situation, the property value, and market conditions. You may not be able to refinance this loan.

Tax Deductions
If you borrow more than this property is worth, the interest on the loan amount above this property's fair market value is not deductible from your federal income taxes. You should consult a tax advisor for more information.

Contact Information

	Lender	Mortgage Broker	Real Estate Broker (B)	Real Estate Broker (S)	Settlement Agent
Name	Ficus Bank		Omega Real Estate Broker Inc.	Alpha Real Estate Broker Co.	Epsilon Title Co.
Address	4321 Random Blvd. Somecity, ST 12340		789 Local Lane Sometown, ST 12345	987 Suburb Ct. Someplace, ST 12340	123 Commerce Pl. Somecity, ST 12344
NMLS ID					
ST License ID			Z765416	Z61456	Z61616
Contact	Joe Smith		Samuel Green	Joseph Cain	Sarah Arnold
Contact NMLS ID	12345				
Contact ST License ID			P16415	P51461	PT1234
Email	joesmith@ ficusbank.com		sam@omegare.biz	joe@alphare.biz	sarah@ epsilontitle.com
Phone	123-456-7890		123-555-1717	321-555-7171	987-555-4321

Confirm Receipt

By signing, you are only confirming that you have received this form. You do not have to accept this loan because you have signed or received this form.

Applicant Signature Date Co-Applicant Signature Date

FICUS BANK
4321 Random Boulevard • Somecity, ST 12340

Save this Loan Estimate to compare with your Closing Disclosure.

Loan Estimate

DATE ISSUED 2/15/2013
APPLICANTS Michael Jones and Mary Stone
123 Anywhere Street
Anytown, ST 12345
PROPERTY 456 Somewhere Avenue
Anytown, ST 12345
SALE PRICE $180,000

LOAN TERM 30 years
PURPOSE Purchase
PRODUCT Fixed Rate
LOAN TYPE ☒ Conventional ☐ FHA ☐ VA ☐ ______
LOAN ID # 123456789
RATE LOCK ☐ NO ☒ YES, until 4/16/2013 at 5:00 p.m. EDT
*Before closing, your interest rate, points, and lender credits can change unless you lock the interest rate. All other estimated closing costs expire on **3/4/2013** at 5:00 p.m. EDT*

Loan Terms

Loan Terms		Can this amount increase after closing?
Loan Amount	$162,000	**NO**
Interest Rate	3.875%	**NO**
Monthly Principal & Interest *See Projected Payments below for your Estimated Total Monthly Payment*	$761.78	**NO**
		Does the loan have these features?
Prepayment Penalty		**YES** • **As high as $3,240** if you pay off the loan during the first 2 years
Balloon Payment		**NO**

SAMPLE

Projected Payments

Payment Calculation	**Years 1-7**	**Years 8-30**
Principal & Interest	$761.78	$761.78
Mortgage Insurance	+ 82	+ —
Estimated Escrow *Amount can increase over time*	+ 206	+ 206
Estimated Total Monthly Payment	$1,050	$968

		This estimate includes	In escrow?
Estimated Taxes, Insurance & Assessments *Amount can increase over time*	$206 a month	☒ Property Taxes	YES
		☒ Homeowner's Insurance	YES
		☐ Other:	

See Section G on page 2 for escrowed property costs. You must pay for other property costs separately.

Costs at Closing

Estimated Closing Costs	$8,054	Includes $5,672 in Loan Costs + $2,382 in Other Costs – $0 in Lender Credits. *See page 2 for details.*
Estimated Cash to Close	$16,054	Includes Closing Costs. *See Calculating Cash to Close on page 2 for details.*

Visit **www.consumerfinance.gov/mortgage-estimate** for general information and tools.

LOAN ESTIMATE PAGE 1 OF 3 • LOAN ID # 123456789

Closing Cost Details

Loan Costs

A. Origination Charges	$1,802
.25 % of Loan Amount (Points)	$405
Application Fee	$300
Underwriting Fee	$1,097

B. Services You Cannot Shop For	$672
Appraisal Fee	$405
Credit Report Fee	$30
Flood Determination Fee	$20
Flood Monitoring Fee	$32
Tax Monitoring Fee	$75
Tax Status Research Fee	$110

C. Services You Can Shop For	$3,198
Pest Inspection Fee	$135
Survey Fee	$65
Title – Insurance Binder	$700
Title – Lender's Title Policy	$535
Title – Settlement Agent Fee	$502
Title – Title Search	$1,261

D. TOTAL LOAN COSTS (A + B + C)	$5,672

Other Costs

E. Taxes and Other Government Fees	$85
Recording Fees and Other Taxes	$85
Transfer Taxes	

F. Prepaids	$867
Homeowner's Insurance Premium (6 months)	$605
Mortgage Insurance Premium (months)	
Prepaid Interest ($17.44 per day for 15 days @ 3.875%)	$262
Property Taxes (months)	

G. Initial Escrow Payment at Closing		$413
Homeowner's Insurance	$100.83 per month for 2 mo.	$202
Mortgage Insurance	per month for mo.	
Property Taxes	$105.30 per month for 2 mo.	$211

H. Other	$1,017
Title – Owner's Title Policy (optional)	$1,017

I. TOTAL OTHER COSTS (E + F + G + H)	$2,382

J. TOTAL CLOSING COSTS	$8,054
D + I	$8,054
Lender Credits	

Calculating Cash to Close

Total Closing Costs (J)	$8,054
Closing Costs Financed (Paid from your Loan Amount)	$0
Down Payment/Funds from Borrower	$18,000
Deposit	– $10,000
Funds for Borrower	$0
Seller Credits	$0
Adjustments and Other Credits	$0
Estimated Cash to Close	$16,054

LOAN ESTIMATE PAGE 2 OF 3 • LOAN ID # 123456789

Additional Information About This Loan

LENDER	Ficus Bank	MORTGAGE BROKER	
NMLS/__ LICENSE ID		NMLS/__ LICENSE ID	
LOAN OFFICER	Joe Smith	LOAN OFFICER	
NMLS/__ LICENSE ID	12345	NMLS/__ LICENSE ID	
EMAIL	joesmith@ficusbank.com	EMAIL	
PHONE	123-456-7890	PHONE	

Comparisons	Use these measures to compare this loan with other loans.
In 5 Years	$56,582 Total you will have paid in principal, interest, mortgage insurance, and loan costs. $15,773 Principal you will have paid off.
Annual Percentage Rate (APR)	4.274% Your costs over the loan term expressed as a rate. This is not your interest rate.
Total Interest Percentage (TIP)	69.45% The total amount of interest that you will pay over the loan term as a percentage of your loan amount.

Other Considerations

Appraisal — We may order an appraisal to determine the property's value and charge you for this appraisal. We will promptly give you a copy of any appraisal, even if your loan does not close. You can pay for an additional appraisal for your own use at your own cost.

Assumption — If you sell or transfer this property to another person, we
- ☐ will allow, under certain conditions, this person to assume this loan on the original terms.
- ☒ will not allow assumption of this loan on the original terms.

Homeowner's Insurance — This loan requires homeowner's insurance on the property, which you may obtain from a company of your choice that we find acceptable.

Late Payment — If your payment is more than *15* days late, we will charge a late fee of *5% of the monthly principal and interest payment.*

Refinance — Refinancing this loan will depend on your future financial situation, the property value, and market conditions. You may not be able to refinance this loan.

Servicing — We intend
- ☐ to service your loan. If so, you will make your payments to us.
- ☒ to transfer servicing of your loan.

Confirm Receipt

By signing, you are only confirming that you have received this form. You do not have to accept this loan because you have signed or received this form.

Applicant Signature   Date   Co-Applicant Signature   Date

LOAN ESTIMATE   PAGE 3 OF 3 • LOAN ID #123456789

Closing Costs

When considering expenses associated with a real estate transaction, people often think about commission, sale price, interest, homeowners insurance, and property taxes. *Any* cost to a buyer or seller can be listed on a settlement statement.

Some items not required by the lender, such as a fee for a professional home inspection or for repairs necessary to close the transaction, may not appear on the settlement statement. However, the escrow deposits that lenders require a buyer to pay to cover future property taxes or homeowners insurance are required to appear on the settlement statement, even if they are considered an out of pocket expense.

When a buyer has paid a charge in advance, it is indicated on the closing statement as P.O.C. (Paid Outside of Closing).

Debits and Credits

To understand the final distribution of money involved in the transaction, real estate licensees must be familiar with the concept of **debits** and **credits**.

- **Debits** (like debts) are *sums of money owed*. A debit is charged to a particular party on a balance sheet to represent money that must be paid out. The settlement statement reflects the total costs the seller must pay and the buyer must pay. These are the debits.
- **Credits** are *sums of money received*. A credit is given to a particular party on a balance sheet to represent money that is paid by another party or that has already been paid. The settlement statement also reflects the total amounts credited to the seller and the buyer.

Debits and credits work together when **reconciling** the settlement statement. All debits owed by the buyer are totaled and added to the purchase price. Then the credits are totaled and subtracted from the total debits to determine *how much money the buyer must bring to closing*. The mortgage amount shows up as a credit to the buyer, since it is the lender who brings that money to closing.

A similar process occurs on the seller's side. All credits due to the seller are totaled and added to the purchase price. All debits owed are totaled and subtracted from the total money due to determine how much money the seller will receive at the closing.

Typical Seller Closing Costs

The costs sellers can expect to pay include:

- **Attorney fees**, which vary depending on the type of representation provided and the amount of work involved.
- **Broker's commission**, which is typically a percentage of the property's sale price. When a buyer's broker is involved in the transaction, the buyer's broker may be paid a percentage of the selling broker's commission through a cooperative arrangement as detailed in the sales contract.
- **Condo or co-op fees** are *assessments for maintenance of common areas and other items associated with a condominium or cooperative*. Before closing, sellers must bring their account current. Co-op owners may also be required to pay a *flip tax* upon sale or transfer of a cooperative. The tax, which may equal 1% to 5% of the purchase price, is not paid to the city or state, but to the cooperative corporation.
- **Existing liens payments**, if there are any on the property, are generally satisfied prior to close, although it is not a legal requirement. For example, in a cash transaction, the buyer has the right to purchase the property subject to outstanding liens.
- **Recording fees** are incurred by sellers when they have to file a discharge of mortgage and/or other satisfaction of judgments through attorneys.

New York State Transfer Taxes

Sellers are also required to pay a **real property transfer tax**, which is simply a *tax on the sale of real property.* The amount of any mortgage being assumed (highly unusual in today's market) is subtracted from the tax owed, and only new funds brought to the transaction are taxed. If the property transfer is the result of a gift, no transfer tax is due. With new construction, the developer may require the buyer to pay the transfer tax.

The transfer tax is $4 per $1,000 of the purchase price. The tax amount is rounded up to the next $2 up to $500. For example, if the purchase price is $120,300, the transfer tax is $483:

$120,300 / $1,000 = $120.30 x $4 = $481.20; rounded up to the next $2 = $483

When the tax is greater than $500, the amount is rounded up to the next $4.

When reviewing older deeds, note that prior to 1983, transfer tax was $1.10 per $1,000 of the purchase price.

Typical Buyer Closing Costs

The costs buyers can expect to pay include:

- **Appraisal, credit report, and survey fees**, typically charged to buyers by lenders as part of the mortgage application process.
- **Attorney's fees** for their own attorney's representation; if the lender has an attorney, the buyers are responsible for paying those fees as well.
- **Bank fees**, which can be a variety of charges payable to the lender upon closing:
    - **Origination fee** to compensate the lender for making the loan
    - **Points** charged by the lender for a variety of reasons, such as to lower the interest rate or to accommodate a higher risk borrower or a higher risk property. A point is equal to 1% of the loan amount.
    - **Escrow** collection for hazard insurance and property taxes
    - **Tax service fees** to offset the cost of monitoring the escrow account for property taxes
    - **Private mortgage insurance** (PMI).
- **Condo or co-op fees**, which the buyer may owe to adjust for assessments paid by the seller for services the buyer will use.
- **Home inspection fees**, which are the buyer's responsibility. Although encouraged, home inspections are not a lender requirement. Lenders do, however, require a **termite inspection**, which the buyer must pay for.
- **Mortgage insurance**, which protects lenders in the event a buyer defaults on the home loan. If the buyer puts down more than 20% of the purchase price, mortgage insurance is usually not required. Federal Housing Administration (FHA) loans always require mortgage insurance.
- **Mortgage recording tax**, which in New York is 0.75% of the mortgage amount. In counties with public transportation, the tax is 1.25%. In counties with the 1.25% tax, the buyer pays 1% of the tax and the lender pays 0.25%.
- **Recording fees** paid to the county clerk for filing the deed, mortgage, and NYS Real Property Transfer Report (Form RP-5217)
- **Title search/title insurance**, which is required by lenders to ensure a good, marketable title.

- **Flood certification fee**, which is required to analyze whether property is in a flood zone and therefore requires flood insurance.

NEW YORK CITY

CLOSINGS IN NEW YORK CITY

Some items related to closings that are relevant for New York City:

- In New York City, real estate documents are filed and recorded in the Register's Office.
- There is a specific New York Real Property Transfer Report form available for New York City (Form RP-5217NYC) that must accompany the deed along with the filing fee when it is recorded.
- In addition to the New York State transfer tax, New York City imposes an additional transfer tax of 1% of the purchase price of residential property up to $500,000. If the purchase price is more than $500,000, the New York City transfer tax is 1.425%.

Proration

Proration is *the division of expenses between buyer and seller in proportion to the actual usage of the item* represented by a particular expense. A proration is also known as an **adjustment**. In order to adjust a cost shared by both buyer and seller, it's necessary to determine whether the expense is accrued or prepaid.

Accrued Expenses

Accrued expenses are the items on a settlement statement for which *the cost has been incurred, but the expense has not yet been paid*. Examples of accrued expenses include unpaid recurring assessments and mortgage interest. Accrued items start from the position that nothing has been paid, so the seller's portion must be calculated so she can be debited and the buyer credited for this amount. For example, a transaction closes on May 31. The neighborhood has a special assessment for sidewalks, and the next assessment payment is due June 30. Since the seller lived in the house for five of the six months covered by the unpaid assessment, that portion will be prorated on the settlement statement as a debit to the seller and a credit to the buyer.

Prepaid Expenses

Prepaid expenses are the *items on a settlement statement the seller has already paid*. Homeowners insurance, association fees, utility bills, and some property or special assessment taxes may be prepaid costs. Since the seller has already paid for these, he is entitled to a credit for the portion paid but that will not be used by him. For example, a transaction closes on July 31. Property taxes in New York are paid in advance, so the buyer will get a tax bill at the beginning of the year. The seller lived in the house for seven months of the year and is therefore responsible for that portion of the tax bill. At settlement, the taxes would be prorated so that the seller is credited for the remaining five months of the property taxes that he has already paid. The buyer's side will show a debit for five months of property taxes.

Other Expenses

Buyers and sellers sometimes share the costs of items such as surveys, inspections, and lender fees. These items are easy to prorate because they are either negotiated or are calculated as a percentage of the item used and not based on days of usage.

Calculating Prorations

When performing proration calculations, it's important to know the factor on which to base the adjustment. Expenses may be prorated using:

- A 360-day year, 12 months of 30 days each.
- A 365-day year, counting the exact number of days in each month (taking leap years into account).

Either way, the steps to calculate the adjustment are similar:

1. Determine if the expense is accrued or prepaid.
2. Divide the expense by the appropriate period to find a monthly/daily rate.
3. Determine how many months/days are affected by the expense.
4. Multiply the monthly/daily rate by the number of affected months/days.
5. Determine which party is credited and which is debited.

CASE IN POINT

Example 1: ***Property taxes of $2,140 are due at the beginning of the year. The transaction closes on September 15.***

(Using a 360-day year)

1. Property taxes are a prepaid item that the seller paid.
2. $2,140 / 12 = $178.33 per month; $178.33 / 30 = $5.94 per day
3. September 15 to September 30 = 16 days; October to December = 3 months
4. (16 days x $5.94 = $95.04) + (3 months x $178.33 = $534.99) = $630.03
5. Seller credit of $630.03; buyer debit of $630.03

Example 2: ***Condominium fees of $275.50 were paid on the first of the month. The transaction closes on July 17.***

(Using a 365-day year)

1. Condo fees are a prepaid item that the seller paid.
2. $275.50 / 31 = $8.89 per day
3. July 17 to July 31 = 15 days
4. 15 days x $8.89 = $133.35
5. Seller credit of $133.35; buyer debit of $133.35

Proration Notes

- Generally in New York, buyers become the owners of the property they purchase *on the closing date.* In practice, the buyer or seller may be charged with that day's fees and expenses. Actual possession of the property may take place several days, weeks, or even months after closing. In these instances, the sales contract should note who is responsible for what expenses until the new owner takes possession.
- In some areas, unless specifically noted otherwise, interest, taxes, utility bills, and similar expenses are calculated using 360 days in a year and 30 days in a month. In other areas, prorations are calculated using the actual number of days

in the calendar month of closing and 365 days in a year. It's important to find out which factor is used.

- In some cases, sellers are expected to pay off special assessments before the transaction can close. Special assessments are usually levied for municipal improvements such as street repairs and the installation of sidewalks and sewers, and are usually payable over several years.
- When rental property is sold, the rent is commonly prorated on the basis of the actual number of days in the month of closing. Buyers often agree to collect any unpaid rent for the current month and remit a share of it to the seller since the property was still the seller's when the rent was actually due. Tenants' security deposits are transferred by the seller to the new property owner. Even though this may be transparent to tenants, it is required by law that they be notified of the transfer of deposit.

SUMMARY

1. **Marketable title** is title that is *free and clear from undisclosed encumbrances or other defects that would affect the purchaser.* A title search to determine ownership and the quality of the title prior to conveyance is usually performed by an abstractor or a title company. It starts with the **chain of title** and results in the creation of an **abstract of title**, a *complete historical summary of title to a piece of property*. If there is a cloud on the title, a **suit to quiet title** may be necessary (**Article 15 proceeding**).
2. A **closing** is *the final stage in a real estate transaction; transfer of real property ownership from seller to buyer occurs according to the terms and conditions in a sales contract.* In most real estate transactions, two closings simultaneously take place: The closing of the buyer's mortgage loan and disbursement of funds, and the closing of the sale. Participants in a closing usually include the buyers and sellers, their attorneys, the real estate agent, and representatives from the mortgage and title companies.
3. The sales contract usually dictates how closing is handled. Documents typically required for closing include: Evidence of title (usually title insurance), mortgage documents, the deed from the grantor, homeowner's insurance, and a settlement statement.
4. The **Loan Estimate**. One of the requirements flowing from the Dodd-Frank Act was to integrate two separate consumer disclosures, the Good Faith Estimate, required by RESPA and the Truth In Lending Statement, required by the Truth In Lending Act, into one, easy to read disclosure form. This form, called the Loan Estimate must be provided to the borrower within three (3) days of a completed application. Loan and settlement costs are disclosed, providing the borrower the ability to shop for the best loan possible. Other loan features are disclosed on this form also. This form is required by the Truth In Lending Act.
5. The **Closing Disclosure**. The new TILA-RESPA Integrated Disclosure (TRID) rules require a Closing Disclosure be delivered to the borrower within Three (3) business days prior to loan consummation. The disclosure combines the former HUD 1 Settlement Statement and the Final Truth In Lending Statement into one form that provides the consumer information about the settlement service provider charges incurred in an easy to read and understand format. These charges are compared with the original charges disclosed on the Loan Estimate and are subject to tolerance change limitations.
6. Information that guides the consumer about a Mortgage Loan is provided in a new format with the integration of the Know Before You Owe Disclosures. The "**Your Home Loan Toolkit**" must be provided to the primary borrower within three (3) business days after receipt of a completed application. Creditors must provide the Toolkit, referred to in the TILA-RESPA Integrated Disclosure rule as the special information booklet, to mortgage applicants as a part of the application process. The toolkit is

designed to replace an existing booklet that creditors currently must provide to mortgage applicants, which was initially developed by the Department of Housing and Urban Development. The updated toolkit is designed to be used in connection with the new Loan Estimate and Closing Disclosure forms that will be effective on August 1, 2015. Creditors must provide the toolkit to mortgage applicants as a part of the application process, and other industry participants, including real estate professionals, are encouraged to provide it to potential homebuyers.

7. A **settlement statement** is a *document prepared by an attorney or closing agent that itemizes all expenses and costs paid by the buyer and seller to close the real estate transaction.* Any cost to a buyer or seller can be listed on the settlement statement. Items can vary from closing to closing because the payment of any item is always negotiable between buyer and seller. Items not listed on a settlement statement are those paid for personally by the buyer or seller prior to closing.

8. Buyers and sellers incur costs necessary to close the real estate transaction. **Sellers** can expect to pay: Attorney's and broker's fees, any existing liens on the property, recording fees, and New York State transfer taxes of $4/$1,000 of the purchase price. **Buyers** can expect to pay: Fees for appraisals, credit reports, and surveys; attorney's fee; bank fees; recording fees; a mortgage recording tax; and title, mortgage, and homeowners insurance premiums. **Debits** (like debts) are *any sum of money that is owed*. A debit is charged to a particular party on a balance sheet to represent money that *must be paid to the other party*. **Credits** are indicated as that sum of money either already paid before closing, paid by a third party, or to be reimbursed at closing, whether it is the buyer or the seller.

9. **Proration** is *the adjustment of expenses between buyer and seller in* proportion to the actual use of the item represented by a particular expense. **Accrued expenses** are *the items on a settlement statement for which the cost has been incurred, but the expense has not yet been paid.* **Prepaid expenses** are *the items on the settlement statement that the seller has already paid, but will not be used because he or she no longer owns the property.* Prorations are calculated based on a 360-day year (12 months of 30 days each) or a 365-day year to account for the specific number of days in the proration period.

7

Estates and Interests

In This Session

You've made the decision to start a new career in real estate. Perhaps you're planning to sell houses. Perhaps you're planning to manage property that is owned by other people. Whatever your plans are, you need to have a clear understanding of exactly what real estate is. After purchasing real estate, people say that they have just bought a house, but the house is only one element that they now own. Other elements include the rights, the land, and the objects attached to the land. In this session, you will see key definitions and discuss concepts related to real property and ownership.

You'll learn:

- The elements and characteristics of real property.
- What constitutes real property and personal property.
- The difference between freehold and leasehold estates.
- Alternate ways people can take ownership of real property.

Key Terms

- Appurtenance
- Beneficiary
- Bundle of Legal Rights
- Chattel
- Emblements
- Fee on Condition
- Fee Simple Estate
- Fixture
- Joint Tenancy
- Land
- Leasehold Estate
- Life Estate/Life Estate Pur Autre Vie
- Littoral Rights
- Parcel
- Partition
- Personal Property
- Possessory Interest
- Qualified Fee
- Real Property
- Right of Survivorship
- Riparian Rights
- Severalty
- Tenancy by the Entirety
- Tenancy in Common
- Trade Fixture
- Undivided Interest
- Unities of Possession, Interest, Time, and Title

The Nature of Property

The law classifies all property as either real or personal. Understanding the rights of real property ownership and the distinction between real property and personal property is essential for real estate licensees. Real property rights and laws are important because they determine what is being sold. Some key definitions:

- **Land** is legally considered to include *the surface of the earth, the subsurface to the center of the earth, and the air above the land within reasonable limits* to permit commercial air travel. Land is unique in that no two **parcels**, or *specific pieces of land or lots,* are the same.
- **Real estate** is defined as the *actual physical land (also known as unimproved land or raw land) and everything, both natural and man-made, that is permanently attached to it.*
- **Real property** is *land and its attachments, as well as all of the rights* associated with the property.
- **Personal property** is most easily defined as *any property that is not real property.* It is moveable, thus not fixed to the land.

Categories of Real Property

Before we look at real property rights that accompany ownership, let's review the different categories of real property:

Residential. As you can imagine, there is a wide range of properties used for dwellings, for example, single family homes, condominiums, apartment buildings, duplexes, cooperatives, mobile homes, townhouses, converted warehouse space, lofts, etc.

Commercial. The term **commercial investment real estate** usually brings to mind multi-million dollar properties with numerous tenants. While these properties certainly exist in our markets, they are usually brokered and leased by commercial real estate firms. The vast majority of real estate investments are of a much smaller scale and are readily available to any licensee who wishes to trade in commercial properties. These investments run the full spectrum, from single-family homes to smaller apartment properties to small single-user and neighborhood multi-tenant retail, as well as office and industrial properties.

Industrial. The classification "industrial real estate" is very broad, and includes warehouses and general storage facilities, which are often purchased by investors. But many times we think of industrial properties as distribution and manufacturing facilities. Since this type of property often has highly specialized features, manufacturing and distribution properties are often purchased by companies or individuals who will use the property.

Agricultural. For the purposes of determining property taxes, New York State defines agricultural property as land and land improvements used for agricultural production. Any structures and buildings located on the property and are used or occupied to perform agricultural production are also included as agricultural property. Housing for employees is an example. Land that is set aside in federal supply management programs or soil conservation programs are included as well. However, the residential property of the owner is not qualified agricultural property. This includes the residence and any associated building, like the garage or shed.

Woodland property is also considered agricultural property if it is used for agricultural production or the production of wood products is used on the farm. Additionally, woodland used for pasture does count as agricultural property. Typically, agricultural property can include croplands, pastures, greenhouses, nurseries, and feed lots.

Special Purpose. Special-purpose properties are considered to have a limited use, and are most often publicly owned. Such a building would require a substantial reinvestment to convert its purpose. Examples of special-purpose properties include, but are not limited to:

- Golf courses
- Schools
- Churches
- Tennis clubs

Bundle of Legal Property Rights

Real property rights that are conferred by ownership are defined in terms of a **bundle of legal rights:**

- **Right of possession.** The right of possession gives the owner the right to *physically occupy the land and to use the land and make it productive*. Owners can use the land in any way they want, as long as it is legal and does not interfere with other people's rights.
- **Right of quiet enjoyment.** The right of quiet enjoyment gives the owner *the freedom to possess and use the land without interference from other people or society*. However, this also includes a responsibility to make sure that their neighbors' enjoyment is not hindered or adversely affected.
- **Right of disposition.** The right of disposal allows the owner to *transfer all or some of the rights to other people*. For example, landowners normally have the right to sell, lease, give away, divide, and retain part of the land or to dispose of it completely. An example of partial disposition would be someone who sells 10 acres of his 100-acre farm. Another example of partial disposition would be a landlord who rents an apartment, allowing someone else to possess part of the property, even if temporarily.
- **Right of exclusion.** The right of exclusion, or restriction, allows the owner to *stop others from using the property or even from entering the property*.
- **Right of control.** The right of control allows the owner to *physically alter or change the property*. For example, a property owner can build a garage, tear down a fence, put in a swimming pool, etc. (Of course, there could be zoning issues related to this.)

Interfering With Real Property Rights

Certain activities can interfere with a property owner's bundle of rights:

- **Trespassing** is a *physical invasion of land by another person who has no lawful right to enter it.* Trespassing interferes with the owner's possessory interest in the land, diminishing the owner's right of use and right of enjoyment since, during the trespass, the owner of the land has less than full possession of it.
- **Encroachment** is a *legal synonym for trespass, but the term refers to objects, such as buildings, whereas trespass refers to people.* Thus, a neighbor's garage built over your property line encroaches on your land. A tree growing over a property line is another example of an encroachment. Legal steps can be taken to force a landowner to remove the encroachment by tearing it down, trimming the tree, or forcing the landowner to buy the land on which it sits.

- A **nuisance** *interferes with the quiet enjoyment of land from outside causes* such as loud noises, unsightliness, and obnoxious odors. A nuisance does not involve possessory rights. To be actionable in court, a nuisance must be a continuing unreasonable use of land by the offending landowner, but a court usually will not support an action if a landowner moved there with knowledge of the nuisance.

Appurtenances

Appurtenances are *rights that go with real property*, for example, access rights, limited air rights, water rights, mineral rights, etc. When real property is sold, appurtenant rights are usually sold along with it. They can, however, be sold separately and may be limited by past transactions. For example, a property owner sells the mineral rights of her property to a mining company. She keeps ownership of the property. Later, when the land is sold, the mineral rights will most likely stay with the mining company (depending on the wording of the contract involved) even though the rest of the bundle of rights associated with the land is transferred to the new owner. The new owner is limited by the past transaction of the previous owner, and may not sell these mineral rights to another party, nor transfer them in a future sale of the land.

In addition to knowing the boundaries of the land and what attachments are considered part of the real property, buyers also need to understand which appurtenant rights are being transferred in a real property transaction. A lender also must know if the entire bundle of rights is being transferred or if there are restrictions or past transactions that may limit the current transfer of ownership in any way. This is important because it may have a great effect on the value of the real property.

CASE IN POINT

For example, Jack inherits 75 acres of land and decides to build a house. A previous owner had found natural gas on the land and sold the natural gas rights to the gas company, so Jack does not inherit those rights.

While the builders are clearing an area for the house, they find coal. Jack changes the location of his home in order to contract with a company to extract the coal. Later, Jack dies and his son, Phil, inherits the property. Phil doesn't want the property or the house, so he sells the property but keeps the coal rights.

Hopefully, you can see how past transactions and ownership rights can be separated for appurtenances. As a real estate agent, you need to know what items will be part of a real estate transaction and disclose as appropriate.

Land

One way to understand the rights that accompany land ownership is to imagine the property as an inverted pyramid, with its tip at the center of the earth and its base extending out into the sky. An owner has rights to the surface of the land within the property's boundaries, plus everything directly over the surface and everything under the land within the pyramid. When defining land in a legal description, only the surface is detailed. The law implies subsurface and air rights are included as part of the land even though they are usually not documented.

Air Rights

A property owner's rights go to the upper limits of the sky. Air rights include the right to undisturbed use and control of airspace over a parcel of land (within reasonable limits for air travel). A property owner may sell air rights over a property separately from the land. Because of air travel, though, the federal government controls U.S. airspace. Property owners still have the right to use the lower reaches over their land, but they may not interfere with air traffic. Owners also have the right not to be harmed by use of the airspace above their property.

Water Rights

Land owners have specific rights to use water on their property. Water rights include:

- **Riparian** and **littoral** rights. The *rights of an owner of land contiguous to a body of water.* If the water in question is flowing, for example, a river or stream, the rights are said to be riparian. If the property is subject to the ebb and flow of the tide, such as an ocean, bay, or large lake, the rights are said to be littoral. The terms riparian and littoral are sometimes used interchangeably, but generally speaking, riparian rights may be defined principally as *the right of access to the water and the right to all useful purposes to which the body of water may be applied.* Ownership rights of the land under the water are usually determined by whether or not the body of water is considered to be navigable.
- **Appropriative** rights. Water rights granted by government permit independent of land ownership. Government permits allow the holder to take water from a particular body of water for a specified use, such as crop irrigation. Appropriated water does not have to be used on riparian or littoral land, but riparian and littoral landowner rights are considered when issuing appropriation permits. Appropriative rights usually cannot interfere with riparian or littoral rights.
- **Percolating** water rights. Involve the *use of underground water*. For example, landowners have the right to install wells to access water for their own use.

Mineral Rights

A landowner owns all the solid minerals in and under the surface of the land. Minerals are considered real property until they are extracted from the earth. A landowner may sell or lease mineral rights separately from the surface land, and many do, especially if they do not have the necessary skill or equipment to mine or drill.

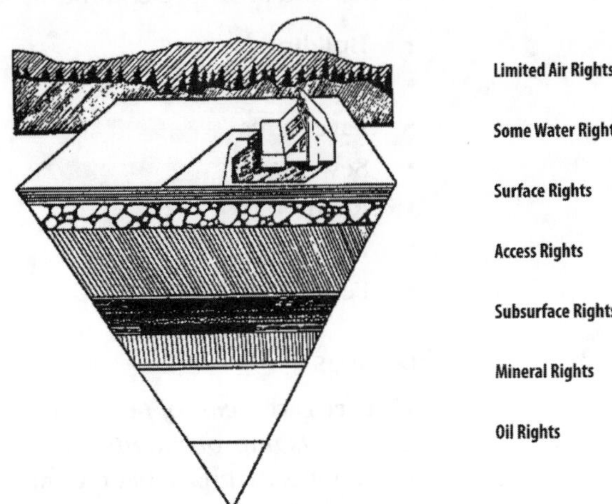

Oil and gas are governed by the **rule of capture**. The **rule of capture** says *whoever drills a well on his or her land owns all the oil or gas the well produces even though it may have migrated from under a neighbor's land*. A landowner can drain oil or gas from beneath his or her own land and from neighboring land because oil and gas flow toward the point of lowest pressure where the reservoir was pierced by the well. The rule of capture is designed to stimulate oil and gas production, since the only way to stop oil or gas from going to a neighbor's well is by drilling your own well.

When considering mineral rights, keep in mind that a landowner also has **supporting rights**. A piece of land is supported by the land that surrounds it. A landowner has a right to the natural support provided by land beside and beneath it. **Lateral support** is support from adjacent land. A neighbor's excavations may make your land shift and settle. In some cases, the neighbor can be held liable for resulting damage if there was negligence. **Subjacent support** is support from the underlying earth. Generally, the mining party is liable for surface damage caused by underground mining even if excavations were performed carefully.

Forces of Nature

We don't normally think about it in this way but forces of nature can affect our ownership of land. The land itself can move or change shape through the forces of nature, which can result in a transfer of title.

- **Erosion** is a gradual wearing away of land by wind, rain, or other natural forces. If eroded soil moves over property lines, X loses title to the soil, and Y gets title to it.
- **Accretion** is a gradual process of waterborne silt being deposited in a river or lakebed or on the shore. These deposits are called *alluvion* or *alluvium*. Riparian or littoral property is increased this way, and the landowner acquires title to the silt.
- **Avulsion** means the land is torn away by flowing water. Avulsion doesn't transfer title if the severed land is identified and reclaimed by the original owner.
- **Reliction** means water recedes exposing more of the bed. In some states, reliction doesn't add to land since owners already have title to the bed to the water's midpoint.

Attachments

The definition of real estate includes **attachments**, the *things attached to the land, whether natural or man-made*. Man-made attachments that are artificially attached to the land are more commonly known as **improvements**. For example:

- Buildings
- Pipelines
- Pavements
- Sewers
- Roads
- Driveways
- Fences

Fixtures

Fixtures are *items of personal property that have been permanently attached to the land or its improvements*, for example, ceiling fans, built-in bookcases, furnaces, etc. Even items that have been temporarily removed from the real property for servicing (e.g., built-in dishwasher at the repair shop on the day of closing) can still be fixtures.

Fixtures start out as personal property but can become real property through one of several methods:

- Becoming **physically attached** to real property, a process called **annexation**
- Becoming attached conceptually because of a **close association** with real property (such as keys to a house)
- Becoming attached through the process of adoption, for example, curtains that were custom-made for an unusual window size or shape or even wall-to-wall carpeting
- Becoming part of the real property through agreement between the parties involved (such as a landlord and a tenant)

Fixtures can be *detached from the land and so revert back to personal property* through the process of **severance** (such as when a chandelier is removed from the ceiling).

Examples of fixtures may include:

- Ceiling fans
- Built-in bookshelves
- Chandeliers
- Custom-made window coverings

That word "may" is critical. The determination of whether or not something is personal property or a fixture that is attached to the land or its improvements can become very involved. Since fixtures and improvements are part of the real estate, one might assume that they are included by implication in the description of the real estate. However, it is a best practice to state everything to be included in the sale in the listing agreement.

TRADE FIXTURES

Trade fixtures are *any equipment or personal property a* ***commercial tenant installs*** *for* ***business purposes***. While these items may be attached to real property, they remain the **personal property** of the tenant. Unless otherwise indicated in the lease, trade fixtures should be removed by the tenant before the lease ends. For example, a tenant who opens a pizza shop can remove the ovens he installed, even though they are attached to the floor. However, the tenant must repair any damage caused by the removal.

Natural Attachments

The definition of "land" also encompasses **natural attachments**, *the plants growing on the land*. Plants such as trees, perennial flowers, and other vegetation are considered to be part of the land, therefore **real property**. Note that plants may be considered to be **personal property** if they are removed. For example, if you plant an apple tree next to your house, it becomes part of the real property and is called *fructus naturales*. However, once you pick an apple from that tree, the apple **becomes personal property**. The proper term for flowers, crops, and other vegetation that are *planted or cultivated annually or seasonally* is *fructus industriales*, meaning fruits of industry. Another word for fructus industriales is **emblements**.

Personal Property

Personal property, also called **chattel,** is *any property that is moveable and not fixed to land*. Personal property can be tangible – something that can be held or touched, such as appliances, cars, furniture, etc. – or intangible – something that cannot be held or touched, for example, savings accounts, stock rights, or intellectual property. The ownership of personal property is generally conveyed in one of two ways:

- When someone sells personal property, its ownership is conveyed by a **bill of sale.**
- When personal property is part of a will, it is conveyed by **bequest**, sometimes referred to as a **legacy**.

The distinction between real property and personal property becomes important when land ownership or possession is transferred. Unless otherwise agreed, all *real property* is included in the transfer, but personal property that happens to be on the land is not necessarily included.

Since a seller and a buyer may not agree on what items are fixtures and are therefore included in the transfer of real property, a real estate agent should take care to make certain that the seller and buyer are clear on this. Is a built-in dishwasher a fixture? Is a shed an improvement? Is a chandelier personal property? Is a satellite dish a fixture? To avoid confusion and even possible legal action, always notate what personal property is included in the sale of a home in your listing agreements. It is also necessary to indicate what is not included. For instance, if the seller will be taking a chandelier or the kitchen appliances, you will want to note this in the listing agreement. That way, potential buyers know up-front what to expect when they take possession of the property.

Perhaps the most reasonable strategy you can suggest to the seller is to remove or replace the item(s) prior to showing the house. This makes it impossible for a buyer to expect a particular item to be included in the sale and resolves all issues regarding whether the buyer saw the item and assumed it would transfer. For example, if the seller intends to take the dining room chandelier to his new home, he should just go ahead and replace it with an appropriate light fixture before ever showing the property.

What if a buyer wants to purchase items that the seller had not intended to sell with the property? For example, a buyer really likes the curtains in the living room and would like them to be sold with the house. If the buyer and seller come to a private agreement on personal items, the best solution is to have the parties draw up a separate bill of sale, which transfers title to personal property (like a deed transfers title to real property). Still, the agents--and the attorneys on both sides--should be made aware of any such separate deals.

Settling Property Disputes

If a seller does not clearly label items as personal property in a listing agreement, it could ultimately result in a legal dispute with the buyer. If these types of disputes end up in court, there are some key legal questions that help determine if an object is a fixture, in other words, **not** personal property:

For example, can the object be removed without damaging the property? Was the item custom made or designed specifically to fit or be used in the property? Physical attachment of an item is taken into account when the court decides if something is a fixture, but it's not decisive. The court still looks at other factors.

One of the most important issues a court considers in deciding whether an item is a fixture is the *intent* of the annexer and purpose of the annexation. The annexer is the owner of the personal property that was brought onto real property. Did he or she intend for it to become part of the real property, or to remain as personal property? Did he or she buy the item to improve the real property or simply for personal use?

In answering these questions, the court will look for objective evidence of the annexer's **intent**. It's not enough to claim that you always intended to remove the item. Other considerations, such as the nature of the item and manner of annexation, are viewed as objective evidence of intent. For example, setting a statue in concrete shows intent to make it a permanent feature; just setting one out on the lawn doesn't.

Relationship of the Parties

Another factor courts often take into consideration in fixture disputes is the relationship of the parties. Between a seller and a buyer of real property, the rules for determining whether an item is a fixture are usually interpreted in favor of the buyer.

Between a landlord and a tenant, the rules tend to be interpreted in favor of the tenant. A tenant who installs a chandelier (or some other ornamental item) usually has the right to remove it at the end of the lease. These rules tie to considering the annexer's intentions; the law presumes a homeowner intends to improve real property, but a tenant installs things only for personal use.

That doesn't mean a tenant is invariably allowed to remove everything he or she installed, especially if it were done without written permission. If a tenant built a deck onto the back of a rented house, it would almost certainly be considered a fixture and part of the landlord's real property. Here's another example: What if a tenant installed a wrought iron railing without the landlord's permission? This, too, might be considered a fixture of real property, especially if there was no agreement between landlord and tenant. As usual, the court would look at the nature of the item, the manner of annexation, and how difficult it would be to remove. Remember: Once a dispute gets to a court, anything could happen!

Written Agreement

Regardless of the previously discussed considerations, if there's a written agreement between the parties stating how an item is to be treated, a court will enforce the agreement. So, when a seller wants to remove items that may be considered fixtures, he or she should inform a buyer by including a statement in the listing agreement naming items that are excluded from the sale. This way, there are no assumptions regarding whether something will or will not be included in the sale. A separate bill of sale should then account for any personal items the buyer wants to purchase from the seller.

Bottom line: Recommend that everything be put in writing, and you can be of genuine assistance to your client or customer should a dispute arise.

Real Property Interests

A person with a *property right or a claim against property* is said to have an **interest** in the property. An interest may be an ownership right (e.g., a life estate), right to use the land (e.g., an easement), or a financial claim against the title (e.g., a mortgage). An **estate** is a *possessory interest in real property*, which entitles the holder to possess the property now (a present interest) or sometime later (a future interest). In addition to being classified as to the time of enjoyment, present or future, interests are also classified as a freehold or leasehold estate.

Freehold Estates

A **freehold estate** is a *possessory interest of uncertain duration*; it may end, but no one knows when. Some events that will end a freehold estate include the transfer of the property to someone else, the death of the owner, foreclosure, confiscation for back taxes, or condemnation under eminent domain. There are different types of freehold estates: Fee simple, qualified fee, fee on condition, and life estates.

Fee Simple Estate

A **fee simple estate** is the *fullest freehold estate interest that exists in real property*. It is also called fee title or fee simple absolute. A person referred to as the "owner" of land usually holds a fee simple absolute interest. The owner of a fee simple absolute has all the bundle of legal rights. Since the fee simple estate is absolute, this implies there are *no conditions on the title*. It is perpetual, inheritable, and transferable. When a fee simple absolute owner deeds an interest in property to someone else, it is presumed the entire estate is transferred, unless the deed language specifies otherwise. This means that the new owner holds the property in fee simple absolute, too.

Qualified Fee Estate

A **qualified fee estate** means that *a grantor puts a condition or requirement in the deed that terminates the estate automatically if the condition or requirement is not met and reverts the title back to the grantor or the grantor's heirs.* For example, deed language may transfer Juanita's land to Darlene, as long as the land is used as a park. If Darlene uses the land for another purpose, the title to the property reverts back to Juanita (or her heirs). A qualified fee estate creates a type of encumbrance on the title because it **runs with the land**, meaning that the restriction is not against the owner but is against the land.

This may also be called a **fee simple defeasible estate**.

Fee on Condition

A **fee on condition estate** means that *a grantor puts a condition or requirement in the deed that gives the grantor the "right of reentry" if the condition or requirement is not met.* In this type of estate, the grantor (or heirs) has the right to terminate the estate, but this does not happen automatically. For example, deed language may transfer David's land to Frank, but if Frank builds a bar, the grantor may take possession or go to court to regain possession. Generally, the grantor would need to **prove in court** that the stated event occurred before regaining title to the property.

The grantor could also include a condition where the grantor retains title to the estate **until** a specific condition occurs. For example, Bill will transfer title of the property to his grandson Will ***if*** Will marries before his 25th birthday.

Life Estates

A **life estate** is a *freehold estate that lasts only as long as a specified person, the "measuring life," lives*. The *holder of a life estate* is called a **life tenant**.

With a **conventional** life estate, *the measuring life and the life tenant are the same person*. For example, grantor Jane owns property in fee simple. She decides to deed that property to grantee David "for life." Although Jane still owns the property, David now has the right to occupy and use the property for as long as he lives. The life estate is measured by the lifetime of the measuring life, which in this case is David, the life tenant. When David dies, the life estate ends.

A life estate may also be *based on a person's life other than the life tenant*, which is known as a **life estate pur autre vie** (for another's life). With this type of life estate, the measuring life and the life tenant are *not* the same. For example, Paul owns property in fee simple. He decides to deed that property to Sue for as long as Mike lives. Sue is the life tenant, and Mike is the measuring life. When Mike dies, the life estate ends and Sue no longer has the right to occupy and use the property.

Both types of life estate are a present interest that *creates a future interest* for the one who will possess the land upon death of the measuring life holds. This future interest may be:

- **Reversionary**. The property *reverts to the grantor*, or the grantor's heirs, upon the death of the measuring life.
- **Remainder**. The grantor grants the life estate to one person, *then to another person*, the **remainderman,** upon the death of the measuring life.

CASE IN POINT

Here's an example of how the concept of a future interest works: Joe grants a life estate to daughter Sue. Joe is called the **reversioner** because he has a reversionary interest in the estate. When life tenant Sue dies, the life estate reverts to Joe. In his will, Joe leaves everything to his son, Bill, who now has a reversionary interest in the estate as well. If Joe dies before Sue dies, the life estate will revert to Bill, Joe's heir, upon Sue's death.

But since son Bill gets everything, according to Joe's will, can Bill kick sister Susan off the property and take complete possession fee simple? No. Susan's life is the measuring life. She can stay on the property until she dies, at which point, Bill would have the property fee simple. And if Bill were to die before Susan, Susan could remain on the property and the estate would go to Bill's heirs upon her death.

Here's a variation of that example: Joe deeds property "to daughter Sue for life, and then to nephew Tim." Tim has a remainder interest and is known as the **remainderman**. In this case, when Sue dies, Tim (or his heirs) takes title to the property in fee simple. This is because the death of life tenant Sue, the measuring life, ends the life estate. If Joe were to die before Sue, Sue would still have the present life estate, and Tim would still have just the future remainderman estate.

A life tenant's interest can be sold, mortgaged, or leased. But a person can transfer only the interest he owns. Someone who buys a life tenant's interest has only a life estate, and that interest ends when the measuring life dies. For example, Larry has a life estate, but he gets a job out of state and will no longer live on the property. He sells his life estate to Barb. Barb can live on the property, but she does not own the property. Her interest ends when Larry dies.

A life tenant may not commit an **act of waste** to the property, which means *using the property in a way that damages it or reduces its market value*. Thus, a life tenant has restricted rights of use that are transferred with the life estate.

Leasehold Estates

A **leasehold estate** is an *interest that gives the holder a temporary but exclusive right to possession of the estate without title.* A leasehold estate is more limited than a freehold estate. The *holder of a leasehold estate* is called the **lessee** or **tenant**. A tenant has the right to exclusive possession of the property but only for a limited time. An *owner who leases property to a tenant* is called the **lessor** or **landlord**. Leased fee interest is **reversionary** in that possession reverts to the landlord when the lease ends.

Specific types of leasehold estates are covered in the chapter on Leases.

Forms of Ownership

Ownership can be divided into two primary forms, depending on whether the property is held by one person or multiple people. Generally speaking, ownership or title to property is created and conveyed in one of these ways:

- By **deed**, which is *a document that transfers ownership of real property*, as when someone sells a house to someone else.
- By **devise**, which is *when real property is transferred because of a will.*
- By **descent**, which is *when real property is transferred to an heir in the absence of a will.*

Ownership can be divided into two primary forms that describe how the property is held: Ownership in severalty and co-ownership.

Ownership in Severalty

Ownership in severalty, also known as tenancy in severalty, is the simplest form of ownership. It is a sole form of ownership, meaning that *only one person or legal entity holds the title to that property*. Don't be confused about the word "severalty." It might sound as though it implies "several" people, but it really means that one owner's interest has been *severed from the interests of all others.*

Co-Ownership

Co-ownership, also known as concurrent ownership, is *any form of ownership where two or more persons or legal entities share title to real property, with each person having an undivided interest in the property*. **Undivided interest** gives *each co-owner the right to possession of the whole property, not just part of it.* Under the law, any number of persons may join in the ownership of real property.

There are three forms of co-ownership: Tenancy in common, joint tenancy, and tenancy by the entirety. Key distinguishing factors include the method in which the interest is created as well as the method by which ownership is passed. The **right of survivorship** means that *the property passes automatically to other co-owners* *when one co-owner dies.* The presence of several conditions, known as **unities**, also defines the form of co-ownership:

- **Unity of possession**. *All co-owners hold the same undivided right to possess the whole property* (as opposed to a designated portion of that property).
- **Unity of interest**. *All co-owners hold equal ownership interests.*
- **Unity of time**. *All co-owners acquired their interests at the same time.*
- **Unity of title**. *All co-owners acquired their interests by the same deed or will.*

A fifth unity must also be considered: The unity of **person**, which means that all co-owners are a *single, indivisible legal unit*. This unity applies to legal spouses.

Tenancy in Common

Tenancy in common is a form of co-ownership with *two or more persons having an undivided interest in the entire land, but no right of survivorship.* Tenancy in common is the most common form of co-ownership and requires **only the unity of possession.** Tenancy in common is the only co-ownership that can be owned in unequal portions. When a tenant in common dies, his interest in the property passes to his heirs.

For example, Mike, Dan, and Sam own a farm. Mike has a 50% interest in the property; Dan and Sam each have a 25% interest in the property. Sam can sell his 25% interest to Mary if he wants. When Mike dies, his 50% interest goes to his heirs, not to Dan and Mary.

If language in a deed does not specify a different type of co-ownership, or if the co-owners are not married to each other, tenancy in common is assumed. If the deed is silent as to the interests of the parties, the shares will be equal.

Joint Tenancy

Joint tenancy exists when *each co-owner has an equal undivided interest in the land and right of survivorship.* Joint tenancy requires the **four unities** of possession, interest, time, and title. A main feature of joint tenancy is that it allows co-owners to take ownership shares of a deceased co-owner automatically. Since survivors take ownership equally and simultaneously, a person can't will or inherit a survivorship estate. A joint tenancy ownership interest may only be conveyed through deed.

For example, Allen, Beth, and Lois take title to property as joint tenants. Each owns a one-third interest in the property. When Allen dies, his interest passes to Beth and Lois automatically, who each now own a half interest.

When a joint tenant *conveys* an interest, the new co-owner is a tenant in common in relation to the other co-owners, and the right of survivorship in that interest ends. For example, Mary, Ted, and Lou co-own a property as joint tenants. Lou sells his share to Lisa. Mary and Ted are still joint tenants, but Lisa is a tenant in common, since there is no unity of time and title. If Mary dies, her interest goes to joint tenant Ted. If Lisa dies, her interest goes to her heirs.

Caution: Generally speaking, joint tenancy always assumes the right of survivorship. In New York, however, the creation of joint tenancy with right of survivorship **must** be explicitly stated in the deed, for example: "Jane and Jack, as joint tenants with right of survivorship and not as tenants in common…" In New York, simply stating the form of ownership as "joint tenants" in the deed would actually be considered tenancy in common, in other words, no right of survivorship.

Partition

Parties to a joint tenancy or tenancy in common have the **right of partition**, which *allows any co-owner to end the co-ownership.* A voluntary partition can be implemented where both parties agree to end the joint venture and divide the property so each owns a piece in severalty, if it can be done equitably. Or, one owner can sue the other to dissolve the co-ownership and divide the property or sell it and divide the proceeds.

Tenancy by the Entirety

Tenancy by the entirety is a *form of co-ownership that involves only owners who are husband and wife with each having an equal and undivided share of the property.* This form of ownership includes the right of survivorship, with property automatically going to the surviving spouse, who would then own the property in severalty.

Tenancy by the entirety requires all five **unities** – possession, interest, time, title, and person -- since spouses are considered a single, indivisible legal person. In New York, husband and wife ownership is assumed to be tenancy by the entirety unless specified otherwise in the deed

This type of ownership can be terminated if:

- Either spouse dies, at which point the surviving spouse becomes owner in severalty.
- Both parties agree to end this type of ownership and both sign a new deed.
- The couple divorces. In New York, distribution of property when a married couple divorces falls under the Domestic Relations Law of the New York Consolidated Laws, which mandates **equitable distribution**, which may or may not be equal distribution. After a divorce, therefore, the couple owns the property as tenants in common.

Co-Ownership

		Tenancy in Common	Joint Tenancy	Tenancy by the Entirety
Unities	Possession	✓	✓	✓
	Interest		✓	✓
	Time		✓	✓
	Title		✓	✓
	Person			✓
Right of Survivorship			✓	✓

CAUTION: It is important to remember as a salesperson that, although you may be familiar with these different forms of ownership, your role is *NOT* to be a lawyer, estate planner, or tax advisor to your clients.

Ownership by Businesses

Ownership in severalty and co-ownership can be further categorized into ownership by business entities, which include nonprofit groups and other organizations. Depending on its form, a business association may be a legal entity separate from its members or owners.

Sole Proprietorship

A **sole proprietorship** is a *business owned by a single individual (or a husband and wife for tax purposes) in severalty.* With this, the owner is personally responsible for any business debts, and personal assets could be attached in the event of default (except for property that is owned with a spouse as tenants by the entirety). A sole proprietorship can operate under the sole proprietor's name or under an assumed or fictitious name, if registered with the state, for example, Joe Smith doing business as (dba) Smith Realty or Patsy Davis also known as (aka) Patsy Cakes.

Partnerships

A **partnership** is *an association of two or more individuals as co-owners of a business, as specified in the partnership agreement.* The Uniform Partnership Act, first established in 1914 by the National Conference of Commissioners on Uniform State Laws (NCCUSL), and adopted by New York State, allows a partnership to take title to property in the name of the partnership as **tenants in partnership**, a *form of co-ownership that gives each partner an equal, undivided interest in the property*. In a tenancy in partnership arrangement, property is purchased and owned by the partnership. Partners may also take title to property in the name of **individual partners** as **tenants in common** or as **joint tenants**. Any of the partners may convey partnership property, but all members of the partnership must agree before any party can sell or assign his interest in partnership property.

The type of partnership determines how much control and liability each individual will bear:

- A **general partnership** is *an association of two or more individuals as co-owners of a business where all partners share in the financial liability both individually and as a member of the partnership.*
- A **limited partnership** is an *association of two or more persons as co-owners of a business with one or more general partners and one or more limited partners.* The rights and duties of general partners in a limited partnership are the same as in a general partnership, but limited partners have no say in partnership matters. Further, the partners' liability is limited to their original investment.

Corporations

A **corporation** is a *legal entity that is created and operated according to the laws of each state.* A corporation could be public (cities, counties, school districts, etc.), private for profit, or private nonprofit. It is regarded by the law as a legal person *separate from the individual stockholders*, and therefore shareholders are not personally liable for the corporation's debts. Within a corporation, property is owned *in severalty* as the legal person.

- A **C Corporation** must pay corporate income tax. Then when profits are distributed to the shareholders, the shareholders pay income tax on the dividends as well, which leads to a situation of double-taxation.
- A **subchapter S Corporation** functions as a corporation, but like a partnership,

it does not pay any corporate income taxes. Instead, the corporation's income or losses are divided among and passed through to its shareholders. The shareholders must then report the income or loss on their own individual income tax returns.

Condominiums, Cooperatives, and Townhomes

Condominiums and other housing alternatives physically and legally combine individual ownership with co-ownership.

- **Condominiums** are *properties developed for co-ownership where each co-owner has a separate fee simple interest in an individual unit and an undivided interest in the common areas of the property*. Common areas are areas of the development that all residents use and own as tenants in common, such as the parking lot, hallways, and recreational facilities.
- **Cooperatives** *are buildings owned by corporations, with the residents as shareholders who each receive a proprietary lease on an individual unit and the right to use common areas*. The title to the cooperative building is held by a corporation formed for that purpose. A person who wants to live in the building buys shares in the corporation, instead of renting or buying a unit, and is given a proprietary lease for a unit in the building.
- **Townhomes** are *properties developed for co-ownership where each co-owner has a separate fee simple interest in an individual unit, including its roof and basement, as well as the land directly beneath the unit, and an undivided interest in the common areas of the property.* The fee simple ownership may extend to a small patio or lawn outside of the unit.

TRUSTS

A **trust** allows the *owner of property, known as the* ***trustor****, to transfer ownership to someone else, the* ***trustee****, in order for them to manage the property for a third party, the* ***beneficiary***. A trust may be an individual or a company and is often established as a way to reduce inheritance taxes or to direct an estate. The trustee's powers are limited by the terms outlined in the trust. When a trust is *established in the trustor's lifetime*, it is known as a **living trust.** A trust *established by will or after the death of the trustor* is a **testamentary trust**. Most states permit real estate to be held in trust, though the laws regarding trusts can be complex and can vary greatly from state to state.

Businesses for Owning Real Estate

There are three more types of business organizations that may be formed for the purpose of owning real estate.

- A **syndicate** (or syndication) is a type of joint participation of individuals, partnerships, corporations in a real estate investment that is not recognized legal entity. A syndicate allows most property ownership forms possible (joint, tenants in common, partnership, corporation, etc.) and is generally used for large-scale, ongoing projects or multiple projects.
- A **joint venture** is an arrangement in which two ore more individuals or companies pool resources in order to engage in one project or a series of projects but not as an ongoing business concern.
- A **real estate investment trust** or **REIT**, is a real estate investment business, with at least 100 investors, organized as a trust where one or more trustees manage

property for the benefit of the beneficiaries. To create a REIT, a trust document vests title to the property in the trustees, who have only those powers expressly granted to them in the trust document. The beneficiaries have no legal interest in the property, but do have power to enforce performance of the trust.

SUMMARY

1. **Real property** is *land and its attachments, as well as all of the rights* associated with the property. The **bundle of legal property rights** includes: The right of possession, the right of quiet enjoyment, the right of disposition, the right of exclusion or restriction, and the right of control. Trespassing, encroachment, and nuisance interfere with these rights.
2. **Personal property**, also called **chattel**, is most easily defined as *any property that is not real property.* A bill of sale transfers title to personal property.
3. A property owner has rights to the surface of the land within the property's boundaries, plus everything directly over the surface and everything under the land. The law implies **subsurface, air, mineral**, and **water** rights are included as part of the land. Water rights include riparian/littoral (adjacent to bodies or water) and appropriative (government permit to use). These rights usually transfer with land but may be sold separately.
4. Man-made attachments refer to **fixtures**, which are *personal property attached to real property that, through the process of* ***annexation****, becomes real property.* Major fixtures are improvements. Fixtures can *revert to personal property* through the process of **severance.** Natural attachments (plants) are real property when in the ground but personal property, or **emblements**, when picked. Attachments stay with the land; personal property doesn't. **Trade fixtures**, *installed by a tenant for business*, are personal property and may be removed before the lease ends.
5. A **freehold estate** is a *possessory interest of uncertain duration*. A **fee simple estate** is the *fullest interest in property*; it is inheritable, transferable, and perpetual ownership. A **qualified fee estate** has certain conditions that, if not met, *revert the title automatically* back to the grantor. A **fee on condition estate** has certain conditions that, if not met, *give the grantor the right of reentry.* **Leasehold estates** give tenants a *temporary right to exclusive possession.*
6. A **life estate** is a *freehold estate that lasts only as long as a specified person, the "measuring life," lives*. The *holder of a life estate* is called a **life tenant**. With a **conventional** life estate, *the measuring life and the life tenant are the same person*. A life estate may also be *based on a person's life other than the life tenant*, which is known as a life estate **pur autre vie** (for another's life).
7. Ownership can be in **severalty** (one person or legal entity) or **co-ownership** (many persons). Types of co-ownership can be defined by the **right of survivorship** and the five **unities**: Possession, interest, time, title, and person. **Tenancy in common** is the undivided *interest in land with no right of survivorship* and requires only the unity of possession. It is the most common type of co-ownership. **Joint tenancy** is the *undivided equal interest* and includes the right of survivorship; it requires all four unities. **Tenancy by the entireties** is a form of co-ownership that *involves only owners who are husband and wife*; it includes the right of survivorship and requires all five unities.

8. There are many different types of ownership by businesses. **Sole proprietorship** is *ownership in severalty.* Business co-ownership includes: Corporations (C Corps and subchapter S Corps), and partnerships (general and limited). **Condominiums** *include fee simple ownership of individual units and undivided interest in common areas.* **Cooperatives** are *owned by corporations with residents as shareholders who get a proprietary lease on a unit.* **Townhomes** include *fee simple ownership of individual units and the land beneath the units, as well as an undivided interest in common areas.*

8

Land Use Regulations

In This Session

It is important for real estate professionals to be aware of land use regulations because they affect the way land can be used and may impact the marketability of property. In this session, you'll learn about private and public land use regulations. You'll also learn what powers are available to local, state, and federal governments regarding land. Finally, you'll see how zoning affects land use.

You'll learn:

- How restrictive covenants are created and terminated.
- The purpose of zoning and how it is classified.
- Regulations related to the subdivision of land.
- How land use regulations are enforced.

Key Terms

- Abutting Property
- Accessory Apartment
- Accessory Use
- Area Variance
- As of Right Zoning
- Census Tract
- Certificate of Occupancy
- Cluster Zoning
- Condemnation
- Deed Restriction
- Demography
- Doctrine of Laches
- Eminent Domain
- Escheat
- Group Home
- Incentive Zoning
- Infrastructure
- Lead Agency
- Moratorium
- New York State Office of Parks, Recreation, and Historic Preservation (OPRHP)
- New York State Uniform Fire Prevention and Building Code
- Nonconforming Use
- Plat
- Police Power
- Restrictive Covenant
- Setback Requirements
- Special Use Permit
- Spot Zoning
- Subdivision Regulations
- Surveys
- Taking
- Topography
- Transfer of Development Rights
- Use Variance
- Vacant Land
- Variance
- Zoning Ordinance

Land Use Regulations

Land ownership in New York can be **absolute**, meaning *the complete bundle of rights belongs to the owner.* Owners have the right to use, enjoy, dispose of, and possess property. However, this does not necessarily mean landowners have the absolute right to use and enjoy the land. How can this be? Restrictions are sometimes placed on the land by the government, private companies, and even individuals in the form of ordinances, deed restrictions, covenants, rules, and regulations.

Land use regulations are continually changing. Many regulations relevant today were of little concern six decades ago. And this will be the case six decades from now. It is prudent for real estate licensees to educate themselves in the land use regulation cases being argued before local, state, and federal courts, and in land use legislation being introduced and passed.

Private Land Use Controls

Individual owners and developers can impose controls on their own real property. The controls, or restrictions, can affect individual deeds, or an entire neighborhood. Often, these controls prohibit uses that zoning laws would permit. For instance, a developer may place a restriction on land that only single-family homes may be built on it. Even though zoning in the area supports any type of residential use, the builder has imposed a strict control on how the land may be used – only for single-family homes. And when a deed restriction and zoning law differ, *the more restrictive use prevails.*

To prevent objectionable land use by new owners, a grantor can put *restrictions on the grantee's title*, known as **restrictive covenants,** which may be in a deed or a separate document. This is common practice when land is subdivided. Restrictive covenants are also created by express agreement between two parties, but to make a restriction enforceable against third parties, *it must be recorded*. Once a covenant is in the recorded chain of title, future buyers take title *subject to* the restriction, even if it is not stated in the deed.

Restrictive covenants can run with the land *only if they touch and concern the land.* They must relate to the use, maintenance, or improvement of the real property. A covenant that prohibits a landowner from smoking obviously cannot run with the land. However, a covenant prohibiting smoking *on* the land does; therefore, it is a valid restrictive covenant.

Deed Restrictions

Deed restrictions are simply *restrictive covenants in a deed that apply to all future landowners.* These restrictions run with the land, which means they move with the title in future conveyances. Deed restrictions are one way an owner can exercise control over a property, which is part of the bundle of rights for property owners.

Deed restrictions may or may not be conditional. For example, a deed may state, "The grantee covenants (promises) never to tear down the barn on the property." The covenant does not make the title conditional. Even if a restriction is violated, the property remains under the ownership of the grantee; it does not revert to the original owner, or go to another owner. However, if the barn is razed, a court may order the grantee to rebuild or pay damages to the grantor – but the grantee will not lose title to the land.

Some deed restrictions are accompanied by conditions. When this is the case, if the grantee violates the deed restriction, the land reverts to the grantor. Consider the previous example. If the deed contained a *restriction and condition* that stated, "The grantee covenants never to tear down the barn on the property and if he violates this promise, title to property is revoked," and the grantee does raze the barn, title reverts to the grantor. This is also known as a *qualified fee estate*.

Terminating Restrictive Covenants

Restrictive covenants may be terminated in a number of ways, including:

- Setting a termination date.
- Releasing the owner from the covenant.
- Abandoning the property.
- Changing the circumstances of the property and/or the owner.

Further, restrictive covenants that become illegal after they were written automatically terminate. For example, a deed restriction indicating people of certain religious beliefs or nationalities may not purchase land may have been legal and enforceable in the past. However, when the Civil Rights Act of 1968 was enacted, religion, national origin, and ancestry became protected classes and these deed restrictions became illegal, thus automatically terminating them.

Subdivision Regulations

Subdivision regulations can be both private and public. *Private* **subdivision regulations** *enable property owners to maintain the quality and consistency of the residences in the subdivision*. A common subdivision regulation is that improvements meet **setback requirements**, which means the structures *are located a specified distance between the front property line to the building line, as well as from the front, rear, and side property lines.*

If a resident does not adhere to the setback requirements, which are covenants, property owners within the subdivision may take legal action. If, on the other hand, property owners do not take legal action to enforce covenants, or they do not take legal action in a timely manner, violators are not subject to a court's orders and the covenant will be terminated. When the *loss of legal rights occurs due to the failure to assert rights in a timely manner*, the **doctrine of laches** has been applied. In New York, property owners who wish to assert their rights have *two years* from the date the violation of the deed restriction occurred.

Government Powers

Public land use restrictions are those *imposed by the government at the local, state, and federal level.* Understandably, the government has a much broader jurisdiction when it comes to land use restrictions than the private sector does. When the government does restrict how land is used, it is an example of its **police power**, which is the *constitutional power of state and local governments to enact and enforce laws that protect the public's health, safety, morals, and general welfare.*

Considering that each county in the state and each municipality in the county has its own land use regulations, it would be impossible to list all of the controls individual municipalities in New York have over land use. Local regulations in New York concern everything from zoning, mobile homes, site plans, and subdivisions to cell towers and shoreline development ordinances.

Power of Taxation

In New York State, property taxes are local taxes and the income is spent locally to finance the government and public schools. Property taxes create a lien on real estate, and in New York, as in other states, real property taxes take priority over all other liens. The amount a landowner pays in property taxes is determined by two things:

- The property's taxable assessment, which is calculated by a local tax assessor
- The tax rate of the locality in which the land is located

Power of Escheat

Another power of the state is **escheat.** *When a person dies intestate—without a will—and has no heirs or creditors, title to property reverts back to the state through the power of escheat.* Escheat assures that land is not ownerless.

Eminent Domain

Eminent domain *is the government's constitutional power to appropriate or condemn private property for public use, as long as the owner is paid just compensation.* Eminent domain is the power, whereas **condemnation** is the actual act of *taking the property for public use through the government's power of eminent domain.*

In New York, condemning authorities include the state and its authorized agencies, municipalities, school districts, railroads, public utilities, and the federal government. Two conditions must be met before the government can exercise its power of eminent domain:

1. The condemned property is for the use and benefit of the public.
2. The property owner is paid fair market value for the property lost. (If the property owner disagrees with the compensation offered, he has the right to a trial in which the court decides if the compensation is just.)

A **taking** *occurs when the government acquires private property for public use by appropriation.* The difference between a taking and eminent domain is that the property is regulated by a government authority to the economic detriment of the owner, *without compensation*.

In 1992, the U.S. Supreme Court ruled that a taking is unconstitutional if it prohibits the building of any habitable or productive improvement on the owner's land and eliminates all economic benefits associated with the land.

Environmental Protection Laws

Federal and state land use controls are increasing as a means to protect the environment. Regulations can involve blocking or restricting use of land where there are environmental concerns. Sometimes this conflicts with a landowner's proposed usage of the land.

The government controls land use in protecting wildlife, endangered species, and wetlands. Federal and state agencies may deem land a safe haven or a protected area that cannot be developed. Of course, the rules may be revised to permit uses perceived as beneficial. These policies are often controversial as the benefits of preservation and conservation are weighed against the benefits of usage.

Interstate Land Sales Full Disclosure Act

The **Interstate Land Sales Full Disclosure Act** protects consumers from fraud and abuse in the sale or lease of land. The Act is regulated through the U.S. Department of Housing and Urban Development (HUD) and attempts to prevent marketing schemes that entice consumers to purchase land sight unseen. Developers of subdivisions with 25 or more nonexempt lots must register with HUD and provide each purchaser with a disclosure statement known as a **property report**. The property report contains relevant information about the subdivision and must be delivered to each purchaser *at least three days before* a contract is signed. Further, if the purchaser does not receive the report, he has two years to cancel the sale.

U.S. Army Corps of Engineers

The Army Corps of Engineers is a division of the U.S. Army made up of civilian and military members. Besides influencing land use through its authority to permit or deny a number of water-related projects, the Corps provides engineering services to the U.S. by:

- Planning, designing, building, and operating water resources and other civil works projects.
- Designing and managing the construction of military facilities.
- Providing design and construction management support for other defense and federal agencies.

New York State Regulations

New York State utilizes several laws, ordinances, and acts to regulate land use.

New York Office of Parks, Recreation, and Historic Preservation

The Field Services Bureau of the **New York Office of Parks, Recreation and Historic Preservation (OPRHP)** *oversees public recreation areas and administers federal and state preservation projects.* Because New York, like most states, has a state register of historic places, the state receives federal grants for historic preservation. The Field Services Bureau oversees the Certified Local Program, which is a nationwide program that supports local preservation and is the link between local communities, as well as state and federal programs.

New York State Article 9-A

Article 9-A of the New York State Real Property Law requires subdividers to file with the Department of State before offering to sell or lease subdivided vacant lands to New York State residents on an installment plan. Filing consists of a filing statement, an offering statement, and a filing fee.

Article 9-A applies *only* to vacant land sold on an installment plan. If the offering consists of lots on which homes exist, no filing is necessary. Deed and mortgage transactions that require a down payment are not included in the Article. Because of these two caveats, most real estate offerings in New York are not required to be filed with the Department of State.

State Environmental Quality Review

The **State Environmental Quality Review Act (SEQR)** requires a state environmental quality review to *assess the environmental impact of any activity or action approved by a state agency or unit of local government*. A state environmental quality review requires the government entity that sponsored or approved the activity to not only identify, but to mitigate, its significant environmental impact.

If a proposed action may significantly impact the environment, an environmental impact statement (EIS) is necessary. The EIS is actually the process that describes and analyzes the proposed action. According to the state, examples of factors considered adverse to the environment include:

- A substantial change in air quality, ground or surface water quality or quantity, traffic, or noise levels.
- A significant increase in solid waste production or the potential for erosion, flooding, leaching, or drainage problems.
- Removal or destruction of vegetation or fauna.
- The impairment of the character or quality of historical, archeological, architectural, or aesthetic resources or of existing communities or neighborhoods.

Environmental concerns affect land use policy on the local, state, and federal levels because government agencies at all three levels approve projects and/or activities with potential environmental risks. If multiple agencies are involved, a **lead agency** *oversees the entire evaluation process*. The lead agency makes the final decision about whether an environmental impact statement is required and, in turn, files the statement.

Transportation

Streets and roads provide access to residential, commercial, and public places, so the state may regulate land use in these cases to benefit the community as a whole. The New York State Department of Transportation (NYSDOT) is responsible for building and maintaining state-owned roadways, bridges, and overpasses. State-owned roads in New York City are the exception, however, because New York City has its own department of transportation.

Municipal Planning

City planning is essential for city growth. Thoughtful and deliberate city planning allows for expansion that is consistent and balanced. Nearly every municipality in New York has a **planning board** that holds public hearings, investigates solutions for the planning issues at hand, and makes recommendations to the appropriate legislative authority.

A planning board is involved in many things that directly affect the growth and development of the city. The major responsibilities of a city planning board include:

- Creating a capital budget.
- Developing and controlling the city's comprehensive plan.
- Regulating plat, density, street, and traffic patterns.
- Controlling subdivision development.
- Reviewing site plans.
- Taking specific zoning actions.

Creating a Capital Budget

Like any household or business, a city must create a budget to determine what money is coming in, and, conversely, what money is going out. City planning boards include in their master plan what money they plan to take in over the long term and how they plan to do so, whether through taxes, or other means. By doing this, they can plan projects, both short and long term, as well as how to finance them.

Creating a Comprehensive Plan

A **comprehensive plan**, or **master plan**, *is a written document that identifies the goals, objectives, principles, guidelines, policies, standards, and strategies for the growth and development of a community.* It is up to the planning board to create the plan, in association with other government agencies and community leaders, and maintain the plan. This may involve making necessary revisions and updates based on a number of factors, including budgetary concerns, new land use regulations, new environmental concerns, and a host of other reasons unique to every community.

The planning board is also responsible for a community's official map. This goes hand-in-hand with creating and controlling the comprehensive plan. The **official map** *is final and conclusive with respect to the location and width of the community's streets, highways, drainage systems, and parks.*

Subdivision and Land Development Regulations

When a subdivision is planned for a community, one of the first things determined is its **density**, which is *the number of families that can inhabit a plot of land*. Planning boards must regulate a community's density to avoid overcrowding in residential areas. Planning boards accomplish this by placing minimums on the lot size, setback, and boundary requirements, as well as on the size of the dwellings on the land.

Subdivision regulations are state and local laws regulating how land may be subdivided. These regulations may govern the size of the lots in a subdivision and the location of streets and sidewalks, and sewer and water lines. Open spaces and recreational areas may also be required through subdivision regulations.

A local government enforces subdivision regulations by requiring developers to submit a *plat* for approval. A **plat** *depicts the arrangements of buildings, roads, and other services for a development*. Plats can be used in determining traffic patterns in a subdivision, since they illustrate the primary roads, through streets, and **cul-de-sacs**, or *dead end streets that do not connect to main roads.* After a plat has been approved, it may be recorded in the county in which the land is located.

Demographic Studies

When a developer proposes to build a subdivision in a community, the city planning board researches the impact the development will have and ultimately grants, or denies, the proposal. The first step the board takes to determine whether the development will be allowed is a demographics study.

Demography *is the study of the social and economic status of a given area or population*. Knowing a community's demographics enables planners to determine whether the community can support new development. In order to study the demographics, planners rely on **census tracts**, which *are relatively small areas used to track the population of the United States by the U.S. Census Bureau.*

The demographic study is important because it reveals whether the city's **infrastructure** – *support facilities and services, including roads, parks, sewers,* *water, schools, as well as police and fire protection* – can sustain the added burden of a new development and all the people it will bring with it.

> **THE ROLE OF THE FHA**
>
> While it is not the responsibility of the planning board, an important component in subdivision regulation is Federal Housing Administration (FHA) approval. The FHA has minimum building standards for properties with FHA-approved mortgages. For homes built in a subdivision with FHA financing, developers must also follow its regulations and guidelines, as well as the municipality's guidelines.

Reviewing Site Plans

Site plans are an integral part of any new development. Developers create site plans for commercial and residential projects and include everything that must be considered before work can begin. In New York, local planning boards can review site plans in order to evaluate the effects the development may have on the community.

When developers create a site plan, they consider the **topography**, or *physical characteristics, of a parcel of land*. Topography includes:

- Water sources.
- Native vegetation.
- Location of trees and rocks.
- Soil type.
- Floodplains.

It is important to know such specific information because it may impact how and where buildings and utilities will be situated, as well as the overall appearance of the new neighborhood. Other considerations include environmental issues, types of structures to be built, the configuration of streets and sidewalks, zoning in surrounding areas, and what utilities are available, along with how easy it will be to put new systems into operation.

Finally, a survey is included in the site plan. **Surveys** *locate and measure the boundaries of a property, and identify improvements, encroachments, and easements associated with the land.*

> **SUNSHINE LAWS**
>
> City councils, town boards, village boards of trustees, school boards, commissions, legislative bodies, and subcommittees fall within the framework of the Open Meetings or "Sunshine" Law, which went into effect in New York in 1977. This law gives the public the right to attend meetings of public bodies. The law also requires that prior notice be given of the time and place of such meetings.

Zoning

Cities, counties, subdivisions, and even streets are typically divided into distinct zoning classifications. The kinds of activities permitted in different zones are regulated to protect the public. **Zoning ordinances** are local laws that divide a city or county into different areas, or zones. They *set forth the type of use permitted under each zoning classification and specify requirements for compliance.*

Each zone generally sets minimum lot size, building height limit, setback, and side yard rules governing building position, and may even limit how much of a lot a building can cover. Zoning laws are also likely to set rules for off-street parking, landscaping, outdoor lighting, and other items.

New York State has some responsibility for determining zoning – mainly for public lands and open spaces. In other areas, however, zoning is the responsibility of local governments. This encompasses everything from subdivision development and building codes to budgeting and site plan review.

Zoning Ordinances

Once the planning board creates a plan, members begin establishing zoning ordinances accordingly. Zoning ordinances have two parts:

1. A zoning map that divides the community into designated districts
2. A text of the zoning ordinance that sets forth the type of use permitted in each zone, including specific requirements for compliance

According to New York State law, municipalities are required to refer certain planning and zoning actions to respective county planning boards for review. When a municipality wishes to add or change zoning in a particular area, planning boards, along with planning department staff, review and prepare a recommendation letter in response to the request.

Planning boards receive numerous requests for zoning actions that can range from minor variances for single-family homes to site plans for major development projects. Requests are assessed by looking at the county's comprehensive plan as well as how the request will impact streets, roads, traffic, parks, services, and the overall well-being of the community and its residents.

Occasionally, planning boards impose a **moratorium** *that temporarily suspends the right of property owners to obtain development approvals while the local legislature takes time to consider, draft, and adopt land use regulations or rules to respond to new or changing circumstances not adequately dealt with by its current laws.* Instances where moratoriums may be instituted include when a comprehensive plan or zoning law is being established and when the municipality cannot provide the services necessary to support the proposed action. It is important to note that when a moratorium is imposed, the municipality is exercising its right of police power. Moratoriums can be used only to protect the public's welfare.

Zoning Classifications

Typical New York zoning classifications include residential, commercial, industrial, institutional, agricultural, public open space, vacant land, and parkland/recreational. Each classification also has numerous subcategories.

Residential

Residential zones are just that – residential, meaning they are *for residences and not commercial buildings*. Residential zones consist of single-family as well as multi-family dwellings. Even though residential zones consist of homes and apartments, accessory uses are common in these areas. **Accessory uses** are *uses or occupancy incidental or subordinate to the principal use or occupancy of a property*. A **home occupation**, *in which a small business or other occupation is carried out in the residence*, is an example of an accessory use. Another example is an **accessory apartment**, which *is simply an apartment within a primary residence.*

A **group home** is *a residential facility in a residential zone for three or more unrelated people.* Group homes serve the special needs of a group, usually the physically or mentally disabled or those recovering from an affliction or dependency. Foster homes, rehabilitation centers, and halfway houses are all examples of group homes. Because of the nature of group homes, there is controversy over whether they should be allowed in residential zones; however, the Fair Housing Act makes it illegal to deny a permit for a home "because of the disability of individuals who live or would live there."

Often, residents in residential areas declare that only "families" can reside in residential dwellings. This, of course, leads to the question, "What is the legal definition of a family?" According to New York State law, a **family** can be:

- *An individual, or two or more people related by blood, marriage, or adoption, living together in one dwelling.*
- *A group of up to three people who are not married, not blood relatives, nor adopted, who live together as a single unit.*
- *One or more people living in a single unit, as distinguished from a group occupying a hotel, club, or fraternity or sorority house.*

Commercial

Another common type of zoning is commercial. Hotels, retail shops, restaurants, malls, salons, and a host of other business entities fit this category.

Industrial

Manufacturing facilities are included in industrial zoning. Whether the facility is for the actual manufacturing of goods, or if it is for storing those goods, it is industrial.

Institutional

Institutional zoning includes schools, college campuses, hospitals, correctional facilities, and courthouses. Institutions may appear in residential or commercial zones, depending on local zoning ordinances.

Agricultural

As the name implies, agricultural zoning is for areas where animals may graze and crops may be grown.

Public Open Space

When land is intentionally left undeveloped, it is considered public open space. Forests, public parks, lakes, bays, and shorelines are examples of public open spaces that can be owned either privately or publicly.

Parklands

Parklands differ slightly from public open spaces in that they are specifically used for recreational activities and maintained for their ecological, aesthetic, and educational value. Local, state, and federal authorities can all exercise their power over land use when it comes to parklands.

Recreational

Recreational areas in New York are owned primarily by municipalities and private citizens. The Department of Environmental Conservation (DEC) and the Office of Parks, Recreation, and Historic Preservation classify recreational areas as:

- Greenways.
- Parks.
- Public fishing areas.
- Shorelines.
- Trailways.
- Waterway access.

Vacant Land

Vacant land *is unimproved land, or land with no buildings on it.* Land that does have a building on it is not necessarily occupied. It still may be considered vacant if that building (or improvement) does not serve a purpose.

Types of Zoning

Just as there are several classifications of zoning, there are also several types of zoning. Some types are specific to a zoning classification, while others may be applied across the board.

As of Right Zoning

Landowners enjoy the bundle of rights associated with the property they own; as of right zoning is implied in this bundle of rights. **As of right zoning** *prohibits discrimination among landowners in a particular zone.* Simply put, if one landowner is permitted, through zoning ordinances, to build a fence on his land, all landowners in that zone are permitted to do the same.

Cluster Zoning

Cluster zoning *allows developers to provide a varied selection of lot sizes and housing choices within a single area.* A common element to areas with cluster zoning is the incorporation of green spaces, or open spaces to add to the development's beauty and for the entire community's enjoyment. The zone may consist of **abutting properties**, which are *directly contiguous parcels, sharing at least one common boundary.*

Cluster zoning may also take the form of a **planned unit development (PUD)**, which is a special type of subdivision in which developers do not have to comply with all standard zoning and subdivision regulations. For example, nonresidential and residential buildings may be combined in the overall plan. Since PUD developers do not have to follow setback and lot size rules, buildings may be closer together, creating large open spaces for public use and enjoyment.

Incentive Zoning

Incentive zoning is *a system by which developers receive zoning incentives on the condition that specific physical, social, or cultural benefits are provided to the community*. Common incentives include:

- Increases in the permissible number of residential units or gross square footage of the development.
- Waivers of the height, setback, and use provisions of current zoning ordinances.
- Affordable housing, recreational facilities, open space, day-care facilities, and infrastructures.

Spot Zoning

The *illegal rezoning of a single parcel or a small area to benefit one or more property owners rather than carry out the objectives of the master plan* is known as **spot zoning**. Rezoning is a revision in zoning law, usually changing a zone from one type to another. When rezoning occurs, the zoning law is actually changed; it is not a variance or exception. Spot zoning is a perfect example of how the rezoning process can be abused. Isolated zoning changes can be illegal because the law is not applied the same way to all landowners.

Transfer of Development Rights

Development rights go hand in hand with zoning because, theoretically, a landowner buys land to develop it. And a landowner's ability to develop property is directly related to zoning ordinances. Often the development rights enjoyed by owners of historic buildings and properties are not exercised because these properties must be preserved. However, that does not mean their right to develop is lost.

A **transfer of development rights** *occurs when a developer buys the development rights from a property owner who cannot use them*. Essentially, owners who do not intend to use their development rights transfer their rights by selling to developers who can use them. For instance, the owner of a home listed on the National Register of Historic Places has development rights – even if she never intends to use them. She could sell those rights to a developer or another individual if she chooses.

The Zoning Board of Appeals

New York State statutes require that a zoning board of appeals be formed when a local legislature adopts its zoning law. The board must consist of three to five members. The essential functions of the zoning board of appeals is twofold:

- To grant variances
- To interpret ordinances

In this capacity, it protects landowners from the unfair application of the laws in particular circumstances. The zoning board of appeals also hears appeals from the decisions of the zoning enforcement officer or building inspector when interpretations of the zoning ordinance are involved.

NEW YORK CITY

PLANNING AND ZONING IN NEW YORK CITY

In New York City, the planning board and the zoning board are one entity known as the Board of Standards and Appeals. It consists of 12 members and one chairperson.

New York City does not have two separate boards for planning and zoning. The two boards are combined and form the Board of Standards and Appeals. There is no separate board of appeals.

Article 78 Proceedings

A zoning board's determinations can be challenged in state courts through Article 78 proceedings. An Article 78 proceeding refers to an article of the New York Civil Practice Law and Rules that allows aggrieved persons to bring an action against a government body or officer, or in the case of zoning disputes, a municipality's zoning board of appeals. This device allows review of state and local administrative proceedings in court.

Exceptions to Zoning Laws

Zoning laws are often controversial because they can have a big impact on the use and value of property. A zoning law is constitutional only if it applies in the same manner to all similarly situated property owners. To prevent undue hardships, zoning laws usually provide for limited exceptions.

Nonconforming Uses

Nonconforming uses *occur when land use does not conform to current zoning laws, but is legally allowed because the land use was established before the new zoning laws were enacted.* Most nonconforming uses are allowed to continue but may not be expanded or enlarged.

Permission to continue nonconforming uses is not tied to the landowner. If the property is sold, the new owner may continue with the nonconforming use. Some localities may have zoning laws that automatically terminate the right to a nonconforming use if the use is discontinued for a certain amount of time, usually one year.

Variances

A **variance** *is a form of administrative relief that allows property to be used in a way that does not comply with the literal requirements of the zoning ordinance.* There are two types of variances: Use and area.

Use variances *allow landowners to use their land in a way that is not permitted under current zoning laws – such as commercial use in a residential zone.* This type of variance is granted only in cases when the current zoning ordinance causes the landowner an *unnecessary hardship*. To prove unnecessary hardship, owners must establish that the requested variance meets four statutorily prescribed conditions, including:

1. The landowner is deprived of all economic use and/or benefit of the property and can provide financial evidence to that effect.
2. The landowner did not create the hardship.
3. The hardship is not common to the area or neighborhood.
4. The variance will not change the nature and quality of the neighborhood.

Area variances *entitle landowners to use land in a way that is typically not allowed by the dimensional or physical requirements of the zoning law.* This type of variance is needed when a building application does not comply with the setback, height, lot, or area requirements of the zoning ordinance. This type of variance is granted only in cases when the current zoning ordinance has *practical difficulty*, affecting the health, safety, or welfare of a community. In order for an area variance to be granted, landowners must demonstrate certain qualifications, including:

- The variance will not create an undesirable change or detriment to neighboring properties.
- The benefit sought cannot be achieved through other means.
- The variance is not substantial.
- The landowner did not create the difficulty.
- The variance would not have an adverse effect or impact on the physical or environmental conditions in the neighborhood or district.

Conditional Uses

Conditional or special uses are allowed in certain zoning districts, but only upon issuance of a **special use permit**, *subject to conditions designed to protect surrounding properties and the community* from a possible negative impact resulting from the permit.

Local Enforcement

Several codes, departments, and individuals serve to enforce the land use regulations within a given community, municipality, city, and even state.

Building Codes

Building codes *protect the public by setting minimum standards and requiring builders to adhere to certain construction standards, including using particular methods and materials, sanitary equipment, electrical wiring, and fire prevention standards.* Landowners must obtain building permits before constructing or renovating residential or commercial property. New York State adopted the International Building Code in July 2003. It applies to all construction when no local code exists, or when local codes are less restrictive.

Building codes are established locally and permits are issued through local government authorities. Typically, an owner who wants to build or remodel a building must submit plans to a local building department for approval. A **building permit** is issued only if the plans comply with the codes. Local inspectors, who can stop work if necessary, inspect the project several times throughout the construction process.

Once construction is complete, a final inspection is conducted, and if the structure meets all building codes, the landowner is given a **certificate of occupancy**, which *is a permit issued to the builder after all inspections have been made and the property is deemed fit for occupancy*. A **certificate of compliance** *is issued for an altered building*. If deficiencies are found during the final inspection, no certificate of occupancy will be issued. It is then up to the landowner and contractor to correct the problems before another inspection takes place.

New York State Uniform Fire Prevention and Building Code

The **New York State Uniform Fire Prevention and Building Code** *sets forth the construction, materials, safety, and sanitary standards for buildings in New York as well as standards for the "condition, occupancy, maintenance, rehabilitation, and renewal of existing buildings*." The code provides minimum standards for all types of buildings – residential and commercial, new and existing. If a local code is more stringent than the state code, *the local code applies*. If, on the other hand, there is no local code, the State of New York code applies.

Building Department

A city or municipality's building department protects residents by seeing that code restrictions are followed and construction and renovations are performed by licensed professionals. Building departments also oversee code enforcement. Investigators, code enforcement officers, and inspectors all work to ensure the public's safety and welfare are protected.

Other state and local agencies work to meet this goal as well. For instance, the New York State Department of Health is not associated with the building department; however, it can also inspect and investigate building code violations that ultimately affect the health and safety of the community.

Professional Service Providers

Land use regulations, zoning ordinances, and building codes, whether they pertain to new construction or existing structures, could not be applied or enforced without the assistance of hundreds of individuals. Among those directly involved in these areas are professionals representing both public and private interests, including:

- Architects.
- Urban designers.
- Project managers.
- Surveyors.
- Engineers.
- Planners.

Local Courts

In New York State, the courts have the responsibility of controlling local land use decisions. If land use decisions are challenged in the courts, the courts typically uphold the decisions made at the local level.

SUMMARY

1. Land ownership in New York can be **absolute**, meaning the complete bundle of rights to the land belongs to the owner. Owners have the right to use, enjoy, dispose of, and possess the land they own; however, restrictions are sometimes placed on the land by individuals, private entities, and the government in the form of deed restrictions, zoning ordinances, and land use regulations.
2. **Private land use controls** are enacted by individual owners and developers. These controls often prohibit what zoning ordinances would typically allow. **Deed restrictions** *are restrictive covenants that apply to future landowners*. The restrictions **run with the land**, which means *they move with the title in future conveyances*. Deed restrictions may be conditional.
3. **Restrictive covenants** may be *implemented when land is subdivided or when two parties agree*. To be enforceable against third parties, they must be recorded. Restrictive covenants can be terminated in a variety of ways, including by: Termination date, release, merger, abandonment, and changed circumstances. If a restrictive covenant becomes illegal after it is written, it is automatically terminated.
4. Private **subdivision regulations** *enable property owners to maintain the quality and consistency of the residences in the subdivision*. A common regulation in a subdivision is that residences must meet **setback requirements**, which means *they are located a specific distance between the front property line to the building line, as well as from the interior property lines.* If subdivision regulations are not followed, property owners within the development may take legal action. If legal action is not taken, or if it is not taken in a timely manner, the restriction will be terminated, which means the **doctrine of laches** has been applied.

5. **Public land use restrictions** are those *imposed by the government at the local, state, and federal level.* When the government restricts land use, it is exercising its **police power**, *the constitutional power of state and local governments to enact and enforce laws that protect the public's health, safety, morals, and general welfare*. Local powers include taxation as well as restrictions dealing with everything from zoning to shoreline development. State powers involve escheatment, environmental conditions, transportation issues, filing requirements, and preservation concerns. Federal powers concern eminent domain, environmental protection laws, disclosure, and HUD funding.

6. **Zoning ordinances** *set forth the type of use permitted under each zoning classification and specific requirements for compliance*. Cities, counties, subdivisions, and even streets can be divided into distinct zoning classifications. The kinds of activities permitted are regulated to protect the public. New York State has some responsibility for determining zoning; however, it is usually the responsibility of local governments.

7. Typical New York **zoning classifications** include *residential*, *commercial*, *industrial*, *institutional*, *agricultural*, *public open space* (intentionally undeveloped land), *parklands*, *recreational*, and *vacant land* (unimproved land). Within these classifications of zoning are **types of zoning**, including *as of right* (gives all landowners the same rights to do as they wish with their property), *cluster zoning* (allows developers to provide a varied selection of lot sizes and housing choices within a single area), *incentive zoning* (gives developers zoning incentives), and *spot zoning* (illegal rezoning to benefit certain property owners).

8. Nearly every municipality in New York has a **planning board** that *holds public hearings, investigates solutions for the planning issues at hand, and makes recommendations to the appropriate legislative authority*. In *New York City, the planning board and zoning board are one entity* known as the **Board of Standards and Appeals**. Planning boards create a capital budget; control the city's comprehensive plan; regulate plat, density, street, and traffic patterns; regulate subdivision development; review site plans; and take specific zoning actions.

9. **Zoning boards of appeals** *grant variances*. In this capacity, the boards protect landowners from the unfair application of the laws in particular circumstances. A zoning board's decisions may be challenged in court through Article 78 proceedings.

10. Zoning laws are constitutional only if they apply in the same manner to all similarly situated property owners. To prevent undue hardships, zoning laws provide for limited exceptions. **Nonconforming uses** *occur when land use does not conform to current zoning laws, but is legally allowed because the land use was established before the new zoning laws were enacted.* **Variances** *allow property to be used in a way that does not comply with the literal requirements of the zoning ordinance.* The two types of variances are **use variances** (*allowing landowners to use their land in a way that is not permitted under current zoning laws*) and **area variances** (*entitling landowners to use land in a way typically not allowed by the dimensional or physical requirements of the zoning law*). **Conditional uses** *are allowed upon issuance of a special use permit subject to conditions designed to protect surrounding property and the community from possible negative impact resulting from the permit.*

11. **Building codes** *protect the public by setting minimum standards requiring builders to use certain construction standards, including particular methods and materials, sanitary equipment, electrical wiring, and fire prevention standards.* New York uses a statewide building code that applies to all construction when no local code exists, or when local codes are less restrictive. The **New York State Uniform Fire Prevention and Building Code** *sets forth the construction, materials, safety, and sanitary standards for buildings in New York, as well as standards for the condition, occupancy, maintenance, rehabilitation, and renewal of existing buildings.* The code provides minimum standards for all types of buildings. Building departments also oversee code enforcement.

9

Construction Basics

- Amperage / Voltage
- Balloon Construction
- Basement
- Beam
- Bearing Walls
- Blueprint
- British Thermal Unit (BTU)
- Building Codes
- Building Envelope
- Building Inspection
- Circuit Breaker
- Concrete Slab
- Crawl Space
- Drywall / Plasterboard / Sheetrock/ Wallboard
- Eave
- Fascia
- Flashing
- Footer
- Foundation Walls
- Fuse
- Girder
- Headers
- Joists
- Lally™ Column
- Percolation Rate
- Pitch
- Platform Framing
- Post and Beam Framing
- Rafter
- R-Factor
- Septic System
- Sheathing
- Siding
- Sill Plate
- Slab-on-Grade Construction
- Soffit
- Studs

Key Terms

In This Session

In this session, you'll be introduced to the basic elements of home construction. You'll see how the construction process works and learn common construction terminology. You'll also develop an understanding of the restrictions, regulations, and codes that affect construction.

You'll learn:

- Which building codes direct construction in New York State.
- The requirements to complete a construction project.
- The major systems that run a home, including heating, cooling, plumbing, electrical, and waste systems.
- The mandated guarantees and warranties for new construction and renovations.

Construction and the Real Estate Professional

Clients look to real estate professionals for help in understanding the many issues surrounding their property purchases. For example, clients may ask about the renovation needs of an older property they're considering or the steps in the construction of a new build. A basic knowledge of construction allows real estate agents to have initial conversations with clients about renovation and construction-related topics. It also helps agents identify situations that require professionals such as contractors, engineers, and inspectors.

Land Use and Construction

It is important for licensees to understand how land use controls pertain to the construction process. Land use controls are any public or private restrictions on how land may be used and are usually government-enacted zoning laws. You cannot construct just any building on any property. Builders must follow specific zoning regulations when developing a property. They also develop specifications, ensure adherence to codes, and obtain the necessary permits.

Specifications

In construction, planning and pre-construction begin with documents called **specifications**, which are *written documents explaining the requirements for the scope of the work, including materials, standards, and expected quality of the finished product.*

Once a lot or parcel has been chosen, a **blueprint**, which is a *detailed building plan used to evaluate design, determine feasibility, and guide construction of a structure,* can be used for obtaining quotes from prospective builders.

Decisions for the finish materials and components for the entire project must also be made. Things such as hardwood floors versus carpet over a subfloor, and type and brand of cabinetry, are detailed in a materials list. After all, a builder cannot bid on a project, nor can an appraiser perform a new construction appraisal assignment, if the quality, type, and quantity of materials have not yet been decided.

Building Permits and Requirements

The next step is getting approval of the building specifications and blueprints by local authorities. A plot plan may also need to be submitted, showing the proposed layout of the property site, including the building's position. This is the first step in obtaining the necessary building permits.

Permits, issued after approval of the builder's initial plans, are *official government documents* obtained from the appropriate government authority that acknowledge that the proposed work meets the department's standards, and grant permission for it to be performed. They also prompt government authorities to monitor projects and follow up with appropriate inspections. In some areas, one building permit may cover the entire new construction, building addition, or renovation project. In other areas, however, separate permits may be needed for the building itself as well as the electrical and plumbing systems. In those cases, different inspectors may be utilized.

Codes and Compliance

Building codes *protect the public by setting minimum standards and requiring builders to use certain construction standards, including particular methods and materials, sanitary equipment, electrical wiring, and fire prevention techniques.* In New York, as with every other state, there are numerous building codes that must be followed when performing any type of construction work. It is important to note that states have minimum building standards, and local jurisdictions could have stricter standards.

In addition to the *International Building Code*, there are several other widely adopted building codes, including the *Uniform Building Code*, the *National Electrical Code*, and the *Uniform Plumbing Code*. Building codes adopted and enforced by local jurisdictions generally allow older work in residential properties to stay in place, as long as the work was up to code at the time it was installed and is presently in safe condition. Often, though, if remodeling or improvements are performed, all conditions must reflect the current code.

Builders should always be up to date on the required compliance regarding accessibility under the Americans with Disabilities Act (ADA). When new, stricter standards are imposed, property owners may have to bring old buildings up to code. Fines and injunctions are often used to enforce these laws and codes.

New York State Energy Code

The **New York Energy Conservation Construction Code** became mandatory in 2002. It provides minimum standards requirements concerning energy efficiencies in new commercial and residential buildings. The Code is intended to save energy costs and make New York's air cleaner by reducing carbon dioxide emissions and acid rain-causing sulfur.

The provisions for *residential* buildings include:

- More stringent insulation in electrically heated homes.
- Reduced infiltration in fireplaces.
- More efficient thermostats, including those with programmable features.
- Basement insulation levels that vary by region and climate.

The provisions for *commercial* buildings include:

- Mandatory high-efficiency transformers.
- A special compliance path for two-piped hydraulic systems, which are common in New York.

Building Inspections

It is critical for licensees to know why building inspections are important. **Building inspection** is the *process whereby government authorities, usually state or local, are charged with ensuring compliance with prevailing building codes.* Since building codes are written to ensure buildings are safe, enforcement of these codes, through inspection, is in the community's best interest. Building inspections, though, differ from home inspections in that building inspectors do not inform a prospective buyer of potential problems with a building, but ensure compliance with current building standards.

Certificate of Occupancy

A Certificate of Occupancy is issued to builders after all inspections have been made and the property is deemed fit for occupancy. According to the New York State Uniform Fire Prevention and Building Code, a certificate of occupancy is required in two instances:

1. For all work for which a building permit was required.
2. Whenever the general occupancy classification for a building is changed.

For altered buildings, a certificate of compliance is issued.

Site Requirements

The state of New York regulates water supply and sewage disposal systems serving subdivisions (under Article 11, Title II of the Public Health Law and Article 17, Title 15 of the Environmental Conservation Law).

New York State On-Site Well Requirements

According to the New York State Department of Health, Appendix 5-B Standards for Water Wells, there are specific standards for well location and construction that must be followed to protect well water from contamination. The following are a few of the guidelines taken directly from the Public Health Law:

- A well shall be located so adequate access for inspection, maintenance repair, renovation, treatment, and testing is provided.
- A well shall be located where it is not subject to seasonal flooding or surface water contamination, or it shall be constructed in such a manner that seasonal floodwater cannot enter the well.
- A well shall be located up gradient of any potential or known source of contamination unless property, boundaries, site topography, location of structures, and accessibility require different locations. There are minimum requirements for horizontal separation distances from potential sources of contamination.
- Acceptable water well construction methods include drilling, driving, boring, jetting, and excavating into an aquifer to obtain groundwater as a supply source.
- A well shall have a minimum casing length extending from one foot above finished grade to 19 feet below finished grade upon completion of well drilling, with the following exceptions:
  - It may exceed 20 feet if geologic conditions are an issue.
  - It may be completed at a depth of less than 19 feet if groundwater availability is an issue.

It is important to note that in order to provide adequate water supply to an average household, wells are expected to produce at least *five gallons of water per minute.*

New York State On-Site Sanitary Waste System Requirements

Wastewater treatment systems are needed so that New York's rivers and steams are not polluted, contaminating the water necessary for marine wildlife to live. Approval from the Board of Health must be obtained before a septic system may be installed. One of two types of sanitary waste systems is usually found in a residential property:

- **Septic system**, which includes a septic tank and soil absorption system. It acts as a sewage treatment system that moves wastewater to an underground storage area where solid waste matter decomposes.
- **Municipal wastewater system**, in which wastewater is drained from the house through pipes into a sewer. The sewer carries the waste to a local wastewater treatment facility.

Section 75-A of the New York Public Health Law covers wastewater treatment standards in detail. Following are several important wastewater treatment standards:

- Where sewage treatment systems are to be located on the watersheds or wellhead area of public water supplies, the rules and regulations enacted by the State Department of Health for the protection of these supplies must be observed.
- When individual sewage systems overlay a drinking water aquifer, local health departments may establish population density limits and minimum lot sizes for residential development with on-site sewage treatment systems.
- There must be at least four feet of usable soil available above rock, unsuitable soil, and high seasonal groundwater for the installation of a conventional absorption field.
- Soils with a **percolation rate**, the *rate at which water moves through soil,* faster than one minute per inch are not suitable for subsurface absorption systems unless the site is blended with less permeable soil.
- Subsurface treatment systems and components of the sewage system shall be separated from buildings, property lines, utilities, and wells to maintain system performance, permit repairs, and reduce the effects of underground sewage flow and dispersion.

Site Use

There are several factors that determine the best use of a site. It is important to consider these factors before beginning a construction project, or even before purchasing a property.

If a client purchases a site and later finds certain factors prohibit him from using the property as he intended, it could blemish a licensee's reputation and may bring potential liability for not using reasonable care to research the information for the client prior to the sale. It is important to look at factors that affect site use.

Drainage

Drainage is the natural or artificial movement of water from a given area. In addition to proper drainage, it is important to make sure the site is properly graded. Grading refers to the slope of the ground or landscape area. Proper drainage and grading are important means of directing rainwater away from a property, avoiding damp foundations, wet basements, and a host of other water issues.

Landscaping

Great landscaping may inspire buyers and help sell a property. In site construction, landscaping is improving a property or land by adding plants, trees, bushes, retaining walls, etc., or otherwise altering the contours of the ground. Landscaping provides privacy, shading, and curb appeal. When constructing a site, a developer may build around existing mature trees, creeks, or woods to add value to the land.

Appurtenances

Appurtenances are rights that go with real property ownership. They are usually transferred with the property, but they may also be sold separately. Appurtenant rights retained or sold separately affect how a site can best be used. For example, the issue of a property's subsurface rights sold separately would affect future use of that property with regard to new construction.

Shading

The amount of shade property receives depends on how a structure is situated on it. For example, if the front of a structure faces east, it will receive a lot of morning sun. Bushes and mature trees create excellent shading and are ideal for reducing heat. Shade can reduce energy bills by lowering the overall temperature of a building. Large trees shading the roof of a home can often reduce the internal temperature 8-10 degrees Fahrenheit, although the actual reduction varies depending on other factors.

Walkways

The U.S. Department of Housing and Urban Development (HUD) sets minimum building standards for housing and mobile homes, and is responsible for enforcing the federal Fair Housing Act for minimum property standards for walkways. The Architectural Barriers Act of 1968 stipulates that buildings must be accessible by those with disabilities. HUD also requires that all states and cities have building codes for accessibility, including walkways and paths. In addition, construction managers should reference blueprints or site plans in the event specific types of walkways (i.e., all-brick) are required in certain neighborhoods.

Zoning

Zoning and other regulated limitations on land usage (i.e., building codes) are implemented to protect the health, safety, and welfare of a community. Land use controls affect real estate because they may limit development and affect property values. For example, land may be more valuable with an office building instead of a house, but zoning laws may not permit such usage.

Structure

After determining an appropriate site to build on, a new owner faces many decisions ahead in the construction of the home. Fundamental components of a basic structure include foundation, framing, roof, exterior finish work, and interior finish work.

Foundation

The **foundation** is *the basic structure on which the rest of the house sits.* A typical foundation system is usually concrete slab, pier and beams, crawl space, or basement. The foundation supports the rest of the structure, so it is important that it is strong and dry. New York building standards require at least *eight inches of visible foundation wall above grade (ground level).*

Foundation walls are the *side walls that support the structure.* They are typically made of poured concrete, concrete block, or brick.

Footer

A **footer** is the *underground base, usually concrete, that supports a foundation.* A trench is dug so concrete can be poured onto solid ground; thus, the footer is wider at the bottom – and wider than the structure it will support. Local building codes dictate how footers must be built (size and placement), based on the characteristics of the ground being built on, type of foundation used, and frost depth common in the area. Footers go below the freeze line, the deepest depth that the ground freezes in winter.

Slab-on-Grade Construction

Slab-on-grade construction is a *concrete foundation built directly on the ground*. A slab-on-grade house or building does not have a basement. In more specific terms, a **concrete slab** is a *foundation made from a layer of poured concrete reinforced with steel rods* (called "rebar"). In some parts of the country, the concrete slab is common, due to the underlying soil or preference. In other markets, however, the concrete slab is considered inferior.

Crawl Space

A **crawl space** is the *unfinished space below the first floor of a house or other structure, but less than a full story in height.* The crawl space is accessed, most times, from an exterior scuttle so the structure can be serviced from beneath. In other cases, a crawl space is the result of a **pier and beam foundation**, with the piers extending out of the ground less than a full story in height and supporting the weight of the structure.

Basement

A **basement** is *part of a house or building partially or entirely below grade, and is used to support the rest of the structure*. Basements are at least one full story in height and are formed as a result of space excavated before a house or building is erected. The walls of a basement sit on concrete footers, and serve as the foundation for the structure.

Framing

The term "building envelope" may be mentioned when a structure is being developed. The **building envelope**, sometimes called a building shell, *refers to the exterior elements* (walls, windows, floor, roof, etc.) *that enclose the interior.*

The framing is the basic, load-bearing skeleton of a structure to which the interior walls, exterior walls, and roof system are attached. Framing also includes the solid support structure surrounding window and door openings. When interior framing is complete, it is possible to walk around the floor plan and experience the structure's layout.

Types of Framing

There are three basic frame construction types:

- **Platform construction,** also called platform framing, is *a type of framing by which the house or building is constructed one story at a time, with each story serving as a platform for the next.* Studs, which make up the vertical wood framing that forms the skeleton of a structure, are cut to the height of each story, with horizontal flooring and support across the top of them. The studs for the next story are then cut and attached to the flooring.

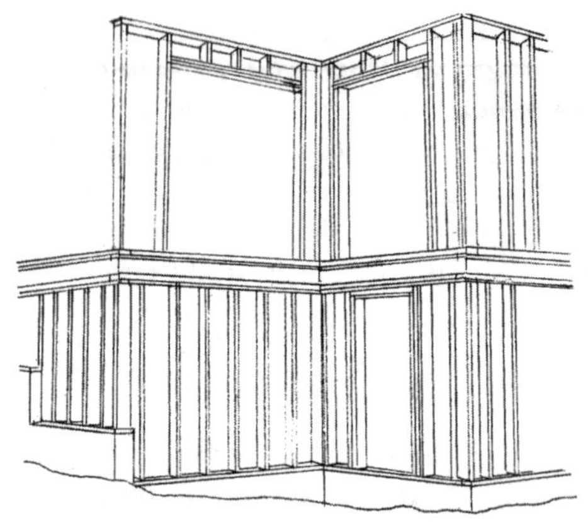

Platform

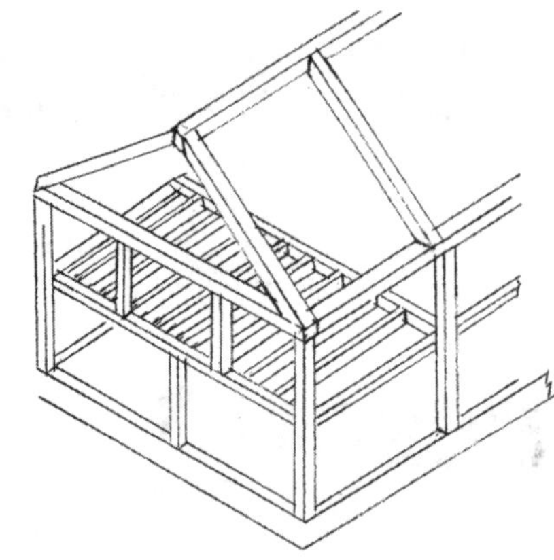

Post and Beam

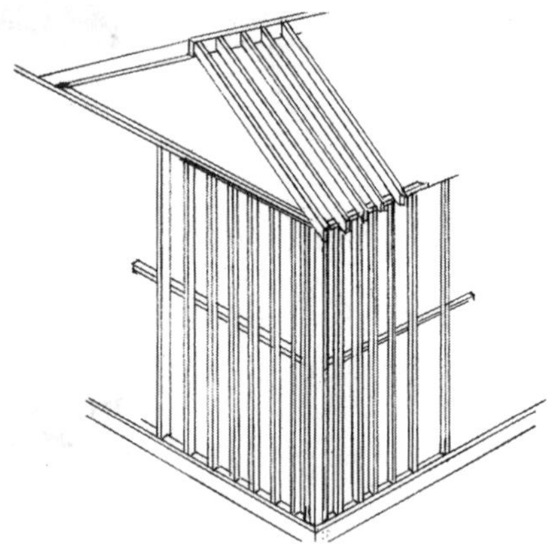

Balloon

- **Post and beam construction**, also called post and beam framing, is *a type of framing with the floor for higher stories (and the roof) supported by beams that sit on top of posts and the outside wall perimeter.* With post supports, not as many interior walls are needed, allowing for larger and more open rooms. Posts, beams, and frame members are heavier than other types of framing and, in the case of wood, may often be left exposed for decorative purposes.
- **Balloon construction**, also called balloon framing, is *a type of framing with long studs going up the entire length of the house, from the foundation to the roof.* Horizontal studs (called ledger boards) are nailed to these tall studs to provide support for the floor and roof joists. Although common in older multi-story brick buildings, balloon construction is rarely used today. It is *no longer permitted* as a construction method by most building codes because of its poor fire-resistant design and the high cost of the long studs.

Beams, Wood-Framing Members, and Flooring

A **beam** is a *long piece of wood, metal, or concrete, etc.* A **stud**, also known as a **wood-framing member**, is *a vertical beam that serves to frame a structure.* Drywall and/or siding are attached to studs. Studs must be at least two inches wide and, when installed as part of a framing system, should not be less than two by four inches in load-bearing partitions.

There are several other important parts that make up a building's frame. A **girder,** *a large, main carrying beam that usually runs horizontally, supports the vertical loads.* **Joists** *are long horizontal beams of wood or steel that span the piers of a foundation* (floor joists*) or load-bearing walls of a roof* (ceiling joists).

The floor joists sit on the ledges or sills of the basement or foundation walls around the perimeter of the building. They are usually supported in the center of the building by the girder (or main beam) and sit on some type of support column or beam that rests on the support column. Support columns may be concrete, wood, metal, or block piers. These piers, in turn, sit on a slab or footer.

Lally™ columns are *steel support columns filled with concrete* and are only for interior use. The **sill plate** is *the bottom piece of a frame that is anchored horizontally to the foundation, and provides a nailing surface for the floor or wall system.* It is the first layer of wood that starts the construction of the house.

Structural Tie-Ins

Wall development begins with **bearing walls**, which *are walls that carry the load for the roof, ceiling, and/or floors. Reinforcements made of wood for door and window placement* are called **headers**, or lintels. Flitch beams, made of two or more timbers cut lengthwise and bundled together, provide additional support for the ceiling and roof.

Roof Framing

Roof framing is also an important part of a structure. A **rafter** is a *sloped support beam that follows the pitch of the roof and serves to hold the outer roof covering.* The rafters are fastened to the roof ridge beam, a horizontal beam at the top of the roof. A lot about the style of a roof can be determined from its *pitch*, or the degree of a roof's slope. More specifically, the **pitch** is a *roof's vertical rise in inches, divided by its horizontal span in feet.*

Common roof styles include:

- Hip (square or rectangular).
- Gable (pitched).

Other roof styles include:

- Mansard.
- Flat.
- Gambrel.
- Shed.
- Saltbox.

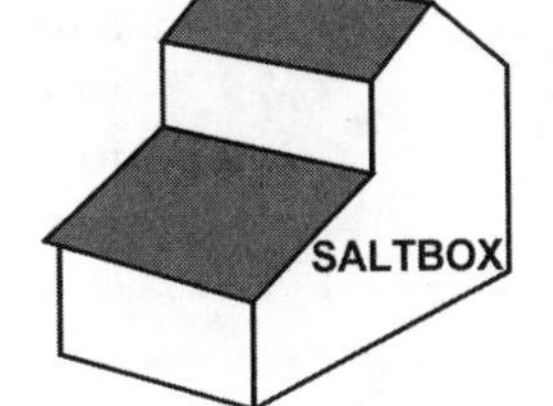

Roof

There are other parts of the roof that are more visible and might be more familiar:

- The **eave** is the *lowest section of the roof that projects beyond the side walls.* It protects the property from the elements.
- The **soffit** is the *underside of an arch, beam, overhang, or eave*. It is often ventilated to provide adequate airflow to the attic.
- The **fascia** is a *panel or board facing the outer edge of the soffit.* If the property has gutters, they are fastened to the fascia. Fascia can act as decorative trim to give the roof a finished look. Victorian and Tudor style homes often feature fascia board, giving them a distinctive look.

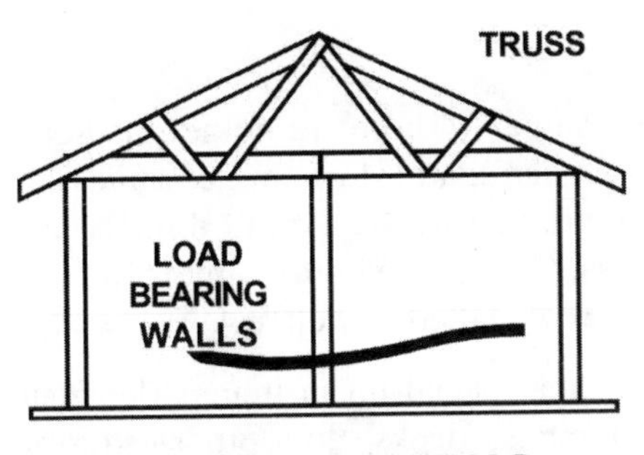

TRUSS ROOFING

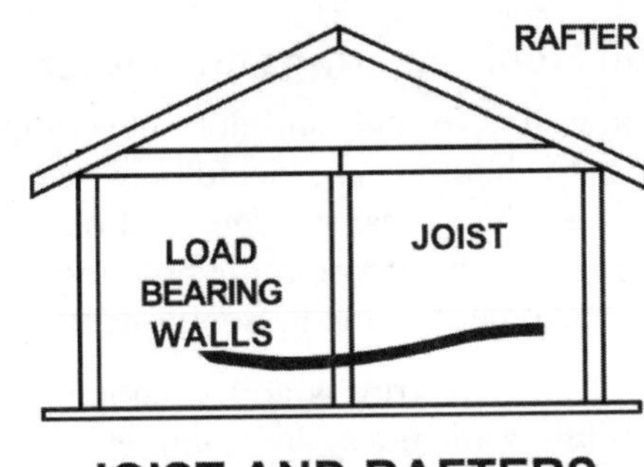

JOIST AND RAFTERS

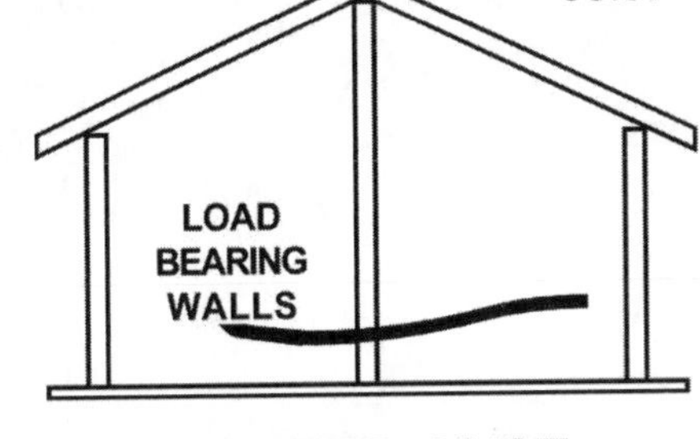

SLOPED JOIST

Flashing

Once the roof is in place, **flashing** is added *to cover joints where two or more types of materials join together for the purpose of preventing water from penetrating the joint* (e.g., metal over the seam between a brick chimney and a shingle roof).

The illustration on the next page gives an overall look at how many of these components work together.

Exterior Finish Work

Exterior finish work, which protects the exposed surfaces from the elements, is completed as soon as final framing is finished. In most cases, *sheathing* is used. **Sheathing** is a *structural covering, often made of plywood, placed over a building frame's exterior wall studs or roof rafters.* For the roof, sheathing is added and covered by a roofing paper and then roofing material, such as asphalt shingles – one of the most common roofing materials used today.

Once the sheathing has been placed on the exterior of the property, siding can be added. **Siding** is the *outer covering for a building's exterior walls, designed to shed water and protect the building from the elements.* It is often made of vinyl, wood, steel, or aluminum. Many other types of exterior coverings are available, including stucco, brick, and stone.

Interior Finish Work

After the exterior finish work is complete, interior finish work begins. Interior finish work includes such elements as rough-ins, wallboard, and wall and floor coverings. In some cases, permits are needed for each type of interior finish work performed. Nevertheless, thorough inspections will follow, usually after each type of work is completed, to ensure it complies with all building codes and safety regulations.

Rough-Ins

The next step in the building process is to begin rough-ins. Essentially, these are items hidden later by finished walls, but are vital to the operation of the house. Rough-ins can include electrical wiring, plumbing, and heating and air-conditioning elements.

Wallboard

A common wall covering called **drywall,** also known as **plasterboard, wallboard,** or **sheetrock,** is *gypsum plaster sandwiched between two layers of coarse paper.* Today's drywall is mold resistant to avoid black mold accumulation. When the drywall is added, the property really begins to take shape.

Wall and Floor Coverings and Other Items

Painting, wall coverings, and floor coverings come next. There are numerous floor coverings to choose from, including wood, carpet, laminate, vinyl, and ceramic tile. Light fixtures, electrical switches and outlets, plumbing fixtures, and cabinetry are also installed at this point in the building process. If there are built-in items such as kitchen equipment or media components, they are installed as well.

Finally, all interior trim is added, along with other special finish items. The final exterior finish includes the completion of porches, decks, and other exterior components.

EXTERIOR PARTS

1. Flashing
2. Fascia
3. Eaves
4. Soffit
5. Siding
6. Lintel
7. Foundation
8. Gutter
9. Downspout
10. Gable
11. Corner Board
12. Porch
13. Shed Roof
14. Post
15. Double Hung Window
16. Window Frame
17. Window Sash
18. Sill
19. Door

INTERIOR PARTS

1. Rafters
2. Studs
3. Beam or Girder
4. Joists
5. Header
6. Bearing Wall
7. Sheathing
8. Drywall, Plasterboard, or Wallboard
9. Basement/Crawlspace
10. Foundation Wall
11. Footer (below grade of foundation wall)
12. Subfloor
13. Sill Plate

Construction Completion

At this point in the construction process, the site should have received its final landscaping with grass seed and straw applied (or sod installed). The contractors have removed their tools and materials. All debris and discarded materials have been removed. The building is complete when the appropriate authorities have approved the structure for final occupancy. A certificate of occupancy is then issued for the property.

Energy Efficiencies and Tie-Ins

Energy efficiency is an important consideration in home building, especially with regard to long-term cost savings to clients. It is also regulated by building codes. A variety of insulation options is available to builders, but certain types work best for specific areas. It is important for real estate professionals to be aware of what type of insulation should be used in each area of a client's property.

R-Factor and R-Value

INSULATION

To help keep property warm in the winter and cool in the summer, insulation is installed. The parts of a structure that need to be insulated include the floor, walls, and ceilings. Insulation is rated by an **R-Factor**, which is a *way to measure the insulating value or resistance to heat flow through a material or an object.* Insulation's **R-Value** is *its R-Factor multiplied by the amount of material.* Thus, the more effective the insulation, the higher the R-Value it will have.

New York State Insulation Regulations

New York State regulates insulation requirements through the New York State Energy Code. This Code includes information on where insulation is to be installed and what materials are used, among other regulations.

Types of Insulation

Insulation is installed once the main structure is complete. There are several types of insulation, including:

- **Blanket insulation.** This insulation often comes in a pre-measured width to pair with standard stud, joist, or rafter spacing. It is made of a mineral fiber, such as fiberglass, enclosed in a paper covering.
- **Foamed-in insulation.** This type of insulation is sprayed into an area. It starts as a liquid, but expands into a plastic solid. It is often made of a polyurethane mixture and works well for insulating irregularly shaped spaces.
- **Loose-fill or blown-in insulation.** This type of insulation is blown into an area, often the attic space. It is made of fiber pellets or loose fibers and is good at filling small, tight areas.
- **Rigid insulation.** Rigid insulation is commonly used on basement walls and can come in a variety of thicknesses. It is made of a fibrous material, such as fiberglass or polyurethane.
- **Reflective insulation.** Reflective insulation is used between roof rafters, joists, or wall studs. It is known for its reflective surface that either contains or resists heat to keep a space warm or cool. It should be exposed to an open air space to work properly.

Major Systems

Real estate licensees might hear questions like, "This furnace looks old. How many years do they last?" and "What are those vents on the roof used for?" The major systems of a well-functioning structure – electrical, plumbing, ventilation, heating, and cooling – are begun in the next phase of the construction process.

Ventilation

Interior air can contain high levels of pollutants and irritants, including dust, pet dander, and chemicals, as well as high moisture levels. These can have a serious health impact on those living in the home, and can also cause problems to the structure itself. Properties need effective ventilation for the occupants' and the building's well-being. *Effective ventilation* means both a controlled ventilation rate and a means of distributing fresh air to habitable spaces.

Ventilation Systems

Ventilation systems are often comprised of an exhaust fan and ducts to remove stale and polluted air from the building. To ensure proper ventilation, the ventilation rate should be sized so the building has a minimum ventilation rate of **15 cubic feet per minute (CFM) per person**. This rate should be continuous when the property is occupied.

Natural ventilation is achieved when properties rely on windows and natural airflow through cracks in the building for ventilation. Even if a property is drafty, it may not have a reliable source of fresh air, since natural ventilation also depends on factors such as temperature and wind. Since outdoor ventilation cannot be controlled, there is no way to ensure fresh air is coming in. In this case, other ventilation options may be considered.

There are many different techniques and strategies for providing proper ventilation. Examples of ventilation systems include:

- **Balanced ventilation.** This type of ventilation system requires the use of two fans: One to remove moist and polluted air, and a second to replace the air being vented with fresh air. Balanced ventilation can be achieved with or without heat recovery as part of the system.
- **Exhaust ventilation.** This system uses an exhaust fan to remove air from the property. An equal amount of fresh air enters either by way of intentional wall ventilation openings or specially designed windows. This type of ventilation may be preferred to other systems in areas with moderate climates.
- **Supply ventilation.** Supply ventilation uses either a supply fan or a forced-air heating/cooling fan to deliver fresh air and, in some cases, can pressurize the property. This type of system may be preferred to other systems during months requiring cooling.
- **Spot or source point ventilation.** This form of ventilation uses bathroom and kitchen exhaust fans. These are generally operated on an intermittent basis for cooking and bathing, and are not necessarily a substitute for occupant ventilation.

Heating Systems

The heating system of a house is comprised of several elements depending on what is in use. These elements can include the following:

- Boiler
- Registers
- Radiators
- Furnace or heat pump
- Flue
- Thermostat
- Ducts and ductwork

Depending on the type of fuel the system uses, there may also be electrical connections, gas lines, or oil/fuel storage.

Today there are many alternative heating systems available, and solar and radiant heating are becoming popular. The three most common heating systems are hot water, steam, and forced warm air (electric heat, oil-fired heat, or gas-fired heat).

Hot Water System

This system consists of a boiler, pipes, and convectors or radiators. It relies on a process of heating and cooling liquid to heat a home. A boiler, typically located in the basement, heats water and sends it to pipes located throughout the walls of the home. The pipes move the water to the convectors or radiators that transfer the heat to the air and warm the rooms in a building.

Steam System

Like the hot water system, the steam system needs a boiler, pipes, and convectors or radiators to operate. Steam is produced in the boiler and moves through the pipes to convectors or radiators that transfer heat into the room. Steam systems are either one- or two-pipe systems. In the one-pipe system, steam and condensation travel through the same pipe. In the two-pipe system, they travel through different pipes. Steam systems are considered less effective than hot water systems and are often found in older buildings.

Forced Warm Air System

Most people are familiar with forced warm air systems, since most buildings today include forced-air furnaces. The components of this system include a furnace (with a blower), a heat source (i.e., gas, oil, wood, electricity, etc.), distribution ducts, and return air ducts. In this system, air is heated in the furnace and moves through ductwork to warm each room. Cool air is then recirculated through return air ducts.

There are three types of heating options available for furnaces:

- An **electric** furnace consists of a cabinet, blower, heating elements, and controls. With this type of furnace, resistance heating elements heat air to warm each room. Most electrical heating in New York does not incorporate a furnace. Each room is individually heated and has its own thermostat. This is called cellular construction and the cost is not much higher than oil or gas.
- The **oil** furnace consists of the cabinet, heat exchanger, burner, fire box, and blower. The air is heated when oil is burned in a chamber and the blower moves air through the ductwork to warm the building.
- The **gas** furnace consists of a cabinet, heat exchanger, blower, gas valve, and burner assembly. Air is heated in a gas-burning chamber and a fan moves it through the ducts to heat a building.

Air Conditioning Systems

In recent years, air conditioning in a home has become less of a luxury and more of a "must have" item. It is becoming standard in new buildings, and older buildings are being retrofitted to include air conditioning.

Air Conditioning Components

Components of an air conditioner include a condenser, condenser fan, compressor, evaporator and blower, and a liquid refrigerant. The condenser needs outside air to operate, thus, air conditioning units are found outside. Basically, to make cool air, the compressor moves the liquid refrigerant to the evaporator where it absorbs heat from air passing over the coils, thereby cooling the air forced through the room.

Air- or Water-Cooled Systems

Air-conditioning units are either cooled by air or water, or a combination referred to as evaporative cooled condensing units. Evaporative systems are most commonly used in commercial construction. Water-cooled systems often use cooling towers to do their job. Air-cooled units rely on expelling heat outside and are most often used in residential construction.

British Thermal Unit Ratings

Determining the correct size of the furnace or air conditioner a house needs can be a difficult task. Not only must the size of the house be taken into consideration, but also the number of windows, type of foundation, amount of ventilation, and how it is insulated.

To determine the appropriate size of the furnace or air conditioning unit needed, knowing how many British Thermal Units the house loses per hour is essential. A **British Thermal Unit (BTU),** the common measurement of heating capacity, is the *amount of heat needed to raise the temperature of one pound of water by one degree Fahrenheit.*

For example, a 2,000-square-foot house loses about 60,000 BTUs per hour. Theoretically, it would require a 60,000 BTU furnace – but then the furnace or air conditioner would have to run constantly. Instead, to save energy and save the homeowner money, HVAC specialists add 20–30% to their estimates. So in this example, the house could have an 80,000 BTU furnace installed.

To determine how long a furnace will run before it reaches the desired temperature, simply divide the BTUs lost by the BTUs the furnace has:

60,000 ÷ 80,000 = 75%

This means the furnace would run about 75% of the time.

Air conditioning calculations are different than those for a furnace because additional factors are considered. Since heat rises and tries to escape, a less powerful air conditioner is needed.

Heat Pumps

Electric heat pumps are an alternative to traditional heating and cooling systems. Heat pumps are more energy efficient than furnaces, and only one unit is needed instead of two.

A distinct disadvantage to heat pumps is that they are effective only in moderate climates. However, in recent years, more refined heat pump systems have been introduced and are an improvement over earlier systems, which lacked efficiency once the outside temperature dropped below a certain level.

Lately, it has been common to combine these systems with traditional forced-air systems, creating a dual system. Other variations of the heat pump include the air-to-air heat pump, which draws on the outside air, even in the winter, as a heat source and the geothermal heat pump system, which utilizes the outside ground temperature to convert to inside heating and cooling.

Plumbing Systems

The plumbing system of a building is comprised of many elements:

- Piping
- Sinks
- Drains
- Toilets
- Tubs
- Vents
- Showers
- Valves
- Hot water tank (gas or electric)
- Faucets

The piping includes cold water lines, hot water lines, and wastewater lines (sewer lines). Gas lines are often included as part of the plumbing system. It is important to understand that supply lines carry water under pressure from the source. Water heaters are specially designed to retain this pressure when delivering hot water.

Water Heating

There are a variety of appliances that can bring hot water into a building, including hot water heaters and tankless water heaters. Most hot water heaters in New York are tank-type heaters in which water is continually kept heated and ready for use. Tank sizes start at 30 gallons, although most homes have a tank between 40-75 gallons. Typically, units holding 30-40 gallons are found in one-bathroom homes, and 50-gallon or more tanks are found in two- to three-and-one-half bathroom homes.

Recently, tankless water heaters have become popular. They do not retain water in a traditional tank. Instead, water is heated by a heating coil when it is needed. Tankless heaters are more energy efficient since they do not heat water continuously, only when hot water is needed.

Types of Piping

Plumbing requires a system of pipes for water supply and drainage. Most jurisdictions allow for several types of piping materials, including:

- **Cast iron.** Used as drainage piping and found in municipal water systems. Cast iron is incredibly durable and lasts for many years. The downside is it can corrode from the inside.
- **Galvanized.** Steel with a protective coating designed to extend its life. It is often used for water lines, but cannot be used for gas lines.
- **Copper.** Ideal for water lines and generally considered superior to other types of piping. It can be expensive, but it is very durable since it rarely, if ever, corrodes.
- **Brass.** Rarely used anymore due to its expense.
- **PVC.** A type of plastic piping popular in plumbing construction and drainage systems, it is economical and resistant to rust and corrosion. PVC pipe cannot be used for hot water – though other types of plastic piping can be used.
- **PEX.** A flexible (cross-linked polyethylene) piping that is popular because it is resistant to bursting if the lines freeze. Plumbers can avoid using a lot of elbows and joints (or other connectors) to make more continuous piping runs.

Older homes may have water lines made from iron, steel, lead, or other galvanized materials. Lead pipes are extremely hazardous since they can contaminate drinking water. Clients should be advised that lead pipes should be replaced.

Domestic Water

Water comes into a building from a series of pipes. The specifics on how the water gets to your home depend on where you live. If you live in a metropolitan city or a suburb near a city, you probably get your water through the public water supply. If you live in an area beyond the city, such as a rural area, you may depend on a well water supply. Water is brought into the pipes through pressure from the main water supply. When repairs are needed, a curb shut-off temporarily cuts off water to your home from the main water supply.

Pipe Sizing for Adequate Pressures

When you take a shower or wash your hands, adequate water pressure is not something you usually think about – until it is not there. Building codes offer standards for maximum and minimum water pressure. A guideline for adequate water pressure is *five gallons of water per minute*. Low water pressure often results from a number of factors, including:

- Problems in the underground lines leading up to the house.
- Mineral deposits on the inside of a pipe.
- Well pumps with low pressure.

Pressure can often be restored by increasing pipe size, or repairing or replacing clogged pipes.

Plumbing Fixture Venting Requirements

Buildings need proper ventilation to prevent harmful gases from coming into living spaces. Building codes provide standards for plumbing system venting requirements. In plumbing, the vent system consists of pipes that provide airflow through wastewater piping. The vent system connects to a pipe on the roof called a vent stack, and releases gases into the air, rather than back into the building.

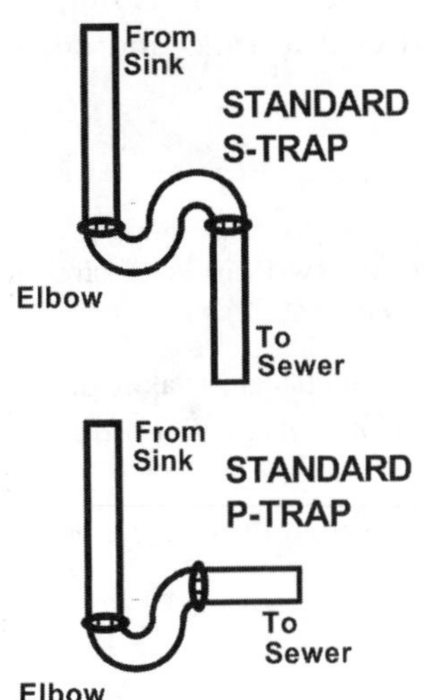

Drain Traps

The purpose of a drain trap is to keep some water in the elbow of a pipe so fumes or gases from the sewer do not escape back into the drain. Older-style S-traps have been replaced in most building codes with **P-traps**. It has been determined that P-traps are better at stopping the backflow of gases and fumes, as an S-trap's water seal can be broken more easily. When the water in the S-trap emits a gurgling sound, it is a sign the water seal is broken and a small amount of sewer gas has escaped back through the drain opening of the sink.

Electrical Systems

Utility companies supply power to buildings by providing electricity through power lines. Power cables are located either underground or aboveground. **Service lateral** is an underground power supply line, and **service drop** is the aboveground supply line going from the service pole to a building. For the most part, homeowners are responsible for everything else (upgrading a breaker box, for example).

A building's electrical system is comprised of several elements:

- Wiring distribution box
- Circuit breaker box and circuit breakers
- Fuses
- Lights, lighting fixtures, and light switches
- Wall outlets

Voltage, Amperage, and Capacity Requirements

Voltage is *a measure of the force that pushes electricity through a wire.* Most residential circuits operate at 110 volts, while larger appliances require 220-volt circuits.

Amperage is *the amount of electricity going through the wire – measured in amps.* Most residential service is a minimum of 100 amps, although newer construction more typically requires 200-amp service. A structure's electric service panel often contains the main disconnect switch (to cut power to the whole structure), as well as individual circuit breakers and fuses. The amperage capacity can usually be found on the main disconnect switch. This number (e.g., 100 or 200) identifies amperage capacity.

Power consumption is measured in **watts** or kilowatts. High-wattage items draw large electrical current. If the wiring is too thin, it may get hot as the device attempts to pull more power. Existing wiring in older houses without updated electrical services often cannot handle microwave ovens, air conditioners, and other high-drain power items common today. Worn or frayed wiring can also significantly reduce the wire's load capacity and increase the risk of fire.

Most building codes also require kitchens and bathrooms to have specially grounded outlets, called **ground fault interrupters** (GFI), which turn off power at the outlet instantly if the device or appliance plugged into it gets wet, shorts out, or malfunctions. These types of outlets are usually required next to sinks and other potentially wet and/or hazardous areas.

Fuses and Circuit Breakers

To reduce the risk of overloading a wire's capacity, there are two kinds of circuit protectors:

- A **circuit breaker** is *a device,* usually located inside the electrical breaker panel or circuit breaker box, *designed to break its electrical connection should an overload occur.*
- **Fuses** are *protective devices for a wiring system that contain a wire designed to melt and open the circuit when overheating occurs.*

Wiring Materials

Various electrical cabling materials are available to serve different purposes. Two of the most common types are aluminum and copper.

Aluminum cabling is a good conductor of electricity and is found in buildings constructed after 1965. It is also used in many power grids and high-voltage transmission lines. Aluminum cable is less expensive than copper and weighs less. **Copper** conducts better than aluminum. It is also easy to bend and can take a high degree of heat without substantial damage.

Other types of wiring include:

- **BX cable.** Armored cable, which is a grouping of wires wrapped in a metallic covering to protect it from damage.
- **Romex.** Cable wrapped in plastic that contains two or more conductors; is relatively easy to install and cost effective.
- **Conduit.** Electric wiring enclosed in a metal or plastic pipe; can be flexible or rigid, with rigid offering more protection.
- **Greenfield.** Flexible conduit, not designed to be used in rainy, wet, or damp areas.

National Electrical Code

The **National Electrical Code**® (NEC) provides for the safe installation of electrical equipment and wiring. The code is a U.S. standard and is part of the **Uniform Fire Code™** created by the National Fire Protection Association (NFPA). The **New York Board of Fire Underwriters** provides inspection services to ensure that installations comply with the NEC.

As of 1962, the NEC required that new 120-volt household receptacle outlets for general-purpose use be both grounded and polarized.

- A **grounded circuit** is connected to the ground for safety, limiting voltage buildup and providing an alternate route for electrical current flow.
- **Polarized outlets** have one slot larger than the other so items can be plugged in only one way. One side is hot (or live) and the other side is neutral. By limiting the path of the electrical current, the risk of electrocution is reduced.

Mandated Warranties and Guarantees

Some homeowners encounter problems during home improvement construction or when building a home. For example, a contractor might not show up at the agreed upon timeframe. And sometimes issues crop up after a home is completed, such as a plumbing problem that happens soon after the owners move in. To better protect homeowners, New York implemented the General Business Law 36-A and B. This law provides regulations that home improvement contractors must follow, and warranties that home builders must extend to buyers.

Home Improvement

New York General Business Law 36-A provides information on laws governing home improvement. A few important points of this law dictate that home improvement contracts exceeding $500 should contain:

- The approximate dates when the work will begin and end and a description of the work to be performed.

- A notice to the owner from the contractor about mechanic's liens.
- A schedule of progress payment, if needed.
- A notice to the owner that the owner has until midnight of the third business day after the contract has been signed to cancel the contract.

Law 36-A also provides information on penalty for fraud, including:

- An owner who signed a contract with fraudulent terms or statements may sue a contractor for a penalty of $500 plus attorney's fees in addition to other damages.
- Contractors who do not deposit funds into an escrow account (or provide a bond of contract of indemnity or irrevocable letter of credit) will be subject to a civil penalty not to exceed $250 per violation or 5% of the contract price (the total penalty will not exceed $2,500 per contract).

New Home Construction

New York General Business Law 36-B provides information on laws governing a new home. The warranties include:

- One year for workmanship.
- Two years for plumbing, heating, electrical, cooling, and ventilation systems.
- Six years for material defects.

New York State law requires the installation of a functioning **smoke detector** and **carbon monoxide detector** in all one- and two-family residential properties as well as residential condominiums and cooperatives.

SUMMARY

1. **Building codes** *set construction requirements.* **Building inspection** is the *process whereby government authorities, usually state or local, are charged with ensuring compliance with prevailing building codes*. A **Certificate of Occupancy** is *issued to the builder after all inspections have been made and the property is deemed fit for occupancy.*
2. The **New York Energy Conservation Construction Code** provides minimum standards requirements of energy efficiencies for new commercial and residential buildings.
3. New York State has specific on-site well and sanitary waste system requirements. One of two types of sanitary waste systems is usually found in a residential property: **Septic system** or **municipal wastewater system**.
4. Builders should take factors such as *drainage, landscaping, appurtenances, shading, walkways, and zoning* into consideration when constructing or renovating a building. These are examples of **site use**.
5. The foundation, which typically consists of walls and footers, is the basis for a structure. A **foundation** can be *concrete slab, pier and beams, crawl space, or basement.* Footers are always below the frost line. Framing, the load-bearing skeleton of a structure, can be made of wood,

concrete block, or metal. **Beams** and **studs** *serve as the building frame*. Studs should not be less than two by four inches in load-bearing partitions. There are three basic types of framing: **Platform construction**, **post and beam construction**, and **balloon construction**. Platform construction is the most popular.

6. The roof is typically added after framing. Roof components include **roof rafters, eaves, soffits,** and **fascia.** A roof's **pitch** is the degree of its slope.

7. Exterior finish work includes **sheathing**, a *structural covering, often made of plywood, placed over a building frame's exterior wall studs or roof rafters,* and **siding**, the *outer covering for a building's exterior walls, designed to shed water and protect the building from the elements.* **Flashing** is added to cover joints where two or more materials join together.

8. Interior finish work comes near the end of construction. It includes **rough-ins**, such as the addition of electrical wiring, plumbing, and heating and air-conditioning elements.

9. **R-Factor** is *a way to measure the insulating value or resistance to heat flow through a material or an object.* **R-Value** is *the insulation's R-Factor multiplied by the amount of material.* There are several types of insulation options, including *blanket, foamed-in, loose-fill, blown-in, rigid, and reflective*. The more effective the insulation, the higher the R-Value it will have.

10. Ventilation systems are often comprised of an exhaust fan and ducts to remove stale and polluted air from the building. To ensure proper ventilation, the ventilation rate should be sized so the building has a minimum ventilation rate of **15 cubic feet per minute (CFM) per person**. Ventilation systems include: Spot or source point, balanced, exhaust, and supply.

11. Common types of heating systems include: Hot water system, steam system and forced warm air system. Furnaces are either electric, oil, or gas.

12. Air conditioning units are either cooled by air or water, or a combination referred to as evaporative cooled condensing units. To determine the appropriate size of the furnace or air conditioning unit needed, knowing how many British Thermal Units the house loses per hour is essential. A **British Thermal Unit (BTU),** the common measurement of heating capacity, is the *amount of heat needed to raise the temperature of one pound of water by one degree Fahrenheit.* Electric **heat pumps** are an alternative to traditional heating and cooling systems. Heat pumps are more energy efficient than furnaces, and only one unit is needed instead of two. It has become common to combine these systems with traditional forced-air systems, creating a dual system.

13. Plumbing requires a system of pipes for water supply and drainage. Water is normally brought to homes through municipal water systems or well water supply. The New York State Department of Health has specific requirements for well construction. Pipes can be made of a variety of materials, including cast iron, galvanized, copper, brass, or plastic piping such as PVC or PEX.

14. Electricity is brought into a home through aboveground or underground cables. **Service lateral** is *an underground power supply line* and **service drop** is *aboveground wire line*. The electrical system is comprised of several elements, which include the wiring distribution box, circuit breaker box, circuit breakers, fuses, lights and lighting fixtures, light switches, and wall outlets. Standard electrical service in New York calls for a minimum of **200 amps**.

15. Aluminum cable is lightweight and used in many power grids and high voltage transmission lines. Copper cable can take a lot of heat without a lot of damage and is often used in building wire systems. Other cabling includes BX cable, Romex, Conduit, and Greenfield.

16. A contractor building or renovating a home must follow specific regulations for home improvements and extend warranties for new home builds under **New York General Business Law 36-A and B**.

9-A

Environmental Issues and Property Concerns

In This Session

In this session, you'll learn how environmental issues affect real estate. You'll review important federal environmental protection laws and learn to recognize common man-made and natural property hazards. You'll also become aware of your responsibility in disclosing environmental hazards and in ensuring that others do, too.

You'll learn:

- What New York State environmental law requires.
- Why the EPA was established and what it does.
- What constitutes wetlands and why they are protected.
- How to recognize common environmental hazards and how to deal with them.
- The real estate professional's obligations related to environmental issues.

Key Terms

- Asbestos
- Carbon Monoxide
- Chlorofluorocarbons (CFCs)
- Due Diligence
- Electromagnetic Fields
- Environmental Impact Statement (EIS)
- External Environmental Hazards
- External Obsolescence
- Freon
- Friable
- Groundwater
- High-Tension Power Lines
- Internal Environmental Hazards
- Methamphetamine
- Mold
- Mycotoxin
- Nuisance
- Radon Gas
- Residential Lead-Based Paint Hazard Reduction Act
- Sick Building Syndrome
- Stachybotrys
- Transformers
- Underground Storage Tanks (USTs)
- Urea-formaldehyde
- Wetlands

Environmental Issues

For many, a property's location determines its value. If a buyer had the choice between a house next to a beautiful lake or a landfill, she would likely choose the lake because the environment in and around a home is important. However, what if the lake is quietly being contaminated by a company using it as a dumping ground for waste byproducts? Suddenly the property is no longer as attractive, even though on the surface, it appears fine.

Federal and state regulations dictate that specific details must be disclosed when potential environmental hazards could be present in and around a property. Real estate professionals must often advise clients to call in environmental scientists, engineers, or environmental attorneys when hazards are suspected.

Environmental Protection at the Federal Level

For many years, people pumped pollutants into streams, lakes, and the air with little thought about how this contaminated the earth. Environmental laws were established out of concern over the deteriorating quality of the air, land, and water.

In 1970, the **National Environmental Policy Act (NEPA)** was enacted to:

Declare a national policy which will encourage productive and enjoyable harmony between man and his environment; to promote efforts which will prevent or eliminate damage to the environment and biosphere and stimulate the health and welfare of man; enrich the understanding of the ecological systems and natural resources important to the Nation; and establish a Council on Environmental Quality (Pub. L. 91-190, Sec. 2 [42 USC § 4321]).

The NEPA requires federal agencies to prepare an **environmental impact statement (EIS)** for any project that would have a significant effect on the environment. An **EIS** *details a project's impact on energy use, sewage systems, drainage, water facilities, schools, and other environmental, economic, and social areas.* The NEPA applies to all federal development projects, such as dams and highways, and to private projects that require a license or permit from a federal agency or a federal loan.

The Environmental Protection Agency

Prior to 1970, environmental concerns such as air pollution, water, solid waste, and radiation were handled by different federal departments, bureaus, committees, and offices. These entities eventually came together to form one independent agency – the Environmental Protection Agency (EPA).

The EPA is tasked with creating and enforcing environmental protection standards, helping others with environmental pollution problems through the use of grants and other means, assisting the Council on Environmental Quality (CEQ) by suggesting policies and procedures for environmental protection, and providing research on environmental issues (such as the effect of pollution on the earth and methods for controlling pollution). Since its inception, the EPA has established many important laws to protect the country's land, air, and water.

Important federal laws to be aware of include:

- Clean Air Act (CAA).
- Clean Water Act (CWA).
- Comprehensive Environmental Response, Compensation, and Liability Act (CERCLA).

- Superfund Amendments and Reauthorization Act (SARA).
- Resource Conservation and Recovery Act (RCRA).
- Safe Drinking Water Act (SDWA).

The Clean Air Act

The Clean Air Act requires the EPA to develop air quality standards for existing pollutants, along with establishing air standards for new sources of pollution. It also regulates air pollutant emissions, determines acceptable levels for emissions, and sets deadlines for compliance.

The Act established the procedures for how the EPA and individual states work together to set and enforce standards. For example, states are required to prepare a *state implementation plan* (SIP) for meeting national air quality standards. States are also authorized to stop projects that interfere with clean air objectives.

The Clean Water Act

Under the Clean Water Act, national water quality standards are determined by the EPA. The Act also created a regulatory structure for the discharge of pollution into waterways and gave the EPA the right to enact control programs. It also set up a permit system whereby anyone who wants to discharge pollutants from a point source needs a permit, and any discharges with unacceptable amounts of pollutants are prohibited.

During the early years of the Act's enforcement, the EPA and governmental entities focused more on specific pollutants and sources of pollutants, such as municipal treatment plants or industries. In recent years, the focus has been on the bigger picture – protecting clean waterways from pollution and revitalizing contaminated waterways.

Comprehensive Environmental Response, Compensation, and Liability Act

The **Comprehensive Environmental Response, Compensation, and Liability Act,** or CERCLA, addresses *what to do with closed or abandoned waste sites.* It created mandatory waste-site requirements and established consequences for when hazardous materials were released at the sites.

Additionally, a tax was created for the chemical and petroleum industries. The tax revenue raised was placed in a trust fund used for cleaning up out-of-control or abandoned hazardous waste sites where no clearly responsible party could be identified. Because of the trust fund, CERCLA is also known as the **Superfund.**

CERCLA gave the federal government broad authority to respond when hazardous materials are released or when there is a threat of release. There were two types of response actions authorized:

- **Short-term** situations require immediate action for removal of hazardous materials because of serious life-threatening issues.
- **Long-term** situations require action to permanently or significantly reduce dangerous exposure to hazardous materials, but are not immediately life threatening.

CERCLA also established that liability for contaminated property be transferred to new owners, thus forcing potential buyers and lenders to conduct **due diligence**, or *an environmental assessment of the property to determine any potential liability*, by having a consultant determine its integrity.

Environmental Assessment

An environmental assessment typically consists of four phases:

- **Phase I: Investigative**. Property is inspected and records pertaining to it for a period of 50 years are reviewed. If no problems are found, the process may end here.
- **Phase II: Testing**. Done to determine the problem (if any) and the severity. If contamination is found, the next phase is begun.
- **Phase III: Cleanup**. At this point, local, state, and federal agencies, and other organizations, may participate in the cleanup effort. After cleanup is complete, Phase IV is initiated.
- **Phase IV: Management** of the site. Includes routine checks to prevent new problems.

The Superfund Amendments and Reauthorization Act

Closely related to CERCLA, is SARA, or the **Superfund Amendments and Reauthorization Act**. SARA amended CERCLA in 1986 as a result of the administration of the fund. The SARA increased the Superfund to $8.5 billion and required review of the standards and requirements in state and federal environmental laws and regulations. It also established new enforcement authorities, increased state involvement in administration of the Act, and created new settlement tools and procedures.

The SARA recognizes hazardous waste sites cause health problems and stresses the need and importance of permanent remedies along with the development and use of new treatment technologies for waste-site cleanup. The scope of involvement for decision making in site cleanup was broadened by the SARA, encouraging greater public participation in determining how sites should be cleaned up. Finally, the Act required the EPA to revise its assessment of the risk to public health and the environment for uncontrolled sites and revised how those sites are ranked for cleanup.

The Act also created a concept called "innocent landowner immunity," which does not hold landowners liable if they did not create the contamination and were not present on the site when the title was taken, providing there is proof – preferably an environmental audit.

The Resource Conservation and Recovery Act

The **Resource Conservation and Recovery Act** (RCRA, pronounced "rick-rah") gave the EPA the authority to control hazardous waste throughout its entire life cycle, including its generation, transportation, treatment, storage, and disposal.

In 1984, Hazardous and Solid Waste Amendments to RCRA require land disposal of hazardous waste to be phased out. Additional amendments in 1986 enabled the EPA to address environmental problems that could result from underground tanks storing petroleum and other hazardous substances. RCRA focuses only on active and future facilities and does not address abandoned or historical sites, which are covered by CERCLA.

The Safe Drinking Water Act

The **Safe Drinking Water Act** (SDWA) established standards for water intended for human consumption that include the amount of contaminants permitted, and how frequently public water sources are tested and reported. The Act requires that public water suppliers report violations to consumers. Public water supplies are tested for different types of bacteria, chemical pollutants, and mineral levels.

Ninety-five percent of New York State's population gets its water from public supplies. The **New York State Department of Health** (NYSDOH) is responsible for regulating drinking water. In cooperation with other agencies, the NYSDOH:

- Ensures the quality and quantity of public water supplies.
- Regulates the operations of suppliers.
- Authorizes plans for new subdivisions.
- Sets standards for private water supplies (well water) and sewage systems (septic systems).

Water supplies serving subdivisions in New York State are regulated under the public health law, which determines water supply requirements, and the environmental conservation law, which includes sewerage service regulations. Installation and approval of individual residential on-site wastewater treatment systems in New York are controlled by the following:

- New York State Department of Health (NYSDOH) for systems of less than 1,000 gallons per day
- New York State Department of Environmental Conservation (NYSDEC) for systems of 1,000 gallons or more per day

Private Water Supplies

The NYSDOH also oversees private well drilling. Well drillers must be licensed by the National Ground Water Association or equivalent, and registered with the Department of Environmental Conservation. The Residential Code of New York State determines the distances wells must be drilled from a potential contamination source. Well drilling includes any excavation done for the purpose of obtaining water, including:

- Drilled wells.
- Dug wells.
- Springs.
- Well points.

Homeowners must send well water samples to a lab for testing. This is the only way to determine if the water is contaminated. The NYSDOH can assist owners of private water sources should the water become contaminated. Experts recommend testing private wells at least once a year for bacteria, mineral content, and pH levels.

Wetlands

Wetlands can have a tremendous impact on the value of surrounding properties – not just individual homes but entire cities and communities. **Wetlands** are *ecosystems where the land is permeated with water, and are commonly referred to as swamps, bogs, and marshes.* The water lies either on or near the surface of the land, creating a highly conducive environment for the growth of plants and wildlife.

No two wetlands are exactly alike. One of the most famous is the Everglades in Florida. Some people think wetlands primarily tend to be in the southeastern portion of the United States, which is not true. Almost every state has some form of wetland.

Benefits of Wetlands

Wetland benefits include:

- Preventing flood damage by acting as a barrier between drier land, absorbing and slowing water that could overwhelm communities.
- Acting as a filtering system, trapping nutrients and sediment that can affect the quality of water, along with interfering with fish reproduction.
- Providing habitats and shelter for various wildlife and aquatic species.

In the past, many people did not understand the benefits of wetlands, viewing them as insect-infested places best converted to usable land. This viewpoint changed as wetland benefits became better understood. And because wetlands are beneficial, the government passed laws to protect them.

Clean Water Act and Wetlands

Federally, wetlands are protected under Section 404 of the Clean Water Act, which deals with the dredging or filling of waters in the United States, including wetlands. Section 404 is intended to minimize adverse actions that could damage wetlands and other areas. The U.S. Army Corps of Engineers regulates and enforces Section 404, with the EPA having ultimate authority.

In some states, the EPA has authorized state environmental protection agencies to work with the Army Corps of Engineers to enforce and monitor wetlands there. Some states have also passed their own wetland protection laws. The New York State Department of Environmental Conservation (NYSDEC) has established the **Freshwater Wetlands Act** and **Statewide Minimum Land-Use Regulations for Freshwater Wetlands** under the Environmental Conservation Law of New York State.

Local governments that voluntarily assume regulatory authority over their wetlands must implement and adhere to the standards outlined in these Acts. Variances can be requested by submitting a proposal to commissioners that explains the social and economic benefits that would result.

Wetlands in New York State

In New York State, a protected wetland must cover an area of at least *12.4 acres, or have unusual significant importance*. Adjacent areas, within 100 feet of the wetland, may also qualify for protection if the area provides security to the wetland. Some activities that are *not* restricted and do *not* require a permit are:

- Trapping.
- Occasional use of motor vehicles.
- Maintaining existing structures.
- Some agricultural activities.
- Establishing walking trails.

Activities that are *not allowed or require a permit* are those that could permanently change or destroy the wetland habitat, including:

- Dredging,
- Draining,
- Clear-cutting,
- Grading,
- Altering a beaver dam,
- Filling, and
- Constructing roads, bulkheads, dams, docks, buildings, and parking lots.

To conform to the standards set by the Freshwater Wetlands Act, the NYSDEC maintains maps showing all protected wetlands. These maps may be obtained at the DEC regional office and other local government offices.

New York Environmental Law

When a person, entity, or government agency wants to initiate a project in New York State, the project must undergo an *environmental impact assessment*. Examples of such projects include the construction of residential developments and roads, as well as work in wetlands and other bodies of water.

Projects requiring an environmental impact assessment are classified as Type I. The process for review is directed by the State Environmental Quality Review Act (SEQR) and mandates that local governments consider the impact on the environment, as well as the social and economic benefits, when determining whether to proceed.

Projects that do not require an assessment are classified as Type II. Examples of these projects include replacing existing structures and minor construction.

Wastewater Treatment Standards

Residential properties with private wastewater treatment systems are regulated under Appendix 75-A by the New York State Department of Health (NYSDOH). Local health department standards must meet or exceed the state-defined standards. The NYSDOH sets standards for sewage flows, soil, and site appraisals, as well as appropriate separation distances from wells, streams, residences, and property lines.

Septic tank requirements are based on the number of bedrooms in the household and the results of percolation tests. Once the site has been "perced," the system can be installed. A soil percolation test, or perc test, determines the permeability of the soil in a particular area to assess the feasibility of a septic system.

Alternative wastewater treatment systems must be designed by a professional who oversees the construction of the system to make sure it is developed according to plan. Local health departments ensure standards are met.

Property Hazards

Devastating environmental accidents like Chernobyl, Three Mile Island, and Love Canal had serious repercussions for community members, such as increased incidences of cancer, and even death. It is clear that any property located near a perceived threat could be negatively associated with external environmental hazards. However, external factors are only half the picture.

Internal threats within a property might not be visible, but they can cause health problems. Many consumers research internal environmental threats before they consider buying a particular home or property. Real estate salespeople also need to stay current on environmental issues.

Nuisances and Environmental Hazards

A **nuisance** is *anything that interferes with the owner's right of quiet enjoyment*. This, by definition, means a nuisance originates from *another person's* property. Thus, a property owner cannot be a nuisance to herself; she can only be a nuisance to her neighbors.

If a nuisance is more or less permanent, it is referred to as an **external obsolescence**, and can affect property values in a neighborhood. Examples are noise from an airport or the stench from a factory farm. Both could hurt property values by making the property less desirable, and contribute to the neighborhood's decline.

By definition, a nuisance cannot contribute to a neighborhood or property values in a positive way. It can be either private or public. A private nuisance affects a private individual, and a public nuisance affects the public as a whole. Based on this definition, an environmental hazard might be classified as a nuisance depending on its specific circumstances. An **environmental hazard** is *a situation that exists with potential for harm to persons or property from conditions that exist outside or within a property.*

External Environmental Hazards

External environmental hazards are *those concerns that exist outside the boundaries of a property, which can have a significant impact on its value*. Visible signs of environmental damage give buyers a fear of contamination and make a property or neighborhood less desirable. Examples include toxic substances in nearby landfills, waterways with high levels of pollution, or thick smog from nearby factories.

Other less-quantifiable hazards may still pose a problem for a property or neighborhood, such as proximity to nuclear power plants or the presence of high-tension power lines. Regardless of the fact that scientific research has not produced conclusive evidence of risk, there is a strong perception among some buyers that these environmental factors are, at best, undesirable, and at worst, unsafe.

Internal Environmental Hazards

For many people, external environmental concerns might be a more serious issue, especially if a property is near a hazard that causes public concern, such as a nuclear power plant. However, **internal environmental hazards** or *hazards within a property* can be as dangerous, or more dangerous, than external hazards. The good news is that property owners and potential buyers have some power over fixing these problems, thus minimizing or eliminating them.

Examples of internal environmental hazards found in residential property or on the premises include the following:

- Asbestos
- Carbon monoxide
- Chlorofluorocarbons (CFCs) or hyfrochlorofluorocarbons (HCFCs)
- Electromagnetic fields
- Insects (ants, termites, bees, etc.)
- Lead
- Methamphetamine (meth) labs
- Mold
- Polychlorinated biphenyls (PCBs)
- Poor air quality
- Radon
- Rodents
- Urea-formaldehyde
- Underground storage tanks
- Uncapped gas wells
- Groundwater contamination

Liability

Any potential environmental hazard can cause great fear among sellers, buyers, and real estate professionals. In addition to concerns about associated health issues, there is also concern about liability. Buyers and sellers must consider future liability if a home is sold with a hazardous condition.

Presently, sellers are generally not held liable if they, in good faith, did not know adverse conditions existed. However, this could change, because some sellers have recently been held liable for environmental hazards they did not know about. Sellers must disclose any known hazard. In some situations, it may be appropriate to call in experts to evaluate the situation.

Man-Made Environmental Hazards

In addition to being external or internal, environmental hazards can be man-made or naturally occurring. Although there is usually a distinction between man-made and natural environmental concerns, some hazards fall into both categories. For instance, asbestos, lead, and electromagnetic fields occur naturally; however, the manipulation and use of these materials by man has made them hazardous.

Regardless of whether a hazard is man-made or natural, it is important to know how to identify it and how to deal with it.

Asbestos

Asbestos is a *fibrous material derived from a naturally occurring group of minerals*. The mining and use of asbestos began in the U.S. in the late 1800s and became more widespread during World War II. In the past, asbestos was commonly found in many building materials because of its insulating and heat- and fire-resistant properties. It was also embedded in various construction materials, such as cement and plastic, and was used to insulate pipes and duct work in older buildings and ceiling tiles. These **friable** materials, which are *easily crumbled or become powdery when manipulated by hand*, are some of the most dangerous asbestos-containing materials.

Asbestos is no longer used in construction, but the U.S. Department of Health and Human Services continues to classify it as a known carcinogen.

Dangers of Asbestos

As the small particles of asbestos are breathed in, they can become trapped in lung tissue or the digestive tract. Over time, the accumulation of particles causes inflammation and scarring. This, in turn, can lead to a variety of breathing problems and an increased risk for developing many different illnesses, including:

- **Asbestosis**. A lung disease that causes shortness of breath and is typically considered an occupational illness as it is caused by extended inhalation of asbestos fibers.
- **Mesothelioma**. A form of lung cancer typically considered an occupational illness, as it is caused by extended exposure to asbestos.
- **Lung and other cancers.**

Symptoms of Asbestos Exposure

It may be decades before a person exposed to asbestos develops symptoms or becomes ill. Common symptoms of exposure are:

- Cough.
- Difficulty swallowing.
- Anemia.
- Shortness of breath or wheezing.
- Swelling of the neck or face.

Testing

Typical testing procedures to determine the presence or level of asbestos (or other airborne contaminants) include:

- **Air testing**. Requires moving a determined amount of air across a filter, then examining captured particles under a microscope.

- **Bulk sampling**. Involves a certified asbestos handler removing a small piece of the suspect material and sending it to a laboratory.
- **Wipe sampling**. Involves gathering particles from a common surface, such as the floor or countertop, by wiping the area with a piece of filter paper.

Management

There is some debate over whether existing asbestos should be removed or left alone. Since it is thought to be a problem only when it becomes airborne, some people believe it is best not to disturb asbestos. Removal is an expensive process and must be done by EPA-licensed contractors. Some choose the option of monitoring and maintaining the asbestos product because, as long as it is kept in good condition, it is not a threat.

Removal of asbestos-containing materials is the only permanent solution to an asbestos problem. However, if the asbestos is in good condition and not likely to be disturbed, there are other methods of managing it in place:

- **Encapsulation** is the *process of applying a sealant to the asbestos-containing material, which penetrates the material's surface, preventing the release of the dangerous fibers.* Encapsulating with a penetrating sealant can make future removal of the asbestos-containing material more difficult. And because the encapsulant may begin to deteriorate, it must be regularly inspected.
- **Enclosure** involves *isolating asbestos material by using a sturdy, airtight barrier and is a possible temporary remedy for some asbestos problems.*

The **New York State Department of Labor** (NYSDOL) regulates the installation, removal, and enclosure of asbestos materials..

Carbon Monoxide

Carbon monoxide (CO), *a natural byproduct of fuel combustion, is a colorless, odorless gas released as fuel sources break down to produce heat*. Thus, CO is emitted by appliances such as furnaces, space heaters, fireplaces, water heaters, and stoves. When these appliances function properly, small, regulated amounts of CO are emitted and then dissipate. Unfortunately, if malfunctions occur, unacceptable levels of CO can be released. Larger amounts of CO can also be released when ventilation is inadequate.

Symptoms of Carbon Monoxide Poisoning

People begin to experience adverse effects as CO enters the bloodstream because it stops the blood from carrying oxygen throughout the body. Overexposure to CO, or CO poisoning, can cause:

- Dizziness.
- Headache.
- Blurred vision.
- Drowsiness.
- Nausea.
- Slowed response time.
- Unconsciousness.
- Death.

CO Detection

Because CO is invisible to the senses, it is difficult to detect and can easily be absorbed into the body. The most effective method to keep track of CO is with a CO detector. In addition to smoke detectors, **New York law requires all new homes to have a CO detector.** The law also requires **existing homes** to have an operable CO detector upon the sale of the home. This includes single- and multiple-family units, condos, and co-ops. New York City requires **all rental properties** to have a carbon monoxide detector.

Prevention

Appliances that produce carbon monoxide as a byproduct should be checked routinely to make sure they are functioning properly, and ventilation should be checked for adequacy. Homeowners with an attached garage should never leave cars running in it. Even with the garage door open, CO can enter the home at deadly levels.

Chlorofluorocarbons

Chlorofluorocarbons (CFCs) are *chemical compounds containing chlorine, fluorine, and carbon atoms, and are known to deplete the ozone layer*. Sold under the trademarked name of **Freon** for many years, the compound was *used as a coolant in refrigerators, air conditioners, and dehumidifiers*. CFCs were also commonly used as a propellant in aerosol cans and in fire suppression systems and devices. Use of these compounds began to be banned in the 1970s, when their detrimental effects on the earth's atmosphere were determined. Scientists therefore added hydrogen to create **hydrochloroflourocarbons (HCFCs)** as a substitute. While HCFCs break down before reaching the ozone layer, they still release some chlorine into the atmosphere, and are considered by the EPA to be a class II ozone-depleting substance and so they, too, are being phased out. These compounds have been replaced by **hydrofluorocarbons** (HFCs) in many current refrigerant/cooling systems. HFCs are less of a threat to the atmosphere since they do not contain chlorine.

Property managers and owners must comply with Clean Air Act regulations regarding these compounds, or face substantial fines. These laws include following proper disposal procedures for old appliances that contain CFCs or HCFCs. Owners must also maintain equipment to prevent coolant leaks. Fines have been assessed to owners who knowingly allow CFCs or HCFCs to leak from damaged equipment. Certified service personnel are required to work on such equipment, and the coolant must be recaptured while working on a unit. Service workers who allow these compunds to freely vent into the air can also face large fines, and even prison time.

Electromagnetic Fields

Electromagnetic fields (EMFs) *are invisible fields produced by electrically charged objects*. An electromagnetic field is similar to a magnet except an electrical current is needed to produce the field. Small electronic equipment in the home, such as hair dryers and computers, produces small electromagnetic fields.

Electromagnetic fields can affect other charged objects nearby. Small appliances are not usually a problem. High-tension power lines (large transmission cables carrying electrical energy), transformers (transferring power from one circuit to another), and secondary distribution lines create larger electromagnetic fields.

Suspected Health Risks

The larger electromagnetic fields created by high-tension power lines are suspected as the cause of hormonal changes, cancer, and behavioral abnormalities. The evidence for these health risks is controversial and, in some cases, contradictory. This does not mean that real estate licensees should ignore high-tension power lines next to a property they are trying to sell, because some buyers may be concerned about them.

The real concern is not health issues, as they have not been proven, but rather the public's perception and fear of health issues related to EMFs and high-tension power lines. Because properties near power lines are stigmatized, as the controversy grows, public fear grows. This fear often results in reduced property values.

Management

Most materials are not effective in blocking electromagnetic fields. Congress' Office of Technology Assessment recommends a policy of prudent avoidance when it comes to exposure to EMFs within the home. Prudent avoidance means:

- Testing areas for the strength of the field.
- Determining which electrical appliances and wiring emit the strongest fields.
- Reducing exposure by increasing distances from the sources by rearranging furniture and beds accordingly.

Other precautions include:

- Replacing electrical appliances with ones that do not use electricity.
- Turning off appliances when not in use.
- Using shields for some items, such as computer monitors and cell phones.
- Avoiding time outdoors beneath power lines.

Lead

Until 1978, lead was added to exterior and interior paint as a drying agent and for pigmentation. Also, lead pipes and solder were commonly used in plumbing systems in homes and businesses prior to the 1930s. Research found that digesting or inhaling lead or lead dust caused various health issues in children and adults.

Lead poisoning occurs via the nose and mouth – it must be breathed in or ingested. You cannot get lead poisoning by skin contact. Still, it is estimated that nearly one million children in the U.S. between the ages of one and five suffer from a high level of lead in the bloodstream.

Suspected Health Risks

The human body cannot differentiate between lead and calcium, so lead acts as calcium in the body and can stay in the bloodstream for weeks. From there, it can be absorbed by the bones, as calcium is, and remain permanently. Lead can cause serious, irreversible health problems. That is why it is discussed so much in the real estate business, and why disclosure is required.

In children, the list of symptoms associated with high or even low levels of lead poisoning is extensive. Some early signs of lead poisoning include chronic fatigue or hyperactivity, loss of appetite or weight loss, difficulty sleeping, irritability, and reduced attention span.

Adults also face serious dangers from lead poisoning, including fertility problems, high blood pressure, nerve damage, memory loss and concentration problems, muscle and joint pain, and birth defects in their children.

Water Contamination

Lead present in water is colorless, odorless, and tasteless. In older homes, it is wise to be alert for lead pipes. There is no remedy other than replacement. Water from lead pipes should be considered non-potable, or undrinkable. Another danger to the water supply in homes is well water contamination. Older pumps made of brass or bronze can leach lead into the water. Also, some wells were once packed with a lead collar, lead shot, or lead wool.

Homes built before 1988 often have copper pipes soldered together with lead-based solder, which can leach into the water. Water from this type of piping is usually considered safe if the water is not stagnant for more than six hours. If this kind of piping is in a home built prior to 1988, it is advised to let the water run for one to two minutes before using it for consumption. This ensures fresh water, less likely to have been contaminated from lead leaching.

In urban locations with municipal water supplies, many people do not realize that the pipe in the yard from the home to the water main is the responsibility of the homeowner. Often, when water pipes are replaced in older homes, the water main pipe is overlooked and should be inspected to ensure it is not made of lead.

Soil Contamination

Issues arise when lead-based paint begins to chip or flake. Paint peeling from the exterior of a property can fall into soil, contaminating it. Then, the soil can be tracked and deposited within the home as dust. Because of the damaging effect of lead and the potential exposure to lead from lead products used in home construction, the Residential Lead-Based Paint Hazard Reduction Act, or Title X, was passed.

Residential Lead-Based Paint Hazard Reduction Act

The **Residential Lead-Based Paint Hazard Reduction Act** *requires sellers, real estate licensees, property management companies, and landlords to disclose known lead paint hazards for homes built before 1978.* EPA and HUD regulations issued to implement these disclosures include:

- Disclosure of any known lead-based paint hazard in homes and any reports available from prior lead tests.
- A pamphlet about how to protect families from lead in homes must be given to buyers and renters.
- Homebuyers have a ten-day period (or other mutually agreed to time) to conduct a lead paint inspection or risk assessment at their own expense.
- Sellers, landlords, and real estate professionals must include certain language in sales contracts and/or lease contracts to ensure disclosure and notification actually take place (included in most standard board of real estate contracts).

Compliance with Title X

Sellers, landlords, and real estate licensees share responsibility for ensuring compliance with lead paint disclosure rules. According to HUD, **real estate *licensees must comply with the law if the seller or landlord fails to do so.*** Licensees are not responsible, however, if owners conceal information or fail to disclose it. As long as they inform the sellers or lessors of their obligations to disclose, they cannot be held liable.

In addition to the lead paint notification language included in many standard contracts brokers and licensees use, the contracts also contain additional lead-based paint disclosure forms as a way to prove compliance with HUD and EPA requirements. This is wise, since the penalty for failure to disclose lead hazards is a fine of up to $10,000 and up to one year in jail plus triple damages. For convenience, brokers and agents frequently use the HUD disclosure form.

HUD Lead-Based Paint Hazards Disclosure Form

The HUD disclosure form concerning lead-based paint is divided into three sections:

1. **Seller's Disclosure**. A place for **sellers** to disclose known lead-based paint issues and any reports
2. **Purchaser's Acknowledgment**. A place for **purchasers** to acknowledge whether they received any reports, the pamphlet, and the right to an assessment period
3. **Agent's Acknowledgment**. A place for **agents** to acknowledge their role in compliance and affirm they informed the sellers of their obligations

The "Protect Your Family From Lead in Your Home" Pamphlet

Sellers and landlords are required to give potential buyers or tenants the pamphlet titled "Protect Your Family from Lead in Your Home," produced by the EPA. The pamphlet explains the facts related to lead hazards, how lead can be ingested, associated health problems, responsibilities of a landlord, seller, or remodeler, and general information about remodeling or removal. **Real estate agents are required to ensure seller compliance in providing the pamphlet.**

Sellers are not required to test for or remove lead paint and/or other lead hazards. The contingency language in a purchase contract should explain what happens if lead paint or lead hazards are found. For example, the contract may allow a buyer or tenant to rescind the contract if unacceptable levels of lead are found, or a seller or landlord may have the right to remove the lead. Other times, lead hazards are negotiated (as a price reduction) like any other property defect or contingency.

Exempt Properties

Some properties are exempt from lead paint disclosure rules:

- Zero-bedroom units, such as lofts or dormitories
- Units leased for less than 100 days
- Housing exclusively for the elderly
- Housing for the disabled (unless occupied by children)
- Rental units inspected and found to be lead free
- Houses sold by foreclosure

Management

The only way to find out for sure if water, soil, or paint is contaminated by lead is to send samples to a laboratory for testing. Lead paint in good condition should be left alone and painted over to seal it. The easiest way to deal with chipping or peeling paint is to cover it up – by installing vinyl siding over the exterior of a house or adding a thin layer of drywall to interior walls, for example. Surfaces with lead paint should not be sanded or scraped, to avoid releasing lead dust into the air.

Disclosure of Information on Lead-Based Paint and/or Lead-Based Paint Hazards

Lead Warning Statement

Every purchaser of any interest in residential real property on which a residential dwelling was built prior to 1978 is notified that such property may present exposure to lead from lead-based paint that may place young children at risk of developing lead poisoning. Lead poisoning in young children may produce permanent neurological damage, including learning disabilities, reduced intelligence quotient, behavioral problems, and impaired memory. Lead poisoning also poses a particular risk to pregnant women. The seller of any interest in residential real property is required to provide the buyer with any information on lead-based paint hazards from risk assessments or inspections in the seller's possession and notify the buyer of any known lead-based paint hazards. A risk assessment or inspection for possible lead-based paint hazards is recommended prior to purchase.

Seller's Disclosure

(a) Presence of lead-based paint and/or lead-based paint hazards (check (i) or (ii) below):

(i) ______ Known lead-based paint and/or lead-based paint hazards are present in the housing (explain).

____

(ii) _____ Seller has no knowledge of lead-based paint and/or lead-based paint hazards in the housing.

(b) Records and reports available to the seller (check (i) or (ii) below):

(i) ______ Seller has provided the purchaser with all available records and reports pertaining to lead-based paint and/or lead-based paint hazards in the housing (list documents below).

____

(ii) _____ Seller has no reports or records pertaining to lead-based paint and/or lead-based paint hazards in the housing.

Purchaser's Acknowledgment (initial)

(c) ________ Purchaser has received copies of all information listed above.

(d) ________ Purchaser has received the pamphlet *Protect Your Family from Lead in Your Home.*

(e) Purchaser has (check (i) or (ii) below):

(i) _____ received a 10-day opportunity (or mutually agreed upon period) to conduct a risk assessment or inspection for the presence of lead-based paint and/or lead-based paint hazards; or

(ii) _____ waived the opportunity to conduct a risk assessment or inspection for the presence of lead-based paint and/or lead-based paint hazards.

Agent's Acknowledgment (initial)

(f) ________ Agent has informed the seller of the seller's obligations under 42 U.S.C. 4852(d) and is aware of his/her responsibility to ensure compliance.

Certification of Accuracy

The following parties have reviewed the information above and certify, to the best of their knowledge, that the information they have provided is true and accurate.

Seller	Date	Seller	Date
Purchaser	Date	Purchaser	Date
Agent	Date	Agent	Date

Lead-Based Paint Hazards Disclosure

Source: The Department of Housing and Urban Development

Methamphetamine

Methamphetamine (meth) is an illegal, man-made drug that is extremely addictive. Like cocaine, it is a stimulant. Since the ingredients are not necessarily hard to find, meth labs are found in homes, apartments, motels, wooded areas, and even cars.

Meth Hazards

Along with a higher risk of fire and explosions from having a meth lab on a property, meth's cooking process creates a dangerous residue, toxic byproducts, and fumes. The residue can contaminate a property, affecting the floors, ceiling, walls, carpeting, air conditioning and heating vents, and blinds, in addition to contaminating personal property such as clothing and toys.

Since the residue permeates the property, it is not always easy to remove; it lingers unless removed by a professional cleaner. Some houses have been demolished as a result of the proliferation of chemicals. Also, many of the toxic byproducts are poured either down the drain or into the soil outside the property. Essentially, the property can become a mini toxic waste site. If a property is not cleaned thoroughly, anyone living in it can develop health problems, ranging from serious respiratory problems, burning in the hands and feet, nausea, headaches, liver damage, to death.

Polychlorinated Biphenyls

Polychlorinated biphenyls (PCBs) are organic compounds that were mainly manufactured as cooling and insulating agents for transformers and capacitors. The compound was also used in adhesives, hydraulic fluid, inks, fire retardants, and many other products. The chemical compound is usually colorless and odorless and can easily permeate skin, vinyl, and latex. PCBs are classified as persistent organic pollutants, which means they are difficult to break down. Therefore, they have an accumulating effect in both the environment and the body.

Improper disposal of PCB-containing materials has contaminated soil and runoff leaches into streams and rivers where the chemicals are absorbed by fish. Contamination is spread further when people eat the fish and drink the water.

Health Risks of PCB Exposure

PCBs have been proven to cause cancer in animals and, therefore, are considered a carcinogen in humans. Besides cancer, PCBs are suspected to have detrimental effects on the immune, reproductive, nervous, and endocrine systems. Short-term exposure can cause spasms and skin, vision, and hearing problems.

Management

The amount of allowable PCBs in water supplies is 0.5 parts per billion (ppb). This standard was set by the EPA and is enforced by National Primary Drinking Water Regulations. Public water suppliers are required to adhere to these standards of water quality and regularly test the water.

PCBs are destroyed physically by incineration, irradiation, and ultrasound. Another method uses microorganisms to do the work. The tiny creatures feed on the carbon in the compound, thus breaking it down into a less toxic substance. Other chemicals are also used to destroy the compound by creating a reaction that decontaminates it.

Poor Air Quality

A building's poor air quality may not exactly be considered hazardous, but it can create problems and discomfort for those who must spend time inside. Many of the hazards covered here can be contributing factors to poor indoor air quality.

Legionnaires Disease, which is caused by airborne bacteria typically distributed by unclean air conditioning systems, can be deadly. This type of contamination is different from **sick building syndrome**, *where people suffer from headaches, fatigue, nausea, sore throat, nose and eye irritation, and other symptoms present only while in a building with poor air quality.*

Poor air quality is usually found in buildings sealed for energy efficiency and lacking adequate ventilation systems, allowing air pollutants to build up. Chemicals released from carpets, furnishings, copy machines, paint, and cleaning products all contribute to indoor air pollution. Adding to the problem are contaminants people bring into the building, such as animal dander, hairspray, dust, etc. The best remedy for poor air quality is to improve airflow throughout a structure.

Underground Storage Tanks

Underground storage tanks (USTs) *store a variety of substances such as heating oil, gasoline, chemicals, and hazardous waste.* New York's property disclosure form requires sellers to disclose the presence of any underground storage tanks or wells.

The EPA has enacted tougher standards for USTs, imposing additional steps that owners and property managers must take to protect USTs against corrosion, spills, leaks, and overfills. What was once a common practice for the storage of fuel or chemicals in rural areas may now be an expensive process of ensuring that tanks do not leak or digging them up and removing them altogether. This can pose even bigger environmental dilemmas for commercial properties, where costs can be much higher.

Exemptions

Some types of tanks are exempt from federal regulations, including:

- Tanks with a capacity of less than 110 gallons.
- Tanks used on farms and residential properties that store less than 1,100 gallons of motor fuel used for noncommercial use.
- Heating oil tanks, where the fuel is burned at the location.
- Tanks that are aboveground or at ground level; these might be in basements or tunnels.
- Septic tanks and tanks that collect storm water and wastewater.

State UST Laws

Some states have more stringent laws for the use of underground storage tanks than the federal government does. In those cases, the stricter laws prevail. In New York State, the Department of Environmental Conservation (DEC) and the Hazardous Substances Bulk Storage Program provide guidelines and controls for the storage of many different hazardous chemicals.

Underground storage tanks can be an internal or external hazard to a property – a leaking storage tank from a neighbor can contaminate your property. New York State requires that tanks be certified by an environmental engineer in order to be filled.

New York State was the first to establish laws to help prevent chemical spills and leaks. Its Environmental Conservation Law requires the NYDEC to regulate chemicals covered under CERCLA and other known hazardous chemicals. The sale, storage, and handling of hazardous materials are regulated by the Hazardous Substances Bulk Storage Act.

The Chemical Bulk Storage Regulation lists more than 1,000 substances that must meet storage guidelines. The regulation requires chemical companies and distributors to supply buyers with proper storage and handling instructions. The regulation also established storage equipment standards and testing and inspection requirements.

Uncapped Gas Wells

In 2007, Section 242 of the Real Property Law was amended to require sellers to inform buyers prior to a sale of the existence of any **uncapped natural gas wells** of which the seller has actual knowledge.

Capping a natural gas well could cost a new property owner thousands of dollars in unforeseen costs if he didn't know about such a well.

Urea-Formaldehyde

Urea-formaldehyde is *a clear chemical used in manufacturing.* It can be used in the production of building materials and home products such as particleboard, plywood paneling, carpeting, and ceiling tiles. Many of these products use urea-formaldehyde resin in adhesives. The EPA regulates the use of formaldehyde and determines appropriate emission levels, especially in the construction of prefabricated and mobile homes.

The biggest concern is the use of urea-formaldehyde foam in insulation. **Urea-formaldehyde foam insulation (UFFI)** is *a type of insulation that can be blown into an existing structure*. The EPA now recommends UFFI *not* be used in residential homes because of potential health risks. Over time, the fumes and release of formaldehyde from the product dissipate, so insulation installed several years ago should not pose a health risk now.

Health Risks of Formaldehyde Exposure

Exposure to formaldehyde can cause:

- Shortness of breath.
- Asthma.
- Cancer in animals; also suspected of causing cancer in humans.
- Wheezing.
- Skin and eye irritation.

Foam insulation is not the only source of formaldehyde inside a home. Building materials such as plywood and fiberboard also use the chemical. Formaldehyde is commonly used in many household products, including furniture cushions, carpet, cabinetry, mattresses, fabric finishes, and cosmetics.

Naturally Occurring Internal Hazards and Pests

Environmental hazards are not always created by man. Internal environmental hazards can also occur naturally. Mold and termites can have extremely destructive effects on a property. It is important to understand these types of hazards, what types of harm they can cause, and how they can be remedied or addressed.

Mold

Mold is *a fungus that can grow anywhere and on any organic material.* In order to grow, mold requires three components:

1. Moisture
2. Oxygen
3. Food source

A leaky roof that goes undetected or serious water damage creates a perfect atmosphere for mold growth. New construction, which creates tightly sealed homes, can pose a problem by allowing moisture to remain trapped in the home. If not found in time, mold can actually consume the substance on which it is growing.

Some molds produce *toxic substances* known as **mycotoxins**. One of these types of mold is **stachybotrys,** or **black mold**, *which is greenish-black in color and grows on materials with high cellulose content such as drywall, ceiling tiles, and wood that is chronically moist*. In some situations, mold can even grow behind the surface of walls or wallpaper.

Health Risks of Mold Exposure

There are many different varieties and types of molds, but not all molds are created equal – some are dangerous to humans; some are not. Mold can produce allergens, which can trigger reactions such as wheezing, eye and skin irritation, and a stuffy nose. For some people, mold can cause asthma attacks.

Suspected health issues caused by mold include:

- Chronic fatigue.
- Flu-like symptoms.
- Digestive problems.
- Immune system problems.
- Neurological problems.

Awareness

The EPA has not specifically required mold disclosure or set standards to measure contamination. Some states, including California and Texas, have passed their own legislation regarding mold issues, and some states now require real estate agents to conduct a thorough visual inspection of properties for the existence of mold. Although New York does not have such requirements, it is a good idea to be alert to telltale signs that mold is present to help protect clients. Some signs indicating a presence of moisture in the home and thereby increasing the likelihood of finding mold are:

- Visible mold growth.
- Plumbing leaks.
- Leaking roofs or windows.
- Strong, musty odors.
- Water stains on ceilings, walls, or floors.
- Warped wood.
- Cracked or peeling paint.
- Peeling dry-wall tape.
- Clogged gutters.

Licensees must be careful not to act as experts or make claims they cannot verify. They should merely inform clients of any suspicions and advise them to seek further information from a specialist or home inspector. Sellers should be encouraged to disclose any problem or potential problem. More and more states are implementing new laws regarding mold and real estate, including disclosure statements that include mold, and new requirements for licensees.

Protecting Clients

There is no proven method of protecting a client from unwittingly ending up with a mold-contaminated property; however, there are some steps licensees can take to help, including:

- Advising homebuyers to purchase separate mold protection insurance policies.
- Having the property inspected specifically for mold and any related problems by a specialist.
- Adding a mold protection clause as part of a standard purchase contract.
- Encouraging the government to expand required disclosures to include toxic mold.
- Encouraging the government to pass state standards and licensing for mold inspection and cleanup.

Homeowners also must be diligent in keeping property thoroughly maintained to prevent mold growth.

Pests

Rodent and insect infestations can cause major physical damage to a property. When working with a client on these issues, it is best to adopt an empathetic and a proactive approach. Experience regarding the proper professional to contact may be the only solution clients need. Licensees should personally check companies' credentials, and it is always wise to recommend three or more.

Bees

To get advice on handling bees, it is advisable to contact a beekeeper, exterminator, or the local county co-operative extension service. In many cases, it is best to contact a beekeeper first. Licensees should never try to resolve bee problems on their own – there can be more than 50,000 bees in one hive or nest.

Often, beekeepers can save the bee colony and the property, and may even save clients money. The beekeepers usually do not cost as much as an exterminator, because they want to keep the bees and the queen. Sometimes bees can be a nuisance; however, it is important to remember honeybees are an important contributor to the food chain and should be saved if possible.

Termites

Termite problems come in all shapes and sizes. The most common type of termite found in homes is the subterranean termite. The good news is that most termite infestations are relatively easy to identify by a trained termite technician or home inspector and, if caught in the early stages, are treatable. Major problems result when termite infestations proliferate over several years. This may even threaten the structural integrity of a home. There are numerous preventive measures available to homeowners, the most inexpensive being the inspection.

Short of a professional inspection, there are some signs that indicate a termite problem. If termites or shed wings are visible inside the home, there is likely an infestation somewhere. As is the case with most pests, for every termite seen, there are typically many more not seen.

Termites can be hard to detect, as they work underneath the wood surface and do not leave behind any sawdust as carpenter ants do. Termites hollow out the wood, leaving the surface appearance intact. Tapping on a suspicious area to see if it sounds hollow is one way to see if termites might be present. Another clue is to look on the outside of the structure's foundation. Termites will leave mud tubes, typically one-quarter to one inch wide, on the foundation. These tubes act as a protective barrier from the ground into their access point.

Carpenter Ants

Many real estate licensees are incredibly relieved when no termites are found during a home inspection, only to discover there is an infestation of carpenter ants. Carpenter ants can be just as destructive as termites, chewing into wood, creating a living habitat, which causes damage.

Carpenter ants look just like the average ant for the most part, only they are very large. If you see an ant that is black, or black and red, and is one-quarter to one-half inch long, it is probably a carpenter ant.

Carpenter ants typically get into a house through openings in the foundation. One sign of carpenter ants is the sawdust they leave behind. Slit-like holes in wood, especially around windows and doors are also indications of an infestation.

Remediation at the colony source is the preferred treatment to extinguish these pests. There seems to be more of a tolerance for carpenter ant infestation remediation disclosures than for termite problems. The public seems less concerned, after treatment has been initiated, than an ongoing termite treatment regimen. Consequently, there are fewer buyer problems associated with carpenter ant issues.

Bedbugs

Bedbugs are small, flat, brownish insects about 1/4-inch long that feed mostly on human blood. Once thought to be more or less eradicated, bedbugs have unfortunately made a comeback in recent years. Many cities—including New York City—have experienced a sharp rise in complaints about bedbug infestations. New York City's bedbug problems are affecting everything: Apartments, theaters, schools, hotels, retail stores, and even the Empire State Building.

The presence of bedbugs is usually detected by tiny blood stains and droppings on upholstered furniture, mattresses and box springs, baseboards of walls, and in various cracks and crevices. Newly hatched bedbugs are nearly transparent, and so very difficult to see. While the bite of the bedbug is not particularly toxic, nor has it been proven to transmit disease, it can cause varying degrees of skin irritation and itching on most people. Perhaps more devastating, however, is the emotional and financial impact of dealing with a bedbug infestation. Getting rid of bedbugs can be an extremely difficult task and almost always requires the services of a licensed pest management professional.

Pest Solutions

What can be done to remedy a rodent or an insect problem? As in most areas discussed here, a proactive approach is more effective than a reactive one. One of the most important services the real estate licensee can provide is recommending a number of reliable termite or pest control companies to clients.

If a seller thinks there may be an insect problem, it's the licensee's responsibility to be proactive and counsel the seller to have the problem exterminated prior to marketing the home. New York State law requires insect damage or infestations to be disclosed. It is better to take care of a problem and disclose than it is to:

- Negotiate around a problem.
- Conceal, or fail to disclose a latent defect.

Unless a real estate licensee is a licensed exterminator, or the homeowner is willing to tackle the infestation problem without a warranty for the repair, a reputable professional should be contacted and all written documentation and receipts should be kept.

New York City landlords must let prospective tenants know in writing if an apartment has suffered a bedbug infestation within the past year, or if there has been a bed bug problem in the building during that time. The proper form is the DBB-N – Owner's Notice to Tenant Disclosure of Bedbug Infestation History.

Radon

Radon is *a naturally occurring radioactive gas that emanates from rocks, soil, and water because of the decay of uranium.* It is the densest gas known and is odorless, colorless, and tasteless. Since it is radioactive, it has been identified as a cancer-causing agent. Indoors, it can present a problem because it can build up to a dangerous level, especially in newer homes built to be more airtight.

The presence of radon can vary from location to location, and from house to house. Thus, one house might have a radon problem, while another on the same street might not. The levels within a house can also vary depending on weather conditions and time of year. Radon enters a home from the ground, usually through cracks or holes in the foundation, but can also creep in from uncovered sump pumps and crawl spaces. It is recommended that every house in a radon-prone zone have a radon test every two years.

Health Risks of Radon Exposure

The Surgeon General of the United States has issued an advisory regarding health risks due to exposure to radon in indoor air. The World Health Organization (WHO) says radon is the cause of up to 15 percent of lung cancer cases worldwide and that more than 20,000 Americans die of radon-related lung cancer each year. Lung

Radon can enter a home from the soil beneath it, through cracks in walls or the foundation, or even through the water supply if a home has well water. The following EPA diagram shows many of the ways radon can enter the home.

EPA RADON DIAGRAM:

How Radon Can Enter A Home

1. **Cracks in solid floors or slabs**
2. **Construction joints (between floors and walls)**
3. **Cracks in walls (especially concrete walls)**
4. **Mortar joints**
5. **Gaps around service pipes**
6. **Drainage system (with interior, exposed sump)**
7. **Exposed dirt in sump pump area**
8. **Gap between exterior brick or siding and top of foundation wall**
9. **Open top of concrete blocks in foundation wall**
10. **Some building materials (e.g. stone, block pores)**
11. **Water supply (usually with well water systems)**

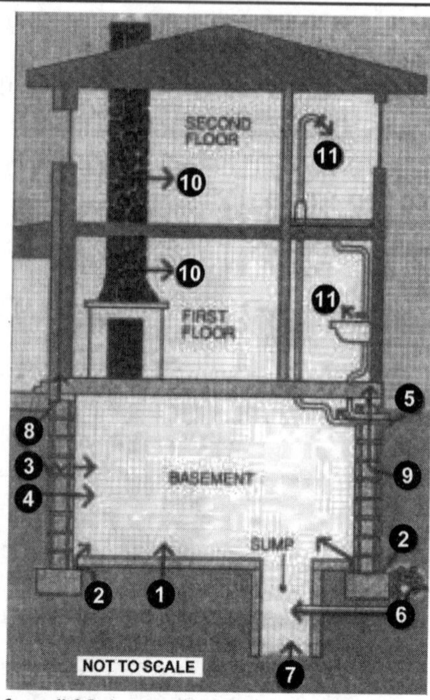

Source: U. S. Environmental Protection Agency

cancer is the primary health concern of extended exposure to radon. But there is the possibility it could contribute to other health issues, such as:

- Allergies.
- Hypertension.
- Diabetes.
- Asthma.
- Birth defects.

Testing for Radon

For a small fee, state residents can request a home radon test kit from the New York State Department of Health. Tests can also be purchased at most home improvement stores. Tests are sent to a certified lab for results.

Another common way to test for radon is with continuous electronic radon monitors, which cost more but are more accurate. These tests should be set up and conducted by professional certified testers. Because they are also more tamper resistant, they are typically used for pending real estate transactions.

The New York Property Condition Disclosure Statement asks if a property has ever been tested for radon. If a test has been conducted, a copy of the test results should be attached to the statement.

Remedy

If radon or another hazardous substance is found, treatment options are dictated and controlled by the purchase contract. First and foremost, these options must be in accordance with EPA, state, and local guidelines and standards. If not currently covered, an addendum may be used, which should be in accordance with the policies of the real estate office, local real estate board, and local laws.

The actual cost of purging a house of radon gas is relatively inexpensive – often less than the cost of eliminating termites. In fact, with low levels of radon, simply sealing cracks may be enough. With higher levels of radon, it may be necessary to install a fan or blower to bring in fresh air and keep air moving through the house. It might also be necessary to vent the radon. Radon remediation systems should be installed by an experienced, licensed remediation company. It is highly recommended that testing be performed after the installation of the removal system, and checked periodically through the years.

Prevention

Many homes built since 1990 in radon-prone zones have incorporated radon proofing into the design. A commonly used construction technique is to place a four-inch layer of clean gravel under a plastic sheathing, then pour a concrete slab foundation on top. The gases cannot penetrate the plastic cover. A vent pipe penetrates through the layers to the gravel, to vent any gases up and out through the roof. This type of construction also includes sealing and caulking all foundation openings.

Groundwater Contamination

Groundwater is *found in subterranean crevices or spaces.* Since groundwater is naturally occurring, it is included here with other naturally occurring hazards. However, most of the time, groundwater contamination is from man-made sources. Dumping toxic waste, such as meth cooking byproducts, can contaminate underground water and the water supply. Groundwater contamination may also come from faulty septic tanks, leaky underground storage tanks, contaminated soil washed into lakes, rivers, and streams, and toxic surface spills. It is also possible for groundwater to be contaminated by naturally occurring elements such as radon, lead, and arsenic.

The contamination of groundwater can also affect people who use private wells as a water supply. Also, many public water systems use groundwater as a water source. On some disclosure forms, sellers are required to indicate where the property's water supply comes from, and some buyers will ask whether the water supply has been tested for contaminants. New York **does require** the seller to disclose the source of the water supply – whether a well, private, or municipal.

Liability for Environmental Hazards

Property owners are being held to a higher standard than ever before when it comes to environmental hazards. With regard to property found to be contaminated with environmental hazards, not only can the past producers and/or dumpers of the contamination be held liable, but so can an innocent, current owner.

Current and past owners might be required to pay for clean-up costs, even if they did not contaminate the property, or even know of the contamination. The law specifically includes liability for owners who knew or should have known of the contamination. Even the lender in a management capacity can be held liable.

Real Estate Professional's Liability

Given today's legal climate, it is important for everyone involved in a transaction to take steps to protect themselves. Although real estate licensees are not required to be technical experts with regard to environmental issues, they do need to understand environmental issues and know how to look for signs of trouble. They also need to stress the need for sellers to be honest and thorough when completing disclosure forms. Improper disclosure can result in a real estate agent being responsible, if it is decided the agent should have known, or helped to conceal information.

Other real estate professionals, such as appraisers, must make an extra effort to ensure they are aware of any potential environmental hazards to a property because the value of a property, and properties in the immediate area or an entire neighborhood, can be severely affected. When in doubt, an expert should be contacted.

SUMMARY

1. The **Environmental Protection Agency (EPA)** is responsible for creating and enforcing environmental protection standards, and providing support and research on environmental issues. Important federal environmental laws to be aware of include:
   - **National Environmental Policy Act (NEPA).** Promotes methods to prevent or eliminate damage to the environment and educate the public of the importance of our natural resources and ecological system. It established the Council on Environmental Quality.
   - **Clean Air Act (CAA).** Regulates air pollutant emissions.
   - **Clean Water Act (CWA).** Sets national water quality standards, and penalties for water pollution violations.
   - **Comprehensive Environmental Response, Compensation, and Liability Act (CERCLA).** Creates requirements for closed or abandoned waste sites, and establishes taxes and fines that provide money for the Superfund.
   - **Superfund Amendments and Reauthorization Act (SARA).** Amended CERCLA and increased the monetary size of the Superfund.
   - **Resource Conservation and Recovery Act (RCRA).** Gave the EPA the authority to control hazardous waste throughout its life cycle, including its generation, transportation, treatment, storage, and disposal.
   - **Safe Drinking Water Act (SDWA).** Established by the EPA; sets standards for water intended for human consumption. The New York Department of Health regulates drinking water in New York State and sets standards for private water supplies and septic systems.
2. **Wetlands** are *ecosystems where the land is permeated with water*, which either lies on or near the surface. Also known as bogs, marshes, and swamps, they provide a habitat for aquatic plants and wildlife, act as a flood barrier, and naturally filter water. Wetlands are protected under the Clean Water Act.
3. A **nuisance** is *anything that interferes with the right of quiet enjoyment* (e.g., airport noise, farm stench). Permanent nuisance can be **external obsolescence**. An **environmental hazard** is a *situation of potential harm to persons or property from conditions that exist in property or external to it.* Examples of **external hazards** are toxic waste dumps, nuclear power plants, and high-tension power lines. Environmental concerns within a property (**internal hazards**) can be dangerous but are often easy to rectify. Sellers must disclose known hazards on property disclosure forms.
4. Common **man-made hazards** are:
   - **Asbestos.** *A fibrous, heat-resistant material once commonly used as insulation.* Inhaled asbestos particles can cause lung cancer.
   - **Carbon monoxide (CO).** *A colorless, odorless gas that is released when fossil fuels are broken down to produce heat.* New York requires all new housing to have CO detectors, and older homes must have one installed in order to be sold. Overexposure to CO can cause dizziness, nausea, and death.
   - **Chlorofluorocarbons (CFCs).** *A chemical compound, commonly known as Freon, used as a coolant in refrigerators, air conditioners, and dehumidifiers.* EPA regulates use and handling of CFCs, and sets fines for misuse.
   - **Electromagnetic fields.** *Invisible fields created by moving electrical currents.* High-tension power lines, transformers, and secondary distribution lines create large electromagnetic fields suspected of causing hormonal changes, cancer, and abnormal behavior. Evidence is

controversial and no remedies have been established, other than to maintain a safe distance from EMF-emitting appliances and power lines.

- **Lead**. *A bluish-white metal added to exterior and interior paint as a drying agent and for pigmentation*. Also used in pipes and solder in the plumbing systems in homes and businesses. Digesting or inhaling lead or lead dust causes neurological disorders and learning disabilities; can contaminate soil. The **Residential Lead-Based Paint Hazard Reduction Act**, or **Title X**, requires disclosure of known lead-based paint dangers. For houses built before 1978, a lead paint brochure must be given to buyers and tenants; buyers must be given time to conduct lead tests (usually a ten-day period), if they desire.
- **Methamphetamine**. *An illegal, man-made drug that is extremely addictive*. Residue from a meth lab can permeate and contaminate property, water, and soil. Currently there are no federal disclosure laws, but some states are passing laws.
- **Urea-formaldehyde**. *A chemical used in adhesive for household materials (particleboard, plywood paneling, carpeting, ceiling tiles), and blown-in foam insulation*. Health risks include shortness of breath, wheezing, asthma, and skin and eye irritation; suspected to cause cancer.
- **Underground storage tanks (USTs)**. *Buried tanks that store heating oil, gasoline, chemicals, and hazardous waste*. Storage guidelines in New York State are set by the Department of Environmental Conservation and the Hazardous Substances Bulk Storage Program. Disclosure of underground storage tanks in New York is required.
- **Uncapped gas wells**. Sellers are required to inform buyers prior to a sale of the existence of any uncapped natural gas wells of which the seller has actual knowledge.

5. Other common environmental concerns are derived from nature. Common **naturally occurring hazards** are:

- **Mold**. *Many different varieties of fungus*; dangerous mold is black mold (stachybotrys). Lawsuits regarding mold issues have branched beyond builders and insurance companies to include sellers, brokers, management companies, and licensees.
- **Radon**. *A naturally occurring, odorless, colorless, and tasteless radioactive gas that emanates from rocks*. Radon can build up to dangerous levels in homes due to inadequate ventilation; prolonged exposure to the gas can cause cancer.
- **Groundwater contamination**. Groundwater *is found in subterranean crevices or spaces*. Dumping of toxic waste into soil, faulty septic tanks, leaky underground storage tanks, and toxic surface spills can contaminate groundwater, which results in the pollution of private wells and public water systems. It is also possible for groundwater to be contaminated by naturally occurring elements found in the earth's soil.
- **Pests**, including rodent and insect infestations, can cause major physical damage to a property. It may be necessary to engage an exterminator certified by the state of New York. Records should be kept to prove that remediation has taken place.

10

The Valuation Process and Pricing Properties

In This Session

In this session, you'll learn about the important process of property valuation, which is much more involved than simply guessing what a property is worth. Proper valuation requires knowledge of all aspects of real estate, research and careful analysis of market trends, an understanding of housing characteristics, familiarity with neighborhoods, and many other factors. Whether one is performing an appraisal or comparative market analysis or evaluating property for some other purpose, knowing how to research the market and analyze the assets and characteristics of property to arrive at a reasonable opinion of value is a critical skill for any real estate professional.

You learn:

- Differentiate between comparative market analysis and appraisals.
- Discuss the definition of market value.
- Explain the difference between value, price, and cost.
- Explain how and why a CMA is used.
- Explain the salesperson's role in the valuation process and pricing properties.
- List the three approaches to determining value.

Key Terms

- Appraisal
- Assessed Value
- Comparative Market Analysis (CMA)
- Cost
- Cost Approach
- Depreciation
- Direct Cost
- Evaluation
- External Obsolescence
- Functional Obsolescence
- Income Approach
- Indirect Cost
- Insured Value
- Investment Value
- Location/Situs
- Mortgage Value
- Plottage
- Price
- Residential Market Analysis
- Sales Comparison Approach
- Valuation

Real Estate Agents and Valuation

Real estate professionals must have some familiarity with valuing homes because it is part of the profession! Accurate valuation is the most important part of a professional Comparative Market Analysis (CMA). It will take new licensees time and experience to extract and use the correct comparables to create the CMA. Even using computer reports, the licensee must first learn the fundamentals of pricing properties. Knowing how to research the market and the characteristics of a particular property will help you do your job and, thus, help your clients get the best results.

Characteristics of Real Property

What is real property?

The law classifies all property as either *real* or *personal*. Simply put, **real property** is *land and everything attached to it*, while **personal property** is *any property that is moveable and not affixed to the land*. Appraisers and real estate agents assign value to *real property.*

There are seven characteristics of real property – four value characteristics and three physical characteristics.

Value Characteristics

The four value characteristics are:

- Demand.
- Improvements.
- Scarcity.
- Location

Demand is *the need or desire for a specific good or service by others.* Demand is an essential element in creating value. Without demand, any amount of supply is meaningless. But, when you have purchasers who want what you have to sell, you command value. Everyone *needs* a place to live; however, some people want more than a basic rentable space—they want to own real estate. That is where desire enters the picture. Determining what someone really wants (and can afford) versus what they need is critical to finding the best property to purchase. A homebuyer, typically, wants to satisfy basic needs or individual wants beyond life's essentials. Along with demand, *effective demand* must also be present to create value.

The **improvements** to land can have a great affect on the value. As every piece of land is improved from a vacant parcel to a dwelling, the appeal increases. Improvements are not just limited to a dwelling, but can include utilities, road access, landscaping. This can help increase the value.

Scarcity is the perceived principle of **supply and demand**: The more supply of goods or service relative to the demand the lower the value. If there is an unlimited supply of something, it is perceived to have little value. People generally perceive real estate to be a valuable commodity because there is a limited supply of it. This notion drives the anticipation that buying a home is an investment that will increase in value as time goes by.

The greatest characteristic and effect on property value is its **location (situs)**. Property located where there is scarcity would command a higher value. If the property is not in an area of accessibility, it would have little demand. Location was and will be for the most part, the number one effect on home sales.

Physical Characteristics

Real estate has three physical characteristics that serve to give land inherent value. The three physical characteristics are:

- Uniqueness.
- Immobility.
- Indestructibility.

These unique characteristics are not present as a group in other types of property. Only real estate has this combination of physical attributes and, as a result, note how the three physical characteristics of real estate are often intertwined with the four value characteristics.

Uniqueness refers to the fact that *every piece of land, every building, and every home is different* – no two are the same. This is also referred to as **non-homogeneity.** Even if two houses or two buildings look the same, they are said to be different because of their locations, even if side by side. Since no more land can be created in any given location, this uniqueness leads buyers to view land as a scarce commodity.

Immobility is the physical characteristic that refers to the fact that *real estate itself cannot move from one place to another.* That is the difference between land and personal property, which can be moved anywhere. Land is fixed and cannot be moved. This is one of the most important reasons why real estate is valuable.

Indestructibility refers to the fact that *real estate cannot be destroyed.* Land is not consumed, nor does it wear out like other goods. Land may be altered or changed in some manner, but it will remain. This is the reason that it is so attractive as an investment.

Appraisal, Valuation, Evaluation, and Value

Appraisal is *an opinion of the value of property, as of a specified date, supported by objective data.* This opinion is supported in writing with collected data and reasoning. An appraiser uses data from three approaches value and applies them: sales comparison, cost and income. Each approach will have a different value it may yield. The appraiser will reconcile the different values applying accepted appraisal methods. Example income approach is not generally used in a single family property.

Appraisers value properties using three different methods:

- Sales comparison approach
- Cost approach
- Income approach

Each approach to value is independent of the others and must be *performed separately* to arrive at an opinion of value. The appraiser's choice in the application of the approaches is driven by the scope of work decision. The *scope of work* is the type and extent of research and analyses needed in an assignment. As a result, the appraiser could elect to use one, more than one, or all three approaches.

Sales Comparison Approach

Generally, the sales comparison approach is the most useful and credible of the three appraisal methods in market value appraisal assignments, especially for non-income-producing residential properties, because it is deeply rooted in actual market activity. A minimum of three comparables is required by most secondary market lenders to ensure an accurate appraisal from sufficient data. These comparables should be as recent as possible, usually having been sold no more than six months or a year prior to the date the appraisal is being performed, and as similar as possible to the subject property.

Remember, an appraisal is just an opinion of value. Only the marketplace can establish the true value of a property. In a market value appraisal assignment, the more actual market data and activity is relied upon, the more credible the appraiser's opinion will be. The appraiser's opinion must be supported by relevant data and proper judgment. In other words, the appraiser must not only understand what the data says, but interpret how to apply it, and how to use it to arrive at a conclusion.

In the sales comparison approach, the appraiser will perform five steps based on scope of work:

1. Identify the market for which the subject is competitive and research the market for comparable data reflecting closed sales
2. Confirm the identified data by verifying accuracy.
3. Choose the units of comparison most applicable to the assignment and the subject property in a manner consistent with how the market would most recognize the comparison (total property price, per square foot, per acre, etc.).
4. Apply adjustments to each property deemed a comparable sale to address significant differences.
5. Reconcile the strengths and weaknesses of the indications resulting from the data analysis to conclude on an opinion of value.

Cost Approach

The **cost approach** is a *valuation method that develops an opinion of value for a property by calculating the cost of building the structure on the land, subtracting any depreciation, and adding in the value of the site and any other miscellaneous site improvements*.

In the cost approach, the appraiser always performs six steps based on the scope of work:

1. Defines the basis for the cost.
   - Reproduction
   - Replacement
2. Chooses a costing method.
   - Comparative unit
   - Unit-in-place
   - Quantity survey
   - Index
3. Estimates depreciation based on physical deterioration, functional obsolescence, and external obsolescence using one of the recognized methods.
   - Age-life
   - Breakdown
   - Market extraction
4. Adds "as is" contributory value of other site improvements.
5. Adds vacant land value, which is developed by accepted methods and based on the land's highest and best use.
6. Concludes on an opinion of value.

Depreciation

Depreciation is *the loss in value to property for any reason*. That loss in value may be attributable to physical deterioration, functional obsolescence, or external (or economic) obsolescence. The common thinking is that depreciation relates exclusively to physical deterioration.

It is important to remember, cost does not always equal value. A house that does not conform to surrounding properties, is over-improved with features the market does not respond to, or one with excessive deterioration would likely have a lesser value than the cost to build a new house.

On the other hand, a new building must have a greater benefit than the actual cost to build it, such as profit for the developer. Without the motive of profit, there would be no new buildings. Buyers do not care what a house costs to build as much as what other houses are selling for in the area. Still, the cost approach sets the theoretical ceiling of value for most properties because of the theory of substitution.

Remember, depreciation is a monetary loss in property value for any reason. Keep in mind that, although the value of land can fluctuate due to external and economic forces that affect its highest and best use, the land itself is said *never* to suffer depreciation. Improvements to the land that make it a site and the enhancements that we place on it can suffer deterioration or obsolescence. Thus, when talking about depreciation, we are talking about the structure on the land and other site improvements. Forces that cause depreciation are:

- **Physical deterioration** is *actual wear and tear due to age, the elements, or other forces*. Regular maintenance can slow the process, and most physical deterioration is repairable, or curable. A depreciation figure for physical deterioration is calculated by taking the new price of the item and subtracting a percentage for the wear and tear.
- **Functional obsolescence** means *a building is less desirable because of something inherent in the structure itself.* Some examples are an outdated style, outdated fixtures, or faulty design. A super over improvement making it to costly for the area. These undesirable features may be curable – fixed at a reasonable cost – or incurable – not able to be fixed without major cost or renovation. Depreciation for functional obsolescence is determined by the cost of curing the undesirable feature or, for incurables, by comparing the difference in sale price of a property with the feature and one without it.
- **External obsolescence** occurs when *something outside the control of the property makes it less desirable.* Some examples are the changes in land-use resulting in air pollution heavier traffic. These external causes are usually incurable. Depreciation for economic obsolescence is determined by comparing the difference in sale price of a property with the feature and one without it.

Other Elements Needed for Cost Approach

There are two additional important elements needed to develop an opinion of value using the cost approach:

- Estimated site value.
- Other site improvement value.

Estimated site value. The site value used in the cost approach always represents the value of the site at its highest and best use. If the current or proposed improvements are not consistent with the highest and best use of the property, it will be addressed as an obsolescence and result in depreciation of the improvements.

Other site improvement value. Most often, the contributory value of other site improvements will be considered "as is," or in their depreciated state. These items are things not already considered in the cost calculations, such as driveways, landscaping, walkways, and, in some cases, utility provisions, stated as an aggregate value.

- **Replacement** is building the functional equivalent of the original building using modern materials, design, and functional layout
- **Reproduction** is building an exact replica of the original building, duplicating the materials, design, functional layout, workmanship, inadequacies, etc.

Income Approach

The **income approach** is an appraisal method that *estimates the value of real estate by analyzing the revenue, or income, the property currently generates or could generate often comparing it to other similar properties.* This approach is most widely used with commercial or investment properties.

There are many ways to analyze real estate income depending on the purpose. The two most common methods are using a **capitalization rate** and **gross rent multiplier**. In the capitalization rate method of income appraisal, we are interested only in the net income or **net operating income**, *income after expenses.* This is important because an investor does not receive money that pays for expenses. The **gross rent multiplier** (GRM; sometimes also referred to as *GMRM or gross monthly rent multiplier*) is a *number derived from comparable rental properties in an area, used to estimate the value of real estate.* The gross rent multiplier is used for only one- to four-unit residential properties. The GRM is based on the total gross monthly rent. With this method, no deduction allowance is made for expenses, vacancies, or collection losses. Because of the complexity of this type of approach, it is beyond our discussion.

Valuation Basics

Value is the worth of the investment. This is what someone is willing to pay for a property at a given moment in time. The value depends on the expected future income of the property. We say "expected" because all tenants (potentially) could move out when their leases are up. We can be reasonably sure, if the property's income is fair in the marketplace, that the income stream is likely to continue into the future (minus a small percentage for vacancy and collection losses).

This value figure does not take into account the fact that the real estate may appreciate in the future. Most investors buy real estate with this in mind, but since this is an uncertain event, it is not included in an appraisal.

Additional types of value with which real estate professionals should be familiar include:

- **Mortgage value,** the amount of money a lender is willing to let someone borrow to finance, or re-finance, property. Mortgage value may also be referred to as loan value.
- **Investment value,** the highest price investors would pay for a property based on how well they believe it will serve their financial goals.
- **Insurable value,** the amount a property can be insured for, usually representing only the replacement cost of the structure and disregarding any value for the land.

- **Assessed value,** the amount used to calculate taxes due, and sometimes representing a percentage of market value.
- **Value in use,** the present worth of the future benefits of ownership.

Evaluation is a *study of the nature, quality, or utility of certain property interests in which a value estimate is not necessarily required* (e.g., highest and best use, feasibility, market supply and demand, etc.).

Highest and best use is *the most profitable, legally permitted, economically feasible, and physically possible use of a property.* This is the most important property-specific factor an appraiser considers before making a determination of value. With most houses, the determination of highest and best use is simple because the houses are in residential neighborhoods. The determination that land is improved to its highest and best use may be obvious since zoning regulations may not allow other uses. Highest and best use becomes a vital consideration when examining vacant land or improved or unimproved properties with changed zoning.

If a house sits on a widened street, surrounded by commercial buildings, it is likely the land would be more valuable if put to commercial use. The zoning laws must permit the intended use, and the owner must be able to build the proposed structure on the land. All of these factors must be considered when valuing real estate.

Land utilization studies are *combining two or more parcels of land into one larger parcel.* This is typically done to increase the usefulness of the land by allowing one larger building to be constructed on the larger parcel that could previously only have held smaller individual parcels. When assemblage results in an actual increase in land value (over simply the combined value of the individual parcels), it is called **plottage,** or plottage value.

Evaluation does not result in a value of property as a valuation will.

Market Value

Market value is *the theoretical price real estate will likely bring in a typical transaction.* A typical transaction may also be referred to as an **arm's length transaction,** meaning the *transaction occurred under typical conditions in the marketplace, and each of the parties is a relative stranger to one another and was acting in their own best interests.*

Market value is the most probable price a property will bring if:

- Buyer paid cash for the property at closing or obtained a mortgage through a lender to pay the seller the agreed upon price at closing.
- Buyer and seller are not related in any way.
- Buyer and seller are both acting in their own best interests.
- Buyer and seller are not acting out of undue haste or duress.
- Buyer and seller are both reasonably informed about the property and its potential uses.
- Property has been available on the market for a reasonable period of time.

Market value implies arm's-length transaction, nonrelated buyer and seller. Sales where one party is in a distress situation or are related parties are not fair market value.

Market Value vs. Market Price

We have defined market value as the theoretical price real estate is most likely to bring in a typical transaction. The *value* of real estate should not be confused with its *price*. **Market value** is the *expected price*; **market price** is *actual price – what someone has actually paid*. Further, both value and price may have nothing to do with what the property actually cost to build.

Value, Price, and Cost

On the surface, value, price, and cost may appear to mean the same thing. That is not the case when it comes to real estate! Again, these terms have different meanings and **cannot** be used interchangeably.

Value

A property's value is not necessarily the same as its price or even its cost. Remember, market value is the *expected price*; market price is the *actual price paid*. And the cost to build and maintain a property is not always tied to its market value and market price.

Price

A property's **price** is the *amount a ready, willing, and able buyer agrees to pay for a property and a seller agrees to accept under the terms of the transaction*. This may or not equal the value. Different circumstances may dictate why a seller accepted less or a purchaser paid more for a property. A seller under duress could be because of a job transfer he must move quickly. Here, price and value are not equal.

Cost

The *total dollar expenditure for the land, materials, legal services, architectural design, financing, taxes paid during construction, interest, contractors' overhead and profit, and entrepreneurial overhead and profit* defines a property's **cost**. There are two types of costs, direct and indirect:

Direct Costs	Indirect Costs
Land, materials, and labor	Real estate taxes during construction
Building permits	Fees:
Equipment costs	• Engineering
Utility installation and cost	• Architectural
Contractor's profit	• Appraisal
Construction site security	• Accounting
	• Legal
	Insurance during construction
	Marketing costs and commissions
	Interest and expenses on any loans during construction

Based on this definition, it is easy to see how the value and price of the property may not correspond with its cost. Depending on many factors, such as the economic climate, real estate market, and the seller's situation, a property could, in fact, sell for *less* than its cost to develop, build, and maintain.

Principles of Value

Substitution means *an informed buyer will not pay more for a home than a comparable substitute.* Although each home is said to be unique, there is a limit to what a buyer will pay. No one really knows where that point is until the home is listed for too much.

The theory of substitution can also be applied to items within a home. When an appraiser determines the value of a home's fireplace in an area where most homes do not have one, she must take into account buyers are not going to pay more for that home than they would for a similar home, plus the cost of adding a fireplace. In other words, if the addition of a fireplace costs $2,500, an appraiser cannot justify adding much more than that to the value of a home.

Conformity means *a particular home achieves its maximum value when surrounded by homes similar in style and function.* This applies to neighborhoods, as well, which are more desirable when there is a general similarity in utility and value for all homes there. A home that stands out as being too different from the rest is worth less than that same home would be if it were in a different, more homogeneous neighborhood.

Contribution means *a particular item or feature of a home is worth what it actually contributes in value to that property.* If a five-bedroom home is typically not desirable, then putting an addition onto a house to add a fifth bedroom does not increase its value. The owner may want or need a fifth bedroom, but he should not expect the addition to add to the home's value when it is sold. The value of an item or improvement is equal *only* to what a prospective buyer is willing to pay for

The Appraisal Process

Regardless of the approach an appraiser uses, a step-by-step process is followed in all cases. The purpose of the process is to ensure the steps leading to the creation of the appraisal report are orderly, and the report itself is thorough, comprehensive, and accurate.

The steps in the appraisal process are:

1. Define the appraisal—state the problem.
2. Define the data and sources necessary to perform the appraisal.
3. Collect and analyze the relevant data.
4. Determine the highest and best use for the subject property.
5. Determine the value of the land separately from the structures.
6. Estimate the value of the subject property using all three approaches.
7. Reconcile estimates of value using all three approaches.
8. Report conclusions of the valuation process, including all data used and the final value estimate.

The Appraisal Report

The final step in the appraisal process is the appraisal report – the primary means of communicating the appraisal results to the client.

The appraisal report not only reports a final opinion of value for the subject property, but also explains the appraiser's reasoning to the client and anyone else authorized to read the appraisal report. With this in mind, the report should be clear and concise, logical and consistent, and supported and documented with market evidence in defense of its conclusions. Remember, the appraiser's opinions must be supported by analytical data.

The **fundamental elements of every appraisal report** are:

1. The report must be clear, accurate, and not misleading.
2. The report must contain sufficient information to be understood properly by the intended users.
3. The appraisal report must disclose any extraordinary assumptions, or other assignment conditions, that directly affect the appraisal.

Comparative Market Analysis

A comparative market analysis **(CMA)** is part of the listing process. It involves recommending a price to the owner that will be the listing price. The price will be determined by comparing other properties that are similar to the subject property. There are usually three sets of properties we will use:

- Recent closed sales,
- Those currently on the market, and
- Recently expired.

As stated at the beginning of the chapter, for new licensees it will take time and experience to be able to pick the right properties to use and how to explain to the homeowner the reasons for their use. No two properties are the same; that is where the experience will come – in choosing the correct properties for your CMA. That is why you will always want to pick properties as similar in all aspects to the subject property. This will save you time when you use properties with the same style, age, lot size, number of bedrooms, and baths, etc.

Remember comparables – the other term used is "comps" – should be as similar as possible to your subject property. Most agents will utilize the MLS system to retrieve the comps they need. They also can be gotten from the office files or town clerk's files. When using an MLS system to generate the CMA, it is basically self explanatory. This is another area that agents will need experience with. The computer will pick listings, but the agent must know which ones to choose.

Agents must understand that any property that they put into the CMA must be explained fully to the owners. The owners may ask why one property sold for one price and another did not sell. This again is where your experience and expertise comes in, explaining the rationale for the sale and why one did not sell. Another important factor in the CMA is **"DOM"** – Days on the Market. This is important because it shows how long it took the different properties to sell, or if there was a price change. It also shows how long expired listings were on the market until expiration. This is one key factor you will address with the owners.

Sample CMA

Shown is a comparative market analysis derived from Multiple Listing Service of Long Island. It is for sample purposes only. A CMA is *not* an appraisal. New York State law specifically states a CMA may *never* be referred to as an appraisal.

Residential Market Analysis

A residential market analysis is an *in-depth study of your listing as it stands on its own, as well as in light of current market conditions*. This is where your expertise

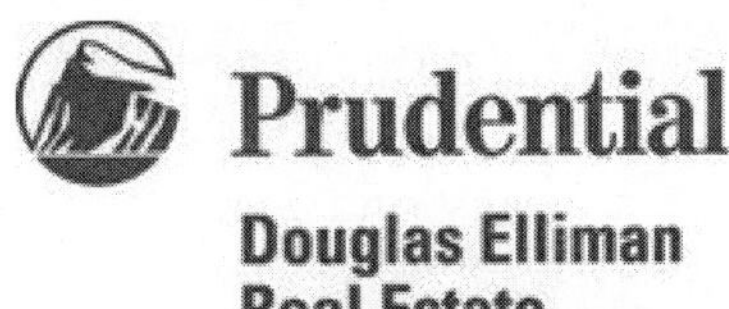

Comparative Market Analysis

Prepared For:

Mr.& Mrs. John & Mary Smith
100 Main Street
Anytown, N. 10000

Prepared By:

William Plunkett
Licensed Sales Associate
bcs927@hotmail.com

Prudential Douglas Elliman RE
2314 Merrick Rd
Merrick, NY 11566
Ph#: (516)623-4500
http://www.prudentialelliman.com

Source: Derived from Multiple Listing Service of Long Island. Reprinted with permission of Bill Plunkett for sample purposes only.

January 8, 2009

Mr.& Mrs. John & Mary Smith
100 Main Street
Anytown, N. 10000

Dear Mr.& Mrs. John & Mary Smith,

Thank you for the opportunity to present this Comparative Market Analysis for 100 Main St. This carefully prepared report of current and past market activity compares this home with other similar homes in the area. The analysis enables you to easily compare the features of this home with others and to determine the best pricing strategy for today's market.

We look forward to working with you in the future. Our firm is committed to providing you with professional and dedicated service. Please do not hesitate to contact me should you require any further information.

Sincerely,

William Plunkett
Licensed Sales Associate

Prudential Douglas Elliman RE

Subject Property Information

Location:
100 Main St
Anytown, NY 10000
School District #: 12

Suggested Price And Taxes:
From: To:
Taxes:

Property Characteristics:
Cape Det 1 Family
7 Rooms, 4 Bedrooms, 2 Baths, 1 Kitchen
Eat In Kitchen: Y Basement: Full Finished Bsmt: Y
Garage: 1 Driveway: Pvt
Fuel: Oil Heat: Hw
Approx. Year Built: 1960 Appearance: Excel

Comments:
Beautiful Cape on tree lined street. All updated

William Plunkett
Licensed Sales Associate

Prudential Douglas Elliman RE
2314 Merrick Rd
Merrick, NY 11566
(516)623-4500

-- Information herein deemed reliable but not guaranteed --

Side By Side Listing Comparison

	Subject Property	On The Market *	On The Market *	On The Market *	Recently Sold
	Photo Not Available				
ML#		2107849	2117676	2120353	2064912
Address	100 Main St	251 Meadowbrook Rd	210 Fox Ct	2076 Bruce Ln	1113 South Dr
Town	Anytown	N. Merrick	N. Merrick	N. Merrick	N. Merrick
School Dist #	12	29	29	29	29
Price		$424,900 *	$449,990 *	$449,990	$345,000
Style	Cape	Cape	Cape	Cape	Cape
# Families	1	1	1	1	1
Det/Att	Det	Det	Det	Det	Det
Rooms	7	7	7	7	6
Bedrooms	4	3	4	4	3
Baths	2	1	2	2	2
# Kitchens	1	1	1	1	1
Eat In Kitchen	Y	N	N *	N	Y
Basement	Full	Full	Full	Full	Full
Fin Bsmt	Y	N	N	Y	N
# Fireplaces	0	1	0	0	0
Fuel	Oil	Oil	Oil	Gas	Oil
Heat	Hw	Hw	Steam	Hw	Ha
Garage	1	2	0	1	1
Driveway	Pvt	Pvt	N	Pvt	Pvt
Pool	N	N	N	N	N
Taxes		$9,596 *	$8,960	$8,849	$8,417
Approx. Year Built	1960	1933	1949	1950	1949
Appearance	Excel	Excellent	Excellent	Good	As-Is
Lot Size	60x100	65 X 179	36 X 138 Irr	38 X 100 Irr	60 X 100
Waterfront	N	N	N	N	N
Waterview	N	N	N	N	N
Waterfront Desc					
Adult Community		N	N	N	N
Minimum Age					
Listing Date		8/14/2008	9/18/2008	9/26/2008	4/4/2008
Contract Date				*	6/25/2008
Title Date					8/27/2008
Exp Date		2/14/2009	12/31/2008 *	3/26/2009	9/14/2008
Days On Market		147	112	104	82
Original Price		$424,900	$449,990	$449,990	$404,900
Listing Price		$424,900 *	$449,990 *	$449,990	$359,910
Sold Price					$345,000
<u>Adjustments</u>					
Price		$424,900 *	$449,990 *	$449,990	$345,000
Adjustment					
Adjusted Price		$424,900	$449,990	$449,990	$345,000

-- Information herein deemed reliable but not guaranteed; * denotes a change in the data --

Side By Side Listing Comparison

	Subject Property	Recently Sold	Recently Sold	Expired From Market	Expired From Market
	Photo Not Available				
ML#		2086260	2109315	2054754	2073188
Address	100 Main St	1671 Stevens Ave	2076 Bruce Ln	1242 Jerusalem Ave	1671 Stevens Ave
Town	Anytown	N. Merrick	N. Merrick	N. Merrick	N. Merrick
School Dist #	12	29	29	29	29
Price		$349,000	$350,000	$429,000	$434,500
Style	Cape	Cape	Cape	Cape	Cape
# Families	1	1	1	1	1
Det/Att	Det	Det	Det	Det	Det
Rooms	7	7	7	6	7
Bedrooms	4	3	4	4	4
Baths	2	2	2	2	2
# Kitchens	1	1	1	1	1
Eat In Kitchen	Y	N	N	Y	N
Basement	Full	Full	Full	Full	Full
Fin Bsmt	Y	Y	Y	Y	Y
# Fireplaces	0	0	0	0	0
Fuel	Oil	Gas	Oil	Oil	Elec
Heat	Hw	Elec	Hw	Ha	Hw
Garage	1	1.5	1	0	1.5
Driveway	Pvt	Pvt	Pvt	Pvt	Pvt
Pool	N	N	N	N	N
Taxes		$8,460	$7,729	$8,867	$8,462
Approx. Year Built	1960	1955	1950	1949	1955
Appearance	Excel	Good	Good	Excellent	Good ++
Lot Size	60x100	50 X 125	38 X 100	58 X 94	50 X 125
Waterfront	N	N	N	N	N
Waterview	N	N	N	N	N
Waterfront Desc					
Adult Community		N	N	N	N
Minimum Age					
Listing Date		6/6/2008	8/20/2008	3/6/2008	4/29/2008
Contract Date		8/8/2008	9/15/2008		
Title Date		10/17/2008	9/24/2008		
Exp Date		12/6/2008	11/18/2008	6/6/2008	5/31/2008
Days On Market		63	26	92	32
Original Price		$399,000	$349,900	$429,000	$234,500
Listing Price		$369,000	$349,900	$429,000	$434,500
Sold Price		$349,000	$350,000		
Adjustments					
Price		$349,000	$350,000	$429,000	$434,500
Adjustment					
Adjusted Price		$349,000	$350,000	$429,000	$434,500

-- Information herein deemed reliable but not guaranteed; * denotes a change in the data --

Side By Side Listing Comparison

	Subject Property	Expired From Market
	Photo Not Available	
ML#		2055502
Address	100 Main St	28 Wellington Rd
Town	Anytown	N. Merrick
School Dist #	12	29
Price		$469,000
Style	Cape	Cape
# Families	1	1
Det/Att	Det	Det
Rooms	7	7
Bedrooms	4	4
Baths	2	2
# Kitchens	1	1
Eat In Kitchen	Y	Y
Basement	Full	Full
Fin Bsmt	Y	Y
# Fireplaces	0	0
Fuel	Oil	Gas
Heat	Hw	Hw
Garage	1	1
Driveway	Pvt	Pvt
Pool	N	N
Taxes		$9,417
Approx. Year Built	1960	1947
Appearance	Excel	Mint
Lot Size	60x100	54 X 120
Waterfront	N	N
Waterview	N	N
Waterfront Desc		
Adult Community		N
Minimum Age		
Listing Date		3/8/2008
Contract Date		
Title Date		
Exp Date		6/30/2008
Days On Market		114
Original Price		$499,000
Listing Price		$469,000
Sold Price		
Adjustments		
Price		$469,000
Adjustment		
Adjusted Price		$469,000

SAMPLE

-- Information herein deemed reliable but not guaranteed; * denotes a change in the data --

Comparable Summary Report

For:

100 Main St
Anytown, NY 10000
1/8/2009

Subject Property

ML#	Address	Town	Style	Rooms	Bedrooms	Baths	Suggested Price
-	100 Main St	Anytown	Cape	7	4	2	

Homes Recently Sold

ML#	Address	Town	Style	Rms	Br	Bth	List Price	Sold Price	% Dif	List Date	Cont Date	Title Date	DOM
2064912	1113 South Dr	N. Merrick	Cape	6	3	2	$359,910	$345,000	4.14	4/4/2008	6/25/2008	8/27/2008	82
2086260	1671 Stevens Ave	N. Merrick	Cape	7	3	2	$369,000	$349,000	5.42	6/6/2008	8/8/2008	10/17/2008	63
2109315	2076 Bruce Ln	N. Merrick	Cape	7	4	2	$349,900	$350,000	-0.03	8/20/2008	9/15/2008	9/24/2008	26
	# Properties: 3				Averages:		$359,603	$348,000	3.18				57

Homes Currently On The Market

ML#	Address	Town	Style	Rms	Br	Bth	Orig Price	List Price	% Dif	List Date	DOM
2107849	251 Meadowbrook Rd	N. Merrick	Cape	7	3	1	$424,900	$424,900 *	0.00	8/14/2008	147
2117676	210 Fox Ct	N. Merrick	Cape	7	4	2	$449,990	$449,990 *	0.00	9/18/2008	112
2120353	2076 Bruce Ln	N. Merrick	Cape	7	4	2	$449,990	$449,990	0.00	9/26/2008	104
	# Properties: 3				Averages:		$441,627	$441,627	0.00		121

Homes Expired From The Market

ML#	Address	Town	Style	Rms	Br	Bth	Orig Price	List Price	% Dif	List Date	Exp Date	DOM
2054754	1242 Jerusalem Ave	N. Merrick	Cape	6	4	2	$429,000	$429,000	0.00	3/6/2008	6/6/2008	92
2073188	1671 Stevens Ave	N. Merrick	Cape	7	4	2	$234,500	$434,500	-85.3	4/29/2008	5/31/2008	32
2055502	28 Wellington Rd	N. Merrick	Cape	7	4	2	$499,000	$469,000	6.01	3/8/2008	6/30/2008	114
	# Properties: 3				Averages:		$387,500	$444,167	-26.43			79

-- Information herein deemed reliable but not guaranteed; * denotes a change in the data --

Recently Sold

1113 South Dr
N. Merrick School Dist# 29
Cape1 Family Det

List Price: **$359,910**
Sold Price: **$345,000**
Taxes: $8,417
Approx. Year Built: 1949

Rooms: 6	Fuel: Oil	Appearance: As-Is
Bedrooms: 3	Heat: Ha	Lot Size: 60 X 100
Baths: 2	Garage: 1	Waterfront: N
#Kitchens: 1	Drive: Pvt	Waterview: N
Eat In Kitchen: Y	Basement: Full	Pool: N
#Fireplaces: 0	Finished: N	Porch:
Dining Room: None	Construction: Frame	Patio:
List Date: 4/4/2008	Contract Date: 6/25/2008	DOM: 82
Title Date: 8/27/2008		ML#: **2064912**

1671 Stevens Ave
N. Merrick School Dist# 29
Cape1 Family Det

List Price: **$369,000**
Sold Price: **$349,000**
Taxes: $8,460
Approx. Year Built: 1955

Rooms: 7	Fuel: Gas	Appearance: Good
Bedrooms: 3	Heat: Elec	Lot Size: 50 X 125
Baths: 2	Garage: 1.5	Waterfront: N
#Kitchens: 1	Drive: Pvt	Waterview: N
Eat In Kitchen: N	Basement: Full	Pool: N
#Fireplaces: 0	Finished: Y	Porch:
Dining Room: Formal	Construction: Siding	Patio: Rear
List Date: 6/6/2008	Contract Date: 8/8/2008	DOM: 63
Title Date: 10/17/2008		ML#: **2086260**

2076 Bruce Ln
N. Merrick School Dist# 29
Cape1 Family Det

List Price: **$349,900**
Sold Price: **$350,000**
Taxes: $7,729
Approx. Year Built: 1950

Rooms: 7	Fuel: Oil	Appearance: Good
Bedrooms: 4	Heat: Hw	Lot Size: 38 X 100
Baths: 2	Garage: 1	Waterfront: N
#Kitchens: 1	Drive: Pvt	Waterview: N
Eat In Kitchen: N	Basement: Full	Pool: N
#Fireplaces: 0	Finished: Y	Porch:
Dining Room: Formal	Construction: Frame	Patio:
List Date: 8/20/2008	Contract Date: 9/15/2008	DOM: 26
Title Date: 9/24/2008		ML#: **2109315**

-- Information herein deemed reliable but not guaranteed; * denotes a change in the data --

On The Market

251 Meadowbrook Rd
N. Merrick
Cape1 Family Det

List Price: **$424,900 ***
School Dist# 29
Taxes: $9,596 *
Approx. Year Built: 1933

Rooms: 7	Fuel: Oil	Appearance: Excellent
Bedrooms: 3	Heat: Hw	Lot Size: 65 X 179
Baths: 1	Garage: 2	Waterfront: N
#Kitchens: 1	Drive: Pvt	Waterview: N
Eat In Kitchen: N	Basement: Full	Pool: N
#Fireplaces: 1	Finished: N	Porch:
Dining Room: Formal	Construction: Sided	Patio: Y
List Date: 8/14/2008		DOM: 147
		ML#: **2107849**

210 Fox Ct
N. Merrick
Cape1 Family Det

List Price: **$449,990 ***
School Dist# 29
Taxes: $8,960
Approx. Year Built: 1949

Rooms: 7	Fuel: Oil	Appearance: Excellent
Bedrooms: 4	Heat: Steam	Lot Size: 36 X 138 Irr
Baths: 2	Garage: 0	Waterfront: N
#Kitchens: 1	Drive: N	Waterview: N
Eat In Kitchen: N *	Basement: Full	Pool: N
#Fireplaces: 0	Finished: N	Porch:
Dining Room: Other *	Construction: Brick/Viny	Patio: Yes
List Date: 9/18/2008		DOM: 112
		ML#: **2117676**

2076 Bruce Ln
N. Merrick
Cape1 Family Det

List Price: **$449,990**
School Dist# 29
Taxes: $8,849
Approx. Year Built: 1950

Rooms: 7	Fuel: Gas	Appearance: Good
Bedrooms: 4	Heat: Hw	Lot Size: 38 X 100 Irr
Baths: 2	Garage: 1	Waterfront: N
#Kitchens: 1	Drive: Pvt	Waterview: N
Eat In Kitchen: N	Basement: Full	Pool: N
#Fireplaces: 0	Finished: Y	Porch:
Dining Room: Formal	Construction: Frame *	Patio: Yes
List Date: 9/26/2008		DOM: 104
		ML#: **2120353**

-- Information herein deemed reliable but not guaranteed; * denotes a change in the data --

Expired From The Market

1242 Jerusalem Ave
N. Merrick School Dist# 29
Cape1 Family Det

List Price: **$429,000**
Taxes: $8,867
Approx. Year Built: 1949

Rooms: 6	Fuel: Oil	Appearance: Excellent
Bedrooms: 4	Heat: Ha	Lot Size: 58 X 94
Baths: 2	Garage: 0	Waterfront: N
#Kitchens: 1	Drive: Pvt	Waterview: N
Eat In Kitchen: Y	Basement: Full	Pool: N
#Fireplaces: 0	Finished: Y	Porch:
Dining Room: None	Construction: Vinyl	Patio:
List Date: 3/6/2008		DOM: 92
Expiration Date: 6/6/2008		ML#: **2054754**

1671 Stevens Ave
N. Merrick School Dist# 29
Cape1 Family Det

List Price: **$434,500**
Taxes: $8,462
Approx. Year Built: 1955

Rooms: 7	Fuel: Elec	Appearance: Good ++
Bedrooms: 4	Heat: Hw	Lot Size: 50 X 125
Baths: 2	Garage: 1.5	Waterfront: N
#Kitchens: 1	Drive: Pvt	Waterview: N
Eat In Kitchen: N	Basement: Full	Pool: N
#Fireplaces: 0	Finished: Y	Porch: None
Dining Room: L-Shaped	Construction: Framed	Patio: Rear
List Date: 4/29/2008		DOM: 32
Expiration Date: 5/31/2008		ML#: **2073188**

28 Wellington Rd
N. Merrick School Dist# 29
Cape1 Family Det

List Price: **$469,000**
Taxes: $9,417
Approx. Year Built: 1947

Rooms: 7	Fuel: Gas	Appearance: Mint
Bedrooms: 4	Heat: Hw	Lot Size: 54 X 120
Baths: 2	Garage: 1	Waterfront: N
#Kitchens: 1	Drive: Pvt	Waterview: N
Eat In Kitchen: Y	Basement: Full	Pool: N
#Fireplaces: 0	Finished: Y	Porch:
Dining Room: Formal	Construction: Brk/Alum	Patio:
List Date: 3/8/2008		DOM: 114
Expiration Date: 6/30/2008		ML#: **2055502**

-- Information herein deemed reliable but not guaranteed; * denotes a change in the data --

Market Statistical Report

For:

100 Main St
Anytown, NY 10000
1/8/2009

	DOM	Price
Subject Property		*Suggested Listing Price*
100 Main St		
Recently Sold	*DOM*	*Sold Price*
2076 Bruce Ln	26	$350,000
1671 Stevens Ave	63	$349,000
1113 South Dr	82	$345,000
On The Market	*DOM*	*List Price*
2076 Bruce Ln	104	$449,990
210 Fox Ct	112	$449,990 *
251 Meadowbrook Rd	147	$424,900 *
Expired From The Market	*DOM*	*List Price*
1671 Stevens Ave	32	$434,500
1242 Jerusalem Ave	92	$429,000
28 Wellington Rd	114	$469,000

-- Information herein deemed reliable but not guaranteed, * denotes a change in the data --

Marketing Plan

For:

Mr.& Mrs. John & Mary Smith
100 Main Street
Anytown, N. 10000

Tentative Date	**Activity**
	I will hold open houses and advertise in local papaer etc!!!!!

Prepared By: **William Plunkett**
Prudential Douglas Elliman RE

comes in. The more knowledge you have of particular areas and markets, the more likely you are to sell the property quickly and for the best price. These conditions will determine how the property should be marketed. Remember a "property priced correctly is half sold."

There are several elements to consider when preparing a residential market analysis, including:

- Recently sold properties
- Assets and drawbacks
- Currently listed competing properties
- Area market conditions
- Recently expired listings
- Recommended terms
- Curb appeal
- Market value range
- Market position

Recently Sold Properties

When researching recently sold properties, choose several located in the same area as your subject property that are similar in style. The comparable properties should be analyzed as to number of days on the market, location to subject property, condition, lot size, listed price, any reduction in price, and final sale price. This is where your time will come into play. As a new licensee you probably will not have any knowledge of these homes. The job is to research the comparables with any means possible – talking to your broker or manager, other agents – you must have an understanding of these properties before you can discuss them with your potential sellers. You will also determine the number of days the properties remained on the market, the list price, and the final sale price. This is the most important part of the job – having a thorough understanding of the sold properties and the reason why they sold for whatever price there is.

Currently Listed Competing Properties

Another important factor in the residential market analysis concerns the properties in competition with your listing. When analyzing competing listings, pay close attention to:

- Number of competing properties on the market
- Length of time the properties have been listed
- Whether the list price has been reduced
- How many times the list price has been reduced

The important point in this factor is that these homes are the competition to your owner's property. This must be explained to them in a professional way. They must understand that everyone feels their property is unique and always better than the competition. The market is the way properties are sold, very rarely through emotion, even though it is an important part of the buying process. You can also use, if needed, properties that are under contract. This will not give you a sold price but an idea of how the property was listed and what transpired with price – if there were any price changes – days on the market, the listed price when it went to contract, which could or not be the selling price.

Recently Expired Listings

As you know, a listing expires when a property does not sell within the time frame stated in the listing agreement. When listings expire because the price was more than market conditions justified, researching these properties can give you valuable insight on what is an acceptable list price. A careful research of these properties is valuable. Again, as the new licensee, you have work to do in discovering the possible reasons for the high prices. There are times when owners are just not motivated to sell at the price they were told is fair market value. This is what you must ascertain: If the property was just overpriced or if there were other reasons it did not sell.

Curb Appeal

Even though this portion of the residential market analysis is subjective, it is still an important part of your research. Since many buyers make a decision on whether they will look at a home simply by how it looks from the street, curb appeal is very important. Items like landscaping, color, building materials, and the distance from the house to the road are all part of curb appeal. Compare your subject property to others in the neighborhood and then work with clients to maximize curb appeal. You may have a property that doesn't have the same appeal as your subject property, but it may offer other amenities that may be better. No matter what, the feeling on curb appeal the first impression is a lasting one.

Market Position

Market position is relatively simple: Compared to your listing, *how many similar properties are for sale in the same neighborhood and for a similar price*? Now, where does your listing fit in among these properties? Once you have determined your listing's market position, you can effectively market it.

Assets and Drawbacks

Your residential market analysis should include a comparison of the assets and drawbacks of your listing relative to competing properties. Your research should reveal how these things affected the sale and/or sale price of the comparable properties. A property in a cul-de-sac or quiet residential street will have more appeal than one on a main road or busy street. Property condition will stand out from inferior ones. Also look at properties with nice landscaping that have been well maintained. This will help you in evaluating your subject property to the comparables. How does the subject property compare to these homes?

Area Market Conditions

The stability and health of the real estate market as a whole directly impacts your business and what your clients can expect – whether they are buying or selling a home. If market conditions are favorable, homes are likely to sell faster than in a slow market. Of course, this determines your marketing strategy and is why researching the area's market conditions is an important component to a residential market analysis. If there are more competing properties it may take longer to sell. Some will look at seasonal conditions, like weather holidays, time of year for school. If the market is favorable, these conditions very rarely will have an impact on the sale.

Recommended Terms of Sale

The terms of your sales agreement may directly affect how long a home is on the market. For instance, your seller gets an offer on her home after it has been on the market for only 11 days. Her new home, however, will not be ready to move into for four months. She did not anticipate selling so quickly. Do the buyers still agree to the sale? What if they are not in the position to live in their current residence four more months? Here, the terms of the sale directly affect the buyer and the seller. Other terms that are often a concern include:

- Interest rates.
- Types of financing available (i.e., seller financing).
- Seller concessions (i.e., paying closing costs).

Market Value Range

After conducting your research, you will want to assign a price range to the listing. At this time, you will want to explain how you arrived at the value range and give your recommendation for the list price.

You will soon find that many sellers think their house is an exception and will garner the highest price you have presented, even if you show them why it is unlikely they will be able to sell it for that price. Use caution in these situations. It may be more prudent for you to walk away from this listing rather than try to sell it for more than the market supports. In the end, your clients will be frustrated their property is on the market longer than expected, and you will be frustrated because your marketing effort is not producing a sale.

The Agent's Roles and Responsibilities

Even though a residential market analysis is not an official appraisal report, real estate salespeople do have a specific role and certain responsibilities when preparing them.

Competence and Confidence

The residential market analysis should be the foundation on which your listing presentation is built. The information contained within the analysis must be justifiable and pertinent to a seller's specific case.

As a real estate professional, you should be competent and confident in all areas of your listing presentation. Your training and experience should be helpful for you to begin working with customers and providing the service they need and deserve. All licensees must have the competence and confidence in themselves when they are presenting the CMA. The salesperson must be prepared to answer any and all questions from the owners, and have the data to justify their answers. Competence is the key to success. Never take shortcuts or give customers an answer you do not know to be true – this will undermine all you have worked for thus far. Remembering generally there were two or three other agents giving their presentation also. That is why the competence and confidence of your presentation will be the key to your success.

Diligence

Working with sellers involves much more than putting a sign in the yard and hoping for the best. It is your responsibility to do everything you can for clients to create a positive experience and help them meet their ultimate goal of selling a home. You can provide outstanding service by continually researching the market, adjusting your marketing strategy, and always working in your clients' best interest. Once you have the listing there is a lot of paperwork involved. The salesperson must constantly stay abreast of the activities involving the listing. Follow through in contacting agents who showed the property and ask for feedback from their buyers. The licensee must always communicate with the sellers regarding anything concerning the listing. The agent should have a schedule when to stop by and discuss with the owners regarding any showings, what was said how the buyers felt about the property whether it is positive or negative you must always be truthful and honest with your sellers. Always give the sellers any change in the activity in the market or competing properties.

Documentation

It may seem elementary, but documentation is extremely important when it comes to the residential market analysis and real estate in general. To better serve clients, always keep good records of the calls you receive and the calls you make regarding any property. You will also want to document who showed your listings and what their clients' impressions were.

Documenting information and statistics on new listings and competing properties is also a good idea, so you can effectively market your own listings.

Communication

Real estate is a team effort between you and your clients, and communication is the key to making the "team" successful. Your clients will expect to hear from you regularly, whether there is anything new to report or not! That is why documentation is so important. You can relay even the tiniest piece of information and, usually, clients will be appreciative of your effort. Regularly update clients on the market activity of their home, as well as information on competing homes. Also, communicate how you are marketing their home. Keep them informed regarding any broker open house you had, and the remarks or suggestions from other agents. Remind them we need the other agents to help sell the home. After any public open houses you have, give them feedback on what, if anything, the customers had said to you. Stay in touch with the agents showing the property and ask for their feedback from their buyers, and relate this to your owners. Keeping your owners abreast of the market activities surrounding their home and any advice you feel is important to marketing the property better will only make you look and sound like the professional you are. Always listen before you speak, this way you will learn much more.

SUMMARY

1. **Appraisal** is an *opinion of value of property, as of a specified date, supportable by objective data.* Appraisals are performed for a variety of reasons, including tax, loan, and insurance purposes. Buyers and sellers want to know how much a property is worth before they make an offer or list a home.
2. Real estate agents need basic knowledge of the appraisal process because customers will have questions. And even though most real estate agents are not equipped to offer official opinions of value in the form of an appraisal, they are responsible for assigning value when listing homes and/or negotiating the sale price for buyers.
3. **Real property** is *land and everything attached to it*, and **personal property** is *any property that is moveable and not affixed to the land*. There are several characteristics of real property—**value characteristics**, including ***demand***, ***utility***, ***scarcity***, and ***transferability***; and **physical characteristics**, including *uniqueness, immobility*, and *indestructibility*.

4. Several factors affect value, including *economic*, *governmental*, and *social factors*. A good appraiser is aware of these and knows how to weigh them when subjective criteria must be applied in an appraisal. The **broad market factors** that affect a property's value are *supply and demand*, and *uniqueness and scarcity*. Additional factors considered when appraising and valuing properties are **highest and best use**, **location**, **substitution**, **conformity**, and **contribution**.

5. **Appraisal**, **valuation**, and **evaluation** are all common terms. It is important to note they do *not* mean the same thing and are *not* interchangeable. **Appraisal** is *an unbiased estimate of the nature, quality, value, or utility of an interest in or aspect of, identified real estate*. **Property valuation** refers to *the actual approaches appraisers use to determine the market value of a piece of property*. **Evaluation** is *a study of the nature, quality, or utility of certain property interests in which a value estimate is not necessarily required* (e.g., determining highest and best use, feasibility, market supply and demand, etc.).

6. **Market value** is the *expected price*; **market price** is the *actual price paid*. Additional types of value include: *mortgage value, investment value, insurable value, assessed value*, and *value in use*. In real estate, value, price, and cost all have separate meanings. **Value** is *expected price*. **Price** is *the amount a ready, willing, and able buyer agrees to pay for a property and a seller agrees to accept under the terms of the transaction*. **Cost** is *the total dollar expenditure for land, labor, materials, legal services, architectural design, financing, taxes paid during construction, interest, contractors' overhead and profit, and entrepreneurial overhead and profit*. There are *two types of costs*—**direct** (land, materials, labor, building permits, equipment, etc.) and **indirect** (taxes, engineering fees, insurance, marketing, etc.).

7. Appraisers value properties using *three different methods*: sales comparison approach, cost approach, and income approach. The **sales comparison approach** *develops an opinion of value by comparing the property being appraised with other properties that reflect a typical buyer's action in a sales transaction*. **Cost approach** *develops an opinion of value by calculating the cost of the building structure on the land, subtracting any depreciation and adding value*. The **income approach** *estimates the value of real estate by analyzing the revenue, or income, the property currently generates or could generate, often comparing it to other similar properties*.

8. **Adjusting** properties is the process of making chosen comparables come as close as possible in features to the subject so meaningful price comparisons can be made. **The subject property never changes**. In order to make adjustments, an understanding of what is significant is required. Among other things, the sale date, lot size, condition, square footage, and terms of sale are all considered significant.

9. **Depreciation** is *the loss in value to property for any reason*. Loss in value can be attributed to *physical deterioration*, *functional obsolescence*, and *external obsolescence*.

10. As part of an appraiser's scope of work decision, she must *determine whether the cost estimate is based on replacing or reproducing the improvements*. **Replacement** is *building the functional equivalent of the original building using modern materials, design, and functional layout*. *Reproduction* is *building an exact replica of the original building, duplicating the materials, design, functional layout, workmanship, inadequacies, etc.*

11. A **comparative market analysis (CMA)** is a *method of determining the approximate market value of a home by comparing the subject property to other homes in the same neighborhood or vicinity that have sold, are presently for sale, or did not sell*. Real estate agents can, and quite often, provide CMAs for their clients. Sellers might need a CMA to determine the home's list price. Buyers might need a CMA to determine a fair price to offer for a home.

12. A **CMA** is not an appraisal. New York State law specifically states a CMA *may never* be referred to as an appraisal.

13. In order to determine how to market a property, a residential market analysis is required. A **residential market analysis** is an *in-depth study of a listing as it stands on its own, as well as in light of current market conditions*. There are several elements to a residential market analysis, including researching: recently sold properties, currently competing listings, recently expired listings, curb appeal, market position, assets and drawbacks, area market conditions, recommended terms, and market value range.

14. As a real estate professional, you have several roles and responsibilities when it comes to the residential market analysis. You must always *demonstrate competence and diligence as well as keep accurate and thorough documentation, and communicate professionally and often with your clients*.

10-A

Real Estate Math

In This Session

Real estate agents are frequently faced with math calculations to determine commission, interest rates, and monthly mortgage payments, profit, and more. While some people are wary of math, it does not have to be challenging. In this session, you will look at basic concepts and formulas necessary to respond to the most typical calculations.

You'll learn how to:

- Measure square footage and acreage.
- Calculate commission.
- Calculate the net to seller.
- Calculate annual interest.
- Calculate percentage of profit and loss.

Key Terms

- Acre
- Commission
- Cubic Feet
- Front Foot / Frontage
- Hectare
- Interest
- Net to Seller
- Perimeter
- Square Feet

Measurements

There will be times when it's necessary to calculate the area of property. For instance, when figuring market values of properties in the area, some properties may list the square footage of a bedroom, others may just provide dimensions. Real estate licensees will have to convert one or the other to make a comparison. The same is true for lot dimensions. Perhaps the dimensions of a lot are listed, but the client wants to know the size in acres. First, here is some key information:

Linear Measurement		
12 inches	=	1 foot
3 feet	=	1 yard
16 1/2 feet	=	1 rod, perch, or pole
5,280 feet	=	1 mile, 80 chains

Cubic Measurement		
27 cubic feet	=	1 cubic yard
1 cubic foot	=	7.48 gallons

Square Measurement		
43,560 square feet	=	1 acre, 10 square chains
2.47 acres	=	1 hectare (10,000 square meters)
640 acres	=	1 square mile
1 square mile	=	1 section
36 sections	=	1 township
9 square feet	=	1 square yard

Area Measurement

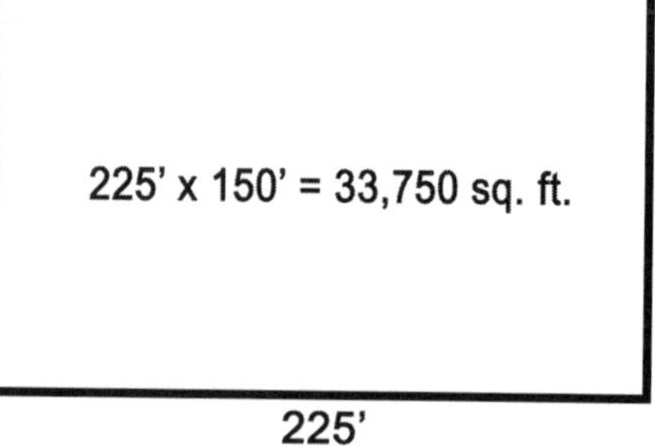

To determine the area of a square or rectangular parcel, the equation is:

Area = Width x Length (AWL)

Area ÷ Width = Length

Area ÷ Length = Width

If given the area and length and asked to find the width, for example, divide the area by the length:

33,750 Square Feet ÷ 225 Feet (Length) = 150 Feet (Width)

Front Feet

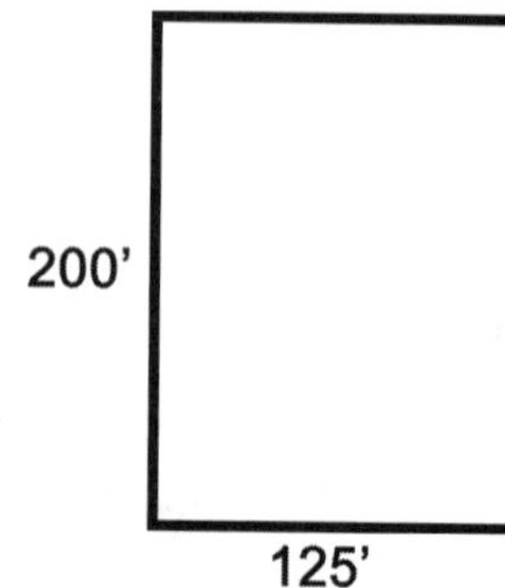

Front feet, or **frontage**, is *that portion of the lot that faces the street.* In a measurement, the frontage is always the *first* number.

In this example, the lot is 125' x 200', so the frontage is 125 feet.

Triangular-Shaped Lots

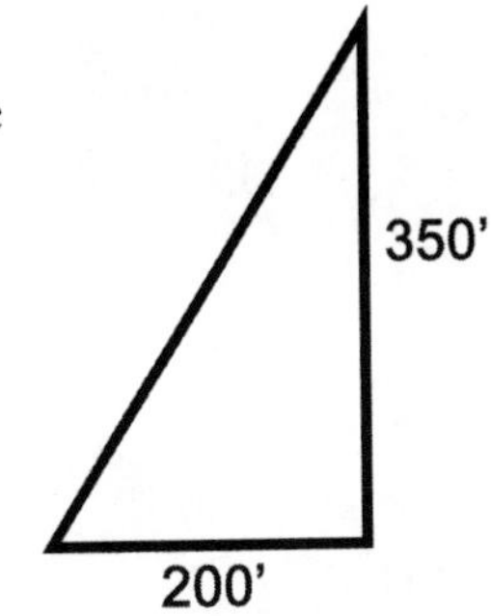

Triangular, or pie-shaped, lots are also fairly common. There are two common ways to figure the square footage of a triangle:

- Multiply **half** of the **base** measurement times the **height:**

  (200 ÷ 2) x 350 = 35,000 Sq. Ft.

- Multiply the **base** times the **height** and divide by 2:

  (200 x 350) ÷ 2 = 35,000 Sq. Ft.

Irregular Lots

Like houses, irregular lots tend to be a collection of many squares, rectangles, and sometimes triangles. In the most basic sense, the total square footage can be determined by separating the house into individual shapes, figuring the square footage for all parts, then adding them together. In this simple example, the total measurement would be 1,775 square feet (1,250 + 150 + 375).

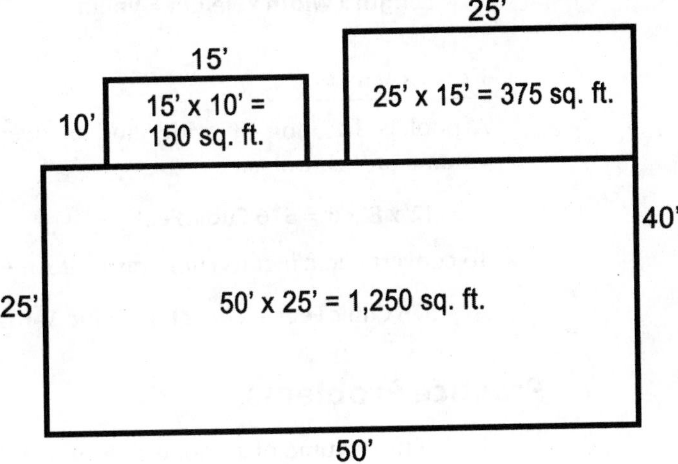

Acreage

There are **43,560 square feet** in an acre. To find the acreage of a lot:

Square Footage ÷ 43,560 = Acres

FOR EXAMPLE:

George and Judy are looking for an empty lot to build a custom home, and they want at least half an acre. You have found a lot that you think is suitable for them. It measures 120' x 200'. Will this lot meet their size request?

First, find the total square footage:

120 x 200 = 24,000 Total Square Feet

Then divide to find the acreage:

24,000 ÷ 43,560 = .55 Acres

Yes! This lot is just over half an acre. George and Judy should be pleased.

Perimeter (Linear Footage)

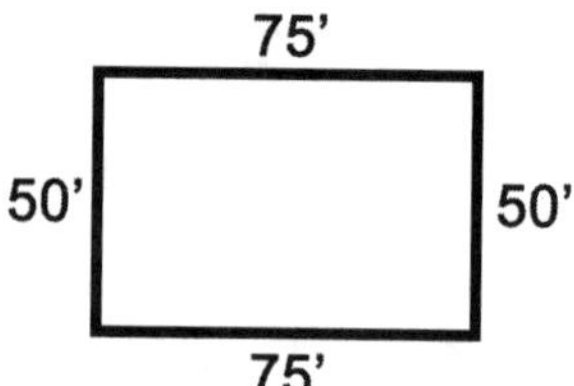

To find the **perimeter** of a lot, *add the length in feet around the outside of all sides of the lot.*

FOR EXAMPLE:

A 75' x 50' back yard would require 250 linear feet of fencing (75 + 50 + 75 + 50).

Cubic Measurement

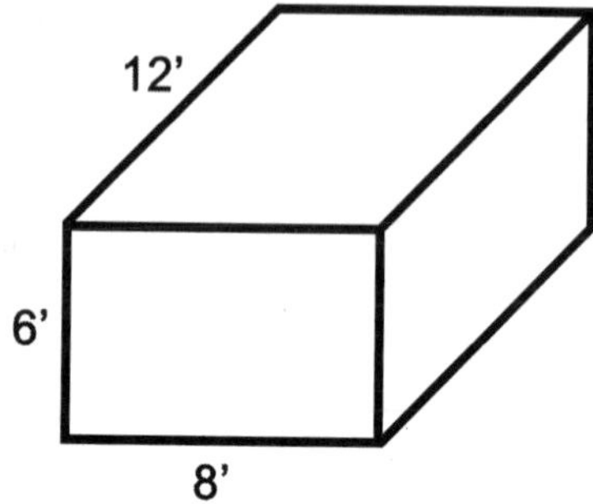

Cubic measurement may be needed to determine the volume of something, for example, the airspace in a room or the amount of water in a pool.

Length x Width x Height = Volume

FOR EXAMPLE:

A pool is 12' long, 8' wide, and 6' deep. The volume of the pool is:

12' x 8' x 6' = 576 Cubic Feet

To convert cubic feet to cubic yards, it's necessary to divide by 27:

576 Cubic Feet ÷ 27 = 21.33 Cubic Yards

Practice Problems

1. If the volume of a pool is 576 cubic feet, how many gallons of water will it take to fill it?

2. What would a commercial lot, 150' x 600', priced at $2,000 per front foot cost? What would it cost at $3.25 per square foot?

3. If a bag of concrete makes 1 cubic yard, how many bags will it take to pour a 60 foot x 4 foot sidewalk that's 4 inches deep?

4. A triangular lot measures 110' across the front and is 80' deep. What is the square footage of the lot?

5. A local nature preserve takes up 42 acres of land. How many square feet is that?

T-Math

Many real estate situations require the ability to calculate percentages, for example, commissions or property assessment. An easy method for solving these problems is called **T-math**. When using T-math, the ***horizontal line means divide*** and the ***vertical line means multiply.***

When calculating percentages, the part goes on the top of the T. The percent goes on the bottom, and the whole goes on the bottom opposite the percent. When you know any two variables, you can easily find the third:

Part
÷ ÷
Percent x Whole

Percent	**x**	**Whole**	**=**	**Part**
Part	**÷**	**Percent**	**=**	**Whole**
Part	**÷**	**Whole**	**=**	**Percent**

Commission

When working with commission, the *commission is the part*, the *commission rate is the percent*, and the *sale price is the whole:*

Sale Price	**x**	**Rate**	**=**	**Commission**
Commission	**÷**	**Rate**	**=**	**Sale Price**
Commission	**÷**	**Sale Price**	**=**	**Rate**

For example:

Albany Real Estate sells one of its listed properties for $211,000. If the commission rate is 6%, what is the total commission?

Commission
÷ ÷
6% x $211,000
OR 7%

.06 x $211,000 = $12,660

The total commission is $12,660.

Practice Problems

1. A property lists for $100,000 and sells in a cooperative transaction for $90,000. The commission rate is 7%, which the brokerages split evenly. How much does each company get?

2. One brokerage sells another brokerage's listing. Both receive half of the 6% commission. If each company receives $6,060, what is the price of the home?

3. An agent sells his own listing; the broker gets half of the commission and the agent gets half, which is $5,122. The home sells for $157,600. What is the commission rate?

4. A property measures 230 feet x 310 feet. If it sells for $14,000 per acre and the commission rate is 6.5%, how much commission will the seller pay?

5. The seller pays a total of $14,000 commission on a sale of $200,000. The cooperating selling broker earns a 3% commission. The listing broker takes 5% of his earned commission off the top of his brokerage's earned commission to pay a franchise fee. Of the remaining balance, the broker keeps 40% and pays the listing agent 60%. How much did the listing agent earn?

Net to Seller

A **seller's share**, or **net to seller**, is an *estimate of the money a seller should receive from a real estate transaction, based on a certain selling price after all costs and expenses have been paid.* This is *not* a guarantee but an approximation of what the seller should receive. The purpose of computing the net to seller is to let the seller know how much money he can expect to make from a transaction after everything has been paid. This is important information when considering both a listing price for the property and deciding whether to accept an offer.

FOR EXAMPLE:

Laney wants to sell her home. She must pay off her existing $35,000 mortgage and pay $3,200 in closing costs. She wants to have $40,000 left so she can buy another home. If she pays a 6.5% commission, what is the minimum offer she can accept?

First, subtract the known commission rate from the total sale price to find the percentage of the sale the seller will net:

100% - 6.5% = 93.5%

Total up the other known expenses:

$35,000 + $3,200 + $40,000 = $78,200

Finally, divide the total expenses by the net to seller percent:

$78,200 ÷ 0.935 (93.5%) = $83,636.36

Laney must sell her house for a minimum of $83,637.

Practice Problems

1. The Joneses are selling their house for $260,000. They have to pay 7% commission and closing costs of $8,900. They have to pay off the balance of their existing loan, which is $115,000. How much money will they have left to use as a down payment on their next home? If they use the entire net to seller to make a 20% down payment, what's the most they could afford to pay for a new home?

2. Joan is selling her home. She needs to pay off a $65,000 first mortgage, a $15,000 second mortgage, and wants $30,000 in cash for herself. If her closing costs total $1,200 and she must pay a 7% commission, for how much must she sell the property?

Principal and Interest

Interest is the *cost of borrowing money*, while **principal** is the *balance of the loan*. The T-math strategy can be used to solve problems involving interest. The annual interest is the part, so it goes on the top. The principal is the whole, so it goes on the bottom with the interest rate. If you know any two factors in the equation, you can easily find the third.

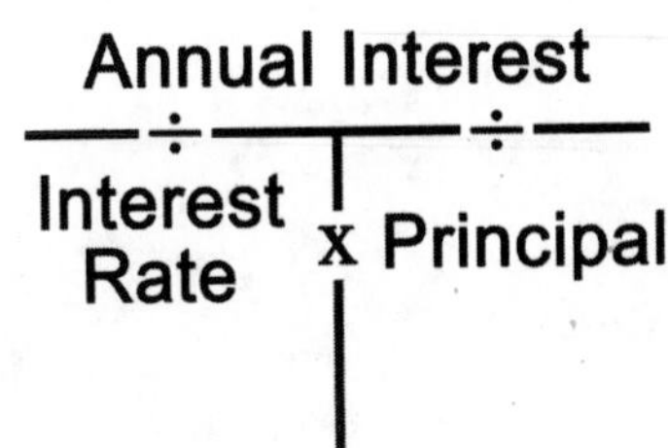

FOR EXAMPLE:

If the loan balance (principal) is $135,000 and the interest rate is 7.5%, the annual interest would be:

.075 x $135,000 = $10,125

That number, divided by 12, indicates the monthly interest on the loan balance. If the borrower makes a monthly mortgage payment of $985, it's possible to see how much of that payment is applied to the principal that month:

$10,125 ÷ 12 = $843.75 Monthly Interest

$985 - $843.75 = $141.25 Applied to Principal

Practice Problems

1. The balance on Lois's loan is $42,000. Of her monthly payment, $297.50 is applied to interest. What is the interest rate on the loan?

2. Geoff takes out a $144,000 mortgage at an interest rate of 6%. When he makes his very first mortgage payment, how much will be applied to interest?

3. Jane has an interest-only loan of $8,000 with an interest rate of 6%. Every month, she pays $40. After 20 payments, what is the balance of the loan?

Return on Investment

If you know the original purchase price of the property and the eventual sale price, you can calculate the return on investment, also known as the percent of profit.

Profit ÷ Original Purchase Price = Percentage of Profit

or

Loss ÷ Original Purchase Price = Percentage of Loss

FOR EXAMPLE:

A parcel of land is purchased for $100,000 and later sold for $115,000. What is the percent of profit?

$115,000 (Sale Price) - $100,000 (Original Price) = $15,000 (Profit)

$15,000 ÷ $100,000 = 0.15 or 15% Profit

Practice Problems

1. A man purchases land for $50,000. He divides it into three lots that are sold for $20,000 each. What is his return on investment?

2. Hal purchases an investment property for $125,000. He later sells it at a loss of $20,000. What is Hal's percent of loss?

3. Bill sold his real estate for $234,900, making a 28% profit. What did he originally pay for the property?

MATH EXERCISES

1. A seller must pay off an existing $42,000 mortgage and pay $1,700 in closing costs. If the seller wants to net $100,000 after paying a brokerage fee of 7%, for how much must the home be sold?

2. An individual purchased two lots last year for $10,000 each. The lots just sold for a total of $25,000. What is the percent of profit?

3. Joe makes a payment of $367.50 on his loan, of which $120 was applied to principal. The balance on Joe's loan is now $36,000. What is the annual percentage rate on Joe's loan?

4. Elisa is going to build a building. It will be 40' x 40' and consist of two floors. If the price per square foot of the building is $90, and the cost of a 150' x 500' lot is $100 per front foot, what is the total cost of the project?

5. A buyer purchased a home for $260,000. Two years later, he had to sell suddenly for $247,000. What was his loss percentage?

6. A developer purchases a lot that measures 348' x 1,000'. If the land cost $5,000 per acre, what is the total cost? (Round up to the nearest dollar.)

7. A house sold for $165,000 and the commission paid was $10,725. What was the rate of commission?

8. A property was listed for $150,000 and sold for 90% of the listing price. Commission was 7% and was split 50/50 between two brokerages. The listing broker then split his portion evenly with a listing salesperson. How much did the selling company get?

9. Quinn is looking at two rectangular lots that are adjacent. According to the plat map, Lot A has a square footage of 46,060, and Lot B has a square footage of 43,005. The common boundary they share is 235 feet long. What is the width of Lot B?

10. Stan buys some farmland to build a small housing development. The land measures 465 feet by 520 feet. If he wants lots to be at least half an acre, how many houses could he build on that land?

11. Lisa paid $154,000 for her property. She wants to make a profit of at least 12% when she sells. What is the minimum selling price she would accept?

PRACTICE PROBLEM SOLUTIONS

MEASUREMENTS

1. 576 x 7.48 = **4,308.48 gallons**
2. 150′ x $2,000 = **$300,000**
   150′ x 600′ = 90,000 square feet
   90,000 square feet x $3.25 = **$292,500**
3. 60′ x 4′ x (4 ÷ 12 = .33′) = 79.2 cubic feet
   79.2 cubic feet ÷ 27 = 2.93 cubic yards or **3 bags**
4. 110′ ÷ 2 = 55′
   55′ x 80′ = **4,400 square feet**
5. 43,560 x 42 = **1,829,520 square feet**

COMMISSION

1. $90,000 x .07 = $6,300
   $6,300 ÷ 2 = **$3,150**
2. $6,060 x 2 = $12,120
   $12,120 ÷ .06 = **$202,000**
3. $5,122 x 2 = $10,244
   $10,244 ÷ $157,600 = **.065 or 6.5%**
4. 230′ x 310′ = 71,300 square feet
   71,300 ÷ 43,560 = 1.6368 acres
   1.6368 x $14,000 = $22,915.20
   $22,915.20 x .065 = **$1,489.49**
5. Commission rate = 7% ($14,000 ÷ $200,000 = .07)
   Listing broker commission = $8,000 ($200,000 x .04 = $8,000)
   Franchise fee = $400 ($8,000 x .05 = $400)
   Listing brokerage commission = $7,600 ($8,000 - $400)
   Listing broker commission = $3,040 ($7,600 x .40 = $3,040)
   Listing agent commission = **$4,560** ($7,600 x .60 = $4,560)

NET TO SELLER

1. $260,000 x .07 = $18,200 (commission)
   $18,200 + $8,900 + $115,000 = $142,100 (expenses)
   $260,000 - $142,100 = **$117,900** (net to seller)
   $117,900 ÷ .20 = **$589,500** (maximum new home price)
2. 100% - 7% = 93% (net to owner)
   $65,000 + $15,000 + $30,000 + $1,200 = $111,200 (known expenses)
   $111,200 ÷ 0.93 (93%) = **$119,569.89**

PRINCIPAL AND INTEREST

1. $297.50 x 12 months = $3,570 annual interest
   $3,570 ÷ $42,000 = **.085 or 8.5%** interest rate
2. $144,000 x .06 = $8,640 annual interest
   $8,640 ÷ 12 months = **$720** applied to interest
3. It is an interest-only loan; therefore, the balance remains the same: **$8,000**

RETURN ON INVESTMENT

1. 3 x $20,000 = $60,000
   $60,000 - $50,000 = $10,000
   $10,000 ÷ $50,000 = **20%**
2. $20,000 ÷ $125,000 = **0.16 or 16%**
3. Selling price: 100% (original price) + 28% (profit) = 128% of purchase price
   $234,900 ÷ 128% = **$183,516**, original purchase price (rounded)
   Double check: $234,900 - $183,516 = $51,384 profit
   $51,384 ÷ $183,516 = .27999 or 28%

MATH EXERCISES ANSWER KEY

1. $154,516.12
2. 25%
3. 8.25%
4. $303,000
5. 5%
6. $39,945
7. 6.5%
8. $4,725
9. 183 feet
10. 11 houses (5.55 acres x 2 houses per acre)
11. $172,480

11

Human Rights & Fair Housing

In This Session

Fair and equitable treatment in housing is a right by law not a choice. In this session, we focus on the mandatory fair housing issues real estate licensees must understand. The United States Congress and the New York State legislature have made it clear that ensuring equal access to housing is an important goal for our society. Real estate professionals need to know what conduct violates anti-discrimination laws. Licensees should also be aware of any laws that may affect their area, where they are practicing.

You will learn:

- Describe the evolution of fair housing laws.
- Identify examples of discrimination.
- Explain federal Fair housing laws and practices.
- Define elements of the Americans with Disabilities Act.
- Utilize acceptable advertising guidelines.
- Identify implications of violating fair housing mandates.
- Describe the elements of New York State law related to fair housing.
- Recognize the authority of the New York Civil Rights Commission.

Key Terms

- Americans with Disabilities Act (ADA)
- Blockbusting
- Cease and Desist List
- Civil Rights Act of 1866
- Department of Housing and Urban Development (HUD)
- Disability
- Discrimination
- Fair Housing Act of 1968
- Familial Status
- Filtering Down
- Marital Status
- New York State Human Rights Law
- Non-solicitation Order
- Public Accommodation
- Real Property
- Reasonable Accommodation
- Redlining
- Steering
- Tester

An Introduction to Fair Housing

Licensees must be educated about discrimination laws. Discrimination in any form can jeopardize your license, plus the liabilities in civil court you may have to defend. The main reason for NOT discriminating it is socially offensive. Try and put yourself in the person's shoes that are being discriminated against. I do not think you will enjoy it, no matter how high the commission is. Treat all clients fairly and equally under the law.

Testers

The only and fair way to police the real estate industry is through a program of testing.

Testers are either volunteers, employees of federal programs, or people from civil rights groups. The main purpose of testers is to visit real estate offices posing as home buyers, they may even pose as sellers. There are often two sets of testers they can be of any race, religion, ethnic background, they will be matched to buyer qualifications such as income, financial reports, they may also be pre-approved. After the visit they will compare notes on the way they were treated. Testing is not just limited to racial steering; it can encompass any of the protected classes, e.g., children.

Investigations by testers have been upheld by the U.S. Supreme Court and the DOS as a legitimate and lawful method to ascertain the actions of real estate licensees and firms with regard to fair housing violations. The only defense against testers is DO NOT DISCRIMINATE!

Equal Housing Today

Despite the passage of the 1866 and 1968 Civil Rights Acts and the amendments added to them, people today believe that discrimination is being resolved. The purpose of the laws, even though they were passed for the good of all, are not really realized in today's society. As a licensee, you must be aware of what you will encounter in your career.

- Discriminatory remarks from renters or buyers about the community.
- Sellers and landlords who only want certain types of people to be shown their housing, e.g., "I only want the *right* people."
- Being asked specific (pointed) questions of discriminatory nature about the community. The only answer to this is: "By law, I cannot answer that."
- Renters and buyers do not want to see property if certain types of people live in that area.
- Concerns over what the people in an area might do or say if you rent or sell to a particular class of people.

Federal Fair Housing Laws

The **Civil Rights Act of 1866** was the first major effort of the federal government to guarantee equal housing to all U.S. citizens. The law prohibits any type of discrimination based on race or color. The 1866 law has a blanket statement that says *all citizens of the United States have the same right in every state to inherit, buy, sell, or lease and convey real and personal property.* **The act also provides no exemptions**. It is enforceable in federal court.

Federal Fair Housing Act of 1968

First enacted as Title VIII of the Civil Rights Act of 1968, the **Fair Housing Act** provided that it is unlawful to discriminate on the basis of race, color, religion or national origin when selling or leasing residential property.

Jones v. Mayer

The second significant fair housing development of 1968 was the Supreme Court decision in the case of ***Jones v. Alfred H. Mayer Co.*** In the ruling, the court held the Civil Rights Act of 1866 was applied, to prohibit any racially based discrimination in housing, private or public, in the sale of and rental of property.

> **Supreme Court Decisions**
>
> The two main decisions regarding the Civil Rights Act of 1866 guaranteeing all people the right to purchase, lease, sell, and convey real and personal property are:
>
> - ***Plessy v. Ferguson.*** The 1896 case the Court ruled that separate but equal was legally acceptable. As long as separate housing or facilities for African-Americans and whites were deemed equal, they were legal.
> - ***Brown v. Board of Education.*** In the 1954 landmark decision, Supreme Court reversed the ruling on *Plessy v. Ferguson*. It found that separate facilities were, by nature, unequal. The Board of Education was in Topeka, Kansas.

New Protected Classes

In 1974 an amendment added the prohibition against discrimination on the basis of *sex (gender)*. Until 1988, the Department of Housing and Urban Development (HUD) was limited to a negotiator, trying to effect an agreement between the parties through persuasion. HUD is the agency where any civil rights violations are reported. In 1988 another amendment added two new classes: Those with *handicaps* and *familial status* (presence of children or minors in the family).

Familial status means a parent or guardian who has legal custody of children under the age of 18 and pregnant women. Title VIII forbids property owners or agents from refusing to rent or sell a dwelling to a qualified person because there are children under 18 in the household. Landlords are prohibited from any advertisement referencing the preference for "adults only" or "no children" in certain situations. Title VIII specifically authorizes the exclusion of children from housing for elderly persons. The exemption was amended by the Housing for Older Persons Act of 1995. The requirements to qualify are:

- At least 80% of the occupied units must be persons 55 and older,
- All units occupied by individuals age 62 and older,
- The housing must publish and adhere to policies that demonstrate an intent to be housing for seniors, and
- The facility must comply with rules issued by the secretary of HUD.

Handicapped status is a physical or mental impairment which limits one or more of a person's life activities. This refers to any physiological disorder or condition, cosmetic disfigurement, or anatomical loss. This includes anyone with the HIV virus, AIDS, and other diseases that cannot be transmitted by casual contact, and also includes alcoholics. The law does not include anyone using illegal drugs or who pose a threat to others. HUD regulations state real estate brokers or agents may not inquire whether a person has a handicap or the extent in evaluating their qualification to buy or rent.

Disabled

Title VIII prohibits owners from refusing to allow tenants to make reasonable structural modifications to a unit, **at the tenant's expense,** to allow the handicapped tenant full enjoyment of the unit. The tenant must return the unit to its original condition upon end of the lease. Landlords must make reasonable accommodations in any rules or regulations governing the development to permit the tenant to fully enjoy the premises, e.g., allowing a guide or service dog in a no-pet building or assigning a parking space to a handicapped person near building entrance.

Accessibility Requirements

The following document was originally published by the U.S. Department of Housing and Urban Development, and is reproduced here with the Department's permission.

Under the federal Fair Housing Act, new multi-family buildings consisting of four or more units that have an elevator and were built for first occupancy on or after March 13, 1991 must provide:

- Wheelchair-width doors and hallways
- Accessible public and common areas
- Accessible routes into and through the unit
- Accessible light switches, electrical outlets, thermostats, and other environmental controls
- Reinforced bathroom walls to allow later installation of grab bars
- Kitchen and bathrooms that can be used by people in wheelchairs

The Fair Housing Act provides that covered multi-family dwellings built for first occupancy after March 13, 1991, shall be designed and constructed to meet certain minimum accessibility and adaptability standards. If any of the structural changes needed by the tenant are ones that should have been included in the unit or public and common use area when constructed, then the housing provider may be responsible for providing and paying for those requested structural changes. However, if the requested structural changes are not a feature of accessible design that should have already existed in the building pursuant to the design and construction requirements under the Act, then the tenant is responsible for paying for the cost of the structural changes as a reasonable modification.

Although the design and construction provisions only apply to certain multi-family dwellings built for first occupancy since 1991, a tenant may request reasonable modifications to housing built prior to that date. In such cases, the housing provider must allow the modifications, and the tenant is responsible for paying for the costs under the Fair Housing Act.

In buildings with four or more units first occupied after March 13, 1991 *without* elevators, these standards apply only to ground units.

What is the difference between a *reasonable accommodation* and a *reasonable modification* under the Fair Housing Act?

Under the Fair Housing Act, a reasonable *modification* is a structural change made to the premises, whereas a reasonable *accommodation* is a change, exception, or adjustment to a rule, policy, practice, or service. A person with a disability may need either a reasonable accommodation or a reasonable modification, or both, in order to have an equal opportunity to use and enjoy a dwelling, including public and common use spaces. Generally, under the Fair Housing Act, the housing provider is responsible for the costs associated with a reasonable accommodation unless it is an undue financial and administrative burden, while the tenant, or someone acting on the tenant's behalf, is responsible for costs associated with a reasonable modification.

Conduct Prohibited by Fair Housing Laws

The following acts are illegal under the law:

- Refusing to sell, rent or otherwise make unavailable a dwelling after receipt of a bona fide offer, based on race, color, sex, religion, national origin, handicap, or familial status.
- Representing that a dwelling is not available when the fact it is, based on prohibited criteria, e.g., telling a family with children the apartment is not available when it actually is.
- Refusing to accept an offer to purchase or rent because the applicant is a member of a protected class.
- Denial of access or participation in a multiple listing service based on prohibited criteria.
- Discrimination in granting requested financial assistance based on prohibited criteria.
- Changing any conditions, services, or terms for different individuals as a means of discrimination.

Group Homes Under Fair Housing

The following document was originally published by the U.S. Department of Housing and Urban Development, and is reproduced here with the Department's permission.

The Fair Housing Act prohibits a broad range of practices that discriminate against individuals on the basis of race, color, religion, sex, national origin, familial status, and disability. The Act does not pre-empt local zoning laws. However, the Act applies to municipalities and other local government entities and prohibits them from making zoning or land use decisions or implementing land use policies that exclude or otherwise discriminate against protected persons, including individuals with disabilities.

What is a group home within the meaning of the Fair Housing Act?

The term "group home" does not have a specific legal meaning. In this statement, the term "group home" refers to housing occupied by groups of unrelated individuals with disabilities. Sometimes, but not always, housing is provided by organizations that also offer various services for individuals with disabilities living in the group homes. Sometimes it is this group home operator, rather than the individuals who live in the home, that interacts with local government in seeking permits and making requests for reasonable accommodations on behalf of those individuals.

The term "group home" is also sometimes applied to any group of unrelated persons who live together in a dwelling -- such as a group of students who voluntarily agree to share the rent on a house. The Act does not generally affect the ability of local governments to regulate housing of this kind, as long as they do not discriminate against the residents on the basis of race, color, national origin, religion, sex, handicap (disability) or familial status (families with minor children).

Does the Fair Housing Act pre-empt local zoning laws?

No. "Pre-emption" is a legal term meaning that one level of government has taken over a field and left no room for government at any other level to pass laws or exercise authority in that area. The Fair Housing Act is not a land use or zoning statute; it does not pre-empt local land use and zoning laws. This is an area where state law typically gives local governments' primary power. However, if that power is exercised in a specific instance in a way that is inconsistent with a federal law such as the Fair Housing Act, the federal law will control. Long before the 1988 amendments, the courts had held that the Fair Housing Act prohibited local governments from exercising their land use and zoning powers in a discriminatory way.

Fair Housing Advertising

Section 804(c) of the Fair Housing Act makes it unlawful to make, print, or publish, or cause to be made, printed, or published, any notice, statement, or advertisement, with respect to the sale or rental of a dwelling, that indicates any preference, limitation, or discrimination because of race, color, religion, sex, disability, familial status, or national origin, or an intention to make any such preference, limitation, or discrimination. However, the prohibitions of the Act regarding familial status do not apply with respect to housing for older persons.

HUD and the National Association of REALTORS®

In 1996, the HUD/NAR® Fair Housing Partnership was created, which allows HUD and the National Association of RELTORS® to work together toward the common cause of fair housing. The principles of the HUD/NAR® Fair Housing Partnership include:

- Sharing responsibility for achieving fair housing.
- Identifying fair housing issues and concerns.
- Developing measurable strategies and actions to address issues and concerns.
- Evaluating the success of actions taken.
- Determining future strategies and actions based on that evaluation.

Nationally, HUD and the NAR® meet regularly to work toward these goals. Local HUD and NAR® associations are also encouraged to form local fair housing partnerships to build on the success of the national partnership.

The Fair Housing Poster

The Fair Housing Act requires fair housing posters to be posted and maintained at any place of business where housing is offered for sale or rent, and they should be prominently displayed. Using the fair housing logo, statement, slogan, and poster declares to the public that the brokerage and its licensees subscribe to the principles of fair housing practices. If a broker or lender is investigated for alleged discriminatory acts, failure to display the poster and use the logo may be considered evidence of discrimination.

Fair Housing Violations

Steering

The federal Fair Housing Act prohibits **steering**, which relates to buyers or renters, and is *channeling prospective buyers or renters to or away from specific neighborhoods*

U. S. Department of Housing and Urban Development

EQUAL HOUSING
OPPORTUNITY

We Do Business in Accordance With the Federal Fair Housing Law

(The Fair Housing Amendments Act of 1988)

It is illegal to Discriminate Against Any Person Because of Race, Color, Religion, Sex, Handicap, Familial Status, or National Origin

- In the sale or rental of housing or residential lots
- In advertising the sale or rental of housing
- In the financing of housing
- In the provision of real estate brokerage services
- In the appraisal of housing
- Blockbusting is also illegal

Anyone who feels he or she has been discriminated against may file a complaint of housing discrimination:
1-800-669-9777 (Toll Free)
1-800-927-9275 (TTY)

U.S. Department of Housing and Urban Development
Assistant Secretary for Fair Housing and Equal Opportunity
Washington, D.C. 20410

Previous editions are obsolete

form HUD-928.1 (2/2003)

based on their race religion, national origin, or other protected class, to maintain or change the character of a neighborhood. For instance, Caucasian customers might be shown homes only in traditionally Caucasian neighborhoods and Hispanic customers shown homes only in traditionally Hispanic neighborhoods.

> **EXAMPLE**
>
> When real estate licensees make assumptions about the types of neighborhood clients would like to live in instead of showing them all available options, they are practicing steering. Never assume you know what is best for your client. Spend time talking about their preferences, and then show them a variety of options that meet their requirements.

Blockbusting

Blockbusting is *inducing or attempting to induce, for profit, any person to sell or rent property based on representations made regarding entry into the neighborhood of persons of a particular race, color, religion, sex, or national origin* and it is prohibited under federal and state law. You may also hear blockbusting referred to as **panic selling** or **panic peddling**.

Before the federal Fair Housing Act, unscrupulous real estate licensees intimidated homeowners into selling their homes by suggesting the ethnic or racial composition of their neighborhood was changing. Homeowners were led to believe their property values would decline, the area would experience higher crime rates, and the quality of schools would suffer.

The apparent motive of these licensees was profit. Through certain techniques, property owners listed or sold properties at a reduced price, and then the licensee turned around and resold the properties at a higher price.

Redlining

Redlining is *discriminating against anyone by a commercial lender in making a loan for buying, building, repairing, improving, or maintaining a dwelling, or in the terms of such financing.* As you can see from the definition, redlining relates to mortgage lending and insurance brokers.

In most instances, homeowners insurance and financing must be obtained in order to buy a house. Redlining is a refusal to make loans or provide insurance on property located in particular neighborhoods for discriminatory reasons (effectively, drawing a red line around an area).

In the past, many lenders assumed an integrated or predominantly African American neighborhood was a place where property values were declining. Based on that assumption, they refused to make loans there. *Since it was almost impossible to get purchase or renovation loans, it was extremely difficult to market, maintain, or improve homes in those neighborhoods, causing values to decline*; a phenomenon referred to as **filtering down**.

Lenders may still deny loans in neighborhoods where property values are declining, but this must be based on objective criteria regarding the condition and value of the property or area. A lender may not simply equate integrated or minority neighborhoods with declining property values.

Federal Fair Housing Exemptions

Although the federal Fair Housing Act covers the majority of residential transactions in the U.S., there are five specific exemptions, including:

1. Owner-occupied buildings.
2. Single-family housing.
3. Housing operated by organizations.
4. Housing operated by private clubs.
5. Housing for older persons (familial status exemptions only).

It is extremely important to note that under the 1866 Civil Rights Act, discrimination based on race or ancestry is prohibited in any property transaction, regardless of exemptions available under the federal Fair Housing Act. **No transaction involving a real estate licensee is exempt.**

1. Owner-occupied buildings
    - The owner occupies one unit as a residence (unless the owner is a real estate licensee).
    - No discriminatory advertising is used.

2. **Single-family Housing**

    The law does not apply to a single-family home sold or rented by a private owner provided that:

    - The owner owns no more than three such homes at one time
    - No discriminatory advertising is used

    To qualify for this exemption, the owner must meet all requirements. If the owner is not the occupant or most recent occupant, they may use this exemption only once every 24 months.

3. **Housing Operated by Organizations**

    In dealing with their own property in noncommercial transactions, religious organizations or affiliated non-profit organizations may limit occupancy, or give preference, to their own members provided membership is not restricted based on race, color, or national origin.

4. **Housing Operated by Private Clubs**

    Private clubs with lodging not open to the public and not operated for commercial purposes may limit occupancy or give preference to members. Membership, however, may not be restricted based on race, color, or national origin.

5. **Housing for Older Persons**

    Familial status protection does not apply to housing for older persons. Exempt senior housing facilities and communities can lawfully refuse to sell or rent dwellings to families with minor children or may impose different terms and conditions of residency.

    The Act defines "housing for older persons" as any housing that is:

    - Provided under a state or federal program designed to assist the elderly.
    - Intended for and solely occupied by persons 62 or older.
    - Designed to meet the physical and social needs of older persons, if management publishes and follows policies and procedures demonstrating an intent to provide housing for those who are 55 or older, at least 80 percent of the units are occupied by at least one person 55 or older, and the facility or community provides HUD with surveys and affidavits confirming the ages of residents.

    Senior housing facilities may not discriminate based on race, color, religion, sex, disability, and national origin. In addition, in communities where families with minor children are permitted, those families may not be segregated in a particular section, building, or portion of a building.

No real estate broker or agent is used to facilitate the transaction.

The Americans with Disabilities Act

Although the federal Fair Housing Act prohibits discrimination against the disabled, Congress further expanded the necessary accommodations with the Americans with Disabilities Act (ADA). At the time the ADA was signed into law in 1990, there were more than 43 million Americans with one or more physical or mental disabilities. Congress found that, unlike other protected classes, individuals with disabilities repeatedly encountered a variety of forms of discrimination and often had no legal recourse.

It is the purpose of this chapter

(1) To provide a clear and comprehensive national mandate for the elimination of discrimination against individuals with disabilities;

(2) To provide clear, strong, consistent, enforceable standards addressing discrimination against individuals with disabilities;

(3) To ensure that the Federal Government plays a central role in enforcing the standards established in this chapter on behalf of individuals with disabilities; and

(4) To invoke the sweep of congressional authority, including the power to enforce the fourteenth amendment and to regulate commerce, in order to address the major areas of discrimination faced day-to-day by people with disabilities.

The **Americans with Disabilities Act** is a *civil rights law that prohibits discrimination based on disability.* In addition to providing a clear and comprehensive national mandate for the elimination of discrimination against individuals with disabilities, the purpose of the Act was to create consistent and enforceable standards.

Besides enforcing workplace equality, a major component of the ADA is ensuring disabled Americans have easy access in new multifamily housing consisting of four or more units. The Act requires accommodations be included to make housing physically accessible to those with disabilities. This includes allowing tenants to make alterations at their own expense. Although it is acceptable for landlords to require the premises be returned to its original state when the tenant vacates the building.

Exemptions for Private Clubs and Religious Organizations

The provisions of this subchapter shall not apply to private clubs or establishments exempted from coverage under title II of the Civil Rights Act of 1964 (42 U.S.C. 2000-a(e)) or to religious organizations or entities controlled by religious organizations, including places of worship.

Illegal Use of Drugs

For purposes of this chapter, the term "individual with a disability" does not include an individual who is currently engaging in the illegal use of drugs, when the covered entity acts on the basis of such use.

Penalties for Violation

The goal of the ADA enforcement program is to work with wrongdoers toward compliance. Alternative means of dispute resolution are encouraged through settlement negotiations, conciliation, facilitation, mediation, fact-finding, and arbitration.

However, there are times when offenders refuse to comply and violations are substantial. In these cases, private individuals or New York's Attorney General may initiate actions, including court orders to stop discrimination. In such cases, the Attorney General may:

- Grant any equitable relief, which may include restraining orders (temporary, preliminary, or permanent), requiring the provision of auxiliary aids or services and modification of policies.
- Award other relief, including monetary damages to aggrieved persons.
- Assess a civil penalty, not to exceed $55,000 for a first violation.

Civil penalties may not be assessed in cases against state or local governments.

CASE IN POINT

The following case is reprinted with the permission of the Department of Housing and Urban Development.

The U. S. Department of Housing and Urban Development announced that it has charged The Townsend House Corp., a private cooperative in New York City, with housing discrimination for refusing to allow a family to obtain an animal that provides emotional support for their autistic child.

The Fair Housing Act makes it unlawful to refuse to make reasonable accommodations in rules, policies, practices, or services, when such accommodation may be necessary to afford a person with disabilities equal opportunity to use and enjoy a dwelling.

Maria Mostajo and Mark Schein are the parents of an 11-year-old boy who has been diagnosed with Autistic Spectrum Disorder and Central Auditory Processing Disorder, which significantly impairs his day-to-day functioning and ability to learn and hear. To treat their son's disorders, the child's doctor prescribed to the parents that they acquire a support animal to provide emotional support for their son. Prior to acquiring an emotional support animal, the parents requested an exception to the co-op's no-pet policy.

After receiving documentation from doctors confirming the child's disabilities and need for an emotional support animal, the co-op agreed to permit the parents to obtain a dog for their son, but subject only to the terms contained in a Pets License Agreement, which was drafted specifically for this family. The parents alleged that the agreement contained unreasonable restrictions. In addition to requiring the parents to obtain insurance providing liability coverage of $1,000,000.00, the Agreement imposed other discriminatory terms, including a ten-pound weight limit; a limit on how long the service animal could be left alone in the apartment; and a requirement that the dog be muzzled when in the co-op's common areas. HUD's investigation confirmed that the Agreement contained unreasonable restrictions that in effect denied the reasonable accommodation to the child.

"It is not right or legal for landlords to dictate the unreasonable terms and conditions by which persons with disabilities should live their lives,"; said Kim Kendrick, HUD Assistant Secretary for Fair Housing and Equal Opportunity. "HUD is deeply committed to enforcing the Fair Housing Act to make sure that this does not happen."

New York Human Rights Law

The federal Fair Housing Act contains the provision that state and local governments may add legislation that increases the protections provided. As is the case in New York, state and local laws often provide broader coverage and prohibit discrimination based on additional classes *not* covered by federal law.

The New York State Division of Human Rights was created to enforce this important law. The mission of the agency is to ensure that "every individual . . . has an equal opportunity to participate fully in the economic, cultural and intellectual life of the State."

New York has the proud distinction of being the first state in the nation to enact a Human Rights Law, which affords every citizen "an equal opportunity to enjoy a full and productive life."

This law prohibits discrimination in employment, housing, credit, places of public accommodations, and non-sectarian educational institutions, based on age, race, national origin, gender, sexual orientation, marital status, disability, military status, and other specified classes.

In New York State, the Division of Human Rights (DHR) enforces Human Rights Law, also called Executive Law. The Human Rights Law of New York extends protected classes beyond those covered in the federal Fair Housing Act. It does so in many ways, such as helping to fight discrimination on the basis of:

- Race and color
- Creed
- National origin
- Sex
- Age
- Disability
- Sexual orientation
- Marital status
- Familial status
- Military status
- Arrest or conviction record
- Predisposing genetic characteristics

Public Accommodations

To remove architectural barriers, and communication barriers that are structural in nature, in existing facilities, and transportation barriers in existing vehicles and rail passenger cars used by an establishment for transporting individuals (not including barriers that can only be removed through the retrofitting of vehicles or rail passenger cars by the installation of a hydraulic or other lift), where such removal is readily achievable; and

Where such person can demonstrate that the removal of a barrier under this paragraph is not readily achievable, a failure to make such facilities, privileges, advantages or accommodations available through alternative methods if such methods are readily achievable. "Readily achievable" means easily accomplishable and able to be carried out without much difficulty or expense. In determining whether an action is readily achievable, factors to be considered include:

- The nature and cost of the action needed
- The overall financial resources of the facility or facilities involved in the action; the number of persons employed at such facility; the effect on expenses and resources or the impact otherwise of such action upon the operation of the facility;
- The overall financial resources of the place of public accommodation, resort or amusement; the overall size of the business of such a place with respect to the number of its employees; the number, type and location of its facilities;

- The type of operation or operations of the place of public accommodation, resort or amusement, including the composition, structure and functions of the workforce of such place; the geographic separateness, administrative or fiscal relationship of the facility or facilities in question to such place.

Some exemptions, permitted under federal law, may not be exemptions under state civil rights laws. New York does not include any exemptions for single-family housing units, as prescribed in the FHA. But, they do allow discounts to people with disabilities and people age sixty-five or older. New York also allows dormitory rooms to be restricted to people of the same sex.

New York Human Rights Law follows the same criteria for reasonable accommodation and accessibility for people with disabilities as stipulated under the federal Fair Housing Act. New York prohibits discrimination in the:

- Sale, rental, or lease of properties, including commercial space and land.
- Terms, conditions, and privileges of the sale, rental, or lease of property; they must be consistent to all interested applicants.
- Advertisements.
- Blockbusting.
- Coercion and retaliation.

Those parties required to adhere to the laws include the following:

- Owners
- Real estate boards
- Lessees
- Real estate brokers
- Sublessees
- Real estate salespersons
- Managing agents
- Employees or agents of any of these named parties

Exemptions

The New York Human Rights Law contains exceptions as like the federal Fair Housing in only certain situations. It has no exception based on race. Some exceptions are:

- Housing for the elderly senior living
- Renting of room or rooms to people of the same gender
- In the renting of a room in a single family home as long as it is by the owner or occupant
- In the rental of a two family home, if the owner or member of their family live in one unit.

New York has no exemptions for the sale of single family housing, unlike the federal law. Where the federal law permitted exceptions for the rental of up to four family units, with the owner occupying one, New York only allows for the rental of a two family owner occupies one unit. Brokers and salespersons may not participate in any exemption.

Commercial, Land, and Credit

The Human Rights Law has a broader range of sanctions regarding discrimination practices in other areas:

- For obtaining credit to purchase, construct, repair, or maintain housing land or commercial space.
- To discriminate in the granting, withholding, extending or renewing, or in the fixing of the rates, terms or conditions of, any form of credit, on the basis of race, creed, color, national origin, sexual orientation, military status, age, sex, marital status, disability, or familial status.

- To use any form of application for credit or use or make any record or inquiry which expresses, directly or indirectly, any limitation, specification, or discrimination as to race, creed, color, national origin, sexual orientation, military status, age, sex, marital status, disability, or familial status.

Filing Complaints

Who may file? Any person or organization claiming to be aggrieved by an alleged unlawful discriminatory practice may, in person or by an attorney-at-law, make, sign and file with the regional office a verified complaint in writing. Assistance in drafting and filing complaints shall be available to complainants' at all regional offices in person, by telephone or by mail. If a complainant lacks mental capacity, the complaint may be filed on his or her behalf by a person with a substantial interest in the welfare of the complainant. The complaint must be filed within one year from the date of the occurrence of the alleged unlawful discriminatory practice. If the alleged unlawful discriminatory practice is of a continuing nature, the date of its occurrence shall be deemed to be any date subsequent to its inception, up to and including the date of its cessation.

In order to ensure that complainants act promptly when they feel they have been discriminated against, the Law imposes a one-year time period for the filing of complaints in the Division. If your claim is older than a year, you should consult with an attorney to see if you are able to file your claim in state court.

New York City Commission on Human Rights

Fair Housing means that you have a right to live wherever you choose and be treated according to the same rules as everyone else. Fair housing laws promote equal opportunity and prohibit discriminatory practices that can unfairly limit the housing choices of numerous groups. The New York City Commission on Human Rights enforces those laws in the five boroughs.

The New York City Human Rights Law is one of the most comprehensive civil rights laws in the nation. The Law prohibits discrimination in employment, housing and public accommodations based on race, color, creed, age, national origin, alienage or citizenship status, gender (including gender identity and sexual harassment), sexual orientation, disability, marital status, and partnership status. In addition, the Law affords protection against discrimination in employment based on arrest or conviction record and status as a victim of domestic violence, stalking and sex offenses. In housing, the Law affords additional protections based on lawful occupation, family status, and any lawful source of income. The New York City Human Rights Law also prohibits retaliation and bias-related harassment.

Unlawful practices of fair housing in the five boroughs of New York City include:

- Refusing to sell or rent housing;
- Misrepresenting the availability of housing;
- Setting different terms, conditions or privileges for the sale or rental of housing;
- Providing different housing services or facilities;
- Posting discriminatory advertising or marketing that indicates a preference, limitation, or discrimination based on a protected class; for example, ads that say "no children" or "married couples only" would be discriminatory;
- Refusing to provide a reasonable accommodation for a person with a disability; steering a potential homebuyer or renter to – or away from – an area on the basis

of race or national origin;

- Pressuring, for profit, homeowners to sell by exploiting ethnic, racial or other demographic changes (blockbusting); and
- Threatening, coercing or intimidating individuals because they exercise their Fair Housing rights or assist others in doing so.

The Human Rights Law also prohibits discriminatory lending by banks, mortgage brokers and other lenders.

Source: New York Commission on Human Rights.

Protected Classes Under the NYC Human Rights Law

The NYC Human Rights Law prohibits discrimination in employment, housing, and public accommodations based on numerous protected classes. These protected classes are:

- Race
- Color
- Creed
- Age
- National origin
- Alienage
- Citizenship status
- Gender (including gender identity and sexual harassment)
- Sexual orientation
- Disability
- Marital status
- Partnership status

In addition, the Law affords protection against discrimination in employment based on:

- Arrest or conviction record.
- Status as a victim of domestic violence.
- Status as a victim of stalking and sex offenses.

In housing, the Law affords additional protections based on:

- Lawful occupation.
- Family status.
- Lawful source of income.

The New York City Human Rights Law also prohibits retaliation and bias-related harassment.

New York City, in addition to the listed protected classes, has added other classes under its Human Rights Laws.

Lawful Source of Income in New York City

In March 2008, the Administrative Code of the City of New York was amended making "lawful source of income" a protected class (Local Law 10/2008) under the City's Human Rights Law.

In general, the law prohibits the owners of buildings in New York City with six or more apartments from refusing to rent or otherwise dispose of property to any person due to their lawful source of income. The amendment defines "lawful source of income" as income derived from social security or any form of federal, state or local public assistance or housing assistance, including section 8 vouchers.

Two examples where the six or more units requirement does not apply include rent controlled apartments where the tenant resided in the apartment when the law took effect (March 2008), and where the owner owns another building in the city that has six or more units. Under these circumstances, regardless of the number of units in the building in question, the housing provider would be required to accept the subsidy.

The Commission interprets this amendment to apply to new, as well as existing, tenants.

The amendment also prohibits the printing of advertisements that are discriminatory in nature; therefore, online or newspaper ads and billboards that state "No Programs" are discriminatory and create a separate cause of action under the law.

Lending Practices

The City Human Rights Law also prohibits discriminatory lending practices by any person, bank, trust company, private banker, savings bank, savings and loan association, credit union, investment company, mortgage company, insurance company, or any other financial institution or lender when you apply for a loan, mortgage or other financial assistance for construction, repairs or maintenance of your property. It is also against the law for financial institutions to redline, the practice of denying mortgages to prospective purchasers in certain communities.

Guidelines Regarding Gender Identity Discrimination

In December 2004, the Commission issued "Guidelines Regarding Gender Identity Discrimination" based on a 2002 amendment to the City's Human Rights Law. These guidelines were created by the New York City Commission on Human Rights with the assistance of a working group from the LGBT community, as well as input from various city agencies and the private sector, to assist individuals and organizations in evaluating and handling gender identity issues.

These guidelines do not constitute legal advice. For specific questions regarding Local Law 3/2002, contact the New York City Commission on Human Rights, consult the Administrative code of the City of New York, or seek legal counsel.

The Provisions Shall Not Apply

1) To the rental of a housing accommodation, other than a publicly-assisted housing accommodation, in a building which contains housing accommodations for not more than two families living independently of each other, if the owner or a member of the owner's family reside in one of such housing accommodations, and if the available housing accommodation has not been publicly advertised, listed, or otherwise offered to the general public.
2) To the rental of a room or rooms in a housing accommodation, other than a publicly-assisted housing accommodation, if such rental is by the occupant of the housing accommodation or by the owner of the housing accommodation and the owner or members of the owner's family reside in such housing accommodation.

The provisions shall not apply if any advertising, real estate listings, public notice, or the services of any real estate broker or salesperson are used.

CIVIL ACTION BY PERSONS AGGRIEVED BY UNLAWFUL DISCRIMINATORY PRACTICES

If you believe you have been the victim of discrimination in the City of New York, you may file a complaint with the Law Enforcement Bureau of the City's Commission on Human Rights, located at 40 Rector Street, 9th Floor, in lower Manhattan or any of our Community Service Centers. The Law requires that the complaint be filed within one year of the last alleged act of discrimination.

The City Commission on Human Rights and the corporation counsel shall each designate a representative authorized to receive copies of complaints in actions commenced in whole or in part pursuant to subdivision (a) of this section. Within 10 days after having commenced a civil action pursuant to subdivision (a) of this section, the plaintiff shall serve a copy of the complaint upon such authorized representatives.

A civil action commenced under this section must be commenced within three years after the alleged unlawful discriminatory practice or act of discriminatory harassment or violence as set forth in chapter six of this title occurred. Upon filing of a complaint with the City Commission on Human Rights or the State Division of Human Rights and during the pendency of such complaint and any court proceeding for review of the dismissal of such complaint, such three year limitations period shall be tolled.

Restrictions on Solicitations

The New York Department of State has designated certain geographic areas as cease-and-desist zones. Residents within the zone can file a notice with the DOS to indicate they do not want to sell, lease, or list their property. Once property owners register on the cease-and-desist list, brokers and salespersons are prohibited from soliciting the property owner. Violation of the cease-and-desist order is considered an act of untrustworthiness or incompetence on the part of the licensee.

In the past, the state could also establish non-solicitation orders for designated geographical areas. A non-solicitation order is an order prohibiting the solicitation of residential property listings and applies to all real estate brokers and agents. The Secretary of State could order additional terms and conditions to the non-solicitation order but generally, it prohibited letters, postcards, phone calls, door-to-door sales, fliers, and postings in public areas. However, the New York State Association of Realtors® challenged non-solicitation orders on the grounds that it violated licensees' First Amendment rights. In 2002, the U.S. Court of Appeals ruled non-solicitation is in fact unconstitutional.

Prohibited Forms of Solicitation

(a) Within a nonsolicitation area, no real estate broker or real estate salesperson shall engage in any form of solicitation where the purpose of such solicitation is, directly or indirectly, to obtain a listing of residential property for sale and where such solicitation is directed at or toward a homeowner or occupant of residential property within a designated nonsolicitation area.

(b) The following are examples of the types of solicitation that are prohibited:

(1) letters;

(2) postcards;

(3) handbills or leaflets or fliers;

(4) direct advertising delivered by mail or other service;

(5) telephone calls;

(6) door-to-door calls; and

(7) postings in public places.

(c) The following is not prohibited by a nonsolicitation order. Advertisements that are published in newspapers of general circulation:

(1) if such newspaper has a general readership throughout the metropolitan New York City area or throughout a substantial portion of the metropolitan New York City area;

(2) if such newspaper is published not less than once per week; and

(3) if such newspaper is sold by subscription or by individual copy and is not distributed free of charge.

CLASSES PROTECTED UNDER FAIR HOUSING LAWS

	Federally Protected Classes	State Protected Classes	NYC Protected Classes
Race	✓	✓	✓
Color	✓	✓	✓
Religion/Creed	✓	✓	✓
National Origin	✓	✓	✓
Familial Status	✓	✓	✓
Disability	✓	✓	✓
Gender	✓	✓	✓
Marital Status		✓	✓
Sexual Orientation		✓	✓
Age		✓	✓
Military Status		✓	✓
Citizenship Status			✓
Partnership Status			✓
Lawful Occupation			✓
Lawful Source of Income			✓

Broker's Responsibility for Agents and Upholding Fair Housing

The broker has a duty and responsibility to train, supervise, and oversee the actions of their agents. Brokers can be held accountable for the actions of agents in any violation of Fair Housing laws. They must be aware of the needs of agents to be fully apprised of all Fair Housing laws. HUD regulations and NAR recommendations should help brokers attain this goal. Brokers must also understand that the potential penalties for violation of fair housing laws are so serious they simply cannot assume the risk. Also they must realize that their errors and omissions policy may be excluded.

Office Environment

To further ensure fair housing compliance, brokers should oversee the training agents are receiving or are not taking. The broker must be aware of the agents who can jeopardize their positions; this will help avoid potential problems that may arise. In addition there should be included in every office manual or policy statement information regarding Fair Housing and the consequences of breaking any of the laws. The firm should be very strict on compliance with these directives. Brokers should have a record-keeping system that will have all pertinent information regarding all prospects. With this system, brokers can monitor their agents to see that all policies are being upheld and if there are any violations of fair housing so that they can address them.

Education and Training

Real estate agents should have regularly scheduled training or seminar sessions to keep updated on all new laws and amendments. The NAR has a course every member must take; it runs every four years. The New York Department of State as of July 1, 2008, has made mandatory everyone taking continuing education must have a three-hour fair housing course as part of the 22.5 hours they must do.

Also critical is educating individual clients, who may put the pressure on a broker to discriminate or steer. Sellers must understand that brokers will not accept any listing on any conditions that violate fair housing laws.

Fair Treatment

Agents must learn and understand how to greet people, obtain listings, prepare and maintain documentation, and conduct open houses. These should be performed in a professional way, so everyone feels they are being treated equally. The needs and wants should be of main concern for agents, i.e., the type of home, price, special features, any special area. The discussions should be kept to only information regarding the properties and if they are financially able to purchase.

Documentation

Licensees must be aware of the importance of maintaining and keeping good records. They should contain any and all information regarding the prospect through the use of any form or one that is provided by the office. It should contain preferred home requirements, financial analysis, properties shown or suggested. They should document all calls to prospects or received calls and the subject of the call. If an agent is confronted with a complaint whether from a customer or a "tester," without a written record to explain their reasons for whatever actions they took they have no basis to say they were treated fairly. Agents are going to meet many people in the course of a day, week, or month. Without a record to show each person they were given equal professional service, they have no defense against a discrimination complaint. Documentation is the strongest defense.

(Back of card)

RECORD OF SHOWINGS			
DATE	ADDRESS	BY	COMMENTS

(Front of card)

PROSPECT INFORMATION CARD

Name		Date
Address		Home Phone
		Bus. Phone
Income(s)	Occupation(s)	# of children
Price Range	Taxes	Type of Financing
Down Payment	Monthly Payment	Estimated Expenses

PREFERRED HOME REQUIREMENTS

Preferred Location	Style of Home	Preferred lot size Frontage Depth	
# Bedrooms	# Baths	Type Heat	Garage

❑ Dining Room ❑ 1st Fl. Laundry ❑ 1st Fl. Family Room ❑ Eat-in Kitchen ❑ Fireplace

List Other Features:

Current Residence ❑ Own ❑ Rent	Referred to us by	Salesperson

Reprinted with permission of Bill Plunkett, New York Real Estate Institute

When dealing with applicants, ask yourself these questions:

- Am I treating this applicant any differently because he or she is a member of a protected class?
- Am I acting in a way that will potentially exclude as residents a higher number of persons belonging to a protected class?
- Does what I am doing have a valid, nondiscriminatory business purpose? Could I accomplish it in a way that would have less impact on a protected class?

Be sure to use the same technique and questions for all applicants:

- Have a list of questions to ensure consistency.
- Don't ask any questions that could be construed as discriminatory.
- Do not record any possibly discriminatory information.

In addition, you cannot refuse or fail to:

- Show an apartment because of a prospect's protected status.
- Provide information about an apartment because of a prospect's protected status.
- Rent an apartment after a bona fide offer has been made because of a prospect's protected status.

The selection process should be explained to each applicant and they should be given an opportunity to review the project's tenant selection procedures. Further, whatever reason is used to reject or accept one applicant must be used to reject or accept another under the same circumstances.

County Laws

Most counties in New York have passed anti-discrimination laws that are in line with those passed by the State. Such laws allow complaints to be filed and handled locally, which generally results in more efficient processing.

For example, both Nassau County and Suffolk County have passed laws that make it illegal to deny a person the opportunity to sell, purchase or lease, rent, or obtain financing for the purchase or lease of housing accommodations because of *actual or perceived* race, creed, color, gender, disability, age, religion, sexual orientation, familial status, marital status, ethnicity, or national origin. Like New York City, Nassau County also recognizes source of income as a protected class (as does Westchester County).

Both Suffolk County and Nassau County have a Commission on Human Rights with the authority to receive complaints, investigate, hold hearings, and impost civil penalties for related violations. Civil penalties for unlawful discriminatory practices may result in a fine of not more than $50,000. Where the Commission finds that an unlawful discriminatory practice was the result of the respondent's "wanton or malicious" act, the Commission or court may impose a civil penalty up to $100,000.

Again, it is critical that you understand the laws in the jurisdictions in which you practice.

Megan's Law: What Licensees Must Know

Despite court rulings, agents should abide by "Megan's Law" requirements.

A New York appellate court has affirmed a lower court's ruling that in New York, sellers and their real estate broker/sales associates do not have a duty to disclose the presence of a convicted sex offender in the neighborhood to a buyer. To read a summary of the lower court's decision which was posted in *The Letter of the Law*, with a more thorough discussion of the facts,

To summarize the facts, Neil and Kerry Glazer ("Buyers") learned after purchasing a home that a convicted sex offender lived across the street. The Buyers brought a lawsuit against the seller ("Seller"), the broker ("Broker") and the salespeople ("Salespeople") who represented the Seller during the transaction. The Buyers' lawsuit claimed that the Seller, the Broker, and the Salespeople fraudulently concealed from the Buyers the presence of the sex offender. The trial court ruled that the Seller, Broker, and the Salespeople had no duty to disclose the presence of the convicted sex offender to the Buyers. The Buyers appealed.

The Supreme Court, Appellate Division, Second Division, affirmed the trial court decision. The court ruled that the Seller, the Broker, and the Salespeople had no duty to disclose information concerning the premises unless a confidential relationship existed between the Buyers and the others. Since there was no confidential relationship between the parties, the Buyers would have had to show that there was an active concealment by the other parties of the fact that a convicted sex offender lived across the street, and they were unable to show this. Further, the court stated that the Buyers had made no effort to discover the character of the surrounding neighborhood, which would have revealed that a convicted sex offender lived there, because this information had been reported in the local media. Thus, the court affirmed the trial court's rulings.

Glazer v. LoPreste, 717 N.Y.S.2d 256, 278 A.D.2d 198 (N.Y. App. Div. 2000).

In New York, Sellers and Their Salespeople Do Not Have Duty to Disclose Presence of Sex Offender to Buyer

A New York State court recently considered whether sellers and their real estate sales associates have a duty to disclose the presence of a sex offender in the neighborhood to a buyer.

In April 1998, the LoPrestes ("Sellers") entered into a contract with Century "21", Marlene Goodman, R.E. ("Broker") to sell their home. Barbara Mazzitelli, Davidine Le Boyer, and Natalya Shvirsky (collectively, "Salespeople") were employed by the broker to effectuate the sale of the Sellers' home.

In July 1998, Neil and Kerry Glazer ("Buyers") closed on their purchase of the Sellers' home. Following the closing, the Buyers learned that a convicted sex offender lived across the street. They brought a lawsuit against the Sellers, the Salespeople, and the Broker for failing to inform them of the sex offender.

The Buyers claimed that all of the defendants fraudulently concealed the presence of the sex offender from them and factually misrepresented the neighborhood to them. They also claimed that the defendants were guilty of intentionally inflicting emotional distress upon them and were liable for punitive damages. The Salespeople filed a motion for entry of judgment in their favor, while the Sellers brought a motion to dismiss the Buyers' complaint.

The Supreme Court for the State of New York, Nassau County, granted both the Sellers' and Salespeople's motions. In reaching its decision, the court did not reference the state's "Megan's Law." Instead, the court first considered the claim of intentional infliction of emotional distress. The court dismissed these allegations because the Buyers had not demonstrated extreme and outrageous conduct by any of the defendants. Extreme and outrageous conduct is necessary to seek recovery for intentional infliction of emotional distress.

Next, the court considered the allegations of fraudulent concealment and factual misrepresentation. In New York, the rule for real estate transactions is "caveat emptor," or "buyer beware." There was no duty on the part of the Seller or Salespeople to disclose this information to the Buyers, unless there had been a confidential relationship (for example, like a trustee/beneficiary relationship) between the parties or an active concealment of a convicted sex offender in the neighborhood. Since none of the parties had a confidential relationship with the Buyers, and there were no allegations of active concealment of the presence of a sex offender, the court found the Sellers and Salespeople did not have a duty to disclose that a convicted sex offender lived across the street from the Sellers' house.

The court further stated that the caveat emptor doctrine requires a purchaser to "prudently" assess the property they are purchasing. Information about the particular sex offender had been publicized in the local media, and so the Buyers could have made themselves aware of his presence. Since these facts were not exclusively known by the Sellers and Salespeople, the court granted the motions brought by both parties. The court allowed the Buyers' lawsuit against the Broker to remain.

Glazer v. LoPreste, Index No. 8238/99 (N.Y. Sup. Ct. January 7, 2000), *aff'd* 717 N.Y.S.2d 256, 278 A.D.2d 198 (N.Y. App. Div. 2000).

SUMMARY

1. The **Civil Rights Act** was the *first federal anti-discrimination statute to have the greatest effect on real estate transactions*. It was enacted in 1866 in an effort to guarantee equal housing opportunities for all U.S. citizens. This Act *prohibited racial discrimination in the sale or rental of all real or personal property* and gave all citizens the same rights with regard to property. **It has no exemptions.**

2. The **federal Fair Housing Act** *prohibits discrimination in the sale or lease of residential property for protected classes*—**race, color, religion, sex, disability, familial status,** and **national origin.** The Act *also prohibits discrimination in advertising, real estate brokerage, lending, and some other services associated with residential transactions; against individuals associated with persons in these protected classes; against U.S. citizens and non-citizens.*

3. Although the federal Fair Housing Act covers the majority of residential transactions in the U.S., there are several **specific exemptions**: some single-family homes rented by a private owner, rentals with no more than four units per dwelling, provided owner occupies one unit, religious and non-profit organizations, and private clubs. The law outlines several practices and activities that violate the federal Fair Housing Act if based on the protected classes. **Steering, redlining,** and **blockbusting** are among these illegal practices. To avoid violations, licensees must be diligent in their knowledge and enforcement of federal and state laws. Discrimination, whether intentional or unintentional, still exists as evidenced in the renting, selling, advertising, and municipal actions examples in this chapter.

4. Licensees should ensure **disclosure**. The agent must *provide information to the client in written form that outlines the fair housing statement*. When a real estate agent goes along with a client's discrimination, consequences can be serious.

5. The **Americans with Disabilities Act** (ADA) gives *civil rights protection to individuals with disabilities.* It guarantees equal opportunity for individuals with disabilities in public accommodations, employment, transportation, state and local governments, and telecommunications. *Title III* requires all public and commercial facilities be 100% accessible to the disabled. Affirmatively furthering fair housing is a requirement for participating in HUD programs. HUD, in conjunction with the private sector, has developed voluntary programs and partnerships, including *Voluntary Affirmative Marketing Agreements (VAMA) and the HUD/NAR® Fair Housing Partnership.*

6. The **Human Rights Law of New York** *extends protected classes* beyond those covered in the Fair Housing Act to include, *age, creed, marital status, military status, and sexual orientation.* Further, **New York City** extends protection to include citizenship status, partnership status, lawful source of income, and lawful occupation. New York City is constantly updating their fair housing laws. Other municipalities and counties have their own fair housing laws.

12

Contracts and Contract Preparation

In This Session

Contract law is important to understand because it touches many aspects of real estate. The basic concepts and requirements are the same whether talking about a listing agreement, a purchase contract, or any other type of agreement. In fact, ***agreement*** is another word for ***contract***. A contract does not need to be a lengthy document, but to be enforceable in a court of law there are some rules for contract formation, which are discussed in this session.

You'll learn:

- Basic concepts of contract law.
- The essential elements of a valid contract.
- How the statute of frauds applies to contracts.
- How contracts may be terminated.
- What information is needed to prepare a sales contract.

Key Terms

- As Is
- Assignment
- Bilateral / Unilateral
- Consideration
- Contingency
- Contract
- Earnest Money Deposit
- Executed / Executory
- Express / Implied Contract
- Forbearance
- Land Contract
- Liquidated Damages
- Meeting of the Minds
- Novation
- Offer / Counteroffer
- Option
- Power of Attorney
- Proprietary Lease
- Rescission
- Rider
- Right of First Refusal
- Sales Contract
- Specific Performance
- Statute of Frauds
- Statute of Limitations
- Time Is of the Essence
- Void / Voidable

Basic Contracts

The primary real estate contracts listed below are subject to the elements of contract law discussed in this session:

- **Listing agreement.** Agency contract between a seller and a real estate broker stipulating the details of their agreement, including the broker's commission with regard to the seller's property
- **Buyer agency agreement.** Agency contract between a buyer and a real estate broker providing the details of their agreement and how the broker will be compensated for representing the buyer in the purchase or lease of property
- **Sales or purchase contract.** Contract between a buyer and a seller detailing the sale of real property
- **Lease.** Contract between a landlord and a tenant stipulating the terms of tenancy, rent, and tenant's rights and obligations
- **Option to buy or lease.** Contract that gives one party the right to buy or lease the property of another at a specified price within a specified time frame

Real estate professionals cannot give legal advice. In New York, it is unlawful to practice law without a license. In fact, the New York Department of State asserts that the real estate broker's license does not grant the right to draft legal documents or give legal advice. If your clients have legal questions regarding a contract, you must advise them to consult an attorney. This will save you, your clients, and your brokerage from possible liability. .

Contract Classifications

A **contract** is an *agreement between two or more parties to do, or not do, something.* Contracts are legally enforceable promises, with the law providing remedies for breach. There are several key terms that are used to more specifically classify contracts:

Classification		Definition	Example
Contract Creation	Express	An agreement expressed in words, either spoken or written	Signing a work order at the garage to have your car repaired in exchange for payment
	Implied	An agreement that has not been put into words, but is implied by actions of the parties	Eating in a restaurant – it is understood you will pay the bill, even if it is not explicitly discussed before sitting down and eating
Contract's Promise	Unilateral	Only one party makes a binding promise to the other	An option is an example of a unilateral contract because one party has the right to do something within a designated amount of time, without obligation to do it
	Bilateral	Each party makes a binding promise to the other	A listing agreement – the seller agrees to pay commission to the broker if she carries out her responsibilities

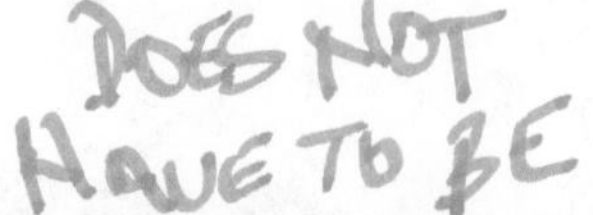

Classification		Definition	Example
Contract Status	Executory	One or both parties have not yet completed performance of their contractual obligations	Party A and Party B sign a listing agreement; the broker is actively seeking a buyer but has not yet fulfilled his side of the contract
	Executed	Both parties have fully performed their contractual obligations (not to be confused with executing a contract, which is merely the act of signing it)	Party A and Party B sign a listing agreement; after a buyer is found, the seller pays the broker's commission at closing
Contract Validity	Valid	The contract is binding and legal, meeting all the essential elements for contract formation	A sales contract that includes all essential elements binds both parties to the terms of the contract
	Void	Lacks one or more of the essential elements for contract formation	A listing agreement to sell a house does not include the signatures of both owners of the property and is therefore lacking an essential element
	Voidable	One party can end an agreement without liability because of lack of legal capacity or other factor such as fraud or duress	A sales contract signed by a minor is voidable by the minor, but not the other party to the contract
	Unenforceable	A contract that may have been valid between the parties but that a court would refuse to enforce	An oral contract for the sale of real estate when one party does not follow through, or a vaguely worded contract whose intent cannot be established

Essential Elements of a Contract

For a contract to be valid, it must have these essential elements:

- Competent parties
- Lawful and possible objective
- Consideration
- Description
- Mutual agreement, also known as meeting of the minds
- Written format and signatures

Competent Parties

For a contract to be valid, each party must be legally competent. This may also be referred to as **contractual capacity**, which requires:

- Legal **age** of majority (18 years old).
- **Mental** competence (sober, mentally sane, etc.).
- Proper **authorization** (when signing a contract on behalf of a corporation or other entity).

When an adult enters into a contract with a minor, the contract is voidable by the minor only. Even if the minor pretended to be over 18, the minor can disaffirm the contract at any time before turning 18 or within a reasonable time thereafter. The minor may choose to enforce the contract and require the adult to perform. The adult does not have the power to disaffirm the contract.

CASE IN POINT

Stewart was only 17 when he signed a contract to buy a house from Pete, who did not realize Stewart was a minor. A few weeks later when the sale was ready to close, Stewart changed his mind and told Pete the deal was off. Pete cannot sue to enforce the contract. But, if the tables were turned and Pete wanted to back out, Stewart could sue him to enforce the contract.

An adult who is incapable of understanding the nature and consequences of a contract also does not have the capacity to enter into a contract. Once a person has been declared incompetent by a court (because of mental illness or senility, for example), any contract this person enters into is considered void and neither party may enforce it. Even if a person has not been declared legally incompetent, if it can be proven he was not of sound mind when the contract was signed, the contract may still be voidable by that person.

Lawful Objective

Lawful objective means the *purpose or objective of a contract must be lawful at the time the contract is made*. When one person promises to pay someone for committing an illegal act, the contract is void. A court may also refuse to enforce an otherwise legal contract if its objective violates public policy.

Many contracts have more than one purpose and are often **severable**, meaning *one part or provision of a contract can be held unenforceable without making the entire contract unenforceable*. The unenforceable part is severed, or cut, from the agreement, but the rest is enforced.

Consideration

Consideration, also called **valuable consideration**, is *anything of value such as money, services, goods, or promises given to induce another to enter into a contract*. Consideration for most contracts is a *promise* to give something of value. Thus, the parties to a contract are sometimes referred to as the **promisor** *(one making a promise)* and the **promisee** *(one who gets the benefit of a promise)*. Consideration can also be *a promise to refrain from doing something*, where it is referred to as **forbearance**.

Exchanging consideration distinguishes a contractual promise from the promise of a gift. A promise is not enforceable in court unless it is a contractual obligation for which both parties exchanged consideration. In a typical real estate contract, the buyer promises to pay the seller money and the seller promises to transfer title to the buyer. These promises create an executory contract; when they are fulfilled (buyer pays seller; seller gives buyer a deed), the contract is executed.

Adequacy

The value of the consideration one party gives does *not* have to be equal to the value of what the other gives. In other words, even if one party struck a bad bargain, both still have an enforceable contract. Of course, grossly unequal consideration may mean there was fraud, undue influence, duress, or a mistake involved. But the contract is enforceable unless any of these things are proven.

Description

Any contract must include a description of what is being contracted. For real property, it could be a legal description or simply the property's address.

Mutual Agreement

Before any contract can be formed, there must be **mutual agreement**, which generally involves an offer and acceptance. Acceptance of the terms of an offer indicates a **meeting of the minds**. In general terms, an **offer** is *one party (the offeror) proposing a contract to another party (the offeree)*. When an offer is accepted, a contract is formed and both parties are legally bound. Neither can back out without legal excuse unless the other is willing to end the contract.

Genuine Assent

Genuine assent means *consent must be freely given* to create a binding contract. Offer and acceptance as an expression of mutual agreement are not freely given under any of these circumstances:

- **Fraud** is *intentional* or negligent misrepresentation of material facts. The fraud results in a contract that would not have been completed had the truth been known.
- **Undue influence** is *excessive pressure on someone, preventing him from making a rational or prudent decision*. A contract is voidable if a person is persuaded to sign it by taking advantage of another's trust or weakness of mind (exhaustion, senility, etc.).
- **Duress** is *threatening violence against or unlawfully confining a person, or any member of that person's family, to force him to sign a document.* Duress can also be a threat of injury to reputation. Economic duress (also called business compulsion) is a threat of taking action that will be financially disastrous to the victim.
- **Mistake** occurs when *one or more parties to a contract are mistaken about a fact or law.* Usually, bad faith and ill will are not involved. If both parties are mistaken about something important to the contract (mutual mistake), either may disaffirm it. If only one party is mistaken (unilateral mistake), the contract is not voidable unless the other party knew of the mistake and did nothing.

Written Format

The **statute of frauds** is *a law requiring certain types of contracts to be in writing and signed to be enforceable*. The purpose of the statute of frauds is to prevent fraudulent claims and false testimony. The New York State statute of frauds, codified in the General Obligations Law (Section 5-703), requires real estate contracts be written and contain all the essential elements for a valid contract. It applies to contracts conveying an interest in real estate, including purchase contracts, options, mortgages, or deeds. The **plain-language requirement**, known as New York's Sullivan Law, states that *written agreements for the sale or lease of residential property must contain words common in everyday usage if the transaction is for $50,000 or less.*

Oral Contracts

The Doctrine of Part Performance allows a New York State court to enforce an oral agreement that should have been in writing if the promisee has taken irrevocable steps to perform her side of the bargain, and failure to enforce the contract would result in an unjust benefit for the promisor. Part performance minimizes unfairness in some cases because one party began to perform his side of the contract, relying on the other party's promises. However, the rule of **parol evidence** provides that *the written agreement overrides any oral agreements.*

POWER OF ATTORNEY

The statute of frauds also applies to any power of attorney authorizing someone to sell another's real estate. A **power of attorney** is *an instrument authorizing one person* (called an attorney-in-fact) *to act as another's agent to the extent stated in the instrument.* Unlike an attorney at law, an attorney-in-fact can be anyone. An attorney-in-fact may be a universal or general agent and his authority is restricted to those things specifically stated in the power of attorney.

A power of attorney conferring the right to sell another's real property must be in writing, signed, witnessed by two competent witnesses, acknowledged before a notary, and recorded with the county recorder in the county where the land is situated to become effective.

Performance and Discharge of Contracts

Once a contract is formed, there are any number of things that affect how it is carried out, or *not* carried out. If one party to a contract performs his or her contractual obligations, the other party is also required to perform.

Breach of Contract

A **breach of contract** occurs when *one party to a contract fails to perform with no legal cause.* The breach does not terminate the obligations of the breaching party. Further, the non-defaulting party may take legal action against the breaching party.

It is not always easy to determine whether a breach of contract has occurred. For example, Curtis does all the things he promised, but Amy feels they were not done well. Or, Curtis does nearly everything promised, but some details are not finished and he takes longer to do it than agreed. In these cases, there is room for argument about whether the contract was breached and whether Amy is required to perform her obligation, which is to pay Curtis. Amy's obligation to perform depends on whether there has been *substantial performance* or a *material breach*.

Substantial Performance

Substantial performance means a *promisor does not perform all contractual obligations but does enough so that the promisee is required to fulfill her obligation.* If Curtis has not fulfilled every detail of a contract but has carried out its main objectives, then it may be treated as substantial performance. Although Amy may be able to sue for damages because of the unfulfilled details, she still must perform as agreed.

Material Breach

Material breach is a *breach of contract important enough to excuse the non-breaching party from performing any contractual obligations.* If Curtis fails to perform some important part of the contract or performs very badly, it is treated as a material breach. If he commits a material breach, Amy may be able to sue for damages and be excused from fulfilling her promises.

Clauses

Contracts may include certain clauses and conditions that impact whether a breach is considered material.

Time Is of the Essence

Many contracts state **"time is of the essence."** The purpose of this phrase is *to emphasize timely performance as an essential part of the contract, and failure to perform on time is a material breach.* When a contract does not provide a "time is of the essence" clause, usually performance within a reasonable time after a stated deadline is not a material breach.

Thus, if "time is of the essence" is *not* in the contract and the buyer was late in performing, then the seller could give the buyer a reasonable time to perform even though the deadline in the contract has passed. The contract is voidable at that point by the seller, and the seller could terminate the contract at anytime.

If "time is of the essence" *is* in the contract, then the contract is void as soon as the deadline has passed; there is a material breach. Depending on the customs of the local market, when a deadline passes, it could be the buyer who is in breach of the contract, or the seller. The only way to save the contract is for the buyer and seller to agree to extend the contract before the deadline passes.

Conditions

Conditions, also called **contingency** clauses, are *contract provisions that make the parties' rights or obligations dependent on the occurrence (or nonoccurrence) of certain events*. Contracts often include one or more conditions. If the event does not occur, the promisor can withdraw without liability for breach of contract. For example, a purchase agreement may be contingent upon the sale of the buyer's current home, or the buyer qualifying for financing.

When a contract is conditional, the promisor must make a good faith effort to fulfill the condition. The promisor cannot deliberately prevent its fulfillment to get out of the contract. However, a condition can be waived by the party it was intended to benefit or protect.

Remedies for Breach of Contract

If one party to a contract does not perform her contractual obligations, or breaches the contract, the non-defaulting party may take legal action by filing suit against the defaulting party in a court of law. Remedies include the following:

- **Cancellation** is the *termination of a contract without undoing acts that have been performed under it.* This can be done without going to court if both parties agree they prefer to cancel the contract. When a contract is canceled, all further obligations are terminated.

- **Compensatory damages** are intended to *compensate the plaintiff for harm caused by the defendant's act or failure to act.* This is the most common remedy for breach of contract. The award is usually the amount that will put the non-breaching party in the same position he would have been in, if the other party had fulfilled the contract.
- An **injunction** is a *court order that requires a party to do or refrain from doing a certain act* (or acts) as opposed to a monetary award.
- **Liquidated damages** reflect *the amount of money specified in a contract to be awarded in the event the agreement is breached.* A liquidated damages clause is included in some contracts to lessen the chance of expensive litigation. Since the parties have agreed in advance to damages of a certain amount or figure using a specified formula, the non-breaching party must accept liquidated damages instead of suing for actual damages. If the breaching party refuses to pay, the case will go to court.
- **Reformation** is *when a court or a judge changes or modifies a contract to reflect the true intent of the parties.* Reformation usually occurs when the parties to the contract enter into it without realizing it contains a clerical error.
- **Rescission** is *the destruction, annulment, or termination of a contract and all parties to the contract must give back anything acquired under it to the other party.* This occurs when one party does not want to enforce the other party's promise; one party did not provide the promised consideration, or a voidable contract is disaffirmed. When a contract is rescinded, all contractual obligations are terminated.
- **Specific performance** is *a legal remedy in which a court orders someone who has breached a contract to perform as agreed, rather than simply paying damages.* This occurs most often when the non-breaching party to a contract cannot be compensated for harm that resulted from the other's breach. In such a case, the non-breaching party has the right to compel the other party to do what was promised in the contract. This is also referred to as a *forced sale.*

Discharge of Contracts

Contracts can be discharged, or terminated, in a number of ways:

- **Agreement of the parties.** When all parties to a contract agree, any executory contract can be discharged, or terminated; this is also known as release of contract.
- **Partial performance.** When both parties agree to accept something different than the terms of the original contract, the original obligation is extinguished.
- **Full performance.** When all parties to a contract have fulfilled their contractual obligations, the contract is executed, and thus released.
- **Impossibility of performance.** When the performance of a contractual obligation becomes illegal because of a change in the law after the contract was created, the contract is terminated.
- **Operation of law.** When the rights and liabilities of the contracting parties are changed by application of the law, a contract can be terminated through:
    - **Alteration of contract.** Intentionally cancelling or altering a contract discharges the agreement.
    - **Bankruptcy.** Contracts in existence as of the date of the bankruptcy filing are terminated.

- **Statute of limitations.** According to New York State law, the time limit to bring legal action regarding a real estate contract is **six years**.

> **ASSIGNMENT AND NOVATION**
>
> In an **assignment**, *one of the parties* (assignor) *transfers rights or interests under a contract to another person* (assignee). Generally, either party can assign the contract without the other's consent, unless the contract states that consent is required. When a contract is assigned, the assignor is ***not*** relieved of liability under the contract. The assignor remains secondarily liable to the other party, and can be sued if the assignee does not perform. This rule applies even when the other party consents to the assignment.
>
> In New York, all contracts are assignable unless the contract states otherwise. One exception concerns contracts for personal services. A party to a personal service contract can assign the contract only with the consent of the other party. *Listing agreements are considered personal service contracts and thus cannot be assigned.*
>
> **Novation** is the *substitution of a new contract for an earlier contract.* The new contract cancels the original contract. A novation may also involve the substitution of a new party for an original party.

Sales Contracts

Sales contracts are ***contracts in which a seller promises to convey title to real property to a buyer in exchange for the purchase price.*** In different areas, these may also be called purchase agreements, sale agreements, earnest money agreements, and other names. A sales contract usually serves three purposes:

- It's the buyer's initial **offer** (and subsequent counteroffers).
- It's the **receipt** for any earnest money deposit.
- It's the **contract** between the buyer and seller.

A sales contract establishes the **terms** and **conditions** of the sale and is the document that communicates the details of the transaction to the mortgage lender, title company, and any other party to the transaction.

Note that a real estate listing is *not* a property owner's offer to sell. By listing the property, the seller is merely soliciting offers from potential buyers. A buyer does *not* create a contract by accepting the seller's listing. Instead, a buyer makes an offer to purchase and the seller accepts or rejects the offer. The listing is an independent contract between a seller and a real estate broker, not a part of the contract between the seller and buyer.

The Offer

When a buyer makes an offer to purchase, it must meet some basic requirements:

- **Intent to contract.** The explicit words and actions of the offeror must reasonably indicate the intention of forming a contract.
- **Definite terms.** The offer must be complete in its terms and details; an offer isn't binding if it's vague or does not include the essential elements of a contract.

Earnest Money Deposit

An **earnest money deposit** made with an offer to purchase is *not* consideration. In fact, earnest money is not required for an offer. Instead, earnest money is *an inducement to have the buyer's offer accepted and a means of showing the seller the buyer is serious and able to follow through with the financing necessary to buy the property.* The amount of the deposit could be a factor in whether or not an offer is accepted, especially if more than one offer is presented to the seller. For instance, if Brian has 10% to put down and Jane has 20%, that makes Jane more secure and, theoretically, makes her offer more attractive.

Earnest money deposits are generally held by the listing broker, selling broker, or the attorney representing the seller and must be maintained in a separate escrow account to prevent commingling of funds.

Termination of an Offer

To create a binding contract, an offer must first be accepted before it terminates. An offer can be terminated by:

- **Lapse of time.** Many offers include a "time is of an essence" clause and/or state they will expire at a certain time, for example, "after five days" or "on March 31." When an offer does not specify an expiration date, it expires after a reasonable amount of time has passed. Even when an offer has an expiration date, however, it may be terminated sooner by death or incapacity or revocation.
- **Death or incapacity.** The death or incapacity of one of the parties makes it impossible to form a contract. This also terminates an offer before a stated expiration date. Suppose an offer made on March 1 states it will expire on March 31. If the offeror dies on March 23, before the offer has been accepted, the offer terminates on that date.
- **Revocation.** An offer is terminated if the offeror revokes or withdraws it before the offeree accepts it. At the point the offer has been revoked, the offeree has lost the chance to accept it.

Requirements for Acceptance

To complete the formation of a sales contract, the offer must be accepted. **Acceptance** – also referred to as **a meeting of the minds** – occurs when *the parties agree on price, down payment, financing method, and other essential terms.* At this point, *the broker has earned a commission* – even if the sale never closes.

There are some basic requirements for acceptance:

- **Acceptance must be communicated to the offeror.** One party may have decided to accept an offer, but until that party lets the other party know it has been accepted, the offer can be revoked. Even if the seller cashed an earnest money deposit check, it is not enough for just the buyer to know the offer was accepted. The seller must communicate acceptance directly to the buyer. An **earnest money deposit** is a *deposit a buyer makes at the time of submitting an offer to demonstrate intent to purchase*.

- **Acceptance must be made in the manner specified.** Many offers specify a certain manner of acceptance (i.e., "in writing," "via fax," or "by delivering a cashier's check"). The offeree's acceptance is not effective unless the instructions in the offer are followed. If the offer states acceptance must be in writing, but the offeree calls and accepts over the phone, it does not create a binding contract; the offeror can still revoke the offer.

  When an offer does not specify how it is to be accepted, any reasonable method of acceptance effectively binds the offeror and prevents revocation. This rule applies to all contracts – even those required by law to be in writing and signed, such as real estate purchase agreements. The *offeror* is bound by an oral acceptance even if the contract is required to be in writing, but only a written, signed acceptance is binding on the *offeree*.

- **Acceptance must not vary the terms of the offer.** To create a contract, the offeree must accept *exactly* those terms offered. The offeree cannot modify them or add new terms. If an offeree makes changes, that response is not an acceptance, it is a *counteroffer*. A **counteroffer** *represents a change*; it is essentially a rejection and a new offer. The offeror becomes the *counterofferee*, and the original offeree is now the *counterofferor*. A binding contract is not created unless the counterofferee accepts the counteroffer.

Contract Preparation

New York State does not dictate the use of a specific form for sales contracts. When a buyer is ready to make an offer, the actual procedure used for preparing the sales contract is typically determined by local customs and practices.

Standardized Sales Contracts

While the law prohibiting real estate licensees from dispensing legal advice applies to contracts, New York's Attorney General has concluded that a broker may use a standardized sales contract form that has been approved by a recognized Bar Association in conjunction with a local Board of REALTORS® as long as it meets certain criteria, including:

- The form requires that the broker fill in only nonlegal provisions such as names of the parties, property location and description, terms of the sale, and date and location of the closing.
- The document clearly and prominently indicates on its face that it is a legally binding document and it is recommended all parties seek an attorney's advice before signing.
- Brokers cannot add any provisions to the standard preprinted contract form unless they make the entire contract subject to the review and approval of the attorneys representing all parties.

In New York, standardized sales contracts are used most often by Upstate brokers, which is typically understood to include anything north of Westchester County.

Binders

A **binder** is sometimes referred to as a "Sales Agreement," "Purchase Agreement," or "Deal Sheet." In the New York City and Long Island areas of New York, this what agents use. These documents – which are generally one page – contain most of the important information that will go in the actual Sales Contract prepared by the seller's attorney.

The basic way it is used:

1. When the agent receives an offer from the buyer, he will fill out the form and present it to the listing agent and seller.
2. Upon acceptance, it is sent to the seller's attorney and the buyer's attorney.
3. The seller's attorney then draws up the Sales Contract and sends this to the buyer's attorney.

The buyer always signs the contract first, and then the seller will sign it, making it an official transaction.

Essential Elements of a Sales Contract

All of the essentials of a valid contract must be present in a sales contract, including the **signatures** of all parties to the transaction. Furthermore, a sales contract must identify the:

- **Parties** to the contract, including the names and addresses of the buyer(s) and seller(s).
- Specific **property** to be sold. Typically, the street address is sufficient, but may include the legal description (section, block, and lot or metes and bounds) or the tax map designation.
- **Interest** in the property to be sold (for example, all of the bundle of rights, just subsurface rights, etc.).
- **Terms** of the sale as clearly as possible, for example: What is and isn't included in the sale, including personal property; how any earnest money deposit is to be distributed if the transaction does not go through; how and when the buyer will take possession of the property; how commission is distributed.
- Total purchase **price** and **method of payment**, for example, the mortgage-related information and down payment.

Data Needed for Contract Preparation

Some specific information or documents that may be needed in order to complete a sales contract include:

- **Survey** of the property's boundaries.
- Evidence of any **encumbrances** such as easements or liens.
- Prior **deed**, which is used to draft a new deed.
- Property **tax bills**, the most recent available, as well as special assessments and water and fuel bills needed to adjust expenses at closing.
- **Certificate of occupancy** to indicate that the property is habitable after local authorities perform required inspections.

This information can be obtained from various sources, including the buyer, seller, and public records. Real estate licensees may facilitate assembling the necessary information.

SALES AGREEMENT

DATE ____________

PURCHASER(S):

______________________ (name)

______________________ address)

______________________ (telephone)

SELLER(S):

______________________ (name)

______________________ address)

______________________ (telephone)

PROPERTY TO BE SOLD

The undersigned purchaser(s), agrees to purchase and the undersigned seller(s), to sell the property known as and by street number

____

Seller acknowledges the receipt of $ ____________ as a deposit on account of the purchase price.

PRICE AND TERMS

Purchase price:	$ ________
Cash on signing more formal contract *(including amount above):*	$ ________
Subject to existing mortgage (approx.):	$ ________
Subject to new mortgage (approx.):	$ ________
Cash on closing of title:	$ ________

MORTGAGE REQUIREMENTS

This agreement may be cancelled if purchaser is unable to obtain a ______________________ first mortgage loan, in the amount of $ ____________ payable in equal monthly payments of principal and interest, over 30 years, with interest at the prevailing rate, within 60 days after the signing of a formal contract. Purchaser agrees to sign any and all papers and documents and furnish all information required by the lending institution to obtain such a mortgage loan.

PERSONAL PROPERTY

Included in the sale are the following items of personal property:

____

____

ACCEPTANCE OF OFFER

The purchaser's deposit is accepted by the broker with the understanding that this offer is not a sales agreement until the owner agrees to the terms of this agreement. If the owner fails to agree to the terms of this agreement, the deposit shall be refunded to the purchaser. If the owner does agree to the terms of this agreement, a more formal contract expressing the above terms and conditions, prepared by the seller's attorney, shall be signed and exchanged by the seller and the purchaser on or

about: ______________________

DATE FOR SETTLEMENT AND DELIVERY OF DEED

The settlement of the obligations of the seller and purchaser under this agreement (closing of title) and the transfer of the deed shall take place on or about ______________________ at the office of the seller's attorney or lending institution.

BROKER'S COMMISSION

The parties agree that ______________________ obtained an offer from the above named purchasers and that the above named sellers have accepted that offer and all its terms.
The commission is due ______________________ is ____________% of the sales price.
Payment of the commission, which is now earned, shall be deferred until closing of title or earlier termination of this sale. Sellers agree to notify broker at least (48) hours prior to closing of title and to pay commission by cashiers check, bank check, or attorney's escrow check.

______________________ (Purchaser)

______________________ (Purchaser)

______________________ (Seller)

______________________ (Seller)

______________________ (licensed Real Estate Agent)

Attorney for Purchaser:

____

Tel. No. ______________________

Fax No ______________________

Attorney for Seller:

____

Tel. No. ______________________

Fax. No. ______________________

Source: Reprinted with permission of Patricia E. Cardinale, Broker/Owner

Contract Provisions

While each specific sales contract is unique, most contain the following sections:

Parties

Identifies the parties to the contract including the buyers' and sellers' names and addresses.

Property Address

Identifies by address the property to be sold as well as the approximate lot size, which may simply say "as per deed" to prevent reliance on estimated dimensions.

Personal Property Included

Lists the items included in the sale. This section lists several items commonly included with the sale of property like window coverings, carpeting, and alarm systems. There is also room to incorporate any other items included in the sale. And unless otherwise noted, all items are sold "as is."

Items Excluded

Lists the items excluded in the sale. Special lighting fixtures, storage sheds, or play sets are common items excluded.

Purchase Price

Indicates the purchase price. The earnest money deposit, as well as any other deposits, is also in-cluded in this section.

Mortgage Contingency

Explains the mortgage contingency. Here is where it is noted that the agreement is contingent on the buyer obtaining approval for a mortgage loan. The loan type desired is noted as well as who should be contacted when financing is approved. The seller's contribution is also noted, along with how it should be applied.

Mortgage Fees

Indicates the mortgage expense and recording fees are paid by the purchaser unless otherwise nego-tiated.

Other Terms

Details other terms of the contract, if any. For example, repair requests or rental conditions could be listed here.

Title and Survey

Explains title and survey findings. This section also binds the seller to provide any available title and survey information to the buyer without cost. However, in some upstate counties, the seller is charged with providing the continuation of the search and the purchaser pays only to insure it. New construc-tion may just require reimbursement of the builder for cost of the survey.

Property Conditions

Indicates the conditions of the premises. Unless otherwise noted, the premises is sold "as is" without warranty as to condition. Two contingencies are included here: 1. termite inspection, and 2. home in-spection.

Title Conditions

Explains any conditions affecting the property's title.

Deed

Indicates the type of deed that will be conveyed. Upstate New York uses a Warranty Deed whereas south of Poughkeepsie the norm is a Bargain and Sale Deed.

Tax Liability

Explains who is responsible for the New York State transfer tax and mortgage satisfaction.

Tax and Other Adjustments

Indicates tax and other adjustments.

Right of Access

Grants the buyer(s) and/or representatives the right to access the property for any tests or inspec-tions required by the terms of the contract. It also gives the buyer(s) and/or representatives the right to inspect the property within 48 hours prior to closing.

Target Closing Details

Lists the target date and proposed location of the closing. Both items are subject to change once con-tract contingencies are met.

Security Deposit

Details deposit procedures; including where it shall be held as well as what happens to the deposit should the seller not accept the offer. In Upstate New York, brokers typically hold deposit money in an escrow account and buyers often put it toward fees at closing. Downstate, on the other hand, attor-neys usually hold deposit money in their Interest on Lawyer Fund of the State of New York account (IOLA account).

Time Limits

Explains the period the offer is valid.

Real Estate Agents

Acknowledges the real estate broker and salesperson (if applicable) who brought about the sale. This section also contains commission information.

Attorney Approval Clause

Refers to the attorneys' approval clause, which states the agreement is contingent upon the buyer(s) and seller(s) obtaining approval of the agreement from their attorneys. This section should always re-flect a date giving each party's attorney time to receive and review the document

Attached Addenda

Lists any attached addenda. For example, New York State law requires property disclosures be at-tached to sales contracts. Addenda should also be sent to each party's attorney for review along with the contract.

Delivery Details

Explains how notices contemplated by the agreement must be in writing and details how they must be delivered.

Disclaimers and Signatures

Contains the entire agreement disclaimer as well as all parties' signatures, including the listing and selling broker.

Other Contract Provisions

Besides the information listed above, sales contracts may include other various disclosures and provisions:

As Is Clauses

An **as is clause** is a *provision in a purchase agreement stating the buyer accepts the property in its present condition*. The implication is the buyer has inspected the property and agrees to accept it as is without requiring the seller to fix any problems or renegotiating after the discovery of a problem. An as is clause does not protect the seller from liability for non-disclosure of latent defects. Also, an as is clause cannot protect sellers or agents if they deliberately conceal a defect from the buyer. An as is clause is not a defense to fraud, because the "as is" must be specifically described.

CASE IN POINT

Broker Sue has a foreclosed house listed. For two months, the home has been vacant and the utilities disconnected. Recently, the basement flooded because the sump pump was not connected. The furnace, electrical services, and other mechanical components are located in the basement and may have suffered water damage.

Sue cannot protect herself and the seller from potential liability simply by stating to potential buyers the property is sold "as is," without apprising them of the water in the basement. She must make prospective purchasers aware of the condition, as she is aware of it.

Escape Clause

Many contracts include an **escape clause**, also known as a kick-out clause or a 72-hour clause or a 48-hour clause. When a buyer has to sell his home in order to purchase the property in the present contract, the seller can request an escape clause be included in the contract, to allow him to pursue other buyers, while giving the offerer the right to perform or cancel, should another contract be considered.

Contingencies and Riders

Contingencies are *conditions that must occur in order for the contract to be performed.* One example would be satisfactory results from certain inspections, such as termites, septic system, home systems, radon, etc. Other common contingencies are:

- Mortgage contingency in which the buyer is able to secure a mortgage for a specified amount at specified terms.
- Contingency stating that the buyer must be able to sell his house before being required to execute the terms of the sales contract.

Riders are simply *amendments to contracts.* For example, when the buyer is using an FHA or VA loan, a rider may be attached to a sales contract that voids the contract if the property appraisal is less than the purchase price. Riders and addenda should be written by an attorney.

Disclosures

Buyers who write a contract on almost any residential property built prior to 1978 must be given a booklet discussing **lead-based paint** hazards. Buyers of pre-1978 residential property are given ten days to investigate potential lead-based paint hazards before the contract becomes binding.

Additionally, New York law requires sellers to provide buyers with a **Property Condition Disclosure statement**. Failure to provide this document results in a credit of $500 to the buyer at closing.

Signing the Contract

A signed sales contract for real property is the final product of negotiations between the buyer and seller or their representatives. A buyer typically signs the initial offer, and assuming it is acceptable, the seller then signs. Contracts are often delivered via courier, agents, mail, or even e-mail without the buyers or sellers ever meeting face to face. Of course, a contract could go back and forth several times before all terms are agreed to and it is signed by all parties to the transaction. Contracts generally require original signatures, in which case each party to the transaction signs multiple copies of the contract so that all can have their own original copy of the signed documents. When changes are made to the original contract, all parties must initial at each change or in the margin of the paper, next to the change.

Other Types of Sales-Related Contracts

While sales contracts for single-family residential property may be the most common type of sales agreement, it is helpful to be familiar with other ways in which property sales may be transacted.

Cooperative Apartment Purchase and Contract

Cooperatives are *buildings owned by corporations with the residents as shareholders who each receive a proprietary lease on an individual unit and the right to use common areas.* **Proprietary leases** have *longer terms than ordinary leases and offer more rights than an ordinary tenant lease does.* Title to the cooperative building is held by a corporation formed for that purpose. When a buyer makes an offer on a cooperative apartment, he actually wishes to purchase shares of stock in the cooperative corporation. It is for this reason the sales contract and financing are different from other types of real estate transactions. One significant difference between the purchase of shares in a cooperative apartment and a typical real estate transaction is that in order to purchase the shares, a board of directors usually interviews potential shareholders and either agrees, or disagrees, to the purchase.

The financing needed to purchase shares in a cooperative apartment is governed by the **Uniform Commercial Code**, *which provides for the lender to retain a security interest in the personal property or chattel until the lender is paid in full.* In a cooperative transaction, the loan is secured not by a mortgage, but by the shares of stock in the corporation.

Options

Options are *contracts that give one party the right to do something, without obligating him to do so*. Thus, an option is a unilateral contract. The most common type of real estate option is a lease with an option to purchase. An option to purchase gives one party (the optionee) the right to buy the property of another (the optionor) at a specified price within a limited time. Within that period, the optionee may choose to exercise the option – that is, enter into a contract to buy the property – but the optionee is under no obligation to exercise the option.

An option is supported by consideration. The optionee pays the optionor for the option right. For example, if an owner tells a prospective buyer she is willing to sell her house for $100,000, the buyer might pay her $1,000 to keep that offer open for a month. The payment of consideration makes the option irrevocable until it expires. If the optionor dies before the option expires, it is still binding on the optionor's heirs.

Right of First Refusal

The **right of first refusal** is *a right to have the first chance to buy or lease property if the owner decides to sell or lease it.* Someone who holds the right of first refusal has the right to purchase the leased property before anyone else does if the owner decides to sell it. Also, if a third party makes an offer and the owner is willing to accept it, the right holder must match the terms of that offer in order to acquire the property.

Installment Sales Contract

Installment sales contracts, also referred to as **land contracts**, are *agreements for which the buyer (vendee) makes payments to the seller (vendor) in exchange for the right to occupy and use the property, but no deed or title is transferred until all, or a specified portion of, payments have been made*. The seller holds title to the land as security.

An installment sales contract is an express bilateral executory contract. The seller and the buyer each have certain obligations and responsibilities. The seller promises to give possession to the buyer during the contract, accept payments toward the purchase of the property, and convey title once all, or a specified portion of, payments have been made. The buyer promises to make the agreed upon payments, pay taxes, obtain insurance, and maintain the property.

There are unique advantages to an installment sales contract for buyers and sellers. For buyers who cannot qualify for a conventional mortgage loan, a land contract may be an option. And for sellers, tax advantages make land contracts attractive because they can still claim depreciation on the property as the owner, even though they do not actually reside on the property. Another benefit to sellers is they are not required to pay lump sum capital gains tax on a home sold under a land contract. They can simply pay a percentage each year as payments are received from the buyer.

SUMMARY

1. Contract law touches many aspects of real estate. Real estate agents must be familiar with several kinds of contracts including *listing agreements, buyer agency agreements, sales contracts, options*, and *leases*. All of these real estate-specific contracts use the basic rules of contract law. Real estate professionals *cannot give legal advice*. A real estate license also does not grant the right to draft legal documents, such as sales contracts.
2. **Contracts** are *agreements between two or more parties to do, or not do, something*. Contracts are legally enforceable promises that can be classified as: **Express** (agreement expressed in words, spoken or written) or **implied** (agreement not put into words but implied by actions of the parties); **unilateral** (one party makes a binding promise to the other) or **bilateral** (each party makes a binding promise to the other); **executory** (one or both parties have not yet completed performance of contractual obligations) or **executed** (both parties fully performed contractual obligations).
3. A contract can be **valid** (binding and legally enforceable), **void** (not enforceable; lacks one or more requirements for formation or defective in some other respect), **voidable** (one party can end without liability because of lack of legal capacity or other factor), or **unenforceable** (court would refuse to enforce). The **essential elements of a valid contract**: 1. Competent parties 2. Mutual agreement 3. Consideration 4. Description of the object being contracted 5. Lawful and possible objective 6. Written format (when required) and signatures.
4. New York's **statute of frauds** is *a law requiring certain types of contracts to be in writing, contain all essential elements of a valid contract, and be signed to be enforceable*. The Sullivan Law, or **plain language requirement**, states that *written agreements for the sale or lease of residential property to be written in a clear and coherent manner with words common in everyday usage if the transaction is for $50,000 or less.*

5. Contracts can be *terminated* by: Agreement of parties, partial performance, full performance, impossibility of performance, and operation of law. When a contract is **assigned**, the assignor *transfers her rights or interests under a contract to another party (assignee)*. When a contract is assigned, the assignor is not relieved of liability under the contract. **Novation** is the *substitution of an original contract with a new contract, or the substitution of one party to the contract to another person, relieving the withdrawing party of liability.*

6. *When a party fails to perform with no legal cause*, it is a **breach of contract**. A breach may be either **substantial performance** (promisor does not perform all contractual obligations but does enough so promisee is required to fulfill his obligation) or **material breach** (breach of contract important enough to excuse the non-breaching party from performing the contractual obligations). An example of a material breach is not complying with a **time is of the essence** statement. Breach of contract **remedies** include: Cancellation, injunction, liquidated damages, reformation, rescission, and specific performance.

7. **Sales contracts** are *contracts in which a seller promises to convey title to real property to a buyer in exchange for the purchase price*. Sales contracts must contain all of the essential elements to be valid. A sales contract usually includes: **Parties** to the contract, including the names and addresses of the buyer(s) and seller(s), **property** to be sold (address or legal description), **interest** in the property to be sold (for example, all of the bundle of rights, just subsurface rights, etc.), **terms** of the sale as clearly as possible (personal property, earnest money liquidation, closing, commission, etc.), total purchase **price** and **method of payment** (for example, mortgage-related information, down payment), and the **signatures** of all parties to the transaction.

8. An **earnest money deposit** is *an inducement to have the buyer's offer accepted and a means of showing the seller the buyer is serious and able to follow through with the financing necessary to buy the property.* Earnest money deposits are generally held by the listing broker, selling broker, or the attorney representing the seller and must be maintained in a separate escrow account.

9. New York State does not dictate the use of a specific form for sales contracts. Contract preparation is typically determined by local customs and practices. Some brokers (mostly Upstate) use **standardized sales contract forms** that have been approved by a recognized Bar Association in conjunction with a local Board of REALTORS®. These forms allow brokers to fill in the details as long as the contract indicates that is legally binding and recommend attorney review. A **binder**, like an offer to purchase, is a *document that accompanies an earnest money deposit for the purchase of real property as evidence of the purchaser's good faith and intent to complete the transaction.* A binder is a written outline of the details and terms of the transaction that are necessary to create a sales contract. In New York, binders are most likely to be used in New York City and other Downstate counties.

10. Sales contracts typically contain certain provisions and disclosures: An **as is clause** is a *provision in a purchase agreement stating the buyer accepts the property in its present condition.* An as is clause cannot protect sellers or agents if they deliberately conceal a defect from the buyer. **Contingencies** are *conditions that must occur in order for the contract to be formed,* for example, certain home inspections, mortgage contingency, contingency if the buyer cannot sell his house. **Riders** are *amendments to contracts* that should be written by an attorney; disclosures include **lead-based paint** hazards (for houses built prior to 1978) and the **Property Condition Disclosure statement** that New York law requires sellers to give to buyers.

11. Certain information is needed to complete a sales contract and carry out a closing, such as the *prior deed, survey, certificate of occupancy, tax bills, and buyer's and seller's personal information.* This information can be obtained from various sources, including the buyer, seller, and public records. Real estate licensees may help facilitate assembling all necessary information in order for the attorneys involved to complete their portion of the contract.

12. Other types of sales-related contracts include: **Cooperatives**, *buildings owned by corporations with the residents as shareholders who each receive a proprietary lease on an individual unit and the right to use common areas,* involve the sale of shares in the corporation. **Options** are *contracts that give one party the right to do something, without obligating him to do it.* An option is a *unilateral contract.* The most common type of real estate option is a **lease with an option to purchase**, which *gives one party (optionee) the right to buy the property of another (optionor) at a specified price within a limited time*. Optionees have the **right of first refusal** in an option to purchase – *the right to the first chance to buy or lease if the owner decides to sell or lease it.* **Installment sales contracts**, or **land contracts**, are *agreements through which the buyer (vendee) makes payments to the seller (vendor) in exchange for the right to occupy and use the property, but no deed or title is transferred until all, or a specified portion of, the payments have been made.*

12-A

Leases

In This Session

This session discusses the contract that creates a leasehold estate, which is a temporary right to possess property, granted from the landlord to a tenant.

You'll learn:

- How to distinguish among the different types of leasehold estates.
- The purpose of different types of lease options.
- How covenants affect lease contracts.
- How leases may be terminated and when it is acceptable to begin the process of eviction.
- The difference between rent control and rent stabilization.

Key Terms

- Actual Eviction
- Assignment
- Constructive Eviction
- Covenant
- Estate at Will
- Estate for Years
- Graduated Lease
- Gross Lease
- Ground Lease
- Holdover Tenant
- Index Lease
- Land Lease
- Lease
- Leasehold Estate
- Lessee / Lessor
- Net Lease / Double Net / Triple Net Leases
- Percentage Lease
- Periodic Estate
- Quiet Enjoyment
- Security Deposit
- Sublease
- Tenancy at Sufferance

Leasehold Estates

A **leasehold estate** is an interest in real estate that *gives the holder a temporary right to possession, without conveying title.* The *holder of a leasehold estate* is known as a **tenant** or **lessee**. The *property owner* is known as the **landlord** or **lessor**. Leasehold estates are created by lease agreements that provide contractual rights and obligations to all parties involved. A leasehold interest is reversionary, meaning that once the lease ends, *possession of the property reverts to the landlord.* There are several types of leasehold estates.

Estate for Years

An **estate for years** is a leasehold estate *set to last for a specific period, after which it automatically terminates.* It is also known as a **term tenancy**. Duration of an estate for years can be any amount of time, even just for one day. An estate for years terminates automatically at the end of the specified rental period and does not require either party to give notice. Unless someone breaches the terms of the lease, neither the landlord nor the tenant can terminate a term tenancy sooner than what is stated in the contract, unless both parties agree. An estate for years is *not* terminated by the death of either party or by the sale of the property.

Periodic Estate

A **periodic estate** is a *leasehold estate that continues for successive equal periods of length until terminated by proper notice from either the lessor or the lessee.* The term of a periodic estate may be any length of time agreed to – such as week-to-week, month-to-month, or year-to-year – and the tenancy automatically renews itself at the end of each period until one party terminates it. In New York State, proper notice of intent to terminate is at least **one month plus one day for either party**, for example, if the rent is due on June 1 and the landlord wants the tenant to vacate by July 1, notice to terminate must be made by May 31. A periodic estate is *not* terminated by the death of either party or by the sale of the property.

Estate at Will

An **estate at will** is a *leasehold estate that does not have a lease to specify the termination date and rental period.* Sometimes no rent is paid (e.g., resident apartment superintendent), or the rent owed has no reference to time periods (e.g., "35% of gross profits"). A common example of an estate at will is someone who rents to a family member who occasionally pays rent, but there is no lease agreement. Either party can end an estate at will at any time with proper notice, which in New York State is **not less than 30 days**. A landlord must either deliver this notice to the tenant in person or post it in a conspicuous place on the premises where it can be read. Unlike the estate for years or the periodic estate, an estate at will *automatically terminates* when either the landlord or tenant dies.

Tenancy at Sufferance

Tenancy at sufferance describes *possession of property by a tenant who came into possession of the property under a valid lease, but stays on after the lease expires without the landlord's permission.* A tenancy at sufferance is ***not a leasehold estate***.

A landlord is not required to give a tenant at sufferance—sometimes called a **holdover tenant**—notice of termination. New York real property law allows landlords to remove holdover tenants by initiating the legal eviction process. Landlords cannot use force to regain possession of the property; only a sheriff can physically remove a holdover tenant.

In New York municipalities that do *not* have rent regulations, if a landlord accepts rent from a holdover tenant, a month-to-month periodic tenancy is automatically created *(New York Real Property Law § 232-c)*.

LEASE CONSIDERATIONS IN NEW YORK CITY

Estate for years. A term tenancy lease that does not specifically state the duration of the term continues until the *first day of October after possession.*

Periodic estate. If a lease contract states the lease will automatically be renewed unless the tenant gives the landlord notice of departure, it is not enforceable unless the landlord gives written notice at least 15 days before the renewal reminding the tenant about this provision.

Monthly periodic estate. A monthly periodic tenancy, or month-to-month tenancy, may be terminated by notice from the landlord **at least 30 days** from the expiration of the term.

Leases

Leases are *contracts in which one party (*the **lessee**) *pays the property owner* (the **lessor**) *rent in exchange for possession of real estate. Thus, a lease is the conveyance of a leasehold estate from the fee owner to a tenant.* Lessees, or tenants, are entitled to **quiet enjoyment** of the property, which is the *right to the use and possession of real property without interference from the previous owner, the lessor, or anyone else claiming title.*

Owners are expected to receive money in the form of rent plus the reversionary interest in the property. *Reversionary interest* means the property will revert to the owner at the end of the lease term.

Standard Lease Provisions

While there is no statutory form of a lease, since the lease is a contract, the essential elements of a valid contract are also necessary for a valid lease. For example, the lease must be stated in plain language. Standard provisions in a lease include:

- **Legal capacity to contract**, in other words, both parties must be competent and over the age of 18.
- A **demising clause**, which grants possession of the property to the lessee.
- **Terms** of the lease, must be clearly stated, including the duration of the tenancy and its expiration date.
- An adequate **description** of the property. For most leases, the street address is sufficient.
- **Consideration**, which usually is a sum of money paid as **rent** in exchange for possession of the property. It should indicate the amount of rent as well as how and when it is paid.

- **Lease renewal**. New York State does not provide for statutory rights of renewal. However, included in many leases is an **option to renew,** which *sets forth the renewal methods and terms of the new lease.*
- A **use provision**. Residential leases typically assert the premises cannot be used for anything other than its intended purpose – a place to live. Commercial leases, unless otherwise noted, usually state the premises may be used "for any lawful purpose," if the purpose does not violate private deed restrictions.
- **The terms listed in writing** if it will last for more than **one year** to comply with the statute of frauds. In New York, an **oral** lease for *less than one year is generally enforceable.*
- **Signatures** of both parties.

LEAD PAINT DISCLOSURE

The Residential Lead-Based Paint Hazard Reduction Act of 1992 applies both to homes that are sold as well as residential leases. From the perspective of rental property, it requires landlords and agents to disclose known lead paint hazards for homes and rental units built **prior to 1978**, with some exceptions, for example, dormitories and leases for less than 100 days, such as vacation rentals. To comply with this law, landlords must:

- Disclose any known lead-based paint hazard in homes and must give tenants any reports available from prior lead tests.
- Give renters a pamphlet about how to protect families from lead in homes.
- Include certain language in leasing agreements, either in the lease itself or as an attachment, to ensure that disclosure and notification actually take place. This disclosure must be signed by landlords, agents, and tenants.

Security Deposit

A **security deposit** is *money the tenant pays to the landlord that provides monetary security in case of damage to the residence or failure by the lessee to comply with the lease agreement*. Usually, lessees receive the deposit back at the end of the lease term, less any deductions for necessary repairs beyond normal wear and tear.

Security deposits must be held in an escrow account, separate from the owner's personal or operating accounts. In New York, it is illegal to commingle security deposit funds with other funds. For properties consisting of six or more units, owners are required to put security deposits in interest-bearing accounts. The interest belongs to the tenant, not the property owner, although a property owner can claim 1% of the amount of the interest annually to cover administrative expenses.

Habitability

According to the **New York State Warranty of Habitability Law**, property owners are required to lease property that is habitable and livable at the beginning of the lease term and to maintain the premises in habitable and livable conditions throughout the lease term. Owners are also obligated not to subject tenants to conditions that are dangerous, or detrimental to their life, health, and safety. To comply with this law, landlords must also provide heat, hot water, and pest control.

Maintenance and Repair

New York's **Multiple Dwelling Law and Multiple Residence Law** require an owner renting a multiple-family dwelling to keep the property in good repair. If the landlord's negligence leads to injury or results in unsafe living conditions, the landlord can be held legally responsible.

The lessee's basic obligation under any lease is to maintain the premises in the same condition it was found at the beginning of the lease term. Normal wear and tear are expected and accepted by landlords. Lessees, however, are responsible for damage caused by their own negligence.

Apartment Sharing

According to New York State Real Property Law, a lease cannot restrict occupants in an apartment to just the tenant named on the lease. When there is more than one named tenant, the landlord must allow the immediate family to share the apartment. If there is only one named tenant, the tenant can share the apartment with immediate family, one additional occupant, and that occupant's dependent children, as long as the apartment is the primary residence of the tenant or tenant's spouse. If the named tenant moves out, those sharing the apartment have no right to continue to stay in the property without the landlord's consent.

Landlords may limit occupancy if the number of people in the apartment violates local occupancy and health laws, however.

Assignment and Subletting

Assignment occurs when the *lease contract is transferred from the present lessee to an assignee.*

Assignment transfers a tenant's entire interest, but it does *not* transfer a tenant's entire liability under the lease. With an assignment, the assignee (the second tenant) and the assignor (the original tenant) *share legal responsibility* for paying rent to a landlord. If the assignee doesn't pay, the landlord has a right to sue both the assignee and the assignor for the rent.

A **sublease** is *when a tenant transfers only part of his right of possession or other interest in leased property to another person for part of the remaining lease term.* Typically, with a sublease, the sublessee pays rent to the lessee, who then pays the lessor. In a sublease, *the original tenant is responsible to the owner for all provisions in the lease.*

Typically, owners prohibit assignment and subleasing without written approval. However, in New York, if owners unreasonably withhold consent to assign lease rights or sublet, tenants may legally be released from the lease, or they may go ahead and sublet.

Covenant of Quiet Enjoyment

Leases often contain **covenants**, which are *promises or guarantees.* A common guarantee in a lease is the **covenant of quiet enjoyment**, which means the property *cannot be interrupted or invaded by anyone, including the property owner, without the lessee's consent.* What this means is property owners do not have the automatic right to enter the premises unannounced. This also applies to contractors employed by the owner to make repairs and/or installations.

Property owners must provide reasonable notice to tenants before they, or contractors they have employed, enter the premises. Usually, 24 to 48 hours is sufficient. The owner *does* have the right to enter the premises in an emergency in order to protect the property.

Lease Termination

Leases can be terminated in a number of ways, most commonly when a lease term **expires**. Upon expiration, if no renewal agreement is in place, lessees are obligated to vacate the premises voluntarily and fully. Possession then reverts to the owner.

Another method of termination is when the *property owner and the tenant mutually agree to cancel a lease agreement prior to its expiration,* called **surrender**. Surrender cancels all parties' duties and responsibilities, and possession reverts to the owner.

Eviction

If a tenant breaches the lease contract, an owner can choose to terminate the contract by evicting the tenant. **Eviction** is *the forced removal, by legal means, of a tenant and the tenant's belongings from a leased premise*. The key word in this definition is *legal*. This process is known as **actual eviction.**

Lease contracts can also be terminated when **constructive eviction** occurs, which is when *a tenant is prevented from the quiet enjoyment of the property*. Inoperable plumbing and lack of heat due to the owner's negligence are examples of constructive eviction. To claim constructive eviction, tenants must vacate the premises while the conditions that make the property uninhabitable still exist. Constructive eviction claims are not automatic and may require litigation.

A **self-help eviction** is when a landlord uses physical force, threats, or other means to get rid of a tenant instead of going through the legal process. This is **illegal** in New York.

Abandonment

If a tenant abandons the premises and the owner re-enters to repossess it, a lease can be terminated. If a tenant does in fact abandon the property, the owner does not have to accept return of the premises and can pursue the lessee for rent, even though the tenant no longer resides there. If the owner chooses to accept return of the premises, he may still pursue the lessee for lost rent under the old lease.

Death of the Property Owner or Sale of the Property

When one party to the lease dies or the property is sold, it does *not* terminate the lease. The heirs or new owner *must honor the existing lease contracts.* However, a tenancy at will leasehold estate *cannot* be transferred to someone else and so it generally *does end on the death* of the landlord or tenant.

Rent Regulations

Many communities throughout New York have rent regulation programs known as **rent control** and **rent stabilization**. Rent regulations are intended to *protect tenants in privately owned buildings from illegal rent increases while allowing property owners to earn enough from rent to properly maintain their buildings and recognize a profit.* The **New York State Division of Housing and Community Renewal** (DHCR) has oversight of state and local rent control and rent stabilization programs.

Rent control is the older of the two systems of rent regulation. It dates back to the housing shortage immediately following World War II and generally applies to buildings constructed before 1947. Rent stabilization generally covers buildings built between 1947 and 1974, as well as apartments that have been removed from rent control. Both types of regulation restrict the amount of rent charged by property owners and restrict the right of an owner to evict tenants. Rent stabilization programs offer additional tenant protections, for example, the right to have their leases renewed.

In New York City, rent control operates under the maximum base rent (MBR) system. A maximum base rent is established for each apartment and is adjusted every two years to reflect changes in operating costs. Outside of New York City, rent stabilization goes by the name ETPA, or the **Emergency Tenants Protection Act** of 1974, and the DHCR determines the maximum allowable rates of rent increases.

Types of Leases

Leases are generally categorized by the method of rent payment. A **gross lease** is one which *the tenant pays a fixed rent, while the owner or landlord pays all ownership expenses,* such as property taxes, repairs, insurance, and sometimes utilities. A **net lease**, on the other hand, is a lease for which *the tenant pays some or all of the ownership expenses in addition to a monthly rent payment.* With net leases, which are typically used for commercial properties, the property owner or landlord has shifted much of the risk for increased costs to the tenants, who get the additional tax benefit of the business expense.

Commercial Leases	Definition
Net lease	The tenant pays some or all of the expenses associated with the property – taxes, insurance, and maintenance – in addition to rent. If the lease requires the tenant to pay one of these expenses, it's called a single net lease. If the tenant is required to pay any two of these expenses, it's a net-net lease, or a double net lease. A triple net, or net-net-net lease, requires the tenant to pay all three of these expenses.
Percentage lease	The tenant pays a percentage of gross sales on the premises, often in addition to a fixed monthly rental payment. This type of lease is most commonly used for retail tenants and may include a clause that allows the owner to reclaim the premises if gross sales fall below a specified point.
Land lease / Ground lease	A tenant leases unimproved land on a long-term basis; this lease typically includes a provision that provides the tenant will construct a building on the property, which the tenant will own upon completion.
Index lease	The amount of the rent is tied to some common index indicator such as the Consumer Price Index or the Wholesale Price Index that neither the landlord nor the tenant controls. As the agreed upon index increases, the rent goes up by the same percent of change.
Graduated lease	Spells out step-by-step rent increases (or decreases), generally paid in installments. An example might be a long-term lease that spells out annual rent increases.

SUMMARY

1. A **leasehold estate** *gives the holder (tenant) a temporary right to possession, without title.* Lease agreements create leasehold estates and provide contractual rights and obligations to all parties involved. There are several types of leasehold estate including: **Estate for years**, which is set to last for a specific period, after which it automatically terminates; **periodic estate**, which continues for successive equal periods of length, such as week-to-week or month-to-month; and **estate at will**, when a tenant is in possession with the owner's permission, but there is no lease and no specific rent terms (terminates at the death of either party). A **tenancy at sufferance** is *not* a leasehold estate but is when a holdover tenant refuses to vacate the property when the lease ends.

2. **Leases** are *contracts in which one party (lessee) pays the property owner (lessor) rent in exchange for possession of real estate,* so, a lease is the conveyance of a leasehold estate from the owner to a tenant. Lessees, or tenants, are entitled to **quiet enjoyment** of the property, which is *the right to the use and possession of real property without interference from the previous owner, the lessor, or anyone else claiming title.* Lessors have a **reversionary interest** in the property, which means *the property reverts to them at the end of the lease term.*

3. Leases must contain all essential elements of a contract to be valid, for example, **terms in writing** if for more than one year, **plain language**, **legal capacity** to contract, a **demising clause** to grant possession of the property to the lessee, well-defined terms for **duration** and **rent**, an adequate **description** of the property, and **signatures** of both parties. Most leases also contain details related to security deposits, lease renewal, use provisions, and sublease and assignment. Residential leases of property built prior to 1978 must include certain language to ensure that disclosure and notification about **lead paint** have taken place.

4. Leases are *terminated* in a number of ways, including **expiration** (if no renewal agreement has been made, lessees are obligated to voluntarily vacate the premises and possession reverts to the owner), **surrender** (property owner and tenant mutually agree to terminate the lease agreement prior to its expiration), and **eviction** (forced removal, by legal means, of a tenant and his belongings from a leased premise). There are two types of eviction: **Actual** (when a property owner removes a tenant from the premises without the aid or control of the court system) and **constructive** (when a tenant is prevented from enjoying the quiet enjoyment of the premises and so vacates the property). Leases are *not* terminated by the death of one party to the lease nor by the sale of the property.

5. **Assignment** occurs when the *lease contract is transferred from the present lessee to an assignee.* Assignment transfers a tenant's entire interest, but it does *not* transfer a tenant's entire liability under the lease. A **sublease** is *when a tenant transfers only part of his right of possession or other interest in leased property to another person for part of the remaining lease term.* In a sublease, *the original tenant is responsible to the owner for all provisions in the lease.*

6. **Rent regulations** protect tenants living in privately owned buildings from illegal rent increases. Two rent regulations are **rent control** and **rent stabilization**. Rent control limits the rent an owner may charge for an apartment and restricts the right of an owner to evict tenants. It also obligates the owner to provide essential services and equipment. Rent stabilization provides these and other tenant protections, such as the right to have their leases renewed.

7. A **gross lease** is one in which the property owner pays all the expenses associated with the property. . With a **net lease**, the tenant pays some or all the expenses associated with the property. Typical commercial leases include: A **percentage lease**, tenants pay a base rent plus an additional monthly rent derived from a percentage of gross sales; **land lease**, tenant leases unimproved land on a long-term basis; **index lease**, the rent a tenant pays is tied to an index; and **graduated lease**, the rent changes throughout the lease term.

13

Overview of Real Estate Finance

In This Session

Most buyers do not have the ready cash on hand to purchase real estate without financing. While a real estate licensee should not give financial advice, it is important to have a solid understanding of the available real estate finance options. In this chapter, you'll learn what types of financing are available to clients, including conventional loans, seller financing, alternative financing, and government financing programs.

You'll learn:

- What instruments are used to finance the purchase of real estate.
- The difference between primary and secondary mortgage markets.
- Types of primary mortgage lenders and their areas of specialty.
- Methods by which a mortgage loan is repaid.
- The purpose of private mortgage insurance and how it works.
- Indicators of predatory lending and how it can be prevented.

Key Terms

- Amortized Loans
- Buydown
- Conforming / Nonconforming Loans
- Conventional Loan
- Discount Points
- Fannie Mae
- Finance Instruments
- Freddie Mac
- Ginnie Mae
- Grace Period
- Home Ownership and Equity Protection Act (HOEPA)
- Hypothecate
- Loan-to-Value Ratio
- Mortgage
- Mortgage Insurance Premium (MIP)
- Mortgagee
- Mortgagor
- Negative Amortization
- Point
- Predatory Lending
- Private Mortgage Insurance (PMI)
- Primary Mortgage Market
- Promissory Note
- Secondary Mortgage Market
- Securitization

Real Estate Finance Instruments

Finance instruments are *legal documents that establish the rights and duties of all parties involved in a transaction.* There are two types of real estate finance documents: The **financing instrument**, which is typically a promissory note, and the **security instrument**, which is usually a mortgage.

Promissory Notes

A **promissory note** is *a written promise to pay*. On the note, the person promising to pay is called the *maker* of the note and is usually the homebuyer or *mortgagor*. The person who is promised payment is called the *payee*, usually the lender but may also be the seller. Promissory notes are basic evidence of debt, showing who owes how much and to whom. They are usually simple documents, often less than a page long, that include:

- The date.
- Names of the parties involved.
- The amount of debt.
- How and when the debt is to be paid.
- What happens in the event of default.
- The signature of the maker.

Negotiable Instruments

Most promissory notes used in real estate are **negotiable instruments**, meaning that they are *freely transferable from one party to another.* A bank or other creditor can sell the note to obtain immediate cash, though the sale is usually at a discount, meaning the note is sold for a cash amount less than its face value.

Negotiable instruments are governed by the Uniform Commercial Code (UCC), which sets certain requirements for contracts and negotiable instruments. If the specific elements noted are missing from a promissory note, it may still be valid between the parties, but it may not be valid if the note is transferred to another party. This is important since most real estate lenders sell their real estate loans to the secondary market. Secondary market investors will buy only a promissory note that is negotiable because they want to be a **holder in due course**, which is *one who acquires a negotiable instrument in good faith and for consideration and has certain rights beyond those of the original payee.*

Mortgage

In most real estate transactions, a promissory note is accompanied by a **security instrument**. A security instrument allows a debtor to **hypothecate** property, meaning a *debtor can pledge property as security for debt without giving up possession of it.* This serves as security for the creditor and motivation for the debtor to make sure the terms of the note are fulfilled and the note is repaid as agreed. Failure to do so could result in loss of possession. Even without a security instrument, the debtor is still obligated to pay the note. The most common security instrument is a mortgage.

A mortgage is a *type of security instrument where the borrower* (called the **mortgagor**) *pledges property to the lender* (called the **mortgagee**) *as collateral for the debt*. Some mortgages offer a **grace period**, *allowing some flexibility or leniency in the payment schedule of the loan.*

For lenders, the main advantage of mortgages is the right to accelerate the debt in the event of default. The main disadvantage is the time and expense involved with judicial foreclosure, which is the process followed in the event of default. For borrowers, the lender's right of **acceleration** may mean a homeowner who misses one or two payments will be faced with the prospect of having to *pay off the entire debt* to save the home. On the other hand, debtors usually have several months to get the money due to the length of time court proceedings take.

Besides making their mortgage payments, mortgagors have other responsibilities. Most mortgage lenders require buyers to:

- Maintain the property adequately.
- Keep up with taxes and assessments.
- Properly insure the property.

The Mortgage Industry

Several events influenced today's mortgage industry. First, the Federal Reserve Act of 1913 created the Federal Reserve System. This Act established a federal charter that permitted banks to make real estate loans. The Federal Reserve Act was an early step in creating a system for which the government could influence interest rates. Other significant banking legislation followed in the 1930s, creating the Federal Deposit Insurance Corporation (FDIC), as well as the Federal Savings and Loan Insurance Corporation (FSLIC). The creation of these corporations allowed banks and savings and loan associations (S&Ls) to have a continued source of funds to make more home mortgage loans.

Primary Mortgage Market

The **primary mortgage market** *consists of lenders who make mortgage loans directly to borrowers*. The primary market is comprised of various lending institutions in local communities. The source of funds for the primary market is largely made up of the savings deposits of individuals and businesses in the local area. Lenders use those savings to make real estate loans.

Commercial Banks

Commercial banks are financial institutions that provide a variety of financial services, including loans. Although banks are the largest source of investment funds in the country today, these institutions tend to focus on relatively short-term commercial and consumer loans.

Savings and Loan Associations

Savings and loan associations are financial institutions that specialize in taking savings deposits and making mortgage loans. In the late 1970s and early 1980s, management mistakes, economic slumps, and (sometimes) fraud led many S&Ls toward insolvency. At that time, S&Ls were not using the uniform qualifying standards set by major secondary market investors such as Fannie Mae and, therefore, they could not sell loans to the secondary markets. Today S&Ls are the leading home mortgage lenders, and they now follow Fannie Mae qualifying standards.

Mortgage Companies

Mortgage companies are institutions that function as the originators and servicers of loans on behalf of large investors such as insurance companies, pension plans, or Fannie Mae. Since these large investors often operate on a national scale, they have neither the time nor the resources to understand the particular risks of local markets or to deal with the day-to-day management of their loans.

While mortgage companies do lend their own money to borrowers, they often fill the gap functioning more as intermediaries than as sources of lending capital. The loans mortgage companies choose are resold to secondary market investors with the mortgage company acting as an agent to service the loans for a fee. Because they invest little of their own money, their activities are largely controlled by the availability of investment capital in the secondary market. In addition, their loan qualification criteria must reflect the standards of the national market to facilitate resale of the loans. Note that unlike mortgage companies, mortgage *brokers* do not lend money.

Credit Unions

Credit unions are nonprofit financial institutions owned and operated entirely by members. By depositing money in a credit union, the depositor becomes a member and has partial ownership in the institution. To join a credit union, members usually must belong to a participating organization (e.g., employer, school, labor union). In addition to offering mortgage loans, credit unions provide typical financial services, including checking and savings accounts, CDs, retirement accounts, and loans.

Finance Companies

Finance companies are organizations that specialize in making higher-risk loans at higher interest rates. Finance companies are often sources of second mortgages and home equity loans made directly to borrowers.

Portfolio Lenders

Portfolio lenders are financial institutions such as mortgage companies, savings and loans, or commercial banks that originate loans and service them in-house instead of selling them on the secondary market.

Mutual Savings Banks

Mutual savings banks are state-chartered that are owned by depositors and operate for their benefit. Conservative by nature, mutual savings banks often hold a large portion of assets in home mortgages.

Secondary Mortgage Markets

The **secondary mortgage market** consists of *private investors and government agencies that buy and sell real estate mortgages*. Secondary mortgage markets were originally established by the federal government in an attempt to moderate local real estate cycles. (Some of these agencies have since been privatized.) The difference between primary and secondary markets is that secondary markets buy real estate loans from all over the country as investments, whereas primary markets are usually local in nature, with local lenders making local loans.

Loans are bought and sold for several reasons. Both primary and secondary markets are trying to maximize returns on investment dollars. As interest rates rise, it is more profitable to sell older loans with lower interest rates so the lender has new money to lend at higher interest rates. Buying and selling mortgages can also make more funds available for loaning again, thus stabilizing local real estate markets.

The availability of funds in the primary market depends greatly on the existence of secondary markets. First, mortgage funds are loaned to a homebuyer by a lending institution in the primary market. The mortgage is then sold to a secondary market agency that may, in turn, sell it to other investors in the form of mortgage-backed securities. Because the primary lender sold the mortgage on the secondary market, the lender can take the money it receives from the sale and make another mortgage loan, then sell that new loan to the secondary market, and continue the cycle.

A mortgage is purchased by the secondary mortgage market only if the primary market lender conformed to secondary market underwriting standards. There are three agencies responsible for most of today's secondary mortgage market activity.

Fannie Mae

The Federal National Mortgage Association, or **Fannie Mae**, was created to *provide a place for banks and other lenders to sell FHA-insured loans*. Supervised by the Department of Housing and Urban Development (HUD), Fannie Mae is a private corporation that purchases conventional mortgages as well as FHA and VA loans. The organization funds its operation by **securitization**, which is *the act of pooling mortgages and then selling them as mortgage-backed securities*. Fannie Mae is the nation's largest investor in residential mortgages.

The creation of Fannie Mae also helped further standardize home mortgage loans made throughout the country. A loan that *meets Fannie Mae and Freddie Mac standards, and thus can be sold on the secondary market* is called a **conforming loan**. Lenders try to make as many conforming loans as possible, because they like the option of being able to liquidate (sell for cash) their real estate loans on the secondary market if more funds are needed. In 2009, Fannie Mae conforming loan limits for single-family homes in most of the U.S. was set at $417,000.

Freddie Mac

The Federal Home Loan Mortgage Corporation, **Freddie Mac**, was created in 1970 as a nonprofit, federally chartered institution controlled by the Federal Home Loan Bank System. Freddie Mac does not guarantee payment of its mortgages; rather, its primary function is to *help S&Ls acquire additional funds for lending in the mortgage market by purchasing the mortgages they already held.*

Freddie Mac may work with FHA, VA, and conventional mortgages. While Fannie Mae emphasizes the purchase of mortgage loans, Freddie Mac also actively sells mortgage loans from its portfolio, acting as a conduit for mortgage investments. The funds generated by the sale of the mortgages are used to purchase more mortgages.

Ginnie Mae

The Government National Mortgage Association, Ginnie Mae, was created in 1968 as a government-owned corporation operating under HUD. Its primary function is *promoting investment by guaranteeing the payment of principal and interest on FHA and VA mortgages through its mortgage-backed securities program.* This program, supported by the federal government's borrowing power, guarantees interest and principal mortgage payments to mortgage holders.

Categories of Mortgage Loans

Mortgage loans can be categorized as either conventional or government-sponsored. Government-backed loans are insured, guaranteed, or in some way sponsored by government dollars. It is important not to confuse government-backed loans with secondary markets.

Conventional Financing

A **conventional loan** is *any loan not insured or guaranteed by a government agency, such at the FHA, VA, or USDA*. Conventional loans are, however, secured by government-sponsored entities (GSEs) such as Freddie Mac and Fannie Mae. It was Fannie Mae who originally established guidelines for borrowing criteria. The terms and conditions of the mortgage loan are negotiable between the lender and the borrower. Anyone who can meet the lender's requirements can get a conventional loan.

Loan-to-Value Ratio

The **loan-to-value ratio** (LTV) refers to *the amount of money borrowed (the mortgage loan amount) compared to the value of the property.* Lenders use LTV to determine how much they are willing to loan on a given property based on its value. The lender will always use the *lower* of the appraised value or the sale price in order to protect its interest. The lower the LTV, the higher the borrower's down payment, which means the loan is more secure.

For example, on an 80% conventional loan for a house with a sale price of $80,000, the most a buyer could borrow would be:

$80,000 x 0.8 = $64,000 loan amount

Subtracting the loan amount from the sale price indicates that the buyer would need a down payment of $16,000.

The 80% loan has been the standard conventional loan for many years. A buyer who does not have enough money for a 20% down payment but still wants a conventional loan can try to get a 90% conventional loan with a 10% down payment. The qualifying standards for conventional loans above 80% LTV tend to be more stringent, and lenders adhere to those standards more strictly even though the loan is insured. The maximum LTV allowed by conventional standards is 95%.

CASE IN POINT

Bill wants to buy a house that costs $160,000. For an 80% conventional loan, he can borrow $128,000 and needs to make a 20% down payment, or $32,000. If the house appraises for less than $160,000 – say $150,000 – then Bill can borrow only 80% of the appraised value ($120,000). Bill has a couple of options if he still wants to buy the home: He can offer the seller the appraised value of $150,000, or he needs to come up with an additional $8,000 as part of his down payment.

Private Mortgage Insurance

Private mortgage insurance (PMI) is *offered by private companies to insure a lender against a borrower's default.* The insurer does not insure the entire loan amount but rather the upper portion of the loan – the loan amount that exceeds the standard 80% LTV. The amount of coverage varies, but is typically 20-25% of the loan amount. Both Fannie Mae and Freddie Mac require third-party insurance on home loans with down payments of less than 20%. The amount of the PMI premium is typically added to the monthly mortgage payment, although some private mortgage insurance companies offer a one-time mortgage insurance premium that is paid at closing.

In the event of default and foreclosure, and the lender will negotiate how best to proceed. For example, the insurer could pay off the loan and take title or allow the lender to foreclose. If the proceedings from the foreclosure action do not fully reimburse the lender for the principal balance, the lender may be able to make a claim against the insurer. If the insurer were to take the loan, the insurer may be able to file for a deficiency judgment against the borrower.

The Homeowners Protection Act of 1998 requires lenders to automatically cancel PMI on conventional mortgage loans closed after July 29, 1999, when the loan has been paid down to **78%** of the home's current or original value, whichever is lower. The law also says that lenders must drop PMI coverage at a borrower's request when the loan has been paid down to **80% or less** of the home's value and mortgage payments are current.

New York State law requires lenders to stop charging PMI insurance once the borrower has **25% equity** in his home. Exceptions include multi-family units, non-owner-occupant homes, mortgages on second homes, and second mortgages.

Points

Lenders often charge **points** for making loans, for example, to pay administrative costs in processing a loan. They may be called a ***loan origination fee, loan fee, service fee,*** or ***administrative charge***. For FHA and VA loans, the loan fee can be no higher than one point. For conventional loans, the loan fee varies, but is often in the one- to four-point range. A point is simply ***1% of the loan amount.*** Points may be paid by the buyer or the seller, although Fannie Mae, Freddie Mac, and the FHA limit points and other contributions paid by the seller (or other interested parties).

A **buydown** is when *additional funds in the form of* **discount points** *are paid to the lender at the beginning of a loan to lower the interest rate and monthly payments.* A buydown can be **permanent**, meaning it *maintains the lower interest rate through the entire life of the loan*, or **temporary**, where points are paid to a lender to reduce the interest rate and payments *early in a loan, with the interest rate or payments rising later in the loan term.*

For example, Ann is buying a house for $200,000. She makes a $40,000 down payment and borrows $160,000 from County Bank. To provide the loan, the bank charges:

- 1 point for the loan origination fee,
- 1 point to service the loan, and
- 4 points to buy down the interest rate by half a percentage.

Ann pays the bank 6% of the mortgage amount, or $9,600, at closing for these points.

When it comes to points, remember:

- Points are computed as 1% of the loan amount, not the sale price.
- Points can be charged for a variety of reasons.

Federal Housing Administration (FHA)

The Federal Housing Administration (FHA) is part of the Department of Housing and Urban Development (HUD). FHA's primary function is to **insure loans**; the FHA does *not* make loans or build homes.

Under the FHA program, there are no income limits to determine who can take advantage of the program. Instead, the government limits the mortgage amount that can be insured. The FHA insures only *first mortgage loans* on one- to four-family units, with the insured loan amount based on a sound appraisal. A mortgage insurance premium (MIP) is required on all FHA loans.

The maximum insured mortgage amount is based on the median price of homes in a particular area. Each county has a loan limit for one- to four-family residential units. Current maximum home mortgage prices for an area can be found by searching the FHA's website at www.hud.gov or by entering location data directly on this page: https://entp.hud.gov/idapp/html/hicostlook.cfm.

Advantages of FHA-Insured Loans

These are among the attractive features of FHA-insured loans:

- They typically require a lower down payment (FHA minimum down payment is 3.5%).
- The qualifying requirements are less stringent.
- There are no prepayment penalties.

The **mortgage insurance premium (MIP)**—not to be confused with PMI for conventional loans—is required for all FHA loans, regardless of down payment size. You may also see this described as UFMIP, or upfront mortgage insurance premium. For most FHA programs, the MIP has an initial premium and an annual premium. The initial MIP on a new home purchase is 1.00% of the loan amount for 30-year loans, with an annual premium of up to 0.90% of the outstanding loan balance, divided into 12 monthly payments.

VA-Guaranteed Loans

The Veterans Administration (VA) **guarantees** repayment of certain residential loans made to eligible veterans. To be eligible for a VA-guaranteed loan, the borrower must have completed a minimum number of days of active duty – generally more than 180 days in peacetime or at least 90 days in wartime – and must not have been dishonorably discharged. Eligibility is validated by the discharge papers (known as DD-214). Veterans must also have a Certificate of Eligibility issued by the VA.

VA loans can be used to buy single-family homes or multi-family residences up to four units. VA loans must be owner-occupied. With single-family units, the veteran must intend to occupy it as his or her residence; with multi-family dwellings, the veteran must occupy one of the units.

The VA does not make loans; it only guarantees lenders against losses for the loan guaranty amount. A VA mortgage loan is made by an approved lender, and terms of the loan are negotiable. If the borrower defaults, the VA will guarantee a portion of the loan to the lender. The VA does charge borrowers a **funding fee** to use the VA home loan program, although disabled veterans may be exempt from this requirement.

Advantages of VA-Guaranteed Loans

These are among the attractive features of VA-guaranteed loans:

- They may be obtained with no down payment (there is a small funding fee assessed to the veteran that can be borrowed).
- There are no maximum loan amounts.
- Secondary financing is permitted.
- There are no prepayment penalties.
- The loan origination fee can be no higher than one point or 1% of the loan amount.
- They may be assumable under certain circumstances.

USDA Rural Development Housing Programs

The USDA Rural Development's direct and guaranteed loan programs provide low-interest, no-down-payment loans to help eligible families living in rural areas purchase homes. The direct loan program is geared toward low-income individuals. Eligible applicants are qualified for a loan amount up to a county-by-county limit based on debt-to-income ratios. In addition, applicants must have an acceptable credit history and adequate and dependable income.

Borrowers must personally occupy the dwelling following the purchase. Dwellings must be structurally sound, functionally adequate, and in good condition. The standard term for a loan in this program is 33 years. Depending on an applicant's income, loans may be subsidized and interest rates may be reduced to as low as 1%. Closing costs may be included in the loan. More information about homeownership financing or other USDA Rural Development programs can be found at www.rurdev.usda.gov.

State of New York Mortgage Agency Programs

The State of New York Mortgage Agency (SONYMA) was created in 1970 to reduce funds shortages from private banks for mortgage lending within the state of New York. It is the only government program that is a *direct lender*. Programs through SONYMA are designed to make housing affordable to low- and moderate-income households and they are funded by the sale of tax-exempt bonds. SONYMA offers:

- Below-market interest rates.
- Low or no down payment requirements.
- No prepayment penalties.
- Closing cost assistance.

New York residents can take advantage of below-market mortgage interest rates offered through SONYMA programs.

Program	Target Audience	Additional Information
Remodel New York	First-time homebuyers and owners in target areas	Help finance the cost of renovations
Achieving the Dream	Low-income, first-time homebuyers	Offers the lowest interest rate of any SONYMA program
Construction Incentive Program	First-time homebuyers purchasing new builds	Offers 100% financing with a stepped interest rate that is lower for the first four years
Homes for Veterans Program	Qualified veterans	Loans require only 3% down

Loan Repayment

A mortgage, like any loan, consists of two components:

- The **principal**, which is *the amount originally borrowed.*
- The **interest**, which is *the charge a borrower pays to a lender for the use of the lender's money.*

Amortization

Amortization is the *reduction of the balance of the loan by paying back some of the principal owed on a regular basis*. **Negative amortization** *occurs when a loan balance grows because payments do not cover the interest on the loan.* Loans may be amortized a number of ways.

Fully Amortized Loans

With a **fully amortized loan**, *regular payments are applied first to interest owed and then to the principal amount over a number of years (the term).* Initially, more of the monthly payment goes to the interest payment and less goes to principal reduction. If all payments are made on time, the loan will be paid off in full with the last scheduled payment.

An **amortization schedule** is a tool that borrowers and lenders can use to *show exactly how much of each payment of a fully amortized loan will be applied toward principal and how much toward interest over the life of the loan.* Some amortization schedules show only a year-to-year schedule, while others show a month-to-month breakdown. All amortization schedules will show the total amount that the loan is costing the borrower over its entire term.

Straight Loans

A **straight loan** is one in which the *regular payments cover only the interest over the term of the loan.* At the end of the term, a lump sum payment of the principal is required.

Partially Amortized Loans

A **partially amortized loan,** sometimes known as a **balloon loan**, has *periodic payments that do not fully amortize the loan by the end of the loan term.* Therefore, the final payment is larger than the others and is known as a balloon payment.

Loan Assumption

Assumption of a loan *means one party agrees to take over payments of another party's debt, with terms of the note staying unchanged*. In an assumption, the buyer can simply agree to take over payment of the seller's debt, and terms of the note remain the same. The property is still security for the loan, but the buyer becomes primarily liable for repayment. In the event of foreclosure, though, the seller remains secondarily liable. Loan assumption is rarely possible with loans written today, though some conventional mortgages allow assumptions if they do not have an enforceable alienation clause. (Clients should be advised to consult the original lender or a lawyer.)

Nonconforming Loans

While conforming loans meet Fannie Mae and Freddie Mac standards, and thus can be sold on the secondary market, **nonconforming loans** *do not meet these standards, and cannot be sold to Fannie Mae or Freddie Mac.* (There are other secondary markets where nonconforming loans can be sold, however.) Lenders who have the option of keeping loans in their own portfolio (mostly banks and S&Ls) can, within the limits of the law, deviate from the standards set by secondary markets.

Two reasons why loans are classified as nonconforming include the size of the loan and the credit quality of the borrower. For example, **jumbo loans** *exceed the maximum loan amount established by Fannie Mae and Freddie Mac for conforming mortgage loans*, so they are classified as nonconforming loans.

Subprime Loans

Subprime loans, also called *B-C loans* or *B-C credit,* have *more risks than are allowed in the conforming loan market.* Until recently, subprime loans were alternative financing tools to help people with questionable credit reach their goal of homeownership. Some lenders and investors were willing to make these riskier loans because they could charge much higher rates. For some borrowers, it was the only way to buy a house and re-establish credit.

With subprime lending, criteria for who is approved – and at what interest rate – can vary greatly, but it is the underwriter who makes the final decision. Prime loans are made to customers with good credit. For these loans, borrowers can typically find interest rates posted in the newspaper. For customers with less-than-perfect credit, however, interest rates are quoted based on the risk the lender associates with the loan. Sometimes larger down payments or secondary owner financing may be required to ensure the collateral can cover the loan amount.

Subprime Lenders

Legitimate subprime lenders offer loans to low-income and risky borrowers, and must charge higher interest rates to accommodate the risk. The higher-than-typical closing and processing fees allow them to take on that risk. Without these lenders, riskier borrowers could not tap into their home equity or even own a home. It is true that subprime lenders have been accused of predatory lending in cases where the allegations are unfounded. This makes it difficult for potential borrowers to discern who is legitimate and who is not.

Subprime lenders may be mainstream lenders also offering conventional loans to borrowers or mortgage brokers specializing in working with the "credit impaired." These lenders usually do not make government-backed loans and, therefore, often operate outside of federal regulations. This lack of regulation has now been criticized as one of the problems in predatory lending schemes.

Predatory Lending and Foreclosure Scams

Predatory lending involves loans that *take advantage of ill-informed consumers through excessively high fees, misrepresented loan terms, frequent refinancing that does not benefit the borrower, and other prohibited acts.* Predatory lending targets borrowers with little knowledge of, or defense against, these practices. New regulations require that complete and clear disclosures be made to borrowers. The law specifically prohibits certain practices, including:

- Packing a loan with credit insurance and other extra fees.

- Extending credit to people with little or no income and who have little chance of repaying the loan (the lender forecloses on the property and keeps the excess equity to cover costs).
- Refinancing the lender's own high-cost loan with another fee-rich loan in less than a year's time (unless a lender can show that the new loan benefits the borrower).

The motive for predatory lending is profit. The goal of a predatory lender is to take the property or strip its equity, or to profit from the exorbitant fees charged. Undoubtedly, the lender claims to help borrowers achieve the American dream of homeownership.

Predatory loans are approved without regard for the borrower's ability to repay. Interest rates are higher than the level of risk justifies. And, lenders may bundle unrelated products – such as a life insurance policy – into the mortgage loan to further their profit.

The Cost of Predatory Lending

Predatory lending costs the borrower in many ways. Although it is understandable a higher-risk borrower would pay higher interest rates than someone with good credit would, it still forces borrowers to pay more than they would for a typical transaction. Because of difficult-to-understand terms, the borrower may be paying:

- Exorbitant loan origination and settlement fees.
- Unreasonable servicing fees.
- Unknown charges detailed in poorly disclosed fine print.
- Unreasonable prepayment penalties.

There may be a dozen or more such fees under a variety of names alleging services that were done on the borrower's behalf. These are often referred to as **junk fees**. Fees greater than 4-5% of the loan amount are usually too much. Some scams have involved fees of 10-20% or more of the loan amount.

Common Predatory Lending Ploys

For many borrowers, but particularly those not well informed, loan documents may be difficult to understand. Legal jargon, small print, and page after page of confusing documentation may be presented for immediate signature. Often, the pressure is on finishing the closing with no time allowed to read the documents carefully. What is the solution for the borrower? Have an attorney review all documents before signing, or get a credit counselor or other expert to review them.

Exorbitant prepayment penalties may lock borrowers into abusive loans that cannot be easily refinanced when credit scores improve. Prepayment penalties may be thousands of dollars and be not be allowable as long as five years into the loan. The reason? To discourage payoff of the highly profitable loan. In reality, the majority of lenders do not charge prepayment penalties or, if they do, only in the first years of the loan.

Skimming equity from borrowers' homes involves lenders making various types of loans knowing the borrower will not be able to make the monthly payments, thus setting her up for foreclosure. The borrower loses everything – the home and the equity in it. Home improvement scams and loan flipping are also forms of equity skimming. In home improvement scams, lenders and contractors share in illegal profits, and loan flipping involves financing a property repeatedly.

Borrowers with extremely high debt in relationship to income are targets of *extreme lending*. Statistically, more than 8% of homeowners put 50% or more of their income toward their mortgage payment. With conventional lending guidelines restricting borrowers to no more than 28% of income toward the mortgage payment, this extreme lending puts borrowers at risk. If this borrower is laid off, loses a job, or experiences unanticipated expenses due to injury or illness, the risk for foreclosure is great because of the high percentage of income going solely to the mortgage loan.

Indicators of Predatory Lending

According to the Mortgage Bankers Association, there are 12 indicators of predatory lending:

1. Steering borrowers to high-rate programs
2. Falsely identifying loans as lines of credit or open mortgages
3. Structuring high-cost loans with unaffordable payments
4. Falsifying loan documents
5. Making loans to mentally incapacitated homeowners
6. Forging signatures on loan documents
7. Changing loan terms at closing
8. Requiring credit insurance
9. Increasing interest rates for late payments
10. Charging excessive prepayment penalties
11. Failing to report good payment history on a borrower's credit report
12. Failing to provide the accurate loan balance and payoff information

Anti-Predatory Lending Laws

Laws have been enacted at the federal, state, and local levels to stop the practice of predatory lending. The **Home Ownership and Equity Protection Act (HOEPA)**, which amended the Truth-in-Lending Act in 1994, *prohibits equity stripping, whereby a homeowner loses equity in a home due to excessive fees, and other abusive lending practices*. It is enforced by the Federal Trade Commission. HOEPA provides the following consumer protections on loans identified as HOEPA high-cost loans:

- **Balloon payments.** Balloon payments are prohibited on HOEPA loans with terms of less than five years. HOEPA-covered loans must also have regular payments to pay down the principal or at least pay interest.
- **Negative amortization**. Loans having any kind of interest or payment adjustment that could result in negative amortization are not permitted. The payment schedule must, at a minimum, pay off interest. Ideally, the payments will also reduce principal. This means that any interest rate changes and payment schedule caps must be coordinated to avoid negative amortization.
- **Pressure tactics**. Another consumer protection provision requires lenders to include text in the disclosure stating the consumer is not required to complete the credit transaction. This disclosure is intended to protect consumers from pressure tactics that imply being locked into the agreement, or that canceling is extremely complex or expensive.
- **Loan pricing.** Several consumer protections set limits on loan pricing. Loans subject to HOEPA must not include more than two advance payments from the loan proceeds. The borrower should get the maximum use of the funds and have a legitimate opportunity to use the loan proceeds.

- **Acceleration clauses.** Acceleration clauses are part of the predatory practices that HOEPA controls. The regulation prohibits increasing interest rates if the customer is in default.
- **Prepayment penalties.** HOEPA places limitations on prepayment penalties. The goal is to avoid unfair practices that lock consumers into loans that may not be, or are no longer, in their best interest. Prepayment penalties generally are prohibited unless limited to the first five years of the loan. Prepayment penalties also are prohibited if the consumer's total monthly debts, including the HOEPA loan, exceed 50% of the gross monthly income verified by the creditor.
- **Loan flipping.** Refinancing a HOEPA loan within a one-year period, which is called flipping, is strictly prohibited unless it is clearly in the borrower's best interest.
- **Demand clauses.** Any provision that would enable the creditor to call the loan before maturity is strictly prohibited. Only certain consumer behavior would permit the lender to call the loan, including fraud, material misrepresentation, default, or damage to the property.
- **Income verification.** HOEPA makes it illegal to make a loan to a customer without verifying that the customer can repay it. HOEPA rules require lenders to compile written income verification and create a written record of ratios, such as debt to income or cash flow analysis.

New York State implemented its own anti-predatory lending law in 2003. The law applies restrictions to high-cost loans that are first or junior lien mortgages. To qualify as a high-cost loan, the loan must be for:

- A principal amount less than the conforming loan size limit for a comparable dwelling as established by Fannie Mae, up to a limit of $300,000.
- Personal or family purposes (not a business loan).
- Real property of one to four units that will be used as the borrower's primary residence.

The law sets additional criteria for what constitutes a high-cost loan. It also bans numerous other practices, such as lending without regard for the borrower's ability to pay.

New York City PACE Program

In 2005, Mayor Michael Bloomberg and the Department of Housing Preservation and Development initiated the PACE program (Preserve Assets and Community Equity) in an effort to fight predatory lending in New York City.

The program includes educating homeowners in targeted segments of the community. Members work with other community-based and nonprofit organizations to assist homeowners who may have already fallen victim to a predatory lending scam. Legal and financial assistance is available through the program, as well as loans, training, and counseling.

Foreclosure Scams

Unfortunately, when foreclosure rates rise, so do the number of scams targeting those in default. Scam artists, also known as rescuers, locate victims in a variety of ways, including finding distressed homeowners through public foreclosure notices in newspapers or at government offices. There are also private companies that sell such lists. The National Consumer Law Center published the report, *Dreams Foreclosed: The Rampant Theft of American's Homes Through Equity-Stripping Foreclosure "Rescue" Scams,* and in it identified the three most common varieties of foreclosure scams:

- **Phantom help.** Ridiculously high fees are charged for minimal help, or the rescuer promises to represent the borrower further, and does not.
- **Bailout.** Homeowners surrender title to their home, believing they will be able to rent it back from the rescuer, and eventually buy it back.
- **Bait and switch.** Homeowners do not realize they are surrendering homeownership in exchange for being rescued.

All are typically heavily promoted, and claim to save borrowers from foreclosure. In reality, the schemes result in the homeowner losing the equity in the home or losing ownership completely.

Foreclosure Fraud Tactics

Why would anyone fall for these scams? Typical reasons why scamming tactics work include:

Trusting the wrong people. A borrower faced with losing a home is emotionally vulnerable. Criminals capitalize on this vulnerability by exploiting the homeowner's belief that the perpetrator is genuine. Even though the rescuer is most likely a complete stranger, the homeowner becomes convinced from appearance alone he can be trusted to help. This is fueled by the homeowner's desire to be saved, and the level of worry about losing a home.

Few or no details of the transaction. Many consumers do not understand the foreclosure process. When this is the case, they are easily exploitable. The rescuer implies the only way the homeowner can be saved is with her help. The homeowner probably has never been through the process before, is unfamiliar with how and when things happen, and what recourse is available.

Fraud and deception. Forgery, lies, fake documents, and blank documents are all common in mortgage fraud. The rescuer takes advantage of the homeowner, lying about the ability to save him, even having the homeowner sign blank or fake documents to give the impression action is being taken and help is on the way. This makes the owner feel secure, thinking all is being taken care of – while signing away the right to the property and/or its equity.

Lack of financial knowledge. Sometimes lack of financial knowledge is the reason consumers are taken in by criminals. They simply do not realize they are falling prey to high-interest loans or exorbitant, unnecessary fees. It is likely the homeowner facing foreclosure is not savvy with regard to financing options, reliable financing sources, or consumer groups that can help.

Desperation. Once the foreclosure process starts, time is of the essence. Fraudulent lenders take advantage of this pressure and the homeowner's panic. Rescuers are experts at creating pressure to act quickly, lying about when the owner will lose the home and have to move. A homeowner's panic is the fraudulent lender's best ally in these scenarios.

Affinity marketing. Here, rescuers market themselves to certain religious groups, senior citizens, and others to foster the belief the rescuer is "one of them." Foreclosure rescuers will even use a business name that makes the homeowner believe they are one of the group, whether religious, fraternal, or age-related.

Saturation marketing. Scam artists make repeated contact with desperate homeowners and saturate them with promises about how they can help. Through this type of marketing, homeowners are persuaded by repeated contact and promises of help.

Avoiding Foreclosure Scams

A report issued by the National Law Center contains sage advice on avoiding foreclosure scams. Real estate licensees should be prepared to advise customers and clients about the variety of scams and educate them on how to avoid becoming a victim. The following advice may be helpful to clients who could be vulnerable to foreclosure scams:

- **Avoid doing business with anyone calling himself a foreclosure consultant**. If you feel the person or business is credible, take time to do further research. Check for references and licensing, and talk to people in the lending business to see if anyone knows the person or business and the work they do.
- **Do not work with anyone who solicits business door to door**, or who advertises to those on pending foreclosure lists.
- **Avoid working with anyone who wants an upfront fee**. Never give anyone mortgage payments to pass along to the lender. Always make payments directly to the lender or loan servicer.
- **Avoid anyone claiming to pay closing costs on a new loan, or who wants to buy a home as is.**
- **Do not sign the title over to anyone to avoid foreclosure**. Do not agree to transfer the subject property to anyone who makes these promises.

SUMMARY

1. **Finance instruments** are *written documents establishing rights and duties of the parties involved in a transaction*. **Promissory notes** are *written promises to pay money*. They are negotiable instruments and are freely transferable so creditors can sell them for cash. Negotiable instruments are governed by the Uniform Commercial Code (UCC). The one promising to pay the money is called the **maker** of the note, usually the homebuyer. The one to whom payment is promised is called the **payee**, usually the lender. A **mortgage** is a type of *security instrument* where the *borrower* (called the **mortgagor**) pledges property to the *lender* (called the **mortgagee**) as collateral for the debt, a concept known as **hypothecation**.
2. The **primary mortgage market** *consists of lenders making mortgage loans directly to borrowers*. Primary lenders include commercial banks, S&Ls, and mortgage companies.
3. The **secondary mortgage market** *consists of private investors and government agencies that buy and sell home mortgages*. It was created to moderate local real estate cycles, providing lenders new money to lend again by selling their mortgages, giving local lenders loans from other areas, and standardizing loan criteria for better quality loans. The **Federal National Mortgage Association (Fannie Mae)** is *the largest investor in residential mortgages*. It is now privately owned and supervised by HUD. Fannie Mae buys loans then sells securities backed by its pool of mortgages. The **Government National Mortgage Association (Ginnie Mae)** was created to replace Fannie Mae when it became privately owned. *It is government owned and managed by HUD. Ginnie*

Mae guarantees payment of principal and interest on FHA/VA loans for its mortgage-backed securities. The **Federal Home Loan Mortgage Corporation (Freddie Mac)** *issues mortgage-backed securities.* Freddie Mac is privately owned but government supervised.

4. **Conventional loans** are *not insured or guaranteed by a government entity.* Traditional conventional loans are long term, fully amortized, and have a fixed rate. Conventional loans can be for 15, 30, or even 40 years. A 15-year loan retires sooner and saves interest, but requires higher payments and, sometimes, a higher down payment. An 80% conventional loan means the **loan-to-value ratio (LTV)** is 80% of the appraised value or sale price of property, whichever is *less*. For an 80% loan, the buyer must make a 20% down payment.

5. **Private mortgage insurance (PMI)** is private insurance for lenders against borrower default and is typically required for conventional loans with an LTV greater than 80%. PMI compensates lenders for lower borrower equity, and shares partial risk (of the upper part) with the lender. Federal law says that loans after July 1999 must drop PMI when LTV is 78% of original property value, or if the borrower requests it and the appraisal is 80% of the original property value.

6. **Buydowns** are *additional money (points) paid to the lender at the start of a loan to lower the interest rate and payments.* A borrower would use **discount points** to buy down the interest rate. One **point** equals *1% of the loan amount.* Points increase the lender's yield and are paid for many reasons.

7. The **Federal Housing Administration (FHA)** *insures mortgage loans.* FHA does not make loans. FHA-insured loans may have lower down payments and less stringent qualifying requirements than conventional loans. FHA loans require a mortgage insurance premium (MIP). The **Veterans Administration (VA)** *guarantees repayment of certain residential loans made to eligible veterans.* The VA does not make loans. VA-guaranteed loans may be obtained with no down payment. The VA charges borrowers a funding fee to use the VA home loan program, although some disabled veterans may be exempt. The **State of New York Mortgage Agency (SONYMA)** *is designed to make housing affordable for low- and moderate-income households.* SONYMA is a direct government lender that offers below-market interest rates and low or no down payment requirements.

8. **Assumption** means that *one party (the buyer) takes over primary liability for the loan of another party (the seller).*

9. An **amortized loan** *has payments applied to principal and interest;* **fully amortized loans** *have total payments over the life of the loan that pay all principal and interest due.* A **straight note** pays interest only over the life of the loan with a lump sum payment of principal at the end. A **partially amortized loan** pays some principal, but includes a balloon payment of the remaining principal at the end.

10. **Conforming loans** meet Fannie Mae/Freddie Mac standards and can be sold on the secondary market. **Nonconforming loans** (due to credit quality or loan size, for example) do not meet these standards and cannot be sold to Fannie Mae/Freddie Mac, but can be sold on the secondary market to other buyers. **Subprime loans** have more risk than generally allowed by the conventional market. Homebuyer assistance programs can consist of down payment assistance programs, subsidized mortgage interest rates, help with closing costs, or a combination.

11. **Predatory lending** involves loans that *take advantage of ill-informed consumers through excessively high fees, misrepresented loan terms, frequent refinancing that does not benefit the borrower, and other prohibited acts.* Predatory lending targets borrowers with little knowledge of, or defense against, these practices. Laws such as the **Home Ownership and Equity Protection Act (HOEPA)** establish disclosure requirements and prohibit equity stripping and other abusive practices. HOEPA also prohibits balloon payments on short-term loans (less than five years) and negative amortization and limits pre-payment penalties and loan flipping on high-cost loans.

12. The result of mortgage fraud is often foreclosure. High foreclosure rates pave the way for rescuers – scam artists who prey on homeowners in dire financial straits. Schemes include phantom help, bailout, and bait and switch. Vulnerable homeowners are victims of saturation marketing, trust scams, fraud and deception, desperation, affinity marketing, and lack of financial knowledge. Many steps can be taken by a consumer facing foreclosure, including contacting the lender and seeking legal advice.

14

Mortgage Basics

In This Session

Many different types of mortgages are available to home buyers and can be defined by repayment method, additional funds, or special purposes. Borrowers must meet specific requirements to qualify for loans, and they are afforded certain protections throughout the loan process.

You'll learn:

- Types of mortgages and their particular uses.
- Typical legal clauses found in mortgages.
- The process of judicial foreclosure and the equitable right of redemption.
- Lending regulations designed to protect borrowers.
- What information is required on a loan application.
- Qualifying standards for conventional, FHA-insured, and VA-guaranteed loans.
- The difference between a mortgage banker and a mortgage broker.
- What the responsibilities of a mortgage broker are.
- The state registration requirements for mortgage brokers.
- New York requirements for dual agency disclosure.

Key Terms

- Acceleration Clause
- Adjustable Rate Mortgage (ARM)
- Alienation / Due on Sale Clause
- Annual Percentage Rate (APR)
- Blanket Mortgage
- Bridge Mortgage
- Construction Mortgage
- Debt-to-Income Ratio
- Default
- Deficiency Judgment
- Equitable Right of Redemption
- Graduated Payment Mortgage
- Home Equity Line of Credit / Home Equity Loan
- Interest Rate Cap
- Judicial Foreclosure
- Mortgage Banker
- Mortgage Broker Dual Agency Disclosure Form
- Mortgage Loan Originator
- Open-End Mortgage
- Package Mortgage
- Payment-to-Income Ratio
- Pre-Approval / Pre-Qualification
- Prepayment Penalty Clause
- Purchase Money Mortgage
- Regulation Z
- Release Clause
- Reverse Equity Mortgage
- Sale-and-Leaseback Financing
- Straight Mortgage
- Subordination Agreement
- Truth-in-Lending Act (TILA)
- Wraparound Mortgage

Types of Mortgage Loans

Mortgage loans come in all shapes and sizes. Even buyers with very specific needs can find a loan to help them achieve their property-ownership goals. Within the broad categories of conventional or government-backed, there are numerous types of mortgages available. Mortgage types can be broken down by how they are repaid, what their purpose is (e.g., refinancing), what collateral is used as security for the loan, and the specific situations for which they may be used.

Mortgages Defined by Repayment Method

Mortgages that differ on how the borrower repays the principal and interest portions of the loan include:

- A **graduated payment mortgage (GPM)**, which *allows the borrower to make smaller payments early in the mortgage*. The lower payments in the early years are not sufficient to cover the interest due on the loan, resulting in a scheduled period of **negative amortization**. At a predetermined point in the loan term, the payments escalate on a scheduled basis until they eventually reach the point in which they are sufficient to fully amortize the loan over the remainder of its term.
- A **straight mortgage,** also called a **term** or **interest-only mortgage**, which enables *the borrower to pay the principal in a lump sum as a balloon payment at the end of a specified term, during which only interest was being paid*.

Mortgages for Additional Funds and Refinance

The following types of mortgages are used to obtain additional funds or refinance a loan to benefit from lower interest rates:

- An **open-end mortgage** *allows borrowers to request additional funds from the lender, usually up to a certain predetermined limit.* In most cases, lenders will not advance funds in excess of the original principal balance of the loan or that exceed a predetermined loan-to-value.
- Loans may be secured by a mortgage on a principal residence. A **home equity loan** is usually *a one-time loan for a specific amount of money* (and often for a specific purpose), whereas a **home equity line of credit** *is money available to the homeowner to use as expenses arise*. Both financing vehicles use the equity in the property by attaching a junior mortgage (unless the property is free and clear) to it.
- A **reverse equity mortgage** is when *a qualified homeowner with only a few or no outstanding liens mortgages his home and, in return, receives a monthly check from the lender*. The mortgage is repaid when the home is sold, the borrower dies, or the borrower does not occupy the home for 12 consecutive months. These mortgages are designed to help elderly homeowners achieve financial security or other financial goals by converting home equity into cash. To qualify, the homeowner must be age **62** or over and have little or no outstanding balance on his mortgage. The amount of money received depends on several variables including the value of the home, age of the homeowner, and the interest rate.

Mortgages for Special Purposes

Mortgages that are used for specific situations include:

- A **construction mortgage** is *a temporary loan used to finance the construction of buildings on land*. When construction is complete, the loan is replaced by permanent financing called an *end loan*.
- A **bridge mortgage**, or **swing loan**, *covers the gap between selling one property and buying another.* Bridge mortgages are usually short term and are used most commonly for construction financing.
- A **blanket mortgage** covers *more than one parcel or lot and is usually used to finance subdivision developments*. These loans usually have a *partial release clause* allowing the borrower to pay a certain amount of money to release one or more lots with the mortgage continuing to cover other lots. The released lots can then be sold to generate income for the developer.
- A **package mortgage** means *personal property, such as an appliance, is included in a property sale and financed together with one contract*. Typically, package mortgages are used for such properties as condos or vacation homes.
- A **no doc mortgage** or **stated doc mortgage** may be available *for those who cannot pass a credit review but have a large down payment, or who cannot prove income stability because they are self-employed.* The lender relies on stated income rather than documentation. These may also be called no ratio or nonconforming loans.
- **Sale-and-leaseback** financing is similar to a land contract and used mostly when long-term leases are involved, such as for commercial or retail properties. In a sale-and-leaseback transaction, *the purchaser, usually a real estate investor, buys the property and leases it back to the seller.* The new owner gains income tax benefits and a guaranteed rental stream; the seller is able to free up capital and still control the property under a lease with the new owner.
- A **wraparound mortgage** describes a financing arrangement in which an *existing loan on a property is combined with a new loan*. For example, a seller keeps the existing loan and continues to pay on it while giving the buyer another mortgage. The total debt (new loan plus existing loan) is treated as a single obligation by the buyer. Essentially, the buyer pays the seller who, in turn, pays the original lender. Wraparound mortgages can be very dangerous for home buyers because, if the seller stops making payments, the property goes into foreclosure. Lenders often include a due on sale clause in a mortgage that would prohibit a property owner from offering a wraparound mortgage.
- **Land contracts** are real estate *installment agreements where the buyer (vendee) makes payments to the seller (vendor) in exchange for the right to occupy and use the property, but no deed or title is transferred until all, or a specified portion of, payments have been made*. The seller holds title to land as security, not just a mortgage lien. Since actual title will be transferred by deed at a future date, the buyer's present interest in a land contract is called *equitable title*.
- A **purchase money mortgage** may generically refer to any mortgage loan used to buy real estate. The term is often used, however, to specifically describe *when a seller finances all or part of the sale price of a property for a buyer*.

Seller Financing

Seller financing is when *a seller extends credit to a buyer to finance the purchase of the property.* This can be instead of or in addition to the buyer obtaining a loan from a third party, such as an institutional lender. A seller may help with financing for several reasons:

- A buyer may be unable to afford the cash necessary for the required down payment for a conventional mortgage.
- A buyer may want to take advantage of the low interest rate on the seller's existing mortgage.
- A buyer is not able to qualify for a loan from a lender for various reasons.
- In tight money markets, sometimes the only way sellers can make a deal is to finance part of the purchase price themselves.

In any case, sellers can often enhance the salability of their properties by offering complete or partial financing.

Mortgage Interest Rates

The interest charged is determined by the **interest rate** that is negotiated between the lender and borrower. The annual interest on a loan can be calculated as shown:

Principal x Interest Rate = Annual Interest

The interest rate a lender charges is not only dependent on the risk factors associated with particular buyers, but also on national and local economic conditions. With any loan, the interest rate may be fixed or adjustable. Note that most states have **usury** laws, which can *limit the maximum interest rate that can be charged.*

Fixed Rate Mortgages

Fixed-rate loans have *interest rates that remain constant for the duration of the loan.* Of course, the biggest advantage for borrowers is that they do not need to worry about rates increasing and, if rates decrease, refinancing is always an option. An advantage from the lender's perspective is that there is a guaranteed rate of return.

Repayment Schedules

For many years, the traditional conventional home loan has been a **30-year fixed rate mortgage** loan. This gives home buyers a reasonable payment amount and the security of a long-term loan to pay off the debt or refinance when they choose. The length of any loan, however, is negotiable and lenders typically offer 20-, 25-, and 35-year payouts as well.

The **15-year, fixed-rate mortgage** is popular with some buyers, primarily because 15-year mortgages save them money. Over the life of the mortgage, the total interest paid on a 15-year mortgage is about one-third less than a 30-year mortgage at the same interest rate. Often, lenders give home buyers a better interest rate on 15-year mortgages, because the shorter term means less risk.

Of course, there are disadvantages to 15-year mortgages. As indicated in the following chart, payments are higher. Also, larger down payments are sometimes required on

15-year mortgages to keep payments manageable, and to qualify buyers. Both of these consume financial resources that could be invested other ways and earn higher returns than the interest rate paid on the mortgage. Plus, the borrower loses the tax deduction more quickly because the home is paid for sooner.

15-YEAR MORTGAGE TO 30-YEAR MORTGAGE COMPARISON OF INTEREST PAID				
LOAN AMOUNT	TERM	INTEREST RATE	MONTHLY PAYMENT	TOTAL INTEREST PAID
$50,000 MORTGAGE	15YR	7%	$449.41	$30,894.54
	30YR	7%	$332.65	$69,754.45
$100,000 MORTGAGE	15YR	7%	$898.83	$61,789.09
	30YR	7%	$665.30	$139,508.90
$150,000 MORTGAGE	15YR	7%	$1,348.24	$92,683.63
	30YR	7%	$997.95	$209,263.35

Note: Typically, rates for a 15-year mortgage are lower than rates for a 30-year mortgage. The same rate was used here for both to illustrate a direct comparison of total interest paid.

Adjustable Rate Mortgages (ARMs)

An **adjustable rate mortgage (ARM)** permits a lender to *adjust the interest rate periodically so that it reflects fluctuations in the cost of money as indicated by a chosen index.* ARMs are popular alternative financing tools because they can help borrowers qualify more easily for a home loan. Many lenders like ARMs because they pass the risk of fluctuating interest rates on to borrowers – if rates climb, payments go up; if they decline, payments go down.

Because ARMs shift the risk to the borrower, lenders normally charge a lower initial rate for an ARM than for a fixed rate loan, although many borrowers prefer the security of a fixed rate (provided the rate is not too high).

The borrower's interest rate is determined initially by the cost of money at the time the loan is made. To determine a current ARM interest rate, the lender designates an **index**, which is *a statistical report that is a generally reliable indicator of the approximate cost of money,* and adds to that its **margin**, which is *the lender's profit*.

Current Index Value + Margin = Interest Rate

So, future rate adjustments for ARM loans are based on fluctuations in the index.

Elements of ARM Loans

In addition to margin and index, there are several elements common to an adjustable rate mortgage.

Rate adjustment period. The rate adjustment period is the interval at which a borrower's interest rate changes. It can range from a few months to many years.

The most common rate adjustment periods are every six months or one year. After checking movement in the selected index, lenders notify borrowers, in writing, of any change in the rate.

Mortgage adjustment period. The mortgage payment adjustment period is the interval at which a borrower's mortgage payment changes. Here, the borrower's actual principal and interest payments change. Like the rate adjustment period, the payment adjustment interval can range from a period of months up to many years, and it is possible for mortgage payment adjustments not to coincide with interest rate adjustments.

Interest rate cap. An **interest rate cap** *limits the number of percentage points an interest rate can be increased during the term of a loan*, helping to eliminate large and frequent mortgage payment increases. This is one way lenders limit the magnitude of payment changes that occur with interest rate adjustments.

Ceiling. The **ceiling** on an adjustable rate mortgage is the *highest interest rate that may be charged over the term of the loan.*

Conversion option. An ARM loan could include a conversion option that allows the borrower to convert to fixed-rate. These options typically have conditions such as higher interest rates.

Typical Mortgage Clauses

Various clauses are used in mortgages to give certain rights to the lender or borrower.

Acceleration Clause	*Gives the lender the right to declare the entire loan balance due immediately because of borrower default or for violation of other contract provisions.* Most promissory notes, mortgages, trust deeds, and land contracts contain an acceleration clause allowing the lender to accelerate the debt upon default as defined in the contract.
Alienation Clause or Due on Sale Clause	*Gives the lender certain stated rights when there is a transfer of ownership.* This is designed to limit the debtor's right to transfer the property without permission of the creditor. Upon sale, or even a transfer of significant interest in the property, lenders often have the right to accelerate the debt, change the interest rate, or charge a hefty assumption fee. FHA and VA loans *cannot* include an alienation clause.
Prepayment Penalty	*Gives lenders the right to charge borrowers a penalty for paying off the loan early* or making substantial principal reductions, essentially depriving the lender of further interest income. Standard Fannie Mae and Freddie Mac notes and mortgages do not have prepayment penalties, and they are prohibited in FHA and VA loans. Subprime loans usually contain these clauses.
Subordination Agreement	*Gives a mortgage recorded at a later date priority over an earlier recorded mortgage.* Normally with mortgages, trust deeds, and other real estate contracts, the first to get recorded has lien priority. In some situations, however, the parties may desire that a later recorded instrument have priority over an earlier one. Subordination agreements are made between lienholders.

Foreclosure

When a borrower is in **default** on a loan, or *fails to make payments*, the lender may accelerate the due date of the debt to the present and give the debtor notice of default demanding that the debtor pay off the entire outstanding balance at once. With a mortgage as security, the collateral is real estate, *so the procedure in the event of default is* **judicial foreclosure**, *which requires a court-ordered sheriff's sale of the property to repay the debt*. The lender initiates a foreclosure action in the county where the property is located. If the court determines the lender is rightfully owed the money, a judge will issue an order of execution directing an officer of the court to seize and sell the property.

In New York, the officer of the court, usually the county sheriff, notifies the public of the place and date of the sale. On the sale date, a public auction is held. Once the property is sold to the highest bidder at or in excess of the minimum bid, the proceeds are used to pay any back property taxes, then the cost of the foreclosure (sheriff, appraisers, transfer tax, auctioneer, etc.), and then the lienholders are paid in priority order (first lien, second lien, etc.). Any surplus funds go to the debtor.

After the sale, a *confirmation of sale* is filed to finalize the transaction. In New York, after the confirmation of sale, the transfer of the property is final. The debtor no longer has the right to redeem the property by paying what is due.

Equitable Right of Redemption

A debtor can redeem (save) her property from the time a *notice of a pending foreclosure*, called a **lis pendens**, is filed until the confirmation of the foreclosure sale. This is done by paying the court what is due, which may include court costs and attorneys' fees. *This right, used in New York, to save or redeem the property prior to the confirmation of sale* is called the **equitable right of redemption.** Some other states use the statutory right of redemption, which allows debtors to redeem themselves after the final sale. Once the redemption is made, the court will set aside the sale, pay the parties, and the debtor gains title to the property again.

One other option debtors have to avoid foreclosure is to make a voluntary conveyance, also called **deed in lieu of foreclosure**. With this action, *debtors still lose the property, but by returning it voluntarily before final court action, they avoid having a foreclosure on their credit record*. After confirmation of sale, however, it is too late.

Deficiency Judgment

If the property does not bring enough money at the sale to pay off the mortgage, the creditor may be able to obtain a **deficiency judgment**, *a court order stating that the debtor owes money to the creditor when the collateral property does not bring enough at a foreclosure sale to cover the entire loan amount, accrued interest, and other costs*. The deficiency judgment is a personal judgment against the debtor that creates a general and involuntary lien against all real and personal property.

Mortgage Lien Priority

A mortgage is a lien against a borrower's property. Some liens have priority, or a higher status, than others. Terms used to indicate lien position include:

- **First mortgage** (senior mortgage). A security instrument with a first lien position. A first mortgage always has priority over all other mortgages, meaning the first mortgage holder is paid first in the event of a foreclosure sale. The only lien that pre-empts a first mortgage is a tax lien.

- **Second mortgage** (junior mortgage). This is also a mortgage instrument that is in a second lien position. Although property is still used as security, the second mortgage lender is in a riskier position because a first mortgage is paid first, out of foreclosure proceedings. If nothing is left, the second mortgage holder gets nothing.

Lien priority is especially important in the event of foreclosure because the proceeds from a foreclosure sale pay the liens in the order they were applied to the property. The only exception is a *tax lien*, which is *always paid first*. The first lien is paid in its entirety; if money remains, the second lien is paid, then the third, and so on, until the money is gone.

Financial Disclosure Requirements

Federal regulations impose disclosure requirements on real estate financial transactions. Lenders who offer credit, including for real estate, must make certain disclosures to consumers before the transaction is finalized.

One of the most pertinent laws regarding lending is the federal Consumer Credit Protection Act, more commonly known as the **Truth-in-Lending Act (TILA)**. TILA was *enacted to prevent abuses in consumer credit cost disclosures, and requires lenders to disclose consumer credit costs in a uniform manner to promote informed use of consumer credit.* The disclosures are required so consumers know exactly what they are paying for, enabling them to compare credit costs and shop around for the best terms.

The specific provisions of the TILA are implemented by **Regulation Z**, which *controls the disclosure of interest rates and other finance charges imposed by lenders.* Disclosures are required in two general areas:

- When lenders offer credit or funds to borrowers
- When credit terms are advertised to potential customers

The provisions of the Truth-in-Lending Act apply to lenders who, in the ordinary course of business, offer or extend credit to consumers primarily for personal residential or agricultural purposes, but not commercial or business use. The provisions include any credit offered subject to finance charges or payable by written agreement in more than four installments.

Annual Percentage Rate Disclosure

For residential mortgages, the most important required disclosure is the **annual percentage rate (APR)**, *the actual interest rate charged, including loan fees and points.* The APR is often higher than the contract interest rate or note rate. For example, a mortgage loan with an 11% interest rate may have an APR of 11.5%, representing the total cost of the loan, including finance charges spread over the life of the loan.

The APR and other required disclosures are made in the form of a standardized **Loan Estimate** that details the actual cost of borrowing money at the time of the loan application or within three business days. This initial form includes:

- Name of the lender/creditor.
- Estimated closing costs, the cash necessary to close the purchase and the Total Interest Percent.
- Finance charge expressed as an annual percentage rate.
- Number, amount, and payment due dates.

- New payment, late payment, and prepayment provisions.
- Description and identification of the security (mortgaged property or other collateral).
- Consideration as to whether the loan may be assumed by a subsequent buyer.
- A statement indicating that the borrower is not required to complete the loan simply because he has been given the disclosure.
- Servicing disclosures and refinance conditions.

Also, note that revisions in the Truth-in-Lending Act in 2009 require a waiting period of seven business days after a borrower is presented with the Loan Estimate and the Truth-in-Lending statement before a loan can close.

Advertising Regulations

Reg Z also regulates the advertising of consumer loans. Prior to the passage of the Truth-in-Lending Act, an advertiser might have disclosed only the most attractive credit terms, distorting the true cost of financing. For example, an ad could have included the low monthly payments (e.g., $75 a month) without indicating the large down payment necessary to qualify for that payment level.

If an advertisement contains any of the terms specified in the Act, it must also include the required disclosures. **Triggering terms** are *words or phrases that describe a loan, including the down payment, terms, and monthly payment.* If an ad uses a trigger phrase, disclosures are needed to tell everything about the loan; if an ad does not use a triggering term, no disclosures are needed.

Triggering Terms (require disclosure)	**Non-Triggering Terms** (do not require disclosure)
"20% down"	"No down payment"
"Pay only $700 per month"	"We'll work with you"
"Only 360 monthly payments"	"Easy monthly payments"
"30-year financing available"	"FHA financing available"
"1% finance charge"	"100% VA financing available"

If an ad contains any triggering terms, all of these disclosures must be included:

- Amount or percentage of down payment,
- Terms of repayment, and
- Annual percentage rate (using that term spelled out in full) as well as indicators if the APR may increase (e.g., for ARMs).

Right of Rescission

Rescind means to *take back or withdraw an offer or contract*, and under Regulation Z, consumers have the right to rescind credit transactions involving the establishment of a security interest (usually a mortgage) in their existing primary residence. This includes, for example, home equity loans, refinancing, or a new mortgage on an existing residence. The right to rescind extends until midnight of the third business day after the transaction closes.

Consumers may *not* rescind a residential mortgage transaction used to finance the purchase or construction a principal residence. This protects builders who may have performed services based on the buyer's commitment, and sellers who may have entered into another contract or purchased a home contingent on the buyers purchasing their present home.

Lenders must inform consumers of their right to rescind in a separate document from the sale or credit document. If a borrower rescinds, she is entitled to a refund of all fees paid in conjunction with the loan.

The Closing Disclosure and Required Waiting Period

An additional consumer protection is mandated by the Truth In Lending Act or Regulation Z in the form of the **Closing Disclosure**. This 5 page document provides the borrower with the final charges for the acquisition of the subject property. This form must be delivered to the borrower a minimum of three (3) business days prior to closing. The closing costs that are finalized on the **Closing Disclosure** are compared with the charges disclosed initially on the **Loan Estimate**. The charges must be in compliance with the tolerance limits that are set by the TRID guidelines. The final Annual Percentage Rate is also disclosed on the Closing Disclosure and if the prescribed tolerance guidelines are exceeded, a corrected Closing Disclosure must be delivered to the borrower and a new rescission period must be provided to the borrower.

Applying for a Mortgage Loan

In the past, buyers completed a mortgage loan application only when they were ready to buy a particular home. Loan applications required detailed information so lenders could make informed decisions about whether to grant credit. Now there is a growing trend toward pre-approving buyers for loans because, among other things, pre-approval can be a useful negotiating tool. However, pre-approval is not the same as pre-qualifying buyers:

- **Pre-qualification** is *the process of determining the size of loan for which a potential home buyer might be eligible*. An agent or a lender can pre-qualify a buyer; however, it does *not* guarantee approval. Pre-qualification is not binding on the lender, which is why the distinction is very important. The lender is only indicating it looks likely the buyer will be approved.
- **Pre-approval** is the *process by which a lender determines if, and for what amount, potential borrowers can be financed.* For pre-approval, a buyer goes through many of the steps in the loan process. With pre-approval, a lender is stating the prospective buyer's situation has been verified, and providing all circumstances stay the same, they will loan a certain amount of money. Sellers often give more weight to an offer from a buyer who has been pre-approved for a loan than to other potential buyers.

The Loan Application

The *Uniform Residential Loan Application*, also called the *1003*, is the form most lenders require potential borrowers to complete. The form includes all the pertinent information about the borrower and subject property, for example:

- Type of mortgage and the terms
- Property information and purpose of the loan
- Borrower's personal, employment, and financial information

Evaluating the Borrower

When evaluating a borrower, a lender usually considers these items:

- **Capacity.** Does the borrower have the financial ability to pay the mortgage along with other debts and obligations?
- **Collateral.** Is the borrower's down payment and property value sufficient for the lender to recoup its money, if foreclosure is necessary?
- **Credit.** Does the borrower's past payment history show a willingness and ability to repay obligations?
- **Character.** Does the borrower have stability in a job and in responsibilities such that, even with setbacks, financial obligations will be honored?
- **Conditions.** Do other factors, such as economic health of the borrower's job field and general economic conditions, look favorable?

Income

Stable monthly income is *the monthly income amount that can reasonably be expected to continue in the future.* This is generally meant to include the borrowers' gross base income from primary jobs, plus earnings from acceptable secondary sources.

Secondary sources of income include bonuses, commissions, secondary job, or investment income. Although lenders may include these sources, a thorough analysis will be conducted. Before deciding if there is sufficient income, the underwriter must decide what portion of the borrower's total verified earnings is acceptable as a part of stable monthly income. This is accomplished by studying the *quality* (dependability) and the *durability* (probability of continuance) of the income source(s). Note that the federal Equal Credit Opportunity Act prohibits discrimination against borrowers whose source of income is from public assistance.

Basic Mortgage Qualifying Standards

Before making real estate loans, lenders evaluate the borrower's income and debt load to determine how much mortgage debt they can comfortably borrow. Qualifying standards can vary from lender to lender, but with lenders' increased dependence on selling their loans to the national secondary mortgage markets, the majority of lenders have incorporated Fannie Mae and Freddie Mac standards into their own conventional loan underwriting criteria. However, FHA and VA guidelines are more liberal than Fannie Mae and Freddie Mac ratios and standards. A borrower considered marginal by Fannie Mae and Freddie Mac might qualify more easily for an FHA or VA loan.

When evaluating a borrower's income, the important ratios to consider are the payment-to-income ratio and debt-to-income ratio.

Payment-to-Income Ratio

The **payment-to-income ratio**, also called the *housing expense ratio*, examines whether a borrower's stable monthly income is considered adequate to cover the proposed monthly mortgage payment of principal, interest, taxes, and insurance (PITI).

For a conventional Fannie Mae mortgage loan, the PITI payment cannot exceed **28%** of stable monthly income. For an FHA-insured loan, the PITI payment typically cannot exceed **31%** of stable monthly income. For example, mortgage loan applicant Ralph has $2,900 in stable gross monthly income. The maximum monthly PITI mortgage payment allowed for a conventional loan would be 28% of that:

$2,900 x 0.28 = $812 maximum PITI monthly payment allowance

> **VA-Guaranteed Loans**
>
> A loan that is guaranteed by the Veteran's Administration does not apply a payment-to-income ratio as a qualifying component, but does look at **residual income**, which is *the amount of income a borrower has left after subtracting taxes, housing, and recurring debt obligations*. The VA has regional guidelines to estimate the average cost of utilities based on the size of the house. Those costs are included as part of the debt obligations.
>
> To be eligible for a VA-guaranteed loan, the borrower must have completed a minimum number of days of active duty (this number differs according to whether served during wartime or peacetime) and must not have been dishonorably discharged. Reservists may also be eligible. A VA-issued certificate of eligibility is required by a lender to establish the veteran's status.

Debt-to-Income Ratio

A second but equally important concern when determining a buyer's qualification for a mortgage loan is the ratio of the borrower's recurring debt to the total PITI payment, known as the **debt-to-income ratio** or the *total debt service ratio*. Recurring debt includes all debt owed with ten or more payments left, such as car payments, credit card debt, other loans, and child support and alimony.

For a conventional Fannie Mae mortgage loan, the total recurring debt cannot exceed 36% of stable monthly income. For an FHA-insured loan, the total recurring debt cannot exceed 43% of stable monthly income. For a VA-guaranteed loan, the total debt including utilities cannot exceed 41% of stable monthly income. After determining the total debt allowed, the known debts must be subtracted to find the maximum monthly mortgage payment. For example, Ralph has $2,900 in stable monthly income and a monthly auto loan payment of $320. For a conventional loan, the maximum monthly mortgage and recurring debt allowance would be:

$2,900 x 0.36 = $1,044, Total Debt Allowed for Ralph

$1,044 – $320 = $724 Maximum Monthly PITI Payment Allowance

A buyer needs to qualify under **both** ratios. Therefore, the **smaller of the two** would be the maximum allowable monthly PITI payment.

Qualifying Income Expense Ratios

	Payment-to-Income Ratio	Debt-to-Income Ratio
Fannie Mae/ Freddie Mac Conventional Loans	PITI Not to exceed **28%** of income	Housing + Debt (10 or more payments) Not to exceed **36%** of income
FHA-Insured Loans	PITI Not to exceed **31%** of income	Housing + Debt (10 or more payments) Not to exceed **43%** of income
VA-Guaranteed Loans	Not considered; instead, looks at residual income	Housing + ALL Debt and Utilities Not to exceed **41%** of income

Note that the qualifying standards discussed here could change. Always check for the most current information.

Credit History

Credit history is a *record of debt repayment, detailing how a person paid credit accounts in the past*. It is a guide to whether she is likely to pay them on time and as agreed in the future. Borrowers must inform a lender of all debts – even things that may not show up on a credit report.

As a part of the loan evaluation, the underwriter analyzes the borrower's (and co-borrower's) credit history by obtaining a credit report from a local and/or national credit rating bureau. **Credit scoring** involves *assigning specific numerical values to different aspects of the borrower*, such as number of open accounts and their credit limit, outstanding debt, late payments, liens, etc. Credit scores are an indication of the strength or weakness of particular borrower: The higher the credit score, the better credit risk a borrower is. Different lenders determine the cutoff scores they will use in qualifying borrowers, and could decline a loan application or charge a higher interest rate for applicants with low credit scores.

Underwriting and Approving the Loan Application

Processing the loan application involves reviewing the information submitted and verifying items as necessary. When the lender receives the credit report, verification forms, and appraisal, a loan package is put together and given to an **underwriter**, *who evaluates a loan application to determine its risk level for a lender or investor.* The primary concern throughout the underwriting process is determining the *degree of risk* a loan represents. The underwriter attempts to answer two fundamental questions:

- Does the borrower's overall financial situation, which is comprised of income, credit history, and net worth, indicate she can reasonably be expected to make the proposed monthly loan payment in a timely manner?
- Is there sufficient value in the property pledged as collateral to assure recovery of the loan amount in the event of default?

Fannie Mae and Freddie Mac refer to loans that meet these two requirements as "investment quality loans."

The underwriting process can be automated or performed by an individual who works for the lender. Both processes apply various qualifying standards. With automated underwriting, computer software makes a recommendation to accept a loan, or refers it to a human underwriter for review. Loan underwriters carefully examine a loan package and decide to approve, reject, or approve the loan with conditions (such as the buyer must bring proof that his previous home was sold and the mortgage is no longer outstanding). The underwriter is usually the final decision maker on loan approval.

Mortgage Bankers and Loan Originators

Key players on the financial side of a real estate transaction are mortgage bankers and mortgage loan originators.

Mortgage Bankers

Mortgage bankers – also referred to as mortgage companies:

- Originate mortgage loans.
- Are the actual lenders of the mortgage monies in the primary market.

- Typically charge the borrower a loan origination fee and annual interest for the use of the money during the term of the loan.
- Make mortgage loans with the intention of selling them to investors in the secondary market.
- Typically continue to service loans for investors who have purchased the loans in the secondary market and charge these investors servicing fees.

The Mortgage Banker Role

Mortgage bankers can work for any of the primary or secondary market institutions. Typically, though, mortgage bankers are involved in the primary market, where lenders make mortgage loans directly to borrowers. In addition to the typical duties and paperwork performed in most office jobs, there are specific functions for mortgage bankers.

Origination is the process of *making or initiating a new loan*. Almost all primary mortgage market entities originate loans. Origination involves taking a loan application, pulling a credit report, ordering an appraisal, and assembling all other forms and documents required by the person or company underwriting the loan.

Underwriting is the process of *evaluating and deciding whether to make a new loan.* This is done by the funding source – usually a primary lender, and almost never by a mortgage broker. Underwriting involves evaluating credit scores, credit history, appraisals, job history, assets, and other measures of strength or weakness in the borrower and collateral. There are specific skills and expertise required of underwriters that go beyond simply evaluating numbers produced by a computer. An employer usually provides training in this area, however, with the creation of automated underwriting, underwriters' roles have changed. In many cases the underwriter does not have the ability to override decisions if the automation gives a negative or positive response. An underwriter's main role is to verify the data entered into the system and verify information provided by the mortgage originator.

Servicing is the *continued maintenance of a loan* after it has been made. This can be done by any entity, with some companies set up solely to perform this function. Servicing involves maintaining direct contact with borrowers, sending mortgage statements, collecting payments, and pursuing late payments. Often primary lenders sell mortgages to the secondary market, but still service them for a fee.

Comprehensive Mortgage Companies

Many mortgage bankers offer a combination of all these functions to their clients. For one loan, they may:

- Originate the loan (find the borrower),
- Underwrite the loan (fund the borrower), and
- Service the loan.

If a lender is not able to provide a loan product that meets the needs of a particular borrower, the lender may act simply as a broker and refer the borrower to another company as a courtesy to its customers, or for a referral fee. Whether a loan is sold by a particular mortgage company or by a lender, many still offer loan servicing because of the lucrative fees generated.

New York Mortgage Banker License

The State of New York requires an individual or entity who *originates at least five mortgage loans in any one year* to be licensed by the **New York State Banking Department.** As with real estate, licenses are mandated primarily in order to protect the citizens of the state. The regulations provide uniformity throughout the residential mortgage lending process, including the application, solicitation, and making and servicing of mortgage loans. The following are among the requirements for a New York mortgage banker license applicant, whether an individual or entity:

- At least **$250,000 in adjusted net worth**, which shall be maintained at all times
- Written documentation of a **line of credit**, provided by a banking institution or an insurance company outside the applicant's corporate structure, in an amount of **not less than $1 million**
- A corporate **surety bond** in a principal amount of **not less than $50,000** or more than $500,000 based on its volume of business
- **Five years of verifiable experience** in the making of mortgage loans on either a retail or wholesale level

In addition to the fees, there are additional application requirements, such as submitting fingerprints, a background check, etc.

Mortgage Loan Originators

Mortgage loan originators do *not* lend monies to borrowers. Rather, a mortgage loan originator *earns a fee to act as an* ***intermediary*** *to bring together borrowers and the lenders who originate the actual loans*. A mortgage loan originator may:

- Solicit,
- Process,
- Place, and/or
- Negotiate residential loans.

A mortgage loan originator may be especially useful in helping borrowers obtain **nonconforming loans**, those that do not follow standards set by Fannie Mae and Freddie Mac. These loans may exceed the maximum loan amount or may not meet the minimum qualifying standards.

Role of the Mortgage Loan Originator

A mortgage loan originator serves as a trusted consultant, helping the borrower through the often confusing process of obtaining a residential mortgage loan. It's the mortgage loan originator's job to help the borrower get the best loan rates and terms available. Mortgage brokers generally assist a buyer with:

- **Pre-qualifying**, which is the process of *pre-determining how much of a loan a potential homebuyer might be eligible to borrow*. An agent or a MLO can pre-qualify a buyer; however, it does not guarantee approval nor is it binding on any lender.
- Helping the borrower gather the necessary documentation to assist the lender with **pre-approval**, the process by which *a lender determines if, and for what amount, potential borrowers can be financed.* The lender gives the buyer the pre-approval information in writing, which is sometimes referred to as a certificate or letter of pre-approval.
- Submitting loan applications to lenders.
- Explaining the terms of various loan options, such as interest rates, discount points, origination fees, etc.
- Negotiating a **rate lock**, which is when *the agreed-upon interest rate and points are frozen until the loan closes*.
- Securing a **mortgage commitment** from a lender, which is *a written letter that confirms the lender's willingness to loan the money*.
- Scheduling the closing of a loan.

New York Lender Disclosure

Disclosure of interest is a familiar concept in the real estate business. A licensee must disclose any interest he may have in a property transaction. The same rules apply to a mortgage broker. Any **regular business relationship** that the mortgage broker maintains with any lender to which he presents loan applications must also be disclosed at the first substantive contact between the mortgage broker and the buyer/borrower.

The exception to this requirement is if the mortgage broker submits the application to more than three lenders.

Mortgage Loan Originator Licensing

As defined by New York Banking Law, a **mortgage loan originator** is an individual—a natural person, *not* an organization or entity—who takes a mortgage loan application or offers or negotiates terms of a mortgage loan for, or in the expectation of, compensation or gain. This definition does *not* include:

- An individual engaged solely as a loan processor or underwriter.
- An individual who performs only real estate brokerage activities and is licensed by applicable New York law, unless that individual is compensated by a lender, a mortgage broker, or other mortgage loan originator.
- A person or entity solely involved in extensions of credit relating to timeshare plans.

A mortgage loan originator must be either employed by or an independent contractor to a licensed or registered originating entity, such as a mortgage brokerage company. An MLO may not be simultaneously employed or affiliated with more than one originating entity.

A **loan processor** or **underwriter** who is an independent contractor of an originating entity may *not* engage in residential mortgage loan origination activities without obtaining and maintaining an MLO license as well as a valid unique identifier issued by the NMLS.

Exemptions

The following are among those who are exempt from requiring a mortgage loan originator license:

- Registered mortgage loan originators. A registered mortgage loan originator is an individual who performs the functions of an MLO, is employed by a depository institution, and who is registered with the NMLS.
- Immediate family loans. Any individual who offers or negotiates the terms of a residential mortgage loan with or on behalf of an immediate family member of the individual. Immediate family members include a spouse, child, sibling, parent, grandparent, or grandchild. This includes stepparents, stepchildren, stepsiblings, and adoptive relationships.
- Loans on an individual's residence. Any individual who offers or negotiates terms of a residential mortgage loan secured by a dwelling or residential real property that served as the individual's own residence.
- Certain attorneys and manufactured home sellers.

Getting an MLO License

No individual can engage in the business of originating a mortgage loan for a dwelling or residential real property in New York without obtaining and maintaining a mortgage loan originator license, unless specifically exempt by New York Banking Law. A mortgage loan originator must demonstrate the financial responsibility, character, and fitness necessary to command the confidence of the community and to warrant a determination that he or she will operate honestly, fairly, and efficiently.

MLO applicants are required to meet the prelicensing education and testing requirements defined by the federal Secure and Fair Enforcement Mortgage Licensing (SAFE) Act and by the State of New York prior to applying for an MLO license.

Prelicensing Education

Anyone applying for a mortgage loan originator is required to complete at least **20 hours** of education with an NMLS-approved program that includes the following:

- Three hours of federal law and regulations
- Three hours of ethics, including instruction on fraud, consumer protection, and fair lending issues
- Two hours of training related to lending standards for the nontraditional mortgage loan marketplace, which is defined by the SAFE Act and in Article 12-E of New York Banking Law as anything *other than* a fixed rate, 30-year mortgage
- Three hours of applicable New York law and regulations
- Nine hours of elective courses related to the mortgage industry

Mortgage loan originator applicants must pass a written test developed by the Nationwide Mortgage Licensing System & Registry (NMLS) and administered by a test provider approved by the NMLS based upon reasonable standards. The portion of the test regarding New York-specific law must be administered by a test provider approved by the Department.

Surety Bonds

Each mortgage loan originator must be covered by a surety bond as defined in Article 12-E of the Banking Law. The surety bond of an originating entity may be used to satisfy the MLO's surety bond requirement, provided that such surety bond contains coverage for each mortgage loan originator not otherwise covered by a qualifying surety bond. For the purpose of determining the appropriate surety bond, it is the volume of loans originated by the MLO in the **prior year**.

License Renewal

MLO licenses expire on **December 31** each year and must be renewed annually. Each licensed MLO shall complete and provide evidence to the Superintendent through the NMLS or otherwise as directed by the Superintendent of the completion of at least ***11 hours*** of annual continuing education (CE) by the annual expiration date of the MLO's license.

New York Dual Agency

When a real estate licensee represents both the buyer and the seller as clients, **dual agency** exists and must be disclosed. When a real estate licensee is also registered as a mortgage broker, the potential for dual agency also exists.

For example, if a buyer asks Lisa, the listing agent, to recommend a mortgage broker to assist him in obtaining financing and Lisa is also a mortgage broker, she must explain the concept of dual agency to both the buyer and seller and **obtain consent from both parties** before taking on that role.

Dual Agency Disclosure

If a mortgage broker dual agency situation arises, Article 12-D of the New York Banking Law requires the mortgage loan originator/real estate agent to present the following disclosure, which must be signed by both parties.

The disclosure may be in writing or via electronic transmission, and the required signatures may be handwritten or digital to the extent such signatures are recognized as binding under New York State law.

As with other documentation of a transaction, a hard or electronic copy of the disclosure form and signed acknowledgment must be maintained by the mortgage loan originator for at least **three years.**

THE FOLLOWING DISCLOSURE AND ACKNOWLEDGMENT APPLY TO THOSE TRANSACTIONS IN WHICH THE REAL ESTATE BROKER REPRESENTING THE SELLER AND THE MORTGAGE BROKER REPRESENTING THE BUYER/BORROWER ARE THE SAME PERSON OR ENTITY.

DISCLOSURE REGARDING DUAL AGENCY ROLE IN RESIDENTIAL REAL ESTATE TRANSACTIONS

I must explain what dual agency means to you.

DUAL AGENCY

1. As a real estate licensee in the pending transaction (Name of Real Estate Broker) represents the seller in the sale of the residential real property and as such the primary responsibility is to the seller.
2. As a mortgage broker (Name of Mortgage Broker) represents the buyer/borrower in the acquisition of the mortgage loan and as such the primary responsibility is to the buyer/borrower.

YOUR RIGHTS UNDER DUAL AGENCY

1. I may represent you only with the knowledge and informed consent of each of you.
2. By consenting to Dual Agency you are giving up your right to undivided loyalty. You should carefully consider the possible consequences of a Dual Agency relationship before agreeing to such representation.
3. Since I am not a legal expert or an attorney you may wish to consult one before signing this form.
4. You the buyer may retain the services of a real estate broker or mortgage broker who will represent only you in the transaction.
5. You the seller may, subject to any existing contract of sale and/or any real estate agreement which you have already signed, retain the services of a real estate broker who will represent only you in the transaction.

☐ I place mortgage loan applications with three or fewer mortgage lenders.

☐ I place mortgage loan applications with more than three mortgage lenders.

ACKNOWLEDGMENT OF PROSPECTIVE BUYER AND SELLER TO DUAL AGENCY

1. I have received and read this disclosure notice.
2. I understand that as a real estate/mortgage broker you may be representing the interests of the seller in the sale of the residential real property and the buyer in the acquisition of the mortgage loan and that you will be unable to offer the full range of fiduciary duties to each of us.
3. I understand that subject to the terms of any existing contract of sale and/or any real estate agreement which I may have already signed I the seller may engage my own broker as a real estate broker who will not act as a mortgage broker for any potential buyer/borrower in this transaction; or that I as a buyer/borrower may engage my own broker as a mortgage broker and/or my own broker as a real estate broker who will not act as a real estate broker for the seller in this transaction.

☐ I understand that you as a mortgage broker will ordinarily place mortgage loan applications with three or fewer mortgage lenders.

☐ I understand that you as a mortgage broker will ordinarily place mortgage loan applications with more than three mortgage lenders.

DATED: ____________________ DATED: ____________________

SELLER: ____________________ BUYER: ____________________

SUMMARY

1. A **mortgage** *creates a voluntary lien against property* as security for debt. Common examples are: **Bridge mortgage**, a temporary mortgage between two others, repaid with a later mortgage; **package mortgage**, includes personal property; **blanket mortgage,** for more than one land parcel; **construction mortgage**, a temporary loan to finance the construction of buildings.
2. **Adjustable rate mortgages (ARMs)** let lenders *adjust interest rates* at periodic intervals throughout the loan term. The lender picks an **index** (*statistical report reflecting the cost of money*), adds a **margin** (*profit margin*), and this is the **rate** paid on the loan. **Negative amortization** can occur if the loan balance increases if payments are not sufficient to cover accrued interest. With a **conversion option**, the borrower can convert to a fixed-rate mortgage.
3. Mortgage clauses give certain rights to the lender or borrower. An **acceleration clause** lets the lender call the loan balance due if in default. A **prepayment penalty clause** lets lenders charge a penalty for paying off a loan early. An **alienation clause** (also called due-on-sale clause) gives lenders some stated rights if the property is transferred. **Subordination agreements** between lienholders let a later-recorded mortgage take priority over an earlier one.
4. The **Truth-in-Lending Act** (TILA) requires lenders to *disclose consumer credit costs* to promote informed use of credit. TILA is implemented by **Regulation Z** and requires a **Closing Disclosure** that details the APR, total payments, payoff terms, etc. **Annual percentage rate** (APR) is total cost of financing including an interest rate, fees, and all other finance charges. TILA also provides a **right to rescind** within three days of closing a loan on an existing primary residence and regulates lender advertising. Ads with triggering terms must include all details, including down payment, terms, and the annual percentage rate. Requires a waiting period of seven business days from when disclosures are given to when a loan can close.
5. Buyers can get *pre-qualified* or *pre-approved*. **Pre-qualification** is when an agent or lender reviews a borrower's history to determine if she is *likely* to get approved for a loan, and for about how much. Pre-qualification is *not binding* on the lender. **Pre-approval** is when a lender determines potential borrowers can be financed for a certain amount and commits to the funds.
6. The **loan application** asks a number of personal and financial questions, along with information about the property the borrower wishes to purchase. Assets and liabilities must all be disclosed, including alimony and child support, if it is an obligation.
7. An additional consumer protection is mandated by the Truth In Lending Act or Regulation Z in the form of the Closing Disclosure. This 5 page document provides the borrower with the final charges for the acquisition of the subject property. This form must be delivered to the borrower a minimum of three (3) business days prior to closing. The closing costs that are finalized on the Closing Disclosure are compared with the charges disclosed initially on the Loan Estimate. The charges must be in compliance with the tolerance limits that are set by the TRID guidelines. The final Annual Percentage Rate is also disclosed on the Closing Disclosure and if the prescribe tolerance guidelines are exceeded, a corrected Closing Disclosure must be delivered to the borrower and a new rescission period must be provided to the borrower
8. The borrower is analyzed and all information is verified. Lenders and underwriters look at: *Capacity* (ability to pay), *collateral* (down payment, home value), *credit* (payment history), *character* (job stability, reserves), and *conditions* (health of job market, economy).
9. Fannie Mae, Freddie Mac, the FHA, and the VA all consider *monthly income stability, quality, and durability.* Bonuses, commission, part-time earnings, and overtime all count if shown to be a consistent part of the borrower's income for the past few years. Lenders will not usually count unemployment, welfare, and temporary income. **Recurring debt** is any money obligation that cannot be cancelled. **Credit history** is a record of debt repayment. Credit scoring is an objective means of evaluating credit. Lenders verify assets and may require financial statements. **Net worth** is assets minus liabilities.

10. The **payment-to-income ratio** is the relationship of the borrower's total monthly housing expense (PITI) to income (stable monthly income), expressed as a percentage. This required ratio is 28% for conventional loans and 31% for FHA loans. VA loans look at regional **residual income** requirements. **Debt-to-income ratio** is the relationship of the borrower's total monthly recurring debt obligations (including housing and long-term debts with more than ten payments remaining) to income (stable monthly income), expressed as a percentage. This ratio is 36% for conventional loans and 43% for FHA loans and VA loans (although VA loans consider all recurring debt including utilities). Qualifying standards could change, so it's advisable to stay current of the guidelines.

11. **Mortgage bankers are the actual lenders** of mortgage monies. Mortgage bankers can work for any of the primary or secondary market institutions. They provide services such as loan origination, underwriting, and servicing loans. Comprehensive loan companies provide all of these functions.

12. The State of New York requires mortgage bankers to be **licensed** by the New York State Banking Department. Requirements for a licensed mortgage banker include: At least $250,000 in adjusted net worth, written documentation of a line of credit in an amount of not less than $1 million, a corporate surety bond in a principal amount of not less than $50,000, and five years of verifiable experience in the making of mortgage loans on either a retail or wholesale level.

13. Mortgage loan originators do not make loans to lenders. **A MLO earns a fee to act as an intermediary** to bring together borrowers and the lenders who fund the actual loans. A MLO may solicit, process, place, and negotiate residential loans. Typical duties of the MLO include pre-qualifying lenders, getting pre-approval, negotiating a **rate lock** in which the agreed-upon interest rate and points are frozen until the loan closes, and securing a **mortgage commitment** from the lender.

14. Mortgage loan originator applicants must complete **20 hours of education** that includes at least 3 hours of state-specific content. They must pass an exam that has a national and a state component. Licenses expire every year on December 31.

15. A real estate agent who is acting as a mortgage loan originator must explain the concept of **dual agency** to both the buyer and the seller and **obtain consent from both parties** before taking on that role. She must also complete the dual agency **disclosure form** and as with other documentation of a transaction, maintain a hard or electronic copy of the disclosure form and signed acknowledgment for at least **three years.**

16. Any **regular business relationship** that the mortgage broker maintains with any lender to which he or she presents loan applications must also be disclosed at the first substantive contact between the mortgage broker and the buyer/borrower. The exception to this requirement is if the mortgage broker submits the application to more than three lenders.

15

Municipal Agencies

DATE FEB 9, 2016

In This Session

An important part of your job as a real estate licensee is being able to answer questions about a virtually endless range of topics. Often the information your clients are seeking can be found through various municipal agencies. Everything from tax assessments, to historic preservation, to zoning is done at the municipal or local level, so this is always the best place to start your search for answers. Understanding municipal agencies will help you to effectively market your listings and assist clients in finding the right property to meet their needs.

You'll learn:

- The administrative divisions within New York State.
- The roles and responsibilities of municipal agencies in New York State.
- How these agencies can help you as a real estate professional.

Key Terms

- Architectural Review Board
- Building Department
- City Council
- Conservation Advisory Council
- County Health Department
- Historic Preservation Office
- Landmarks Preservation Commission
- Municipal Engineer's Office
- Planning Board
- Planning Department
- Real Property Tax
- Receiver of Taxes
- Tax Assessor
- Village Board of Trustees
- Zoning Board of Appeals

New York Counties

As in most states, the primary administrative division in New York is the **county**. A county is considered a regional form of government. Every county has a county seat, often a populous or centrally located city or village, where the county government is located.

In New York, some counties have an executive, such as a county administrator. Other counties have only a legislative body, which may be called a board of supervisors, board of representatives, or county legislature, for example. Counties also have their own courts with their associated judges and county prosecutors.

Generally speaking, a county has the authority to provide police services and social services, among other functions, to the areas within its borders that have not already been specifically delegated to more specific administrative divisions, such as cities.

New York Municipalities

The next administrative division is a **municipality**. These designations are not as much a matter of population as the form of government under which they operate.

- A **city** is a self-governing incorporated area with great authority to provide services and have taxing jurisdiction over its residents. Cities are established by an act of the state legislature and are organized and governed by their unique charters. Most cities in New York have a mayor and a city council. Larger cities also have municipal courts.
- A **town** is the major division of each county. A town contains all unincorporated areas and could contain villages within its borders. Therefore, everyone in New York who does not live in a city or on an Indian reservation lives in a town. A town is comparable to a township in other states. Towns often provide some services to village residents and most services to residents of unincorporated areas.
- A **village** is an incorporated area, usually within one town. A village could overlap multiple town or county borders, however. A village is intended to provide local services, such as garbage collection and street maintenance. Some villages have police and other services. Generally, a village is no more than five square miles and must have at least 500 residents.
- A **borough** is an administrative division only in New York City, resulting from the towns, villages, and cities in a county merging into one entity.

City Council

Many municipalities have city councils that form the city's legislative body. Typically, **city councils** *set policies, approve budgets, and pass ordinances and resolutions* that affect everything from land use to campaign finance. They often partner with the mayor in governing the city.

The responsibilities of city council members, no matter what city they are in, are vast. Their ultimate goal is to represent the best interests of the constituents in their districts. They do this using the legislative process, passing laws and resolutions.

Town Boards

According to New York State Town Law, a **town board** governs each town. A town board has both executive and legislative authority. It is the legislative, appropriating, governing, and policy-determining body of the town. Towns have a supervisor, council members, a town clerk, an assessor, a receiver of taxes and assessments, and other employees as needed. Towns also have a judiciary in some form, such as town justices.

Village Board of Trustees

A **village board of trustees** *governs the village.* Like a city council, a village board of trustees *consists of elected officials whose main purpose is to serve the constituents who elected them.*

A board of trustees usually includes a mayor, village administrator, or town supervisor, as well as several trustees. The number of trustees on the board depends on the size of the village. Like city council members, trustees are typically responsible for the village's budget, programming, land use regulations, and services. Passing laws, ordinances, and resolutions are also within the scope of a village board of trustees.

NEW YORK CITY

The Legislative Process in New York City

To understand fully how a city council, village board of trustees, or any legislative body adopts laws and ordinances, it's helpful to review how a bill becomes a law. The legislative process outlined here is for New York City. It is important to keep in mind there may be slight differences to the process for different municipalities. In order for a bill to become a law in New York City, the following steps are taken:

1. A city council member files a bill, which is simply proposed legislation, with the council speaker's office.
2. The bill is introduced into the council during a stated meeting and referred to the appropriate committee. One or more public committee hearings may be held on the proposed legislation.
3. The bill may be amended after public testimony and committee debate.
4. The committee votes on the final version of the bill.
5. If the committee passes the bill, it is sent to the full council for more debate and a final vote.
6. If at least 26 members of city council vote "yes," the bill is then sent to the mayor, who also holds a public hearing.
7. The mayor either signs the bill or vetoes it.
8. If the mayor signs the bill, it immediately becomes a local law and is entered into New York City's Charter of Administrative Code.
9. If the mayor vetoes the bill, he must return it to the city clerk along with his objections by the next scheduled stated meeting.
10. The council then has 30 days to override the mayor's veto.
11. If the council re-passes the bill by a two-thirds vote (at least 34 of the 51 members vote affirmatively), it is considered adopted and becomes a local law.
12. If the mayor does not sign or veto the bill within 30 days of receiving it from city council, it is automatically approved.

Adoption of Budgets and Property Tax Rates

In New York State, the **real property tax** *is a tax based on the assessed value of real property*. Cities, counties, villages, towns, school districts, and special districts all raise money through real property taxes. The money funds schools, pays for police and fire protection, maintains roads, and funds other services enjoyed by residents. Since municipalities and school districts collect property taxes, which are one of their largest sources of income, property taxes and assessments are administered locally rather than by the state.

Property tax rates are determined by **tax levies**. And in order to settle on the tax levy, a local budget must be adopted. To create and adopt a budget, local entities establish where all sources of revenue come from, other than property taxes. These revenues are subtracted from the original budget, and the remainder becomes the tax levy, which is raised through real property taxes.

Whether a city, town, or village is governed by a city council or board of trustees, or has a mayor or administrator, that local governing body is responsible for determining property tax rates based on its annual budget.

Property Taxes and Assessments

It is important to note that property taxes are *not* the same as property assessments. In fact, the two are determined by two different entities. Property taxes are set by boards – school, town, village, and the like. Each board determines the total amount of taxes it needs to raise, and then divides that by the total taxable assessed value of the jurisdiction to determine the tax rate. A property owner's share of the tax is calculated by **multiplying the tax rate by the property's assessed value, minus exemptions**. Assessors, not municipal legislators, figure a property's assessed value.

A property's **assessment**, on the other hand, *is a percentage of its market value*. Market value is simply how much a property would sell for under normal market conditions. Assessments should be based on market value.

The Tax Assessor's Office

The tax assessor's office is mainly responsible for determining the *assessed value* of property. The assessor also processes exemption applications and keeps a close watch on the local real estate market. *The tax assessor's office does not determine property taxes*. That is the responsibility of school boards, town boards, village boards, and county legislatures. The assessor's office does have an effect on an individual's property taxes, however, if the assessed values in the municipality are not recorded correctly, fairly, and equally.

Tax assessors *are elected or appointed local officials who independently estimate the value of real property.* Assessing units follow county, city, town, or village boundaries. Assessors estimate the value of real property in a number of ways, based on the sale prices of similar properties or on the depreciated cost of materials and labor required to replace it.

No matter where property is located, every parcel of real property in an assessing unit is assessed, no matter how big or how small it is. Even though all real property is assessed, it is *not* all taxed. Property owned by a church or temple or by the government, may be totally exempt from property taxes. And veterans may receive partial exemptions.

Municipal tax assessor offices **monitor improvements on properties for reassessment** and **keep records** on a variety of things, including:

- Location of parcels.
- Property ownership.
- Tax information.
- Sales information.
- Tax maps.
- Exemptions.

Challenging an Assessment

In some cases it may be necessary to challenge an assessment, for example, if a property owner believes the assessment is excessive (exceeds the market value), unequal (relative to other similar properties), unlawful, or misclassified. The steps to challenge an assessment are:

1. Meet with the assessor to voice concerns and request adjustments.
2. File a complaint with the local Board of Assessment Review on or before the day the board meets to hear complaints.
3. Seek a judicial review by commencing a *tax certiorari* in New York State Supreme Court or by filing a Small Claims Assessment Review (SCAR).

Possible outcomes of challenging an assessment are full denial, full reassessment, or partial reassessment.

The Office of Receiver of Taxes

Tax departments in New York municipalities are called the office of receiver of taxes and *the elected official who oversees this office is the* **receiver of taxes**. Typically, the **office of receiver of taxes** *is responsible for collecting taxes, disbursing funds, keeping tax records, and other accounting functions.*

The office of receiver of taxes is strictly an administrative office, not a policymaking office. The office does *not* set tax rates; it simply collects them, among other financial duties.

The Planning Board

Nearly every municipality in New York has a **planning board** *that holds public hearings, investigates solutions for the planning issues at hand, and makes recommendations to the appropriate legislative authority.*

Besides advising all other boards on land use matters and ensuring the requirements of the State Environmental Quality Review Act are followed, planning boards are involved in many activities that directly affect the growth and development of a city. The major responsibilities of a city planning board include:

- Creating a capital budget.
- Developing and controlling the city's comprehensive plan.
- Regulating plat, density, street, and traffic patterns.
- Regulating subdivision development.
- Reviewing site plans.
- Taking specific zoning actions.

New York City Board of Standards and Appeals

In New York City, the planning board and the zoning board are one entity known as the **Board of Standards and Appeals**. It consists of 12 members and one chairperson. In many New York municipalities, planning board members are appointed by the mayor or trustees, or equivalent, for a term ranging from one to several years. Planning board members ensure that city growth is orderly and that the city can support the growth.

The Planning Department

On the surface, planning departments may seem identical to planning boards. While the overall mission of each body may be the same – to maintain and enhance the communities they serve through the organized and deliberate planning of how land is used – the day-to-day activities are different.

A **planning department** *is an office of a jurisdiction with employees who carry out administrative functions.* Besides providing professional advisement to many agencies and boards within a community, planning departments are responsible for a wide range of activities and operations. Some of the most common responsibilities of planning departments include:

- Comprehensive municipal planning
- Grant implementation
- Transportation planning
- Zoning referrals review
- Long-range economic development
- Water resource management
- Capital improvements development

As you can see, these responsibilities are somewhat different from those of a municipal planning board. Planning boards approve or reject proposals for subdivisions based on the municipality's comprehensive plan. A planning department, on the other hand, would not approve such plans. Instead, they help carry plans out, once they are approved by the board.

Another major difference between a planning board and planning department is that a planning board consists of community members appointed by a town mayor, county supervisor, village administrator, or the like.

The Zoning Board of Appeals

A local **zoning board of appeals** *hears and decides requests for variances and special permits brought before the board.* Interpreting zoning laws is another function of the zoning board of appeals. New York State statutes specifically give the zoning board of appeals the power to hear appeals seeking interpretation of provisions of local zoning ordinances.

The Architectural Review Board

A local **architectural review board** *determines the effects a proposed building or other structure, or alteration to an existing structure, will have on the desirability, property values, and development of surrounding areas.* Members of architectural review boards are usually appointed and serve terms of various lengths.

The purpose of a local architectural review board is to conserve the value of property and to encourage the most appropriate land use within the community by upholding municipal ordinances. Applications for building, sign, and fence permits are often referred to the architectural review board. The construction of any structure visible from any street, or alterations that will affect the exterior appearance of a building fall under the realm of the architectural review board.

The Conservation Advisory Council

Another important municipal agency is a city's **conservation advisory council**, *which studies matters affecting the environment, preservation, development, and use of a city's natural and physical features and conditions with regard to ecologic integrity, aesthetic appeal, and quality.*

Conservation advisory councils are created by local legislatures to advise in the development, management, and protection of the community's natural resources and to prepare an inventory map of open spaces. Another major function of local conservation advisory councils is to ensure environmental issues prevalent in the community are handled according to municipal ordinances. Members of local conservation advisory councils are appointed by city mayors, town administrators, or village boards of trustees for terms of various lengths.

The Historic Preservation Office

Historic preservation offices *identify, evaluate, preserve, and revitalize the municipality's historic, archaeological, and cultural resources.* The purpose of this office is to provide advice and guidance to property owners and government agencies regarding historic preservation in the community, as well as recommend properties for preservation.

The historic preservation office typically consists of a board composed of members familiar with historic preservation. Members are usually appointed and may include architects, historians, archaeologists, and archivists. In many cases, other city or village departments, such as planning, tourism, and the historical society are represented on historical preservation boards.

Reviewing and commenting on any projects that could affect historic properties are within the scope of the historical preservation office. Many boards, in conjunction with the respective building inspector, review applications requesting to demolish all or any substantial part of any building in the municipality and decide whether the building appears to be one with significant historical value.

New York City Landmarks Preservation Commission

New York City's Landmarks Law requires potential landmarks to be at least 30 years old and possess "a special character or special historical or aesthetic interest or value as part of the development, heritage, or cultural characteristics of the city, state, or nation" before it is designated a landmark.

The **Landmarks Preservation Commission (LPC)** *is the New York City agency responsible for identifying and designating the city's landmarks,* which may include buildings, bridges, parks, cemeteries, fences, sidewalk clocks, *building lobbies, and even trees.* As long as it meets the Landmarks Law criteria, it may be considered for designation as a landmark. The commission also regulates changes to already designated landmarks.

The Building Department

Landowners must obtain building permits before constructing or renovating residential or commercial property. New York uses a statewide building code that applies to all construction when no local code exists, or when local codes are *less* restrictive. Local **building departments** *are responsible for issuing building permits* *and for seeing that code restrictions are followed and construction and renovation are done by licensed professionals.*

Building codes are established locally, and permits are issued through local government authorities. Typically, an owner who wants to build or remodel a building must submit plans to a local building department for approval. (Copies of building permits are also sent to the municipality in which the property is located to provide the local assessor notice of the improvements for reassessment.)

Building permits are issued only if the plans comply with the codes. Building departments are essentially the gatekeepers of any construction project. Local inspectors, who can stop work if necessary, inspect the project several times throughout the construction process to ensure the work is up to code.

The Municipal Engineer's Office

The planning, design, and construction of New York's public works facilities and projects are all within the scope of a **municipality's engineer's office**. Typically, the office is headed up by a city (or county, village, town, etc.) engineer, who oversees and manages engineering services and support staff. City engineers are usually civil engineers by trade.

A municipal engineer's office designs capital improvement projects, such as roadways, sewer systems, and water connections. Other important functions the office performs include:

- Evaluating applications for subdivisions and land development.
- Preparing and updating ordinances pertaining to construction standards.
- Evaluating and making recommendations regarding drainage, grading, and water retention.
- Reviewing site plans for commercial, industrial, and multi-family properties.
- Conducting engineering research work.
- Communicating with the municipality's legislators, administrators, and constituents regarding public works projects.

The County Health Department

Each county in New York State has its own **health department**, *which is a human service and regulatory agency that administers public health programs and activities within the county*. Most importantly, health departments assess the health status of the community and then develop policies and plans to meet the needs identified in the assessment.

Essential services many municipal health departments provide include:

- Monitoring the health status of the community to solve chronic health problems.
- Educating the community about healthy living and preventive care.
- Enforcing laws and regulations to protect the health and safety of the community.
- Connecting community members to needed health services.
- Training public health care providers.
- Continually evaluating and updating public health programs.
- Researching solutions to health problems common in the community.

Some responsibilities that fall under the supervision of a county health department are not as obvious. For instance, this department is responsible for approving **septic and other sanitation systems**. Health departments also regulate food service establishments, tanning salons, swimming pools, and environmental health concerns.

Land use regulations, public health, public works, maintaining historical integrity, taxes, public education, zoning, and passing legislation all involve a municipal agency. Really, just about anything you can think of, no matter how big or how small, falls within the realm of a municipal agency. For this reason, you will want to keep up to date on the municipal agencies in the communities where you work.

It is worth the time to get to know local officials, become involved in local organizations, and keep abreast of local legislation. By doing this, you'll know whom to turn to when customers and clients have questions. Superior customer service leads to referrals, which are essential to the growth of your business.

SUMMARY

1. **City councils** typically *set policies, approve budgets, and pass ordinances and resolutions that affect everything from land use to campaign finance*. City councils usually partner with the mayor in governing the city. City council members are elected by constituents in the areas they serve for terms of varying lengths.
2. In some areas of New York, a **village board of trustees** *governs the village instead of a city council.* The entities are similar in the fact that they both consist of elected officials whose main purpose is to the serve the constituents who elected them. A board of trustees usually includes a mayor, village administrator, or town supervisor, as well as several trustees. Trustees are responsible for the village's budget, programming, land use regulations, and services.
3. In New York State, **real property tax** is *based on the value of real property*. Cities, counties, villages, towns, school districts, and special districts all raise money through real property taxes. Money earned from taxes funds schools, police and fire protection, road maintenance, and other services enjoyed by residents. Property taxes are administered locally rather than by the state. Tax rates are determined by tax levies. In order to settle on a tax levy, a local budget must be adopted. Taxes are *not* the same as property assessments.
4. Municipal **planning boards** *hold public hearings, investigate solutions for planning issues at hand, and make recommendations to appropriate legislative bodies.* Planning board members are appointed by the mayor, trustees, or equivalent, for terms of varying lengths. Planning board members are involved in creating a capital budget, creating and controlling the city's comprehensive plan, regulating plat, density, street, and traffic patterns, regulating subdivision development, reviewing site plans, and specific zoning actions.

5. **Planning departments** *focus on the day-to-day operations of a municipality*. The overall mission of planning boards and planning departments is the same, which is to maintain and enhance the communities in which they serve through the organized and deliberate planning of how land is used.

6. The **zoning board of appeals** *hears and decides requests for variances and special use permits.* Interpreting zoning laws is also a function of the zoning board of appeals. New York State statutes specifically give zoning boards of appeals the power to hear appeals seeking interpretations of provisions of local zoning ordinances.

7. A local **architectural review board** *determines the effects a proposed building or other structure, or alteration of an existing structure, will have on the desirability, property values, and development of surrounding areas*. The purpose of local architectural review boards is to conserve the value of property and to encourage the most appropriate use of land within the community.

8. **Conservation advisory councils** *study matters affecting the environment, preservation, development, and use of a city's natural and physical features and conditions in regard to ecologic integrity, aesthetic appeal, and quality*. A major function of the council is to ensure environmental issues prevalent in the community are handled according to municipal ordinances.

9. The purpose of local **historic preservation offices** is to *identify, evaluate, preserve, and revitalize the municipality's historic, archaeological, and cultural resources*. Historic preservation offices provide advice and guidance regarding historic preservation in the community as well as recommend properties for preservation.

10. The **Landmarks Preservation Commission (LPC)** is *the New York City agency responsible for identifying and designating the city's landmarks.* The LPC also regulates changes to already designated landmarks.

11. **Building departments** *issue building permits and see that code restrictions are followed, and construction and renovation is done by licensed professionals*. Building codes are established locally and permits are issued through local government authorities. A building permit is issued only if the plans comply with codes.

12. The **tax assessor's office** is mainly *responsible for determining the assessed value of property*. Assessors also process exemption applications and keep close watch on the local real estate market. The tax assessor's office does *not* determine property taxes.

13. *Tax departments in New York* are called the **office of receiver of taxes**. The elected official who oversees this office is the receiver of taxes. This office is strictly administrative; it does not make policies. The office of receiver of taxes does *not* set taxes; it simply collects them.

14. The *planning, design, and construction of New York's public works facilities and projects* are all within the scope of the **municipal engineer's office.** This office designs capital improvement projects, including roadways, sewer systems, and water connections.

15. Each county in New York State has its own **health department**, which *is a human service and regulatory agency that administers a number of public health programs and activities within the county*. Health departments assess the health status of the community and then develop policies and plans to meet identified needs.

15-A

In This Session

Property insurance is a consideration that factors into the purchase of both residential and commercial real estate. In this session, you'll learn the basic information you need in order to advise clients about property insurance: How it's marketed, what types of policies are available, typical costs, and what protections insurance affords them.

You'll learn:

- The purpose of having property insurance.
- How insurance is obtained.
- What types of policies are available to property owners and what they cover.
- Why a property insurance mortgage clause is required by lenders.

Key Terms

- Actual Cash Value (ACV)
- Deductible
- Direct Loss
- Indirect Loss
- Liability
- Liability Insurance
- Monoline Policy
- Mortgage Clause
- Package Policy
- Peril
- Property Insurance
- Replacement Cost Basis
- Umbrella Policy

The Purpose of Property Insurance

Property insurance is *coverage that indemnifies a person with an interest in the property for a loss caused to the property by a covered peril.* Fire insurance is just another name for property insurance, which can cover building structures (real property), contents (personal property), or both on the same policy.

A dwelling policy is sold to owners or owner-occupants of dwelling structures, so a person who owns a dwelling structure and rents it to others can qualify, as well as the person who owns a dwelling structure and lives in it. The insured may also be a renter who wants personal property covered, but not the building.

Insurance Agents

Insurance companies generally market insurance:

- Through insurance agents, or
- By selling directly to consumers through mass marketing

The majority of insurance policies are sold through agents. Insurance agents may be employees of a company or independent agents (contractors). Ownership of the policy expirations varies by company.

- **Independent agents** sell policies that best fit the clients' needs, from among the many insurers they represent, and are paid a commission for each sale. They own the expirations of the policies sold, meaning they may place that business with another insurer on renewal if it is in the best interest of the client.
- **Exclusive agents** represent only one company, and may be paid a salary or be compensated by commissions. Exclusive agents *do not* own the policy expirations.
- **Direct writing companies** pay salaries to employees whose job function is to sell the company's insurance products. The insurance company owns the expirations and the agents' businesses.
- **Insurance brokers** do not represent any particular company and are not employees of any insurance company. They are representatives of the customer and secure quotes and policies from an agent or insurance company on behalf of the customer.

Types of Policies

Insurance coverage may be purchased as a **monoline policy** to cover *property both real and personal.* "Mono" means *one,* and "line" means the *specific type of property.* This policy is designed to cover one specific area – *property.*

Insurance may also be purchased to handle more than one line of coverage. A customer may also wish to include **liability** (casualty), *which is coverage in case of a lawsuit filed by another person claiming bodily injury or damage to property.* **Liability insurance** *insures the individual for financial losses that may arise out of the person's responsibilities to others imposed by law or contract.*

When *two or more coverage parts are combined into one policy,* the resulting contract is considered a **package policy.** Most insurance contracts are purchased as package policies, since customers typically look for more than one area of coverage. It is up to the insurance agent to advise which type of policy best suits his customer's needs. The two most frequently used policy types are **dwelling** and **homeowners.**

Dwelling Policies

Dwelling policies *cover a direct loss to physical property as well as an indirect loss that results because the insured cannot use the property after it is damaged.* It can be written for a one-, two-, three-, or four-family structure. There are two important points to remember about dwelling policies:

- There is **no theft** coverage on contents.
- There is **no liability** coverage.

Direct and Indirect Losses

A **direct loss** is *one that happens suddenly due to a covered peril* – such as fire, lightning, wind, hail, etc. An **indirect loss**, also known as a consequential loss, is one that *occurs as a consequence of the direct loss.* For example, on the dwelling policy, fire is covered as a direct loss. However, since the policy *also covers loss of rental income as an indirect coverage,* lost rents due to a fire in the dwelling are also covered.

Purchasing a Dwelling Policy

The dwelling policy is unique because coverage can be purchased based on an individual policyholder's needs. For example, if building coverage is needed, the customer buys it; the same with other structures, contents, and fair rental value. Not only can policyholders pick which coverage they want, they can also decide *how much* coverage they want.

A **peril** *is anything that can cause a loss,* such as fire, wind, hail, etc. There are two ways to cover property against perils:

- **Named peril policy**. Each peril is listed and named. If property is damaged and the peril that caused it is **not** listed and named, then there is **no** coverage.
- **All risk policy.** The insured has coverage for all direct risk of physical loss; therefore, **everything** is covered unless the peril is specifically **excluded**.

Dwelling Policy Forms

Dwelling policies can be issued using a DP-1, DP-2, or DP-3 coverage form.

Dwelling Property (DP) Forms	
Basic Form (DP-1)	A named peril form that covers the property for 11 named perils. If the peril causing the damage is not listed and named, then there is no coverage. The perils covered are: • Fire • Damage done by aircraft • Smoke, sinkhole collapse, and sprinkler leakage • Lightning • Explosion • Wind or hail • Volcanic action • Riot or civil commotion • Damage done by vehicles other than the insured's Vandalism and malicious mischief (VMM) coverage is optional.
Broad Form (DP-2)	The name Broad Form speaks for itself – the coverage is much broader than on the Basic Form. It is still a named peril policy, so the rules of coverage do not change. Customers who purchase a DP-2 get protection from all of the perils of the DP-1 plus: • Weight of ice and snow. • Water damage (caused by accidental discharge from a plumbing device). • Damage from falling objects. • Freezing of plumbing (if the heat is left on).
Special Form (DP-3)	The DP-3 Special Form offers all risk coverage on Coverage A (the dwelling) and Coverage B (the other structures). Except for contents coverage, unless the peril is specifically excluded somewhere in the policy contract, it is covered. This is why the DP-3 contains many more exclusions. The DP-3 still contains a list of named perils that apply to Coverage C (contents) only; the list of named perils is the same as the DP-2 (Broad Form). The DP-3's new exclusions to Coverage A (dwelling) and Coverage B (other structures) include all risk exclusions, such as wear and tear, pollutants, and mold.

General Exclusions

Dwelling policy forms contain general exclusions that apply to the policy as a whole. All three dwelling policy forms exclude:

- **Ordinance or law.** The insurer will not pay for loss to property caused by enforcement of any law or ordinance regulating the use, construction, repair, or demolition of the structure.
- **Earth movement.** Although the policy covers volcanic eruption, this clause excludes earth movement caused by land shockwaves or tremors before, during, or after a volcanic eruption, as well as a variety of other causes of earth movement.

- **Water damage.** Flood, tidal waves, and water that backs up through sewers or drains, or is below the ground's surface and seeping through basement walls, etc., are not covered.
- **Power failure.** Failure of power or other utility service is not covered if the failure takes place off the premises.
- **Neglect, war and nuclear hazard, intentional loss.** There is no coverage for these items.

Selected Endorsements to Dwelling Policies

Policyholders can add selected endorsements for an additional premium, including theft coverage and personal liability.

Broad theft coverage. Since dwelling policies do not cover theft of contents, some policyholders add this endorsement for an additional premium. The peril of theft, defined as any act of stealing, is added, providing coverage for theft both on and off the premises. A **limited theft endorsement** (usually purchased by landlords) can also be added, covering theft occurring only on the premises.

Comprehensive personal liability. Since dwelling policies do not cover personal liability, a policyholder could add this coverage by endorsement for an additional premium. If comprehensive personal liability is added, the policy provides liability coverage for activities or events occurring *both* on and off the premises. Coverage applies if the injury to someone else or damage to someone else's property is caused by the insured's negligence. **Premises liability** (usually purchased by landlords) can also be added, but the liability coverage is limited to situations occurring only on the premises.

Homeowners (HO) Policies

The Homeowners (HO) policy is a package policy with two parts:

- Section I, which covers property
- Section II, which covers liability

The HO property section is similar to the dwelling forms. In fact, the HO-1 Basic Form, HO-2 Broad Form, and HO-3 Special Form basically parallel the DP-1, DP-2, and DP-3 forms; however, they are completely separate policy sets. In addition to these three forms, there are HO policies to cover renters, condominium owners, and older dwellings. Most differences in the various HO policies relate to the property sections.

Note that the information regarding dwelling policies and perils also applies to homeowners policies. In the property area, the major difference between DP and HO forms is that none of the DP forms covers theft of contents or personal liability to others, but all HO forms cover theft, personal liability, and medical payments to others.

The HO liability section covers the homeowner's personal liability to others in the areas of bodily injury and property damage due to the insured's negligence. Section II coverages – personal liability and medical – are uniform on all HO policies.

HO Forms

There are a number of different homeowners policy options available:

Homeowners (HO) Policy Forms	
HO-1 Basic Form	A named peril form on both dwelling structures and contents; vandalism and theft are included
HO-2 Broad Form	A named peril form on both dwelling structures and contents; theft is included
HO-3 Special Form	All risk coverage on the dwelling and other structures; contents are named peril
HO-4 Renters or Tenants Form	Coverage for insureds who do not own the premises they inhabit; contains no structures coverage
HO-5 Comprehensive Form	All risk coverage on both the structure and contents
HO-6 Condominium Unit Owners	A small amount of coverage for the interior space owned by the insured, but not the condo building structure or common areas
HO-8 Modified Form	Named peril on structures and personal property; specially designed for older homes for which the replacement cost of the dwelling exceeds market value

The Cost of Homeowners Insurance

Homeowners insurance rates are based on:

- Property location.
- Construction materials.
- Amount of insurance requested.

Insurance Policy Deductibles

A **deductible** *is usually a dollar amount the insured must pay on each loss. The insurance company pays the remainder of each covered loss up to the policy limits.* Deductibles help control the cost of insurance and are contained in most property insurance policies. They are also used to prevent overutilization of the policy.

The client selects the deductible at the time the policy is purchased. The higher the deductible is, the lower the premium will be. Most deductibles apply on **a per occurrence basis**, meaning if more than one type of property is damaged in a single event, only one deductible applies for the entire loss. Policyholders must satisfy the deductible on each and every claim.

Liability coverage is usually written without any deductible, but certain policies may include one. **Dwelling and homeowners** liability policies are **written without deductibles**.

The deductible is stated as a dollar amount on the declarations page. New York insurance statutes require a disclosure notice be sent to the insured if the policy also contains a hurricane deductible. **Hurricane deductibles** can be a flat amount, but most are stated as a percentage of the coverage amount on the dwelling. The notice must also state, in clear and plain language, the circumstances under which the hurricane deductible applies.

How Much Insurance Is Needed?

Standard policies require policyholders to carry enough insurance to cover at least **80 percent** of the cost to replace the structure. Some insurance carriers now require the insured to carry **100 percent** of the cost to replace the dwelling as the minimum to receive all policy benefits. If the insured does not carry the required amount, there could be a substantial reduction or even a penalty imposed at the time of a loss.

Partial Loss Versus Total Loss

Most claims filed are for **partial losses**, where the cost to replace or repair the damage does not exceed the limit of insurance. These situations are affected most by inadequate coverage. If the insured does not carry the required amount of insurance, the amount paid for a partial loss could be substantially less than the amount needed to repair or replace the damaged property.

A **total loss** occurs when the cost to repair or replace exceeds the limit of insurance on the policy. If the damage to the property is considered a total loss, then the policy limit is paid out and the claim closed.

Settling Claims

Claims can be settled in two ways, depending on the contract wording and/or the amount of insurance carried:

Actual cash value (ACV) *is calculated by determining the replacement cost of the damaged property at today's prices (not including the land) and then subtracting any depreciation, based on the property's age and its use over time*. The formula for determining ACV is:

Replacement Cost (RC) – Depreciation = ACV

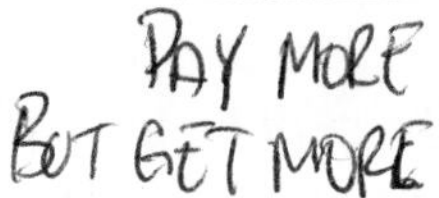

Instead of ACV, better policies pay claims on a **replacement cost basis,** which are *paid in full without any depreciation, up to the policy limits, less any deductible*. However, dwelling policies that contain replacement cost coverage also require the insured's coverage be at least 80% of the replacement cost value for that coverage to apply. If the client is underinsured and carries less than 80%, a penalty may follow. Most clients prefer replacement cost coverage versus actual cash value.

The New York Insurance Underwriting Association

The **New York Property Insurance Underwriting Association** (NYPIUA), created in 1968, developed the FAIR Plan (**F**air **A**ccess to **I**nsurance **R**equirements) to ensure that affordable property insurance is available without consideration of location, provided the property meets minimal underwriting insurability standards.

The NYPIUA insures:

- Buildings (dwelling and commercial properties).
- Contents of commercial premises.
- Household furnishings and personal property.

The NYPIUA provides five types of coverages:

1. Fire, lightning, and explosion
2. Extended coverage, including these perils:
   - Windstorm
   - Hail
   - Riot
   - Civil commotion
   - Aircraft
   - Vehicles
   - Smoke
3. Vandalism and malicious mischief
4. Sprinkler leakage (commercial property only)
5. Time element coverages

The NYPIUA does *not* offer liability, flood, or theft coverage.

Cancellation and Nonrenewal of Policies

During the first 60 days a covered policy is in effect, a notice of cancellation must be accompanied by a statement of the **specific reason(s) for cancellation**. After the policy has been in effect for 60 days, or upon the effective date if the policy is a renewal, cancellation or nonrenewal can take effect only based on specific reasons, including nonpayment of premium.

A **written notice** of nonrenewal must be sent at least 45-60 days prior to the nonrenewal date. The specific reason(s) for nonrenewal must be stated in the notice. If the notice is not sent according to guidelines, the insured may request renewal of the policy on timely payment of the proper premium to the carrier or its agent.

Rather than cancel a policy, an insurer may change limits or eliminate coverage not required by law. To do this, the insurer must provide notice to the insured at least 20 days prior to the effective date of the action.

Flood Insurance

Property insurance does not cover damage caused by the peril of flood. Consumers who want flood coverage must purchase flood insurance from the National Flood Insurance Program (NFIP) or from an insurer participating in the Write Your Own program, which provides essentially the same coverage as the policy sold through the federal program.

Coastal Residents Assistance

The Coastal Market Assistance Program (C-MAP) was established by the State of New York Insurance Department and is administered by the NYPIUA. Its purpose is to assist homeowners living in New York's coastal areas in obtaining homeowners insurance. Applicants to C-MAP may apply directly, or through their insurance brokers or agents. Homeowners are encouraged to use the services of professional brokers and agents to assist them in these transactions. Applicants must meet certain eligibility requirements to participate in C-MAP.

Other Types of Property Insurance

Commercial property owners may purchase coverage for buildings and/or business personal property in the same way as an individual property owner. Coverage can be written on a monoline basis – providing protection for only one type of property – or coverage can be packaged together into a commercial package policy to cover the physical property owned by the business, as well as property that may be in transit via land conveyance or on or over water via boat or airplane.

Often, specialized policies exist to cover the breakdown of equipment, such as:

- Boilers.
- Pumps.
- Motors.
- Refrigeration and air conditioning units.

These can also be included in a package policy designed especially for a business. Commercial property policies may be tailored to cover property on a blanket or specific basis.

Blanket property insurance provides a single amount of insurance that may apply to different types of property or to different locations. Clients may select a single limit of insurance that may apply to:

- All types of property at a specified location.
- One type of property at more than one location.
- All types of property at various locations.

In contrast, **specific property insurance** provides a specific amount of insurance for specific types of property at a specific location.

Umbrella Policies

Although a policy may cover or be endorsed to cover liability, there is still a demand for **umbrella policies,** which provide very *high limits of liability and broad coverage for a very reasonable premium charge.* Umbrellas are written to provide excess liability coverage – over and above other liability policies. The primary policies (home or commercial) act as a deductible for the umbrella, which pays only in the event the primary coverage is exhausted.

Most underwriters require that underlying (primary) policies be written with uniformly high limits. If the primary policy pays a claim up to that amount, the umbrella policy takes over, usually providing at least another $1 million or more of coverage for bodily injury and property damage. Umbrellas do not have anything to do with property coverage. Some umbrellas are designed to cover gaps in coverage in the underlying policies.

Property Insurance and the Real Estate Professional

The State of New York Insurance Department website has a unique section for property owners, which answers important questions about the purpose and costs of property insurance. This is an excellent reference tool if a buyer does not have an insurance agent to handle these important aspects of becoming a property owner. The website is available at: http://www.ins.state.ny.us

The Lender's Interest

Lenders have an insurable interest in the property and will require that the proper **mortgage clause** be added to the property policy *to cover the lender's interest in preservation and reconstruction of the property after a loss.* If the customer does not comply with the lender's insurance requirements, the lender has the right to place insurance on the property to cover its interest in the event of a loss.

This forced insurance by lenders covers only the loan value in case of a covered loss to the structure. It does not provide for any contents or personal property coverage for the insured. It also will not provide any liability protection in case of a lawsuit against the property owner.

Most lenders require buyers to pay the first year's insurance premium in full *prior* to closing. The lender incorporates the annual insurance cost, along with current property taxes, into an escrow account. The insurance cost and property taxes are then prorated over the next 12 months to determine a monthly insurance and property tax payment amount, which is added to the monthly principal and interest due for loan repayment. Upon payment each month, the insurance and taxes are deposited into the client's escrow account. When property taxes and insurance become due, the lender forwards the payment to the respective recipients on behalf of the property owner.

The Buyer's Liability

In the event of a cash sale with no lender involvement, buyers should obtain insurance on the property at closing. At this point, the buyer has ownership and an insurable interest in the property and its preservation. Buyers – at the moment of closing – *could also be held liable for any injury or property damage to others caused by their actions and/or occurring on their property*. It is in the buyer's best interest to obtain insurance immediately at closing, even if the seller is allowed to remain on the property for a period of time.

The buyer's insurance policy would not cover personal property belonging to the seller. However, if the seller's personal property is damaged due to the negligence of the buyer, a lawsuit could develop and the buyer would need the proper protection from an insurance policy.

SUMMARY

1. **Property insurance** is *coverage that indemnifies a person with an interest in the property for a loss caused to the property by a covered peril.* **Fire insurance** is just another name for *property insurance, which can cover building structures* (real property) *or contents* (personal property), *or both in the same policy.*

2. Insurance coverage may be purchased as a **monoline policy** to cover *property both real and personal.* It can include **liability** (casualty), which is *coverage in case of a lawsuit filed by another person claiming bodily injury or damage to property*. **Liability insurance** *insures the individual for financial losses that may arise out of the person's responsibilities to others imposed by law or contract.* When *two or more coverage parts are combined into one policy*, the resulting contract is now a **package policy**.

3. A **dwelling policy** *covers a direct loss to the physical property as well as an indirect loss that results because the insured cannot use the property after it is damaged*. There is **no** theft coverage on contents, *and* **no** liability coverage on a dwelling policy. A **peril** is *anything that can cause a loss,* such as fire, wind, hail, etc. A policy can be either a **named peril** policy, in which *each peril is listed and named in the policy,* or an **all risk** policy, with *coverage for all direct risk of physical loss;* therefore, ***everything*** is covered ***unless*** the peril is *specifically excluded.*

   Dwelling policies can be issued using **DP-1**, **DP-2**, or **DP-3**. **DP-1** – Dwelling Property Basic Form covers up to 11 named perils. **DP-2** – Dwelling Property Broad Form covers all perils from the basic form, plus four more. **DP-3**—Dwelling Property All Risk Form covers all perils unless specifically excluded somewhere in the contract (and except for contents coverage). All three dwelling policy forms exclude: Ordinance or law, earth movement, water damage, power failure, neglect, war, nuclear hazard, and intentional loss. For an additional premium, insureds can add **Broad Theft Coverage** and **Comprehensive Personal Liability** to dwelling policies.

4. A **homeowners policy** has two parts: **Section I**, which covers *property,* and **Section II**, which covers *liability.* The HO Property section is similar to the dwelling forms. The **HO-1 Basic Form** is a named peril form on both dwelling structures and contents, and vandalism and theft are included. The **HO-2 Broad Form** is also a named peril form on both dwelling structures and contents, and theft is included. The **HO-3 Special Form** provides the best coverage for the money and is all risk on the dwelling and other structures. The contents are still named peril. The **HO-4 Renters or Tenants Form** provides contents coverage for insureds who do not own the premises they inhabit. The **HO-5 Comprehensive Form** provides all risk coverage on both the structures and contents. The **HO-6 Condominium Unit Owners Form** is very similar to the HO-4, *except* it includes a small amount of coverage for the dwelling unit, which is the interior space owned by the insured. The **HO-8 Modified Form** is designed for older homes for which the replacement cost of the dwelling exceeds market value.

5. **Standard policies** require the insured to carry at least **80%** of the cost to replace the structure as the minimum amount of insurance on the property. Most claims filed are for **partial loss,** where *the cost to replace or repair the damage does not exceed the limit of insurance.* A **total loss** is *where the cost to repair or replace exceeds the limit of insurance on the policy*. Claims can be settled for **actual cash value** (*replacement cost minus depreciation),* or **replacement cost basis** (*paid in full without any depreciation)*. The property coverage on homeowners policies is very similar to dwelling policies; however, these coverages **stack** on an HO policy, meaning *each coverage is added to the other(s).* The policy amount is stated as the Coverage A (dwelling) and Coverage B (other structures); C (contents/personal property), and D (loss of use) are *in addition* to that.

6. The **New York Property Insurance Underwriting Association** (NYPIUA) designated a FAIR Plan (fair access to insurance requirements) to write certain types of property insurance. The association currently offers fire, extended coverage, vandalism and malicious mischief, sprinkler leakage, and time element coverage. The NYPIUA insures buildings (dwelling and commercial properties), contents of commercial premises, and household furnishings and personal property.

7. Property insurance does *not* cover damage caused by the peril of **flood**. Consumers who want this coverage need to purchase flood insurance from the National Flood Insurance Program (NFIP) or from an insurer participating in the Write Your Own program.

8. The **Coastal Market Assistance Program** (C-MAP) was established by the State of New York Insurance Department and is administered by the New York Property Insurance Underwriting Association (NYPIUA) to assist homeowners living in New York's coastal areas in obtaining insurance for their homes. C-MAP has specific eligibility requirements.

9. **Homeowners insurance rates** are based on *property location, construction materials, and amount of insurance requested.* A **deductible** is *usually a dollar amount the insured must pay on each loss to which the deductible applies.* The insurance company pays the remainder of each covered loss up to the policy limits. Deductibles help control the cost of insurance and prevent overutilization of the policy.

10. Commercial property owners may purchase **blanket property insurance** that *provides a single amount of insurance that may apply to different types of property or to different locations* or **specific property insurance** to *provide a specific amount of insurance for specific types of property at a specific location.* **Umbrella** policies provide *high limits of liability and broad coverage for a very reasonable premium charge.*

11. The lender has an *insurable interest* in the property and will require that the proper **mortgage clause** be added to the property policy *to cover the lender's interest in preservation and reconstruction of the property after a loss.* If the customer does not comply with the lender's insurance requirements, the lender has the right to place insurance on the property to cover its interest should there be a loss.

16

Real Estate Taxes and Assessments

In This Session

Nearly all property listed for sale is affected by taxes and assessments. As a licensee, you'll need to understand property taxes to complete comparative market analyses. It is also your responsibility to let buyers know how taxes will affect their mortgage payments. In this session, you'll see how property tax is managed in the State of New York, and look at the process of assessing specific property for tax purposes.

You'll learn:

- The purpose of property taxation.
- Who may be exempt from property taxes.
- How properties are assessed and by whom.
- How to calculate property taxes.
- How equalization affects property taxes.
- The process property owners follow to challenge assessments.

Key Terms

- Ad Valorem
- Administrative Review
- Appropriation
- Approved Assessing Unit
- Assessed Value
- Assessing Unit
- Assessment
- Assessment Roll
- Board of Assessment Review
- Equalization
- Equitable Right of Redemption
- Homestead
- In Rem
- Judicial Review
- Level of Assessment
- Lien
- Non-Homestead
- Reassessment
- Special Assessment
- Special Assessment Districts
- Statutory Right of Redemption
- Tax Levy
- Tentative Assessment Roll
- True Tax

The Purpose of Taxation

Taxes and assessments go hand in hand with land ownership. Anyone who owns land can expect to have their property assessed and then pay taxes on the assessed value. Tax rates in New York State vary depending on the city, town, or county in which the land is located.

Real property tax is an **ad valorem tax**, which refers to *taxes based on the assessed value of property*. This means two owners of real property of equal value should pay the same amount in property taxes. Or, the owner of more valuable property should pay more in taxes than the owner of less valuable property.

Why Tax Property?

The reasons local governments choose to impose real property taxes rather than raise the sales and/or income tax include:

- Property taxes are relatively **easy to administer** because they are imposed on a known, stable tax base.
- Property taxes are **predictable** – municipalities can count on a steady stream of income from the time a property is assessed until it is reassessed.
- Property taxes are somewhat **protected** in slow economies when compared to other types of taxes.
- Property taxes do not distinguish between resident and nonresident home and business owners – all land is taxed whether it is owned by resident or not, so **no one is missed** in the process.
- Property taxes are the one **identifiable local revenue source** for municipalities and schools, which makes local government directly accountable for executing operations and programs in a cost-effective manner.

You do not have to be an expert at calculating taxes and understanding assessments. You should, however, be able to direct clients when they have questions you are not qualified to answer. In the case of taxes and assessments, the municipality's tax assessor and office of receiver of taxes are the best places to start.

New York Property Tax Administration

The money earned through the taxes pays for municipal services. Funding schools, maintaining roads, paying for police and fire protection, and covering the expense of other services and amenities residents benefit from are all examples of how real property taxes are used. Several entities raise money through real property taxes, including:

- Counties.
- Cities.
- Towns.
- Villages.
- School districts.
- Special assessment districts.

Property taxes in New York State are administered *locally* to finance local governments and public schools. In fact, real property taxes are the largest single revenue source for the support of municipal and school district services and more than $26 billion is raised in local property taxes across the state annually. The state does *not* collect or receive any direct benefit from real property taxes.

Who Pays Property Taxes?

All real property may be subject to property taxes. That includes the land itself and any improvements on the land, including houses, factories, barns, stores, apartments, hotels, restaurants, office buildings, etc. It does not matter if it's a small cabin or a large industrial park; nearly every property owner is responsible for paying taxes on her property.

Exemptions

Some entities, organizations, and even individuals are exempt from all or part of property taxes. Property tax exemptions fall into two categories – complete and partial. Tax exemptions are commonly given to:

- Colleges and universities.
- Schools.
- Parks.
- State governments.
- Federal governments.
- Religious organizations.
- Hospitals.

In order to be granted complete tax exemptions, a *property must be used for tax-exempt purposes*. If it is not being used in this capacity, the land is subject to tax.

Partial Exemptions

In the State of New York, some others may be granted partial exemptions for property tax if they meet the qualification standards for their specific taxing authority. Examples include:

Disabled. In New York, local governments and public school districts have the authority to grant a reduction in property taxes to qualifying persons with disabilities. To qualify, one must be able to produce documented evidence of their disability. In addition, there is generally a minimum income necessary to qualify for an exemption, and possibly other criteria as identified by the taxing authority.

Veterans. Qualified veterans may receive a partial exemption on the value of a primary residence, excluding cooperatives. Those who served in combat are eligible for an *additional* exemption. The exemption, which renews automatically each year, applies to general municipal taxes, not school taxes.

Elderly. Homeowners who are 65 or older with modest incomes may be eligible for a partial exemption from property taxes on their primary residence. Depending on income levels, exemptions can range from 10% to 50%. Application is made through local village, town, or city assessors' offices and must be renewed yearly. This special tax treatment is known officially by the title Senior Citizens' Exemption and is an option that only towns, counties, and school districts may adopt.

Farmers. In specific agricultural areas, exemptions may be offered to encourage the continuation of agricultural uses. Farmers may claim exemption from school taxes for part, or all, of their acreage.

Gold Star Parents. Parents who have lost a child in combat may be eligible for a partial exemption on their property taxes.

STAR Program Homeowners. All homeowners in the State of New York are entitled to school tax relief (STAR), which permanently reduces school taxes on a primary residence. Enhanced STAR programs are available to elderly homeowners who meet certain income requirements. The STAR exemption applies *only* to school district taxes. It does not apply to county, city, town, or other municipal taxes unless the schools are funded through those municipal property taxes.

If questions arise regarding whether a client is eligible for an exemption or partial exemption, contact the tax assessor's office in the area where the property is located. Licensees must also be mindful when telling potential buyers the tax amounts on any given property. You will want to give them the **true tax**, which is *the amount that would be paid before any exemptions held by the present owner are subtracted*. This is because the new owner may not qualify for the same exemptions.

Special Assessments

Special assessment districts are *geographic areas designated to pay for infrastructure costs for a specific project*. Likely projects include the addition or repair of items, such as:

- Sidewalks.
- Ornamental street lighting.
- Curbs.
- Driveway approaches.
- Traffic lights.
- Boulevard landscaping.

Property owners or local governments identify possible projects and follow a protocol to get them approved. The projects involve **special assessment taxes**, which are *taxes or levies against real property for improvements*. Special assessments are not imposed on all residents of a community, but only to the owners of the properties who will benefit from the improvement.

After a project is proposed, hearings are held and notices are given to the owners whose property is affected. An ordinance may be adopted that outlines the project, including its nature and benefits, how much it is expected to cost, and a description of the area that will be specially assessed. The special assessment is then spread among the parcels of land that will benefit from the improvement. Special assessments often vary because not all parcels of land will benefit equally.

Property Assessment

Unlike income taxes and sales taxes, property taxes do not depend on how much money a person earns or spends; instead, property taxes depend solely on how much the property is worth. **Market value** – the price most people would pay for the property in its current condition – is used as the basis for property assessments.

The Tax Assessor's Role

A **tax assessor** is a *local government official who estimates the value of real property within a city, town, or village's boundaries*. The property within these boundaries is known as an **assessing unit**.

The tax assessor's job is to assess every parcel of land within her assessing unit. Like an appraiser, a tax assessor estimates the market value of property, but not with the expectation of the property being sold, of course. An assessor needs that value so that she can **proportion the tax burden** over all the property owners in her jurisdiction so that each pays a fair share of the total tax amount.

Assessed Value

Once an assessor arrives at a determination of market value for a property, that value is converted to the assessed value, or assessment. An **assessment** *is a government's valuation of property for tax purposes*. And, a property's **assessed value** is *the value placed on land and buildings by a city, town, or county assessor for use in levying annual real estate taxes*. It is a percentage of a property's market value.

Once an assessor estimates the market value of a property, the total assessment is calculated by multiplying the market value by the **uniform percentage** for the assessing unit. So, if a property is determined to have a market value of $200,000 and the uniform assessment rate for that municipality is 20%, the property would be assessed at $40,000. If the landowner is not entitled to any exemptions, this property's taxable assessed value is $40,000. It is crucial to note this is *not* the tax bill. The tax bill depends on the tax rate for the municipality.

While the state does not require municipalities to assess at 100% of market value, it does provide an incentive to local assessing units who assess at 100% market value by making them eligible to be *certified by the State Board of Real Property Services* as **approved assessing units** and receive state aid for each parcel of land in the assessing unit.

Exception to Uniform Percentage of Market Value

According to New York State law, all property within an assessing unit must be assessed at the same uniform percentage of market value. In New York City and Nassau County, however, class assessing (assessing based on property type) is allowed.

Assessor Property Records

The tax assessor maintains property records for every property in her jurisdiction that includes information such as:

- Lot size.
- Square footage of the structure(s).
- Property features, such as number of bedrooms, baths, type of heat, etc.
- Condition of the property.

Every year, assessors must update the records of any property that has been sold or that has changed in some way. Where does an assessor get the information for the property records? They look at building permits, examine deeds and surveys, and utilize data collectors to make actual visits to the property. Sometimes an assessor has no choice but to observe the outside and guess about the inside of a property, because a property owner is *not* obligated to let an assessor inside to inspect.

Assessment Rolls

Assessors gather all the information and assess each property in their assessing unit to create annual assessment rolls. An **assessment roll** is *a public record that lists the assessed value of each property*. Every municipality sets a specific date for the following milestones:

- The assessor completes, certifies, and files a **tentative assessment roll** containing **level of assessment** (*the percentage at which the properties are assessed relative to market value*) and the proposed assessed values for each property in the assessing unit. Any property owner whose assessment or tax status was changed will receive a notice.
- The public will have a certain amount of time in which to inspect the tentative assessment roll, concluding with **grievance day,** which is the day on which the local Board of Assessment Review hears complaints from property owners seeking reductions in their tentative assessments.
- The assessor signs and files a **final assessment roll** that contains the final assessments, including all changes.

Annual Reassessments

Assessments change because of new construction, fires, additions or improvements, demolition, and periodic community-wide assessment updates necessary to maintain an equitable assessment roll. These *new assessments* are known as **re-evaluations**.

Real property is assessed annually in New York. In order for properties to be assessed at a uniform percentage of current market value every year, assessments must be reviewed and adjusted when necessary. To accomplish this, an assessor analyzes and evaluates the market and then revises assessments each year to maintain current market value.

New Construction

In New York, assessors are required to add value to the property with new construction that increases the value of the property. When value for new construction is added, the taxable value of the remainder of the property does not change; the value of the new construction is simply added.

Typically, building permits are required to construct new buildings and renovate or alter existing buildings on a parcel of land. Assessors are notified of new construction or changes to structures when they receive a copy of the submitted building permit, and inspect the property prior to the tentative assessment roll deadline to determine its status as of that date. At that time, the assessor updates the information in the property records, evaluates the cost of the improvements, and upgrades the assessment accordingly.

New construction not fit for occupancy at the time of annual reassessments is assessed at a value reflecting the percentage of completion as of the reassessment date. Once the new construction is complete, it is assessed at its full value beginning the month following completion.

Undeclared Improvements

While not all improvements to property are assessable, it is possible that significant improvements could be made to a property and then go undiscovered for several months, or even years. This usually happens when the owner does not obtain a permit for the work and the municipality has no idea it occurred. If in the course of annual reassessments the improvements are discovered, the assessor will adjust the assessment accordingly and the new rate will be applied going forward. Property owners are not typically responsible for the back taxes the improvements may have added to the value of the home. However, the assessor's office may notify code enforcement officers that an improvement may have been constructed without a building permit. In some cases, fines are then issued against the property owner.

Selective Reassessment

Selective reassessment occurs when a municipality is not in the midst of a municipal-wide reassessment, yet specific parcels, various portions of an assessing unit, or certain types of property are reassessed without regard to the relative uniformity of assessments within the municipality.

Selective reassessment is a violation of the Equal Protection Clauses of the United States Constitution and New York State Constitution. Unless there is a planned re-evaluation, or a comprehensive plan to review the assessments of all the parcels in an assessing unit, selective reassessment is *illegal.*

Tax Rates

A municipality's tax rate is not an arbitrary number – many factors go into determining the rate. Tax rates are a direct result of the **tax levy**, *which is the formal action taken to impose the tax*. There are several steps involved in establishing the tax levy. Taxing jurisdictions must:

1. Develop and adopt a budget.
2. Evaluate the revenue from all sources other than property taxes (state aid, sales tax, user fees, etc.).
3. Subtract the revenues from the original budget.

After completing these steps, the number that remains is the tax levy. And it is the amount of the tax levy that is raised through the property tax. Before a tax levy can be introduced to the community at large, **appropriation** occurs, which *authorizes the expenditure of funds and provides for the sources of the money.*

Determining Tax Rates

Tax rates are calculated by *dividing the total amount of money raised from the tax levy by the taxable assessed value of taxable real property* in a municipality. In the State of New York, taxes are expressed in dollars per hundred dollars.

CASE IN POINT

Let's say Township ABC has a $2 million tax levy and a total taxable assessed value of $40 million, which is the sum of the assessments of all taxable properties:

Total Tax Levy ÷ Total Assessed Value = Tax Rate

$2 million ÷ $40 million = 0.050

The tax rate, then, for Township ABC would be $5 for each $100 of taxable assessed value. To figure the actual tax owed for a home in Township ABC assessed at $40,000:

(Home's Assessed Value ÷ 100) x Tax Rate = Tax Owed

($40,000 ÷ 100) x $5 = $2,000

Sample Tax Assessment Roll Key

A. SWIS (State Wide Information System): A six-digit number assigned by the State as a unique identifier for every municipality in the state. The first two digits define the county, the second two the city or town, and the last pair the village, if any.

B. Uniform Percentage of Market Value: New York State law requires that all properties in a municipality be assessed at the same percentage of market value. In this case, 95% means that the municipality is assessing property at 95% of market value.

C. Valuation Date: In each municipality, property is assessed based on what its market value would have been on this date, given its condition on the taxable status date. In most towns, Valuation Date is July 1 of the year prior to the roll. (Confirm the date in your municipality with your assessor.)

D. Taxable Status Date: The assessment reflects the ownership and physical condition of the property as of this date. In addition, most exemption applications must be filed with the assessor by this date. In most towns, Taxable Status Date is March 1 of the year in which the roll is filed. (Please confirm the date in your municipality with your assessor.)

E. Tax Map Parcel Identification Number: (Also known as the Section-Block-Lot or SBL.) This number will match the number on the tax bill, and is used when applying for exemptions and assessment review.

F. Property Location & Class: The code identifies the parcel's category (i.e., 210 falls within the 200 range, indicating a one-family residence):

100's = agricultural

200's = residential

300's = vacant

400's = commercial

500's = recreation / entertainment

600's = community service

700's = industrial

800's = public services

900's = wild / forested / conservation lands / public parks

School District: The parcel's school district and school district code.

Parcel Size: The parcel's frontal and depth dimensions.

Grid Coordinates: The parcel's identification by geographical coordinates, used for mapping purposes.

Deed Book: The volume number of the book (liber) and page number where deeds are recorded.

G. Land Assessment: The assessed value of the land without the addition of improvements (permanent structures). By law, only the total assessment **(H)** may be reviewed or (grieved).

H. Total Assessment: The total assessed value of the property, including the land and improvements.

I. Full Market Value: What a willing buyer would pay a willing seller under normal circumstances. This should approximate the dollar amount for which the property could be sold. In places where the uniform percent of market value is 100%, this is the same as the assessed value; otherwise market value multiplied by the uniform percentage of value **(B)** will be the total assessed value **(H)**.

J. Exemption: The name of the exemption and the exemption code (in this case Basic STAR 41854), followed by the amount of the exemption for each taxing jurisdiction (i.e., STAR B is the Basic STAR exemption and applies only to school tax, thus the taxable value of the exemption for county and city is zero).

K. Tax Description: Taxing jurisdictions include counties, cities, towns, school districts, villages and special districts (fire, sewer, water, etc.).

Taxable Value: The value, after exemptions are applied, upon which your tax bill will be calculated (**H** minus **J** = **K**). In this case, the school taxable value is different from the others due to the STAR exemption.

L. Assessor's Oath: This is only listed on the last page of the roll. The assessor signs the roll to indicate that all assessments are uniform at the stated percentage of market value.

A Closer Look at the Tentative Assessment Roll

STATE OF NEW YORK
COUNTY - Big County
CITY - Anywhere
SWIS - 999999 **A**

2 0 0 6 TENTATIVE ASSESSMENT ROLL
TAXABLE SECTION OF THE ROLL - 1

UNIFORM PERCENTAGE OF VALUE IS 95% **B**

C VALUATION DATE - JULY 1, 2005

D TAXABLE STATUS DATE - MAR 01, 2006

TAX MAP PARCEL NUMBER / CURRENT OWNERS NAME / CURRENT OWNERS ADDRESS	PROPERTY LOCATION & CLASS / SCHOOL DISTRICT / PARCEL SIZE/GRID COORD	ASSESSMENT LAND / TOTAL	EXEMPTION CODE / TAX DESCRIPTION / SPECIAL DISTRICTS		-------------COUNTY--------- TAXABLE VALUE	CITY----- ACCOUNT NO.	SCHOOL
**********						57.63-2-79	**********
57.63-2-79 **E**	3 Main St **F**		STAR B	41854	0	0	30,000 **J**
Archer, John	210 1 Family Res						
Acher, Louise	School 111111	5,000 **G**					
3 Main St	FRNT 60.00 DPTH 93.50		COUNTY	TAXABLE VALUE	145,400		
Anywhere, NY 00000	EAST-0647310 NRTH-0966910	145,400 **H**	CITY	TAXABLE VALUE	145,400		
	DEED BOOK 2509 PG-260		SCHOOL	TAXABLE VALUE	115,400 **K**		
	FULL MARKET VALUE	153,053 **I**					
**********						57.63-2-78	**********
	5 Main St						
57.63-2-78	210 1 Family Res		VETERANS	41121	17,357	17,357	0
Baker Janice	School 111111	3,700	STAR E	41834	0	0	50,000
5 Main St	FRNT 45.00 DPTH 113.00	115,700					
Anywhere, NY 00000	EAST-0647290 NRTH-0966860		COUNTY	TAXABLE VALUE	98,343		
	DEED BOOK 2605 PG-355		CITY	TAXABLE VALUE	98,343		
	FULL MARKET VALUE	121,789	SCHOOL	TAXABLE VALUE	65,700		
**********						57.63-2-77	**********
	7 Main St						
57.63-2-77	421 Restaurant						
Cook, Ima	School 111111	2,660					
310 George Street	FRNT 75.00 DPTH 113.00	129,900	COUNTY	TAXABLE VALUE	129,900		
Somewhere, CA 55555	EAST-0647290 NRTH-0966800		CITY	TAXABLE VALUE	129,900		
	DEED BOOK 2670 PG-640		SCHOOL	TAXABLE VALUE	129,900		
	FULL MARKET VALUE	136,737					

L I, the undersigned, do depose and swear that, to the best of my knowledge and belief, I have set forth in the tentative assessment roll attached hereto or filed herewith all the real property situated in the assessing unit in which I am assessor and, with the exception of assessments made by the State Board of Real Property Services, I have estimated the value of such real property at the sums which I have determined to be in accordance with the provisions of section three hundred five of the Real Property Tax Law. ______________

Source: New York State Office of Real Property Services

Homestead and Non-Homestead Property

The Homestead Tax Option allows approved assessing units to apply separate tax rates to different categories of property:

- **Homestead** properties are *dwellings of four or fewer units, owner-occupied mobile homes, residential condominiums, farms, and vacant land suitable for qualified buildings*.
- **Non-homestead** properties *consist of industrial and commercial parcels and most vacant land.*

The Homestead Tax Option is locally established and administered, and prevents a large shift of the property tax burden to residential property owners after reassessments occur.

Equalization

The New York State Office of Real Property Services (ORPS) is obligated by law to administer an equalization program to ensure equitable property tax allocation among all the taxing jurisdictions in New York. **Equalization** *attempts to measure the relationship of locally assessed values to a fluid real estate market*. The only instances where equalization does not apply are when full-value assessments are conducted.

For example, consider Town A and Town B, which share School District XYZ. This school district needs to raise $1 million through property taxes. Since both towns have a total assessed value of $10 million each, one might think that the tax burden could simply be shared equally. But if the assessors for each town used a different level of assessment, there must be a way to distribute taxes equally based on the *market value* of each town.

An equalization rate is the state's measure of a municipality's **level of assessment** (LOA). To find this, ORPS first analyzes the level of assessment that is published by each assessor, and if they find the LOA meets appropriate standards, the assessor's LOA becomes that jurisdiction's equalization rate. If ORPS cannot confirm or accept the assessor's LOA, they then calculate an equalization rate based on property sales. Once the equalization for every specific assessing unit is established, the state can then estimate the total market value of the entire taxing jurisdiction.

CASE IN POINT

Both Town A and Town B have an assessed value of $10 million.

- Town A has an equalization rate of 33.33, which means its total market value is $30 million (10 / .3333 = 30).
- Town B has an equalization rate of 50.0, which means its total market value is $20 million (10 / .5 = 20).
- The total market value of both towns is $50 million ($30 million + $20 million).

Town A is responsible for 60% of the tax burden (30 / 50 = 60%), and Town B is responsible for 40% of the tax burden (20 / 50 = 40%).

Challenging an Assessment

If homeowners believe their property has been assessed incorrectly, they have the right to challenge the assessment. Taxpayers in New York have four grounds on which to challenge a tax assessment:

- **Excessive assessment**. The property's assessment exceeds its full market value or is excessive because of the denial of all or a portion of a partial exemption.
- **Unequal assessment**. The property is assessed at a higher percentage of its full market value than all other properties of the same class on the assessment roll.
- **Unlawful assessment**. The property is wholly exempt; is located entirely outside the boundaries of the taxing unit it is designated as being located in; has been assessed and entered on the assessment roll by a person or entity without authority to make the entry; and various other technical grounds.
- **Misclassified assessment**. The real property is misclassified. For example, in an approved assessing unit, a residential property is accidentally classified as an industrial property and so has a higher level of assessment.

The *amount* of a tax bill is *not* grounds for filing a grievance because the total tax bill depends on several factors, many of which assessors have no control over; the assessor merely establishes a value for the property.

Challenge Process

To challenge an assessment, a property owner should take the following steps:

1. **Meet with the assessor** to voice concerns and request adjustments. Homeowners should gain an understanding of the factors that went into the assessment.
2. If, after talking with the assessor, homeowners still disagree with the assessment, they may **file a complaint,** or grievance, with the local **Board of Assessment Review**, which *hears complaints and can lower or raise assessments based on the evidence provided.* This **administrative review** is a *prerequisite to a judicial review.* The complaint must be filed on or before the day the board meets to hear complaints. The assessment on the current **tentative assessment roll**, which is the *document containing each property assessment in the municipality* completed by the local assessor, is the only one that may be reviewed. Separate complaints must be filed for each assessed parcel in question in the city or town in which the property is located.

   Possible outcomes of an administrative review are: Full denial of claim, full reassessment of property, or partial reassessment of property.

3. Taxpayers who are still dissatisfied following an administrative review may seek a **judicial review** by commencing a *tax certiorari* (legal action challenging an assessment) in New York State Supreme Court or by filing for a Small Claims Assessment Review (SCAR), which is a municipal hearing.

   Either of the procedures, whether it is a tax certiorari proceeding in the Supreme Court or a SCAR, must be initiated within 30 days of the filing of the *final assessment roll* or notice of such filing, whichever is later. Failure to file complaints on time terminates the homeowner's right for administrative and judicial review of the current year's assessment. Additionally, the burden of proof in both arenas rests on the taxpayer – not the assessor.

Small Claims Assessment Reviews

A SCAR is an option only for owner-occupants of one-, two-, or three-family residences and owners of vacant land not large enough to accommodate a one-, two-, or three-family dwelling. Property owners must complete a petition for a hearing obtained from the county clerk's office.

In order to establish the market value of their property, owners can include the following information on the SCAR petition:

- Purchase price of the property, if recent
- Offering price of the property, if recently offered for sale
- Professional appraisal of the property
- Cost of construction or improvement, if recent
- Amount for which the property is insured
- Purchase price of comparable properties recently sold

Possible outcomes of a SCAR are the same as those of the Assessment Review Board: Full denial, full reassessment, or partial reassessment. The hearing officer may determine the final assessment to be the same as or less than the original assessment, but cannot reduce the assessment to an amount lower than what the property owner claimed on the petition.

If a taxpayer has exhausted his options and is still dissatisfied, he may continue to appeal by commencing an Article 78 proceeding in New York State Supreme Court.

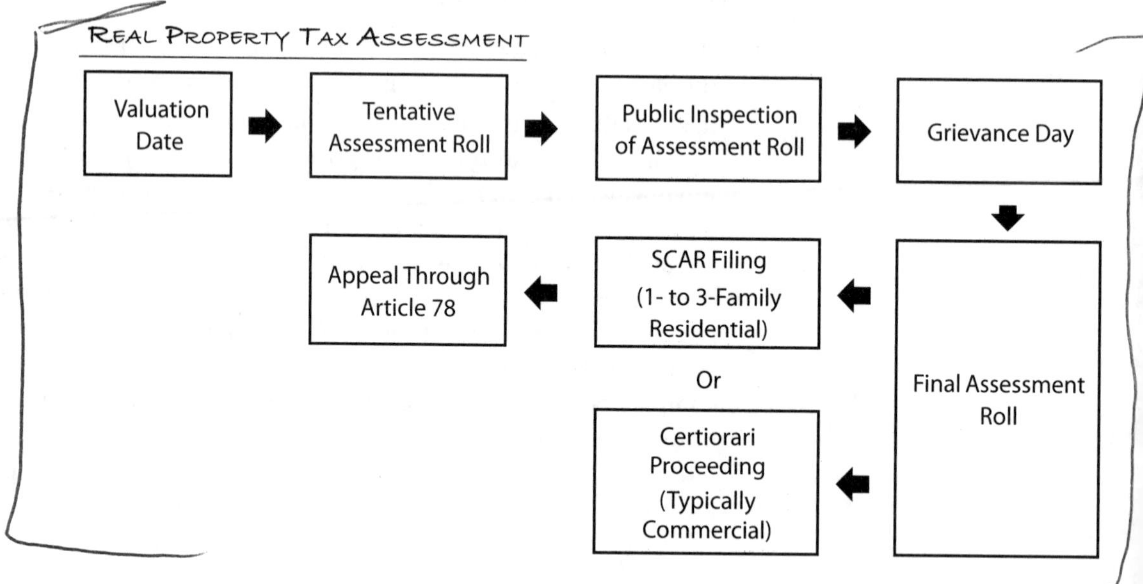

Disputes Involving Commercial Property

Commercial property owners in New York State may also take assessment disagreements to the Board of Assessment Review. The procedure used is the same one for residential property owners, including the four grounds on which to challenge a tax assessment.

Commercial property owners may *not* request a SCAR if they disagree with a property assessment. Rather, commercial property owners may seek judicial review by commencing a **tax certiorari** proceeding in New York State Supreme Court.

Tax Liens

It is generally common knowledge that local governments impose taxes on real estate to fund their many services and programs. Because real estate is permanently fixed and ownership is nearly impossible to hide, governments naturally assume they will be able to collect the tax money owed to them. Taxes are actually liens on property titles. A **lien** is *a nonpossessory interest in property, giving a lienholder the right to foreclose if the owner does not pay a debt owed to the lienholder.*

Enforcing Tax Liens

In order to be enforceable, the taxes creating the lien must be legitimate, which requires them to be properly levied, used for legal purposes, and equitably applied to all landowners. When landowners default on tax payments, the money owed can be collected through **tax foreclosures** or **tax sales**.

Property tax liens always have a higher priority over other previously recorded liens. This is why many mortgage lenders prefer to maintain an escrow account to cover property taxes. The lender is assured that the property taxes will be paid, thus keeping themselves in line as the first position in the priority of liens.

Tax Foreclosure

When a homeowner defaults on their property tax payments, the taxing authority may foreclose on the property. Tax foreclosures are similar to mortgage foreclosures. Many tax foreclosures are **in rem**, which are *lawsuits or legal actions directed toward property, rather than toward a particular person*. These are considered *specific liens*. In rem foreclosures are binding to all persons who claim title to the property.

In the case of property tax foreclosures, municipalities are the lienholders that go to court and subsequently take title to the property for which taxes are delinquent. The lienholder, or municipality, may keep the property or dispose of it by sale.

Tax Sales

Tax sales are comparable to sheriff's sales, which occur when a mortgagor defaults on his mortgage loan. After notice has been published, a tax collector conducts a tax sale.

Once the property is sold to the highest bidder at or in excess of the minimum bid, the proceeds are used to pay any back property taxes, then the cost of the foreclosure (appraisers, transfer tax, auctioneer, etc.), and then the lienholders in priority order. Any surplus funds go to the debtor.

The delinquent taxpayer *may* **redeem** *the property prior to the sale by paying the delinquent taxes plus interest as well as any penalties* associated with the delinquency. This is known as an **equitable right of redemption**.

New York State laws also grant a *period of redemption after a tax sale*, known as a **statutory right of redemption**, if the delinquent taxpayer pays the amount owed at the tax sale along with interest and penalties. No matter how the property is redeemed, once it has been sold, the delinquent taxpayer is usually free of any personal liability for the unpaid taxes. Each county establishes its own allowable period of redemption.

When working with clients, an agent will undoubtedly be asked, "How much will my house payment be?" Or, "What are the property taxes on this property?" Professionally answering either of these questions requires some knowledge of how property taxes are calculated and how land is assessed.

At a minimum, real estate licensees should be familiar with the following information to be able to respond to clients' questions. And for inquiries that go beyond their scope of knowledge, they should contact the office of assessment where the property in question is located.

Property Taxes	Property Assessment
✓ Contact information for local assessors and receivers of tax ✓ How to calculate real property tax ✓ The true tax on a particular parcel ✓ What exemptions are available ✓ Why mortgage payments increase if property taxes increase	✓ Contact information for local assessors ✓ The market value at which homes are assessed in the areas you work ✓ The assessment appeals process ✓ How new construction and improvements to existing structures are assessed ✓ How assessments may increase property values, thus increasing property taxes and mortgage payments

SUMMARY

1. In New York State, real property tax is an **ad valorem** tax, *based on the value of real property*. This means the owner of more valuable property should pay more in taxes than the owner of less valuable property.
2. Money earned through taxes pays for municipal services such as schools, road maintenance, police and fire protection, etc. Property taxes are raised **locally** by counties, cities, towns, villages, and school districts, but *not by the state*. Practically everyone who owns land is responsible for paying real property taxes.
3. **Special assessment districts** *are geographic areas designated to pay for infrastructure costs for a specific project*, such as sidewalks, curbs, traffic lights, etc. Special assessments are imposed on only those who will benefit from the improvements.
4. **Tax exemptions** are commonly given to certain entities, organizations, and individuals. Veterans, the elderly, farmers, homeowners, religious organizations, government entities, hospitals, and colleges are among those who typically receive partial, or even full, property tax exemptions.
5. **Tax assessors** *are local government officials who estimate the value of real property within a city, town, or village's boundaries* (an assessing unit). The market value is converted to an assessment, which is one component in the calculation of real property taxes. New York State law obligates assessors to maintain assessments at a uniform percentage of market value each year. The uniform percentage can be any percentage not exceeding 100%.
6. A property's **assessed value** is the *value placed on land and building by a city, town, or county assessor for use in levying annual real estate taxes*. Once an assessor estimates the market value of a property, the assessed value is calculated by multiplying the market value by the uniform percentage for the municipality.
7. **Reassessments** *occur annually and when new construction, additions or other improvements, fires, and demolition happen*. The benefits of annual assessments include: The elimination of uncertainty in tax rate changes due to equalization, stable tax rates, better communication between

local governments and taxpayers, and equal distribution of property taxes. Annual reassessments do not mean a landowner's assessment will change each year.

8. **Selective reassessment** *is when a municipality is not in the midst of a municipal-wide reassessment, yet specific parcels, various portions of an assessing unit, or certain types of property are reassessed without regard to the relative uniformity of assessments within the municipality*. Selective reassessment is a violation of the Equal Protection Clause of the federal and New York State constitutions.

9. An assessing unit's tax rate is a direct result of a **tax levy**. Among the steps involved in establishing a tax levy are: Developing and adopting a budget, evaluating the revenue from all sources other than property taxes, subtracting the revenues from the original budget, and appropriating the funds. **Tax rates** are calculated by dividing the total amount of money raised from the tax levy by the taxable assessed value of taxable real estate in the assessing unit.

10. In New York, separate tax rates may be applied to homestead and non-homestead property. **Homestead property** is a *dwelling of four or fewer units, owner-occupied mobile homes, residential condominiums, farms, and vacant land suitable for qualified buildings*. **Non-homestead property** *consists of industrial and commercial parcels and most vacant land*. The Homestead Tax Option is locally established and administered and prevents a large shift of the property tax burden to residential property owners after reassessments occur.

11. **Equalization** *attempts to measure the relationship of locally assessed values to a fluid real estate market*. The New York State Office of Real Property Services (ORPS) is obligated by law to administer an **equalization program** in order *to ensure equitable property tax allocation among all taxing jurisdictions in New York*. Equalization does not apply when full-value (100%) assessments are conducted.

12. If landowners believe their property has been assessed incorrectly, they should first discuss it with the assessor. Taxpayers in New York have four grounds on which to challenge a tax assessment: 1. Excessive assessment, 2. Unequal assessment, 3. Unlawful assessment, and 4. Misclassified assessment.

13. The first step in the complaint process is to examine the tentative assessment roll then file a complaint to be heard by the board of assessment review on **grievance day.** After final assessment rolls are produced, there are two types of review for property assessment disputes – **administrative** and **judicial**. Complainants must file an administrative dispute before they can file a judicial dispute. Judicial disputes include Small Claims Assessment Review (SCAR) hearings and tax certiorari proceedings in New York State Supreme Court. Commercial landowners cannot file a SCAR.

14. Taxes are actually **liens** on property titles and *always have a higher priority over previously recorded liens*. When landowners default on tax payments, the money owed can be collected through tax foreclosures or tax sales. **Tax foreclosures** are similar to mortgage foreclosures. Many are **in rem**, meaning they are *lawsuits or legal actions directed toward property, rather than toward a particular person*. Municipalities in foreclosure cases are the lienholders who go to court and subsequently take title to the property for which taxes are delinquent. **Tax sales** are comparable to sheriff's sales. Purchasers in tax sales must pay, at least, the delinquent tax and penalties associated with the delinquency.

16-A

Income Tax Issues in Real Estate

In This Session

Home ownership comes with many benefits, including tax deductions. This session provides an overview of taxation issues related to real estate. You'll learn about the classifications of income as defined by the Internal Revenue Service (IRS) and see how various tax deductions are handled.

You'll learn:

- The tax benefits and deductions available to real estate owners.
- How capital gains and losses are calculated.
- The tax breaks available to property owners, such as like-kind exchanges.
- How property is depreciated.
- The advantages of investment properties, including low-income housing.

Key Terms

- Active Income
- Adjusted Basis
- Appreciation
- Basis
- Boot
- Capital Gain
- Capital Loss
- Depreciation
- Home Acquisition Debt
- Home Equity Debt
- Passive Income
- Portfolio Income
- Recaptured Depreciation
- Straight-Line Depreciation
- Tax-Deferred Exchange

Tax Benefits of Home Ownership

While most will agree that buying property can be exciting, knowing there are excellent tax advantages that go along with home ownership makes it even better. There are several provisions written into the tax code to encourage home ownership:

- **Paid property taxes** are deductible if deductions are itemized.
- **Interest paid on a mortgage** is deductible.
- **Interest paid on home equity loans** used to improve property is deductible.
- Individual Retirement Account (IRA) funds can be tapped to help purchase a first home without any tax consequences. The Internal Revenue Code allows $10,000 toward the purchase without having to pay income taxes or early withdrawal penalties.

Tax Benefits of Owning a Second Home

Property taxes and mortgage interest on a second home are also deductible. As long as the home is not rented for more than 14 days during the year, any rental income can be excluded and taxes and interest can be deducted.

Many New York homeowners rent their homes to tourists, and the rental income may be tax-free. The situation becomes complicated if the home is rented for 15 days or more throughout a single year. If the property is rented for 15 days or more, the income is taxable and expenses are deductible, but they are allocated between the number of days for personal use and the number of days for rental use.

Sale of a Principal Residence

It is probably no surprise that taxes come into play during the sale of a principal residence. Losses on the sale of a personal residence are not realized since it is a personal asset. However, gains from the sale are normally taxable. **The Taxpayer Relief Act of 1997** created a provision for this with **Section 121** of the Internal Revenue Code. Section 121 provides some relief to taxpayers by exempting most, if not all, of the gain.

Section 121 Conditions

Specific conditions must be met for the rules of Section 121 to apply. For example, the taxpayer must have owned and used the property as a principal residence for at least **two of the last five years** prior to the date of sale. It does not have to be the principal residence on the date of sale.

Generally, the provisions of Section 121 of the Taxpayer Relief Act can be invoked only once every two years. There are special circumstances provided in the Code that allow the provisions, including:

- **Change in place of employment.** A change in employment can qualify taxpayers for the eligible moving expenses deduction, but there is a specific requirement. The location of the new place of employment must be at least 50 miles farther from the old residence than that residence was from the former job.

- **Health considerations.** In order for health exceptions to apply, reasons for the sale of the home must include obtaining a change in residence to provide for the diagnosis, cure, or treatment of a disease, illness, or injury; or to obtain or provide medical or personal care for someone suffering from a disease, illness, or injury. Some examples include:
  - Moving because a person is unable to care for herself.
  - Moving to a climate that will minimize the effects of a disease.
  - Moving closer to a recognized treatment facility.
- **Unforeseen circumstances.** Occasionally, circumstances arise that are beyond the taxpayer's control. The last set of provisions makes exceptions for these conditions. The most common are:
  - Involuntary conversion (eminent domain).
  - Disaster.
  - Death.
  - Cessation of employment.
  - Divorce.
  - Multiple births.

Exclusion Limits

There are limits on the total allowable exclusions under Section 121. The exclusion amount for:

- A single person is $250,000.
- A married couple filing joint tax returns is $500,000.

There are some additional requirements to be eligible for the $500,000 exclusion:

- One or both spouses must have owned and used the property as their primary residence for two of the last five years.
- Neither spouse has sold another principal residence within the last two years.

In the event of the death of a spouse, the maximum exclusion on the sale of a primary home by the unmarried surviving spouse is $500,000, as long as joint filing requirements were met prior to the death and the sale occurs no later than two years following the spouse's death.

Calculating the Realized Gain

The exclusion is applied to the realized gain, not the sale price of the property. To calculate the realized gain, you must subtract the **adjusted basis**, or *the original cost plus capital improvements*, from the amount realized, or *the sale price minus selling expenses*. Next, the Section 121 exclusion is subtracted from the realized gain.

The exclusion amount may seem extraordinarily large; however, lawmakers considered **appreciation,** or *the increase in value of an asset over time,* when they drafted the law. It prevents most people from an enormous tax burden simply because they have lived in a home for many years.

CASE IN POINT

Kent sold his primary residence for $325,000. His selling expenses were $22,000 (commission, fees, lawyer, etc.) so the amount realized ($303,000) represents the sale price minus selling expenses. His original investment in the home was $150,000. He renovated the kitchen for $14,000 (capital improvement), and so his adjusted basis is $164,000. Kent meets all the conditions for the Section 121 exclusion. What is Kent's recognized gain?

Amount Realized	**(Sales Price – Selling Expenses)**	$303,000
Adjusted Basis	**(Original Cost + Capital Improvements)**	($164,000)
Realized Gain		$139,000
Section 121 Exclusion		($250,000)
Recognized Gain		$ 0

Since the amount of the Section 121 exclusion is greater than the realized gain, there is no recognized gain for tax purposes. However, the excess amount is lost and cannot be rolled over into future transactions.

Partial Exemption

Although there are circumstances where the two-year rule could be waived, even under those conditions, only a portion of the exemption may be used. The exemption amount is multiplied by a fraction to determine the appropriate exemption amount.

The numerator of the fraction is the number of qualifying months and the denominator is 24 (number of months in the two-year period).

$$\frac{\textbf{Qualifying Months}}{\textbf{24}}$$

CASE IN POINT

Dave and Sarah moved to Knoxville in June 2006. They used the Section 121 provision to eliminate any gain on the sale of their home. They purchased a new home for $275,000. In October 2007, Sarah received a promotion and was required to relocate to Indianapolis. Due to a strong housing market, they were able to sell the home in Knoxville for $575,000. What, if any, gain must they recognize?

Step 1: Calculate the realized gain on the sale by subtracting the adjusted basis from the amount realized.

Amount Realized – Adjusted Basis = Gain
$575,000 – $275,000 = $300,000

Step 2: Calculate the amount of the Section 121 exclusion. Dave and Sarah were in the home 17 months, so the fraction is 17/24. Multiply this by the standard exclusion amount of $500,000.

$$\frac{17}{24} \times \$500{,}000 = \$354{,}167$$

The amount of the exclusion equals $354,167, which is more than the gain realized by Dave and Sarah. Therefore, they have no recognized gain for tax purposes.

Special Considerations

There are other factors and circumstances to consider when a primary residence is sold. If a taxpayer depreciates a portion of his home by converting it to a home office, he cannot apply the Section 121 exclusion to the depreciation – it must be recaptured as income upon the sale of the home.

The same applies if he uses the Section 121 exclusion on a rental or vacation home for which depreciation expenses were claimed in the past. **Recaptured depreciation** most commonly occurs on a *personal asset used for business purposes when that asset is sold*. Since a benefit from the asset has occurred in a prior period, taxpayers cannot benefit from the expense twice, and the *previous depreciation must be included as normal income when the asset is sold*.

By understanding the principles behind Section 121, real estate professionals can help clients avoid large tax bills, in addition to allowing them to move as their circumstances require. However, **clients should always be encouraged to consult with tax professionals for tax advice.**

IRS Rules on Acquisition and Financing

The federal government imposes rules on deductions related to the acquisition of a mortgage, home equity loans, home improvement loans, and construction financing.

Home Acquisition Debt

Home acquisition debt is *a mortgage a taxpayer takes out to buy, build, or substantially improve a qualified home*. The loan must be secured by the home. The amount of the mortgage used to calculate qualified interest is limited to the value of the home plus any substantial improvements.

Mortgage interest paid by any property owner in any given tax year is deductible up to certain limits. On home acquisition debt, owners may deduct interest on up to $1 million when the homeowners are married filing jointly ($500,000 if married filing separately). An amount over those limits may qualify as home equity debt.

Property owners may deduct mortgage interest on refinanced loans when replacing the previous loan with an amount equal to or less than the previous loan.

Points

Points, also called discount points, are a type of prepaid interest that mortgage borrowers can purchase to lower the amount of interest they will have to pay on subsequent payments. Each discount point is generally 1% of the total loan amount.

Points paid on a home loan may be fully tax deductible *in the year paid* if they meet all of the following IRS criteria:

1. The loan is secured by the homestead, defined as the home lived in most of the time.
2. Paying points is an established business practice in the area where the loan was made.

3. The points paid were not more than the points generally charged in that area.
4. The **cash method of accounting** is used. This means *income is reported in the year received and expenses are deducted in the year paid*. Most individuals use this method.
5. Points were not paid in place of amounts ordinarily stated separately on the settlement statement, such as appraisal fees, inspection fees, title fees, attorney fees, and property taxes.
6. The buyer paid the points at or before closing without using funds that were borrowed from a lender or mortgage broker.
7. The loan is used to buy or build a principal residence.
8. The points were computed as a percentage of the principal amount of the mortgage.
9. The amount is clearly shown on the Closing Disclosure as points charged for the mortgage. The points may be shown as paid from either the buyer's or seller's funds.

The points paid to **refinance** a mortgage *are not fully deductible* in the year paid. However, if part of the refinanced proceeds are used to improve the primary home and meet the first six criteria, those points can be deducted and the remainder can be deducted over the life of the loan.

Home Equity Debt

Home equity debt is *a loan that does not qualify as home acquisition debt and is secured by a qualified home*. The amount of home equity debt on which interest is deductible is limited to the smaller of $100,000 ($50,000 if married filing separately) or the home's fair market value reduced by the amount of home acquisition debt.

The purpose of the home equity loan is not considered to qualify the loan. Individuals often take out home equity loans to pay for tuition expenses, medical expenses, or high credit card balances. When the amounts meet the threshold amount, interest is fully deductible. Interest on credit card debt is *not* deductible.

Home Improvements and Construction Financing

After the first six IRS conditions are met, points and interest paid for financing home improvements and new construction are deductible. In the case of new construction, expenses incurred over a 24-month period are the only ones to qualify for the loan that generates deductible expenses.

Prepayment Penalties

Penalties are often imposed on homeowners who pay off mortgage loans early. These penalties can be deducted as home mortgage interest if they are not for a specific service performed or costs related to the mortgage loan.

Income Categories

To differentiate income for tax purposes, the IRS requires taxpayers to separate income into three broad categories:

1. Active income *is income received from services performed* and includes earnings from any of the following sources:

- Wages, salaries, commissions, bonuses, and other payments for services rendered

- Profit from a trade or business in which the taxpayer is an *active* participant
- Gain on the sale or disposition of assets used in an *active* trade or business
- Income from intangible property if the taxpayer played a significant role in the creation of the property

2. Portfolio income *includes earnings derived from the following activities:*

- Interest, dividends, annuities, and royalties not derived from the ordinary course of business
- Gain or loss from the disposition of property that produces portfolio income or is held for investment purposes

3. Passive income is defined in Section 469 as *earnings derived from the following activities*:

- Any trade, business, or income-producing activity in which the taxpayer does not materially participate (such as rental property or a limited partnership business)
- All rental activities, subject to certain exceptions:

  Exception 1: Real Estate Professionals

  Requires the taxpayer to be a real estate professional and meet the following criteria:

  - More than half of the personal services the taxpayer performs in trade or business are performed in real property trades or businesses in which the taxpayer materially participates.
  - The taxpayer performs more than 750 hours of service in these real property trades or businesses as a material participant.

  Exception 2: Operators of Small Rental Activities

  This exception is much broader and usually applies to those who operate smaller rental activities. With this exception, the taxpayer is *not* required to be a real estate professional.

  - The taxpayer may deduct up to $25,000 of losses related to real estate rental activities.
  - The deduction is phased out by 50% above an adjusted gross income (AGI) of $100,000 and is completely phased out when AGI reaches $150,000.
  - To qualify for the exception, a taxpayer must actively participate in the activity and must own 10% or more in value of all interests in the activity during the current tax period while the taxpayer was involved.

Generally, passive losses (such as loss from a rental property or limited partnership) can be used only to offset passive income. Any unused passive losses are carried forward to offset against future passive income. The one exception is when a taxpayer ceases to engage in the passive activity. At that point, all current losses and any losses carried forward may be used to offset active and portfolio income.

Capital Gains and Losses

A **capital asset** is something that is owned long-term. Examples are land, buildings, and machinery. Typically, we think of capital assets as items that appreciate over time. Financial investments can also be considered capital assets. Common capital assets are:

- Stocks and bonds.
- Real property (e.g., a home).

- Collectibles, such as paintings, coins, or rare antique cars.

According to the IRS, the major categories of non-capital assets are:

- Property held for resale in the normal course of business (inventory).
- Trade accounts.
- Notes receivable.
- Depreciable property.
- Real estate used in a trade or business (Section 1231 assets).

Capital gains and losses are generated when a capital asset is sold. A **capital gain** *is the profit made from an investment*. A **capital loss** *occurs when an investment decreases in value*. The change in value over time is inconsequential until a sale or exchange occurs. Capital gains and losses are categorized as **short-term** if held for 12 months or less, or **long-term** if held for more than 12 months.

Depreciation

Depreciation is the *recovery of the cost of a capital asset over time by expensing a set portion of it each year*. Depreciation, instead of expensing, is done to make expenses even over time. If depreciation was not used, a firm could expense the original cost of a new piece of equipment or office building all in one year, causing income to fluctuate greatly from one year to the next.

Straight-line depreciation assumes *an equal amount of an asset's price will be expensed each year of its useful life*. **Only the improvements on property held for business and investment purposes can be depreciated.** Land cannot be depreciated. For depreciation purposes, investment property is classified as either *residential rental* or *nonresidential.* These two classes use a modified straight-line depreciation method:

- *Residential rental* real property is depreciated over **27.5 years**.
- *Nonresidential (commercial)* real property is depreciated over **39 years**.

Any improvements to the two classes are depreciated using the *improvement's* useful life – not the real property's useful life (e.g., new carpeting has a useful life of five years and is depreciated separately using the rules for a five-year class asset).

It is important to note that while depreciation normally decreases the amount of expenses you can currently claim, you can deduct expenses over a longer period, especially when you might have higher income levels.

Depreciable Basis

Often, the amount depreciated is simply the amount paid for an asset. Occasionally, amounts may be added to, or deducted from, the asset's actual cost to determine its **depreciable basis**.

One major deduction to determine depreciable basis is the *value of land associated with property*. Because land is ***never*** depreciable, any property value attributable to the land *must be deducted from the price paid* to determine its depreciable basis. The assumption of debt causes the depreciable basis to increase above the cash paid for an asset.

Settlement costs, such as survey fees, title insurance, legal fees, and recording fees, are also included in the depreciable basis. Any improvements or impairments between the purchase date and the date the property is placed into service also create adjustments to the depreciable basis.

Like-Kind Exchanges

The Internal Revenue Code **Section 1031** allows a taxpayer to sell an investment property and purchase another investment property in its place **without paying taxes on the proceeds** from the sale. In essence, the taxpayer has more buying power in the second purchase because he can use the funds that otherwise would have been paid in taxes for part of his purchase. These types of transactions are called **like-kind exchanges**, and are nontaxable exchanges of property provided certain conditions are met:

1. The transaction must be an exchange and not a sale (i.e., actual property must be exchanged not solely for cash).
2. Transactions are structured as **tax-deferred exchanges**, or *exchanges where taxable gain is deferred until a later date.*
3. Property received and property transferred must be held either for use in a trade or business or for investment.
4. Properties must be similar or like-kind.

Personal-use property, inventory, partnership interests, and securities are *not* eligible for treatment under this section. A like-kind exchange is also known as a nonrecognition provision because the realized gain or loss usually never disappears; rather, it typically carries over into the new asset. If the taxpayer wishes to recognize a gain or loss, the transaction *must* be structured as a sale.

A **reverse exchange** is another way in which a taxpayer might defer tax. In a reverse exchange, the replacement property is acquired prior to transferring the relinquished property. A reverse like-kind exchange could be useful if a taxpayer has identified property that he wants, or if the seller of such property wants to close the sale quickly, but the taxpayer must wait before he can transfer the relinquished property.

Like-Kind Exceptions

Like-kind can be interpreted very broadly. Generally, any real property (realty) can be exchanged for any other real property, regardless of improvements. Personal property (chattel) can be exchanged for any other personal property. Three transactions *cannot* be treated as like-kind exchanges:

1. Livestock of different sexes
2. Personal property for real property (and vice versa)
3. Realty in the United States for realty in a foreign country

Restrictions and Time Limits

Another provision regarding exchanges applies to **related parties** (as defined under Section 267(b)). Related parties may conduct a like-kind exchange, but the property may not be disposed of for a period of **two years**. If the property is disposed of *prior* to the end of the two-year period, the postponed gain is recognized on the date of disposition.

A further restriction is placed on **depreciable tangible personal property**. These business assets must be within the same general business asset class to be treated as a like-kind exchange. Some typical business asset classes are:

- Office furniture.
- Computers and peripheral equipment.

- Airplanes.
- Automobiles and taxis.
- Light general-purpose trucks.
- Heavy general-purpose trucks.

A like-kind exchange of property can be either delayed or nonsimultaneous. However, there are **time limits** within which the exchange must be completed:

- The new property must be identified within **45 days** of the date of the exchange of the old property.
- The new property must be received **180 days** before the date when the old property was exchanged, or the due date for the tax return covering the tax year of the transfer.

Possible Taxable Realized Gain

Occasionally, *property that is not like-kind can be a part of a like-kind exchange to make up for a pricing disparity between the like-kind properties*; this *extra, non-like-kind property* is called **boot**.

To determine whether a gain must be realized, the entire transaction must be analyzed to determine if any gain occurs. Receiving boot will generally trigger a recognized gain in the amount of the lesser of the fair market value of the boot received or the realized gain.

Determining Basis

Basis is *the price paid for the property, including any expenses or gains*. When property is exchanged, the basis must be adjusted to reflect any postponed gain or loss. The traditional view of determining basis can be somewhat confusing even to trained professionals. Fortunately, the Code provides an alternative method for calculating the basis of property received.

Adjusted Basis of Surrendered Like-Kind Property

\+ Adjusted Basis of Boot Given
\+ Gain Recognized
\- Fair Market Value of Boot Received
\- Loss Recognized

Basis of Like-Kind Property Received

This approach uses the *recovery of capital doctrine* (any amount taxed in the exchange is added to the basis of the new property since that amount has already been taxed and should not be taxed in a future transaction). These amounts are the *recognized gains*. Any amount not taxed must be deducted, since the new owner has already received the benefit of deferring tax on those amounts. These amounts are the *recognized losses*.

The value of property should also reflect any amount given or received to make it of equivalent value to the exchanged property. This amount is related to the boot given or received. If the buyer transferred boot, then he, in essence, paid more for the property and his basis should increase. If he received boot, then he was compensated for a lesser-valued property and the amount should decrease the property's basis. In this case, the *basis of the property with the gains and losses from taxes and boot calculated into the figure* results in the **adjusted basis**.

Holding Period and Qualified Intermediaries

The **holding period** of new property includes the holding period of the old property. For example, if a client owned a property for five years, exchanged it, and held the new property for three years, the total holding period of the new property is eight years. The holding period for any boot received starts on the date of the exchange.

Assistance from a **qualified intermediary** is required for Section 1031 exchanges. The qualified intermediary is responsible for safeguarding the assets of each party throughout the exchange process, especially in the case of delayed exchanges. A qualified intermediary:

- Prepares the appropriate documentation.
- Receives, holds, and distributes funds related to the exchange.
- Advises or consults with participants to ensure compliance with all treasury regulations and rulings.

Qualified intermediaries are not required to be bonded, insured, licensed, audited, or regulated. Real estate professionals should help clients choose qualified intermediaries very carefully and advise them to do appropriate research before making a final decision on whom they choose.

Low-Income Housing Incentives

The federal government offers incentives for the development of low-income housing. Low-income housing is defined by the IRS as a project where at least 20% of the units have rents affordable to, and are occupied by, households with incomes no greater than 50% of the area's gross median income, or at least 40% of the units are affordable to, and occupied by, families with incomes no greater than 60% of the area's gross median income.

The major incentive to building and maintaining housing for low-income individuals and families is the **low-income housing tax credit (LIHTC)**, which provides a credit against tax liability (a dollar-for-dollar reduction in tax liability). These credits can be claimed as one of the leading sources of capital subsidies for the development of affordable rental housing.

Most projects, both new construction and rehabilitation, are eligible for a 9% tax credit equal to 9% of qualified costs each year for 10 years. Some projects financed through tax-exempt bonds may qualify for an automatic 4% tax credit. These credits are often sold to outside investors to raise capital for the project.

SUMMARY

1. There are several **tax deductions** available that provide *incentives to purchase a home.* Main deductions include mortgage and home equity loan interest, and property taxes. These deductions can also be counted on a second home or vacation property, provided the home is not rented for more than two weeks during a year.
2. The **Taxpayer Relief Act of 1997** provides an *exemption from capital gains taxes for the sale of a principal residence for those who qualify*. To qualify, the seller must have resided at the property for two of the last five years. This exemption can be claimed only once every two years, unless the seller has had a change in place of employment, health considerations, or unforeseen circumstances. A single person can exclude up to $250,000; a married couple filing jointly can exclude up to $500,000.
3. Mortgage interest paid by any property owner in a given tax year is deductible up to certain limits. Loans for reasons other than to buy, build, or substantially improve a home may qualify as **home equity debt**. Interest paid on home equity debt is also deductible up to certain limits. **Points** paid on a home loan may be fully deductible *in the year paid* if they meet all IRS criteria.
4. According to the IRS, there are three different types of income: **Passive**, **active**, and **portfolio**. The IRS permits certain expenses to be deducted from gross income, thereby exempting the expense from income tax. The **adjusted gross income (AGI)** is the *gross income minus allowable deductions*. The IRS taxes higher levels of income at a higher rate.
5. **Capital gains** and **losses** are *generated when a capital asset is sold*, and are categorized as *long-term* or *short-term* gains and losses, determined by how long an asset is held.
6. **Depreciation** is the recovery of the cost of a capital asset over time by expensing a set portion of it each year. **Straight-line depreciation** assumes an equal amount of an asset's price will be expensed each year of its useful life. **Only the improvements on property held for business and investment purposes can be depreciated.** Land cannot be depreciated. For depreciation purposes, investment property is classified as either residential rental or nonresidential. These two classes use a modified straight-line depreciation method: Residential rental real property is depreciated over **27.5 years**. Nonresidential (commercial) real property is depreciated over **39 years**.
7. One of the major deductions to determine **depreciable basis** is the *value of land associated with a property*. Land is ***never*** depreciable, so any property value attributable to land must be deducted from the price paid to determine its depreciable basis. The assumption of debt causes the depreciable basis to increase above the cash paid for an asset. Settlement costs are also included in the depreciable basis. Improvements or impairments between the purchase date and the date the property is placed into service will also create adjustments to the depreciable basis.
8. **Section 1031** of the IRS Code *allows similar properties to be exchanged without being taxed*. This is called a **like-kind exchange**. Personal property, inventory, partnership interests, and securities do not qualify, and must be sold. If the taxpayers wish to claim a gain or loss, the transaction must be a sale. There are other exceptions, restrictions, and time limitations imposed on like-kind exchanges.
9. The IRS provides certain **tax credits** for building and maintaining low-income housing. A *low-income housing project* must meet occupancy and rent requirements set by the IRS to qualify for credits.

17

Condominiums and Cooperatives

In This Session

In this session, you'll learn about what constitutes a condominium and the legal framework for its creation. You'll also see how condominiums differ from cooperatives and learn how a condop, a hybrid of the two, is created. Familiarizing yourself with the requirements for the purchase or sale of a condo or co-op, as well as the restrictions and benefits that go along with ownership, will help you to better assist your clients.

You'll learn:

- What a condominium is, how it is developed, and how it operates.
- Considerations with condominium purchase and ownership.
- Requirements for the sale and purchase of cooperatives.
- How condos and co-ops differ.
- How a condop is created.

Key Terms

- 80/20 Rule
- Alteration Agreement
- Assigning a Contract
- Board Package
- Bylaws
- Common Areas
- Condominium
- Condominium Act
- Condominium Declaration
- Condop
- Cooperative
- Cooperative Policy Statement #1 (CPS-1)
- Covenants, Conditions, and Restrictions (CC&Rs)
- Flip Tax
- Flipping
- Horizontal Property Acts
- House Rules
- Letter of Intent
- Limited Common Areas
- Maintenance Fees
- Offering Plan
- Proprietary Lease
- Recognition Agreement
- Right of First Refusal
- Share Loan
- Simultaneous Closing
- Sponsor

Condominiums

Condominiums, or condos, have become a common real estate ownership option. Some single, younger buyers want a condo to get established and build equity. Many empty nesters enjoy condo living since it offers freedom from lawn chores and home maintenance in a downsized, easy-to-manage living space. Condo living offers all of that and more, but condo ownership is different than residential home ownership in many ways.

A **condominium** is a *property developed for co-ownership, with each co-owner having a separate interest in an individual unit, combined with an undivided interest in the common areas.* Most condominiums are residential; however, they can also be commercial or retail, such as a multi-unit skyscraper or a community of buildings with three or four units.

Condos are considered *real property* and owners hold a fee simple deed to their individual condo unit. Condos are structured (physically and legally) to combine individual ownership with co-ownership. Condos are non-controlling and are considered separate entities because the interior space of each condo unit is owned individually. This differs from cooperatives, which are discussed later.

The other areas of the property are common areas. **Common areas**, also called common elements, are the *land and improvements in a condominium, planned unit development, or cooperative that all residents use and own as tenants in common,* such as the parking lot, hallways, and recreational facilities.

Some condominiums and co-ops also have **limited common areas** *owned* by all but *used* by only one owner. An example of a limited common area is a balcony that extends out into the air owned by all, but is actually used by only the unit owner. Designated parking spaces are another example of a limited common area. The word *designated* or *assigned* informs the owner that this space is exclusively for her use, even though all other unit owners own the land.

Maintenance fees (also referred to as common area expenses) are *monthly fees, paid by each condo owner or cooperative shareholder, for common area expenses* like utilities, management, building maintenance, and upkeep. Unpaid maintenance fees can result in a lien against a specific unit.

In the event of default on the mortgage, an individual owner's lender can place a lien against the specific unit and undivided interest in common areas. If a lien holder forecloses, only that unit and its undivided interest are affected, not the entire condominium. Property taxes are also levied against each unit separately and thus do not affect the whole property.

When a condominium unit is sold, an undivided interest in common areas and membership in the owners association are automatically transferred, too. Individual units cannot be sold without transferring interest in the common areas.

Condominium Development and Operation

Every state has passed laws that create the legal framework for creating a condominium form of ownership. Known collectively as **Horizontal Property Acts,** these *laws make it possible to define actual ownership rights.* This, in turn, makes it possible for lenders to provide mortgages on condominiums, and for tax authorities to assess property taxes, among other things.

Condominium Act (Article 9-B of the Real Property Law) is *New York State's law governing the establishment of condominiums*. Some stipulations include:

- Condo unit owners must comply with specific bylaws.

- Copies of bylaws and floor plans must be made available to unit owners.
- Information on the election of board manager and duties of the board (through the bylaws) must be made available.
- Information on expenses charged to unit owners must be communicated.

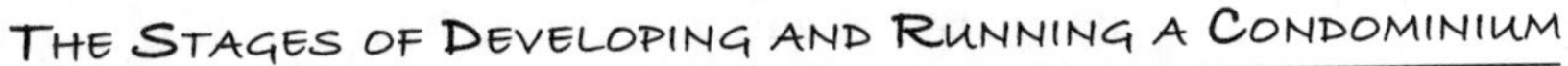

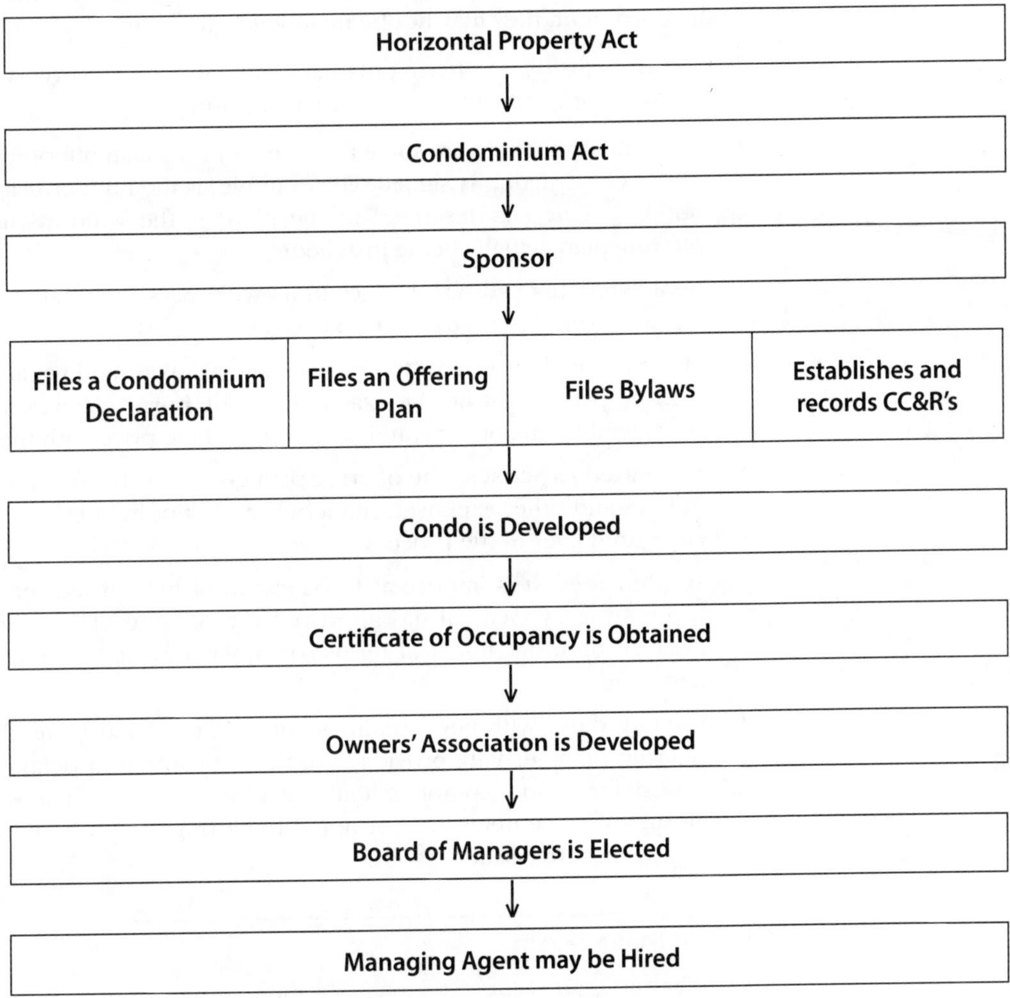

New Condo Development

Property can be developed as a condominium, or an existing building can be converted to a condominium. The **sponsor**, also known as the developer, is the *person, corporation, or other entity that is part of the sale and development of the condo or co-op property.* Sponsors (or developers) begin by filing a condominium declaration and an offering plan.

A **condominium declaration** is the *document that must be filed for record when a property is developed as, or converted to, a condominium*. The sponsor files the condominium declaration with the county auditor. The declaration describes the project in detail and includes a set of drawings showing the land and floor plans of the building(s).

An **offering plan,** *provided by the sponsor, offers detailed information regarding the condo or co-op property being developed.* According to the New York Attorney General's office, an offering plan must be developed and presented *before* a building is developed. Offering plans can be extensive documents containing information on floor plans, estimated expenses, building materials, etc.

Although it is often time consuming for real estate professionals and buyers to sort through offering plans, it is a necessary step before making an offer. Do not rely on word of mouth or advertising to explain the offering plan. If amenities are not listed in the document, they may not be included in the unit.

Important items on an offering plan are listed below; however, you should suggest that your client review the details with an attorney.

- **Special risks**. There are some risks a buyer runs if an offering plan for a building under construction is signed. For example, is the builder using the high-quality building materials described in the plan? Is the window model listed in the offering plan actually being installed?
- **Real estate tax validation**. Each unit owner pays real estate taxes separately and can write off the interest on his taxes.
- **Floor plans**. Due to construction variables, layout and square feet listed in the offering plan might not be exactly what the buyer receives. If the difference is considerable, the buyer could try to renegotiate price with the sponsor.
- **Estimated expenses**. The offering plan gives an estimated cost of items, such as utilities and other expenses, but a buyer will not have exact knowledge of these costs until later in the process.
- **Hidden fees**. It is important to be aware of hidden fees on the project. Even if the Attorney General has approved the offering plan, it does not mean the price of the unit, financial terms, or other aspects of the building have been approved.
- **Closing date**. With new buildings, move-in dates have a tendency to slide, and offering plans usually provide room for construction delays. Advise clients to note defects and incomplete items on a list during the final walk-through before closing. If these items are not noted in writing, it may be more difficult for the buyer to get the issues resolved.

THE MARTIN ACT

The Martin Act, Article 23 of the General Business Law, applies to the sale of condos and co-ops. It requires a full description of the property in the offering plan. The Attorney General's office regulates and reviews all plans.

Eviction and Non-Eviction Plans

When a sponsor converts a building into a condominium or cooperative, what happens to the tenants who currently rent and live in the building? Sponsors offer them either an eviction plan or non-eviction plan. Tenants have rights, and certain requirements must be met in order for a sponsor to move forward with a development plan. Eviction plans vary from building to building.

Eviction plan. If a sponsor files an eviction plan and an existing tenant chooses not to purchase, the tenant may be evicted after a specific period of time. According to the New York Attorney General:

> *For an eviction plan to be declared effective, 51 percent of the bona fide tenants in the occupancy (excluded from the calculation are eligible senior citizens and disabled tenants) of all the dwelling units on the date the Attorney General accepts the offering plan for filing, must sign purchase agreements.*

Non-Eviction plan. If a sponsor files a non-eviction plan, non-purchasing tenants may be able to continue renting the unit. According to the New York Attorney General:

> *For a non-eviction plan to be declared effective, at least 15 percent of the dwelling units must be sold to bona fide tenants or non-tenant purchasers who intend, or whose family members intend, to live in the unit. The percentage may include sales of vacant and occupied apartments. However, an outside purchaser of an occupied apartment may not evict the tenant living in the apartment. The tenant may continue in occupancy as a rent-stabilized or rent-controlled tenant, paying rent to the outside purchaser or the sponsor, who must provide all the services required under applicable laws.*

Bylaws and CC&Rs

Sponsors also record bylaws for the unit owners' association. **Bylaws** are the *rules and regulations that govern the activities of the condominium and cooperative associations.* These include the purpose of the building, rules for elections and voting, and frequency of board of directors or shareholders meetings. Bylaws also set the rules about when sponsors are required to turn over management of the condominium or co-op to board members. According to the Attorney General's regulations:

Sponsors promise in the offering plan they will give up control of the board of managers after they sell more than 50 percent of the common interest, or after five years have passed since the first closing, whichever comes first.

Condominium developers also establish and record a declaration of **covenants, conditions, and restrictions (CC&Rs),** which *create a general plan of private restrictions for a subdivision.* CC&Rs might stipulate that owners cannot paint their front doors certain colors, cannot install a satellite dish, can use only white holiday lights outside, or can have only a certain type of patio furniture. The purpose of CC&Rs is to keep the community attractive and uniform, and to protect its market value.

For a condominium development, CC&Rs dictate the rules unit owners and their guests are required to follow. CC&Rs are binding on all unit owners and are usually enforced by a condominium association. Penalties for violating the condominium's CC&Rs could include fines, lawsuits by the condo association, or forced compliance.

Cooperative Policy Statement #1

Cooperative Policy Statement #1, also referred to as **CPS-1**, is *applicable to cooperatives, condominiums, and homeowners associations and is used to test the market, explore the venture, and determine the needs to meet a variety of conditions*. Key conditions include:

- The sponsor files an *application to test the market* with the Real Estate Financing section of the New York State Attorney General's Office.

- Market testing begins only after the sponsor receives a letter from the Attorney General stating that the application to test the market has been granted, or oral notification of acceptance.
- No reservations, binding or non-binding, are accepted until an offering plan has been accepted for filing by the Attorney General.
- No deposits are accepted until an offering plan has been accepted for filing by the Attorney General.
- All advertisements and advertising literature used by the sponsor need to be cleared by the Attorney General before use. All advertisements and advertising literature should contain the Attorney General's CPS-1 legend and reference should be made to the Attorney General's CPS-1 advertising guidelines. Any proposed advertisement or advertising literature, which was not part of the sponsor's original application to test the market, should be submitted to the Attorney General at least 48 hours prior to needing the approval.
- The application to test the market is effective for 120 days after acceptance. The Attorney General may extend this period for an additional 60 days if an application of extension is filed, explaining why the test period was inadequate. This application should be made at least seven days before the 120-day expiration period.
- An application to test the market will not be granted if the sponsor has submitted an offering plan for filing with the Attorney General.

The CPS-1 also states that the application to test the market shall be accompanied by the following:

- A filing fee of $225, in the form of a check payable to the Department of Law
- A transmittal letter signed by the attorney who prepared the application and affirmed several things under penalty of perjury, including the street address, zip code, and that the attorney has no actual knowledge of a violation of Article 23-A of the General Business Law
- A true copy of the sponsor's deed, option, or contract, if any, to purchase land for the site
- A true copy of the mortgage commitment, if any, of a lending institution
- A copy of floor plans for the building (site plans should be included for homeowners associations)
- A completed statistical information card

Price Changes

It is not unusual for sponsors or developers to amend the original offering plan and raise prices on a condo or co-op as the building is constructed; however, a developer cannot change its offering plan on a whim. Offering plans in New York are highly regulated by the Attorney General's office and any amendments to an offering plan are also regulated.

There are a variety of reasons why sponsors or developers raise prices. Prices often begin increasing from the time the land is purchased to the time the units are ready for occupancy. Reasons for a price increase include:

- **Land and material costs**. Land prices as well as material and labor costs are always increasing, and developers need to offset those costs by raising prices on condo or co-op units.
- **Developer costs**. If there are a lot of front-end costs or financing is not secured until a certain number of units are sold, developers want to ensure sales of some

APPLICATION TO TEST THE MARKET

STATE OF NEW YORK)
: SS.:
COUNTY OF NEW YORK)

___________________________, being duly sworn deposes and says:

1. I am the ______________________ of the _____________________
(Office of Deponent) (Name of Sponsor)
Corporation (hereinafter called "Sponsor"), a domestic corporation with its office at _______ _________________. (If Sponsor is not a corporation set forth appropriate facts concerning the identity of Sponsor.)

2. Sponsor is the owner of (or, has entered into a contract, or has an option to purchase) a parcel of land consisting of __________acres located in the State of ________ _____, County of _________, being more particularly described as follows: (Insert description of exact location of land, including street address and zip code. If Sponsor has an option or contract to purchase add "Annexed hereto is a true copy of the option or contract to purchase the land".)

3. Sponsor intends to erect a housing development on said parcel of land to be owned cooperatively under the laws of the State of ______. (If a condominium, add "and to submit same to the provisions of the Condominium Laws of the State of __________.") Said project will consist of ____
Number and type of units, such as Garden Apartments,
_________________________________ apartments (units) to be located in ________
Townhouses, Attached or Detached, etc. (Number)
structures.

The project will include _____________ (set forth details concerning common elements, including parking spaces, swimming pool or other recreational area, roads, lawns, etc. and any other noteworthy features of the project including the status of construction).

4. The development is a new construction (or rehabilitation) project. If any portion of any building which is the subject of this application is currently occupied by tenants, or is expected to become occupied, so state.

5. Sponsor anticipates that an offering plan, if ultimately submitted for filing to the Attorney General of the State of New York, will be submitted pursuant to Title 13 NYCRR Part _________________________.
(Specify Part 20, 21, etc.)

7/96

Source: New York State Attorney General, Investor Protection Bureau

6. Sponsor has received a mortgage commitment of $_______from __________
___________________ to finance construction of the project. Annexed hereto is
(financing institution & address)
a true copy of such commitment. If such commitment has not been received, so state.

7. Sponsor has received a commitment of $_________ from ________________
_________________ for the granting of permanent mortgages to purchasers of
(financing institution & address)
units. Annexed hereto is a true copy of such commitment. If such commitment has not been received, so state. Alternatively, Sponsor has made a commitment of $__________for the granting of permanent mortgages to purchasers of units.

8. The estimated purchase price for each unit, the number of rooms in each unit, and the estimated monthly carrying costs (or maintenance) for each unit are as follows:

Unit Designation	Estimated Purchase Price	No. of Rooms	Estimated Monthly Maintenance Costs

9. Sponsor requests permission to solicit, for a period of 120 days, indications of interest in the above project. No cooperative interest in realty or condominium unit will be offered for sale and no reservations, binding or non-binding, will be made until an Offering Plan has been accepted for filing by the Attorney General of the State of New York. No deposits will be accepted by Sponsor until an Offering Plan has been accepted for filing.

10. Sponsor intends to solicit interest in the above project in the following manner:

____
(newspaper advertisement, brochure, etc.)

11. All advertisements and advertising literature utilized by Sponsor will comply with Cooperative Policy Statement No. 1 and with the Rules and Regulations of the Attorney General of the State of New York. No advertisements or advertising literature, including but not limited to classified advertisements and signs exhibited at the site, will be utilized by Sponsor unless first submitted to and cleared by the Attorney General of the State of New York. All such advertisements and advertising literature shall contain the Attorney General's Cooperative Policy Statement No. 1 legend.

12. Copies of all proposed advertisements and advertising literature to be utilized by Sponsor, including classified advertisements, signs exhibited at the site, questionnaires to be completed by prospective purchasers, and information cards to be completed by prospective purchasers, are annexed hereto.

13. Sponsor certifies that its assets, together with the proceeds of firmly committed construction financing, are or will be sufficient to meet Sponsor's unsecured obligations under an Offering Plan to complete all work and meet Sponsor's obligations for unsold units.
7/96

14. If Sponsor is not a resident of or was not incorporated or organized in the State of New York, add the following: "Sponsor hereby designates the Secretary of State as its agent to receive the service of process in any action or proceeding in connection with this application or the offering or sale of the aforementioned."

15. Sponsor will file with the Attorney General, on or by the 180th day following the granting of the Application To Test The Market, an affidavit stating the following: (i) if the property is located in New York, that Sponsor has accepted no purchase agreements prior to the acceptance for filing of an Offering Plan by the Attorney General; (ii) if the property is located outside the State of New York, that Sponsor has accepted no purchase agreements from New York residents prior to the acceptance for filing of an Offering Plan by the Attorney General.

WHEREFORE, Sponsor requests permission to test the market in the manner set forth above for a period of one hundred and twenty (120) days pursuant to Cooperative Policy Statement No. 1 of the Attorney General of the State of New York.

____
(Signature of Sponsor or Officer)

Sworn to before me this
day of , 200 .

____
NOTARY PUBLIC

7/96

of the units. Developers might offer incentives or a "first look" special preview as a way to attract buyers. A good preview or great incentives usually result in units sold. Therefore, developers might lower prices initially, and raise them later, once units start to sell.

- **Popularity drives demand**. Many factors drive the demand for a condo or co-op, including location, great views, and incredible amenities.

The price of a condo, just like the price of residential property, will always reflect what the market can bear. Different developers have different financing plans with banks and other partners backing their projects, making factors for raising prices inconsistent across the board. In general terms, a seller's market may bring higher prices for developers since there is high demand. In turn, a buyer's market may hurt developers since a glut of condos may be on the market.

Certificate of Occupancy

In New York, all buildings built *after* 1938 are required to have a permit, called a **certificate of occupancy**, which is issued to the builder or developer after all inspections have been made and the property is deemed fit for occupancy. This certificate describes the legal use and occupancy of the building.

According to New York's Uniform Fire Prevention and Building Code, a certificate of occupancy is required:

- For all work for which a building permit was required.
- Whenever the general occupancy classification for a building is changed.

In New York, a certificate of occupancy is issued by the Department of Buildings. To obtain a certificate of occupancy, the building's developer or representative contacts the department to schedule necessary inspections, including electrical, plumbing, construction, etc. A certificate of occupancy can be issued only after:

- The construction matches submitted plans.
- All applicable laws, ordinances, and regulations have been followed and approvals obtained.
- Necessary paperwork has been completed.
- Department fees have been paid.

There are two types of certificates of occupancy:

- A **final** certificate of occupancy
- A **temporary** certificate of occupancy (TCO)

Both types must be stamped "DOB Certified" to verify that they are an authentic Department of Buildings document.

Most transactions involving residential real estate, including condo development, have a clause in the contract of sale that stipulates property must be in compliance with the certificate of occupancy. The Department of Buildings has information on the status of individual properties with regard to certificates of occupancy.

Although there have been cases where developers were able to obtain mortgage financing without a final certificate of occupancy, it is not the norm, since it is a huge financial risk and poses other potential issues.

Appointment and Role of Board Managers

A condominium's owners' association is made up of all unit owners. The association's board members (known collectively as the board of directors or board of managers) are elected by association members and are responsible for following the condo's bylaws and making decisions on behalf of the condo owners. For example, a board of directors is responsible for the common areas of the condominium, including maintenance, repairs, utilities, taxes, and insurance. Some issues are referred back to the association as a whole for a vote.

The board of directors, through the power of the Condominium Act, has the power to levy assessments to pay for maintenance fees. If a unit owner fails to pay an assessment, a lien may be placed against the unit by recording a certificate of lien.

The board of directors usually does not handle the day-to-day duties of the condominium. Most properties have a **managing agent** who directly oversees building activities, manages building staff, and takes care of maintenance issues.

Purchasing a Condominium

The developer may ask a buyer to sign a letter of intent to purchase a condo unit. A **letter of intent** signifies *two or more parties agree to do business together*. It is a useful document as a transaction develops as it often includes a specific time frame and a set of agreeable terms for both parties. This letter will likely be required when a buyer wants to reserve a specific unit.

The buyer will probably put down an initial deposit as well, often as little as $1,000. The buyer now has the right of first refusal, and during this phase can terminate the agreement and still get the deposit back. If a buyer moves forward with the sale, she will sign a binding contract on the condo unit. A letter of intent is usually non-binding, but you should read the fine print to make sure.

- A **non-binding letter of intent** most likely *signifies the parties' intent to move forward with a transaction and is not meant to be enforceable*. These letters may include information on the closing date, purchase price, or other basic terms of the transaction. Just as the buyer is not obligated to purchase, the seller – which for a new condo is probably the developer – is not obligated to firm pricing yet. Again, read the fine print to be sure your buyer is not obligated to something that was not anticipated.
- A **binding contract** is *a valid contract that is enforceable*. These contracts often contain more details of the transaction, such as conditions that must be met prior to closing. They usually require a sizable deposit – often 20% of the purchase price. Binding contracts obligate parties to complete the transaction or face breaching the contract. Some contracts may allow a rescission period during which the buyer can withdraw from the contract without obligation.

When considering documents drafted by a developer, such as a letter of intent or a binding contract, potential buyers should consult with an attorney with experience in this area.

Financing Considerations

Lenders have **income parameters** for co-op and condo admission that include:

- Acceptable and non-acceptable income.
- Earnings-to-debt ratios.
- Loan-to-value ratios (LTV).

A lender looks at a variety of items on the loan application before deciding to make the loan, including **income and assets**. The types of income a lender typically considers before approving a loan include salary and commissions or bonuses. As long as applicants can prove it is permanent, other income can be counted.

Lenders also like to make sure potential buyers have assets that can be converted into cash. They want to be sure buyers have money for the down payment and closing costs and assets to guard against unexpected bills or a temporary loss of income.

Income	Assets
• Interest	• Stocks
• Dividends	• Bonds
• Capital gains	• Mutual funds
• Alimony	• T-bills
• Rental income	• Trust funds
• Trust funds	• Collectibles
• Social Security	• Retirement assets
• Income from a business	• Real estate

Closing on a Condominium

It is important to be familiar with the terms *flipping, assigning a contract,* and *simultaneous closing* when it comes to property closings.

Flipping means *purchasing property, and quickly reselling it for a profit, usually after fixing it up.* Flipping is also called **assigning a contract** and means *assigning the purchase rights to property or a condo unit to another buyer before that property or unit is closed.* For example, investors may want to flip condo units pre-construction.

Simultaneous closing is a seller-financing technique in which *the investor or seller creates a private mortgage note and then simultaneously closes with the buyer on the same day*. The Department of Housing and Urban Development (HUD) has regulations about predatory flipping with regard to Federal Housing Authority (FHA) single-family mortgages.

Some developers do not allow flipping for a variety of reasons. First, developers do not want to compete against flippers for sales of remaining condo units. Second, while investors may let the property sit empty, buyers who live on the property and maintain it continue to drive the value up and attract more people. For these reasons, developers often prefer buyers to investors who intend to flip property.

Condominium Title Issues

Since a condo unit owner also shares common areas with other tenants and has an undivided interest in the common areas of the property, when a unit is sold, interest in the common area is also sold. To review three key terms:

- **Title** is the actual lawful ownership of real property and refers to holding the bundle of rights conveyed.
- **Title search** is an inspection of the public record to determine all rights and encumbrances affecting the title to a piece of property.
- **Deed** is an instrument that conveys a grantor's interest, if any, in real property. It is also known as a conveyance.

Prior to closing, a title search is completed to resolve any issues the seller has involving the title to the condo unit being sold. Any issues with title must be resolved before closing. Like all deeds, the deed of the condo unit conveys title to real property, and at closing the title is sold and transferred to the buyer.

Closing Costs

The closing transaction for a condo is similar to that for other residential property. The best way to evaluate closing costs is by looking at the Closing Disclosure. A Closing Disclosure, is a document that presents a final, detailed account of a real estate transaction, listing each party's debits and credits and the amount each will receive or be required to pay at closing. Closing Disclosures, which are required by the Truth In Lending Act, are prepared by closing agents, and in some cases by the creditor (for the borrower's Closing Disclosure) to:

- Determine the total amount of money owed to, and by, the seller and buyer.

The Truth In Lending Act also requires that a creditor provide the borrower a Loan Estimate within three (3) business days of a completed application.

RESPA applies to all one- to four-family residences or condominiums that use federally regulated loans and loans made by lenders that invest more than $1 million in residential mortgages. RESPA laws were created to allow buyers to compare costs of services from different lenders or closing agents.

Following is a list of typical condo closing costs for the buyer, seller, and sponsor in New York. Costs listed here are common and are simply an estimate for example purposes. As a real estate licensee, advise clients to consult with an attorney regarding costs, since they will vary from closing to closing.

Buyer's Costs

Attorney Fees	$1,600+
Bank Fees – Points	0%-3% of loan amount
Property Appraisal	$300+
Tax Escrow	Two to six months
Short-term Interest	Maximum of one month
Mortgage Tax	Varies, but approximately 1.8% of the mortgage amount on loans under $500,000, or 1.925% on loan amounts over $500,000
Mortgage Title Insurance	Varies, but approximately $200 per $100,000 of mortgage amount
Fee Title Insurance	Varies, but approximately $450 per $100,000 of mortgage amount
Mortgage Bank Attorney Fees	$500+
Recording Fees	$200-$500
Bank Fees (application, credit report, processing fee, etc.)	$500-$2,000+
Managing Agent Fees	$250+
Municipal Search	$350+
Common Charge Adjustment	Prorated for the month of closing
Real Estate Tax Adjustment	One to six months
Mansion Tax	1% of entire purchase price when property price is $1 milion or more
Move-in Deposit	$500+

Seller's Costs

Attorney Fees	$1,500+
Managing Agent Fees	$450+
Move-out Deposit	$500-$1,000
Bank Attorney Fee	$450+
Various Title Fees and Title Close Fees	$500+
New York City Transfer Tax	1% of sale price up to $500,000, or 1.425% of sale price if $500,000 and over; plus $25 administrative fee
New York State Transfer Tax	$4 per $1,000 of sale price of 0.4% of the purchase price

Sponsor's Fees

If purchasing a unit from the sponsor or developer, the purchaser usually pays these additional fees:

New York City Transfer Tax	1% of sale price up to $500,000, or 1.425% of sale price if $500,000 and over; plus $25 administrative fee
New York State Transfer Tax	$4 per $1,000 of sale price of 0.4% of the purchase price
Sponsor's Attorney Fees	$1,500, estimated
Contribution to Working Capital Fund	$1,000, estimated

Other Buyer Concerns

Other topics addressed in the closing process include:

- **Tax deductions**. The advantage of owning rather than renting is the tax deductions available. While they cannot write off closing costs, condo unit owners can write off mortgage interest, among other things.
- **Right of first refusal**. Some condo contracts contain a **right of first refusal**, which is *the right to have the first chance to buy or lease property if the owner decides to sell or lease it*. This clause allows the condo association the first opportunity to purchase a unit when it is for sale.
- **Title insurance** is also required for condominiums. A title insurance policy protects the lender (and sometimes the property owner) against loss due to disputes over the ownership of a property and defects in the title that were not found during the search of the public record. Defects could be liens or claims against title, and may be recorded or unrecorded.

Cooperatives

The purchase of a cooperative is different from other types of real estate transactions. **Cooperatives** (co-ops) are *buildings owned by corporations with the residents as shareholders who each receive a proprietary lease on an individual unit and the right to use common areas.* A **proprietary lease** is *an exclusive, longer-term lease given to a person who lives in and owns stock in a cooperative.*

A co-op owner's shares are considered personal property. This differs from a condominium purchase, which is a fee simple transaction where the unit owner receives a deed to the property. Like a condo, a co-op is a type of structured ownership known as a legal entity. Unlike a condo, which is a non-controlling entity, a co-op is member-controlled and owned.

A cooperative shareholder pays a prorated share of the building's expenses, including property taxes for the whole building. If a resident does not pay her share of expenses, the entire cooperative may be threatened with foreclosure, unlike a condo, where one resident's actions do not threaten the entire community.

Title to a cooperative building is held by a corporation formed for that purpose (owned in severalty). Even though shares, rather than property, are sold, the transaction is similar to the sale of real estate. The shares and the apartment are transferred to the purchaser along with assignment of the proprietary lease. However, the co-op agreement may provide that a shareholder cannot transfer an interest without the other shareholders' consent.

Since 1996, married couples who own co-ops can take title as tenants in the entirety. This allows them to own the co-op with a 100% undivided interest. This also gives spouses survivorship rights and prevents one party from selling his own share without consent of the other.

Financing a Co-op

Co-op shareholders typically have a **share loan,** which *is a co-op loan signifying a buyer is purchasing shares in a corporation rather than a mortgage for ownership of property.* Co-ops often include a **flip tax,** which is *a fee imposed by the co-op board on the seller for the transfer of ownership during the sale of the unit.*

Before purchasing shares in a co-op, buyers should read between the financial lines to make sure the co-op is in good financial standing. Prospective tenants should look at bills that have not been paid and uncollected maintenance fees. These are signs that the building finances may not be well managed. It's also a good idea to look at reserve funds and the co-op's underlying mortgage.

Financial Statement

The Attorney General's regulations stipulate that every shareholder has the right to view the building's annual financial statement. A financial statement gives every tenant information on how the building's money is being managed.

A Co-op Board's Minutes

According to New York State's Business Corporate Law, co-op corporations must keep minutes of their monthly board meetings. Board minutes are another way to learn about the state of a cooperative.

The board minutes may include information about the building's reserve funds and underlying mortgage. Either of these could be leveraged to pay for unexpected repairs or finance capital improvements or renovations that could increase maintenance fees. The minutes may also include information regarding noise or pet issues with specific tenants.

A client's lawyer should consult both the board minutes and the financial statement before a purchase of shares is made.

Co-op Sale and Purchase Documents

Several documents are needed for the sale and purchase of cooperatives. In addition, there are documents that must be reviewed and understood pertaining to closing, moving in, and making changes to the unit. Common documents include:

Stock certificates and proprietary leases. When a buyer purchases shares in a cooperative, a stock certificate and proprietary lease are issued. Since there is no place to publicly record the stock certificate and lease, the original documents are needed for the transfer agent to complete the sale with the new buyer(s). After closing, the lender typically takes possession of the stock certificate and lease.

Co-op lien search. If liens exist against a co-op seller or her shares, they must be cleared before a new buyer can purchase the shares. During the purchase process, the attorney for the co-op buyer will often complete a lien search to make sure there are no open liens against the seller or seller's shares. This helps ensure a smooth closing.

Lender/Co-op recognition agreements. A **recognition agreement** is *an agreement between three parties – the lender, the co-op, and the shareholder – that recognizes the rights of lenders who finance the shareholder.* This agreement says that the lender, co-op, and shareholder will all be notified in the event of default. This gives the lender time to pay past-due maintenance fees, if so desired, in an attempt to avoid foreclosure. Foreclosure is an expensive prospect, and most co-op boards and lenders want to work with shareholders to avoid it.

Offering plan. As with condominiums, an **offering plan** for a co-op is *a document provided by the sponsor, which offers detailed information regarding the property.* In addition to reviewing the financial statements and board minutes, before a co-op closing, the buyer's lawyer reviews the offering plan. After the lawyer has done due diligence and is satisfied with the results, the contract can be signed.

House rules. House rules are *the rules and requirements established for condo or co-op tenants.* They often address rules for common areas, parking, noise, pets, and use of the recreation room. House rules are usually not drafted by an attorney or backed by a specific law, but are expected to be followed. Board members can amend and change house rules if they have a majority vote from shareholders.

It is important for real estate agents to be aware of the house rules in buildings their clients are considering buying, in case they would alter the decision to purchase. For example, a dog lover would never want to buy shares in a co-op that restricts pets.

Alteration agreement. An **alteration agreement** is a *written agreement, signed by co-op shareholder tenants, before any renovations, modifications, repairs, or alterations can begin.* An agreement should be considered for structural and non-structural alterations. It should take into consideration and provide regulations for:

- Demolition, especially with regard to uncovering and dealing with lead paint and asbestos.
- Electrical, including hiring a licensed electrician.
- Plumbing, heating, and HVAC, including hiring licensed contractors and making sure all installations are approved by the building engineer.
- Environmental issues.
- Certificate of occupancy issues.

The residential Management Council of the Real Estate Board of New York, along with the New York City Bar Association, developed a form that standardizes the alteration agreement.

Cooperative Board Package

Another important part of a cooperative purchase, aside from the financing, is the board package. A **board package** is *presented to the co-op (or sometimes condo) board of directors and often includes financial qualifications, employment verification, letters of reference, and other material requested by the board.* The buyer's real estate agent completes or assists the buyer with the completion of the board package. The package is then forwarded to the managing agent of the building, who confirms it is complete and does any necessary fact checking before forwarding it to the board of directors.

Remember that if a resident of a co-op does not pay his share of maintenance fees, the entire cooperative may be threatened with foreclosure, so the board wants to know up front if a buyer will be financially responsible for the unit, as well as a good neighbor.

Condo owners and homeowners have no control over who becomes their new neighbor, but co-op boards generally have the ability to vote whether to allow a particular person to buy into the cooperative. As long as the board does not discriminate against members of a protected class, it can approve or reject any candidate for a variety of reasons. Remember, the main purpose is to find a good fit for the building as a whole.

CASE IN POINT

There have been several well-known people, such as Madonna and former President Richard Nixon, who did not receive board approval to live in a specific co-op building. Why would the board turn down someone like Madonna? Probably because it wanted its tenants to be able to get in and out of the building easily. If Madonna lived in the building, there most likely would be paparazzi and fans in the lobby and around the entrances, making it loud and crowded (and potentially unsafe) much of the time. On the other hand, if former President Nixon or Madonna wanted to buy the house next door to yours, what would happen? You would have no say and they could buy it. As you can see, owning shares in a co-op is quite different than owning actual property.

The Board Package Checklist

The co-op board requires specific, detailed information from prospective tenants. There is no standardized board package, so there may be differences in how boards want information presented or how many copies are needed. It's important to work with clients to follow the board's specifications exactly. All information must be supported by documentation. Common board package requirements include:

Requirement	Description
Purchase application form	Provides basic information, including the buyer's name, Social Security number, occupation, the name and phone number of current landlord, length of residency in current residence, broker and attorney names, contact information, names of family members who will occupy the building, number and types of pets, and the license plate number of the buyer's and occupant's automobiles.
Fully executed contract of sale	Often prepared by the seller's attorney for the buyer's attorney. With the signing of the contract, the buyer produces the down payment. For co-ops, down payments can easily be 25% or more. The down payment goes into escrow.
Financial statement	Typically asks about assets, liabilities, and net worth. Buyers must provide documentation to verify this information. It is wise to suggest clients rely on a financial professional to make sure this type of information is current. Could include information about real estate owned, retirement funds, cash on hand, bank statements, stocks and bonds owned, and other financial obligations.
Letters of personal reference	Several letters are usually required to give the board insight into the personality of buyers and how well they will fit with current owners. Letters should come from people the buyer has known for an extended length of time.
Employment verification letter	Letter from the buyer's employer verifying occupation and position within the company, length of employment, and salary.
Business letters of reference	Should come from business associates, supervisors, or management with whom the buyer has worked closely. Letters should contain specific information and references about the buyer. This gives the board an idea of how the buyer is viewed by colleagues.
Tax returns	Most boards expect to see three years of federal, state, and city tax returns. The board wants to make sure a potential buyer's taxes are paid on time and whether any tax-related issues exist that might affect the cooperative or the buyer's ability to pay timely maintenance fees or loan payments.
Authorization to perform a credit search	Boards run a credit check on each potential buyer. This requires the signing of a credit release form.
Appropriate New York State disclosure forms	Buyers are required to sign disclosures, including one relating to lead-based paint and lead-based paint hazards.

The Board Interview

Besides preparing a board package, prospective owners are required to interview with the co-op board. A real estate licensee can help prepare a potential shareholder-buyer for the co-op board interview. This is a key part of the process and should not be taken lightly.

Boards usually hold interview meetings once a month and potential buyers may have to wait for these monthly time slots. Most boards expect to meet everyone who will be living in the co-op, including children. The board will notify the buyer or agent/broker of the exact date and time of the meeting.

Buyers should be prepared to handle personal and financial questions. While the buyer should not speak poorly of current neighbors, landlords, jobs, or financial situations, it is imperative to be honest and forthcoming. The buyer should offer more than just total financial disclosure and employment verification. For example, maybe the buyer runs a home-based business, owns a dog, or likes to practice guitar at home. Any of these situations might be prohibited and need to be discussed with the board.

Co-op Shareholder Considerations

Shareholders in a co-op have a stake in the way subletting, sponsor shares, and occupancy are handled. These considerations can have an impact on taxation and future sales.

Subletting Co-ops

In a sublease, a tenant transfers only part of his right of possession or other interest in leased property to another person for part of the remaining lease term. Typically, when a sublease occurs, a sublessee pays rent to a lessee who then pays the lessor. In a sublease, the original tenant is responsible to the owner for all provisions in the lease. There are pros and cons to subletting a shareholder's unit, and they affect everyone involved – from the board, to the shareholders, to potential buyers.

Some cooperative buildings allow subletting and some do not. When a co-op board considers subletting, they start with the proprietary lease. Some leases deny subletting, but, more often than not, the lease gives the board the right to sublet. In buildings that do allow subletting, there are usually specific policies and fees for doing so.

While there are many advantages to subletting, there are also a number of disadvantages. People tend to like cooperatives because of the community feeling and the fact that renters are not constantly changing. If the building has enough sublets in it, it can begin to feel like a rental property instead of a home.

There is a concern that those who sublet will not take care of the building as well as shareholders, producing more wear and tear. Boards also know that too many sublets can cause difficulty for the cooperative or prospective buyers when it comes to borrowing money or refinancing. On the flip side, a cooperative building's shareholders do need to sublet from time to time. Reasons may include the need to move for a job. Many co-op boards understand this and many permit subletting – on their terms.

It is important to adhere to any bylaws regarding sublet fees. While the rules for subletting vary, many buildings require the following fees:

- Move-in and move-out fees
- Sublet fees
- Application fees

There are also requirements for subletting. These vary from building to building, but common requirements include:

- A shareholder must occupy a unit for a specific number of years before subletting is allowed.
- An apartment can be sublet only for a certain number of years.
- Only a certain number of units in the building can be sublet at one time.
- There must be specific reasons for subletting (e.g., financial hardship).

If subletting is managed correctly, it can actually provide extra revenue for the building for improvements or the reserve fund.

Sponsor Shares

Sponsors must give up control of the board after five years or after 50% of the shares in the building are sold. Most sponsors comply with the directions laid out in the original offering plan and the building eventually converts to the board. But what if the sponsor decides to ignore the offering plan and stops selling shares? If the rental market is good, some sponsors want to keep their shares in the unit and sublet. Other times, sponsors do not want to give up control of the board, since that means they cannot nominate their own members. In addition, some sponsors do not take the same care of repairs and maintenance. All of this makes it more difficult for current shareholders to sell.

Usually, there are no problems with original sponsors, but board members should make sure sponsors follow through with their obligations to avoid future problems.

Holder of Unsold Shares

The **holder of unsold shares** is an *investor in a co-op building who is not using it as a primary residence*. The holder of unsold shares, like the original sponsor, for example, is typically *exempt* from the usual fees, including flip taxes and subletting fees. The holder of unsold shares can also sell or sublet a unit to whomever they want without board approval.

CASE IN POINT

Sponsor Nicholas sold to investor/shareholder John. Both knew John was not planning to live in the co-op building but, rather, bought shares for investment purposes. John assumes since he is not taking up residence in the building, he has the same rights and exemptions as Nicholas. Does he? It depends. The proprietary lease defines the unsold shares. Just because John *owns* unsold shares does not mean he is considered the *holder* of unsold shares. Nicholas may need to designate John as the holder of unsold shares. What this means is Nicholas would have to cover John if financial issues arise.

Sold Shares

It seems logical that a cooperative building with 100% occupancy would be the best scenario for banks and shareholders alike. However, a lot depends on who owns the shares that have been sold and who is occupying the units.

For example, if a building is 40% owner occupied, and the rest is occupied by sublets and sponsors or investors, the bank may be hesitant to lend money to that cooperative. Banks consider subletting a risk. They are also hesitant to lend money to potential new shareholders if there are a high number of sublets in the building. Sometimes it is in the best interest of banks, boards, and potential shareholders to keep subletting at a low percentage of the building's occupancy, yet still allow the option for shareholders who need it. It's a fine line for all parties involved.

Condops

A **condop** is *a building that has been divided into at least two condos. The first is the co-op residential units that are considered one condo unit. The second unit is the professional and commercial unit.* The term condop has been misused recently, with many people believing a condop is simply a co-op that lacks the rules and board approval requirements. This is not the case.

When a condop is purchased, owners still purchase shares in a corporation rather than real property, so in that way, a condop is like a cooperative. A condop is also like a condo, since residential co-op units are incorporated into one condo unit. Consider the following example:

A ten-story condop is made up of three condo units. The three condo units in the ten-story consist of:

- An underground garage (considered one condo unit).
- Commercial space on the first floor (considered a second condo unit).
- Residential co-op apartments above (considered a third condo unit).

80/20 Rule

There are several reasons for converting a building into a condop, but the main reason involves Section 216 of IRS code that is commonly referred to as the 80/20 rule.

The **80/20 rule** says that *no more than 20% of the co-op's yearly income can come from non-shareholder sources, in order for individual shareholders to continue to be able to write off yearly taxes and mortgage interest.* Non-shareholder sources include retail or other commercial tenants.

If considering converting to a condop to avoid the 80/20 rule, the cooperative should be aware of a few pitfalls:

- The cost of conversion can be very expensive and not worth it.
- Once that commercial space is sold, the co-op board may lose control over it and any tenant could move in. If that tenant is loud and disruptive, that could upset shareholders and, eventually, decrease the value of the condop.

SUMMARY

1. **Condominiums** are *property developed for co-ownership, with each co-owner having a separate interest in an individual unit, combined with an undivided interest in the common areas of the property.* The **Condominium Act** (Article 9-B of the Real Property Law) is *New York State's law governing the establishment of condominiums.*
2. Condos have **common areas**, such as hallways and recreational facilities that all tenants own and use. **Limited common areas** are areas outside of a unit that are reserved for the specific use of one unit owner, for example, a parking space. **Maintenance fees** (also referred to as common area expenses) are *monthly fees required of each condo owner or co-op shareholder for such expenses as utilities, management, building maintenance, and upkeep.*
3. A **sponsor,** *also known as the developer, is the person, corporation, or other entity that is part of the sale and development of a condo or co-op property.* Sponsors establish a condominium by filing a **condominium declaration**. They also file **bylaws** and establish the **CC&Rs** for the unit owners' association. They have control of the board until they sell more than 50% of the common interest in the building or after five years have passed, whichever comes first. The owners' association is comprised of all unit owners, who elect a **board of managers** (also called a board of directors) from among themselves. The board follows the bylaws and makes decisions on behalf of owners.
4. An **offering plan** is *a document provided by the sponsor that offers detailed information regarding the property,* such as special risks, real estate tax validation, floor plans, price increases, hidden fees, and closing date. This plan can be amended, and developers can raise prices for a variety of reasons, including land and material costs, developer costs, and increased interest in the property. A building can be converted to a cooperative or condominium by the sponsor under an **eviction plan** or **non-eviction plan.**
5. A **letter of intent** signifies *two or more parties agree to do business* together, often used to reserve a particular unit. Most are **non-binding**, which means they are *usually unenforceable*. A **binding contract** to buy a condo is a *valid contract that is enforceable.* A **Cooperative Policy Statement #1 (CPS-1)** is applicable to cooperatives, condominiums, and homeowners associations and is used to test the market.

6. Most mortgage lenders stipulate a property must be in compliance with the **certificate of occupancy**, which is issued after the property is deemed fit for occupancy.

7. **Flipping** means *purchasing property, and immediately reselling it for a profit, usually after fixing it up.* Flipping is also called **assigning a contract** and *means assigning the purchase rights to property or a condo unit to another buyer before that property or unit is closed.* **Simultaneous closing** *is when the investor or seller creates a private mortgage note and then simultaneously closes with the buyer on the same day.* HUD has regulations regarding predatory flipping.

8. Buyers and sellers pay a variety of fees at closing. A **settlement statement** provides a detailed accounting of these. The New York City and State Transfer Tax is paid by the seller, unless the buyer is purchasing directly from the sponsor. In that case, those taxes are paid by the buyer. Any title issues should be resolved before closing. Lenders look at the buyer's income and assets before approving a loan.

9. A **cooperative**, referred to as a co-op, is *a building owned by a corporation, where the residents are shareholders in the corporation. Each shareholder receives a proprietary lease on an individual unit and the right to use the common areas.* A co-op is usually purchased with a **share loan,** which is *a type of co-op loan signifying a buyer is purchasing shares in a corporation, rather than a mortgage for ownership of property.* Co-ops often include a **flip tax** when sold, which is *a fee imposed by the co-op board for the transfer of ownership during the sale of the unit.* An original stock certificate and lease are required for the sale of a co-op. A closing agent usually cannot close the sale without the actual documents, since a missing certificate or lease might indicate a lender is holding them as evidence of a lien.

10. Before purchasing a co-op, the buyer and buyer's attorney should review the financial statement to view how the building's money is being managed. They should also consult the board meeting minutes and reserve funds to find out if upcoming repairs are needed and how they might be paid for, and the *underlying mortgage*, since co-op tenants pay for it in their monthly maintenance fees.

11. **House rules** are not drafted by an attorney or backed by a specific law, but they are the *rules and requirements established for the condo or co-op tenants. These could include rules for common areas, parking, noise, pets, use of recreation room, etc.* The house rules are listed in the co-op's proprietary lease or the condo's bylaws. An **alteration agreement** is *a written agreement, signed by co-op shareholder-tenants, before any renovations, modifications, repairs, or alterations can begin.*

12. To purchase shares in a co-op, a buyer must complete a **board package,** which typically includes complete financial disclosure, including tax returns and credit history, as well as employment history, personal and business references, and an interview. This package is sent to the managing agent and reviewed by the board of directors. Co-op buyers will also need to attend a **board interview**.

13. Some co-ops allow subletting and some do not. If a co-op does allow it, there are a variety of fees and requirements. The **holder of unsold shares,** often the original sponsor, is typically exempt from fees such as flip taxes and subletting fees. A sponsor who sells to another investor might designate his shares to an investor, so that the investor will not pay fees.

14. A **condop** is *a building that has been divided into at least two parts: 1. The co-op residential units that are considered one condo unit and 2. the professional and commercial units that are considered the second unit.* Condops are often created because of an IRS rule, referred to as the **80/20 rule**, which states that *no more than 20% of the co-op's yearly income can come from non-shareholder sources (such as commercial tenants) in order for individual shareholders to continue to be able to write off yearly taxes and mortgage interest.*

18

Property Management

In This Session

Property management is a growing field, and there is a demand for trained and licensed property managers. In this session, you'll see that property managers do more than just collect rent. You'll learn about the functions and responsibilities of property managers, as well as the types of properties they manage.

You'll learn:

- Licensing requirements for property managers in New York.
- What skills are necessary to be a successful property manager.
- What comprises the management agreement used to set up and support property management.
- Which budgets and reports property managers must develop and analyze.
- How to effectively advertise, market, and lease managed properties.

Key Terms

- Actual Eviction
- Anchor Tenant
- Building Manager
- Capital Expense
- Capital Reserve Budget
- Constructive Eviction
- Corrective Maintenance
- Cosmetic Maintenance
- Fiduciary
- General Agent
- Lessee
- Lessor
- Management Agreement
- Management Proposal
- Operating Budget
- Preventive Maintenance
- Principal
- Property Management
- Property Management Report
- Property Manager
- Rent Roll
- Resident Manager
- Risk Management
- Stabilized Budget
- Variable Expense

Property Management

A **property manager** is *a person hired by a real property owner to administer, market, and maintain property – especially rental property.* To become a property manager in the state of New York, one must have a real estate salesperson or broker license.

In a basic sense, **property management** is *the leasing or renting, or the offering to lease or rent, the real property of others for a fee, commission, compensation, or other valuable consideration pursuant to a property management employee contract*. However, property management goes beyond leasing apartments and office buildings. A property manager is considered the custodian and supervisor of an owner's property.

Although property management is a specialized field, property managers today have a variety of options. For example:

- Owners might look for property managers with experience in historic buildings to serve the needs of preservation and renovation.
- With the advancements in technology, some owners may be looking for managers skilled in overseeing technological campuses.
- Some property management companies may specialize in one field, like absentee ownership, and may promote their company to handle complex finances and property monitoring without the owner present.

Functions of a Property Manager

Property managers have different roles, depending on the type of property they oversee:

- **Property manager**. Usually oversees the management of a number of properties for various owners.
- **Building manager**. The manager of just one building.
- **Resident manager**. Represents a property management firm and may live on the premises of the building being managed

Property managers need a diverse set of skills, regardless of the type of property they manage. For example, everyone in the property management field must:

- Have an understanding of leasing regulations to collect rents, and basic construction knowledge to ensure routine maintenance is performed.
- Know how to develop a management proposal.
- Create and manage reports and budgets for property owners.
- Have exceptional communication skills.
- Understand basic marketing principles.

Types of Properties Managed

No matter what type of tenant occupies the space in a building, property managers have the same mission – *to market and rent space effectively, maintain the property in good condition, comply with government regulations, and keep operating costs low.* There are many types of properties a property manager can specialize in, including commercial office, commercial retail, residential, special-purpose, or industrial.

Commercial Office Buildings

Office space may be located downtown, in a suburban office park, or on a street lined with stores. The space can be a small, single-story building or a high-rise complex. Some buildings feature tenants specific to one industry, like medical professionals, while others have mixed-use tenants.

Property managers should familiarize themselves with competing office spaces throughout the area, so they can establish appropriate rental rates and standards for design and structural elements, like window treatments and phone jacks. It is helpful to set a base rent for a typical office space in the building, and then adjust the rent for other office spaces compared to the base rent.

Negotiating an office lease is more complex than negotiating other kinds of leases. From remodeling to escalation clauses, everything is a bargaining point. The right of tenants to sublet in case their business slumps is a crucial issue. Before starting negotiations, a property manager should be very clear about the owner's priorities.

Usually, tenants who request special alterations to their space, like adding or removing walls, special wiring, etc., need to get permission and pay for their alterations themselves. Of course, special alterations can also be a negotiating point between property owners and potential tenants. If the only way to fill non-leased space is by modifying it, the property owner may elect to do so rather than let it sit empty.

Commercial Retail Property

Although small strip shops can be relatively easy to manage, large shopping malls present a range of unique challenges for property managers. A shopping center may have several anchor tenants. An **anchor tenant** is *a major department or chain store strategically located within a shopping center to give maximum exposure to smaller satellite stores*. When assigning spaces, property managers need to be careful not to place stores selling the same goods side by side.

Percentage leases are often used with retail spaces. There may be restrictions on the hours a business can operate and the kinds of alterations that can be made to the space. Qualifying tenants for retail space is generally more detailed. Parking needs and customer requirements should be considered.

Property managers have to be diligent with maintenance issues to avoid lawsuits. Liability for accidents is complicated in shopping malls. It is often difficult to determine who is liable for an accident that occurs in a common area, like the center of the mall's food court or a fountain.

Liability insurance is most effective when the property manager, owners, tenants, and merchants are co-insured. If there is an accident, property managers should notify the insurance company immediately because a consequence of delay can result in a loss of coverage for that accident.

Residential Property

Residential property includes:

- Single-family homes.
- Apartments.
- Condominiums and cooperatives.
- Mobile home parks.
- Retirement communities (these can also be considered special-purpose properties).

Whether it is a single-family home or a large apartment complex, **pricing and marketing** are key elements in successfully renting residential housing. It is helpful for property managers to carefully survey the local market and take into account supply and demand to determine the right amount to charge for rent.

Managing a condominium is similar to managing multi-family residential properties. Tenants should purchase their own insurance, and condo owners should also be insured. Property managers of subsidized housing funded through HUD need to follow HUD's rules and standards.

Both condos and cooperatives have an owners' association called the board of directors or board of managers, and a property manager works with those boards.

Special-Purpose Properties

Property managers may have the opportunity to manage special-purpose properties, including:

- Hotels
- Theaters
- Places of worship
- Planned unit developments
- Motels
- Schools
- Housing for the elderly

The design of the special-purpose building often mirrors the activities that take place there. For example, a theater could probably never function as commercial office space; it was designed specifically to function only as a theater. These types of facilities often have someone on staff who serves as the building manager.

Housing for the elderly includes independent living, assisted living, and nursing homes. These facilities are highly competitive, so smart marketing is essential. Property managers work with elderly tenants plus medical personnel and social workers. The facility itself must have adaptations that meet the needs of this special population.

Property managers should also have some knowledge of **planned unit developments** (PUDs), *special types of subdivisions that may combine non-residential uses with residential uses, or otherwise depart from ordinary zoning and subdivision regulations*. In some PUDs the lot owners co-own recreational facilities or open spaces as tenants in common.

Industrial Property

Industrial property includes manufacturing facilities and warehouses. Because of the heavy equipment, traffic patterns geared for trucks and other specialized vehicles, and storage, industrial tenants are generally long-term, and the space they occupy is usually built or altered specifically for their use. Industrial spaces move slowly on the market. They are often located near each other and may be clustered together in an industrial park.

Industrial properties usually have net leases, requiring tenants to pay a greater percentage of property expenses than most leases do. Industrial tenants usually pay for and perform their own maintenance.

Property Manager and Owner Relationship

A property management company is in an *agency relationship* with a property owner, and owes the property owner the same fiduciary duties of obedience, loyalty, disclosure, confidentiality, accountability, and reasonable care owed to all clients. A **fiduciary** is *a person in a position of trust, held by law to high standards of good faith and loyalty*.

Typically, a property manager is in a **principal-agent relationship**, with the principal being the owner and the agent being the property manager. Here, though, a property manager or property management company is a general agent because of the broad range of duties performed. A **general agent** is *an agent authorized to handle all of the principal's affairs in one area or in specified areas.*

For example, an important part of a property manager's job is managing leases and understanding all documents that need to be signed and maintained. As a general agent, a property manager can handle these types of requirements for the owner. In contrast, a real estate salesperson is classified as a special agent because duties are restricted to *one area* of performance.

Obligations to the Property Owner

One of the most important jobs a property manager has is to understand the goals of the owner. An effective property manager is a true asset for a property owner, maximizing an owner's income and minimizing expenses.

A property manager's three main jobs are to:

1. Fulfill the goals and objectives of the owners.
2. Create income for the owners.
3. Maintain or increase the property's value.

A good property manager must see an individual property within the context of the total real estate picture. Although linked to the general economy, the real estate market experiences its own fluctuations.

Effective property managers make the most of real estate cycles and create opportunities or minimize challenges. Property managers can adjust those factors within their control, for example, offering a free month of rent to entice new renters during a tight market. Assessing the market and planning ahead are essential for fulfilling the owner's goals and for success as a property manager.

The Management Agreement

The **management agreement**, also called the **property management employee contract**, is a *written agreement that governs the relationship between the property owner/investor and the property manager.* This agreement details the duties, responsibilities, and compensation of the property manager. The management agreement is a contract that should be signed, and contains some or all of the following components:

Description of the property. An exact address must be part of the agreement and sometimes a full legal description is necessary. It is also important to establish the perimeters of the property, including any ancillary buildings, or structures. For example, is the landscaping out front or the gift shop in the lobby yours to manage? If not, those exclusions need to be written in the contract.

Length of agreement. The time of the agreement varies from property to property and from owner to owner, and is negotiated between the property manager and owner. One year is a common term. If the owner and property manager are satisfied with the relationship after one year, a longer term can be negotiated, and the contract can be renewed.

Management authority. Management authority outlines what a property manager is authorized to handle in leasing property. Typically, duties include:

- Selecting tenants and leasing units.
- Collecting rents.
- Returning security deposit.
- Evicting tenants.

Management authority also authorizes property managers/agents to sign leases. Some owners limit the amount of authority to a specific time frame or amount. Those limits are listed in the management agreement.

Management fee. Since so many factors can affect the profitability of a property, there is not a single hard-and-fast way to compute management fees. Property managers should determine both the direct and indirect costs associated with their job. They can use this information to arrive at an agreement with the property owner on the management fee they charge.

Management fees may be fixed (flat) or a percentage. A *flat fee* is a specific fee paid out at specific increments. A *percentage fee* is based on the operation's gross collectible income. The percentage fee could also be a fixed percentage of rent or a bonus when a certain number of leases is signed. Note that if there are two leasing agents for the property, the fee is sometimes split.

Insurance and risk management. Risk **management** is *identifying, managing, and minimizing the potential risks on a property.* The property manager must be skilled at risk management to protect the building from loss and insulate the owner from liability with appropriate insurance policy recommendations.

To protect owners from major expenses, property managers need to make certain they have blanketed the property with insurance to cover the greatest risks, purchased at the most economical rates. Necessary coverage might be included for issues such as:

- Damage from fire, flood, wind, and other acts of nature.
- Workers' Compensation claims.
- Liability for contractors, etc.
- Loss of income and loss of occupancy.
- Equipment and machinery.
- Automobiles owned by and used for the property.

Property managers have the responsibility to identify and reduce risks on their property. Some dangers can be avoided or fixed, and others cannot. Property managers need to minimize risks when they can and establish emergency or crisis plans for when they cannot. These plans should be coordinated with local government authorities, security personnel, and tenants.

Accounting responsibilities and reports. Accounting for all income and expenditures is more involved than it sounds. Property managers are responsible for **setting rents** that cover all expenses associated with operating the building and to return a profit. Usually distributed on a monthly basis, **property management reports** are *prepared by property managers to inform owners of the status of the property, often including income, expenses, and disbursement information*. The management agreement should clearly explain when the report must be distributed and to whom.

Owner's responsibilities and objectives. An owner's responsibilities vary, and should be listed in the management agreement. This could include information on who oversees payroll and insurance, as well as information on monthly, quarterly, and yearly payments the property manager needs to make.

Management agreement termination. Details about the termination of the owner-manager relationship should be spelled out in the management agreement. In case an owner wishes to cancel an agreement early, information about the property manager's compensation for negotiated leases and contracts not yet executed should be stated.

Property Management Responsibilities

The daily, weekly, and yearly duties of property managers may vary, but these responsibilities should be familiar to all property managers:

- Developing the management proposal
- Reporting
- General accounting
- Managing office operations
- Understanding building systems and construction
- Landlord-tenant relations
- Leasing space
- Advertising and marketing
- Adhering to codes and regulations
- Negotiating with unions
- Purchasing
- Environmental awareness

Developing the Management Proposal

After the owner's objectives are understood and a management agreement is signed, developing a well-thought-out management proposal is the next step. A **management proposal** is *the plan created by the property manager for overseeing the property. It includes an analysis of the market and a variety of financial reports, including an operating budget.*

The management proposal should lay out an effective strategy for meeting the owner's financial and operational goals. If a plan is already in place, you may be revising it or giving input on it.

A management proposal should include a:

- One-year operating budget.
- Five-year plan.
- Market analysis, which includes:
    - Regional analysis
    - Neighborhood analysis
    - Property analysis

The market analysis information allows property managers to gain an understanding of economic factors, population, zoning regulations, transportation, and other factors pertinent to the managed building's location.

Reporting

Property managers are expected to communicate precisely to owners the condition and financial status of the property. This is typically outlined in the management proposal and the property management reports. All financial reports generated should meet the criteria and specifications agreed upon by the owner and property manager.

In order to develop a one-year and five-year plan for the management proposal and to complete the regular financial reporting to the owner, the property manager develops budgets, reports and statements, and recommendations.

Operating Budget

An **operating budget** is *created to project the income and expenses for the property over a one-year period.* In this report, you will usually find:

- **Total income.** Gross rental income and other income are listed and added together. Losses from vacant spaces, evictions, uncollected rents, etc., are subtracted from that income, in order to determine the total income.
- **Expenses.** *Fixed expenses* are ongoing operating expenses that do not vary based on occupancy levels of the property (e.g., property taxes and insurance). *Variable expenses* are operating expenses necessary to the property, but dependent on the property's occupancy level (e.g., repairs and maintenance, income taxes, salaries, and utilities).
- **Net operating income.** Income after expenses are deducted.

SAMPLE ANNUAL OPERATING BUDGET

Income	
Net rentable area (sq. ft.)	35,000
Rent per square foot	$23.50
Potential gross income	$822,500
– Vacancy and Collection = 10%	$82,250
Effective Gross Income	$740,250
Expenses: Fixed	
Real estate taxes	$91,350
Insurance	$2,450
Expenses: Variable	
Utilities	$81,900
Maintenance	$40,950
Repairs	$14,000
Management fees	$8,400
Other	$1,750
Reserves 5% of EGI (roof, HVAC)	$37,100
Total Expenses	$277,900
Net Operating Income	$462,350

Other Reports and Statements

Property managers must consistently track expenses. They accomplish this by creating and using additional reports, as well as looking at past data.

Capital expenses are *used to improve the property and increase its value*. Sometimes they are preplanned, but other times they are needed to replace something on the property that is no longer working, such as a roof or an air conditioning unit. These expenses are different from regular maintenance expenses. Capital expenses are generally for long-term investment components. Also, some large remodeling expenses are considered capital expenses and are amortized over several years. Those costs may be reflected in the annual operating budget.

The **capital reserve budget** is *a budget for capital expenses that are not fixed (variable expenses)*. The reserve budget is often incorporated into the annual operating budget as an annual average cost of replacing various building components.

After creating an operational budget with fixed and variable expenses, property managers should look toward developing a **stabilized budget**, which is *the income and expenses averaged over a five-year period*. This long-term forecast takes a variety of factors into consideration, such as potential growth, market trends, etc.

Budget comparison statements *compare the actual working budget with the budget developed at the beginning of the year*. These comparisons should be calculated for both the month and year-to-date income and expenses. This comparison can confirm trends as well as identify areas that need extra work to meet expectations.

A **profit and loss statement** is *a brief statement issued at regular intervals, presenting gross receipts, minus operating expenses, minus total mortgage payment, plus mortgage loan principal to equal net profit*.

A **cash flow report** is usually issued on a monthly basis and gives the owner a detailed financial picture of the property. The following formula is used to find the sum of operating cash, which will be a key component of the cash flow report.

Income – Expenses – Debt Services = Operating Cash

Recommendations

After all property management reports have been generated, the property manager should be able to develop the management proposal and then make recommendations to the owner about the property. For example, after reviewing the reports, property managers may recommend adding a pool to a residential apartment complex or renovating the lobby of a commercial building.

General Accounting

As a property manager, it is important to have some knowledge of appraisal, finance, money markets, depreciation techniques, financial trends, and local market conditions to produce useful reports and accomplish the owner's overall objectives and goals. It is also important to understand real estate licensing laws related to financials, such as avoiding the commingling of personal and business funds in any way.

Owners want to know the financial picture of their business and have an understanding of the trends occurring in the marketplace. This helps them decide, for example, when is a good time to sell existing property or add to their portfolio. Property managers should keep on top of this information so they can continue to be a valuable asset to owners.

Management Office Operations

Whether managing a property that is industrial, retail, or residential, a designated office space for the property manager is often necessary. The most logical site for a management office is in the building itself, since easy access and convenience are important. However, the office should not be located in a space that has a potentially high rental value. Space should be allocated for a reception area, file storage, and for desks and equipment for staff.

A well-stocked, well-organized manager's office has these items on hand or readily available:

- Leases
- Correspondence (dating back three years)
- Financial reports (dating back ten years)
- Canceled checks, receipts, etc.
- Annual profit/loss records
- Monthly income/expense reports
- Project bids from companies competing for construction or service work (dating back one year)
- Basic information (property records including mortgage information, title, legal description, management contract, and labor contracts are kept as long as the owners have the property)

- Insurance (checked regularly to ensure coverage is still sufficient and to monitor expiration dates; expired policies are kept for five years)

Supervising Others

In addition to handling owner-tenant relations, most property managers manage a variety of people, so effective communication skills are necessary. A property manager might manage an assistant property manager, tenant services coordinator, or administrative assistant, depending on the size of the property. And a large, multiple-tenant facility may require the manager to oversee any number of contractual employees, including maintenance and janitorial services, security, and landscaping.

Rent Roll

Rent roll is a *spreadsheet or listing of key information about a property* such as the number of units, tenant names with apartment numbers, lease dates, and the rent each tenant pays on a unit. This is helpful for the property manager to manage the level of vacancies and occupancies and to keep tabs on local rent rates.

SUBJECT'S RENT ROLL

Unit	Monthly Rent	Tenant	Unit Sq. Ft.	Original Lease Date	Escalation Provision	Current Lease Term	Term Remaining
1-A	$1375	Roberta Glass	840 sq. ft.	2/15/95	No	3 Years	5 Months
1-B	$1400	John Taylor	840 sq. ft.	7/5/99	No	3 Years	10 Months
2-A	$1250	Brady Hill	840 sq. ft.	6/30/03	No	1 Year	9 Months
2-B	$1300	Roger Stafford	840 sq. ft.	9/1/97	No	3 Years	36 Months

Building Systems and Construction

Property managers should have a general knowledge of the following building systems and components:

- Electrical
- Waterproofing
- HVAC
- Security
- Elevators
- Structural Engineering
- Plumbing
- Gas
- Maintenance

Having a basic understanding of these systems and/or components enables property managers to effectively plan for preventive maintenance and work with maintenance staff, as well as talk with contractors and builders.

Maintenance

Maintenance costs should be carefully scheduled and controlled because they represent a relatively large part of a property's operating budget. There are three types of maintenance property managers are concerned with:

- **Preventive maintenance** includes *routine maintenance and inspections to keep equipment and the property in good working order.* This could include scheduled inspections and the replacement of parts before they fail.
- **Corrective maintenance** *restores broken or failed equipment to a specified condition.* Repair work may be a less frequent expense, but property managers need to line up qualified repair people they can call at a moment's notice.
- **Cosmetic maintenance** *increases a property's appeal.* Adding new wallpaper to a lobby or planting flowers next to a walkway can attract new tenants.

In order to effectively maintain a property, the property manager should:

- Have a thorough understanding of the property.
- Keep a written inventory of property elements with maintenance records.
- Evaluate the cost to perform maintenance and purchase necessary parts and items to keep in supply.
- Determine who will perform the maintenance.
- Keep a detailed schedule for preventive maintenance work.
- Develop a list of qualified contractors and workers, maintain records of work performed, and keep records of competitive bids.

Appraisal

An **appraisal** is *an opinion of the value of property, as of a specific date, supported by objective data.* When a building is appraised, the property manager is the one who interacts with the appraiser. Therefore, it is important to have an understanding of the appraisal process. The condition of the property and the maintenance of building systems can have a large impact on a property's value.

Landlord-Tenant Relations

Creating good relationships with tenants is a key aspect of a property manager's work. Often, property managers who maintain good relationships with tenants have fewer problems and lower turnover.

Spelling out the rules so tenants understand and respect them is basic, but important. For example, tenants need to know all of the landlord's policies, including how to pay their rent and how to place requests for maintenance. Complying with federal, state, and local regulations and communicating them to tenants when necessary are other important parts of a property manager's job.

Leasing Space

Another part of a property manager's job is leasing space. The **lessee** is *a person who leases property* – a tenant, and a **lessor** is *a person who leases property to another* – a landlord. Tenants can be found through effective marketing. Once a tenant has been found, and before the lease is signed, the property manager makes sure the layout of the space is well suited to the tenant's needs. For example, if an advertising agency wants to sign a lease, will the design of the space fit its needs and be functional as well as aesthetically pleasing to the clients? What if the agency signs a major account and needs to expand the company and the space? Is that possible? This is all part of good communication.

Leases

A lease is a binding document and should include:

- Names and signatures of all parties entering into the agreement.
- Date the tenant can assume occupancy.
- Description of the space, including the address and identifying information, such as unit numbers; for example, a commercial space might include a floor plan with the area to be leased highlighted.
- Terms of the lease, including beginning and termination dates, and a statement of the time period covered.
- Valuable consideration, including a statement of the exchange of promises (owner promises to allow tenant to occupy premises, tenant promises to pay rent), amount of rent to be paid, and when and where the tenant should pay.
- Escalation clauses may be added that stipulate any automatic rent adjustments.
- All parties' rights and obligations.
- Any restrictions on the use of the rental space.
- Stipulation that illegal activities on the premises are grounds for immediate termination.

The most common leasehold estate is a **tenancy** (or **estate**) **for years**, which *lasts for a definite period (e.g., one week, three years), which ends automatically when the lease term is up.*

Eviction

Property managers may find they have to evict a tenant who does not pay the rent, breaks the rules, or is involved in criminal behavior. **Actual eviction** is the ***legal process*** *of dispossessing or expelling someone from real property, allowing a landlord to regain possession of the property from a tenant who is otherwise unwilling to give it up.* **Constructive eviction** is *when a landlord's act (or failure to act) interferes with the tenant's quiet enjoyment of the property or makes the property unfit for its intended use, to such an extent that the tenant is forced to move out.* To claim constructive eviction, the tenant must actually vacate the property.

In the case of rent delinquency, the property manager may decide to offer a grace period to try and correct the situation. Property managers who find they do have to evict a tenant need to work with an attorney to bring an eviction suit. It is best to choose an attorney who has performed evictions before.

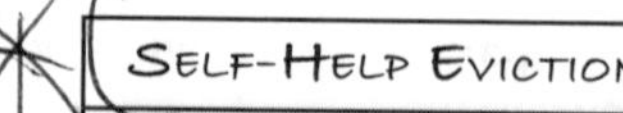

Landlords can certainly become frustrated with bad tenants, but they must resist the temptation to take matters into their own hands. A **self-help eviction**, sometimes called a **lock-out** or a **freeze-out**, is when a landlord uses physical force or other means to get rid of a tenant instead of going through the legal process. Although some commercial leases may include a clause giving the landlord the right to retake possession without going through the legal process if the tenant defaults, a residential landlord is not allowed to force tenants off the property by any means other than the legal process. It's **illegal** for the landlord to:

- Threaten the tenants.
- Change locks or otherwise lock them out.
- Shut off utility services to make them leave.
- Introduce noise or other nuisance to make them leave.

Advertising and Marketing

A solid marketing and promotional plan is needed to attract tenants. A good marketing campaign helps property managers reach a pool of preferred tenants, and can help to convince prospects to sign leases. By deciding whom they need to reach and the best ways to reach them, managers can build an effective campaign.

All advertising should comply with federal, state, and county laws, and city civil rights and fair housing guidelines. Display ads should include the equal housing logo and all ads must be non-discriminatory.

Components of a Marketing Campaign

First, managers should do what they can, within the budget, to make the property more attractive to potential lessees. Then they need to assess the supply and demand in the area and decide, based on prevailing conditions, how much of a marketing effort is needed. For example, if there is a high-vacancy rate, they will need a more aggressive marketing campaign than if there is a single vacancy in a high-demand market.

There are several routes a property manager can take to advertise a property available for rent. Common strategies include:

Word of Mouth

- Word of mouth is a powerful marketing tool, and current tenants are an excellent source for referrals.
- Managers should offer a bonus for good referrals.

Advertisement

- A property manager should determine which publications the target audience reads to get the most out of print advertising dollars.
- Classified ads are less expensive, but display ads deliver greater impact.

Signage

- Signs should specify the kind of unit available, the management firm, and a phone number.

Brochures

- Brochures should be designed and written to appeal to the target audience. Keep copy brief, include attractive photos, and use a clean layout to give the brochure appeal.

Direct Mail

- Fliers can be mailed to a list that includes prospective tenants and targeted real estate brokers.
- Usually less expensive than brochures, fliers can be written and designed more casually.

Online

- A website with easy-to-navigate photos and information is convenient and cost effective.

Press Release

- If a property has special features, a press release highlighting the property's significance, along with a photo, is a good form of advertisement.
- If a publication chooses to run the release, it is an extremely cost-effective way to promote the property.

	Type of Advertising						
Property Type	Word of Mouth	Ad	Signage	Brochure	Direct Mail	Online	Press Release
Commercial	✓	✓ Display ad	✓	✓	✓	✓ For a unique property	
Residential	✓	✓ Newspaper ad	✓		✓	✓	
Industrial	✓	✓ Trade publication ad		✓			
Specialized	✓	✓ Ad choice depends on the property		✓		✓	✓

Evaluation

Whether you choose a simple classified ad or a full-scale campaign, marketing space can be expensive. Property managers need to give owners an idea of how effective their marketing effort is at attracting prospects. By tracking how prospective tenants heard about an open unit, property managers can begin to get a handle on what is working. To calculate the costs and results of each method, note how much each promotional effort costs and how many prospects responded.

CASE IN POINT

A basic formula to track marketing costs most likely includes the **cost per prospect** approach. For example, you are leasing a space in a commercial building for $3,000 a month and you have taken out an ad that costs $800. To determine the cost per prospect, factor in how many prospects viewed the space before it was leased. For this example, assume 10 people walked through the space before a lease was signed.

$800 (Cost of Ad) ÷ 10 (Number of Prospects) = $80 Cost Per Prospect

Advertising Costs Plus Vacancy

In addition to the cost of the advertising, you may also need to factor in how many days, weeks, or months it takes to lease a space. To determine advertising costs plus vacancy, property managers must figure not only how much advertising a unit costs, but also how much it is costing to have empty space. For this example, let's assume a unit was empty for two weeks and the manager took out one classified ad for each of those weeks.

$100 (Cost of Ad) x 2 (Weeks) = $200 in Advertising Costs

Then consider the money lost by *not* renting the space:

$3,000 (Per Month Rent) x 12 Months = $36,000 Total Rent Per Year

$36,000 ÷ 52 (Weeks in a Year) = $692.31 Rent Per Week

$692.21 x 2 (Weeks the Space Sat Empty) = $1,384.62 in Lost Income

Now, add the cost of advertising plus the lost rent.

$200 (Advertising) + $1,384.62 (Lost Income) = $1,584.62 Total Cost

Other Responsibilities

It may seem as though a property manager's job never ends. In addition to the responsibilities already mentions, a property manager must stay on top of federal, state, and local laws, as well as his obligations as a real estate licensee.

Adhering to Codes and Regulations

Another part of a property manager's responsibility is understanding codes and restrictions. In New York State, the New York Multiple Dwelling Law is in effect. Some of its provisions include:

- Each living unit must have an operational carbon monoxide detector and a smoke detector approved by state fire prevention and building codes.
-  From October 1 – May 31, heat must be available.
- Lights of at least 40 watts must be installed in every rear yard, side yard, front yard, and court.

In addition to the New York State law, landlords must comply with:

- Federal Fair Housing laws and the Americans with Disabilities Act.
- Local occupancy laws.
- Environmental laws that spell out requirements for trash disposal (number of trashcans or bins allowed, etc.).
- Health and building department laws.
- Zoning regulations.

Essentially, landlords must secure the premises for the enjoyment of the tenants, keep it clean and free of garbage, and keep it safe. This means property managers may be required to stop noisy parties, add security features if needed, rearrange parking to make it safer, add lights, and take other actions to ensure tenants are safe and happy.

Union Negotiations

As a property manager in the state of New York, it is important to be aware of and have an understanding of union contractors. Maintenance staff, or other building service staff, may be part of unionized labor, which has different needs and schedules than non-union labor staff members.

Purchasing

No matter how big or small a property is, or how many people there are to manage it, all property managers should have an understanding of purchasing. It is not unusual for property managers to be responsible for purchasing supplies, writing purchase orders, and paying a wide variety of contractors. Many larger companies have purchasing departments that can assist the property manager in these duties.

Environmental Awareness

There has been a national movement toward running homes and businesses in environmentally friendly ways. In fact, some buildings are specifically designed to be energy efficient and less taxing on the environment. Depending on the market and the specific property you are assigned to, it is important to be aware of ways you can save energy and/or money on electric, gas, water, and landscaping.

Continuing Education and Designations

Several associations and groups offer professional designations and specialized course work in the property management field. These designations and accreditations increase the knowledge, skill base, and marketability of property management professionals. These associations include:

- **Building Owners and Managers Association International** (BOMA). Offers professional development courses for property managers.
  - *Real Property Administrator* (RPA) is awarded to those completing training courses offered by the BOMA.
- **Institute of Real Estate Management** (IREM). A National Association of REALTORS® (NAR) affiliate group – Provides education and designations in the property management field, including:
  - *Accredited Residential Manager* (ARM). For those specializing in residential property management.
  - *Certified Property Manager* (CPM). For those who meet certain requirements.
- **National Association of Residential Property Managers** (NARPM). Offers designations including:
  - *Professional Property Manager* (PPM).
  - *Master Property Manager* (MPM).

SUMMARY

1. A **property manager** is *hired by a real property owner to administer, market, merchandise, and maintain property, especially rental property.*

2. **Property management** is *the leasing or renting, or the offering to lease or rent, real property to others for a fee, commission, compensation, or other valuable consideration pursuant to a property management employee contract.* A property manager is a **general agent**, *an agent authorized to handle all of the principal's affairs in one area or in specified areas.* He has fiduciary obligations to the owner. The main objectives of a property manager are to fulfill the owner's goals, create income, and maintain or increase the property's value.

3. There are four main types of properties that need to be managed: 1. **Residential property** (single-family homes, apartments, condominiums, co-ops, mobile home parks, and retirement communities); 2. **Commercial property** (retail and office space); 3. **Industrial property** (manufacturing facilities and warehouses); and 4. **Special-use properties** (hotels, theaters, schools, places of worship, PUDs, and nursing homes).

4. A **management agreement** is *a written agreement that governs the relationship between the property owner/investor and the property manager, and outlines the responsibilities of each party.* The agreement typically contains a description of the property, length of agreement, management authority, management fee, accounting responsibilities and reports, insurance and risk management, owner's objectives, and management agreement termination.

5. **Management fees** may be fixed (flat) or a percentage. A **flat fee** is *a specific fee paid out at specific increments.* A **percentage fee** is *based on the operation's gross collectible income.* **Risk management,** an important skill for property managers, is *identifying, managing, and minimizing the potential risks on the property.* **Property management reports** are prepared by the property manager to inform the owner on the status of the property, often including income, expenses, and disbursements information.

6. Property managers have a variety of responsibilities, starting with the **management proposal,** which is a plan created by the property manager for overseeing the property and involves analysis of the market and financial reports, including an operating budget. Property managers need to provide regular reporting and financial analysis to their owners, including an **operating budget**, created to project income and expenses for the property over a one-year period, and a **stabilized budget,** which is the income and expenses averaged over a five-year period. The property manager also keeps track of the capital reserve budget, capital expenses, variable expenses, fixed expenses, budget comparison statements, profit and loss statements, and cash flow reports.

7. Property managers supervise others, interact with appraisers if necessary, and manage the office operations and the rent roll. They also monitor building systems, construction, and maintenance. **Preventive maintenance** includes *routine maintenance and inspections to keep equipment and the property in good working order.* **Corrective maintenance** *restores broken or failed equipment to a specified condition.*

8. Property managers maintain landlord-tenant relations and lease space. Property managers may have to evict a tenant. **Actual eviction** is the ***legal process*** *of making a tenant vacate the property.* **Constructive eviction** is *when a landlord's act (or failure to act) interferes with the tenant's quiet enjoyment of the property or makes the property unfit for its intended use to such an extent that the tenant is forced to move out.* **Self-help** evictions are illegal.

9. Property managers must also develop an advertising and marketing campaign, which may include word of mouth, advertisements, signage, brochures, direct mail, online and website marketing, and press releases. Property managers need to follow codes and regulations and must secure the premises for the safety and enjoyment of tenants. According to the New York Multiple Dwelling

Law, heat must be available from October 1 – May 31. Other responsibilities of property managers include understanding union negotiations, purchasing, and finding environmentally friendly ways to run a property.

10. There are a variety of professional organizations, like the Building Owners and Managers Association (BOMA) and the Institute of Real Estate Management (IREM) for property managers. A property manager can earn many designations, including Accredited Residential Manager (ARM), Certified Property Manager (CPM), and Real Property Administrator (RPA).

19

Commercial and Investment Properties 1

In This Session

Commercial real estate is a challenging and exciting specialty within the real estate field. Of the total number of licensed real estate professionals in the United States, numerous studies have indicated that only about two of every ten agents practice commercial real estate. More agents may explore commercial real estate further if they had some basic information to get started. In this session, you will see how commercial real estate can be defined and take a first step toward understanding the language of commercial real estate.

You'll learn:

- License requirements for commercial real estate.
- Considerations for different types of investment properties.
- How rent is calculated on commercial space.
- How commercial leases are structured.

Key Terms

- Amenity Purchaser
- Anchor Tenant
- Clear Span
- Common Area Maintenance
- Consumer Price Index (CPI)
- Escalation Clause
- Loft
- Loss Factor / Load
- Market Value
- Net Lease
- Pass-Through
- Porter's Wage Escalation Formula
- Pro-rata Share
- Rentable Square Footage / Gross Square Footage
- Retail Investment Property
- Usable Square Footage / Net Square Footage

Working in Commercial Real Estate

Just what is "commercial" real estate? How is that different from "investment" real estate? For all intents and purposes, both terms refer to the same thing: Property that is used for investment purpose. If a single-family home is going to be used for investment purposes, then it, in effect, becomes commercial real estate. Multi-family properties, office, retail, industrial, land – it doesn't really matter what the property is. If someone intends to use that property as an investment, it all falls into the category of commercial real estate.

License Requirements

Contrary to what many people assume, practicing commercial real estate does **not** require a special license. The New York State real estate broker's or salesperson's license is all-encompassing, which means the license permits an agent to conduct business in the brokerage of practically any type of real estate. The basic provisions of agency law, contract law, real property law, and license law are almost identical in commercial real estate and residential real estate.

All In a Day's Work

Working with commercial clients and customers usually means working the hours they work, often nine to five and rarely on the weekend. There are exceptions to this rule, however, as in smaller markets or with those who deal in both residential and commercial properties. And like any real estate professional, it's up to the licensee to generate business. So, while they may not be working directly with clients after typical working hours, or on the weekends, they may be busy generating marketing material, making phone calls, and engaging in other business-building activities.

Learning the Language of Commercial Sales

What many agents find attractive about commercial real estate is the creativity required to put transactions together. Because of this, negotiations are often more time consuming and sophisticated. Commercial transactions are often riskier and more complicated than typical residential transactions. Commercial real estate investments usually require specialized knowledge and expertise different from residential transactions.

By necessity, the commercial real estate industry has developed its own language to describe the market and properties for sale. Therefore, many of the concepts and the vocabulary used by developers and investors have been adopted into the commercial real estate lexicon. The language of commercial real estate may contain some unfamiliar real estate terms, but most of it should be familiar.

Civil Rights and Fair Housing

Licensees working in commercial real estate must understand that the laws of the United States, State of New York, and New York City related to civil rights and fair housing also apply to commercial properties in New York City:

- The **Civil Rights Act of 1866** prohibits public and private racial discrimination in any property transaction in the United States. The Civil Rights Act of 1866 applies to all property – real or personal, residential or commercial, improved or unimproved.
- The federal **Fair Housing Act** makes it illegal to discriminate based on race, color, religion, sex, national origin, disability, or familial status in the sale or lease of residential property, including vacant land intended for residential housing. The Federal Fair Housing Act applies to commercial housing, such as apartment buildings or complexes of more than four units.
- The **American with Disabilities Act** prohibits discrimination against the disabled and has a tremendous impact on commercial properties, especially in connection to accessibility and accommodation requirements.

Types of Investment Property

Commercial investment real estate often brings to mind large buildings such as skyscrapers, shopping centers, or large apartment complexes with hundreds of tenants. These properties certainly do exist within the commercial market; however, the vast majority of commercial investment real estate transactions are of a much smaller scale. Commercial investments run the full spectrum from single-family homes to small single-user retail or office buildings to large industrial properties and/or multi-family residential complexes. One thing to keep in mind is that regardless of the type of property, the investor's goals remain the same: To generate an **acceptable return on investment** and to **minimize the risk** in any transaction.

Unimproved Land

When a person purchases a parcel of land, he is actually acquiring a bundle of rights: Possession, quiet enjoyment, disposition, exclusion, and control. Each right represents a separate and distinct interest and benefit derived from the ownership of property. Most people think of real estate as the actual land, and maybe the bricks and mortar – the surface rights. But there is much more to it than that, which is one of the elements of real property that makes it such a unique commodity. Other rights include:

- Subsurface rights (mineral rights).
- Air rights.
- Water rights.

When an owner sells his land, he can only convey that which he still owns of the original bundle of rights. For example, if a landowner sells a property that she previously leased or sold the mineral rights to, only what is still controlled may be sold. Therefore, the new owner does not receive those previously sold mineral rights as part of the purchase of the fee simple ownership.

Land Usage

There are many things to consider when analyzing a parcel of land. As with most categories of real estate, location is usually the first item considered. There is a long list of site considerations to evaluate as well, including zoning, environmental requirements, and characteristics of the land itself, such as topography, to determine how much of the land is *usable*. All of these can impact the investor's decision whether to purchase the property and at what price.

When the property is analyzed, it usually is surveyed and perhaps receives an engineering or environmental report. Then potential investors generally evaluate the property's **highest and best use**, which is *the legal use of that property that will yield its highest present value* (greatest net return) so long as the use is:

- Physically possible.
- Financially feasible.
- Legally permissible.
- Maximally productive (most profitable).

Other Considerations

Some of the other considerations that will impact the development on unimproved land include:

- **Setbacks.** The distance that a building (or the building area including parking) must be placed from a street, a property line, or an adjacent property.

- **Floor Area Ratio (FAR).** The total maximum size of a building permitted on a development; typically stated as a percentage of the total square footage of the property.
- **Access roads and curb cuts.** Access to the area in which the property is located as well as the actual access from the road to the property. Most localities require approval of any curb cuts. Engineers usually evaluate traffic patterns to determine where curb cuts may be located.
- **Utilities and sanitation services.** Access to water, electricity, gas, sewers, and waste removal. If utilities are not on the property yet, how far away are they? What is the cost to the owner to bring utilities in? What type of sanitation service is required?
- **Green space.** Any vegetated land or water within or adjoining an urban area; it may include vacant land, rivers, playgrounds, bike trails, etc. Many local governments regulate the amount of green space to be maintained as part of land development.
- **Sidewalks.** Many communities are requiring developers to install sidewalks that extend across the entire frontage of a land site. The widths and materials used can vary from area to area.

Residential Property

An investor in a residential property typically does not intend to live at the property but instead chooses to rent it out to tenants for the production of income. Investors have an array of residential property from which to choose, from single-family homes to large multi-family apartment buildings. Each has its own set of considerations.

Single-Family Residences

Many real estate professionals start their commercial careers selling single-family investment property. And many beginning investors own one or more single-family investment residences. Some of the perceived advantages to single-family properties include comparatively smaller management requirements, the stability of the market for rental homes, and the fact that it's a more liquid commodity than other types of investment property. However, the market value of single-family investment property tends to be influenced by general market conditions instead of generally accepted methods of determining investment values. Often, single-family homes may not be able to produce sufficient rental income to justify the price an investor would have to pay to own them. Another consideration: A single-family residential property is either 100 percent occupied or 100 percent vacant.

Small Multi-Family Residences

Small apartment buildings – consisting of two to four units – are still relatively affordable and attractive in the marketplace. An advantage to this property type over single-family homes is that the risk of a full vacancy is somewhat diminished. In a building with two units, if one tenant moves out, it is still 50 percent occupied and consequently still bringing in some income. Some factors to consider with these properties that are not present with single-family homes include utility metering, maintenance of common areas, tenant privacy and compatibility, soundproofing between units, and accessibility issues.

Large Multi-Family Properties

As the number of units in an apartment property increases, so do the management considerations and complexity of investment analysis. While the basic principles do not change, many additional criteria must be analyzed. Typical investors are often larger companies adept at acquiring and managing these properties. Considerations when analyzing large multi-family properties include market conditions and rent levels, overall condition of the property, amenities and services available to tenants, parking, maintenance and security of common areas, rent control laws, insurability, and liability issues.

Office Buildings

An office building is simply a building that contains office space. Office properties range from former single-family homes converted into commercial space, to small buildings with a few office suites, to large buildings in research office parks, to skyscrapers. The determination of when an office building is called a high-rise or skyscraper is usually dependent on the specific locality.

Office property can be highly specialized, and tenants often have very specific needs for this type of space. Some considerations that affect the value of office property include the following:

- Location
- Compliance with the American with Disabilities Act (ADA)
- Accessibility – ingress (entrance) and egress (exit)
- Visibility – building and signage
- Adequacy of parking (generally five to six cars per 1,000 square feet of space)
- General market conditions and rent levels
- Common areas and facilities
- Tenant profile
- Ease of tenant improvements (TI)
- Type and adequacy of mechanical systems
- Special maintenance requirements
- Security and lighting in common areas
- Staffing and management requirements
- Appearance and market appeal
- Ancillary services, such as vending, on-site cafeteria, or child care
- Technology issues, such as cable lines, satellite, or fiber optics

Classes of Office Property

In many markets, office buildings are often rated or categorized by the building's **class**, which is usually based on a combination of building characteristics, such as age, lease rates, architectural design, occupancy, location, tenant profiles, management, and building amenities and services.

- **Class A** buildings are usually the newest and most desirable buildings in a particular market with the best design, superior construction, amenities, and features. These buildings command the highest rental rates and set the standard for the rest of the local market.
- **Class B** buildings have good location, appearance, amenities, and are still desirable, but not quite the top of the market, primarily due to age.
- **Class C** properties are older and still functionally viable, but not as favorably located or maintained. Tenants are typically price-driven.

- **Class D** buildings are the balance of the older, functionally obsolete buildings needing extensive renovation. These are prime candidates for rehabilitation projects or teardown.

Each community has its own standards for these designations. What might be a Class A building in one market might only be a Class B building in another.

Retail Property

Retail properties are diverse and unique when compared to other types of real estate investments, with a wide range of property types available to investors. In the retail market, the ability of a property to produce an acceptable income stream depends on a number of factors, some of which are unique to retail space. The location and its demographics of the customer base are critical, as are these factors: Market appeal, access to public transportation, traffic flow, parking (generally three spaces for each 1,000 square feet), visibility and signage, competition, tenant mix, and anchor tenants. An **anchor tenant** is *a magnet store strategically located in shopping centers to generate traffic for smaller stores.*

Types of Retail Property

Retail investment property ranges from freestanding stores to enormous shopping malls. Retail property may be classified by purpose and size as follows:

- **Strip centers** typically contain a minimum of three stores with a total gross leasable area of up to 30,000 square feet. A wide range of tenants occupy strip centers and provide goods such as groceries and services such as dry cleaning.
- **Neighborhood centers** are typically built around a supermarket anchor tenant and range in size from 30,000 to more than 100,000 square feet.
- **Community shopping centers** have multiple anchor tenants providing a much wider range of goods and services and range from 100,000 to 300,000 square feet.
- **Regional malls** provide a broad range of general merchandise, apparel, home furnishings, appliances, and electronics, as well as an array of services, restaurants, and recreational facilities. Enclosed or not, regional malls range in size from 250,000 to more than 900,000 square feet.
- **Super regional** or **mega malls** are often built around three or more full line department stores as well as many smaller stores offering new every good and service imaginable. They range in size from 500,000 square feet to well over 1.5 million square feet.
- **Specialty shopping centers** are characterized by the lack of a traditional anchor tenant and have a group of tenants clustered together to fill the role of the anchor, for example, festival centers, which are a mixed-use blend of specialty retail with a wide variety of restaurants and food vendors, a strong entertainment component, and even hotel, convention, and meeting facilities.
- **Power centers** take on the unique appearance of a cluster of very large "big box" retailers on the same property with few or no small stores.
- **Outlet centers** consist of several smaller stores that are either attached, detached, or a combination of both styles. The stores are usually restricted to major name retailers and manufacturers selling merchandise that is considered "seconds," "irregulars," or discontinued lines at a discount.

Industrial and Manufacturing Properties

Industrial real estate is a very broad category and includes properties considered as distribution, manufacturing, and research facilities. Unlike office space, this type of property is often purchased by an investor who will also *use* the property since it often has highly specialized features. Therefore, industrial properties must be assessed individually based upon the intended use and perhaps the overall adaptability. Industrial properties are typically handled by an industrial specialist or an industrial broker who specializes exclusively in industrial properties. Institutional investors, including pension funds, life insurance companies, and real estate investment trusts, often purchase industrial property, which can be categorized based on use or property type, for example:

- Warehouse
- Service center
- Wholesale trade
- Distribution/transit warehouse
- Research and development center
- Factory (light or heavy assembly, high tech)

Structural and Site Considerations

There are a number of features to consider in almost all industrial properties, including:

- **Floor load capacity**, how many *pounds per square foot the floor can support.*
- **Ceiling height**, which determines what processes or equipment can be used in the space.
- **Clear span**, which is the *open distance between inside faces of support members,* is especially important for distribution warehouses or manufacturing processes that require wide open spaces for large machinery, assembly lines, or conveyor belt systems.
- **Loading docks**, shipping, and receiving areas.
- **Accessibility and proximity to transportation**, such as highways, railroads, airports, and shipping.
- **Mechanical systems**, including type and adequacy.
- **Environmental concerns**, almost always requiring an environmental impact statement (EIS).

Another consideration related to industrial properties is community opposition. There may be resistance to certain types of industrial businesses that fall into the "NIMBY" category, that is, "Not in my back yard!"

Mixed-Use Buildings

Mixed-use buildings are those that do not fall into a single-use category. A mixed-use building could, for example, combine retail and office space on the first floor with residential on the floors above, or combine industrial, office, and retail. The possibilities and combinations are numerous and depend largely on local zoning laws and ordinances.

A common example of a mixed-use building is a loft. **Loft** buildings are characterized by the fact that *most of the building's interior is left unfinished, or minimally finished*. A loft building or loft space can also refer to an open space design of the tenant's usable area. Traditionally, loft space was used for lower cost or budget manufacturing or distribution operations. Today, however, lofts are often seen in older multi-story buildings that have been converted into multiple creative use designs for retail, restaurant, office, and residential areas. Because the space is unfinished, the rent rate for a loft lease is often lower than for finished space.

Buying Versus Leasing

When business owners are deciding whether to buy or to rent commercial property, they must evaluate the relative merits of owning versus leasing.

Owning Property

Fee simple ownership is the fullest freehold interest in property. It includes all the bundle of rights (possession, quiet enjoyment, disposition, exclusion, and control). This means that a fee simple estate is inheritable and transferable. Some of the *advantages* of owning include:

- Tax savings.
- Income.
- Appreciation.
- Control of the property.

Of course, there are potential *disadvantages* to owning property, including:

- Initial capital outlay.
- Financing.
- Liability.
- Management requirements.
- Legal compliance.
- Inflexibility.

Amenity Purchasers

When working with commercial buyers, you may hear the term "amenity purchaser" and wonder how that differs from an investor. Although there is some overlap of the two, an investor and an amenity purchaser will not find the same value in the same property:

- The **amenity purchaser** is most likely an owner/user who is *motivated to find a location from which to house and operate a business.* This buyer values a property based on its ability to fulfill his specific business needs and may be more concerned about factors such as space, location, potential for expansion, etc.
- The **investor** *desires to place money where it will earn more money.* Investors value a property based primarily on its investment return and are more concerned with vacancy rates, income stream, etc.

Leasing Property

The alternative to acquiring fee simple ownership is obtaining a leasehold interest in property. Leasing is the means of acquiring occupancy rights, physical and partial economic use of property for a specific period. Some of the *advantages* of leasing include:

- Flexibility.
- Lower up-front cash requirement.

- Some tax relief (property taxes, rent, and other expenses are deductible).
- Lower risk of obsolescence.
- Stability of costs.
- Mobility.
- Fewer management distractions.
- Better return on inventory turnover as opposed to tying up capital in ownership.

And some of the possible *disadvantages* to leasing include:

- Inability to take advantage of appreciation.
- Lack of control over property.
- Lack of operational control and changes.
- Limited tax relief.
- Contractual penalties.
- Actual total cost of leasing is often more expensive per square foot than ownership.

Sale-and-Leaseback

Practically every aspect of a business operation can affect the own versus lease decision process. An agent and her clients need to analyze the proposed acquisition to assess the relative merits of the investment value. The ultimate goal is to make the client comfortable with the available alternatives that best satisfy the requirements of his business. But an agent shouldn't narrow the possible solutions she can offer a client to just a straight purchase or lease.

For example, in a sale-and-leaseback arrangement, a company will construct a building that suits its needs, and then sell the building to an investor, who becomes the landlord. This allows the tenant company to have more liquid assets to invest in product or other resources, rather than having all assets tied up in the real estate. There are also tax advantages for both the company lessee and the investor lessor.

Commercial Leases

Leases are *binding contracts that set forth the terms and conditions under which a space can be occupied by a tenant.* Common lease terms include rental payment, permitted uses of the space by the tenant, who is responsible for maintenance and utilities, and how much, if any, rent will increase over the term.

The commercial lease spectrum is simply the wide range of possibilities that exist for constructing rental payment arrangements and cost recovery in different types of income properties. A triple net lease is at one extreme of the spectrum, and a gross lease, or full service lease, is at the other end. In between the two extremes is where most rental negotiations take place.

Gross Leases

A **gross lease** is a *straightforward exchange of rent for occupancy.* With a gross lease, also called a **full service lease**, the tenant pays a fixed rent, while the owner or landlord pays all ownership expenses, such as property taxes, repairs, janitorial services, insurance, and sometimes utilities.

In a modified gross lease arrangement, tenants may be responsible for utilities, trash removal, and cleaning. The landlord pays the taxes and obtains damage and liability insurance and also maintains heating, ventilation, and air conditioning (HVAC) systems as well as security for the building.

Office Leases

Having a full service lease for an office building means the tenant's rent includes his pro-rata, or proportional, share of operating costs. This is based on the percentage of square feet of the entire building the tenant occupies. A typical lease states an estimate for annual operating costs, and the rental payment is a monthly proration of that figure. At the end of the year, the landlord totals the actual costs, and if the actual costs are less than what the tenant paid, the tenant will receive a credit throughout the coming year. If the actual annual costs are more than the estimated costs, the tenant will most likely receive a bill from the landlord for the unpaid excess costs.

Lease terms for office buildings are typically from one to ten years but can, for a major tenant in some markets, be as long as 40 years, with options to extend the term further. In addition to options to extend the term, tenants occasionally negotiate provisions referred to as **accordion clauses**, which *give the tenant the flexibility to expand and contract the amount of space occupied.*

Net Leases

A **net lease** is a lease for which *the tenant pays some or all of the costs of ownership, except mortgage interest and principal, in addition to the agreed upon rent.* With net leases, the property owner or landlord has shifted much of the risk for increased property costs to the tenants, who get the additional tax benefit of the business expense. A net lease means lower rent for the tenant, but higher costs. Net leases may be categorized by the extent of the tenant's responsibility for paying these ownership costs:

- Taxes
- Insurance
- Common area maintenance (CAM)

If the lease requires the tenant to pay *one* of these expenses, it's called a **single net lease**. If the tenant is required to pay *any two* of these expenses, it's a net-net lease, or a **double net** lease. A **triple net**, or net-net-net, lease requires the tenant to pay *all three* of these expenses. A triple net lease is also sometimes referred to as an **absolute net lease**.

Warehouses and Industrial Building Leases

Triple net leases are common for industrial commercial space where single tenants lease entire warehouses. The tenant takes responsibility for all expenses related to maintenance, repair, utilities, taxes, and sometimes even the roof and structure of the building, as well as the parking lots and grounds upkeep.

Of course, the rental payment to the landlord is much smaller on a per-square-foot basis, but the income to the landlord is usually dependable, without the vagaries of bills and unexpected costs. Lease terms for warehouses and other general-purpose industrial properties can be as short as a few months for multi-tenant buildings or as long as several decades for single tenant facilities.

Of course, the terms of a lease are negotiable; therefore, there is a myriad of commercial property lease arrangements to suit individual circumstances. For example, the lease may be a modified net lease arrangement whereby the landlord is responsible for some of the property expenses such as maintaining the building's exterior walls and foundation, as well as any common areas, such as parking lots and main signage. The tenant, then, is usually responsible for other property expenses such as utility payments and trash removal, plus a pro-rata share of the property taxes and common area maintenance (CAM) charges. Because every element of a lease is negotiable, you should always read the entire lease carefully to examine its specific terms.

Percentage Leases

A **percentage lease** is a gross or net lease in which *the tenant pays a fixed monthly base rent as well as a percentage of gross sales achieved by the tenant over and above a predetermined level of sales known as the "breakpoint."* This type of lease, most commonly used for **retail tenants**, allows the landlord to share in the tenant's success and may include a clause that allows the owner to reclaim the premises if gross sales fall below a specified point.

Base rent for retail is usually:

- Figured on an annual basis.
- Paid on a monthly basis.
- Quoted on a per-square-foot basis.

Breakpoint

The **breakpoint** is *the sales volume above which a retailer makes a profit.* For instance, a jewelry store owner agrees to a base rent of $80,000 per year, payable monthly, plus extras (such as common area maintenance charges, security, marketing, etc.). Furthermore, the owner agrees to pay 8% overage. The breakpoint can be determined by dividing the annual base rent by the agreed upon overage percentage. In this example, the breakpoint would be:

$80,000 Base Rent ÷ .08 Overage = $1 Million Breakpoint

If the jewelry store's annual sales exceed $1 million, then each dollar in sales over the breakpoint would cost the tenant another 8% in overage rent. For example, if the store had annual gross sales of $1.1 million, the overage rent would be payable on the $100,000 above the breakpoint. Overage rent would therefore be $8,000 ($100,000 x .08).

Most retail tenants who have percentage rent arrangements calculate the amount of pro-rata percentage rent due and pay it on a monthly basis, adjusting for any discrepancies at year-end when audited records are available.

Residential Property Leases

Leases for apartments might be classified as modified gross leases, with the landlord paying the cost of taxes, insurance, maintenance, repairs, landscaping, and security. Tenants may be responsible for paying utilities in addition to rent. Residential leases are typically for one year.

Single-family residential rentals usually employ net leases or modified net leases. Tenants usually pay most of the cost of utilities and regular maintenance as well as minor repairs, while the landlord covers the cost for major repairs or replacement of equipment such as air conditioning and water heaters. The landlord also typically pays the property taxes and property liability insurance.

Ground Leases

Ground leases, also referred to as **land leases**, *enable tenants to lease only the land (often an unimproved parcel of land), not any structures or improvements on the land.* This type of lease is structured to separate the ownership of the land from the ownership of the buildings and improvements on the land. Rent, therefore, reflects only a base rental amount for the land alone.

A good long-term ground lease enables tenants to have physical control over the parcel, and then finance improvements over the term of the ground lease, including the ability to amortize and/or depreciate the improvements. Most land leases are on an absolute net basis and require the tenant to pay all of the expenses normally associated with ownership of land, such as property taxes, maintenance, and insurance.

Often, the lease term for a ground lease is in the form of an initial term with several options to renew. For example, an initial lease term could be ten years with four five-year options. This would enable the tenant to control the property for an extended period – at least 30 years. This is extremely important because upon expiration of the ground lease, the land, and the building erected upon it, reverts to the landowner, not the lessee.

Lease Clauses

Each and every clause of a lease is a negotiating point between a landlord and a tenant. The following lease clauses, although not all-inclusive, represent some of the most common.

Use Clause

The **use clause** *specifically defines what type of business or use can be conducted by the tenant on the premises.* For example, a commercial lease for a space in an office building might state the leased premises will be used "only for general business office purposes, and for no other use or purpose," or contain words of similar import or intent. This clause is commonly seen in leases for retail or commercial space. Often mall leases may even state what type of products may or may not be sold by the tenant in that space.

Tenants usually want use clauses to be as flexible as possible so they can add other goods and services. Landlords, on the other hand, want to ensure tenants do not compete with each other, so they want use clauses to be specific. If the lease does not have a use clause or does not state a specified purpose, the tenant may use the space for any lawful use.

Attornment

An **attornment clause** *establishes tenancy with a new owner and defends current tenants against claims for rent from the former property owner.* This clause provides that, in the event of foreclosure or termination, for example, the lease shall continue, in force, as if the new owner or mortgagee were the landlord for a term equal to the unexpired term of the lease, and upon the same terms and provisions.

Estoppel

An **estoppel certificate** is a legal instrument that *prevents a person from taking a position, denying a fact, or asserting a fact inconsistent with previous conduct or statements*. Most standard commercial leases contain a clause whereby all tenants agree to comply with the request to complete an estoppel document upon request of the landlord.

For example, an investor who purchases rental property may have current tenants sign an estoppel certificate acknowledging their obligation to pay the agreed upon rent and to confirm the terms of their existing leases.

Subordination and Nondisturbance

When someone is purchasing commercial property, the lender may not be willing to accept the property as security for the loan if it is burdened by an existing leasehold interest with a higher claim against the real estate. A **subordination** agreement *makes the existing lease junior to that of the new mortgage on the leased property.* For example, when a subordination clause is in the lease, the tenant will grant a waiver of his priority in favor of the new lender in the event of foreclosure of the landlord's loan. Those rights of recovery and protection in a leasehold would be subordinate to the rights of the lender, which means the lender could cancel the lease when taking over the tenant's building.

The tenant's protection to a subordination request is a **nondisturbance** agreement from the landlord's lender. This clause requires lenders to sign a document agreeing to honor and not terminate the tenancies of lessees who are current with their rent and who are complying with all provisions and obligations of their leases.

Right of First Refusal Clause

If a tenant thinks that she may wish to buy the building or the property in the future, she may negotiate to have a **right of first refusal** clause placed in the lease. This clause, also called a right of preemption:

- Gives the tenant the right to have the *first opportunity* to buy or lease property *if* the owner decides to put it up for sale or lease.
- Cannot be exercised until the owner gets a bona fide offer from a third party. The owner must then make the property available to the person holding the right at the same terms as the bona fide offer.

Note that a right of first refusal is an inheritable interest and it also creates a cloud on the title and should be recorded in the public record.

Utility Clauses

Utility expenses are often addressed by specific lease clauses. This may, of course, depend on whether the lease is a full service lease or a triple net lease. However, even in a full service lease, utilities may be treated as a separate category. The monitoring of utility usage may be determined by:

- Direct metering by the utility company, where each tenant is separately metered and pays the utility company.
- Sub-metering by the landlord, who pays the utility bill and monitors individual private meters, billing the tenants.
- Pro-rata based on percentage of space occupied.

Disposal of Leased Space

The commercial real estate leasing market is influenced by various economical cycles and is usually most noticeable when the economy experiences a downturn. Tenants may experience these shifts in their own businesses, and their space needs may change accordingly. For instance, if a tenant faces the need to downsize or eliminate a local office, she will likely need to dispose of the leased space. There are four options available to do this, depending upon the terms of the lease:

Close down. Tenants may elect to close down the operation but continue to pay the obligated rental payment until the end of the current term and not exercise their renewal option. By doing this, tenants eliminate paying additional operating expenses. This option is viable only if a nominal amount of time is left on the lease term; if the lease still has several years, the tenant may wish to explore another option.

Buyout. Tenants may elect to approach the landlord with a buyout proposal, in the form of a lump sum paid to terminate the existing lease early. For instance, consider a tenant who is at the end of the second year of a five-year lease and wants to close his business. The current lease obligates him to pay $50,000 per year, or $4,167 per month, in rent. The tenant may offer to pay the landlord a lump sum of one year's rent, or $50,000, in exchange for being released from the remaining three years of his obligation.

Sublease. Tenants may sublease their space to another tenant, if the lease permits it. A sublease exists when a tenant leases his leasehold interest, in whole or in part, to another party. The original tenant remains liable and is entirely responsible for lease payments and all other obligations.

Assignment. Tenants may assign their lease if they no longer wish to occupy the property. When tenants assign a lease, they transfer leasehold interest, rights, and obligations to another party. Tenants holding a leasehold interest can sell their interest or give it away freely, provided the original lease provisions allow assignment. Upon transferring leasehold interest, original tenants no longer make lease payments, but may still be liable for rent and other obligations in the event the assignee defaults.

Good-Guy Clause

Leases often contain a rider known as a "good-guy clause" that limits the liability of the personal guarantor for a tenant when a lease is terminated early. So if a tenant defaults on the lease but is current on rent payments and surrenders the property in good condition, the landlord will not seek payment from the guarantor. A good-guy clause could take the form of a simple paragraph or could be a multiple-page addendum. An example is shown below:

> *The undersigned Guarantor(s) guarantees(s) to Owner, Owner's successors and assigns, the full payment, performance and observance of all the agreements to be performed and observed by Tenant in the attached Lease to XYZ Corp.; including the "Rules and Regulations" as therein provided,*

and including the payment of any of Landlord's legal expenses pertaining the Landlord's legal actions against Tenant, without requiring any notice to Guarantor(s) of nonpayment of, nonperformance, or proof, or notice of demand, to hold the undersigned responsible under this guaranty, all of which the undersigned hereby expressly waive and expressly agree that the legality of this agreement and the agreements of the Guarantor(s) under this agreement shall not be ended, or changed by reason of the claims to Owner against Tenant of any of the rights or remedies given to Owner as agreed in the attached Lease. The Guarantor(s) further agree(s) that in any action or proceeding brought by either Owner or the Guarantors against the other on any matters concerning the Lease or of this guaranty that Owner and the undersigned shall and do waive trial by jury. Notwithstanding the provisions of this guaranty, Guarantor(s) shall be relieved of all liability under this Guaranty upon Tenant's surrendering actual possession of this demised premises to the Owner and retunrning to the Owner the keys to the premises and assigning to Landlord all claim and title to the security deposit held by Landlord under the Lease and paying to Landlord all rents and additional rents and any other charges due to Landlord up to the the date of the surrender of the premises.

Determining Rent for Commercial Properties

In most markets, annual **base rent** is typically calculated as "per square foot." For example, if the rent is quoted as "$8 per square foot," a space with 6,000 square feet would result in $4,000 per month in rent:

$8 x 6,000 Sq. Ft. = $48,000 Annual Rent

$48,000 ÷ 12 = $4,000 Monthly Rent

Understanding space measurement, therefore, is exceptionally important when considering commercial real estate.

Rentable Square Footage

Rentable square footage is generally considered to be the *total floor area of a building.* This measurement, also called **gross square footage**, takes into account all tenant space as well as common areas or service areas such as the lobby, corridors, elevators, restrooms, and stairwells, which are used by two or more tenants and/or third parties and are not under the control of any one tenant.

Rentable square footage is the calculation used to determine a **lease payment** for many types of commercial property, such as office and warehouse space. The tenant pays for a specific space and a prorated share of the identified common areas.

An easy way to remember that rent payments are based on the gross (rentable) square footage is to envision the word "gross" as GRO$$. $$ is paid for GRO$$ square footage.

Usable Square Footage

The **usable square footage**, also referred to as **net square footage** or **carpetable square footage**, is the *amount of actual space within the perimeter of the tenant's premises.* This figure is critical so that the tenant can determine if the space will meet her specific needs for furniture, equipment, and personnel.

Be aware that there are a number of methods for calculating rentable and usable square footage. For example, some property owners or markets may consider the common areas used by tenants, such as lobby and restrooms, as part of the rentable square footage, but *not* consider space taken up by critical structural elements such as fire stairs and elevators. Another property owner may consider the entire gross square footage as rentable square footage for the purpose of rent calculations.

With usable square footage, for example, is space measured to the middle of an interior wall, or just to the wall surface? Make sure you understand the elements of the calculation for each specific property.

Loss Factor

To adequately cover a property owner's loss of rent for common areas that are *not* part of the usable square footage, for example, lobbies, elevator shafts, stairwells, common restrooms, etc., it is necessary to calculate the **loss factor**, sometimes called the **load**. Loss factor is *a ratio of rentable space to usable space.*

(Rentable Sq. Ft. – Usable Sq. Ft.) ÷ Rentable Sq. Ft. = Loss Factor

For example, a building has 10,000 square feet, of which 8,000 square feet are usable:

(10,000 Sq. Ft. – 8,000 Sq. Ft.) ÷ 10,000 = .20, or 20% Loss Factor

When a tenant's rent is calculated, that loss factor – in this example, 20% – is *added on* to the usable space to account for the tenant's share of the common areas. So, if a tenant is leasing 2,000 usable square feet of that 10,000 square foot building, the rent per square foot calculation would be:

2,000 Usable Sq. Ft. x .20 Loss Factor = 400 Sq.Ft. Common Area

2,000 Usable Sq. Ft. + 400 Sq. Ft. = 2,400 Rentable Sq. Ft.

If the landlord charged $22.50 per square foot, then the tenant's annual rent would be:

$22.50 x 2,400 Sq. Ft. = $54,000

Building Efficiency

The flip side of the loss factor is **building efficiency**, which is the *ratio of usable square footage to rentable square footage.* So, that office building with 10,000 rentable square feet and 8,000 usable square feet has a building efficiency of 80%.

Usable Sq. Ft. ÷ Rentable Sq. Ft. = Building Efficiency

8,000 Sq. Ft. ÷ 10,000 Sq. Ft. = 0.80 or 80% Building Efficiency

It is critical to know and understand the language of real estate. Commercial real estate, in particular, requires that you be very specific about how you discuss things:

- When you have a new client who asks you about square footage, don't assume that he knows the difference between net square footage and gross square footage.
- Make it clear that when you quote a price per square foot the prospective tenant knows that it's based on the gross or rentable square footage.
- Explain that when you say "net-net-net" you're discussing the terms of a lease where he will be responsible for paying insurance, property taxes, and common area maintenance.

Lease Escalation Clauses

Leases often contain an **escalation clause** that *allows landlords to raise rent at an agreed upon time during the term of a lease.* These clauses, sometimes called escalators, protect a property owner's profit from rent and, in some cases, may prevent the erosion of their expected return due to inflation.

Base Year

Escalators typically kick in after the **base year** that is identified in the lease. The base year, often the first year of the lease, establishes the operating expenses and taxes. If there is no historical data that supports specific figures for these costs, the indicated base year might not be the first year of the lease. For example, a tenant in a new development has a five-year lease. Since there is no historical data in a new development, the base year indicated in the lease might be year two, so the rent increases will begin in year three.

Pro-Rata Share

Much commercial property includes common space and amenities shared by all the tenants, who are expected to pay for their share of the property's expenses. Some leases determine that share of common expenses on a **pro-rata share** or *proportional basis* of the building's total area.

Tenant's Usable Area ÷ Building's Total Usable Area = Pro-Rata Share

For example, if a tenant occupies 10,000 square feet of a 40,000 square foot building, the tenant is expected to pay a pro-rata share of 25% of the building's expenses:

10,000 Sq. Ft. ÷ 40,000 = .25, or 25%

By evaluating costs occurring in each comparison year with the cost of the same expenses during the base year, increases or decreases in those expenses can be calculated. The determination of the base year and its actual operating costs is necessary to calculate the tenant's pro-rata share. The statement of the base year, operating costs, and the proportionate share should always be clearly defined in a lease to avoid misunderstandings between tenants and landlords.

Pass-Throughs

Many leases allow landlords to *pass along unexpected increases in operating costs to tenants*. These charges are referred to as **pass-throughs**. For example, a lease may contain a provision where the landlord agrees to operating costs up to a maximum rate per square foot or a maximum dollar amount of certain operating expenses with the remainder being passed through to the tenants.

In theory, tenants may be subject to an unlimited number of added expenses that could be passed through by their landlords. Therefore, tenants often negotiate a lease clause that places a maximum on their expense liabilities, which is referred to as an **expense cap** or **expense ceiling**.

Insurance and Property Tax Payments

Insurance and ad valorem property taxes are often handled in the same manner as other operating expenses. A separate clause in a lease may be included to refer to a negotiated amount at which the owner's contribution to property taxes stops. For example, if property taxes were $4 per square foot and the owner had a stop of $3 per square foot, the owner would pay $3 per square foot and tenants would pay $1 per square foot.

Step Increases

With a negotiated contractual **step or bump increase**, *base rent is scheduled to step up or bump up at a predetermined negotiated percentage or pre-established dollar amount* (no matter what happens to actual operating expenses). This is also known as a **graduated lease**.

Such fixed percentage adjustments are commonly effective on each anniversary of the lease or at the beginning of each calendar year. Often, landlords find that lenders are more willing to finance buildings with the income certainty of step increases, as opposed to the fluctuations of other indexed increase methods.

Index Leases

An adjustment mechanism frequently used in the commercial rental market is to link escalation clauses to a readily available **index** based on changes in the marketplace.

Consumer Price Index

The most commonly used index is the **Consumer Price Index (CPI)**. The CPI is an index published monthly by the United States Bureau of Labor Standards (BLS) and is considered *by many to be the basic indicator of inflation in the U.S.* CPI calculations exist for the U.S. as a whole and for regions, states, and even individual markets. By basing rental increases on the increase (or decrease) in the CPI, landlords and tenants can be reasonably sure the amount of rent being paid at the beginning of the lease retains its effective purchasing power no matter what happens to the value of the U.S. dollar due to inflation.

Porter's Wage Escalation Formula

The **Porter's Wage Escalation Formula**, which is used in many New York City buildings, ties the rent escalation to the wages of the building's cleaning and building maintenance personnel (called "porters"). The formula *provides that tenants' rent will increase a specific amount per square foot for a specified increase in the porters' hourly wages*.

Commercial Commissions

There are no fixed or established commission schedules; in fact, any attempt or effort by a group of real estate practitioners to create a standard commission schedule would be construed as a violation of antitrust laws. In commercial real estate, fees may be paid when the transaction closes or in installments, as with a long-term lease. The type and amount of compensation and the payment schedule are always negotiable.

Sales

Fixed percentage. The negotiated commission rate is based on the actual sale price of the property: Sale Price x Commission Rate = Commission.

Graduated percentage. The commission rate is adjusted to the property sale price. For example, 7% on the first $500,000; 6% on the next $500,000; and 5% on anything over $1 million.

Fixed fee. A fixed dollar amount is paid for the performance of specific real estate services. To be paid, the fee arrangement generally requires the successful completion of the transaction.

Retainer or hourly fee. A retainer (in advance) or a fee based on hours worked to perform specified tasks may be paid even when transactions do not close.

Leases

Lump sum. Commission is paid either at the time of execution of the lease (signing of the lease by both the landlord and the tenant) or upon the tenant taking occupancy of the leased premises. This commission is often based on a percentage of the *total rental value of the lease*, known as the **aggregate lease amount**.

Per square foot fee. Commission is based on a dollar amount per square foot of leased space.

Flat fee. Commission is based on a fixed dollar amount for leasing the space regardless of square footage.

Procurement fee. A fee typically paid for finding space for a tenant. Procurement fees are often fixed fees but could be percentage based.

SUMMARY

1. The terms "commercial" real estate and "investment" real estate refer to the same thing: Property that is used for investment purpose. Nearly any type of property could be considered commercial property: Unimproved land, residential property, office buildings, retail, industrial, manufacturing, and mixed-use buildings.
2. Practicing commercial real estate does **not** require a special license or special course work. The basic provisions of agency law, contract law, real property law, license law, and civil rights and fair housing laws are almost identical in commercial real estate and residential real estate.
3. When business owners are deciding whether to buy or to rent commercial property, they must evaluate the relative merits of owning versus leasing. Advantages to owning include tax savings, appreciation, and control. Advantages of leasing include flexibility, lower costs, and less risk.
4. An **amenity purchaser** is most likely an owner/user who is *motivated to find a location from which to house and operate a business.* This buyer values a property based on its ability to fulfill his specific business needs and may be more concerned about factors such as space, location, potential for expansion, etc. An **investor** *desires to place money where it will earn more money.*

Investors value a property based primarily on its investment return and are more concerned with vacancy rates, income stream, etc.

5. Commercial leases reflect a wide range of possibilities for constructing rental payment arrangements and cost recovery. A **gross lease**, also called a **full service lease**, is a *straightforward exchange of rent for occupancy.* A **net lease** is a lease for which *the tenant pays the agreed upon rent and one or more of these ownership costs: Taxes, insurance, or common area maintenance (CAM).* A **single net lease** covers one of these expenses; **double net**, or net-net, covers any two; **triple net**, or net-net-net, covers *all three* of these expenses. A triple net lease, sometimes referred to as an **absolute net lease**, is typical with industrial property.

6. A **percentage lease** is a gross or net lease in which *the tenant pays a fixed monthly base rent as well as a percentage of gross sales achieved by the tenant over and above a predetermined level of sales known as the "breakpoint."* This type of lease, most commonly used for **retail tenants**, allows the landlord to share in the tenant's success and may include a clause that allows the owner to reclaim the premises if gross sales fall below a specified point.

7. **Ground leases**, also referred to as **land leases**, *enable tenants to lease only the land (often an unimproved parcel of land), not any structures or improvements on the land.* This type of lease is structured to separate the ownership of the land from the ownership of the buildings and improvements on the land. Rent, therefore, reflects only a base rental amount for the land alone.

8. Common lease clauses include: **Use** clause (defines use of the leased space), **attornment** (establishes tenancy with a new owner and defends current tenants against claims for rent from a former property owner), **estoppel** (affirms tenants' obligations to lease terms), **sublease** and **assignment** (used when tenants need to dispose of their leased space), **subordination** and **nondisturbance** (places the existing lease in an order junior to that of the new mortgage on leased property), and **electric service** (direct metering, sub-metering, or pro-rata).

9. **Rentable square footage**, also called **gross** square footage, is the *total floor area of a building,* including shared common areas such as hallways, elevators, lobbies, etc. **Usable square footage**, also called **net** square footage or **carpetable** square footage, is the amount of actual space within the perimeter of the tenant's premises. Commercial real estate rent is calculated based on rentable/gross square footage.

10. The **loss factor**, sometimes called the **load**, is *a ratio of rentable space to usable space.* When a tenant's rent is calculated, that loss factor is *added on* to the usable space to account for the tenant's share of the common areas. A loss factor of 20% means for every 100 square feet on which the tenant pays rent, only 80 square feet is actually their usable space. The flip side of the loss factor is **building efficiency**, which is the *ratio of usable square footage to rentable square footage.*

11. Rent is often increased when a lease is renewed or extended. If a lease includes an **escalation clause**, rent may be adjusted, or escalated, during the lease term to add value to the property and/or cover increased costs of operating the building. Escalators typically kick in after the **base year** that is identified in the lease.

12. Some leases determine the share of common expenses on a **pro-rata share,** or *proportional basis* of the building's total area. Many leases allow landlords to *pass along unexpected increases in operating costs to tenants,* referred to as **pass-throughs**. Tenants may negotiate a lease clause that limits their expense liabilities, referred to as an **expense cap** or **expense ceiling.** A **graduated lease** is where the *base rent is scheduled to step up or bump up at a predetermined negotiated percentage or pre-established dollar amount* (no matter what happens to actual operating expenses). An **index lease** links rent escalation to a readily available index based on changes in the marketplace, such as the Consumer Price Index (CPI) or the Porter's Wage Escalation Formula.

13. Commission on commercial transactions can be figured in several ways. On commercial sales: Fixed percentage, graduated percentage, fixed fee, or retainer/hourly fee. On commercial leases: Lump sum percentage of the aggregate lease amount, per square foot fee, flat fee, or procurement fee. Commission may be paid at closing or paid periodically on a long-term lease.

20

Commercial and Investment Properties 2

In This Session

There is no shortage of investment opportunities in the marketplace, such as savings accounts, stocks and bonds, certificates of deposit, money market accounts, precious metals, fine art and collectibles, commodities futures, and, of course, real estate. no matter what the investment, investors select the opportunities they believe closely meet their financial goals. This session explores the elementary factors to consider when investing in real estate.

You'll learn:

- Characteristics of real property investment.
- How risk affects property investment.
- The components of the cash flow model and how it is applied to most investment opportunities.
- How to evaluate the income potential of an investment property and determine its value to an investor.

Key Terms

- Before Tax Cash Flow
- Capitalization Rate
- Cash Flow
- Cash-on-Cash Return
- Debt Service
- Effective Gross Income
- Fixed Expenses / Variable Expenses
- Gross Income
- Leverage
- Liquidity
- Market Value
- Net Operating Income
- Operating Statement
- Pro Forma
- Rate of Return
- Return Of / On Investment
- Risk

Characteristics of Real Property Investments

There is no shortage of investment opportunities in the marketplace, such as savings accounts, stocks and bonds, certificates of deposit, money market accounts, precious metals, fine art and collectibles, commodities futures, and, of course, real estate. No matter what the investment, investors select the opportunities they believe most closely meet their financial goals.

Of course, a primary goal of any investor is the **preservation** of the capital invested; in other words, the investor wants some assurance that there will be a return ***of*** the initial investment. Another attraction of investing in real estate, however, is its capability of producing or earning an acceptable return ***on*** his investment while it is at risk or "tied up" in the property. When a purchaser invests in real estate, he is trading a lump sum of capital in the present for the expectation of one or more of the following:

- Receiving a **continuing stream of income**.
- Creating a **tax shelter**, which *gives owners certain income tax advantages*, such as deductions for property taxes, mortgage interest, and depreciation.
- Building **equity** in the investment through leverage and appreciation.
- Earning a **return on the investment** when the property is sold.

Since a return of the total investment is often not realized until the real estate is sold, it is necessary to analyze the investment for the entire ownership period. There are a number of fundamental investment characteristics that affect how an investor views any investment opportunity. Three important characteristics to consider are risk, liquidity, and leverage.

Risk

Actual events in the market may differ from what investors anticipated at the time property was purchased and so impact an investor's actual rate of return. For example, vacancy rates may be higher than anticipated, or market rental rates at the time of lease renewals may be lower than predicted.

We can view **risk** as *the degree of probability the actual rate of return earned will differ from the return expected when the investment was made.* The amount of expected profit is directly related to the risk inherent in the investment. Low-risk investments are expected to generate low profits; high-risk investments are expected to generate high profits.

Because investors have many outlets for investing their money, real estate must compete with alternative investments; further, the expected returns from real estate must be comparable to returns from other investments with similar risk. An investor's tolerance for risk will have a great impact on her willingness to invest in real estate, because an acceptable level of risk means different things to different investors. Knowing the sources of risk that can affect a particular investment is the first step in risk analysis.

- **Space market risk** is the risk that the *demand for space will affect rents, vacancy rates, and net operating income* (NOI). This can result from either a change in the demand for space by users or changes in the supply of space from new construction.
- **Capital market risk** is the risk that *changes in the market for capital will affect the value of real estate.* Note that this differs from changes in the market for space. Capital market risk is affected by changes in the level of interest rates,

changes in the availability of mortgage and equity capital, and changes in the rate of return for alternative investment opportunities.

- **Financial risk** results when *debt is used to finance an investment.* An investor's return on equity increases if the leverage or the use of credit to enhance speculative capacity increases. Investors expect leverage to be positive when they purchase and finance property. Due to unexpected changes in market conditions, however, the leverage may be negative. The use of debt also increases the risk of default on a mortgage. The degree of financial risk increases with the amount of debt.

Other types of risk can factor into an investment decision, for example **environmental** risk that the value of a property will be influenced by factors that affect the owner's ability to develop or lease the space; **legislative** risk that changes in laws and regulations will affect the market value of the property; or **management** risk that property management can affect the performance of a property.

Liquidity

Liquidity is *the ability to convert an asset into cash quickly without the loss of principal.* Similar to liquidity is **marketability**, which is *the ability to quickly convert a commodity to cash at any price.*

Some investments, such as publicly traded stocks, are highly marketable and therefore relatively liquid. Real estate, on the other hand, may require extended periods to sell and is affected by an unpredictable market. So, the full value of a real estate investment property is usually *not* immediately convertible to cash without some loss of total value. This characteristic of real estate makes it one of the more non-liquid, or illiquid, of the various investment alternatives.

Leverage

Leverage is *the effect borrowed funds have on investment returns.* Leverage may increase or decrease an investor's return that would otherwise have been received had she purchased property on an all-cash basis. Usually, an investor borrows money for a purchase with the expectation that the investment's financial return will increase to such an extent she will realize a profit not only ***of*** her own invested funds (typically the down payment), but will also make a profit ***on*** the borrowed funds. This use of leverage, also called the "use of other people's money" (OPM), is one of the biggest draws for real estate investors.

The use of OPM allows investors to compound their own buying power, thus enabling them to purchase a much larger property or perhaps more property than they otherwise could if they had to use only their own funds for the entire purchase.

Leverage can be positive or negative:

- **Positive leverage** is when borrowed funds are invested at a rate of return higher than the cost of those funds to the borrower, resulting in a profit on the borrowed funds.
- **Negative leverage** occurs when borrowed funds are invested at a rate of return lower than the cost of those funds to the borrower; for example, the interest rate charged by the lender for the borrowed funds is greater than the rate of return the investment is generating on those borrowed funds. In this instance, investors incur a loss on the borrowed funds.

CASE IN POINT

Here is a very simple example of positive leverage. Will buys a rental property for $150,000. He puts $40,000 down and mortgages the remaining $110,000 at 6%. A year later, he's earned $12,000 income from the rent. Without taking into account any tax advantages he may have gained by owning the property, after subtracting the interest paid on the loan – let's say $6,000 – his net profit is $6,000, for a 15% return on investment:

$6,000 ÷ $40,000 = .15 or 15%

If Will had ***not*** financed the purchase of the property:

$12,000 ÷ $150,000 = .08 or 8%

That's the beauty of leverage: Using other people's money to make money.

Evaluating an Investment Property

Investors are typically not emotional about their buying decisions, and like to have objective means to compare properties. Therefore, it's necessary to have a "yardstick" by which to measure the property. One such yardstick is called the **cash flow model**.

An investor uses this model to prepare a **pro forma**, also called **annual property operating data (APOD)**, to show the *hypothetical projection of income and expenses for this first full year of ownership.*

Preparing a pro forma requires investors to first compile a great deal of financial information. The typical investor's thought process when making a buying decision includes weighing:

- Historical information and trends.
- Current supply and demand.
- Factors affecting such trends.
- Anticipated events such as competition from other developments under construction.

Most investors start by requesting a copy of the present owner's recent tax returns and/or their **operating statements**, which are *used by property owners to illustrate total revenues generated and expenses for a given period as a means of evaluating the property's performance.*

Operating Statement Example

While there are many similarities between the present owner's operating statement and the investor's pro forma, there are also many important differences to understand. To compare the two, below is an example of a previous year's operating statement for a small apartment complex:

Operating Statement	
Monthly Rent Roll	
9 Apts. @ $520.00 Month	$56,160.00
8 Apts. @ $610.00 Month	$58,560.00
Annual Rent Roll	$114,720.00
Gross Annual Revenue	$111,320.00
Other Income (Laundry)	$2,400.00
Total Operating Income	$113,720.00
Expenses	
Owner's Salary	$20,000.00
Mortgage Interest	$25,806.00
Owner's Health Insurance	$4,850.00
Travel and Entertainment	$2,025.00
Repairs/Maintenance	$4,237.00
Accounting/Legal	1,100.00
Advertising	$593.00
Electric	$1,585.00
Water Fees	$546.00
Snow Removal	$1,250,00
Lawn Care	$825.00
Heating Oil	$2,344.00
Trash Removal	$1,775.00
Property Taxes	$21,430.00
Pest Control	$1,200.00
Property Insurance	$4,450.00
Miscellaneous	$500.00
Depreciation	$14,546.00
Total Expenses	**$109,062.00**
Earnings Before Taxes (EBT)	**$4,658.00**

Adjusting for a Pro Forma

By reviewing the operating statement, the investor can develop a good understanding of the financial requirements of owning the property, but should not rely solely on the data provided. When the investor prepares a pro forma using the cash flow model, he will:

- Add new line items that pertain solely to the financial needs of the investor/buyer.
- Make use of some of the line items, but will adjust the financial data.
- Omit line items that pertain only to the present owner and are irrelevant to an investor/buyer, for example:
    - Owner's salary (unless the owner is engaged in some required property management that he would have to be hired to do)
    - Personal insurance (medical, 401(k))
    - Travel and entertainment
    - Car and related expenses
    - Debt service
    - Depreciation

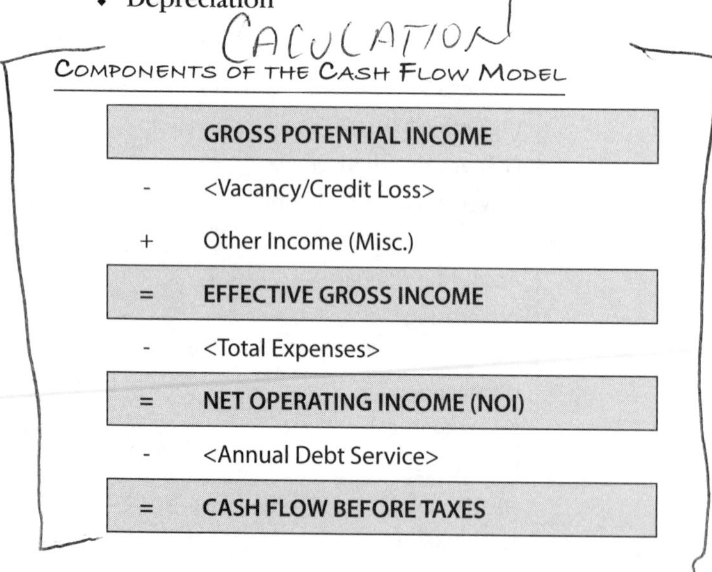

Gross Potential Income

Gross potential income is the *total income, both cash and non-cash, received from an investment or business before any expenses are paid or losses accounted for*. This may also be referred to as **gross revenue**.

A property owner is always challenged to charge market-appropriate rents while maintaining an acceptable occupancy level. If the occupancy level is consistently 95 percent, the rent might be too low, for example. The gross income line on an owner's operating statement will reflect the current rent roll, called the **contract rent**.

A potential buyer would be more interested in determining the **economic rent**, also called the **market rent**, which is the *rent that would be possible to charge if adjusted to appropriate market levels.*

If the market rent is different from the contract rent, an adjustment may be made on the pro forma. However, if the tenants in the property have **long-term leases**, the pro forma should project the current rent roll. Market rent should *not* be used to project gross potential income if the landlord is not in a position to raise the rent.

Vacancy and Collection Losses

Gross potential income also assumes that every space in the building is leased all year with ***no vacancies***. Furthermore, it assumes that everyone is not only paying rent, but also paying on time. Unfortunately, ideal gross income conditions are not always attainable. Every landlord, at some time or another, will experience some period of vacancy during the year and occasionally some tenants will fail to pay.

The cash flow model makes provisions for an allowance for vacancy and collection losses on a pro forma. It is a generally accepted accounting practice that some vacancy losses are expected to be shown here, even if minor, because no property is expected to always be 100 percent occupied. This may be adjusted up or down based on circumstances and perceived risk. Data for anticipating vacancy losses can come from:

- Historical data from existing operating statements.
- Projections based on current market conditions in the area, such as unemployment, etc.
- A market analysis to determine the vacancy losses of comparable properties.

Since the vacancy loss figures so importantly into the equation for finding the net operating income, a conservative investor would want to err on the side of caution when creating a pro forma.

Miscellaneous Income

Some commercial properties generate income for their owners other than rent, such as the change collected at an apartment complex's coin-operated laundry or the vending machines in an office building's break room. Parking income, storage space fees, rooftop antennas, and other income sources are also categorized as miscellaneous income. Any money earned other than rent and rent-related items, such as tenant reimbursements for taxes or utilities, should be itemized and added in as miscellaneous income.

Effective Gross Income

The **effective gross income** is the *estimated rental income the owner anticipates collecting and that will be available to pay the expenses of owning the property.* To calculate the effective gross income, subtract the allowance for vacancy and collection losses, and add the miscellaneous income from the gross potential income.

Expenses

Owning and managing income-earning property costs money. Expenses may be broadly classified as fixed or variable:

- **Fixed expenses** are defined as *expenses that occur on a regular basis, have regular payment amounts – such as property taxes and insurance, landscaping, and other service contracts – and generally do not vary in response to changing levels of occupancy*. These expenses occur whether the property is vacant or fully leased.
- **Variable expenses** are defined as *expenses that are necessary to maintain the income stream of the property and provide services to the tenants*. Variable

expenses tend to be tenant driven. They occur regularly, but may vary based on occupancy levels as well as amounts. For instance, expenses for maintenance, repairs, advertising, pool inspections, city business licenses, and utilities may occur regularly but vary in amount. Variable expenses generally depend on a number of issues including the type, size, age, and condition of the property.

Reserve for Replacements

Reserve for replacements is *money that a property owner sets aside regularly in anticipation of needing to fund capital improvement projects or to pay for extraordinary repairs.* An investor evaluating a property for possible purchase should not neglect this as an expense category on a pro forma.

Reserve for replacements is to the pro forma what depreciation represents to the operating statement. A property owner does not actually pay depreciation as an expense, and so there's not necessarily an absolute correlation between the depreciation and the amount an investor might want to consider as reserve for replacements. The depreciation, however, does provide a reasonable figure to use in a pro forma when evaluating an investment property.

Net Operating Income (NOI)

Net operating income (NOI) is the *annual income from a property or business that remains after annual operating costs are paid.* The NOI is calculated by deducting operating expenses from effective gross income. Because property has value independent of any financing an investor might obtain to acquire it, the net operating income (NOI) does ***not*** take into consideration any expenses associated with the financing of property.

The NOI is one of the first indicators of the real value or worth of an investment and is the most important component in valuing income-producing properties. The NOI measures the ability of an investment property to produce an income stream or cash flow from its operations. Once an investor determines the NOI, he can use it to determine how much he would be willing to pay for the property.

Capitalization Rate

Investors use the **capitalization rate method** to *estimate the present value of future income.* This rate is essentially equal to the rate of return an investor would expect to earn in a real estate investment. Since the capitalization rate for a real estate investment is not guaranteed, an investor will expect a larger rate of return than he or she can get from safer investments.

The capitalization calculation, called the **IRV formula**, relies on three variables: **I**ncome, **R**ate, and **V**alue.

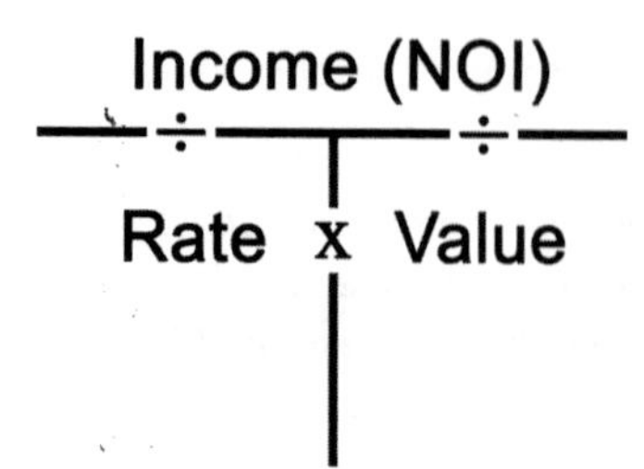

I = **Income**, the property's annual **net operating income** (NOI), may be based on the prior income the property produced or on the projected income demonstrated in a pro forma. Although it's impossible to predict every variable, if the property's income is fair in the marketplace, it's reasonable to expect the income stream to continue into the future.

R = **Rate**, the capitalization rate, represents the *amount of return the investor expects to earn from the investment.* Investors determine what rate of return is acceptable. For example, one investor may be looking for a 10% return, while another would be content with an 8% return.

V = **Value**, the value of the property, is the amount an investor would be willing to pay for the property.

When any two factors are known, it is possible to calculate the third, for example:

Income (NOI) ÷ Rate = Value

Income (NOI) ÷ Value = Rate

Given the same level of NOI, as the desired rate of return (cap rate) increases, the value decreases. Or, as the price of the property (value) rises, the cap rate decreases. This illustrates one of the basic rules affecting cap rates. Referred to as an inverse relationship, the value and cap rates move in opposite directions.

CAPITALIZATION RATE EXAMPLE

When creating the pro forma, the investor revised the numbers from the operating statement by raising rent and adjusting expenses to arrive at a net operating income of $50,690. If he wants to see an 8% cap rate, he would theoretically be willing to pay $633,625 to purchase the property.

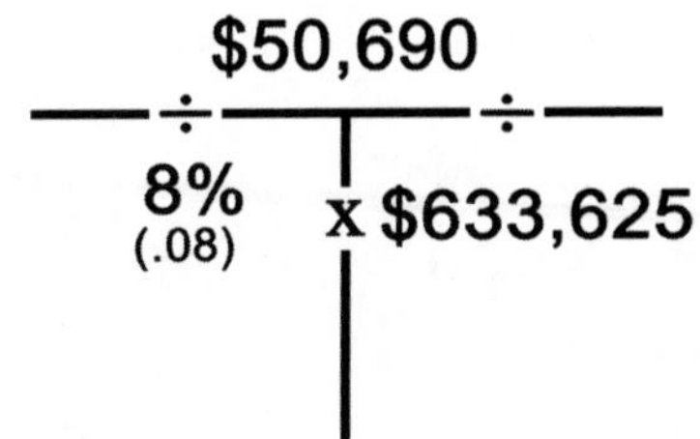

What would he be willing to pay if he accepts a 7% cap rate? How much if he needed to see a 10% cap rate?

Using Cap Rates to Find the Asking Price

The IRV formula can also be used when working with a *seller* to determine the asking price of the property. Instead of considering individual investor goals, it's more common for an agent to evaluate the market and determine what an appropriate cap rate would be by looking at other comparable properties that have sold in the area. If the selling price of a property is known and the NOI can be found, it's possible to determine a reasonable cap rate for that property. Other factors to consider include:

- The location of the property.
- The economic situation of the area.
- The current prime interest rate.

Pro Forma Example

Investors play a "what if" game when preparing a pro forma: "What if I finance at 6%? What if I put $150,000 down? What if I cut expenses? What if I increase rent rolls?" A savvy investor knows not only what questions to ask, but how to reasonably make the adjustments on the pro forma so that there are no unpleasant surprises when he reviews the actual numbers on his first year operating statement.

This pro forma example was prepared using the sample operating statement and adjusted with additional market-driven data. Note the differences from the operating statement.

Annual Property Operating Data - Pro Forma	
Property Address:	**100 Main Street** Anywhere, NY
Market Rent Projection	
9 Apts. @ $575.00 Month	$62,100.00
8 Apts. @ $660.00 Month	$63,360.00
Gross Potential Income	$125,460.00
Vacancy/Credit Loss @ 3%	($3,764.00)
Other Income (Laundry)	$2,400.00
Effective Gross Income (EGI)	**$124,096.00**
Expenses	
Repairs/Maintenance	$6,000.00
Accounting/Legal	$1,100.00
Advertising	$600.00
Electric	$1,775.00
Water Fees	$546.00
Snow Removal	$1,250,00
Lawn Care	$825.00
Heating Oil	$3,425.00
Trash Removal	$1,910.00
Property Taxes	$23,025.00
Pest Control	$1,200.00
Property Insurance	$5,100.00
Reserve for Replacement	$15,000.00
Miscellaneous	$500.00
Management @ 10% of EGI	$12,400.00
Total Expenses	**$73,406.00**
Net Operating Income	**$50,690.00**
Annual Debt	**$31,934.00**
Cash Flow	**$18,756.00**
Cash-on-Cash	**18.76%**

After finding the NOI, this investor decided he could purchase the property for $500,000, anticipating a 20% down payment and a $400,000 mortgage at 7% for 30 years. That would make the annual debt service $31,934. Once he knows that, he can find the cash flow.

Cash Flow

Cash flow is *a measurement of both income and expense items associated with operating the property*. Cash flow before taxes, therefore, is the gross amount of income available before considering taxes. Positive cash flow means more money is coming in from the investment than is leaving it. Negative cash flow is the opposite.

If the property was purchased with cash, cash flow would be equal to the net operating income. If the purchase is financed, however, investors must consider the effect that **debt service**, *the amount of money required for the payment of current interest and principal on a long-term debt,* has on cash flow.

Debt service typically has two components:

- The **interest** due on the outstanding balance.
- The amortization (or reduction) of the balance by paying back some of the **principal** owed on a regular basis.

When annual debt is subtracted from the net operating income, any amount remaining would be considered the cash flow.

Cash-on-Cash Return

Cash-on-cash return, also referred to as "cash in on cash out," is the *ratio of income generated by the property to the cash investment in the property*. Once the before tax cash flow is determined, cash-on-cash return is found by dividing that number by the **out-of-pocket cost** to purchase the property:

Before Tax Cash Flow ÷ Purchase Costs = Cash-on-Cash Return

As shown on the sample pro forma, the investor anticipates a before tax cash flow of $18,756. He expects to make a $100,000 down payment and get a $400,000 mortgage. He could therefore calculate the cash-on-cash return as shown:

$18,756 Cash Flow ÷ $100,000 Down Payment = 18.76% Cash-On-Cash

CASE IN POINT

When calculating the first year cash-on-cash return, many investors choose to include not only the down payment but *all* of the costs associated with purchasing the property, for example, those nonrecurring closing costs such as appraisal fees, attorney fees, title insurance, recording fees, financing fees, etc. This will give a more accurate picture of the return.

If the investor estimates closing costs of $9,800, the total out-of-pocket cost to purchase this property is $109,800. A more realistic estimate of cash-on-cash return for this property would be 17.1%:

$18,756 Cash Flow ÷ $109,800 Total Purchase Cost = 17.1% Cash-On-Cash

Taxable Income

Taxable income is simply the amount of income on which an investor must pay taxes. Property investment gives owners certain income tax advantages when deductions – such as expenses, property taxes, mortgage interest, and depreciation – exceed the cash flow. This, in effect, can "shelter" the owner's other income from taxes. A property owner can deduct any legitimate expense items from his bottom line to find the taxable income. For investment property, that includes mortgage interest as well as depreciation.

Depreciation

Depreciation can be thought of as the *loss of value to a property over the time during which it is expected to be useful.* When considering investment property, depreciation may be determined for tax purposes only; it is **not** a true reflection of the property's actual value and is not considered an out-of-pocket expense. The Internal Revenue Service allows an accounting deduction that reflects the economic fact that buildings do depreciate. This type of depreciation can also be called **cost recovery**. Federal income tax laws set the so-called recovery periods as follows:

- Residential investment property: 27 1/2 years
- Commercial property: 39 years

A residential investment property depreciates faster according to the IRS than a nonresidential investment and therefore results in a larger annual deduction. The annual depreciation is calculated by dividing the value of the improvement (*not* the value of the land on which the improvement sits) by the designated recovery period.

Improvement Value ÷ Recovery Period = Annual Amount of Depreciation

When establishing depreciation values, many investors allocate as much value to buildings as legally possible.

CASE IN POINT

Assume that a year has passed and the investor is preparing his first operating statement on the apartment property he purchased. If the land value of the property is $100,000 and the building itself is valued at $400,000, the annual amount of depreciation would be:

$400,000 ÷ 27.5 = $14,546 Annual Depreciation

If the total property value is $500,000 but the value of the land is greater than $100,000, would the amount of depreciation the property owner could expense be higher or lower?

For tax purposes, the amount of depreciation is treated as a line item **expense** on an operating statement, even though the owner did not have to actually pay the depreciated amount to anyone. Since the depreciation amount, like other line item expenses, is **subtracted** from gross revenues, earnings before taxes will, in effect, be reduced by the depreciated amount.

Loan Interest

Typically, when a property owner prepares an operating statement, he includes the mortgage interest payment as a line item expense.

For example, on the first year of that $400,000 mortgage loan, the owner paid $31,934 in total debt service. Of that amount, $27,871 is interest and $4,063 is principal. If the owner includes *only the interest portion of the mortgage payments* on the operating statement, which is the more proper strategy, then no further calculation would be needed to determine taxable income.

If, however, the owner had included the *entire* mortgage payment as a line item expense in his operating statement, it would be necessary to *add the principal portion* of the payments back to the bottom line in order to determine taxable income, since that aspect of debt service is taxable.

Like depreciation, subtracting the amount paid in interest on the mortgage reduces the owner's earnings on which taxes would be calculated, thereby lowering the owner's tax burden.

SUMMARY

1. A primary goal of any investor is the **preservation** of the capital invested. Investors trade a lump sum of capital in the present for the expectation of one or more of the following: Receiving a **continuing stream of income**; creating a **tax shelter**, which gives owners certain income tax advantages; building **equity** in the investment through leverage and appreciation; and earning a **return on the investment** when the property is sold.
2. **Risk** is *the degree of probability the actual rate of return earned will differ from the return expected when the investment was made.* Sources of risk include: Space market risk (related to the demand for space), capital market risk (related to interest rates and availability of financing), financial risk (related to using debt to finance an investment), as well as environmental, legislative, or management risk.
3. **Liquidity** is the *ability to convert an asset into cash quickly without the loss of principal.* The long-term nature of commercial real estate investments makes it one of the least liquid of investments. **Leverage** is the *effect that borrowed funds (other people's money) have on investment returns.* Leverage can be positive or negative.
4. Investors often use the **cash flow model** to evaluate the earning potential of a property. The cash flow model is: Gross Potential Income – Vacancy Loss + Miscellaneous Income = Effective Gross Income – Expenses = Net Operating Income – Annual Debt Service = Cash Flow Before Taxes.
5. The cash flow model allows investors to prepare **pro forma statements**, which show the *hypothetical projection of income and expenses for this first full year of ownership.* A pro forma requires a great deal of financial data, some of which may be available from the current owner's **operating statement**, which shows *total revenues generated and expenses for a given period as a means of evaluating the property's performance.* The investor will adjust that information as necessary to arrive at an estimate of the property's performance.
6. The most important component of the cash flow model is the **net operating income (NOI)**, which *measures the ability of an investment property to produce an income stream or cash flow from its operations*. Investors use the **capitalization rate method** to *estimate the present value of future income.* The capitalization calculation, called the **IRV formula**, relies on three variables: **I**ncome (NOI), **R**ate, and **V**alue. When an investor knows the NOI and knows what capitalization rate is acceptable, he can determine how much he is willing to pay for a property (Value = Income ÷ Rate).
7. **Cash flow** is *a measurement of both income and expense items associated with operating the property.* This figure allows an investor to find the **cash-on-cash return**, the *ratio of income generated by the property to the cash investment in the property*. Once the before tax cash flow is determined, cash-on-cash return is found by dividing that number by the **out-of-pocket cost** to purchase the property.

8. **Depreciation** is the *loss of value to a property over the time it is expected to be useful.* The Internal Revenue Service allows investors to deduct depreciation as a line item expense to reduce the taxable income. The annual depreciation is calculated by dividing the value of the improvement (*not* the value of the land on which the improvement sits) by the designated recovery period: **27 1/2 years** for residential investment property and **39 years** for other commercial property.

Glossary

The definitions given here represent how the terms are used in real estate. Some terms have additional meanings, which can be found in a standard dictionary.

80/20 Rule Rule that says in order for individual shareholders to continue to be able to write off yearly taxes and mortgage interest, no more than 20 percent of a co-op's yearly income can come from non-shareholder sources.

A

Abandonment The failure to occupy and use property, which may result in a loss of rights.

Abutting Property Directly contiguous properties, sharing at least one common boundary.

Abstract of Title A brief summary of the history of title to a property, listing all recorded documents that affect the title.

Acceleration Clause Contract clause giving the lender the right to declare the entire loan balance due immediately because of default, or other reasons stated in the contract.

Acceptance Agreeing to the terms of an offer, thereby creating a binding contract; taking delivery of a deed.

Accession Gives property owners the right to everything produced by their land. *See:* **Accretion; Annexation; Reliction.**

Accessory Apartment An apartment within a single-family dwelling.

Accessory Use The use or occupancy incidental or subordinate to the principal use or occupancy of a property.

Accord and Satisfaction An agreement to accept something different (usually less) from what the original contract required.

Accountability In an agency relationship, the agent's fiduciary duty to account to the principal.

Accretion The gradual addition of land by the forces of nature.

Acknowledgment The act of signing a document before a notary public, stating it was signed voluntarily.

Actionable Fraud Fraud meeting certain criteria, so a victim can successfully sue. Victim/plaintiff must prove the defendant concealed material facts or made false statements (intentionally or negligently) with intent to induce the victim to enter a transaction, and that the victim was harmed by relying on these misrepresentations.

Active Income Earnings received from any of the following: wages, salaries, commissions, bonuses, and other payments for services rendered; profit from a trade or business where the taxpayer is an active participant; gain on sale or disposition of assets used in an active trade or business; income from intangible property if the taxpayer played a significant role in creating the property.

Act of Waste When a possessor who holds less than fee ownership (i.e., tenant, vendee, and mortgagor) misuses or abuses the property.

Actual Annexation Personal property physically attached to land. *See:* **Fixture.**

Actual Authority Authority intentionally given to an agent by the principal, either expressed or implied.

Actual Cash Value (ACV) The cost to replace a property item at the time of loss, less an allowance for depreciation. Often used to determine the amount of reimbursement for a loss (replacement cost minus depreciation).

Actual Eviction Physically forcing someone off property, preventing someone from re-entering property, or using the legal process to make someone leave. *Compare:* **Constructive Eviction.**

Actual Fraud Intentional misrepresentation or concealment of a material fact; when a person actively conceals material information or makes statements known to be false or misleading. *Also called:* **Deceit.**

Actual Notice Actual knowledge; that which is known.

Adequate Consideration Consideration comparable in value to that which the other party to the contract is giving.

Ad Valorem Tax Tax based on the assessed value of property.

Adjustable Rate Mortgage (ARM) Mortgage that permits the lender to periodically adjust the interest rate so it reflects fluctuations in the cost of money.

Adjusted Basis Original cost of property, plus gains and minus losses.

Administrative Agency Government agency (federal, state, or local) that administers an area of law, adopting and enforcing detailed regulations that have the force of law.

Administrative Discipline The New York Department of State's enforcement of license laws through reprimand and denial as well as the suspension and revocation of licenses.

Administrative Review Initiated when a taxpayer files a grievance with his municipal assessing unit; prerequisite to judicial review.

Administrator Person appointed by probate court to manage and distribute a deceased person's estate when no executor is named in the will, or when there is no will.

Adverse Possession Acquiring title to someone else's real property by possession of it. Possession must be open and notorious, hostile and adverse, exclusive, and continuous for a prescribed number of years (e.g., in New York, 10).

Affiant A person who makes an affidavit.

Affidavit A sworn statement that is written and acknowledged. It may be submitted as evidence in a trial.

Affirm An appeals court ruling that the lower court's decision was correct, rejecting the appellant's arguments.

Affirmative Action Government policies that collectively sought to redress past discrimination.

After Tax Cash Flow Cash flow from income-producing property, less income taxes, if any, attributable to the property's income. If a tax loss provides a tax savings from the shelter of income earned outside the property, that savings is added to the property's earned cash flow.

Agency Relationship of trust created when one person (principal) gives another person (agent) the right to represent him in dealings with third parties.

Agency Coupled with an Interest Situation in which the agent has a personal interest in the subject of the agency, as when one co-owner has been authorized by the other to sell her property.

Agency Disclosure Statement Form that states whether an agent is representing the seller, buyer, or both in a transaction.

Agency Relationship The representation of a party in a real estate transaction.

Agent Person licensed by the state of New York to represent another in a real estate transaction and a member of the National Association of REALTORS®; a person authorized to represent another (principal) in dealings with third parties.

Age of Majority Age at which a person gains legal capacity. *Compare:* **Minor.**

Agency Disclosure Form Form used to disclose the agency relationships permitted, the agency relationships a brokerage practices, payment to/from brokers who do not represent the broker's client, and required fair housing language.

Air Rights The right to undisturbed use and control of airspace over a parcel of land (within reasonable limits for air travel); may be transferred separately from the land.

Alienation Transfer of ownership or an interest in property from one person to another, by any means.

Alienation Clause Contract clause giving the lender certain stated rights when there is a transfer of ownership in the property.

Allodial System System of land ownership under which anyone can own land.

Alluvion Solid material deposited along a shore by accretion.

Alteration Agreement Written agreement, signed by co-op shareholder-tenants, before any renovations, modifications, repairs, or alterations can begin.

Alternative Financing When real estate is financed with terms and/or concessions other than those typical for conventional loans.

Amenity Purchaser Person who values a property based on its ability to fulfill his specific business needs, unlike investors who value a property based primarily on its investment return.

Americans with Disabilities Act (ADA) Civil rights law that prohibits discrimination based on disability; creates consistent and enforceable standards regarding discrimination based on disability.

Amortization When a loan balance decreases because of periodic installments that pay down both principal and interest.

Amortized Loans When monthly payments retire the debt over the life of the loan instead of leaving the borrower with a large balloon payment at the end of the loan term.

Amount in Controversy Amount of money at issue in a lawsuit; used as a limitation on the jurisdiction of some courts.

Amperage Amount of electricity going through electric wires, measured in amps.

Anchor Tenant Major department or chain store strategically located at shopping centers to give maximum exposure to smaller satellite stores. A center may have several anchor tenants.

Ancillary Trustee A trustee appointed to conclude the business of a broker who has died.

Annexation Attaching personal property to land so the law views it as part of the real property. *See:* **Fixture.**

Annual Percentage Rate (APR) Total cost of financing a loan in percentage terms, as a relationship of total finance charges to total amount financed.

Anticipatory Repudiation When one party to a contract informs the other before the time set for performance that he does not intend to perform as agreed. *See:* **Tender.**

Antitrust A business activity that attempts to monopolize, contract, or conspire (or any of these things together) in a way that negatively affects another's ability to do business.

Apparent Agency 1. When someone acts as if she is a person's agent even though she has not been authorized to do so. 2. When an agent acts beyond the scope of her authority, giving a third party the impression the acts are authorized. *Also called:* **Ostensible Agency** or **Apparent Authority**.

Appeal Process by which a higher court reviews a lower court's decision or an administrative tribunal.

Appellant Party who files an appeal because of dissatisfaction with the trial court's decision. *Also called:* **Petitioner.**

Appellate Jurisdiction Authority to hear an appeal as opposed to conducting a trial.

Appellee In an appeal, the party who did *not* file the appeal. *Also called:* **Respondent.**

Appraisal An opinion of the value of property, as of a specified date, supported by objective data.

Appraisal Report The primary means of communicating appraisal results to the client.

Appraiser A person who is specially trained to offer an unbiased value of real property.

Appreciation The increase in value of an asset over time.

Appropriation 1. The authorization of the expenditure of funds and the source of those funds. 2. Taking private property for public use, through the government's power of eminent domain. *Also called:* **Condemnation**.

Appropriative Rights Water rights allocated by government permit according to an appropriation system. It is not necessary to own property beside the body of water in order to apply for an appropriation permit. *Also called:* **Prior Appropriation**. *Compare:* **Littoral Rights**, **Riparian Rights.**

Approved Assessing Unit An assessing unit certified by the New York State Board as having completed a revaluation program implementing a system of real property tax administration, which was or would be eligible for state assistance, based upon the latest completed assessment roll.

Appurtenance A right that goes with real property ownership; usually transferred with the property, but may be sold separately.

Appurtenant Easement An easement that benefits a particular piece of property (dominant tenement). *Compare:* **Easement in Gross.**

Arbitration An alternative to a court proceeding where parties agree to submit facts and evidence to an impartial third party.

Architectural Review Board Determines the effects a proposed building or other structure, or alteration of an existing structure, will have on the desirability, property values, and development of surrounding areas.

Area Variance Permission to use land in a way typically not allowed by current zoning laws.

Arm's Length Transaction A transaction that occurs under typical conditions in the marketplace, with each party acting in his or her own best interest.

Article 12-A Article of New York Real Property Law, which contains most of the laws relevant to real estate brokers and salespeople.

Article 78 Proceeding Refers to an article of the Civil Practice Law and Rules that allows aggrieved persons to bring an action against a government body or officer.

Asbestos Fibrous material derived from a naturally occurring group of minerals commonly used in insulation. Asbestos fibers released into the air are carcinogenic.

Asbestosis A lung disease caused by extended exposure to asbestos.

"As Is" Clause Provision in a purchase agreement stating the buyer accepts the property in its present condition.

As of Right Zoning Prohibits discrimination among landowners in a particular zone.

Assessed Value Value placed on property to which a local tax rate is applied to calculate the amount of real property tax.

Assessing Unit City, town, or county department of assessment with the power to assess real property.

Assessment A percentage of a property's market value.

Assessment Review Board Local board that hears complaints regarding property assessments and property exemption determinations.

Assessment Roll Public Listing of the assessed value for all real property in a municipality.

Assessor Elected or appointed local officials who independently estimate the value of real property.

Assign 1. To transfer a right or interest to another; 2. A tenant transferring his right of possession or other interest in leased property to another for the remainder of the lease term. *Compare:* **Sublease.**

Assignee Person to whom a right or interest has been assigned.

Assigning a Contract Assigning the purchase rights to property or a condominium unit to another buyer before that property or unit is closed.

Assignment One party (assignor) transferring rights or interests under a contract to another person (assignee). In New York, all contracts are assignable unless the contract states otherwise.

Assignor Person who assigns a right or interest to another.

Associate Broker A real estate broker who works for another broker.

Assumption One party taking over responsibility for the loan of another party; usually lender approval is needed.

Attachment Court-ordered seizure of property belonging to a defendant in a lawsuit to satisfy a judgment. In the case of real property, attachment creates a lien. *Also called:* **Order of Attachment.** *See:* **Attachment Lien.**

Attachment Lien A lien intended to prevent property transfer pending the outcome of litigation.

Attestation Witnesses signing a legal document to affirm the parties' signatures are real; the act of witnessing the execution of a legal document (such as a deed or will). *Compare:* **Acknowledgment.**

Attorney-in-Fact Any person authorized to act for another by a power of attorney (not necessarily an attorney-at-law).

Avulsion When real property is lost due to sudden acts of nature like tornadoes or earthquakes.

B

Balloon Construction Type of framing with long studs going up the entire length of the house, from the foundation to the roof. No longer permitted as a construction method by most building codes. *Also called:* **Balloon Framing**.

Balloon Mortgage Loan repaid with small, periodic payments until a specified date, then either the balance comes due in a single, lump payment or the payment amount rises significantly.

Balloon Payment Final payment at the end of a loan term to pay off the entire remaining balance of principal and interest not covered by payments during the loan term.

Bargain and Sale Deed Deed without any warranties against liens or other encumbrances but does imply grantor has the right convey title.

Basement Part of a house or building partially or entirely below grade (ground level) and used to support the rest of the structure.

Basis Accounting procedure used to determine the capital gain or loss after the sale of property. It is equal to purchase price, plus capital improvements, less depreciation.

Bearing Wall A wall that carries the load for the roof, ceiling, and/or floors.

Before Tax Cash Flow Gross amount of income available before considering taxes.

Beneficiary Person designated to receive benefits from a certain act.

Bequeath The act of giving personal property to another by will.

Bequest A gift of personal property by a will.

Bilateral Contract A contract in which each party promises to do something. *Compare:* **Unilateral Contract**.

Bill A proposed law, formally submitted to a legislature for consideration.

Bill of Sale Document used to transfer title to personal property from one person to another.

Binding Precedent A precedent that a particular court is required to follow because it was decided by a higher court in the same jurisdiction.

Bi-weekly Mortgage A fixed rate mortgage, similar to a standard mortgage, but with payments due every two weeks instead of every month.

Blanket Mortgage 1. Mortgage that covers more than one parcel of real estate. 2. Mortgage that covers an entire building or development, rather than an individual unit or lot.

Blind Ad An ad in which a broker attempts to advertise a property for sale without disclosing the fact she is a licensed real estate broker, or when a broker attempts to mislead the public into believing a property is for sale by owner. Blind ads are illegal in New York.

Blockbusting Illegal practice of inducing owners to sell their homes (often at a deflated price) by suggesting the ethnic or racial composition of the neighborhood is changing, with the implication that property values will decline as a result. *Also called:* **Panic Selling** or **Panic Peddling**.

Blueprint Detailed building plans used to evaluate design, determine feasibility, and guide a structure's construction.

Board Package A package presented to the co-op (or sometimes condominium) board of managers/directors from a potential shareholder or buyer. It often includes financial qualifications, employment verification, letters of reference, and other material requested by the board.

Bona Fide In good faith; genuine.

Bond-type Securities Mortgage-backed securities issued by Ginnie Mae, which are long term, pay interest semi-annually, and provide for repayment at a specified date.

Boot Extra, non-like-kind property that can be a part of a like-kind exchange to make up for pricing disparity between like-kind properties.

Boundary Perimeter or border of a parcel of land; the dividing line between one property and another.

Breach Violation of a contract obligation, duty, or law.

Breach of Contract Failure to perform according to the terms of a contract.

Bridge Loan Short-term mortgage loan that covers the gap between selling one property and buying another.

British Thermal Unit (BTU) Amount of heat needed to raise the temperature of one pound of water by one degree Fahrenheit. Used as a measure of furnace or air conditioner capacity.

Broker One who is licensed to represent one of the parties in a real estate transaction.

Broker Protection Clause Provides the broker is still entitled to commission if the property is sold during a certain time under certain circumstances.

Brokerage The business of bringing together buyers and sellers of real property and assisting in negotiating such transactions.

Broker's Agent Engaged and works directly for the broker—a broker's agent is not a subagent of the seller or buyer. Still owes the same fiduciary duty to the broker's seller or buyer the broker does.

Budget Mortgage A mortgage agreement where payments include principal and interest on the loan, plus 1/12 of the year's property taxes and hazard insurance premiums.

Building Code The Uniform Fire Prevention and Building Code, as modified by local amendments. Governs the construction details of buildings and other structures in the interest of the safety of the occupants and public.

Building Department Protects a municipality's residents by seeing that code restrictions are followed, and construction and renovation are done by licensed professionals.

Building Envelope Sometimes called a building shell, the building envelope refers to the exterior elements—walls, windows, floor, roof, etc.—which enclose the interior.

Building Inspection The process whereby government authorities, usually state or local, are charged with ensuring compliance with prevailing building codes.

Building Manager Oversees the management of one building for a property owner.

Building Permit Official documents from a local government or other authority that allow the beginning of a construction or remodeling project.

Bump Clause Provision in a purchase agreement that allows the seller to keep the property on the market until a condition in the contract is fulfilled.

Bundle of Rights All real property rights conferred with ownership, including right of use, right of enjoyment, and right of disposal.

Burden of Proof Responsibility for proving or disproving a particular issue in a lawsuit. The plaintiff usually has the burden of proof.

Business Cycles General swings in business activity, resulting in expanding and contracting activity during different phases of the cycle.

Business Name Certificate Partnership document listing the names and addresses of all partners, which must be filed in the county where the partnership office is located before property can be held in a partnership's name.

Buydown Additional funds in the form of points paid to a lender at the beginning of a loan to lower the loan's interest rate and monthly payments.

Buyer Broker Contract A written agency contract between a buyer and a real estate broker stipulating the broker will be paid a commission when the buyer purchases real estate.

Buyer's Agent Represents and owes all loyalty to the buyer in a real estate transaction.

Buyer's Broker When an agency relationship with a buyer is exclusive.

Buyer's Market A situation in the housing market giving buyers a large selection of properties at favorable prices from which to choose. *Compare:* **Seller's Market**.

Bylaws Rules and regulations that govern the activities of condominium and cooperative associations, including the purpose of the building, rules for elections and voting, and frequency of board of directors or shareholders meetings.

C

Call Provision Clause that lets the lender demand full payment of a loan immediately (*verb:* **call a note**).

Cancellation Termination of a contract without undoing the acts already performed under it. *Compare:* **Rescission**.

Capacity Legal ability to perform some act, such as enter into a contract or execute a deed or will.

Capital Asset Any asset not specifically excluded by the Internal Revenue Code.

Capital Expense An expense incurred to improve property.

Capital Gain Profit made from an investment.

Capital Loss Monetary loss resulting from an investment's decrease in value.

Capitalization Rate Rate of interest considered a reasonable return on investment; commonly used in the process of determining value based on net income. *Also called:* **Rate**.

Capital Reserve Budget A budget for expenses that are not fixed (variable).

Carbon Monoxide (CO) Colorless, odorless gas that is a natural byproduct of fuel combustion.

Case Law Rules of law developed in court decisions, as opposed to constitutional law, statutory law, or administrative regulations.

Cash Flow Money available after subtracting all expenses. Positive cash flow means more money is coming in than going out. Negative cash flow is the converse.

Cash on Cash Return The bottom line of any investment expressed as a percentage by dividing the investment's cash flow by the deposit and settlement costs.

Caveat Emptor Latin phrase meaning, "let the buyer beware." The rule that says a buyer is expected to examine property carefully instead of relying on the seller to point out problems.

Cease and Desist List List on which property owners in a cease and desist zone can register and once they do, brokers and salespersons are prohibited from soliciting them.

Cease and Desist Zone Certain areas designated by the New York Department of State in which property owners can file notice indicating they do not want to sell, lease, or list their property.

Census Tract Relatively small areas used by the U.S. Census Bureau to track the population of the United States.

Certificate of Eligibility Certificate issued by the Veterans Administration to establish the status and amount of a veteran's eligibility to qualify for a guaranteed loan.

Certificate of Judgment Summary of the provisions of a court judgment; when recorded, it creates a lien on all the debtor's real property in the county where recorded.

Certificate of Occupancy Permit issued to a builder after all inspections have been made and the property is deemed fit for occupancy.

Certificate of Title Document prepared by an attorney after performing a title search and reviewing public records stating the status of the title to a property.

Certificate of Transfer Document issued by a probate court showing transfer of title from a deceased person to her heirs or devisees.

Chain of Title Chain of deeds and other documents transferring title to land from one owner to the next, as disclosed in public records.

Chattel Personal property.

Chattel Real Personal property closely associated with real property, such as a lease.

Checker Person who poses as a customer or client attempting to secure real estate services to ensure fair housing is practiced. *Also called:* **Tester**.

Chlorofluorocarbons (CFCs) Chemical compounds containing chlorine, fluorine, and carbon atoms. Sold under the trademarked name of Freon for many years and used as a coolant in refrigerators, air conditioners, and dehumidifiers. Now known to contribute to the depletion of the ozone.

Circuit Breaker A device, usually located inside the electrical breaker panel or circuit breaker box, designed to break its electrical connection should an overload occur.

City Council Municipal legislative body responsible for public policy including approving budgets, and passing laws, ordinances, and resolutions.

Civil Law Body of law concerned with the rights and liabilities of one individual in relation to another; includes contract, tort, and property law. *Compare:* **Criminal Law**.

Civil Litigation Lawsuit in which one person sues another for compensation.

Civil Penalties When a government body seeks financial compensation for damages. These are not considered punishment but restitution.

Civil Rights Fundamental rights guaranteed to all persons by law. The term is primarily used in reference to constitutional and statutory protections against discrimination.

Civil Rights Act of 1866 The first major legislation to directly affect equal rights to ownership of real property.

Clean Air Act (CAA) Government Act requiring the EPA to develop air quality standards for existing pollutants, along with establishing air standards for new sources of pollution. Also regulates air pollutant emissions, determines acceptable levels for emissions, and sets deadlines for compliance.

Clearspan Open distance between inside faces of support members.

Clear Title Title free of encumbrances or defects; marketable title.

Client Person who employs a broker, lawyer, or other professional. Real estate clients can be sellers, buyers, or both. *See:* **Fiduciary**.

Closing Transfer of real property ownership from seller to buyer, according to the terms and conditions in a sales contract or escrow agreement; final stage in a real estate transaction.

Closing Costs Expenses incurred in the transfer of real estate in addition to the purchase price (i.e., appraisal fee, title insurance premiums, broker's commission, or transfer tax).

Closing Disclosure A document that presents a final, detailed account of a real estate transaction, listing each party's debits and credits and the amount each will receive or be required to pay at closing.

Closing Statement Document prepared by the closing agent itemizing all expenses and costs paid by the buyer and seller to close the real estate transaction. *Also called:* **Settlement Statement** or **Closing Disclosure.**

Cloud on Title Claim, encumbrance, or defect that makes title to real property unmarketable. *Compare:* **Marketable Title**.

Cluster Zoning A varied selection of lot sizes and housing choices within a single area.

Code of Ethics and Standards of Practice Referred to simply as the Code of Ethics; a standard of conduct required by New York State license law and the National Association of REALTORS®.

Codicil Addition to or revision of a will. It must be executed with the same formalities as a will.

Codification Collection and organization of various laws into a comprehensive statutory code.

Coercion An act of force used to get a person to comply.

Collusion Agreement between two or more persons to defraud someone.

Color of Title Title that appears to be good but that, in fact, is not.

Commercial Banks Financial institutions that provide a variety of financial services.

Commercial Property Land zoned and used for business purposes, such as warehouses, restaurants, and office buildings (as distinguished from residential, industrial, or agricultural property).

Commingling Illegally mixing money held in trust on behalf of a client with personal funds. *See:* **Conversion**.

Commission Compensation paid to a broker for services provided in a real estate transaction.

Common Areas Land and improvements in a condominium, planned unit development, or cooperative all residents use and own as tenants in common, such as the parking lot, hallways, and recreational facilities; individual apartment units or homes are not included. *Also called:* Common Elements.

Common Grantor Person who owned two or more neighboring properties then sold them to different buyers.

Common Law 1. Early English law. 2. Long-established rules based on English law, still followed in many states. 3. Case law.

Common Law Dedication Dedication resulting from the owner's intention to donate land for public use, along with the government's acceptance of the donation. Common law dedication is actually involuntary in some cases; if an owner acquiesces to public use of his property, intention to dedicate the property may be implied.

Community Property Co-ownership limited to husband and wife; not acknowledged in New York State. *Compare:* **Separate Property**.

Comparables Other similar, recently sold properties in the same market area as the subject property.

Comparative Market Analysis (CMA) A method of determining the approximate market value of a home by comparing the subject property to other homes that have sold, are presently for sale, or did not sell in a given area. *Also called:* **Competitive Market Analysis** and **Comparable Market Analysis.**

Comparative Negligence Rule When parties share liability based on partial fault or negligence in causing the injury or tort.

Compensatory Damages Award, usually money, intended to compensate the plaintiff for harm caused by the defendant's act or failure to act. *Also called:* **Actual Damages.**

Competent 1. Of sound mind, for the purpose of entering a contract or executing a will; not suffering from mental illness, retardation, or senility. 2. Of sound mind and having reached the age of majority.

Complainant Party that files a formal charge in a court of law.

Complaint Document a plaintiff files with the court to begin a lawsuit.

Comprehensive Plan Written document prepared by a city's planning board that identifies the goals, objectives, principles, guidelines, policies, standards, and strategies for growth and development of a community. *Also called:* **Master Plan.**

Concrete Slab A foundation made from a layer of poured concrete reinforced with steel rods.

Concurrent Jurisdiction When more than one court has jurisdiction over a case and a plaintiff may choose in which court to file suit. *Compare:* **Exclusive Jurisdiction.**

Concurrent Ownership Ownership by more than one person; co-ownership.

Condemnation The act of taking property for public use through the government's power of eminent domain.

Conditional Fee A type of defeasible fee; title may be terminated by the former owner if conditions stated in deed are not met. Former owner has a power of termination. *Also called:* **Fee Simple Subject to a Condition Subsequent**. *Compare:* **Fee Simple Determinable.**

Conditional Use Land use that does not comply with the general zoning rules for the zone in which it is located, but is permitted because it benefits the public; for example, a hospital in a residential neighborhood. *Also called:* **Special Exception.**

Condominium Property developed for co-ownership, with each co-owner having a separate interest in an individual unit, combined with an undivided interest in the common areas of the property. *Compare:* **Cooperative.**

Condominium Act New York State law governing the establishment of condominiums.

Condominium Declaration Document filed for record when property is developed as, or converted to, a condominium.

Condop A building that has been divided into at least two condominiums. The first is the co-op residential units considered one condominium unit. The second unit is the professional and commercial units. *Compare:* **Condominium** or **Cooperative.**

Confirmation of Sale Document filed by the court to finalize the sale of property at foreclosure, and after which time the equitable right of redemption is no longer available to the original defaulting borrower.

Conforming Loans Loans that meet Fannie Mae/Freddie Mac standards and, thus, can be sold on the secondary market.

Conformity Theory that a particular home (or neighborhood) achieves maximum value when it is surrounded by homes similar in style and function.

Consensual Dual Agency Occurs when 1. the broker and all licensees are dual agents for both parties in the transaction, or 2. the buyer and seller each appoint a designated agent, who fully represents them. The broker, however, would (with consent) act as a dual agent in the transaction.

Conservation Advisory Council Studies matters affecting the environment, preservation, development, and use of a city's natural and physical features and conditions regarding ecologic integrity, aesthetic appeal, and quality.

Consideration Anything of value such as money, goods, services, or promises, given to induce another person to enter into a contract. *Also called:* **Valuable Consideration**.

Constitution Fundamental document establishing a government's structure and setting limits on its power.

Constitutional 1. Pertaining to or based on a constitution. 2. Not in violation of the U.S. Constitution or a state constitution.

Constitutional Law Law derived from the Constitution.

Construction Mortgage Temporary loan used to finance a construction project.

Constructive Annexation Personal property associated with real property in such a way that the law treats it as a fixture, even though it is not physically attached to the real property.

Constructive Eviction When a landlord's act (or failure to act) interferes with the tenant's quiet enjoyment of the property, or makes the property unfit for its intended use, to such an extent the tenant is forced to move out.

Constructive Fraud A negligent misrepresentation or concealment of a material fact; when a person carelessly fails to disclose material information, or makes false or misleading statements. *Also called:* **Negligent Misrepresentation**.

Constructive Notice Provides protection to a landowner against all unrecorded titles.

Consumer Price Index (CPI) An index published monthly by the United States Bureau of Labor Standards (BLS) considered by many to be the basic indicator of inflation in the U.S.

Contingency Clause Provision in a contract or deed that makes the parties' rights and obligations depend on the occurrence (or nonoccurrence) of a particular event. *Also called:* **Condition**.

Contract Agreement between two or more parties to do, or not do, a certain thing. The requirements for an enforceable contract are **capacity**, **mutual consent**, **lawful objective**, and **consideration**.

Contribution Theory that a particular item or feature of a home is worth only what it actually contributes in value to that property.

Conventional Loan Mortgage loan not insured or guaranteed by a government entity.

Conversion 1. Misappropriating property or funds belonging to another. 2. Changing an existing rental apartment building into a condominium.

Conversion Option Borrower's right to convert from an adjustable rate mortgage to a fixed rate mortgage one time during the loan term, provided certain conditions are met.

Conveyance Instrument that conveys a grantor's interest, if any, in real property. *Also called:* **Deed.**

Cooperating Broker A broker from another company who brings the other party (the buyer or the seller) to a transaction.

Cooperative A building owned by a corporation, where residents are shareholders in the corporation; each shareholder receives a proprietary lease on an individual unit and the right to use the common areas. *Also called:* **Co-op** or **Stock Cooperative**. *Compare:* **Condominium**.

Cooperative Policy Statement #1 (CPS-1) Applicable to cooperatives, condominiums, and homeowners associations and is used to test the market, explore the venture, and determine the needs to meet a variety of conditions.

Co-ownership Any form of ownership in which two or more people share title to a property, holding undivided interests. *Also called:* **Co-tenancy** or **Concurrent ownership**. *See:* **Community Property; Joint Tenancy; Statutory Survivorship Tenancy; Tenancy by the Entireties; Tenancy in Common; Tenancy in Partnership.**

Corporate Resolution Action passed by a corporation authorizing the sale or purchase of real estate.

Corporation An association organized according to strict regulations in which individuals purchase ownership shares; regarded by the law as an artificial person, separate from the individual shareholders. *Compare:* **Partnership**.

Correction Deed Deed used to correct minor mistakes in an earlier deed, such as misspelled names or errors in the property's legal description.

Corrective Maintenance Repairing or restoring broken or failed equipment to a specified condition. *Compare:* **Cosmetic Maintenance**, **Preventive Maintenance**.

Cosmetic Maintenance Maintenance that increases a property's appeal. *Compare:* **Corrective Maintenance**, **Preventive Maintenance**.

Cost Money needed to develop, produce, buy, or build something.

Cost Approach Appraisal method that estimates the value of real estate by figuring the cost of building the house or other improvement on the land, minus depreciation, plus the value of the vacant land.

Cost Inflation An increase in the cost of goods or services. *Compare:* **Demand Inflation**.

Cost Manuals Books that give estimated construction costs for various types of buildings/structures in different regions of the country.

Cost Manuals Method Cost approach appraisal method that uses cost manuals to arrive at an estimate of value for property.

Cost of Money The interest rate people or businesses pay to use another's money for their own purposes.

Co-tenant Anyone who shares ownership of a property with another. Forms of co-ownership include joint tenancy, statutory survivorship tenancy, tenants in common, tenant by the entireties, or tenant in partnership.

Counteroffer A response to an offer to enter into a contract, changing some of the terms of the original offer; a rejection of the original offer (not a form of acceptance).

County Health Department A human service and regulatory agency responsible for public health programs.

Covenant 1. A contract. 2. A promise. 3. A guarantee (express or implied) in a document such as a deed or lease.

Covenants, Conditions, and Restrictions (CC&Rs.) A declaration of covenants, conditions, and restrictions, usually recorded by a developer to create a general plan of private restrictions for a subdivision.

Covenant of Quiet Enjoyment Guarantee that a buyer or tenant has the right to exclusive, undisturbed possession of a leasehold estate and will not be disturbed by the previous owner, lessor, or anyone else claiming interest in the property.

Crawl Space Unfinished space below the first floor of a house or other structure that is less than a full story in height.

Creditor Person or other entity, such as a bank, who is owed a debt.

Credit Money received for an obligation given,

Credit Scoring A means by which the lender makes a determination regarding the creditworthiness of potential borrowers; involves a lender assigning a numerical value to different aspects relating to a borrower's financial situation.

Credit Union A non-profit financial institution owned and operated entirely by its members. By depositing money in a credit union, the depositor becomes a member and has partial ownership in the institution.

Criminal Law Body of law concerned with crimes, an individual commits against society. *Compare:* **Civil Law.**

Criminal Litigation Lawsuit in which the government sues someone to punish the wrongdoer and protect society.

Cure To remedy a default by paying overdue money or by fulfilling other obligations.

Curtesy A husband's interest in his wife's property; in many states, curtesy has been abolished and replaced by dower rights. **Note:** New York does not recognize either curtesy or dower rights.

Customer A party in a transaction to whom an agent does not have a fiduciary duty or relationship, but to whom an agent must still be fair and honest.

D

Damages An amount of money a defendant is ordered to pay a plaintiff.

Debit An expense or money applied against a credit.

Debt Recurring monetary obligation that cannot be cancelled.

Debtor A person or other entity, such as a company, who owes money to another.

Debt Service Amount of money needed to meet the periodic payments of principal and interest on an amortized loan or debt. If the periodic payments are constant and equal, then a portion will pay off accrued interest with the remainder reducing principal.

Decedent A person who has died.

Dedication Gift of land from a landowner to the government. *Also called:* **Dedication by Deed.**

Deductible A dollar amount the insured must pay on each loss. The insurance company pays the remainder of each covered loss up to the policy limits

Deed An instrument that conveys a grantor's interest, if any, in real property. *Also called:* Conveyance.

Deed in Lieu of Foreclosure A deed given by a borrower to the lender to satisfy the debt and avoid foreclosure. *Also called:* **Voluntary Conveyance.**

Deed of Trust An instrument creating a voluntary lien on real property held by a third party as security for the payment of a note. *Also called:* **Trust Deed.** *Compare:* **Mortgage.**

Deed Restrictions Limitations on real property use imposed by an owner through language included in the deed.

Default Failure to fulfill an obligation, duty, or promise, as when a borrower fails to make payments, a tenant fails to pay rent, or a party to a contract fails to perform.

Defeasance Clause 1. Clause used to defeat or cancel a certain right upon the occurrence of a specific event (e.g., on final payment, words of grant in a mortgage are void and the mortgage is thereby cancelled and title is revested to mortgagor). 2. Clause used to give a borrower the right to redeem real estate after default on a note by paying the full amount due plus fees and court costs.

Defendant 1. Person being sued in a civil lawsuit. 2. Accused person in criminal lawsuit.

Deferment Permission to delay fulfillment of an obligation (e.g., paying taxes) until a later date.

Deficiency Judgment A court order stating the debtor owes money to the creditor when the collateral property does not bring enough at the foreclosure sale to cover the entire loan amount, accrued interest, and other administrative costs.

Delivery The legal transfer of a deed (or other instrument). A valid deed does not convey title until it has been delivered to the grantee. *See:* **Donative Intent.**

Delivery and Acceptance Delivery of the deed by the grantor with the intention of transferring title and acceptance by the grantee receiving the land. When a deed has been properly executed, both have occurred.

Demand Inflation Too much money chasing too few goods. *Compare:* **Cost Inflation.**

Deposit 1. Money offered as an indication of good faith regarding the future performance of a purchase agreement. *Also called:* **Earnest Money.** 2. A tenant's security deposit.

Demography Study of the social and economic status of a given area or population.

Department of Housing and Urban Development (HUD) The government agency charged with overseeing housing related issues and projects. Among other things, HUD sets minimum building standards for housing and is responsible for enforcing the federal Fair Housing Act.

Deposition In a lawsuit, the formal, out-of-court testimony of a witness or a party taken before the trial; used as part of the discovery process to determine facts of a case, or if the witness is not able to attend the trial. A transcript of a deposition can be introduced as evidence in the trial.

Depreciate To decline in value.

Depreciation A loss in value for any reason.

Designated Agency When a supervising broker assumes the role of dual agent and each affiliated licensee represents his client as vigorously as possible.

Designated Heir Chosen heir. By filing a document with probate court, a person can choose anyone to be his heir in the eyes of the law.

Devise 1. Real property transferred in a will. 2. To transfer real property by will. *Compare:* **Bequest; Bequeath; Legacy.**

Devisee Recipient of real property by will. *Compare:* **Legatee.**

Direct Cost The cost in labor and materials.

Direct Index An index kept by the county recorder, with each recorded document listed in alphabetical order according to grantor's last name. *Also called:* **Grantor/Grantee Index.**

Direct Loss Referring to homeowner's insurance, a sudden loss due to a covered peril—such as fire, lightening, wind, hail, etc.

Disability A physical or mental impairment that substantially limits or curtails one or more major life activity.

Disaffirm The act of asking a court to terminate a voidable contract.

Disclosures Points or facts in a real estate transaction that must be revealed.

Disclosure Statement A detailed accounting of all financials associated with a residential mortgage loan.

Discount Points Amount paid to a lender when a loan is made to make up the difference between the current market interest rate and the rate a lender gives a borrower on a note. Discount points increase a lender's yield on a note, allowing the lender to give a borrower a lower interest rate. *See:* **Points.**

Discrimination Treating people unequally because of their race, religion, sex, national origin, age, or some other characteristic of a protected class.

Disparate Impact When a law that is not discriminatory on its face but has a greater impact on a minority group than other groups.

Doctrine of Emblements Rule that allows an agricultural tenant to re-enter the land to harvest crops if the lease ends, through no fault of the tenant, before the crop can be harvested (applies only to the first crop).

Doctrine of Laches Loss of legal rights because of failure to assert those rights in a timely manner.

Domestic Corporation A corporation doing business in the state in which it was created.

Domicile The state in which a person has a permanent home.

Dominant Tenant A person with easement rights on another's property; either the owner of a dominant tenement, or someone who has an easement in gross.

Dominant Tenement Property that receives the benefit of an appurtenant easement.

Donative Intent Intent to immediately and unconditionally transfer title to real property.

Double Declining Balance An accelerated method of deprecation.

Dower The interest held by a married person in the real property owned by a spouse. **Note:** dower is not recognized in New York.

Down Payment A lump sum cash payment paid by a buyer.

Drywall Gypsum plaster sandwiched between two layers of coarse paper. *Also called:* **Plasterboard, Wall Board,** or **Sheetrock.**

Dual Agency Occurs when a broker or salesperson represents both parties (buyer and seller) in a transaction; written consent from both parties is required before this can occur.

Dual Agent A licensee who represents both the seller and buyer in the same transaction.

Dual Licensure When real estate licensees hold more than one license at a time (e.g., when a broker wishes to also be an associate broker with another firm; or, when a salesperson wishes to work with more than one broker.)

Due Diligence Investigation to discover facts or liabilities about a property prior to its purchase.

Due on Sale Clause Mortgage clause that prohibits assignment by making the entire mortgage balance due when property is sold.

Duress Threatening violence against or unlawfully confining someone and forcing him to sign a document; or, threatening or confining a signer's spouse, child, or other close relative.

E

Earnest Money Deposit 1. Money offered as an indication of good faith regarding the future performance of a purchase agreement. 2. A tenant's security deposit. *Compare:* **Deposit.**

Easement A right to use some part of another person's real property. An easement is irrevocable and creates an interest in the property.

Easement Appurtenant An easement that grants access. *Compare:* **Right of Way.**

Easement by Condemnation 1. Taking private property for public use through the government's power of eminent domain. 2. A declaration that a structure is unfit for occupancy and must be closed or demolished.

Easement by Grant An easement granted to another in a deed or other document.

Easement by Express Reservation An easement created in a deed when a landowner divides property, transferring the servient tenement, but retaining the dominant tenement.

Easement by Implication An easement created by operation of law (not express grant or reservation) when land is divided, if there is a longstanding, apparent use that is reasonably necessary for enjoyment of the dominant tenement. *Compare:* **Implied Easement.**

Easement by Necessity A special kind of easement by implication that occurs when the dominant tenement would be useless without an easement, even without a longstanding, apparent use.

Easement by Prescription An easement acquired by prescription. *See:* **Prescription.**

Easement for Light and Air A view easement; considered a negative easement. In the case of negative easement, the dominant tenement can prevent the subservient tenement from doing something on the land because it could affect the dominant land.

Easement in Gross An easement that benefits a person instead of land; there is a dominant tenant, but no dominant tenement. *Compare:* **Appurtenant Easement.**

Eave The lowest sections of the roof, which project beyond the sidewalls.

Economic Base Main business or industry supporting and sustaining a community. A good economic base is critical for strong home values.

Economic Duress Threatening to financially harm a person to coerce him into signing a contract.

Effective Age Age of a structure based on actual wear and tear, not necessarily its actual age.

Effective Gross Income Potential gross income minus vacancy and collection losses.

Electromagnetic Fields (EMFs) Invisible fields produced by electrically charged objects.

Eminent Domain Government's constitutional power to appropriate or condemn private property for public use as long as the owner is paid just compensation.

Employee Someone who works under the direction and control of another. *Compare:* **Independent Contractor.**

Encroachment Physical object intruding onto neighboring property often due to a mistake regarding boundary lines.

Encumbered Property Property with mortgages, liens, or other restrictions against it, which prevent or restrict its transfer.

Encumbrance Non-possessory interest in property; a lien, easement, or restrictive covenant burdening the title.

Environmental Hazard A situation that exists with potential for harm to persons or property from conditions that exist outside or within a property. *See:* **Internal Environmental Hazard, External Environmental Hazard.**

Environmental Impact Statement (EIS) Study required by the National Environmental Policy Act for all federal and federally related projects, which details a development project's impact on energy use, sewage systems, drainage, water facilities, schools, and other environmental, economic, and social areas.

Equal Credit Opportunity Act (ECOA) Federal law that prohibits discrimination in granting credit to people based on sex, age, marital status, race, color, religion, national origin, or receipt of public assistance.

Equal Protection Requirement under the fifth and fourteenth amendments to the U.S. Constitution, all citizens are entitled to equal protection of the laws; no law may arbitrarily discriminate between different groups, or be applied to groups in a discriminatory manner.

Equalization Attempts to measure the relationship of locally assessed values to a fluid real estate market.

Equitable Remedy A judgment granted to a plaintiff that is something other than an award of money (damages); for example, an injunction, quiet title, rescission, and specific performance. *Compare:* **Legal Remedy.**

Equitable Right of Redemption The right of a debtor to save (redeem) property from foreclosure proceedings prior to confirmation of sale. *Compare:* **Statutory Redemption.**

Equitable Title An interest created in property upon the execution of a valid sales contract, whereby actual title will be transferred by deed at a future date (closing). Also, the vendee's (buyer's) interest in property under a land contract. *Also called:* **Equitable Interest.**

Equity 1. An owner's unencumbered interest in property; the difference between the value of the property and the liens against it. 2. A judge's power to soften or set aside strict legal rules, to bring about a fair and just result in a particular case.

Erosion Gradual loss of soil due to wind or water.

Errors and Omissions Insurance (E&O) Professional liability insurance that protects real estate professionals from mistakes or negligence.

Escalation Clause Lease clause that allows an increase in rent for increases in expenses paid by the landlord, such as real estate taxes, operating costs, and cost of living expenses.

Escheat When property reverts to the state after a person dies without leaving a valid will and without heirs, or when property is abandoned.

Escrow System in which things of value (e.g., money or documents) are held on behalf of parties to a transaction by a disinterested third party (escrow agent) until specific conditions have been satisfied. *Also called:* **In Escrow.**

Escrow Account 1. An account maintained by a broker for the deposit of client's money (i.e., good faith deposits). *Also called:* **Trust Account.** 2. An account maintained by a lender for the deposit of borrowers' extra 1/12 monthly deposits to cover next year's insurance and tax payments. *Also called:* **Reserve Account.**

Escrow Closing A closing by a disinterested third party, often an escrow agent.

Escrow Instructions Contract that authorizes an escrow agent to deliver items deposited in escrow once the parties have complied with specified conditions; can be the real estate purchase contract or a separate document.

Estate 1. Possessory interest in real property; either a freehold estate or leasehold estate. 2. The real and personal property left by someone who has died.

Estate at Sufferance Possession of property by a tenant who came into possession of the property under a valid lease, but stays on after the lease expires without the landlord's permission.

Estate at Will A leasehold estate with no specified termination date and with no regular rental period.

Estate for Years Leasehold estate set to last for a definite period (e.g., one week, three years), after which it automatically terminates. *Also called:* **Term Tenancy.** *Compare:* **Periodic Tenancy; Tenancy at Will.**

Estate of Inheritance Estate that can be willed or descend to heirs, such as a fee simple estate.

Estoppel Legal doctrine that prevents a person from asserting rights or facts inconsistent with earlier actions or statements.

Evaluation Determining the usefulness or utility of property without specifying an estimate of value.

Eviction Dispossessing or expelling someone from real property.

Exclusionary Zoning Zoning law that effectively prevents certain groups from living in a community.

Exclusive Agency Listing agreement between a broker and seller that provides the broker the exclusive right to represent the seller in the sale of the seller's property and the broker will be compensated if he or any other person or entity (excluding the seller) produces a purchaser in accordance with the listing agreement.

Exclusive Jurisdiction When there is only one court in which a particular type of case can be filed, that court has exclusive jurisdiction. *Compare:* **Concurrent Jurisdiction**

Exclusive Right to Sell Listing agreement that entitles the broker to a commission if anyone, including the seller, finds a buyer for the property during the listing term.

Execute 1. To sign. 2. To perform or complete. *See:* **Executed Contract**

Executed Contract Contract under which both parties have completely performed their contractual obligations.

Executor/Executrix Person named in a will to carry out its provisions, including disbursement of land.

Executory Contract A contract under which one or more parties have not yet completed performance of their obligations.

Exemption Provision holding that a law or rule does not apply to a particular person, entity, or group (e.g., a company with a property tax exemption does not have to pay property taxes).

Express Stated in words (spoken or written).

Expressed Agency Agency relationship based on an expressed agreement, either written or oral.

Express Contract Contract that has been put into words, either spoken or written.

Extension Clause Listing agreement clause providing for a specified time after a listing expires when a broker is still entitled to a commission if the property is sold to someone the broker dealt with during the listing term. *Also called:* **Carryover Clause, Safety Clause.**

External Environmental Hazard Concerns that exist outside the boundaries of a property, which can have a significant impact on its value.

External Obsolescence Any influence that falls outside the actual property site and negatively affects a property's value. *Compare:* **Functional Obsolescence.**

F

Failure of Purpose When the intended purpose of an agreement or arrangement can no longer be achieved, and in most cases, releases the parties from their obligations.

Fair Housing Act Common name for Title VIII of the Civil Rights Act of 1968.

Fair Market Value The price a buyer and seller agree upon in a competitive market and under normal circumstances. *Also called:* **Market Value.**

Familial Status A protected group under the federal Fair Housing Act and New York State law, making it illegal to discriminate against a person because she is the parent or guardian of a child less than 18 years of age.

Family An individual, or two or more people related by blood, marriage, or adoption living together in one dwelling; or a group of up to three people not related by blood, marriage, or adoption living together as a single housekeeping unit; or one or more people living together in a single housekeeping unit in a hotel or club.

Fascia A panel or board facing the outer edge of the soffit.

Fee on Condition Defeasible fee that may be assigned and terminated by the grantor upon the occurrence of an event.

Federal Discount Rate Interest rate charged by Federal Reserve banks on loans to member commercial banks.

Federal Funds Rate The Federal Reserve's target for short-term interest rates.

Federal Home Loan Mortgage Corporation (Freddie Mac) Non-profit federally chartered institution that functions as a buyer and seller of savings and loan residential mortgages.

Federal Housing Administration (FHA) Government agency that insures mortgage loans.

Federal National Mortgage Association (Fannie Mae) Nation's largest, and privately owned, investor in residential mortgages.

Federal Open Market Committee (FOMC) Body that controls the Fed's sale and purchase of government securities, and that is made up of the seven members of the Federal Reserve Board, plus the President of the Federal Reserve Bank of New York, and four other Federal Reserve Bank presidents.

Federal Reserve Board (the Fed) Body responsible for U.S. monetary policy, maintaining economic stability and regulating commercial banks.

Fee An estate of inheritance; title to real property that can be willed or descend to heirs.

Fee Simple Defeasible A fee estate in real property that may be defeated or undone if certain events occur or conditions are not met. *Also called:* **Defeasible Fee.** *See:* **Conditional Fee, Fee Simple Determinable.**

Fee Simple Determinable A defeasible fee that automatically terminated if certain conditions occur. *Also called:* **Determinable Fee.** *Compare:* **Fee, Conditional.**

Fee Simple Estate The greatest estate one can have in real property; freely transferable and inheritable, and of indefinite duration, with no conditions on title. *Also called:* **Fee Simple, Fee Title,** or **Fee Simple Absolute.**

Feudal System System of land ownership under which a king or queen owns all land and all others are merely tenants.

Fiduciary Person in a position of trust held by law to high standards of good faith and loyalty.

Fiduciary Deed Deed executed by a trustee, executor, or other fiduciary, conveying property the fiduciary does not own but is authorized to manage.

Fiduciary Duties What is owed to all clients in an agency relationship—obedience, loyalty, disclosure, confidentiality, accountability, and reasonable care.

Fiduciary Relationship A relationship of trust and confidence, in which one party owes the other (or both parties owe each other) loyalty and a higher standard of good faith than is owed to third parties. *See:* **Client.**

Filtering Down When one practice has negative residual effects. *See:* **Redlining, Blockbusting.**

Finance Company Financial institution that usually specializes in making higher risk loans at higher interest rates.

Finance Instrument Legal documents that establish the rights and duties of all parties involved in transaction.

Financing Statement A brief document that, when recorded, gives constructive notice of a creditor's security interest in an item of personal property.

Finder's Fee Referral fee paid for directing a buyer or seller to a real estate agent.

First Lien Position The lien with highest priority when there is more than one mortgage or other debt or obligation secured by the property.

First Mortgage Security instrument with a first lien position, meaning the first mortgage holder is paid first from a foreclosure sale's proceeds.

First Substantive Contact An event triggering agency disclosure (e.g., prior to entering into a listing agreement, prior to showing a property, at an open house when a buyer displays serious interest, etc.).

Fiscal Policy Government's plan for spending, taxation, and debt management.

Fixed Expenses Occur on a regular basis and have regular payment amounts; occur whether the property is vacant or fully leased, and generally do not vary in response to changing levels of occupancy. *Compare:* **Variable Expenses.**

Fixed Rate Loan Loan with an interest rate that remains constant for the duration of the loan.

Fixture A man-made attachment; an item of personal property attached to or closely associated with real property in such a way that it has legally become part of the real property.

Flashing Material used to cover joints where two or more types of materials join together for the purpose of preventing water from penetrating the joint (e.g., metal over the seam between a brick chimney and a shingle roof).

Flip Tax A fee, imposed by the co-op board, for the transfer of ownership during the sale of the unit.

Flipping 1. Purchasing a property and immediately reselling it for a profit. 2. When a condominium owner assigns his purchase rights to another buyer before the sale of that property or unit has closed. *Also called:* **Assigning a Contract.**

Flitch Beams Two or more timbers cut lengthwise and bundled together to provide additional support for the ceiling and roof.

Footer The underground base, usually concrete, that supports a foundation.

Forbearance A legally binding promise to refrain from doing a particular act.

Foreclosure When real property is involuntarily transferred because the owner defaulted on debts secured by the property.

Foreclosure Action A lawsuit filed by a creditor to begin foreclosure proceedings.

Foreign Corporation A corporation doing business in one state, but created (incorporated) in another state.

Forfeiture Loss of a right or something of value because of failure to perform an obligation or condition.

Formal Will A written, witnessed will.

Foundation The basic structure on which a house will sit. A foundation can be concrete slab, pier and beams, crawl space, or basement.

Foundation Walls The sidewalls that support a structure, typically made of poured concrete, concrete block, or brick.

Framing The basic load-bearing skeleton of a structure to which the interior walls, exterior walls, and roof system are attached.

Fraud Intentional or negligent misrepresentation or concealment of a material fact; making statements that a person knows, or should realize, are false or misleading.

Freehold A possessory interest in real property of uncertain (and often unlimited) duration; an ownership estate in real property; either a fee simple or a life estate. Holder of freehold estate has title. *Compare:* **Leasehold Estate.**

Freon The brand name for the chemical compound CFC used as a coolant in refrigerators, air conditioners, and dehumidifiers; now known as a contributor to the depletion of the ozone.

Friable Characteristic of asbestos in which it can crumble easily or become powdery when manipulated by hand, releasing particles into the air.

Full Covenant and Warranty Deed Contains the strongest and broadest form of guarantee of title of any type of deed, and provides the greatest protection of any deed to the grantee. In this type of deed, the grantor makes various covenants, or warranties.

Fully Amortized Loans Loans for which the total payments over the life of the loan pay off the entire balance of principal and interest due at the end of the loan term.

Functional Obsolescence Loss in property value resulting from changes in tastes, preferences, or market standards.

Fuse A protective device for a wiring system that contains a wire designed to melt and open the circuit when overheating occurs.

Future Interest An interest in real property that may become or will become a possessory interest at some point in the future. *See:* **Remainder Interest; Reversionary Interest.**

G

General Agent A person authorized to handle a principal's affairs in one area or in specified areas.

General Lien A lien against all property of a debtor, instead of just one particular property.

General Partner A partner who has the authority to manage and contract for a general or limited partnership and who is personally liable for the partnership's debts.

General Partnership A partnership in which each member has an equal right to manage the business and share in the profits, as well as equal responsibility for the partnership's debts. All partners are considered general partners.

General Warranty Deed A deed in which the grantor warrants title against defects that might have arisen before or during his period of ownership. *Compare:* **Limited Warranty Deed.**

Girder The main support beam of a structure spanning the foundation walls.

Government National Mortgage Association (Ginnie Mae) Government-owned corporation that guarantees payment of principal and interest to investors who buy its mortgage-backed securities on the secondary market.

Government Survey System Legal description for land referencing principal meridians and base lines designated throughout the country.

Grace Period The time a borrower has after a payment is due to make the payment without incurring penalties.

Graduated Lease A lease in which the rent changes throughout the lease term. The contract specifies how much as well as when the rent will change.

Graduated Mortgage Mortgage that allows a borrower to make smaller payments in the early years of the loan term with payments increasing over time.

Graduated Payment A buydown plan for which payment subsidies in the early years keep payments low, but payments increase each year until they are sufficient to fully amortize the loan.

Grant To transfer or convey an interest in real property by means of a written instrument.

Grantee The person who receives a conveyance of real property in a real estate transaction.

Granting Clause Deed clause stating a grantor's intent to transfer an interest in real property. *Also called:* **Words of Conveyance.**

Grantor The person who transfers title to real property in a real estate transaction.

Gross Income Total income, both cash and non-cash, received from an investment or business, before expenses are paid.

Gross Income Multiplier (GIM) A number derived using annual income figures from comparable commercial properties in an area, which is used to estimate the value of real estate. *Compare:* **Gross Rent Multiplier.**

Gross Lease A lease in which the lessor pays all operating and maintenance costs associated with the property.

Gross Rent Multiplier (GRM) A number derived from comparable rental properties in an area, which is then used to estimate the value of real estate. The GRM is only used for one- to four-unit residential properties. *Compare:* **Gross Income Multiplier.**

Ground Lease A lease in which a tenant leases unimproved land on a long-term basis and typically include a provision that provides the tenant will construct a building on the property, which he will own upon completion. The lessor retains the rights to the land. Essentially, ownership of the land and improvements (building) are separated. *Also called:* **Land Lease.**

Groundwater Naturally occurring water found in subterranean crevices or spaces.

Group Home A residential facility in a residential zone for three or more unrelated people (i.e., foster homes, rehabilitation centers, and halfway houses).

Guardian Court-appointed person who administers the affairs of a minor or someone who is incompetent.

H

Habendum Clause Clause within a deed that describes the type of estate granted; it must always agree with the granting clause.

Hazardous Material Any type of product with toxic, corrosive, flammable, or reactive qualities.

Headers In construction, reinforcements made of wood for door and window placement. *Also called:* **Lintels.**

Heir Someone entitled to inherit another person's real or personal property under the laws of intestate succession.

Highest and Best Use The most profitable, legally permitted, feasible, and physically possible use of a property.

High-tension Power Lines Large transmission cables carrying electrical energy.

Historic Preservation Office Identifies, evaluates, preserves, and revitalizes any given city's historic, archaeological, and cultural resources.

Holder in Due Course One who acquires a negotiable instrument in good faith and for consideration and, thus, has certain rights above the original payee.

Holdover Tenant A lessee who remains in possession of property after the lease has expired; a tenant who refuses to surrender possession of property at the tenancy's end.

Home Acquisition Debt A mortgage a taxpayer takes out to buy, build, or substantially improve a qualified home.

Home Equity Debt A loan that does not qualify as home acquisition debt but is secured by a qualified home.

Home Equity Line of Credit A credit line secured by a second mortgage on the homeowner's principle residence. Home equity lines of credit are available to the homeowner as expenses arise and payments are made according to the credit terms. Interest is usually tax deductible. *Compare:* **Home Equity Loan.**

Home Equity Loan A loan secured by a second mortgage on the homeowner's principle residence. Home equity loans are usually one-time loans for a specific amount of money obtained for a specific, and often non-housing-related, expenditure. Payments are made according to the loan terms and interest is usually tax deductible. *Compare:* **Home Equity Line of Credit.**

Home Occupation Small business or other occupation conducted in a residence.

Homebuyer Assistance Programs Alternative financing programs through which lenders may offer borrowers as tools to help them qualify more easily, get a larger loan, or pay less of a down payment.

Homeowners Association Nonprofit association comprised of homeowners, responsible for enforcing the subdivision's CC&Rs and managing other community affairs.

Homestead Dwellings of four or fewer units, owner-occupied mobile homes, residential condominiums, farms, and vacant land suitable for qualified buildings that may be eligible for a separate tax rate.

Homestead Laws Laws that protect property owners from lien foreclosure by exempting some their equity in real estate. In New York, homestead protection is limited to $10,000 individually and $20,000 for land co-owned by a married couple.

Homestead Protection Limited protection for a debtor against claims of judgment creditors; applies to property of the debtor's residence.

Horizontal Property Acts Laws that create the legal framework for creating a condominium form of ownership and make it possible to define actual ownership rights.

Hostile and Adverse Possession or use of land without the owner's permission and against the owner's interests; one condition necessary for an easement by prescription and adverse possession.

House Rules The rules and requirements established for condominium and/or co-op tenants. These could include rules for common areas, parking, noise, pets, use of recreation room, etc.

Housing Expense Ratio The relationship of total monthly housing expense to income, expressed as a percentage: Total Housing Expense ÷ Income = Ratio %.

Hypothecate To make property the security for a loan without giving up possession of it (as with a mortgage). *Compare:* **Pledge.**

I

Identifiable Grantee The person, to whom real property interest is to be conveyed, identified in such a way so as to reasonably separate that person from all others in the world.

Illiquidity Assets that cannot easily be converted to cash.

Immediate Delivery Program Program giving sellers up to 60 days to deliver mortgages Freddie Mac has agreed to buy on the secondary market.

Immobility Physical characteristic of real estate referring to the fact that it cannot move from one place to another.

Implied Agency Agency relationship created through the behavior (actions or words) of one or both parties. *Compare:* **Expressed Agency.**

Implied by Law Required by law to be part of an agreement and treated by a court as part of an agreement even if it contradicts the express terms agreed to by the parties.

Implied Contract A contract not put into words, but implied by the actions of the parties.

Implied Warranty Guarantee created by operation of law, whether or not the seller intended to offer it.

Implied Warranty of Habitability An implied guarantee that the property is safe and fit for human habitation; treated by law as an implicit provision in every residential lease, regardless of the express terms of the lease.

Improvements Manmade additions to real property; substantial fixtures, such as buildings.

In Rem A lawsuit or legal action directed toward property, rather than toward a particular person. Judgments are binding to all persons who claim title to the property.

Incentive Zoning A system by which developers receive zoning incentives on the condition that specific physical, social, or cultural benefits are provided to the community.

Income Approach Appraisal method that estimates the value of real estate by analyzing the amount of revenue, or income, the property currently generates or could generate, often comparing the subject property to other similar properties.

Incompetent Not legally competent; not of sound mind; mentally ill, senile, or feebleminded.

Independent Contractor Individual who is self-employed. *Compare:* **Employee.**

Index Statistical report that is a generally reliable indicator of the approximate change in the cost of money, and is thus often used to adjust the interest rate for ARMs.

Index Lease Method used to determine rent for long-term leases.

Indirect Cost Costs associated with a construction project, other than labor and materials.

Indirect Loss A loss that occurs as a consequence of the direct loss. For example, regarding property insurance, on a dwelling policy, fire is covered as a direct loss. *Also called:* **Consequential Loss.** *Compare:* **Direct Loss.**

Inflation Increase in the cost of goods or services; or, too much money chasing too few goods.

Informed Consent Written evidence that a client is aware of and has given permission to an agent to perform a specific action or take on a specific role in the client agent relationship.

Infrastructure The support facilities and services for a community, such as roads, parks, sewers, water, schools, trash collection, etc.

Ingress and Egress 1. Entering and exiting; usually refers to a road or other means of access to a property. 2. An easement that gives the dominant tenant access to the dominant tenement.

Inherit In strict legal usage, to acquire property by intestate succession; commonly used to mean acquiring property either by intestate succession or by will.

Injunction Court order prohibiting or compelling an act. *See:* **Equitable Remedy.**

Inquiry Notice When circumstances indicate a possible problem prompting further investigation, a person may be held to have had notice of the problem even if he does not have actual knowledge of it.

Installment Note A note that calls for payments of principal only during the term of the note, with a balloon payment to pay off the balance.

Installment Sales Contract Agreement for which the buyer makes payments to the seller in exchange for the right to occupy and use the property, but no deed or title is transferred until all, or a specified portion of, payments have been made. *Also called:* **Land Contract.**

Instrument Any document that transfers title (such as a deed), creates a lien (such as a mortgage), or gives a right to payment (such as a contract).

Insured Value The amount for which property can be insured, usually representing only the replacement cost of the structure and disregarding any value for land.

Intangible Appurtenance An appurtenant right that does not involve ownership of physical objects, for example, easements as opposed to mineral rights, which involve tangibles.

Integration Clause Contract provision stating the document contains the entire agreement between the parties.

Interest 1. A right or share in something. 2. A charge a borrower pays to a lender for the use of the lender's money.

Interest Rate Cap A limit on the amount of interest rate increase that can occur with an adjustable rate mortgage.

Internal Environmental Hazard An environmental hazard that occurs within a property.

Intestate Dying without leaving a valid will.

Intestate Succession Distribution of property to the heirs of a person who died intestate.

Invalid Not legally binding or legally effective; not valid.

Inverse Condemnation Action Court action by a private landowner against the government, seeking compensation for damage to property that resulted from government action.

Investment Value The highest price an investor would pay for a property based on how well it will serve her investment goals.

Involuntary Alienation When title to property is transferred during the owner's lifetime without his consent.

Involuntary Lien A lien that arises by operation of law, without the consent of the property owner.

Irrevocable Consent Subjects out-of-state licensees to the jurisdiction of the courts of the state of New York.

J

Joint Tenancy A form of co-ownership in which the co-owners have equal undivided interests and the right of survivorship.

Joists Long beams of wood or steel that span the piers of a foundation (floor joists) or the load bearing walls of a roof (ceiling joists).

Joists and Rafters (Roofing) A type of roof frame with joists supported by the outer load-bearing walls, and a central load-bearing wall that acts as the beams do for the floor joists. The ceiling joists run horizontally, parallel to the floor; the ceiling rafters begin on the outer load-bearing walls, but rise as they come to center peak of the roof (sloped joist).

Judgment 1. A court's binding determination of the rights and duties of the parties in a lawsuit. 2. A court order requiring one party to pay the wronged party damages.

Judgment Creditor A person who is owed money as a result of a being awarded a judgment in a lawsuit.

Judgment Debtor A person who owes money as a result of a judgment in a lawsuit.

Judgment Lien A general lien against a judgment debtor's property, which the judgment creditor creates by recording a certificate of judgment in the county in which property is located.

Judicial Foreclosure A lawsuit filed by a lender or other creditor to foreclose on a mortgage or other lien; a court-ordered sheriff's sale of property to repay the debt.

Judicial Opinion A court's written statement outlining the facts of a particular case and explaining the legal basis for the decision.

Judicial Partition A court action to divide real property among its co-owners so each owns part in severalty, or (if it is not practical to physically divide the property) each gets a share of the sale proceeds.

Judicial Review When a court considers whether a statute or regulation is constitutional.

Jumbo Loans Loans that exceed the maximum amount established by Fannie Mae and Freddie Mac for conforming mortgage loans, making them nonconforming loans.

Junior Lienholder Secured creditor with a lower priority lien than another lien on the same land.

Junior Mortgage Any mortgage with a lower lien position than another mortgage.

Jurisdiction The extent of a particular court's authority.

Just Compensation Appropriate or fair value for private land taken by the government for public use. *See*: **Eminent Domain**.

K

Kickbacks Paying part of the proceeds of a sale to another party that helped secure the sale, but is unlicensed.

L

Lally™ Columns Steel support columns filled with concrete.

Land The surface of the earth, the area above and below the surface, and anything attached to the surface.

Land Contract A real estate installment agreement where a buyer makes payment to a seller in exchange for the right to occupy and use property, but no deed or title transfers until all, or a specified portion of, payments have been made. *Also called:* **Installment Land Contract**, **Installment Sales Contract**, and **Land Sales Contract.**

Land Lease Lease in which a tenant leases unimproved land on a long-term basis.

Land Patent An instrument conveying public land to an individual.

Land Use Controls Public or private restrictions on how land may be used (e.g., zoning).

Landlocked Property 1. Land without access to a road or highway. 2. Land not beside water.

Landlord A landowner who has leased property to another. *Also called:* **Lessor.**

Landmarks Preservation Commission (LPC) The New York City agency responsible for identifying and designating the city's landmarks.

Latent Defect One that is not visible or apparent; a hidden defect that would not be discovered in a reasonably thorough inspection of property. *Compare:* **Patent Defect.**

Lawful Objective A legal purpose.

Lead A toxic metallic element found in paint, dust, water, and the ground.

Lead Agency The agency under the State Environmental Quality Review Act principally responsible for determining whether an environmental impact statement is required in connection with the action and for the preparation and filing of the statement if required.

Lease Conveyance of a leasehold estate from the fee owner to a tenant; a contract where one party pays the other rent in exchange for possession of real estate. *See:* **Gross Lease; Net Lease; Percentage Lease; Land Lease.**

Lease Escalation Clause Clause that allows landlords to raise rent to protect their margin of profit and, in some cases, prevent the erosion of their expected return due to inflation.

Leasehold Estate An estate that gives the holder (tenant) a temporary right to possession, without title. *Also called:* **Less-than-Freehold Estate.**

Lease/Option When a seller leases property to someone for a specific term with an option to buy the property at a predetermined price during the lease term, usually with a portion of the lease payments applied to the purchase price.

Legacy Receiving money by will.

Legal Description A precise description of a property. *See:* **Lot and Block; Metes and Bounds; Government Survey System.**

Legal Remedy Money awarded to the plaintiff in a civil lawsuit; damages. *Also called:* **Remedy** or **Common Law Remedy**. *Compare:* **Equitable Remedy.**

Legal Title 1. The interest in property held by the rightful owner. 2. The seller's interest in property under a land contract.

Lessee Person who leases property; a tenant.

Lessor Person who leases property to another; a landlord.

Letter of Intent Signifies two or more parties agree to do business together.

Letter of Opinion A letter accompanying the abstract of title issued by an attorney regarding the status of title to a property.

Level of Assessment The ratio of total assessed value to the municipality's total market value

Level Payment A buydown plan where the interest rate reduction (and hence the payment) is constant throughout the buydown period.

Leverage The use of borrowed funds to purchase property with the anticipation of a return on the funds invested, such that the investor sees a profit not only on his own investment, but also on the borrowed funds.

Levy 1. Verb: to impose a tax. 2. Noun: the tax itself.

Liability Insurance Insures individuals against financial losses resulting from the person's responsibilities to others imposed by law or contract.

Liable Legally responsible.

License Revocable, non-assignable permission to enter another person's land for a particular purpose. *Compare:* **Easement.**

Lien A non-possessory interest in property giving a lienholder the right to foreclose if the owner does not pay a debt owed the lienholder; a financial encumbrance on the owner's title.

Lien Priority The order in which liens are paid out of the proceeds of a foreclosure sale. Tax liens always have the highest priority.

Lien Theory States States in which a mortgagee holds only a lien against property (not actual title) until the loan is repaid, and the mortgagor holds the actual title. *Compare:* **Title Theory States.**

Life Estate A freehold estate lasting only as long as a specified person does lives. That person is referred to as the **measuring life**.

Life Estate Pur Autre Vie A life estate "for the life of another," where the measuring life is someone other than the life tenant. *Also called:* **Pur Autre Vie.**

Life Tenant Someone who owns a life estate; the person entitled to possession of the property during the measuring life.

Lifetime Cap/Ceiling The maximum increase or decrease in the periodic payment allowable over the life of an adjustable or variable rate mortgage.

Limited Common Areas Areas in a condominium or co-up owned by all but used by only one owner (i.e., a designated parking space.)

Limited Partner A partner in a limited partnership who is primarily an investor and does not participate in the management of the business, and who is not personally liable for the partnership's debts.

Limited Partnership A partnership comprised of one or more general partners and one or more limited partners.

Limited Warranty Deed A deed in which the grantor warrants title only against defects arising during the time he owned the property and not against defects arising before that time of ownership. *Also called:* **Special Warranty Deed**. *Compare:* **General Warranty Deed**.

Lineal Descendants A person's children, grandchildren, great-grandchildren, and so on.

Liquid When an investment can easily be converted to cash.

Liquidated Damages A sum of money the parties to a contract agree in advance (at the time of entering into the contract) will serve as compensation in the event of a contract breach.

Liquidity The ability to convert an asset into cash quickly without the loss of principal.

Lis Pendens Recorded notice stating a lawsuit is pending that may affect title to the defendant's real estate.

Listing Agreement A written agency contract between a seller and a real estate broker, stating the broker will be paid a commission for finding (or attempting to find) a buyer for the seller's real property. *Compare:* **Exclusive Agency; Exclusive Right to Sell**.

Litigant A party to a lawsuit; a plaintiff or defendant.

Litigation Lawsuit(s).

Littoral Rights Water rights of a landowner whose property is adjacent to a lake or contains a lake. *Compare:* **Appropriative Rights; Riparian Rights**.

Loan Origination Fee Points charged to a borrower to cover the costs of issuing a loan.

Loan-to-Value Ratio (LTV) The amount of money borrowed, compared to the value (or price) of the property.

Loan Value The amount of money a bank is willing to lend someone to finance property.

Location The exact position of a property.

Location Survey Survey that determines if a property's buildings encroach on adjoining property, or any adjoining property's buildings encroach on the subject property.

Loss Factor The difference between rentable square footage and usable square footage.

Lot A parcel of land; especially, in a subdivision.

Lot and block A type of legal description used for platted property. The description states only the property's lot number and block number in a particular subdivision.

M

Magnet Store A major department or chain store strategically located within a shopping center to give maximum exposure to smaller satellite stores.

Mailbox Rule Acceptance of a contract offer is effective the moment it is mailed, even though one party has not yet received it.

Maintenance Monthly fees paid by condominium owners or co-op shareholders for common area expenses like utilities, building maintenance, and upkeep. *Also called:* **Common Area Expenses** or **Maintenance Fees.**

Management Agreement A written agreement that governs the relationship between a property owner/investor and the property manager and outlines the duties of the property manager. *Also called:* **Property Management Employee Contract.**

Management Proposal A plan created by the property manager for overseeing the property, including market analysis, and developing a variety of financial reports including the operating budget.

Margin Difference between the index value and interest rate charged to the borrower with an ARM loan.

Market Price The actual open market price paid in an arm's length transaction.

Market Position The position an agent's listing is in compared to similar homes in the same neighborhood at a similar price.

Market Value The theoretical price a property is most likely to bring in a typical transaction.

Marketable Title Title free and clear of objectionable encumbrances or defects, so that a reasonably prudent person with full knowledge of the facts would not hesitate to purchase the property.

Material Breach A breach of contract important enough to excuse the non-breaching party from performing his contractual obligations.

Material Fact An important fact; one that is likely to influence a decision.

Materialman A person who supplies materials, equipment, or fuel for a construction project. *See:* **Materialman's Lien.** *Compare:* **Mechanic.**

Materialman's Lien Similar to a mechanic's lien, but based on a debt owed to someone who supplied materials, equipment, or fuel for a project (as opposed to labor).

Measuring Life A person whose life determines the length of a life estate. *See:* **Life Estate.**

Mechanic A person who performs work (construction, remodeling, repairs, or demolition) on real property. *See:* **Mechanic's Lien**. *Compare:* **Materialman.**

Mechanic's Lien A specific lien claimed by someone who performed work on property (construction, repairs, or improvements) and has not been paid. This term is often used in a general sense, referring to materialmen's liens as well as actual mechanics' liens.

Merger Uniting two or more properties by transferring ownership of each to one person.

Mesothelioma A form of lung cancer caused by extended exposure to asbestos.

Metes and Bounds A land survey process whereby a licensed land surveyor starts at an easily identifiable point of beginning (POB) and describes a property's boundaries in terms of courses, (compass directions), and distances, ultimately returning to the point of beginning.

Methamphetamine An illegal, man-made drug that is extremely addictive. Residues left in a residence from the manufacturing process can be toxic.

Mineral Rights Rights to the minerals located beneath the surface of a property.

Minor A person who has not yet reached the age of majority; n New York, that is age 18.

Misdemeanor A misdeed triable in a court of special sessions.

Misrepresentation A false or misleading statement. *See:* **Fraud.**

Mitigation When the non-breaching party takes action to minimize losses resulting from a breach of contract.

Mold A fungus that can release toxins into the environment causing allergic reactions in some people.

Monetary Policy The means by which the government can exert control over the supply and cost of money.

Monoline Policy Insurance coverage designed to cover one specific area—*property.*

Monuments Fixed physical objects stated as points of reference in a metes and bounds description.

Moratorium Suspends the right of property owners to obtain development approval while local legislatures consider, draft, and adopt land use regulations or rules to respond to new or changing circumstances not adequately dealt with by current laws.

Mortgage An instrument that creates a voluntary lien on real property to secure repayment of a debt. The parties to a mortgage are the mortgagor (borrower) and mortgagee (lender).

Mortgage Banker One who originates, sells, and services mortgage loans, and usually acts as the originator and servicer of loans on behalf of large investors, such as insurance companies, pension plans, and FANNIE MAE.

Mortgage Broker One who, for a fee, places loans with investors, but typically does not service such loans.

Mortgage Clause Clause that states in order to get a mortgage loan, property insurance must be obtained prior to closing. The mortgage clause covers the lender's interest in preservation and reconstruction of the property after a loss.

Mortgage Companies Institutions that function as originators and servicers of loans on behalf of large investors, such as insurance companies, pension plans, or Fannie Mae.

Mortgagee A lender who accepts a mortgage as security for repayment of the loan.

Mortgage Insurance Premium (MIP) Insurance offered through the FHA to insure a lender against default on a loan by a borrower.

Mortgage Payment Adjustment Period The interval at which a borrower's actual mortgage payments change with an ARM (adjustable rate mortgage).

Mortgage Payment Cap A limit on the amount of mortgage payment increases that can occur with an adjustable rate mortgage.

Mortgage Value The value of an asset for purposes of securing a mortgage loan.

Mortgagor A person who borrows money and gives a mortgage to the lender as security.

Multiple Listing Service® (MLS) A service whereby local member brokers agree to share listings, and further agree to share commissions on properties sold jointly. The MLS generally consists of online computer services and a regularly published book.

Municipal Engineer's Office The municipal agency responsible for the planning, design, and construction of New York's public works facilities and projects.

Mutual Consent When all parties freely agree to the terms of a contract, without fraud, undue influence, duress, or mistake, and achieved through offer and acceptance. *Also called:* **Meeting of the Minds.**

Mutual Mistake When both parties to a contract were mistaken about a fact or a law.

Mutual Mortgage Insurance Plan The name of the FHA's insurance program for residential mortgages.

Mycotoxin A toxic substance produced by some molds.

N

Narrative Report A type of appraisal report that provides the most detailed analysis, as it allows the appraiser to comment fully on the opinions and conclusions of the appraisal.

National Association of REALTORS® (NAR®) America's largest trade association, representing 1.3 million members involved in all aspects of the residential and commercial real estate industries, including brokers, salespeople, property managers, appraisers, and counselors.

Natural Attachments Things growing on a piece of land, such as trees, shrubs, or crops; considered part of real property while growing and personal property when removed. *Compare:* **Fixture.**

Negative Amortization The balance of a loan growing due to deferred interest and resulting in an even larger balloon payment for the borrower.

Negative Amortization Cap A limit on the amount of negative amortization that can occur with an adjustable rate mortgage.

Negative Easement An easement that prevents the servient tenant from using her own land in a certain way (as opposed to allowing the dominant tenant to use it). *Compare:* **Restrictive Covenant.**

Negligence Conduct that falls below the standard of care a reasonable person would exercise under certain circumstances; an unintentional breach of a legal duty resulting from carelessness, recklessness, or incompetence. *See:* **Tort.** *Compare:* **Strict Liability.**

Net Lease Lease for which a tenant pays all taxes, insurance, etc., plus utilities and rent.

Net Listing Agreement A listing agreement in which the seller sets a net amount acceptable for a property; if the actual selling price exceeds that amount, the broker is entitled to keep the excess as commission; illegal in New York.

Net Operating Income (NOI) Income left after all operating costs are paid.

Net to Seller An estimate of the money a seller should receive from a real estate transaction, based on the selling price after all costs and expenses are paid.

Net Worth Value of a person's assets less liabilities.

New York State Association of REALTORS® All New York Real Estate boards fall under this state board; a member of the NAR®.

New York State Human Rights Law Extends protected classes beyond those covered in the Fair Housing Act to include, age, creed, marital status, military status, and sexual orientation.

New York State Office of Parks, Recreation, and Historic Preservation (OPRHP) Oversees public recreation areas and administers federal and state preservation projects.

New York State Uniform Fire Prevention and Building Code Sets forth the construction, materials, safety, and sanitary standards for buildings in New York as well as standards for the condition, occupancy, maintenance, rehabilitation, and renewal of existing buildings.

Nonconforming Loans Those that do not meet Fannie Mae/Freddie Mac standards and, thus, cannot be sold on the secondary market.

Nonconforming Use Land use that does not conform to current zoning laws but is legally allowed because the land use was established before the new laws were enacted. Most nonconforming uses are allowed to continue but may not be expanded or enlarged.

Non-homestead Property that consists of industrial and commercial parcels as well as vacant land.

Non-judicial Foreclosure Foreclosure by a trustee under the power of sale clause in a deed of trust without the involvement of a court; not used in all states.

Non-possessory Interest An interest in property that does not include the right to possess and occupy the property; an encumbrance, such as a lien or easement.

Non-solicitation Order Prohibits the solicitation of residential property listings, and applies to all real estate brokers and agents; ruled unconstitutional by the U.S. Court of Appeals.

Notary Public An official whose primary function is to witness and certify the acknowledgment made by one signing a legal document.

Notice to Quit A notice to a tenant demanding he vacate the leased property. *Also called:* **Notice to Vacate.**

Novation 1. When one party to a contract withdraws and a new party is substituted with the consent of all parties, relieving the withdrawing party of liability. 2. The substitution of a new obligation for an old one.

Nuisance Interference with the right of quiet enjoyment of property.

O

Objective Intent What the offeror in a transaction says and does. *Compare:* **Subjective Intent.**

Observable Depreciation Any loss of value an appraiser attributes to physical deterioration, functional obsolescence, or economic obsolescence.

Obsolescence The loss in property value caused by economic and/or functional factors.

Offer When one person proposes a contract to another. *See:* **Acceptance.** *Compare:* **Counteroffer.**

Offer of Compensation The commission that will be paid on the sale of property.

Offer of Cooperation An open invitation to other brokers to sell property listed by another broker.

Offeree A person who receives an offer or to whom an offer is made.

Offering Plan A document provided by the sponsor (of a condominium or co-op) that offers detailed information regarding the property. *Also called:* **Offering Statement.**

Offeror A person who makes an offer.

Office Manager A licensed associate real estate broker who elects to work as an office manager under the name and supervision of an individual broker or another broker who is licensed under a partnership, trade name, limited liability company, or corporation.

Office of Fair Housing and Equal Opportunity (FHEO) A division of HUD, which is responsible for the administration and enforcement of federal laws.

Official Map A final and conclusive map with respect to the location and width of a municipality's streets, highways, drainage systems, and parks.

Open and Notorious When possession or use of land is obvious and unconcealed; one of the conditions necessary for easement by prescription.

Open-end Mortgage Mortgage loan that allows borrowers to request additional funds from the lender, up to a certain pre-determined limit, even re-borrowing part of the debt that has been repaid (at the lender's discretion) without having to re-negotiate the loan.

Open Listing A nonexclusive listing given by a seller to as many brokers as he chooses. If the property is sold, the broker who was the procuring cause of the sale is entitled to the commission.

Operating Budget A budget created to project the income and expenses for a property over a one-year period.

Operating Expenses The cost associated with running a building and/or business not including debt service or depreciation.

Operating Statement Document that illustrates total revenues generated for a given period based on rent rolls and management style.

Option A contract giving one party the right to do something within a designated period without obligation. *Compare:* **Right of First Refusal**.

Optionee Person to whom an option is given.

Optionor Person who gives an option.

Option to Purchase A contract giving an optionee the right, but not the obligation, to buy property owned by the optionor during a specified period.

Option to Renew Renewal methods and the terms by which a renewed lease will exist.

Oral Contract A spoken agreement.

Oral Report A type of appraisal report given in person or over the phone often without supporting documentation.

Order of Execution Legal process in which a court orders an official (such as a sheriff) to seize and sell property of a judgment debtor to satisfy a judgment lien.

Ordinance A law passed by a local legislative body. *Compare:* **Resolution**.

Origination The process of making or initiating a new loan.

Ostensible Agency Occurs when an agent is *perceived* as the principal's fiduciary by a third party and the principal does not declare otherwise.

Ownership Title to property, dominion over property; the rights of possession and control of real or personal property.

Ownership in Severalty Ownership by a single individual, as opposed to co-ownership. *Also called:* **Severalty**.

P

Package Mortgage A mortgage where personal property, like furniture, is included in the property sale and financed together with one loan.

Package Policy Two or more lines of coverage combined into one insurance policy. A Homeowners policy is a true package policy because it combines property insurance with liability insurance.

Parcel A lot or piece of real estate particularly a specified part of a larger tract.

Parol Evidence Evidence concerning negotiations or oral agreements not included in a written contract that alter or contradict the terms of the written contract.

Participation Plan A loan when the buyer and another investor (or seller, lender, etc.) enter into a partnership, with the buyer paying an equity share in lieu of interest. *Also called:* **Shared Equity Plan** or **Mortgage**.

Partition Allows any co-owner to end a joint tenancy.

Partnership Association of two or more people to carry on business for profit. Law generally regards a partnership as a group of individuals, not as an entity separate from its owners. *Compare:* **Joint Venture**; **Corporation**.

Partnership Property The property partners bring into a business at the outset, or later acquire for the business; property owned as tenants in partnership. *See:* **Tenancy in Partnership**.

Part Performance The legal doctrine that allows a court to enforce an oral agreement that should have been in writing when the promisee has taken irrevocable steps to perform his contractual obligation and failure to enforce the contract would result in an unjust benefit for the promisor.

Party Wall A wall shared by two separate properties; the owners on each side share the right of use.

Passive Income Defined in Section 469 as earnings derived from any trade or business or income-producing activity in which the taxpayer does not materially participate.

Pass-through Securities Mortgage backed securities issued by Ginnie Mae, which pay interest and principal payments on a monthly basis.

Patent The instrument used to convey government land to a private individual.

Patent Defect A visible, apparent defect that can be seen in a reasonably thorough inspection of property. *Compare:* **Latent Defect**.

Payee The one promised payment in a note.

Payment Cap Protects borrowers from large payment increases in their mortgages.

Percentage Lease Lease under which a tenant pays a percentage of gross sales in addition to rent.

Percolation Rate The rate at which water moves through soil.

Periodic Estate A leasehold estate that continues for successive equal periods of time (i.e., week-to-week or month-to-month) until terminated by proper notice from either the lessor or the lessee. *Also called:* **Periodic Lease** and **Periodic Tenancy**.

Peril Anything that can cause a loss (i.e., fire, wind, and hail).

Permanent Buydown When points are paid to a lender to reduce the interest rate and loan payments for the entire life of the loan.

Permit System System used by state and local governments to monitor compliance with, and enforce building codes and other regulations.

Personal Property Tangible items that (usually) are not permanently attached to, or part of, the real estate. *Also called:* **Personalty** or **Chattel**.

Personalty Personal property.

Pitch A roof's vertical rise in inches, divided by its horizontal span in feet.

PITI Typical payment on a mortgage loan that includes principle, interest, taxes, and insurance,

Plaintiff The party who brings or starts a civil lawsuit; the one who sues.

Planned Unit Development (PUD) A special type of subdivision that may combine nonresidential uses with residential uses, or otherwise depart from ordinary zoning and subdivision regulations; some PUD lot owners co-own recreational facilities or open spaces as tenants in common.

Planning Board Holds public hearings, investigates solutions for the planning issues at hand, and makes recommendations to the appropriate legislative authority. In New York City, the planning board and the zoning board are one entity known as the Board of Standards and Appeals.

Planning Commission A local government agency responsible for preparing a community's comprehensive development plan.

Plaster Board Gypsum plaster sandwiched in-between two layers of coarse paper. It iscommonly used in homes as a wall covering. *Also called:* **Wall Board**, **Dry Wall**, or **Gypsum Board**.

Plat A detailed survey map of a subdivision recorded in the county where the land is located. Subdivided property is often called platted property. *Also called:* **Plat Map**.

Plat Book A large book containing subdivision plats; kept at the county recorder's office.

Platform Construction A type of framing used to build a house or building one story at a time, with each story serving as a platform for the next. *Also called:* **Platform Framing.**

Pledge When a debtor transfers possession of property to the creditor as security for repayment of the debt. *Compare:* **Hypothecate**.

Pledged Account Mortgage An escrow account established with part of a buyer's down payment. The borrower/buyer's lender then withdraws money from the account each month and applies it to the monthly payment.

Plottage An increase in value (to cover the cost of acquiring the parcels) by successful assemblage usually due to use.

Pocket Cards Contains a licensee's photo, name, and business address as well as the name and address of the affiliated broker; prepared, issued, and delivered by the Department of State in cooperation with the Department of Motor Vehicles.

Point of Beginning (POB) The starting point and ending point for a metes and bounds description.

Points One percent of the loan amount. Points can be charged for any reason but are often used for buydowns. *Also called:* **Discount Points**.

Police Power The constitutional power of state and local governments to enact and enforce laws that protect the public's health, safety, morals, and general welfare.

Polychlorinated Biphenols (PCBs) Organic compounds manufactured as cooling and insulating agents for transformers and capacitors used in industry.

Porter's Wage Escalation Formula Ties rent escalation to the wages of a building's cleaning and maintenance personnel (called "porters"). The formula provides tenant's rent will increase a specific amount per square foot for a specified increase in the porter's hourly wages.

Portfolio Income 1. Earnings from interest, dividends, annuities, and royalties *not* derived from the ordinary course of business. 2. Gain or loss from the disposition of property that produces portfolio income or held for investment purposes.

Portfolio Lenders Financial institutions that make real estate loans, which they keep and service in house instead of selling them on the secondary markets.

Positive Easement An easement that allows the dominant tenant to use the servient tenement in a particular way.

Possession 1. The holding and enjoyment of property. 2. Physical occupation of real property.

Possessory Interest Interest that entitles the holder to possess and occupy property, now or in the future; an estate, which may be either a freehold or leasehold.

Possibility of Reverter The interest held by a grantor (or grantor's heirs) who has transferred a fee simple determinable. *Also called:* **Reverter.** *Compare:* **Power of Termination.**

Post and Beam Construction A type of framing with the floor for higher stories (and the roof) supported by beams that sit on top of posts and the outside wall perimeter. *Also called:* **Post and Beam Framing.**

Potential Gross Income The potential income a property would produce in an ideal situation including no vacancy and collection losses.

Power of Attorney An instrument authorizing one person (called an attorney in fact) to act as another's agent to the extent stated in the instrument.

Power of Sale Clause A clause that allows a trustee to sell trust deed property without court supervision if the terms of the trust deed are violated.

Power of Termination The right to terminate a conditional fee estate if the estate holder fails to meet the required conditions. *Also called:* **Right of Re-entry**. *See:* **Conditional Fee.** *Compare:* **Possibility of Reverter**.

Practical Difficulties One reason for issuing a zoning area variance—the zoning prevents the owner from making permitted use of the property.

Pre-approval Process by which a lender determines whether potential borrowers can be financed through the lender for a certain amount of money.

Predatory Lending Practice of making loans with excessively high fees and misrepresented loan terms; predatory lenders often target borrowers who are financially unstable and who do not qualify for conventional loans.

Prepayment Penalties Additional money charged by a lender for paying off a loan early.

Pre-qualification Process by which an agent or lender reviews potential borrowers to determine if they are likely to be approved for a loan and for approximately what amount.

Prescription Acquiring an interest in property (usually an easement) by using it openly and without the owner's permission. *See:* **Easement by Prescription**. *Compare:* **Adverse Possession.**

Preventive Maintenance Routine maintenance and inspections that keep equipment and the property in good working order.

Price The amount a ready, willing, and able buyer agrees to pay for a property and a seller agrees to accept.

Price Fixing An antitrust violation in which competitors set a standard commission rate.

Primary Markets Lenders who make mortgage loans directly to borrowers. *Also called:* **Primary Mortgage Markets**. *Compare:* **Secondary Markets.**

Principal 1. A person who grants another person (an agent) authority to represent him in dealings with third parties. 2. One of the parties to a transaction (such as a buyer or seller), as opposed to those who are involved as agents or employees (such as a broker or escrow agent). 3. With regard to a loan, the amount originally borrowed, as opposed to the interest.

Private Mortgage Insurance (PMI) Insurance offered by private companies to insure a lender against borrower default.

Private Restriction A restriction imposed on property by a previous owner or the subdivision developer; a restrictive covenant or a condition in a deed.

Probate A judicial proceeding in which the validity of a will is established and the executor is authorized to distribute the estate property; or, when there is no valid will, a judicial proceeding in which an administrator is appointed to distribute the estate to heirs according to the laws of intestate succession.

Probate Court A court that oversees the distribution of property under a will or intestate succession.

Procedural Law A law that establishes a legal procedure for enforcing a right. *Compare:* **Substantive Law**.

Procuring Cause The real estate agent who is primarily responsible for bringing about a sale, such as by introducing the buyer to the property or by negotiating the agreement between the buyer and seller. Sometimes more than one agent contributes to a sale. *See:* **Open Listing**.

Proforma Statement A schedule of the projected income and expenses for a real estate investment over a given period.

Promisee A person who has been promised something; a person who is supposed to receive the benefit of a legally binding contractual promise.

Promisor A person who has made a contractual promise to another.

Promissory Estoppel A doctrine applied when someone makes a technically unenforceable promise, but another person acts in reasonable reliance on the promise. If the person who relied on the promise will suffer harm unless it is enforced, a court may enforce it.

Promissory Note A written, legally binding promise to repay a debt.

Property Insurance Coverage that indemnifies a person with an interest in the property for a loss caused to the property by a covered peril.

Property Management Leasing or renting, or offering to lease or rent real property of others for a fee, commission, compensation, or other valuable consideration pursuant to a property management employee contract.

Property Management Report A report prepared by property managers to inform owners on the status of their property, often including income, expenses, and disbursements information.

Property Manager A person hired by a real property owner to administer, market, merchandise, and maintain property, especially rental property.

Proprietary Lease Exclusive, longer term lease given to a person who lives in a cooperative and owns stock in the cooperative.

Pro-rata Share A proportionate share.

Proration The division of expenses between buyer and seller in proportion to the actual usage of the item represented by a particular expense. *Also called:* **Adjustments.**

Public Accommodation Title III of the Americans with Disabilities Act requiring all public and commercial facilities are100% accessible to the disabled.

Public Grant When land owned by the government is transferred to an individual.

Public Nuisance A land use that threatens public health, safety, morals, or welfare, or constitutes a substantial annoyance to the public.

Public Record The official collection of legal documents filed with the county recorder. *See:* **Constructive Notice; Recording**.

Public Restriction A law or regulation limiting or regulating the use of real property.

Puffing Superlative statements about the quality of a property that should not be considered assertions of fact.

Punitive Damages Court-ordered monetary award meant to punish the defendant for malicious or outrageous conduct and discourage others from engaging in similar acts. *Also called:* **Exemplary Damages.**

Purchase Agreement A contract in which a seller promises to convey title to real property in exchange for the purchase price. *Also called:* **Purchase and Sale Agreement**, **Purchase Contract**, or **Earnest Money Agreement**.

Purchase Money When the seller finances all or part of the sale price of a property for a buyer.

Q

Qualified Fee When a grantor puts a condition or requirement in the deed and limits the title to real property. *Also called:* **Conditional Fee, Determinable, Fee Simple Defeasible**, or **Defeasible Fee.**

Quantity Survey Method A cost approach appraisal method where the appraiser counts the number and type of each part and material used to construct a building, and add the cost for labor, profit, permits, etc.

Quiet Enjoyment Use and possession of real property without interference from previous owners, the lessors, or anyone else claiming title. *See:* **Covenant of Quiet Enjoyment.**

Quiet Title Action A lawsuit to determine who has title to a piece of property or to remove a cloud from the title.

Quitclaim Deed Conveys any interest in a parcel of land the grantor has at the time the deed is executed; conveys whatever right, title, or interest the grantor holds in the property without representation that there is any interest at all.

R

R-Factor A way to measure the insulating value or resistance to heat flow through a material or an object. The more effective the insulation, the higher the R-Value it will have.

Radon A naturally occurring radioactive gas that emanates from rocks, soil, and water because of the decay of uranium.

Rafter Sloped support beams that follow the pitch of the roof and serve to hold the outer roof covering. *See:* **Joist and Rafters.**

Range Lines North-south lines running parallel to principal meridians at six-mile intervals in the government survey system.

Rate Adjustment Period The interval at which a borrower's interest rate changes with an ARM (adjustable rate mortgage).

Rate Cap Used with ARMs to protect borrowers from large interest rate increases.

Rate of Return The rate at which an investor recaptures his investment in income-producing property.

Ratification Confirmation or approval of an act not authorized when it was performed.

Ready, Willing, and Able Making an offer to purchase on terms acceptable to the seller, and having the financial ability to complete the purchase.

Real Estate Land and everything permanently affixed to it.

Real Estate Appraiser A person who is specially trained to offer an unbiased value of real property.

Real Estate Broker A person who is licensed to represent one of the parties in a real estate transaction for compensation.

Real Estate Owned (REO) Property acquired through foreclosure and held in inventory by a lending institution.

Real Estate Contract 1. A purchase agreement. 2. A land contract. 3. Any contract having to do with real property.

Real Estate Cycles General swings in real estate activity, resulting in increasing or decreasing activity and property values during different phases of the cycle.

Real Estate Investment Trust (REIT) A real estate investment business with at least 100 investors organized as a trust.

Real Estate Salesperson A licensed real estate professional associated with a broker and, as such, who may perform most of the acts as a broker, on behalf of him.

Real Estate Settlement Procedures Act (RESPA) Requires lenders, mortgage brokers, or servicers of home loans to provide borrowers with pertinent and timely disclosures of the nature and costs of the real estate settlement process.

Real Estate Tax An annual tax levied on the value of real property. *Also called:* **Property Tax** or **General Real Estate Tax.**

Real Estate Transfer Tax A tax levied on the transfer of real property.

Real Property The physical land and everything attached to it as well as the rights of ownership (**bundle of rights**). *Compare:* **Personal Property.**

Realtist A real estate licensee who is a member of National Association of Real Estate Brokers.

REALTOR® Any real estate licensee who is a member of the National Association of REALTORS® and its affiliated boards; only members may use the term REALTOR® as it's a registered trademark of the NAR®.

Realty Real property.

Reassessment The new assessment of a percentage of a property's market value.

Recaptured Depreciation Occurs on a personal asset used for business purposes when the asset is sold.

Receiver of Taxes Municipal official responsible for managing the day-to-day operations of the Office of Receiver of Taxes, which collects local taxes. Other functions include tax billing and collection, banking, record maintenance, mail and accounting functions.

Reciprocity When states agree to allow licensees from other states to sell real estate in their own.

Recognition Agreement An agreement between three parties—the lender, the co-op, and the shareholder—that recognizes the rights of lenders who finance the shareholder.

Reconciliation Verifying debits and credits have been added and subtracted correctly on a real estate settlement statement.

Reconveyance An instrument that releases security property from the lien created by a deed of trust. *Also called:* **Satisfaction of Mortgage.**

Recording Filing a document at the county recorder's office so it is public record.

Redlining When a lender refuses to make loans secured by property in a certain neighborhood because of the racial or ethnic composition of the neighborhood.

Reduction Option Mortgage A fixed rate mortgage that gives borrowers a limited opportunity to reduce the interest rate once during the course of the loan, provided certain conditions are met.

Referee Someone who is empowered by the court to exercise judicial power to convey land.

Referee's Deed Deeds that contain no covenants or warranties although ownership is implied.

Reference to a Plat A description on a deed that includes the property's location on a plat map.

Referendum When citizens vote on an issue.

Reformation A legal action to correct a mistake, such as a typographical error, in a deed or other document.

Regression When the value of the "best" home in a given area is negatively affected by other homes in the area.

Regulation 1. A rule adopted by an administrative agency. 2. Any governmental order having the force of law.

Regulation Z Federal guidelines under the Truth-in-Lending Act that require full disclosure of all credit terms for consumer loans.

Release 1. To give up a legal right. 2. A document in which a legal right is given up.

Release Clause A clause in a mortgage agreement for a subdivision that allows the borrower to pay a certain amount of money to release one or more lots with the mortgage continuing to cover the other lots.

Reliction When a body of water gradually recedes, exposing land that was previously under water. *Also called:* **Dereliction.**

Remainder Interest: A future interest that becomes possessory when a life estate terminates and that is held by someone other than the grantor of the life estate. *Compare:* **Reversionary Interest.**

Remainderman The person who has an estate in remainder.

Remedy The means by which a court enforces a right, imposes a penalty, or makes some other order to impose its will. *Compare:* **Equitable Remedy** and **Legal Remedy.**

Renewal Premium Recurring fee to continue an insurance policy.

Rent Consideration paid by a tenant to a landlord in exchange for possession and use of property.

Rentable Square Footage The amount of space used in calculating a lease payment; rentable square footage is larger than the actual space tenants occupy because it includes their share of the property's service areas like the lobby, corridors, and other common areas.

Rent Control Governmental restrictions on how much rent a landlord can charge.

Rent Roll Spreadsheet or listing of key information about a property (i.e., total number of units, tenant names and apartment numbers, lease dates, and the rent each tenant pays).

Renunciation When someone who has been granted something or has accepted something later gives it up or rejects it; as when an agent withdraws from the agency relationship. *Compare:* **Revocation.**

Replacement Building a functional equivalent of an original building. *Compare:* **Reproduction.**

Replacement Cost (R/C) The cost, for insurance purposes, of replacing property without deduction for depreciation.

Reproduction Building an exact replica of an original building, duplicating the materials, design, functional layout, workmanship, and even inadequacies.

Reproduction Cost The cost to build an exact replica of an original building, giving the new structure the same look and feel as the original.

Rescission When a contract is terminated and each party gives anything acquired under the contract back to the other party (verb form is **rescind**). *Compare:* **Cancellation.**

Reservation A document a condominium buyer signs to reserve a particular unit. *Also called:* **Reservation Request** and **Intent to Purchase Agreement.**

Reserve Account 1. An account maintained by a broker for the deposit of client's money (i.e., good faith deposits). *Also called:* **Trust Account.** 2. An account maintained by a lender for the deposit of borrowers' extra 1/12 monthly deposits to cover next year's insurance and tax payments. *Also called:* **Escrow Account.**

Reserve Requirements The percentage of customers' deposits commercial banks are required to keep on deposit, either on hand at the bank or in the bank's own accounts; money the bank cannot lend to other people.

Resident Manager Represents a property management firm and may live on the premises of the building she manages.

Residential Lead-based Paint Hazard Reduction Act Requires sellers and landlords to disclose known lead paint hazards for homes built before 1978.

Residential Market Analysis In-depth study of a listing as it stands on its own, as well as in light of current market conditions.

Residual Income The amount of income a borrower has left after subtracting taxes, housing expenses, and all recurring debts and obligations (used for VA loan qualifying).

Restitution Restoring something to a person of which she was unjustly deprived.

Restriction A limitation on the use of real property. *Compare:* **Public Restriction; Private Restriction.**

Restrictive Covenant 1. A limitation on real property use, imposed by the owner. 2. A promise to do, or not to do, an act relating to real property.

Retail Investment Property Where a specific type of business activity occurs—retail sales and related business activities.

Retaliatory Eviction When a landlord evicts a tenant in retaliation for complaining about code violations or violations of the Landlords and Tenants Act, or for participating in a tenants' rights group.

Return on Investment A saver/investor's expectation that he will eventually get back the interest paid while the equity was invested.

Reverse To overturn a lower court's decision on appeal, ruling in favor of the appellant. *Compare:* **Affirm.**

Reverse Equity Mortgage When a homeowner over age 62 with little or no outstanding liens, mortgages her home to a lender and, in return, receives a monthly check. *Also called:* **Reverse Mortgage.**

Reversionary Interest A future interest that becomes possessory when a temporary estate (such as a life estate) terminates, and is held by the grantor (or grantor's successors in interest). *Compare:* **Remainder Interest.**

Revocation When someone who granted or offered something withdraws it, as when a principal withdraws the authority granted to the agent, an offeror withdraws the offer. *Compare:* **Renunciation.**

Rezone An amendment to a zoning ordinance, usually changing the uses allowed in a particular zone. *Also called:* **Zoning Amendment.** *Compare:* **Spot Zoning.**

Rider An amendment to a contract.

Right of Disposal A right to transfer all or some of a person's ownership interest in real property.

Right of Enjoyment A right to enjoy the benefits of land ownership without outside interference. *See:* **Quiet Enjoyment.**

Right of First Refusal A right to have the first chance to buy or lease property if the owner decides to sell or lease it. *Also called:* **Right of Pre-emption.** *Compare:* **Option.**

Right of Survivorship A characteristic of statutory survivorship tenancy, joint tenancy, and tenancy by the entireties; surviving co-tenants automatically acquire a deceased co-tenant's interest in the property.

Right of Use The right landowners have to make property productive (part of bundle of rights).

Right of Way (ROW) An easement giving the holder the right to cross another person's land.

Right to Rescind The consumer's right to rescind any credit transaction involving her principal residence as collateral (except first mortgages), up to midnight of the third business day after the transaction.

Riparian Rights The water rights of a landowner whose property is adjacent to or crossed by a river (or any body of water). *Compare:* **Appropriative Rights; Littoral Rights.**

Risk The probability that events will not occur as expected.

Risk Management Identifying, managing, and minimizing the potential risks on the property.

Rough-ins Items hidden by finished walls, but that are vital to the operation of the house.

Running with the Land Binding or benefiting the successive owners of a piece of property, rather than terminating when a particular owner transfers his interest. Usually refers to easements or restrictive covenants.

R-Value Insulation's R-Factor multiplied by the amount of material. *See:* **R-Factor**

S

Safe Drinking Water Act (SDWA) A government act established by the EPA that sets quality standards for water intended for human consumption.

Sale and Leaseback A method for financing commercial or industrial properties in which a company constructs the building then becomes a tenant by selling the building to an investor.

Sales Associate Any licensed real estate salesperson associated with a broker; sales associates never act independently, they act on behalf of the broker. *Also called:* **Salesperson.**

Sales Comparison Approach An appraisal method that estimates the value of real property by performing a market analysis of the area where the subject property is located. Data is collected and adjustments made for differences.

Sales Contract Contracts in which a seller promises to convey title to real property to a buyer in exchange for the purchase price. *Also called:* **Purchase Agreements, Sale Agreements, Purchase and Sale Agreements, Offers to Purchase,** and **Earnest Money Agreements.**

Satisfaction of Mortgage The document a mortgagee gives the mortgagor when the mortgage debt is paid in full acknowledging the debt has been paid and the mortgage is no longer a lien against the property.

Savings and Loan Associations (S & L) Institutions that specialize in taking savings deposits and making mortgage loans.

Scarcity Characteristic of real property that says there is a limited supply of real estate.

Second Mortgage A security instrument in a second lien position.

Secondarily Liable When a party is not completely released from liability of an obligation; thus if the lender cannot recover the loan from the new party, the party who is secondarily liable may still be pursued.

Secondary Markets Private investors and government agencies that buy and sell mortgages. *Also called:* **Secondary Mortgage Market.** *Compare:* **Primary Markets**

Secret Profit A financial benefit an agent takes from a transaction without authorization from the principal, nor informing the principal of the benefit retained. *See:* **Self-dealing.**

Section A one-mile-by-one-mile square within a township used for the government survey system; one section equals 640 acres, 36 sections equal one township.

Sectional Index An index that lists recorded documents under the tax parcel number of the property they apply to, grouping together all recorded documents affecting a particular property. *Also called:* **Tract Index.**

Secured Creditor A creditor with a lien on specific property that enables him to foreclose and collect the debt from the sale proceeds if it is not otherwise paid.

Securitization Act of pooling mortgages and then selling them as mortgage-backed securities.

Security Deposit Money a tenant gives a landlord at the beginning of tenancy to ensure the tenant will comply with the terms of the lease. The landlord may retain all or part of the deposit to cover unpaid rent, repair costs, or other damages, if necessary.

Security Instruments Instruments (i.e., mortgages and trust deeds) that give a creditor the right to have the collateral sold to satisfy the debt if the debtor fails to pay according to the terms of the agreement.

Security Interest The interest a creditor may acquire in the debtor's property to ensure that the debt will be paid.

Seizen The possession of a freehold estate; ownership. *Also spelled:* **Seisin** or **Seizin**.

Self-dealing When a real estate agent buys the principal's property (or sells it to a relative, friend, etc., or to a business the agent has an interest), without disclosing that fact to the principal, then sells it for a profit.

Self-help Eviction When a landlord uses physical force, a lockout, or a utility shutoff to remove a tenant, instead of the legal process.

Seller Financing When a seller extends credit to a buyer to finance the purchase of the property instead of or in addition to the buyer obtaining a loan from a third party.

Seller's Agent The agent who is representing only the seller in a transaction and owes, all loyalty to that seller/client.

Seller's Market A situation in the housing market when there are more buyers than there are properties for sale.

Senior Mortgage Any mortgage that has a higher lien position than another mortgage.

Separate Property In states with a community property system, any property owned by a married person that is not held jointly with the spouse as community property. *Compare*: **Community Property**.

Septic System A type of private sewage disposal system used in areas that do not have public sewers.

Servicing The continued maintenance of a loan after it has been made (e.g., collecting payments, keeping records, and handling defaults).

Servient Tenant The owner of a servient tenement; that is, someone whose property is burdened by an easement.

Servient Tenement Property burdened by an easement; the owner of the servient tenement (the servient tenant) is required to allow someone who has an easement (the dominant tenant) to use his property.

Setbacks Provisions that require residences be located a specified distance between the front property line to the building line, as well as from the interior property lines.

Settlement 1. An agreement between the parties to a civil lawsuit, in which the plaintiff agrees to drop the suit in exchange for a sum of money or the defendant's promise to do or refrain from doing something. 2. Closing.

Settlement Statement A document prepared by the buyer's and seller's attorney or bank representatives that itemizes all expenses and costs paid by the buyer and seller to close the real estate transaction.

Severable When one part or provision in a contract can be held unenforceable without making the entire contract unenforceable.

Shared Equity Mortgage Loan for which the buyer and another investor (or seller, lender, etc.) enter into a partnership, with the buyer paying an equity share in lieu of interest.

Shareholders Stockholders in a corporation.

Share Loan A type of co-op loan signifying a buyer is purchasing shares in a corporation, rather than a mortgage for ownership of property.

Sheathing A structural covering, often made of plywood, placed over a building frame's exterior wall studs or roof rafters.

Sheriff's Deed A deed issued by the court to a property purchaser from a foreclosure sale.

Sheriff's Sale A foreclosure sale held after a judicial foreclosure. *Also called:* **Execution** or **Execution Sale.**

Sick Building Syndrome When poor air quality in a building causes symptoms of headache, fatigue, nausea, sore throat, nose and eye irritation, etc. among its occupants.

Side Yard The area between a building and one side boundary of the lot on which it is located.

Siding The outer covering for a home's exterior walls, designed to shed water and protect the home from the elements.

Sill Plate Bottom piece of a frame horizontally anchored to the foundation providing a nailing surface for the floor or wall system.

Simultaneous Closing A seller financing technique used when an investor or seller creates a private mortgage note and then simultaneously closes with the buyer on the same day.

Sit Down Contract When all negotiating is conducted in one place at one time with all parties to the contract and their attorneys present.

Site A plot of land with enhancements that make it ready for a building or structure.

Situs Place where something exists; an area of preference thus giving it economic attributes (value).

Slab-on-grade Construction A concrete foundation built directly on the ground level. A slab-on-grade house or building does not have a basement.

Soffit The underside of an arch, beam, overhang, or eaves.

Special Agent An agent with limited authority to act on behalf of the principal.

Special Assessment A tax or levy against real property for improvements; not imposed on all residents of a community, but only to owners who will benefit from the improvement.

Special Assessment District A geographic area designated to pay for infrastructure costs for a specific project. Properties within the district each pay a portion of the total project cost. Creates a **special assessment lien** (an involuntary lien).

Special Purpose Real Estate Properties considered having a limited use, such as a church or tennis club.

Special Use Permit Permit issued in certain zoning districts when conditions designed to protect surrounding properties are met.

Specifications In construction, specifications are written documents explaining the requirements for the scope of the work including materials, standards, and expected quality of the finished product. *Also called:* **Plans.**

Specific Lien A lien that attaches only to a particular property. *Compare:* **General Lien.**

Specific Performance A legal remedy in which a court orders someone who has breached a contract to perform as agreed rather than simply paying monetary damages.

Specific Tax Policies Tax laws that can encourage or discourage a particular behavior or activity.

Sphere of Influence People you know and whom you can ask for referrals.

Sponsor Also known as the developer, a sponsor is the person, corporation, or other entity that is part of the sale and development of a condominium or co-op property.

Sponsoring Broker The broker for whom a licensee works.

Spot Zoning The illegal rezoning of a single parcel or a small area to benefit one or more property owners rather than carry out the objectives of the master plan.

Stabilized Budget A property's income and expenses averaged over a five year period.

Stable Income Income that can reasonably be expected to continue in the future.

Stachybotrys A type of mold known as "black mold" that produces mycotoxins.

Stare Decisis Legal doctrine requiring judges to follow precedents (from the same jurisdiction) to make laws consistent and predictable.

State Action In constitutional law, action by a government (federal, state, or local) rather than by a private party.

State Implementation Plan (SIP) Study required by the Environmental Protection Agency to help states meet national air quality standards.

State of New York Mortgage Agency (SONYMA) Offers programs funded by the sale of tax-exempt bonds and designed to make housing affordable to low- and moderate-income households.

Statute A law enacted by a state legislature or the U.S. Congress. *See:* **Statutory Law.** *Compare:* **Ordinance; Resolution.**

Statute of Frauds A law that requires certain types of contracts to be in writing and signed to be enforceable.

Statute of Limitations A law requiring a particular type of lawsuit to be filed within a specified time after the event giving rise to the suit occurred.

Statutory Employee Independent contractors specifically classified as employees by statute for Social Security and Medicare taxes.

Statutory Law Laws adopted by a legislative body (Congress, state legislature, or a county or city council), as opposed to constitutional law, case law, or administrative regulations.

Statutory Life Estate A life estate held by a person whose dower rights have vested (because a person's spouse sold property without a dower release, and subsequently died).

Statutory Non-employee Direct sellers and licenses real estate agents; treated as independent contractors for all tax purposes if certain conditions are met.

Statutory Redemption Allows a mortgagor to redeem property for a set period of time after a foreclosure sale regardless of the timing of other events. *Compare:* **Equitable Right of Redemption.**

Statutory Survivorship Tenancy A form of co-ownership, used in some states, to replace joint tenancy and tenancy by the entireties; each co-tenant has an equal undivided interest in real property and the right of survivorship.

Steering Channeling prospective buyers or tenants to particular neighborhoods based on their race, religion, national origin, or ancestry.

Stigmatized Property Properties that do not have any physical defects but have become less marketable because they were the scene of a crime, suicide, or other undesirable event. .

Straight Line Depreciation Simple depreciation method that takes the total cost of a building and divides that by the number of years the building is expected to be useful.

Straight Mortgage A loan that comes due on a specified date, often before the periodic payments would pay it off. *Also called:* **Term Mortgage**

Straight Note A note that calls for payments of interest only during the term of the note, with a balloon payment at the end to pay off the principal balance.

Strict Foreclosure Foreclosure with a strict deadline, past which a mortgagor can no longer reclaim interest in the real property out of the foreclosure proceedings by bringing the mortgage current.

Strict Liability When someone is held legally responsible for an injury to another, even though he did not act negligently. *Compare:* **Negligence.**

Studs The vertical beams that serve to frame the house. Drywall and/or siding are attached to studs.

Subagency Created when an offer of subagency is accepted (e.g., when a listing broker offers compensation to other brokers as a subagent, the cooperative broker agrees to represent the interest of the seller).

Subagent An agent of an agent; a person that an agent has delegated authority, so the subagent can assist in carrying out the principal's orders.

Subdivision 1. Land divided into two or more parcels. 2. A residential development.

Subdivision Regulations State and local laws with which developers must comply before the land can be subdivided.

Subjacent Support The support land receives from the land beneath it.

Subjective Intent What the offeror in a transaction is actually thinking but necessarily what he does. *Compare:* **Objective Intent.**

Subject Property Property for which a value estimate is sought.

Subject To When property is transferred to a buyer along with an existing mortgage or lien, but without the buyer accepting personal responsibility for the debt. The buyer must make the payments to keep the property, but only loses her equity in the event of default. *Compare:* **Assumption; Novation.**

Sublease When a tenant transfers only part of his right of possession or other interest in leased property to another person for part of the remaining lease term. *Compare:* **Assignment.**

Subordination Clause A contract that gives a mortgage recorded at a later date priority over an earlier recorded mortgage. *Also called:* **Subordination Agreement.**

Subpoena Document ordering a person to appear at a deposition or court proceeding to testify or produce evidence.

Subprime Loan A loan with a higher interest rate than a conventional loan.

Subsequent Good Faith Purchasers Later grantees of a deed who paid consideration for it and they are given some protection from claims not recorded).

Substantial Performance When a promisor does not perform all of his contractual obligations, but does enough so the promisee is required to fulfill his obligations. *Compare:* **Material Breach.**

Substantive Law A law that establishes a right or duty. *Compare:* **Procedural Law.**

Substitution Theory that an informed buyer will not pay more for a home than a comparable substitute.

Subsurface Rights The implication that a landowner has rights to the land below the surface to the center of the earth, even though it is not documented.

Successor in Interest A person (i.e., a buyer or an heir) who has acquired property previously held by someone else.

Superfund Amendments and Reauthorization Act (SARA) Act that amended the CERCLA, designated more money to the Superfund trust, and established new environmental laws and regulations.

Supply and Demand Law of economics that says for all products, goods, and services, when supply exceeds demand, prices will fall, and when demand exceeds supply, prices will rise.

Support Rights The right to have one's land supported by the land adjacent to and beneath it.

Surrender Giving up an estate (such as a life estate or leasehold) before it has expired.

Survey The process of locating and measuring the boundaries of a property, and indentifying improvements, encroachments, and easements associated with the land.

Suspension A real estate agent's license being temporarily withdrawn. Usually, reactivation is automatic the day after the suspension is lifted. *Compare:* **Revocation.**

Syndicate An association of people or entities formed to operate an investment business. A syndicate is not a recognized legal entity; can be organized as a corporation, partnership, or trust.

T

Tacking When successive periods of use or possession by more than one person are added together to equal the 21 years required for prescription or adverse possession.

Takeout Loan A loan that is used to pay off a construction loan when construction is complete.

Taking When the government acquires private property for public use by appropriation. The difference between a "taking" and eminent domain is that the property is regulated by a government authority to the economic detriment of the owner, without compensation.

Tax An annual tax levied on the value of real property.

Tax Assessor An official who evaluates property for the purpose of taxing it.

Tax Deductibility The ability to write-off a portion of interest from a loan on the amount of taxes owed to the government.

Tax Depreciation Calculating depreciation that can be used to determine any expense that can be deducted from income to determine net profit.

Tax Levy Determine tax rates by developing and adopting a budget, evaluating the revenue from all sources other than property taxes (state aid, sales tax, user fees, etc.), and then subtracting the revenues from the original budget.

Tax Lien A lien on real property to secure the payment of taxes.

Tax Sale Sale of property after foreclosure of a tax lien.

Tax Shelter Any method used to reduce taxable income, thereby reducing the amount of tax paid to a government.

Taxation The process of a government levying a charge on people or things.

Tax-deferred Exchanges Exchanges where taxable gain is deferred until a later date.

Temporary Buydown When points are paid to a lender to reduce the interest rate and payments early in a loan, with interest rate and payments rising later.

Tenancy Lawful possession of real property; an estate.

Tenancy at Sufferance Possession of property by a holdover tenant.

Tenancy at Will When a tenant is in possession with the owner's permission, but with no definite lease term and no rent being paid (or rent is not paid on a regular basis); e.g., a landlord lets a holdover tenant remain on the premises without paying rent until a new tenant is found.

Tenancy by the Entireties A form of property co-ownership by husband and wife, in which each spouse has an undivided one-half interest and the right of survivorship, with neither spouse able to convey or encumber his or her interest without the other's consent.

Tenancy (or Estate) for Years *see:* **Estate for Years**

Tenancy in Common A form of co-ownership in which two or more persons each have an undivided interest in the entire property (unity of possession), but no right of survivorship.

Tenancy in Partnership The form of co-ownership in which general partners own partnership property, whether or not title to the property is in the partnership's name. Each partner has an equal undivided interest, but no right to transfer the interest to someone outside the partnership.

Tenant Someone in lawful possession of real property, especially, someone who has leased property from the owner; can also refer to sublessees.

Tender An unconditional offer by one party to a contract to perform his or her part of the agreement; made when the offeror believes the other party will breach to establish the offeror's right to sue if the other party doesn't accept it. *Also called:* **Tender Offer** or **Tendering Performance.**

Tenements Everything of a permanent nature associated with a piece of land and ordinarily transferred with the land. Tenements are both tangible (buildings, for example) and intangible (air rights, for example).

Tentative Assessment Roll The public record listing assessed value for all real property in a municipality.

Term A prescribed period of time; especially, the length of time a borrower has to pay off a loan, or the duration of a lease.

Termites Wood eating insects that can undermine the structural integrity of a building.

Territorial Jurisdiction The geographical area over which a particular court has authority.

Testate Refers to someone who has died and left a will. *Compare:* **Intestate.**

Testator A man who makes a will.

Testatrix A woman who makes a will.

Tester *See:* **Checker.**

Tie-in Arrangements Requiring the consumer, as a condition of a transaction, to use, or not use a particular service or product.

Time is of the Essence A contract clause that means performance on the exact dates specified is an essential element of the contract; failure to perform on time is a material breach.

Time Share An ownership interest that gives the owner a right to possession of the property only for a specific, limited period each year.

Time Value of Money (TVM) The relationship between time, money, a rate of return and earnings growth.

Title The actual lawful ownership of real property and refers to holding the bundle of rights conveyed. Title is not a document, but rather a theory pertaining to ownership.

Title Closing The final stage in a real estate transaction; transfer of real property ownership from seller to buyer occurs, according to the terms and conditions in a sales contract or escrow agreement.

Title Insurance An insurance policy that protects the lender (and sometimes the property owner) against loss due to disputes over the ownership of a property and defects in the title that were not found in the search of the public record.

Title Plant A duplicate (usually microfilmed) of a county's public record, maintained by a title company at its offices for use in title searches.

Title Report A report issued by a title company, disclosing the condition of the title to a specific piece of property.

Title Search An inspection of the public record to determine all rights and encumbrances affecting title to a piece of property.

Title Theory States States in which a mortgagee holds actual title to property until the loan is repaid. *Compare:* **Lien Theory States.**

Topography The physical characteristics of the contour a parcel of land.

Torrens System Title registration system administered by the state, which guarantees indefeasible title to those included in the register; adopted in New York and other states, but is costly and rarely used.

Tort A breach of the standards of reasonable conduct imposed by law (as opposed to a duty voluntarily taken on in a contract) that causes harm to another person, giving the injured person the right to sue the one who breached the duty. *Also called:* **Civil Wrong** (in contrast to a criminal wrong, a crime). *See:* **Negligence; Strict Liability.**

Total Debt Service Ratio Relationship of total monthly debt obligations to income, expressed as a percentage.

Touch and Concern the Land Legal doctrine that says restrictive covenants must be related to actual landuse to be enforceable.

Township Lines East-west lines that run parallel to base lines at six-mile intervals in the government survey system.

Townships Square divisions of land, 6 miles by 6 miles, in the government survey system. One township contains 36 sections.

Trade Fixture Equipment a tenant installs for use in his or her trade or business, and which can be removed by the tenant before the lease expires.

Transfer of Development Rights The exchange of zoning privileges from areas with low population needs to areas of high population needs.

Transformer Transfer power from one circuit to another.

Trespass An unlawful physical invasion of property owned by another.

Trial The fundamental court proceeding in a lawsuit, in which a judge (and in some cases, a jury) hears evidence presented by the plaintiff and defendant and issues a judgment. *Compare:* **Appeal.**

Trial Record All documents and transcripts from a trial.

Trigger Phrase A word or phrase that describes a loan, including the down payment, terms, and monthly payment. If an ad uses a trigger phrase, disclosures are needed to tell everything about the loan.

Triple Net Lease A lease in which the tenant pays *all* the expenses associated with the property, including rent.

True Tax The amount that would be paid before any exemptions held by the present owner are subtracted.

Trust A legal arrangement in which title to property (or funds) is vested in one or more trustees who manage the property (or invest the funds) on behalf of the trust's beneficiaries, in accordance with instructions set forth in the document establishing the trust.

Trust Account A bank account, separate from a real estate broker's personal and business accounts, used to segregate trust funds from the broker's own funds.

Trustee A person appointed to manage a trust on behalf of the beneficiaries.

Trust Funds Money or things of value received by an agent, not belonging to the agent but being held for the benefit of others.

Trustee's Sale A non-judicial foreclosure sale under a deed of trust.

Trustor the borrower who owes payment of a note on a deed of trust.

Truth-in-Lending Act Act that requires lenders to disclose consumer credit costs to promote informed use of consumer credit.

U

Umbrella Liability Policy Provides broad coverage for an insured's liability over and above liability covered by underlying contracts.

Unconstitutional Violating a provision of the U.S. Constitution or a state constitution.

Underground Storage Tanks Holding tanks that can used to store chemicals, fuels, toxic wastes and other substances. Regulated by the EPA.

Underwriter A person who evaluates a loan application to determine its risk level for a lender or investor.

Underwiting The process of evaluating and deciding whether to make a new loan.

Undisclosed Dual Agency Occurs when both principal parties in the same transaction are represented by a fiduciary without full disclosure to and approval from all parties in the transaction.

Undivided Interest A co-tenant's interest, giving him or her the right to possession of the whole property, rather than a particular section of it. *See:* **Unity of Possession.**

Undivided Loyalty This is given up by the buyer and seller when they consent to dual agency.

Undue Influence Exerting excessive pressure on someone to overpower the person's free will and prevent him or her from making a rational or prudent decision; often involves abusing a relationship of trust.

Unencumbered Property Property whose seller has clear title free of mortgages or other liens.

Unenforceable Contract A contract that a court would refuse to enforce. For example, a contract may be unenforceable because its contents cannot be proven, or because it is not in writing, or because the statute of limitations has run out.

Uniform Commercial Code (UCC) Sets out certain requirements for negotiable instruments.

Uniform Residential Appraisal Report (URAR) A standard appraisal report form used by lenders and appraisers because it has been developed and approved by secondary mortgage market players Fannie Mae and Freddie Mac.

Uniform Standards of Professional Appraisal Practice (USPAP) Professional appraisal standards developed by The Appraisal Foundation, and now recognized throughout the United States as accepted standards of appraisal practice.

Unilateral Contract When only one party makes a legally binding promise and the other has not. The promise will become legally binding if the other party chooses to accept it (similar to an offer). *Compare:* **Bilateral Contract.**

Unilateral Mistake When only one of the parties to a contract was mistaken about a fact or a law.

Uniqueness Characteristic of real property that says each piece of land, each building, and each house is a different piece of real estate. *Also called:* **Non-homogeneity.**

Unit Owners Association The organization that manages the operation of a condominium, imposing assessments and arranging for the maintenance of the common areas. The association's members are the unit owners and they usually elect a board of directors. *Also called:* a **Condominium Association.**

Unities of Interest, Possession, Time, and Title Four unities required to form a joint tenancy whereby all owners share equally and simultaneously in these conditions.

Unity of Interest Each co-owner having an equal interest (equal share of ownership) in a piece of property.

Unity of Possession Each co-owner being equally entitled to possession of the entire property, because the ownership interests are undivided. *See:* **Undivided Interest.**

Unity of Time When each co-owner acquired title at the same time.

Unity of Title When each co-owner acquired title through the same instrument (deed, will, or court order).

Universal Agent An agent authorized to do everything that can be lawfully delegated to a representative.

Unjust Enrichment An unfairly obtained benefit by one party at the expense of another.

Unlawful Detainer Action A summary legal action to regain possession of real property; especially, a lawsuit filed by a landlord to evict a defaulting tenant and regain possession of the property. *Also called:* a **Forcible Detainer Action.**

Unnecessary Hardship Reason for a zoning use variance if permitted uses of the property are not economically feasible and the property cannot be used without the variance.

Untenantable Not fit for occupancy (used to describe rental property).

Urea-Formaldehyde A clear chemical that is used in manufacturing including building materials such as particle board, plywood paneling, carpeting, and insulation.

Urea-Formaldehyde Foam Insulation (UFFI) A type of housing insulation used in the 1970's. It was banned because of the formaldehyde fumes it released that caused a myriad of symptoms among homeowners who had it.

Usable Square Footage The amount of actual space within the perimeter of the tenant's premises, including walls, columns, and airshafts; the floor area where tenants can actually lay carpet and place furniture.

Use Variance Allows landowners to use their land in a way that is not permitted under current zoning laws. This type of variance is granted only in cases of unnecessary hardship. To prove unnecessary hardship, owners must establish that the requested variance meets four statutorily prescribed conditions.

Usury Laws limiting the maximum interest rate that can be charged.

V

Vacancy and Collection Losses Estimate as to how much future income may be lost when a building isn't fully occupied or tenants don't pay rent.

Vacant Land Unimproved land or land with no building on it.

Valid The legal classification of a contract that is binding and enforceable in a court of law.

Valid Contract A binding, legally enforceable contract.

Valuation The process of gathering and analyzing information to determine the value of a piece of property.

Value Amount of goods or services offered in the marketplace in exchange for something.

Value in Use The present worth of the future benefits of ownership.

Variable Expense Expenses that are not consistent and regular amounts, and depend on issues including the type, size, age, and condition of a property.

Variance A form of administrative relief that allows property to be used in a way that does not comply with the literal requirements of the zoning ordinance. There are two basic types of variances: use variances and area variances.

Vendee A buyer or purchaser; particularly someone buying property under a land contract.

Vendor A seller; particularly, someone selling property by means of a land contract.

Vendor's Lien A lien to secure payment of the purchase price balance, held by a real estate seller if the buyer does not pay the seller in full at closing (unless the buyer gives the seller a mortgage for the balance).

Vested When a person has a present, fixed right or interest in property, even though he or she may not have the right to possession until sometime in the future. For example, a remainderman's interest in property vests when it is granted, not when a life estate ends.

Veto When the president or governor formally rejects a bill that Congress or the legislature has passed. The bill will not become law unless the legislature votes to override the veto.

Veterans Administration (VA) Government agency that guarantees mortgage loans for eligible veterans.

Vicarious Liability When one person is responsible for the actions of another.

Village Board of Trustees Serve as the primary governing bodies of New York villages.

Violation An action which goes against specific rules or regulations set by national, state or local government and those set by specific governing bodies of a trade or profession. Such as when a licensee goes against any Act set forth in Article 12-A.

Void Having no legal force or effect.

Voidable Contract A contract that one of the parties can disaffirm, without liability, because of a lack of legal capacity or a negative factor such as fraud or duress.

Void Contract A contract that is not an enforceable contract because it lacks one or more of the requirements for contract formation, or is defective in some other respect.

Voltage A measure of the force that pushes electricity through a wire.

Voluntary Affirmative Marketing Agreements (VAMA) These programs are designed to affirmatively promote fair housing to all home seekers through a series of commitments and shared responsibilities.

Voluntary Alienation When title to property is transferred voluntarily through a sale, gift, dedication, or grant.

Voluntary Conveyance When a debtor returns property to the lender in lieu of foreclosure. Generally, the debtor does not receive any compensation for surrendering title to the property, but does avoid foreclosure.

Voluntary Lien A lien placed against property with the consent of the owner; a mortgage (or, in other states, a deed of trust).

Voluntary Partition When co-owners agree to terminate their co-ownership, dividing the property so each owns a piece of the property in severalty.

W

Waiver The voluntary relinquishment or surrender of a right.

Warranty Deed A deed carrying warranties (guarantees) of clear title and the grantor's right to convey. *See:* **General Warranty Deed; Limited Warranty Deed.**

Waste, Act of Destruction, damage, or material alteration of property by someone in possession who holds less than a fee estate (such as a life tenant or lessee).

Water Rights The right to use water in or from a river, stream, or lake. *See:* **Appropriative Rights; Littoral Rights; Riparian Rights.**

Wetlands Ecosystems where the land is permeated with water, which either lies on or near the surface of the land.

Will A person's legally binding instructions regarding how his or her estate should be disposed of after death. *Also called:* **Testament**.

Words of Conveyance A clause in a deed that states that the grantor intends to convey title to the land. *Also called:* **Granting Clause**.

Women's Council of Realtors (WCR) An organization devoted to addressing the issues, needs, and concerns of women in the real estate profession. (Now affiliated with the NAR.)

Wraparound Mortgage When a seller keeps the existing loan and continues to pay on it, while giving the buyer another mortgage. *Also called:* **Wraparound Financing.**

Writ of Execution A court order directing a public officer (often the sheriff or marshal) to seize and/or sell property to regain possession for the owner and/or satisfy a debt.

Writ of Possession A court order issued after an unlawful detainer action, informing a tenant that he must vacate the landlord's property within a specified period or be forcibly removed by the sheriff.

Wrongful Eviction When a landlord evicts a tenant in violation of the tenant's rights.

Y

Yield The total amount of money that can be made from an investment.

Z

Zoning Board of Appeals By issuing variances protects landowners from the unfair application of zoning laws in particular circumstances. Hears appeals from the decisions of zoning enforcement officers and building inspectors when interpretations of zoning ordinances are involved.

Zoning Ordinance Sets forth the type of use permitted under each zoning classification and specific requirements for compliance.

Index

O

P

Q

R

S